# GRANT

# GRANT

## A BIOGRAPHY

## WILLIAM S. McFEELY

W · W · Norton & Company

*NEW YORK · LONDON*

First published as a Norton paperback 1982

Frontispiece: Photograph of Ulysses S. Grant taken in Mathew Brady's studio.
*Library of Congress*

Library of Congress Cataloging in Publication Data
McFeely, William S.
Grant: a biography
Bibliography: p.
Includes index.
1. Grant, Ulysses Simpson, Pres. U..S., 1822–1885. 2. United States—History—Civil
War, 1861–1865—Campaigns and battles. 3. United States—Politics and government—
1869–1877. 4. Presidents—United States—Biography.
E672.M15 1981        973.8′ 2′0924 |B|        80–25279

**ISBN 0-393-32394-3 pbk.**

W. W. Norton & Company, Inc.
500 Fifth Avenue, New York, N.Y. 10110
www.wwnorton.com

W. W. Norton & Company Ltd.
Castle House, 75/76 Wells Street, London W1T 3QT

1 2 3 4 5 6 7 8 9 0

For Jennifer, Eliza, and Drake and
in memory of their grandfather, who
drove an ambulance in another American war
and in 1919 came home from France
on the S.S. *President Grant*.

# Contents

# Preface

MANY PEOPLE helped me while I was working on this book, and I am troubled that I will not succeed in naming them all. I have been the beneficiary of assistance from skilled archivists across the country, and I particularly want to mention the help of Sara Jackson and Oliver Orr. Librarians at Mount Holyoke College—Anne Edmonds, Nancy Devine, Phyllis Joyce, Irene Cronin, and Dorothy Fiegenbaum—were of immeasurable assistance.

I have had generous financial support from the American Council of Learned Societies, the National Endowment for the Humanities, and the Faculty Grants Committee of Mount Holyoke College. I spent particularly enjoyable and productive periods of work at the Huntington Library and the Institute of Historical Research and I am grateful for the differing but equally excellent hospitality in California and London.

Everywhere I went, the surprisingly large and heterogeneous community of fans of Ulysses Grant encouraged me. My interpretation of Grant will not please all of them, but I hope the fact that I have taken him seriously will. While disagreeing with his policy with respect to access to materials, I am much indebted to John Y. Simon, who has done a splendid job as editor of the published papers of Grant's early career.

It is a particular pleasure to say a word of thanks to the students in my Civil War and Reconstruction seminar. As they have climbed across our immense (and sturdy) table refighting Shiloh they have taught me much about Grant. Several of them have done prodigious and useful research on particular aspects of his career, and I especially want to mention Judi Sanzo, Christopher Clarke, Nancy Ledogar, Andrea Roschke, Michael Tomana, Harriet Winer, Carol Ann Drogus, Andrea Mattei, Brenda Tinker, and Monique Chireau. Another historian, Eliza McFeely, contributed much to the book's preparation, as did Kathleen Heath and Dorothy Snow.

Conversations with historians like Russell Weigley, Robert Schwartz, and Willie Rose, in sometimes brief but often critically important moments, were of great assistance. R. Hal Williams and Howard C. Westwood read the whole of the manuscript in an earlier draft, and their patient and thorough criticism was immensely valuable, as was that of Adolf Wood. My editors at Norton have been excellent; James Mairs has been wonderfully steadfast and Esther Jacobson's disciplined hand greatly strengthened the book. Joseph Ellis's candid and constant encouragement was indispensable, and Sarah Youngblood, Marjorie Kaufman, and Mary McFeely labored over the manuscript with more skill and love than its author deserved.

W.S.M.

_York, Maine_
_August 1980_

# Introduction

... it is not right for a writer to enjoy or not enjoy her characters. A writer writes what she sees.

— *Lillian Hellman*

W H Y  G R A N T ?  This question was asked of me many times while I was writing this book. Ulysses Grant is, after all, a curious choice for the subject of a biography if the writer is not an admirer of warfare and is not inordinately fascinated by political corruption. I came to him neither because I had discovered some extraordinary mass of evidence that would enable me to greatly revise accounts of the events of his career nor because I had manufactured an intricate theory that would enable me to claim that I had found a "new" Grant. No amount of revision is going to change the way men died at Cold Harbor, the fact that men in the Whiskey Ring stole money, and the broken hopes of black Americans in Clinton, Mississippi, in 1875.

As the reference to Clinton suggests, one subject of great interest to me that did draw me to Grant was that of race relations. Black people were, in overwhelming numbers, enthusiastic partisans of his, and the immensely popular president went into office with a Supreme Court and a Congress also of his party. The opportunity for Reconstruction would seem to have been immense. I have never been satisfied with existing explanations of why hopes for Negro advancement were so high when Grant moved into the White House, and so low eight years later. In the book considerable attention is given to discussing how it was that the opportunity for Reconstruction was not, in the main, taken; but even the examination of Grant's role in racial matters, as important as I believe it to be, is not justification for a biography.

What I found compelling about Grant as a subject for a biography was the man himself. I liked the way he looked; the picture of the mild, rather small person slouched comfortably in front of a tent suggested neither the fierce killing warrior nor the bumbling and perhaps crooked politician that I had often read about. Looks can be deceiving, of course, but they are not necessarily so. There is almost no glamour in the figure; despite the attempts of countless eulogists, he cannot be made into a Wellington or a Napoleon. It is significant that Grant himself was nicely crotchety about such comparisons, particularly those to Napoleon, whom he detested. There was in Grant neither the sensuous power of the Corsican nor the force of the Iron Duke. He was a more relentless warrior than either and yet remained the ordinary man seen in his pictures.

What was such a man doing commanding the armies of the Republic and then serving as its president? There are historians who, when asked to contemplate Grant, insist that he must have had some secret greatness, hidden within him, that allowed him to accomplish what he did. They speak of the quality almost as if it were some special organ implanted in the bodies of a particular few. I leave to others the problem of accounting for a Mozart or a Marx, but I am convinced that Ulysses Grant had no organic, artistic, or intellectual specialness. He did have limited though by no means inconsequential talents to apply to whatever truly engaged his attention. The only problem was that until he was nearly forty, no job he liked had come his way—and so he became general and president because he could find nothing better to do.

This seemingly flippant remark is made out of respect for the dilemma posed by Ulysses Grant. He had, all along, ideas and a sense of himself that he could make no one notice. Those who search the past exclusively for greatness are frequently unmindful of the extent to which ideas fill the minds of ordinary people. Those who look at such men and women collectively may be aware of the general needs and aspirations of various groups, but only the best of the social historians and the historians of local politics seem conscious of the complexity of concern of the individuals within the groups and of the attendant frustration when that concern cannot be heard. People assume that had fame not come to them, Ulysses and Julia Grant—being unheard— would have had nothing to say.

The Grants never thought of themselves as ordinary. They endured humiliating personal defeats, and yet they ached to be reckoned with. But neither in St. Louis in the 1850's nor in Galena in 1860 did it seem at all likely that Grant would find a reprieve from the listlessness that people, if they noticed him at all, saw in his face. To Julia it did seem likely, and by rights this book should be a joint study of both of them. Unfortunately, Grant does not seem to have saved his wife's letters, and we have information about her life in too disproportionate a share to make a joint study valid. But I hope the importance of Julia in the Grant story is nowhere lost.

It is, finally, a story of the quest of an ordinary American man in the mid-nineteenth century to make his mark. Grant failed as a peacetime army officer, a farmer, a minor businessman, a store clerk—and still he wanted to be taken into account. So he went to war, as did hundreds of thousands of men like him. Luck (his more or less accidentally having gone to West Point), the ruthlessly realistic common sense of someone who never had any patience with theory, and an uneven but remarkable degree of self-confidence enabled Grant to make a very great mark in the terrible American Civil War. The resources, hitherto useless, on which he drew to win the war had been within him all along. What was lacking in Grant—and its absence, paradoxically, may have been what enabled him to be sufficiently ruthless with his soldiers' lives to achieve the victory—was an ability to speak for the men of his army, who were just as trapped as he had been. Nevertheless, those who had gone off to war with him could see in his success a glimmer of their own hopes. They were celebrating their own dreams when they cheered Grant—and gave him the presidency.

I would not argue that the Civil War was fought so that Grant and his colleagues could have a purposeful activity, but I do think Americans should face the perhaps unattractive fact that whether it was fought to end slavery or to preserve the Union, that war was also an outlet for emotional—animal, if you will—energy, an outlet that the society otherwise failed to provide in sufficient measure. Grant's story yields a troubling picture of an America, often represented as in a period of boundless opportunity, that offered him and thousands of men like him no chance for fulfillment other than war. If his story gives us a troubling look at society, it also forces us to look at the individual and ask what he himself did and did not bring to his quest, for once Grant gained attention, he dared not go back into the ranks and make common purpose with the men from whom he came. He had been so close to total failure that having moved out front, he could not risk giving up an inch for fear that he might fall all the way back. Once he had become general, he had to go on to be president, and once his time as president was up, he had, again, no idea what to do with himself. But the difference was that he had heard those cheers and he could not do without them.

# G R A N T

---

. . . he is the concentration of all that is American.
— *Theodore Lyman, 1864*

No American has carried greater fame out of the White House
than this silent man who leaves it today.
— *James A. Garfield, 1877*

# *I*

# CROWDS AND FAMILIES

When the General finishes . . . those who have bellowed themselves
hoarse, make themselves still hoarser.
                    — *Newcastle Daily Chronicle, September 24, 1877*

U L Y S S E S  G R A N T loved the sound of a crowd. The strangely silent
hero heard its roar perhaps more often than any other American and in places
all around the world. Once, on September 22, 1877, in Newcastle, in the
north of England, some eighty thousand working people crowded special
trains, jammed the railroad station, and pressed through the streets and out
onto the town moor to become part of a great parade in honor of the American. Miners from the collieries with pictures of pit boys on their banners,
tailors with pictures of Adam and Eve on theirs, metalworkers from the ship-
yards, carpenters, masons "massive in physique, strong in numbers, and
walking solidly and steadily four abreast like trained soldiers," sawyers, and
tanners marched past the visiting general. The painters carried a "picture
representing the breaking of the chains of slavery, with the inscription, 'Welcome to the Liberator' . . . adorned with bunches of fresh, green fern." The
people came to welcome one of their own. In their England democracy had
not yet been perfected, but here among them was a man who looked like
them and who had left the stink of a tannery to lead the hosts of secular righ-
teousness against the holders of slaves. First as general and then as president,
Grant had been at the head of a nation they imagined to be a beacon of
goodness ready to call in all who sought to live in freedom.[1]

At last Ulysses Grant was loved as he needed to be loved. He stood "open-browed, firm-faced, bluff, honest and unassuming," before huge crowds of people and "everybody at once settled in his own mind that the General would do. The cheers became warmer as that quiet, strong, thoroughly British face grew upon them; and as they increased General Grant, who had at first merely touched his hat to the multitude, bared his head, as an unmistakable every-body-joins-in-it 'Hurrah' roared out from fifty thousand throats, and rattled to the astonished birds circling overhead."[2]

Only a few could hear his quiet voice as he rose, to "return thanks to the working men of Tyneside." To the meeting's chairman he said, "I accept from that class of people the reception which they have accorded me, as among the most honorable I can receive. We all know that but for labor we would have but very little that is worth fighting for, and when wars do come, they fall upon the many, the producing class, who are the sufferers. They not only have to furnish the means largely, but they have, by their labor and industry, to produce the means for those who are engaged in destroying and not in producing." The local newspaper reported his speech as follows: " 'I was always a man of peace, and I have advocated peace, although educated a soldier. I never willingly, although I have gone through two wars, of my own accord advocated war. (Loud Cheers) I advocated what I believed to be right, and I have fought for it. . . .' " Grant had seldom been so outspoken, even with platitudes, but seldom had the call to speak been so compelling. Although there had often been great crowds, there had been none as giving as this one: "The vast concourse, still rushing up from the turnpike . . . estimate the unheard speech after their own thoughts, and applaud every now and again with might and main. When the General finishes . . . those who have bellowed themselves hoarse, make themselves still hoarser. . . ."[3]

These were indeed his people. He was one of them. But Grant had fooled them all. He had been denying them—denying himself—all his life. He believed that if he did not make that denial, he would be nothing but an anonymous failure lost in some similar American crowd. Instead of remaining with them, he had forced himself out of the world of ordinary people by the most murderous acts of will and had doomed himself to spend the rest of his life looking for approval for having done so. It was not that Ulysses Grant did not like other ordinary people. On the contrary, he was always entirely comfortable with them, whether among the crowds in Newcastle or in an army camp. He had the remarkably rare gift of being able to talk to any other man who happened to be sitting on a log along a wartime road. The problem was that he did not trust himself to remain in conversation with the man whose language he could speak. He did not dare embrace the comradeship of those marchers, those producers, those people, because he was afraid they would march off and leave him behind. So he had to push past them all, and when he had gone by them, he was very lonely.

In his *Memoirs* Grant chose to open his version of his lifelong struggle with a firm declaration: "My family is American, and has been for generations, in all its branches, direct and collateral." This was his way of saying that the rock on which he built was steady. He was trying, from the start, to put off anyone who might doubt that his life was solid. He had been trying for all his years to convince himself of that uncertain fact. It was as if having asserted firmly, in print, that he was confident of the world from which he came, he would at last be comfortable in the place which he had reached. Or, at least, he hoped to persuade us that he was.[4]

The *Memoirs* was meant to suggest constant strength, generation after generation. His deft genealogical sketch is accurate until the point in the chronicle when his own memory intrudes. Then, with his account of his grandfather, he begins to get the story wrong, and the ground shifts under him. The Grants had not been constantly successful; instead of a steady generation-by-generation movement ahead, the family had experienced terrifying decline, and Grant spent his life erecting defenses against a repetition of that collapse in his own life. More often than not, his defenses crumbled. The image of a man, stolid and of infinite poise, that he put before the public fooled almost everyone save Grant himself. Courageously, at the end of his life, when failure was again a reality, he tried one last time to achieve solidity. He wrote a fine book—but it was the only truly firm stone in the building.

Before he got to the book, he had been through a lifetime of great contrasts between anonymous failure and vast public acclaim, and only a relentless plunge into the obscene exhilaration of war enabled him to achieve what others perceived to be a steady grasp on the world. This ordinary American man, with seven generations of Americans behind him, had thus gotten his grip at a terrible cost to a great many other ordinary Americans. What was more, the country that his war had so greatly changed was as uncertain of its ground as Ulysses Grant, the man who best symbolized it, was of his.

He was correct in suggesting that the Grants had made their start in America with assurance. Matthew and Priscilla Grant came on the *Mary and John* in 1630. Matthew Grant, in his twenties, helped mark out the lands of his town, Dorchester (now a part of Boston), and himself owned land and two cows and was in full communion with the church. Less than five years later, however, joining fellow townspeople, Grant traveled through the wilderness of central New England to found a second town, Windsor, on the Connecticut River. There he held two essential public posts, those of town clerk and surveyor. His hand gave people their place in the records of the world; his eye established the limits of their land. For forty years, according to "Rules which I have larned by experanc in practis for helpes in measuring land," he marked the boundaries of farms as families increased and lots had to be multiplied in number and divided in size. Litigious New Englanders were beholden to their town surveyor, who established their property lines; Matthew Grant was an important man. What was more, his will suggests that his farm was profitable.[5]

Matthew Grant was also a man of intellect. His diary is an elegant record of a Puritan grappling with his relationship to God through his own poetry, and—in orderly notes—through the sermons of learned clergymen like Thomas Hooker, of nearby Hartford. Matthew Grant had a long life—he died in 1681—and no one in the family since has matched his ability to define, with intellectual precision, the boundaries of his world. When, two hundred years later, Ulysses Grant wrote about the Mexican War and the Civil War, his control of a martial world was as firm as Matthew's had been of Heaven and Windsor, but he lacked his ancestor's range of contemplation. The theological and intellectual world Matthew Grant had lived in so intensely was gone.[6]

Matthew's eldest son, Samuel, as a member of the second generation, had to find his land outside town, to the east. There, in East Windsor, Matthew's grandson, a second Samuel, and his great-grandson, Noah, were born. In 1718 this first Noah Grant was among the men who moved still farther from the river onto the beautiful but rocky Connecticut hills which resist farming. In their town, which they called Tolland, two more generations of Grants were born.[7]

The family continued to hold a relatively secure place in these communities until one of its men went to war. The Grants had been lucky in avoiding King Philip's War, but eighty years later the second Noah Grant left his wife, Susanna Delano, and went off with his bachelor brother, Solomon, to fight in the French and Indian War. Captain Noah Grant led a company of Connecticut men—"Solo[mo]n Sipio and Jupiter Negro, Caleb Talcutt and Thomas Ellsworth" among them—through the bitter cold of the winter of 1755–56 to northern New York, on the Crown Point expedition. Fine storytelling has given this hazardous expedition historical glamour; contemporaries honored the men as well. In the spring of 1756 the Connecticut legislature passed a special bill awarding Noah Grant and Israel Putnam thirty and fifty Spanish dollars, respectively, for "Ranging and Scouting the winter past; for annoyance of the Enemy near Crown Point & Discovering their motives." Putnam's luck held till another war, but the Grants' did not. Solomon was killed in June 1756, and the following September, Noah died in action. His widow was left so destitute that she took her children—among them her eight-year-old eldest son, the third Noah, Ulysses' grandfather—to live with relatives across the mountain in Coventry.[8]

That Noah Grant was given an important place in adulatory biographies of his grandson, in which he was presented as a hero of the Revolution and hence could be seen as a fit ancestor for the hero of the War of the Rebellion. Grant himself placed his grandfather at both Lexington and Concord and credited him with having "served through the entire Revolutionary War." Other writers speak of him as having "fought gallantly." But although his grandson remembered tales that stretched from Bunker Hill to Yorktown, it is unlikely that Noah Grant of Coventry, Connecticut, ever went off to fight against King George at all. Whether the stories of his military adventures were originated by Noah or were made up for him is not clear. In the frequently repeated accounts of Noah as Captain Noah Grant of the Revolutionary War, the details are always vague. The references to him as captain are probably the result of confusion arising from his father's having held that rank in the French and Indian War, for the carefully maintained records of the Connecticut State Library reveal no service in the Revolution by this Noah Grant. The equally complete records of the National Archives tell of only one Noah Grant who fought in the Revolution, a militiaman from Lyme, New Hampshire, who took part in the attack on Quebec in 1775. The New Hampshireman's distant cousin, Ulysses Grant's grandfather—"Captain Noah" only in legend—apparently stayed in Coventry.[9]

Noah Grant is mentioned only nominally in the town-meeting records of Coventry. He was born in 1748 and married Anne Richardson, who bore two sons. He is said to have been a cobbler as well as a farmer, and in the precarious economy of the 1780's, he speculated in land in Coventry and, possibly, in the Susquehanna Lands in Pennsylvania to which Connecticut men held claims. On September 24, 1788, the sheriff of Tolland County was ordered "to take the body of said [Noah Grant] and commit unto the keeper of the gaol" until he paid a fifty-three-pound debt, plus costs. A sentence to debtor's prison, the grim certificate of failure feared by hill-town farmers throughout western New England, had come to Noah Grant. In December he sold his farm to a relative for four hundred pounds and, presumably, cleared either the debt for which he was jailed or a second one incurred to escape jail. He owned other lands as well but lacked the cash to farm them, and by early 1790 he had sold ten parcels, worth nine hundred pounds, and moved west. He left behind his grown elder son and the grave of his wife, high on beautiful Grant Hill.[10]

Taking with him his younger son, Peter, Noah Grant traveled across Connecticut and New York to Pennsylvania, where he settled in Westmoreland County, near Greensburg. There in 1792 he married Rachel Kelly. They had five children, the second of whom was Ulysses Grant's father, Jesse Root Grant, born January 23, 1794. In 1799, with Rachel pregnant with her sixth child, the family traveled down the Monongahela and the Ohio rivers past Pittsburgh to settle across the Ohio border in East Liverpool. There two more children were born. In 1804 Noah moved the family again, to Deerfield, Ohio, and a year later, Rachel Kelly Grant died. Her grave is "in the cemetery at the Center"; if there was a stone, it does not survive. In Deerfield, Noah made shoes, and he is said to have worked alongside Indians, still numerous at that time in this region of northeastern Ohio. Legend has it that he drank with them as well.[11]

With the death of Rachel Kelly Grant came a collapse of the family myth that the stability of Connecticut was maintained in the move west. The Grants were so poor that the family had to be broken up. Noah Grant could not provide for his children, and they were either put in the care of more prosperous relatives or, as Jesse was at age eleven, apprenticed. This disruption had long-reaching effects on the relationship between Noah's son Jesse and Jesse's son Ulysses. Jesse lived first with George Tod of Youngstown, a contentious, vigorous politician from whom he may have gotten his taste for political argument. But apparently, the apprentice was free to detach himself from his arrangements with Tod, for he left Ohio and went down the river to join his half brother Peter Grant, who was prospering in the tanning business in the busy town of Maysville, Kentucky. Jesse had almost no formal schooling. He became apprenticed to Peter, learned the business, and continued in it as an adult.[12]

Jesse Root Grant used the land differently than had his father and their forebears. He neither speculated in properties nor farmed, but instead extracted from the land that which was commercially valuable. Gone was his father's handicraft of shoemaking, and in its place was the manufacture of leather. Jesse and his fellow Ohio Valley tanners were classic examples of the transformation of American frontier settlers from subsistence farmers dependent on village co-operation to entrepreneurs in a capitalist economy of distinct functions and competitive marketing. He worked hard and made other men work equally hard tanning leather cheaply and selling it profitably. Having learned from his half brother in Maysville not only the process but more importantly the business, he returned to Deerfield to work in a tannery, then moved to Ravenna, where the signboard "Jesse Grant, tanner" marked the place of his business, and then went far down the river to Point Pleasant, Ohio.[13]

Business came first for the bachelor; he established his tannery in Point Pleasant. Then, at age twenty-seven, he married Hannah Simpson and settled in a small attractive house near the river. From its front door one looks to the right for a splendid prospect of the Ohio at one of its loveliest points. There, on April 27, 1822, was born Jesse and Hannah's first child, who was given the name Hiram Ulysses Grant. When the boy was eighteen months old, the family moved to the new town of Georgetown, away from the river and near good supplies of tanning bark.

Jesse Grant was always struggling to establish himself. Because of his early experiences, the comfortable idea that a family is a secure joining of people in a relationship of mutual affection was foreign to him. His boyhood had demonstrated just the opposite—that relatives could not be trusted to provide security—and for him a family became a form of property, necessary for achieving economic stability. As a deserted person, Jesse had to fight to build an economic base to keep him safe in the world. When his children were grown, he both expected them to sustain him and doubted that they could be relied on to do so. He used the children, and his wife, to consolidate his grasp on his small but tightly held economic position, and he was always suspicious that they would disappoint him in this enterprise. Two of his sons joined him

*Grant's birthplace, Point Pleasant, Ohio.* LIBRARY OF CONGRESS

in the leather business, and none of his daughters married until their brother Ulysses was so prominent that they no longer had to be kept tied to family duties. Then they found ambitious husbands. Then, too, Jesse could at last look to his eldest son for support. This son, Ulysses, spent his life alternately repudiating Jesse Grant's bleak world and trying to prove himself worthy of it.

Georgetown, a new county seat, was being developed when Jesse Grant moved there. On Cross Street, down the slope from the courthouse square (the courthouse itself was yet to be erected) he built his tannery and, very close by, his small but sturdy brick house. Business was good, but tanning was not a dainty trade. Hides came from animals which had been butchered and from aged animals which were penned, slaughtered, and skinned at the tanyard, with their carcasses then hauled away. The hides were cured in salt for storage, soaked in lye to loosen the hair, and placed in tubs of tannic acid to render them flexible and durable. The animals screamed as they died; the premises across a narrow street from Ulysses Grant's bedroom stank. The boy detested the tannery and often said so; his hatred of it was not merely a sentiment attributed to him by later genteel writers seeking to give their heroic Ulysses noble sensibilities.

The brick house Jesse originally built across the street from the tanyard consisted of a bedroom on top of a kitchen. Five years later he added a wing

larger than the original house, with a solidly respectable parlor and a hall in
which a straight-banistered staircase rose to two bedrooms above. This was
Ulysses Grant's home for sixteen years. Here too his sisters and brothers
were born: Samuel Simpson (known as Simpson) on September 23, 1825;
Clara Rachel on December 11, 1828; Virginia Paine (Jennie) on February 20,
1832; Orvil Lynch on May 15, 1835; and Mary Frances on July 30, 1839.

As the family grew, so too did Jesse Grant's interest in politics. Once a
Democrat (and always a Jacksonian), Jesse broke with the party and became a
Whig. He clashed on personal grounds with the dynamic red-headed Democratic congressman Thomas Hamer, whose promising career was ended by
his death in the Mexican War. Jesse was a Master of the Masonic lodge in
1830, and wrote doggerel about local politics for an abolitionist newspaper,
the Castigator. The writings are curiously revealing, with self-deprecation
disguising an off-pitch but fervent plea to be taken seriously. Occasionally he
was; he served one term (1837–39) as mayor of generally Democratic Georgetown.[14]

If we know something of Mayor Grant and his charmless, ambitious, contentious, and sometimes successful activities—both in business and, briefly,
in politics—we know remarkably little about his wife. Jesse Grant married
up when he married John and Rebecca Simpson's daughter, Hannah. The
Simpson family, which owned six hundred acres in the Ohio Valley, remained in close contact with their firmly established relatives in Berks
County, Pennsylvania, west of Philadelphia; by mail and with visits they retained their ties with the past in ways in which the Grants did not. The
Simpsons had let neither their gentility nor their deeply rooted piety lapse in
the move to the Ohio Valley. They were lettered people; indeed it was Hannah Simpson's stepmother—a splendid grandmother of whom Ulysses was
fond—who, inspired by her reading of a translation of Fénelon's neoclassic
epic Telemachus, provided the name for her Grant grandson.[15]

We actually know more about Ulysses Grant's maternal grandparents and
his uncles and aunts than we do about his mother. As general and president,
Grant was the subject of an enormous number of biographies and biographical sketches. His mother was alive all through the period of his active public
life—she died only two years before he did—and yet she is remarkably absent from these accounts. Her reserve, a trait her son was often said to have
derived from her, will not suffice to explain the fact that in America, with its
reverence for motherhood, the mother of a president of the United States
failed to visit the White House once while her son lived there. Yet in those
years she traveled from the Ohio Valley to New York. Reserve or even independence of spirit is insufficient to explain the absence of a visit so essential
as a demonstration of a son's respect for his mother. Neither is Jesse Grant's
description of his wife as "a plain unpretending country girl" convincing as
evidence that Hannah Grant felt too plain to be comfortable at 1600 Pennsylvania Avenue. Even if she had been rustic, plainer people than Hannah

Simpson have overcome their awe of the Executive Mansion; certainly, the Simpsons were not as crude as Jesse Grant, who himself enjoyed the White House.[16]

While Grant was president, a Cincinnati reporter crossed the river to Covington to interview his mother. No one had done so successfully, and the newspaperman was determined to get a story. He found the Grants' house, close to the curb of a narrow street, and rang; Hannah Grant, home alone, answered. She was dark-haired, slender, erect—and grimly severe. The reporter's excuse for the call was to get her to sign a tinted portrait of her son and thus certify the accuracy of the coloring. This she did, but he could not even report on the timbre of her voice; he heard only a yes and a no. Undaunted by the chill, he grew fulsome: "I think, madame, I am favored. . . . There are multitudes . . . who would be highly gratified to have an interview with the mother of General Grant." It did not work: "Not by a word or an expression . . . did she show that she even heard me."[17]

More gregarious souls than Hannah Grant have sometimes wished, after an interview, that they had handled reporters similarly. But one fears that she revealed something other than natural reticence or quick-witted wisdom in this encounter. There was something strange about her—something no one mentioned. Conceivably she was simple-minded, although it is difficult to imagine Jesse marrying a simple-minded woman and at the time of her death, one of her daughters made a point of mentioning that she had read her daily newspaper the day she died. Possibly Hannah Grant had a psychosomatic disorder; certainly she was shielded from the public by the family. Late in her life, Grant did take his children to visit "Grandma," proving that no acrimony had permanently separated her from him. Nevertheless, an uncommon detachment existed in the relationship of son to mother.[18]

Grant's *Memoirs* gives an uneven picture of his boyhood. He wrote no recollections of his mother's activities to balance his recital of those of his father—such as the story of a trip Jesse made to Connecticut to attempt, unsuccessfully, to reclaim after seventy years a bequest from his great-uncle Solomon, who had died in the French and Indian War. Other of Jesse's efforts to negotiate, which had indifferent success, caught Ulysses' pained attention, but there is little discussion in the book of what the parents hoped their children would achieve. Once his children were grown, Jesse Grant demanded much of them, and depended on them to enhance his sense of importance, but there is no evidence that while they were children he exploited their labor to the detriment of their education. They had time to go to school and to roam the countryside. Grant recorded no parental scolding or punishment, and Jesse would seem to have indulged the boy's disgust with his business and accepted the fact that he "did not like to work," at least to the extent of allowing him to substitute chores involving draft horses for tasks in the tannery. "When I was seven or eight years of age," recalled Grant, "I began hauling all the wood used in the house and shops. I could not load it on the wagons, of course, at that time, but I could drive, and the choppers would load, and some one at the house unload." By the time he was eleven he was plowing, and from then until he left home he did "all the work done with horses." He also farmed, sawed firewood, and each fall hauled a year's supply of wood for the house and tanyard "while," as he pointedly added, "still attending school."[19]

Grant went regularly to schools in Georgetown, which required the payment of tuition. One of the schools was across the street and a bit up the hill; another was a few blocks farther away. In 1836–37 he stayed with relatives in Maysville while attending the Richardson and Rand academy, competently conducted in the prosperous Kentucky river town by two schoolmen—one from New England, the other from Virginia. In 1838–39, he studied in Ripley, Ohio. His was a standard and sturdy education, remarkable neither for deficiencies nor excellence. He was sure-footed in arithmetic, recited, "A noun is the name of a thing . . . until [he] had come to believe it," and, generally, mastered a solid curriculum. Not his studies, however, but horses were Ulysses' greatest interest. Jesse regarded horses as a source of hides for his business; the boy saw them as wonderfully differentiated individuals. He could size up each animal that he encountered: master this one's truculence and urge that one to a feat of strength in hauling rock. His temperament was perfect for handling horses. There is a family legend that as a very young child he was able to toddle between horses' legs and flick their tails without making the sharp sounds or moves that caused such a practice to be dangerous for other children. His skill lay in controlling the animals and through ingenious and sensitive guidance getting them to perform varied tasks. Although it is clear that he rode well, there are fewer stories of Ulysses in the saddle for headlong dashes or feats of great endurance. He retained his unromantic understanding of horses throughout his life. He could exercise masterful control over them as he could not over himself or other people.[20]

One boyhood experience haunted Grant all his life. He referred to it often, usually giving the appearance of laughing it off; but something that must be laughed off repeatedly cannot be dismissed. It is recorded in his *Memoirs:*

> . . . a Mr. Ralston living within a few miles of the village, . . . owned a colt which I very much wanted. My father had offered twenty dollars for it, but Ralston wanted twenty-five. I was so anxious to have the colt, that after the owner left, I begged to be allowed to take him at the price demanded. My father yielded, but said twenty dollars was all the horse was worth, and told me to offer that price; if it was not accepted I was to offer twenty-two and a half, and if that would not get him, to give the twenty-five. I at once mounted a horse and went for the colt. When I got to Mr. Ralston's house, I said to him: "Papa says I may offer you twenty dollars for the colt, but if you won't take that, I am to offer twenty-two and a half, and if you won't take that, I am to give you twenty-five." It would not

require a Connecticut man to guess the price finally agreed upon. This story is nearly true. I certainly showed very plainly that I had come for the colt and meant to have him. I could not have been over eight years old at the time. This transaction caused me great heart-burning. The story got out among the boys of the village, and it was a long time before I heard the last of it. Boys enjoy the misery of their companions, at least village boys in that day did, and in later life I have found that all adults are not free from the peculiarity. I kept the horse until he was four years old, when he went blind, and I sold him for twenty dollars. When I went to Maysville to school, in 1836, at the age of fourteen, I recognized my colt as one of the blind horses working on the tread-wheel of the ferry-boat.[21]

In the *Memoirs*, Grant presented this incident as having provided a lesson well learned in his education as a maturing businessman, but actually it functioned in the opposite way. It reminded him every time he had business to do that he was not good at it, that he was still an embarrassable boy. What was more, he had been humiliated and mocked not for being discovered secretly doing something nasty, but for being innocent and open; in effect, he had been told that grown-up things, business things, were the affairs of men who laughed at boys who were direct about what they wanted. The mockery came not from the horse, but from the boys in town who feigned sophistication, from the owner of the horse, and very probably from his father, who without malice but with great ability to harm, may have laughed at the boy's ingenuousness. If the story is seen as demonstrating a second point, Ulysses' love of horses, the blinding of the animal sours the effect. "My colt"—that unspoiled beautiful mount—became a broken animal, and in the terrifyingly cruel end to which the creature had come Grant saw himself. The blinded beast walked nowhere in ceaseless drudgery. Trivial though the story of the purchase of the horse may seem, Grant spent a lifetime not getting over the transaction with Mr. Ralston.

As a boy—indeed, all his life—Grant was restless. He liked to get out and away from home often, and his competence with horses provided the means of doing so. If a Georgetown family had to make a trip, he was frequently hired as the driver. Sometimes by boat, and as often as possible when driving horses, he visited Louisville, Chillicothe, Maysville, and Cincinnati. Once, while taking a neighbor to Flat Rock, Kentucky, Ulysses spotted a fine horse and traded one of his own team for it on the spot, although the young animal had never been harnessed to a team. On the return trip, the new horse behaved until it was frightened by a dog. Ulysses calmed it and they went on, but on the turnpike into Maysville the horse became terrified by the twenty-foot embankment and began shaking uncontrollably. At this point the passenger (not surprisingly) hitched a ride with a freightman, and Ulysses, left alone, quieted the animal by blindfolding it with his bandanna. There was no sentimental wooing of the beautiful horse; instead he overcame his fear, and perhaps his dislike, by subduing the beast. And, in telling this tale of self-reliance, he pointed no moral about business acumen. His act was simply and importantly an assertion of power.[22]

These trips put Ulysses Grant in contact with slaves and slavery across the river in Kentucky. Years later his father claimed that he had refused to live in the slave South and had left Maysville, Kentucky, in order to raise his family on free soil, but the only contemporary evidence we have of Jesse's sympathies with the antislavery cause is the fact that he wrote for the *Castigator*. The paper was edited by David Ammen, whose son Daniel was Ulysses' schoolmate and friend. Ammen was a close associate of John Rankin, the staunch abolitionist who from his house in Ripley, high on a bluff overlooking the Ohio River and Kentucky beyond, aided runaway slaves. It was in this house that Harriet Beecher Stowe is said to have heard the story of one woman's wintertime escape on which she based the episode of Eliza crossing the ice in *Uncle Tom's Cabin*. But though this powerful literary image may have originated close by, there is no evidence that the slavery question was a critical one in the Grant household. The fact that Jesse Grant moved to Covington, in slaveholding Kentucky (after Ulysses had left home, to be sure), saps his claim of lifelong fervent avoidance of contamination by the peculiar institution.

Jesse Grant was largely self-taught, and it has been suggested that he was determined to give his eldest son the advantages he had lacked, to enable him to succeed through education. The extent of Ulysses' schooling, and his matriculation at West Point, tend to confirm this view. Yet Jesse seems not to have had similar aspirations for his other children, preferring that his daughters stay at home and that his other sons go into his business instead of continuing their education. He seems, in fact, to have admired them for so doing more than he admired his army-officer son. Indeed, apparently he despaired of making a tanner of Ulysses, wondered just what to do with him, and saw in the United States Military Academy a prestigious solution. When his overtures to Senator Thomas Morris for Ulysses' appointment failed, Jesse swallowed his pride and turned for help to his political rival Congressman Thomas Hamer. Perhaps he was less concerned about securing his son's future than about demonstrating his ability to pull strings in attaining the place. According to Grant, his father arranged the appointment without telling him that he was doing so and, when he did tell him, was not entirely sure the boy would accept it. "He thought I would go," Grant stated. West Point had a mixed press in Georgetown: Daniel Ammen's elder brother Jacob taught there; Bartlett Bailey, the richest boy in town, had been dismissed (and had been refused permission to come home by his father as a result). It was this dismissal that gave Ulysses his opportunity. West Point had undoubted charms for Jesse Grant. It was free, and it seemed to provide a secure future for his son. For Ulysses, going to the academy represented less the fulfillment of a career aspiration than a chance to get out of Georgetown: "I had always a great desire to travel."[23]

# II

# CADETSHIP AND COURTSHIP

I don't think we should ever dip into the professional military field for
our Presidents. . . . Their education does not fit them for the job at all.
To a graduate at West Point there is one prime objective in his training,
and that is how much that hill out there is worth in terms of casualties
to hold or to capture.

— *Alfred M. Landon*

You can have but little idea of the influance you have over me Julia,
even while so far away. If I feel tempted to do any thing that I think is
not right I am shure to think, "Well now if Julia saw me would I do so"
and thus it is absent or present I am more or less governed by what I
think is your will.

— *Ulysses S. Grant*

WHEN ULYSSES GRANT reached West Point in 1839 he was still a
boy. At seventeen he weighed 117 pounds and was five feet one inch tall. His
hair was sandy brown; his fair skin was freckled. His hands and feet were
small, and then, as later, his body was not tightly muscled but smoothly
turned. The journey to the academy had been exciting, with a canalboat portage of the Alleghenies and a first trip on the railroad from Harrisburg to
Philadelphia. There, in his first large city, he stayed with Simpson relatives
for five days, walking "about every street" in town and going to the theater.
Then, alone, he went on to New York, where he again walked the intriguing
streets. The experience was exhilarating, but he confessed later that he was
"dallying" because "I had rather a dread of reaching my destination at all."
When, finally, he made the trip up the Hudson Valley to West Point,
Ulysses Grant was as fresh faced and innocent looking as any new boy who
had ever walked into Roe's Hotel.[1]

Grant took advantage of his new start in life to tinker with his name. He
had always been called Ulysses—pronounced *U-lis-sis*—and so he now gave
his middle name first billing and wrote "U. H. Grant" on the hotel register.
He continued to use the name Ulysses H. Grant for some time after a congressman's haste had changed it for him. Thomas Hamer had had little time

in which to respond to Jesse Grant's urgings and make the appointment. He knew the boy as Ulysses and, needing a middle initial but forgetting that his name was Hiram, apparently recalled Mrs. Grant's maiden name and sent in an appointment for "Ulysses S. Grant." When the boy walked up from the hotel to register at the academy, he found on the roster appointments for two Grants—an Elihu Grant from New York State and a U. S. Grant from Ohio. He claimed the latter. Possibly he thought of correcting the name later, but he never did. Long before graduation and commissioning he was, irrevocably, U. S. Grant.[2]

The cadet from the little town in southern Ohio was strikingly unnoticeable, a not inconsiderable advantage for a plebe. His slight frame somehow did not invite the taunts of the more pernicious hazers. Unlike the many cadets who found the first year torture, Ulysses Grant complained merely that it was "wearisome and uninteresting." James Longstreet, proud of his massive physique, called Grant "delicate" and recalled that the man who became his powerful adversary in war had been too small to excel at any sport save riding, which he did exceedingly well. Grant amazed himself by doing well in his studies also. The thought of the academy had been intimidating and he had expected great rigor, but he passed his entrance examination "without difficulty, very much to my surprise" and in his courses did comfortable middling work. He did best in mathematics and least well in French, and in his second year at the academy stood tenth in a class of fifty-three. His

*West Point.* LIBRARY OF CONGRESS

performance is summed up well in his own words: "I never succeeded in getting squarely at either end of my class, in any one study during the four years."[3]

There was little intellectual incentive to do anything ambitious with the dreary courses. The curriculum was sluggish partially because no one had a clear picture of what the education of soldiers was all about. French, taught badly by rote, was studied so the cadets could read untranslated treatises on war by Napoleonic experts, but there was no course in which these works were systematically investigated. In classic American fashion, West Point, while giving some recognition to the need for military leadership, refused to face up to the fact that the ultimate aim of this leadership was to get men to kill. Only subversively, in a highly popular course on engineering, did Dennis Hart Mahan edge into this aspect of a military education. In 1843, the year Grant graduated, the term "Science of War" appeared in the course listings for the first time, but the subject was still taught as an adjunct to Mahan's course, in which the excitable high-voiced instructor preached his enthusiasm for war. He held a view of military history as progressive: since Thucydides, wars had been getting bigger and better, and finally his hero, Napoleon Bonaparte, had perfected the science. Mahan's interpretations were dependent largely on those of Antoine Henri Jomini, a Swiss student of war, and the professor's good students, most notably Henry Wager Halleck, with whom Grant later contested, learned from this authority to see the battlefield as a chessboard on which opposing forces, in complex deployment, faced each other. It was an abstract concept of war, and to the later good fortune of the United States Army, Ulysses Grant seems not to have been interested in the cold theories of Jomini and was repelled by Jomini's and Mahan's hero; perhaps he perceived in the small, controlled, frightening, foreign Bonaparte something too close to his own urges for comfort. Later he detested hearing himself likened to him. Professor Mahan was president of the Napoleon Club, of which George B. McClellan was an enthusiastic member; Grant did not join.[4]

Class distinctions at West Point were not troubling. Far from being a last bastion of aristocratic values, West Point seems to have had very few values at all. James Lunsford Morrison has pointed out that the cadets in Grant's time were drawn not from a rural gentry, but from the small-town bourgeoisie. Ulysses Grant, the Ohio town boy, was a more typical man of the academy than was Robert E. Lee of tidewater Virginia. West Point men were from families that were trying to gain advancement in position or to prevent slippage from a precarious place by having a son achieve—free—prestige that would open new doors. Some of both motivations were involved in Jesse Grant's decision to send his son to the academy. Initially, Ulysses also tried to see West Point in this light, declaring, in a comfortable letter to his cousin, written in his first fall at West Point, "On the whole I like the place very much. . . . The fact is if a man graduates here he safe fer life." Later that year his enthusiasm waned. Congress was debating abolition of the academy, and Grant hoped that it would be shut down.[5]

There was no action on this proposal in his first year, and by the time the legislation was introduced again, and failed, Grant no longer favored abolition. His change of mind, however, is not evidence that he had been reached by West Point's greatest lesson; he had not been converted to the academy's religious commitment to Duty, Honor, Country. The more devout West Point men saw the duties of their calling as apart from and above those of other pursuits in the Republic, but Grant would not have known what George S. Patton meant when he called West Point "a holy place." Of his years at the academy Grant wrote, "A military life had no charms for me," and in the West Point sense, it never did. Unlike many, Grant did not tangle himself emotionally in a knot of hatred and love for the great fortress of military virtue. He liked neither West Point nor peacetime army posts. It was war itself, not army life, that aroused Grant.[6]

"My pants sit as tight to my skin as the bark to a tree. And if I do not walk *military*, that is if I bend over quickly or run, they are very apt to crack with a report as loud as a pistol," he told his cousin, and there were other aspects of military life that were still more trying. Grant found the officer-class mentality unattractive, and was uncomfortable when he had to be the witness who quoted the offending words at the court-martial of a cadet who had called an officious cadet officer "a d....d shit ass." The pompous taking of such testimony in a pretentious trial exemplified, for Grant, the hollowness of the place. He himself became, of course, one of West Point's most illustrious graduates, but Grant Hall was named after him in the face of the fact that he had seldom been happy there. Years later, at a sour moment in the White House, he wrote a friend that he would "hail" the day he left public office "as the happiest of my life, except possibly the day I left West Point a place I felt I had been at always and that my stay had no end."[7]

Since he did not leave West Point, he had to find his own private escape within the school. In his *Memoirs* he wrote, "I did not take hold of my studies with avidity, in fact I rarely ever read over a lesson the second time during my entire cadetship. I could not sit in my room doing nothing. There is a fine library connected with the Academy from which cadets can get books to read in their quarters. I devoted more time to these than to books relating to the course of studies. Much of the time, I am sorry to say, was devoted to novels, but not those of a trashy sort." Here with his characteristic balance of boldness and conventionality, Grant credited himself with intellectual initiative and then, as quickly, apologized for it. Those books mattered to him; he felt it important to record his debt to them. They were good books, and reading them was fun. Grant read "all of Bulwer's [novels] then published" (which means, if the library was keeping up with the prolific Edward Bulwer-Lytton, nine historical novels), James Fenimore Cooper, Washington Irving, the naval adventure stories of Frederick Marryat, and the lively anecdotal novels of Charles Lever, the Irishman who wrote about exuberant young men traveling in Europe. Either the library's collection of Lever disappointed Grant, or (like the duke of Wellington) he enjoyed the Lever so much that he wanted his own copies of the novels. In the spring of his last year at the academy Grant twice urged Lever's American publisher to fill his order for *Charles O'Malley* and *Harry Lorrequer*. [8]

It is difficult to know how important this world of imaginative literature remained for Grant. In later life he disliked discussing literary matters, perhaps because of his lack of formal training or possibly because he liked the books themselves better than the talk about them. He was, for example, unwilling to admit his familiarity with literature in order to establish his intellectual credentials, even with a college president. His wife was both amused and dismayed when her famous husband returned from "a gentlemen's dinner party and . . . telling me of the events and bright witticisms of the evening, as he invariably did, . . . said: 'I am afraid I have ruined myself in the estimation of President —— [his host, whose name Julia left blank], who sat next to me at dinner . . . [and] at once began talking of books, mentioning one or two familiar names, and I—well, I looked as though if I had read that particular book I had forgotten it. After a while, he made some allusion to a character of Dickens. I was equally ignorant of poor little Oliver. So the old gentleman gave me up, and I enjoyed the rest of the evening.' " Julia Grant may have enjoyed her husband's account of his escape from a tedious conversation, but she knew it would carry a price: "You will hear of this, remember!" Julia was correct: ". . . sure enough, within a year after General Grant's death, Mr. —— did announce to his class that General Grant was no reader, citing the . . . incident as evidence."[9]

If Grant was at home with good novels, he never revealed in what ways they stirred him. We can only infer, from their contents, what his mind was invited to explore. Luckily, we have better evidence of where he was carried by another expression of his imagination, drawing and painting. In his second year Grant took a required course with one of the most remarkable teachers ever to be part of the West Point faculty—Robert Walter Weir, the drawing master between 1834 and 1876. Weir had two talented sons, John Ferguson Weir, a baby when Grant knew him, and Julian Alden Weir; all three were painters of greater ability than has been generally recognized. Robert Weir was an attractive man and a consummate teacher. His studio was a creative haven in the sterility of West Point routine. The cadet was required to study art so that as an officer he would be able to sketch the bridge needed to cross a river, and to render the lay of the land when planning a battle, but for Grant, at least, these reasons for the course fell away. Neither he nor Weir seems to have worried about the military usefulness of his drawings; not even perspective got much of a nod.

Weir's studio provided a road away from West Point concerns for a few hours. (Sometimes his students made the recess last; ten years after Grant's time, Weir taught James McNeill Whistler, who chose a deficiency in chemistry rather than great proficiency in art as his permanent route out of the academy: "Had silicon been a gas," he announced, "I would have been a major general.") A good many cadets drew well, and Grant was one of them. There is no more beautiful prospect than that seen from the bluff—the Plain—at West Point: the hills to the north grandly plunge down to the Hudson, "that beautiful river" as Grant put it, "with its bosom studded with hundreds of snow white sails." The view is one thing; the seemingly endless succession of nineteenth-century renderings of it is another. By 1840 Weir, recognizing how banal repeated representation could make even the most beautiful of places, appears to have directed his students to subjects farther away. Too bad. It would have been interesting to see how the river looked to Grant and more interesting still to see how the activities and the people of West Point appeared to him.[10]

Instead, Grant turned his imagination (and his pencil) toward Europe, no doubt under the influence of his teacher. Copying was the respectable way to learn drawing and painting, and Weir had studied in Rome and Florence. Grant had an aptitude for rendering, with considerable grace, Italianate landscapes and crowded marketplaces that bore little kinship to Georgetown, Ohio, or Maysville, Kentucky. There is a lack of originality, but not of curiosity, in his sketches of Old World towers and bridges, and there is a good deal of movement in the people, figured often at too great a distance for clarity, who move through his towns. But not all of his sketches were so genteel. Occasionally technical skill and an affinity for a subject came together well, as in the simple circular sweep of the shoulders and arms of an Indian woman holding a nursing child. (Both the trader and the Indian brave in this painting look surprisingly like the artist.) Another instance is his straightforward, witty painting of a draft horse. Although the legs of the little animal and the cart he pulls have the too charming look of a scene of peasant life one might bring back as a souvenir from Europe, the horse's head, bent low into a feeding bag, conveys the heft of a real animal. This is neither the gleaming stallion of a romantic vision nor a picturesque Sicilian donkey, but rather an overharnessed little beast that Ulysses Grant has under perfect control.[11]

A horse that gave Grant at least equal pleasure was the one his father gave him to ride during the summer furlough after his second year at West Point, a time "I enjoyed beyond any other period in my life." His family had moved to Bethel, Ohio, and the change was disconcerting for Grant, who had known no home other than Georgetown, twelve miles away. His father had bought an unbroken horse for him to master and ride while on leave. Here was a challenge and an opportunity for some fun. Knowing no one in Bethel save his siblings and parents, he used the horse as an excuse not to spend much time there. Instead, with old friends in Georgetown and a powerful young animal saddled beneath him, he had a perfect world. His home became not a place of confinement, but a comfortable base from which to roam, and he found "these ten weeks shorter than one at West Point."[12]

*Painting done by Ulysses S. Grant while a cadet at West Point, now at the United States Military Academy.* PHOTOGRAPH COURTESY LIBRARY OF CONGRESS

With Grant's immense fondness for horses, there can be little doubt that he was disappointed when upon graduation he was not assigned to the branch of service which was his first choice, the cavalry. He held up the tailor, hoping, to the last minute, that he could order a dragoon's uniform rather than the less splendid clothes of an infantry officer. Grant feared making a fool of himself in negotiations and except for an unforceful letter written in the fall after graduation, requesting, unsuccessfully, a transfer to the cavalry, he did no politicking for the preferred assignment. Once, that fear of asserting himself ineptly had spoiled a fantasy. General Winfield Scott, six feet five and massive, in splendid uniform and with vast military dignity, had been reviewing the corps of cadets. "I thought him the finest specimen of manhood my eyes had ever beheld," Grant wrote, "and the most to be envied. I could never resemble him in appearance, but I believe I did have a presentiment for a moment that some day I should occupy his place on review. . . ." Grant quickly dispatched the dream: "My experiences in a horse-trade ten years before, and the ridicule it caused me, were too fresh in my mind for me to communicate this presentiment to even my most intimate chum." Minor childhood agonies were not after all minor.[13]

In Grant's view, his graduation from West Point did not establish his life's work. Almost immediately after receiving his commission, he was planning to resign from the army after the obligatory tour of duty as a second lieutenant (a customary practice of West Point graduates), but he had neither the assurance nor the inclination to enter his father's world of business. Taller now—he had grown six inches and stood five feet seven—he was, at graduation, not in good health. When he got home to Ohio, he was down to the 117 pounds he had weighed four years earlier and was suffering from a respiratory ailment that made him fear tuberculosis, which had killed two uncles. The illness proved unimportant, however, and soon Grant put the splendor of West Point to the test. He dressed in his well-cut new uniform for a visit to Cincinnati and rode proudly down into town. On the main street, a little boy looked up and Grant expected admiration. Instead the child mocked the splendid warrior: "Soldier! will you work? No, sir-ee; I'll sell my shirt first!!" Grant never again counted on a smart uniform to give him self-confidence.[14]

Although Ulysses Grant had been comfortable among the men with whom he lived at West Point, he developed no prescient friendships with those who were later famous. William Tecumseh Sherman and George H. Thomas were in their fourth year when Grant was in his first, and he was in his fourth year when George B. McClellan and Thomas J. Jackson entered. But Grant had no instinct or capacity for cultivating useful people, and those who had such inclinations did not find him worthy of their efforts. However, the parade of personalities did not escape his notice; Grant took in more than people realized, and he remembered things about men who, for their part, never noticed him at all. What he retained was not a sense of how to make these men useful to him, but rather a feeling for their capabilities. After Grant himself became famous, awkward claims of intimacy with him were made by many army officers whose remarks exposed them as unable even to recall his face. The evidence of later intimacy suggests that Grant may have been close to Simon Bolivar Buckner, a year behind him, and he roomed with the not very illustrious Rufus Ingalls, who later capitalized a bit on their long friendship. In his last year at West Point, Grant shared a room with Frederick Tracy Dent, and after graduation, both Grant and Dent were assigned to the Fourth Infantry Regiment, stationed at the Jefferson Barracks, outside St. Louis. The assignment pleased Dent since his family's place, White Haven, was nearby. There was a great deal of free time, and Ulysses Grant soon was spending most of it with Fred Dent—and his sister Julia—at White Haven. Eventually, honoring an old American custom, he married his roommate's sister.

Julia Dent during her lifetime turned White Haven in her imagination into a kind of Tara. She wrote in her *Memoirs* of an Edenic world on the family plantation:

> . . . my time and sister Nellie's was passed mostly out-of-doors. I had my nurse, dear old black Kitty, and Nell had Rose, a pretty mulatto. Besides, we always had a dusky train of from eight to ten little colored girls of all hues, and these little colored girls were allowed to accompany us if they were very neat. . . .

*Lieutenant Grant at twenty-one.* LIBRARY OF CONGRESS

Once, when I was nine years old, I . . . had wandered far up the brook and deeper than usual into the woods when we came upon a beautiful, shadowy, moss-covered nook. My little maids exclaimed: "Oh! Miss Julia! Have this for your playhouse, and we will mark it out with all the pretty stones we can find." Hastening to the brook they gathered all the "petrified honeycomb" and round boulders they could find, placing these so as to mark the supposed walls of my mansion.[15]

An intensely romantic vision of the past was of enormous value to Julia Grant. She was determined to make people see her as the center of a luxurious world in which she could command absolute attention. It was critical to her image of herself that people not recognize the plain truth of her life, about which she had never complained but against which she had relentlessly struggled. If she could make her girlhood beginnings at White Haven seem idyllic, then perhaps people would think the troubles she faced as a young woman had been just a minor interlude before all dreams came true for her in the White House. Julia sought to justify her hunger for that glamorous place by suggesting that her origins made it inevitable that she be there. Her need to be thought of as someone who had always counted was similar to Ulysses' even if she expressed it in very different rhetoric. While he spoke in his own plain speech, she surrendered her personal voice and spoke instead with the intense sentimentality with which women of her class and time disguised rather than revealed their feelings.

Julia knew she was expected to be a dutiful daughter, and her references to her parents were entirely respectful. Ellen Bray Wrenshall Dent and Frederick Dent—"my gentle, beautiful mother and noble father, of whom I was always *so* proud"—had reached Missouri before 1820. According to family legend, they came part of the way along the Ohio River from Pittsburgh on a flotilla of rafts on which cabins had been built as living quarters. The rafts were manned by Dent, his good friend George Tracy, and two slaves. The rest of the way, it was said, they came in a fine carriage. White Haven, twelve miles outside St. Louis, where Julia grew up, was thought of as an ancestral Maryland home transferred west—along with all the mores and some of the slaves! "Most of our old colored people were from Virginia and Maryland, and papa used to buy for them great barrels of fish—herring from that part of the country." With her bow to her father's generosity, Julia sought to make her readers understand that her family had been rich enough to own and command slaves and kindly enough to treat them with whimsical largesse.[16]

Actually, the Dents were at least two generations removed from the old South; Julia's grandfather lived in the western town of Cumberland, Maryland, and the aristocratic transfer to White Haven was preceded by detours into trade in Pittsburgh and again in St. Louis, where the money was made to buy the farm. Julia liked to see her origins as above commerce. She recalled her father as saying, "My daughter, the Yankees that have come west have reduced business to a system. Do you know now if a man wants a loan of a few thousand dollars for a few days—God bless you!—they want a note and interest." (He was describing her future father-in-law with precision.) Colonel Dent, for his part, loved the "repose of a country life." He was, in fact, a splendidly lazy old codger.[17]

But Julia's mother "hated the country and this place [White Haven] especially." In this one phrase the canvas is cut from the frame and the idyllic picture of Ellen Dent as the happy chatelaine of White Haven is gone. She had expected better than a Missouri farm, having ridden on horseback from Pittsburgh to Philadelphia, in its greatest days, to go to school. The trip, after all, did not take her to a great future. However, en route she did move into a world of romance. The story goes that she stopped exhausted at a tavern only to find Aaron Burr and his traitorous men already there: "Mamma, though much fatigued, was very loath to lie on the settle, or bench, before them all to rest until they pressed around and made for her a bed and a pillow of their cloaks and begged her to rest, telling her she would be just as safe there as in her mother's arms. Lying down at last, they covered her with another martial cloak, and she slept as soundly as the princess in the fairy tale." (Safe in the keep of the most lustful prince of American history? It was an odd reverie.) Deprived of Colonel Burr, Ellen Wrenshall went back to Pittsburgh after her schooling and settled for Colonel Dent, who later, at White Haven, "gave up all occupation and passed his time in the summer months sitting in an easy chair reading an interesting book, and in the winter, in the chimney corner beside a blazing hickory fire, occupied in the same way." When not reading, he could be counted on to pontificate on politics. As the years went on, praise for Jackson and Benton yielded to apologias for the Confederacy, and these grew no less fervent when, in his eighties, he moved in with the enemy at 1600 Pennsylvania Avenue.[18]

The colonel's daughter, Julia, attended the Misses Mauros' boarding school in St. Louis, studied a bit of philosophy and history, and read not only Oliver Goldsmith's *Vicar of Wakefield* but some of the same novels that Ulysses read at West Point. But Julia was not well educated. In her *Memoirs* and in conversation she could introduce an interesting line of thought, but she could not sustain it. She did have a pleasant manner of speaking, and getting along with people was no problem; a perceptive granddaughter called her "childishly intense." Physically, she was powerful; although she felt compelled to pretend a fluttering femininity, her fondest recollections were of an open outdoors world. She engaged in conventional competition with her sister Ellen (Nellie) in flirting with suitors, but it was her brothers whom she most admired and wanted to emulate: "My four dear brothers, John, George, Fred and Louis,* were brave fellows . . . and they were wonderful athletes too—such leaps, handsprings, pitching of quoits, as papa, mamma, Nell and I used to witness from the front piazza!"[19]

Julia got off the piazza as often as a girl could. She loved to fish. "Oh! what happiness to see that nibble," she wrote, remembering her very early childhood, "to feel the pull, and to see the plunge of the cork; then the little quivering, shining creature was landed high on the bank." Quickly and carefully, in her *Memoirs*, she re-established her femininity by noting that there was always a slave or a brother present to remove the fish from the hook. As she got older, she fished and hunted with her brothers and rode horseback with her sister. Once, coming to the Gravois when it was swollen with rain, they "stood confounded, watching the waters fairly laughing at us." Julia said they could ford the stream on faith. Nellie asked what faith was; Julia, replying, "Little goose, believe you can and you can," pushed her horse ahead through chest-high water and "went on . . . to the other side and scrambled up the bank. . . ."[20]

The first of Fred Dent's sisters whom the pleasant-looking sandy-haired

*Julia chose the French form of her brother's name when referring to Lewis Dent.

young lieutenant met was Ellen, but when Julia got back from St. Louis she set her cap for Ulysses. Julia was no beauty; even at seventeen her figure was stumpy, she had more neck than chin, and she suffered from strabismus. A malfunctioning muscle caused her right eye to move up and down involuntarily. She was no match for her mother in appearance, and she knew it. As she was putting on a new dress one day, the "colored maids said . . . 'Oh, young Missus, you are looking very pretty, but you never will come up to Old Missus in looks.' " But Julia was lively and, when Ulysses arrived, determined. "Such delightful rides we all used to take!" she recalled; the "Lieutenant rode a bonny little brown steed with flowing wavy mane and tail. He called him Fashion. My horse was a beauty, a chestnut brown, and as glossy as satin, and such pretty ears and great eyes. She was part Arabian, and I named her Psyche. Such rides! in the early spring, the tender young foliage scarcely throwing a shadow." The two were together daily. As Julia remembered it: "He was always by my side, walking or riding." Ulysses recalled (with a bit of unexpected humor) social visits which had been their excuse for going off together: "We would often take walks, or go on horseback to visit the neighbors, until I became quite well acquainted in that vicinity."[21]

They were in love. They barely knew what that meant until a day came when, on the next, they would not be able to see each other. Ulysses was going to Ohio on leave, with the prospect that his regiment would soon be given a new assignment. Julia recalled that before leaving Missouri, Ulysses "spent the whole day. . . . As we sat on the piazza alone, he took his class ring from his finger and asked if I would not wear it." Julia first responded with the passivity of the flirtatious Southern belle: "Oh, no, mamma would not approve of my accepting a gift from a gentleman." But later she leaped to determined action to establish the relationship; after Grant had gone from her house but before she was certain he had actually left the post, she "felt very restless," ordered her horse, and "rode alone toward the Barracks, not feeling afraid." There, she wrote, "I halted my horse and waited and listened." But Grant was indeed gone: "So I rode slowly and sadly home."[22]

At home she found friends who had come to spend the night: "When we young ladies retired, Josephine S. and I slept in my new bed and, according to custom, named the bedposts, and of course my absent friend was not forgotten." Seventy years later, D. W. Griffith, as innocent of Freud as Julia had been, used this same image—the grasping of a stout tall bedpost—for Lillian Gish's declaration of sexual arousal in *Birth of a Nation;* nineteenth-century life anticipated twentieth-century art. That earlier night, as Julia remembered it, "I did dream of Mr. Grant."[23]

When Grant returned from his brief leave in Ohio, he found that his regiment had left for Louisiana. He immediately headed for White Haven. The Gravois Creek, which he had to cross, usually had less water in it than it takes "to run a coffee mill," but it was now swollen from springtime rains. Grant's recollections of that day reveal not only his ardor for Julia but a fundamental philosophy that goes far in explaining the Grant of Vicksburg and Petersburg—and of Appomattox and the gaining of the presidency: "One of my superstitions had always been when I started to go anywhere, or do anything, not to turn back, or stop until the thing intended was accomplished. I have frequently started to go to places where I had never been and to which I did not know the way, depending upon making inquiries on the road, and if I got past the place without knowing it, instead of turning back, I would go until a road was found turning in the right direction, take that, and come in by the other side. So I struck into the stream. . . ."[24]

The water stood higher than his horse, but Grant's control was firm. As the animal swam, Grant headed him toward the opposite bank, and once the horse gained solid ground, he rode on to White Haven. There the young man borrowed clothes from his future brother-in-law, and when Julia came down, Grant in civilian clothes—not in the role of the dashing lieutenant—was the man she wanted. She told him she had dreamed he would come back this way; she told him, too, that her bedpost carried his name. He spoke of marriage. At nineteen, Julia claimed, she was too young, and she requested that he not ask her father for her hand. However, she did now accept his class ring ("and wore it until he replaced it by the little band of gold I have worn so long"). She both did and did not want to be engaged.[25]

Although she was forced by her upbringing and the age she lived in to speak in the most sentimental of tongues, Julia was as tough and determined as a person could be. She and Ulysses Grant were of equal strength, not only in the figurative sense of having a similar balance of positive and negative elements of character but also in the literal sense of having equivalent physical capacity. Julia was a strong woman. There is a legend in the family that one day, while Ulysses and Julia were sitting on the porch at Long Branch, their son Buck ran out of the house and ignoring the porch stairs, hopped the railing. Amused, the general asked his wife what she would do if there were a fire and the railing ran clear around the porch. Without a word, Julia got up, walked to the railing, grasped it with both hands, and vaulted to the ground below.[26]

The story is believable. The countless photographs of Mrs. General Grant stuffed into silk and seemingly immobile say more about the clothes than about the woman who wore them. They were designed to demonstrate that the social goal of uselessness had been reached, that the general's lady was important enough not to have to do anything. But the woman who wore them was sturdily healthy. There is evidence of only the most transient and minor illness in her lifetime; she bore four children with no record of difficulty, and lost none. She lived for seventy-six years. When as tourists at the Paris exposition in 1878 the Grants tested an elaborate scale that was on display, Ulysses weighed 165 pounds, Julia 175 pounds. By then she had to watch her weight if she were not to make a mockery of the chat about fashion and fabrics that filled her letters to relatives. But what all that stuff strained to contain was a body of considerable power. There was a will to match. She was known in the family as "the boss." Behind the façade of a demure, diffident helpmate was a person of great determination, resolved to make much of her life even if the vehicle for the effort was a not very promising husband.[27]

And so Ulysses Grant was going to marry up. He sought in a new family the strength he had not felt in his own. He had not found in his father or mother "the influence," the power and direction he needed. He could not articulate it alone; he needed to find some way to be himself—some path of action that expressed Grant. In the Dents he saw, he thought, a family sure of itself. He liked Fred Dent, he was impressed by old Colonel Dent, he was welcomed by Mrs. Dent. Julia embodied all that these people offered and, of course, more. There is every suggestion that over the years theirs was a close and rich sexual relationship. Ulysses was an attractive man physically, and graduation from West Point had given him (as it had Fred Dent) a certain importance that compensated for lack of money. Julia probably would have married him for his given name alone, but luckily, her family found him worthy of a woman whose family's social ledgers contained both legends of ancient Maryland and actualities of prosperity in Missouri. The young lieutenant would do for the energetic but unlovely Dent daughter. But from the time of their engagement it was up to Ulysses to prove that Julia Dent had not made a mistake.

Once engaged, Julia and Ulysses still had to do a good deal of waiting before the marriage took place. Their courtship continued by correspondence for four years, while he was stationed in army posts in Louisiana and Texas, and with the invading American forces in Mexico. However, this long period in their lives was not a void. The eroticism of hesitation was a vital component of protracted Victorian engagements. Julia's letters do not survive, but from Ulysses' responses, which do exist, we can see that she teased him with talk of other suitors. He in turn sent her precise descriptions of the intriguing people he met, as in this account of his first trip up the Red River: "The boat was quite small and considerably crouded with passengers and they not of the most pleasant sort; a number of them being what are usually called *Black Legs* or Gamblers; and some of them with very cut throat appearances. There was some of them that I should very much dislike to meet unarmed, and in a retired place, their knowing I had a hundred dollars about me. . . ." Grant's evocations of place were richer than his character studies; of the same trip up the Red River he wrote, "The first hundred miles looks like a little deep and winding canal finding its way through a forest so thickly set, and of such heavy foliage that the eye cannot penetrate." He shared his new worlds with Julia, but his letters were given over less to such descriptions than to pleading that she gain her parents' consent to their marriage even though he was on active duty in the army.[28]

To overcome parental objections to Julia's living on army posts, he offered to resign from the army and take an instructorship in mathematics in a college or work for his father in the new leather-goods store and distribution center in Galena, Illinois. Grant was a determined lover and overcame Julia's sometimes flagging interest with no-nonsense reminders of the times they had spent together: "But why should I use to you here the language of flattery Julia, when we have spoken so much more plainly of our feeling for each other?" It was not his fault that their marriage was long delayed. When—to get ahead of the story—he came home from the Mexican War, he went to St. Louis to see Julia and then after a brief visit to his own family returned, without either of his parents, for the wedding. Julia Dent and Ulysses Grant were married on August 22, 1848, not in a bower at White Haven, but in the Dents' house in town.[29]

The couple were seldom again apart. Only in 1852–54, when Grant was stationed on the West Coast, were they once more separated as they had been in the long engagement years. They could not endure this separation, and for the rest of their lives—including the years of the Civil War—they were rarely apart for more than a few weeks. Already in the correspondence of their courtship, Grant expressed not only his need for Julia but his dependence on her. From New Orleans in 1845, just before he went off to Mexico and his first war, he wrote, "You can have but little idea of the influance you have over me Julia, even while so far away. If I feel tempted to do any thing that I think is not right I am shure to think, 'Well now if Julia saw me would I do so' and thus it is absent or present I am more or less governed by what I think is your will."[30]

# III

# THE MEXICAN
# WAR

. . . I have known a few men who were always aching for a fight when
there was no enemy near, who were as good as their word when the
battle did come.

— *Ulysses S. Grant*

The Mexican War was our romance.

— *Simon Bolívar Buckner*

G R A N T ' S  A C C O U N T of the Mexican War is a classic in the literature
of war. In his *Memoirs*, he told the story of an invasion he regarded as unwar-
ranted with critical detachment, and in according the Mexican War much
space, he underscored its importance for him. He awakened in Mexico. In assessing the war, Grant was amused and half won over by the logic of the
Mexicans who celebrated as victories two gallantly fought but lost battles,
Chapultepec and Molino del Rey. It would, he agreed, save trouble, and
blood, simply to declare success in war rather than bother to fight. But Grant
had little faith in fanciful stories. His purpose was simple: "I would like to see
truthful history written." That is what he wrote.[1]

The narrative is masterly, but Grant is jealously protective of his feelings
about war. Where the account becomes personal, it is restrained. Instead, his
emphasis is on presenting objective military history of the first order. The
work is so intellectually unpretentious that one can easily miss the sophistication of his study of Generals Winfield Scott, Zachary Taylor, and William J.
Worth. In its analysis of strategy, Grant's work is still fresh; it is in full conversation with the best modern work on the subject, *The American Way of
War*, by Russell F. Weigley. This 1973 study, controversial because of its

thesis that Americans have come to think of war as annihilation, a concept derived from Grant's way of fighting the Civil War, agrees basically with Grant's analysis of the Mexican War. In 1885 the old politician was careful to be tactful in his discussion of the volunteers (i.e., voters) so maligned by those who saw the Mexican War as a classic argument for a professional army. But such controversies did not interest him greatly; his eye was always on the progress of the war itself. Grant's *Memoirs* demonstrate, as do his letters of this period, that the young lieutenant, silently, unnoticed, studied the moves of his commanders with a critical, but never insubordinate, eye. And in recording what he saw he wrote history, not a treatise on the science of war. He told the story of the Mexican War.[2]

In September 1845 the Fourth Infantry Regiment went, in sailing ships, from New Orleans to Corpus Christi, on the Texas coast. The town, really just a cluster of buildings around a ranch, was at the mouth of the Nueces River, in territory disputed by Mexico and the United States, which had annexed the Republic of Texas earlier that year. The chief industry of Corpus Christi was smuggling American tobacco into Mexico, where it was sold below the price set by the government monopoly. General Zachary Taylor's force of three thousand men, once called the army of observation as it watched from Louisiana the process of the American annexation of Texas, was now styled the army of occupation. The infantry brigades and cavalrymen set up a totally exposed camp of orderly rows of tents along the shore. To brighten dull evenings, James Longstreet directed plays in which fresh-faced Ulysses Grant "looked very like a girl dressed up," but the Othello of the company found that Grant's Desdemona "did not have much sentiment."[3]

Inland, the country was magnificently untamed; a huge herd of wild horses roamed the area, and was preyed upon by men seeking new mounts and a break in the boredom of camp. Traveling through sparsely inhabited country to San Antonio and on to Austin, Grant saw an abundance of deer and antelope. Hunting was the most common pastime, but not for him: "I had never been a sportsman in my life; had scarcely ever gone in search of game, and rarely seen any when looking for it." On this trip, a companion persuaded him to go after the turkeys that fed in flocks on nut trees along the streams: "We had scarcely reached the edge of the timber when I heard the flutter of wings overhead, and in an instant I saw two or three turkeys flying away. These were soon followed by more, then more, and more, until a flock of twenty or thirty had left from just over my head. All this time I stood watching the turkeys to see where they flew—with my gun on my shoulder, and never once thought of levelling it at the birds." There was in Grant a quiet and unsentimental gentleness that was expressed best in his relationships with animals and, later, with his children, but it was a quality that had to be suppressed if he was to make himself heard in a world of men and war. Grant was embarrassed by his unwillingness to kill the birds and spoke of himself as a "failure" as a hunter. But he chose not to forget the incident.

The fascinating—and funny—sight of the turkeys was indelibly in his mind, as was the fact that he had had no urge to shoot them.[4]

Grant also had his eye on the politics of warmaking. All of the considerable literature devoted to explaining how the Mexican War came about might be boiled down to his one sentence: "We were sent to provoke a fight, but it was essential that Mexico should commence it." This said, Grant proceeded in the *Memoirs* to a brief essay on how wars are begun in America. His point loses no force in the twentieth century for having been written in the nineteenth:

> It was very doubtful whether Congress would declare war; but if Mexico should attack our troops, the Executive could announce, "Whereas, war exists by the acts of, etc," and prosecute the contest with vigor. Once initiated there were but few public men who would have the courage to oppose it. Experience proves that the man who obstructs a war in which his nation is engaged, no matter whether right or wrong, occupies no enviable place in life or history. Better for him, individually, to advocate "war, pestilence, and famine," than to act as obstructionist to a war already begun.

This is prophecy; it says much about war in general and about how Grant analyzed the Civil War in particular. He knew that in American wars a general could do only what a president would allow him to do and that something in the politics of war ordained that, once started, a war had a life that could stop only when, somehow, it reached its own end.[5]

Unfortunately for President James K. Polk, the augmentation of the smugglers' camp at Corpus Christi did not provoke the Mexicans to attack. So General Taylor was ordered to march 150 miles south to the Rio Grande. Grant was one of the men who did not relish the role of provocateur. He had not liked the lie, told the troops back at Camp Salubrity, that the United States Army had been moved to this outpost on the western border of Louisiana to stop American filibusterers from entering Texas. He knew the army was there "really as a menace to Mexico in case she appeared to contemplate war," and he "was bitterly opposed to the measure." Grant continued to "regard the war, which resulted, as one of the most unjust ever waged by a stronger against a weaker nation. It was an instance of a republic following the bad example of European monarchies, in not considering justice in their desire to acquire additional territory."[6]

Grant accepted the thesis that the war was the result of a "conspiracy" to create new slave states, and was troubled still more by the United States' having invaded a foreign country, even though he recognized that the prize was great—Texas and the far southwest. He knew this was "an empire and of incalculable value," but thought "it might have been obtained by other means." The means, in his view in the 1880's, was commercial investment. Looking back to the 1840's in a voice rare to Grant, he pronounced a moral judgment and discovered retribution: "The Southern rebellion was largely the outgrowth of the Mexican War. Nations, like individuals, are punished for their transgressions. We got our punishment in the most sanguinary and expensive war of modern times."[7]

The move to the Rio Grande succeeded in provoking war. Polk's action was analogous to that of a bullfighter who torments his prey until, in exasperation, the animal is driven to an attack. The baited bull, on May 3, 1846, was General Mariano Arista, who knew that General Taylor had gone to the coast for supplies and additional recruits with which to goad further the Mexican force stationed in the town of Matamoros. At daybreak Arista's artillery fired, and the Americans, north of the river, returned the fire. Twenty-five miles away at Point Isabel, Lieutenant Grant lay in his tent at the edge of the sea and listened to the sound. He had never heard a "hostile gun before" and "felt sorry" that he had enlisted. He got up and wrote Julia a calm letter about the deaths of certain men, which had been the immediate acts provoking the battle. "As soon as this is over," he added, "I will write to you again, that is if I am one of the fortunate individuals who escape. Don't fear for me My Dear Julia for this is only the active part of our business."[8]

Grant put it in a one-sentence paragraph in his *Memoirs:* "The war had begun." On the way back to Fort Texas, the besieged American outpost across from Matamoros, he fought in his first battle. There was an antique quality to the confrontation at Palo Alto, about eight miles north of the Rio Grande. The Americans, coming across the plain through shoulder-high grass "almost as sharp as a darning needle," faced Mexicans ready for them in front of the trees; their "bayonets and spearheads glistened in the sunlight formidably. The force was composed largely of cavalry armed with lances." The Mexicans outnumbered Taylor's three thousand men, who were armed "with flint-lock muskets, and paper cartridges charged with powder, buckshot and ball. At the distance of a few hundred yards a man might fire at you all day without your finding it out." In addition to these aged arms, Taylor did have howitzers, which were mobile, could be aimed with precision, and shot explosive shells rather than cannon balls. As the shells savagely decimated the Mexican ranks, other men quickly filled the vacancies. The Mexicans did not retreat, but neither did the slashing sabers of their officers compel an attack.[9]

The Mexicans had cannon, though not howitzers, and Grant's company caught the fire. Three days after the battle he wrote Julia, "Although the balls were whizzing thick and fast about me I did not feel a sensation of fear until nearly the close of the [afternoon-long] firing a ball struck close by me killing one man instantly, it nocked Capt. Page's under Jaw entirely off and broke in the roof of his mouth. . . . Capt. Page is still alive." Albert D. Richardson, telling of the event in 1868, reported that the unnamed enlisted man had had his head blown off, "scattering his brains and blood in the faces of his comrades." Whether Grant was one of these comrades we are not told; he was surely nearby. In his *Memoirs*, Grant (using precise details that occasionally give a tone of high macabre humor to his recollection of war) recalled that "the splinters from the musket of the killed soldier, and his brains and bones, knocked down two or three others, including one officer, Lieutenant Wallen,—hurting them more or less." Ulysses Grant had seen a man die.[10]

Of Grant's private response to the death of one man and the mutilation of another we have no indication beyond the preciseness with which he reported and recalled the event. Outwardly, at least, he seems to have been devoid of emotion. As for fighting, he responded by coming back for more. The next day, at Resaca de la Palma, nearer still to the Rio Grande, the Americans again met the Mexicans, this time in a dense thicket. Grant, a quartermaster and not in command of a company, was at the front of the line and took the lead in a charge: "I at last found a clear space separating two ponds. There seemed to be a few men in front and I charged upon them with my company. There was no resistance. . . ." In the *Memoirs* he was modest about the initiative he had taken: "The ground had been charged over before. My exploit was equal to that of the soldier who boasted that he had cut off the leg of the enemy. When asked why he did not cut off his head, he replied: 'Someone had done that before.' "[11]

The humility is engaging, but Grant's bit of humor is almost too appropriate to the way the man next to him died. Speaking of this second day in a letter to Julia, he did not even mention having led a charge. Instead he gave general credit to the Americans for bravery in charging straight into the mouths of the Mexican cannon, and once again the quartermaster, told her of his task in language that is tightly controlled: "After the battle the woods was strued with the dead. Waggons have been engaged drawing the bodies to bury. How many waggon loads . . . would be hard to guess. I saw three. . . ." He thought the victory important: "No doubt you will see accounts . . . in the papers. There is no great sport in having bullets flying about one in evry direction, but I find they have less horror when among them than when in anticipation. Now that the war has commenced with such vengence I am in hopes my Dear Julia that we will soon be able to end it. In the thickest of it I thought of Julia." Neither here nor elsewhere did he write of killing anyone himself. It was probably not the actual experience of killing, but the general activity of battle that had so powerfully aroused him.[12]

The Mexicans were driven across the river, and Fort Texas (later named Brownsville, after a man killed in the bombardment) was relieved. Next, Matamoros, in indisputably Mexican territory, was taken. What had been first the army of observation and then the army of occupation was now the army of invasion, and in August 1846 Taylor marched to Monterrey, the leading city in the interior of northeastern Mexico. The heat made night marches essential, and the recalcitrance of the pack and wagon mules tested

Grant's patience. His vivid description in the *Memoirs* of his struggles with these exasperating animals ends with a passage that is at once an example of the discouraging lapses into conventional diction that take the fire out of so many of his stories and a clue to his personality: "I am not aware of ever having used a profane expletive in my life; but I would have the charity to excuse those who may have done so, if they were in charge of a train of Mexican pack mules at the time." Though the politeness of Victorian letters leaves us fewer samples of the vernacular than are available to historians of the twentieth century, there is absolutely no doubt that rich language in ornate combinations was used in both the Mexican War and the Civil War; yet many observers have confirmed Grant's statement that such was not his style of expression. His speech was terse, unimpassioned, detached, and not earthy.[13]

Talking about war did not stimulate Grant; participating in it did, as is shown by his conduct when the attack on Monterrey began: "My curiosity got the better of my judgment, and I mounted a horse and rode to the front to see what was going on. I had been there but a short time when an order to charge was given, and lacking the moral courage to return to camp [where, as quartermaster, he belonged] I charged with the regiment." About a third of the men in the charge were killed or wounded in the assault on the Black Fort that protected the city; the survivors moved away from the fort to another position facing the city. Grant, the frustrated cavalryman, had been the only mounted man in the charge; as they reorganized themselves he yielded his horse to another officer and commandeered a fresh one from a soldier in his quartermaster corps. They began another charge: ". . . and the next place of safety from the shots of the enemy that I recollect . . . was a field of cane or corn to the north-east of the lower batteries. The adjutant to whom I had loaned my horse was killed, and I was designated to act in his place." Momentarily, in the middle of a fight, Grant had shed the grocery-clerk guise of the quartermaster and forced his way into a position of small authority in a battle.[14]

Students of the Mexican War from Grant onward agree that Taylor's attack on Monterrey was a tactical disgrace. There was, for example, no reason not to bypass the first gate rather than charge it, with resulting slaughter of the American attackers. On entering the city, the surviving Americans were fired on from rooftops by the defending Mexicans, but fought on block by block toward the main plaza. That open square had been brought into accurate range by one battery of Taylor's artillery, and the cannoneers, methodically waiting for their weapon to cool between firings, were lobbing a ball into the square every twenty minutes. After the initial shot, this bombardment had little effect on the Mexicans safe behind sandbags on rooftops around the plaza, but did prevent the Americans from storming this central point.[15]

Grant was among the men who had darted from house to house, crossing the intervening streets at the risk of being shot. Halted two blocks from the plaza, his group realized they were short of ammunition, and Grant, probably still riding the unfamiliar horse, volunteered to go back. With his arm around the neck of the horse, his left foot up behind the saddle, his right in the stirrup, and his body protected by the right side of the horse, he rode at full run past the Mexicans shooting at him. Stopping briefly at one house, in American hands, he found some badly wounded men, one with a probably fatal head injury, another partly disemboweled, and promised to send them help. Then, on the horse again, he made it out of the city. As he was starting back with ammunition and support troops, he met the remnant of his force running out of the city in retreat, but General Worth's men, entering the city from the opposite direction, soon reached its center. Because Taylor refused to resume his attack, he has been blamed for the absence of a decisive victory. Under a negotiated settlement General Pedro de Ampudia and his men left Monterrey armed. There were other costs; Grant observed that no one got back to the "poor wounded officers and men I had found, [they] fell into the hands of the enemy during the night, and died."[16]

During the armistice following the battle Grant became acquainted with Monterrey. Something of the West Point artist returned. In perhaps his finest letters he deftly situated the "beautiful city enclosed on three sides by the mountains with a pass through them to the right and to the left," and with lush economy captured the fragrant quality of Monterrey before it was industrialized, still "so full of Orange Lime and Pomgranite trees that the houses can scarsly be seen until you get into the town." He paid Monterrey a left-handed compliment—"If it was an American city I have no doubt it would be concidered the handsomest one in the Union"—and in his next letter spoke of it with no chauvinism at all: "This is the most beautiful spot that it has been my fortune to see in this world." But he added, his passion for Julia overthrowing his orthography, "Without you *dearest* a Paradice would become lonesom."[17]

The sensual richness of the Mexican city stimulated Grant's desire for Julia. If he described the city as "beautiful" twice in his first letter to her, he mentioned his "love" five times over. And one senses how hard it was for him to put down on paper what he meant by love. Surely he was not just observing forms of social address when he wrote to her, "Julia is as *dear* to me to-day as she was the day . . . more than two years ago, when I first told her of my love. From that day to this I have loved you constantly and the same and with the hope too that long [before] this time I would have been able to call you *Wife*." He yearned for the day when they would be other than "*mere lovers*" corresponding.[18]

Julia knew what he meant. It was time to go to bed. In the long months of their engagement she kept her recollections of him alive in private talks with her sister and in dreams. In one of these dreams, about which she wrote him, her still fresh-faced Ulysses had a beard. There was a whiff of the erotic in this fantasy, as well as a hint of the slow maturation of the not-so-young soldier. We cannot know, of course, but something suggests that he had had very little sexual experience and sought to deny an excess of innocence by taking Julia's hint. Five months later he wrote a male friend, "If you were to s[ee] me now you would never recognize me in the world I have a beard more than four inches long and it [is] red."[19]

Enough men were killed in the battle of Monterrey, in September 1846, for the newspapers in the United States to conclude that it had been a glorious victory for Zachary Taylor. And they began talking about him for the job of president, then held by Polk, a Democrat. Polk was in a quandary. He had given the command to Taylor, a Whig, to keep it away from a more prominent member of the opposition party, Winfield Scott. Looking back, Grant claimed, disingenuously, that Taylor had had no aspirations to be president; at the time, calculating Democrats, dreading a Whig war hero, no doubt sought comfort in Taylor's obscurity. But that comfort was shattered by his three successive victories in battle.[20]

Meanwhile, the army's ranking general, Winfield Scott, was chafing to get into the war, in which he was being upstaged. Scott, an impressive and competent soldier, made no secret of his ambition to move up a notch and become commander in chief. His authority and experience went all the way back to the War of 1812, and he could not be kept out of battle indefinitely; keeping him out became less useful to Polk and the Democratic party after Taylor's flamboyant successes. (Polk's—and Scott's—worries were well grounded, of course. Taylor was nominated and elected president in 1848; Scott, in many ways a more promising candidate in a decade of vacillating presidents, got his unsuccessful try at the presidency only in 1852.)[21]

These domestic aspects of the foreign war were not lost on Grant as he looked back on the events in his *Memoirs:* "The Mexican War was a political war, and the administration conducting it desired to make party capital out of it." He disapproved of the politics that lay behind the Mexican War and found those of the Civil War more congenial, but he took politics for granted in both wars. By 1885 Grant had been both general and president, and the seasoned Republican dismissed his pre–Civil War allegiance to the Democratic party and accepted the Whigs as the forebears of Republicans. The Mexican War, he concluded, was a mistake of the Democrats, who were trying to extend slavery. Paradoxically, it was also a war that Whig generals won, thereby bestowing on their party a mantle of patriotism. But for the ordinary soldiers there was less elation. Looking at the bedraggled veterans of one battle, Grant wrote, "I thought how little interest the men before me had in the results of the war, and how little knowledge they had of 'what it was all about.' "[22]

Scott, allowed to go to Mexico at last, moved in March 1847 directly to Veracruz, the port serving Mexico City. He spurned Taylor's strategy of attacking cities and towns in the relatively unimportant northeastern area of

Mexico in favor of a direct assault on the nation's capital. Grant's was one of
the regiments rushed to Veracruz to support Scott's siege of the port. This
action was conducted with such skill and with so few casualties that newspaper accounts did not accord it the importance given to Taylor's gaudier victory at Buena Vista, in February 1847, in a battle Grant missed. With Veracruz taken, Scott boldly left his sources of supply, and with a vastly
outnumbered force, started for Mexico City. The effectiveness of this risky
maneuver—of moving swiftly, unencumbered by supply lines—was not lost
on Grant, who was to do the same in the Vicksburg campaign and, later,
when he encouraged Sherman to leave Atlanta and head for the sea.[23]

Scott conducted the invasion, along a mountainous route, with great skill.
Thus, in an assault on the mountain stronghold of Cerro Gorde, where the
terrain was so steep that animals could not be used and men moved artillery
pieces into place for the attack, the "surprise of the enemy was complete; the
victory overwhelming." Grant's enthusiasm was unrestrained: ". . . perhaps
there was not a battle of the Mexican War, or of any other, where orders
issued before an engagement were nearer being a correct report of what afterwards took place." And for this staff support of Scott, Grant credited,
among others, Robert E. Lee, Pierre Gustave Toutant Beauregard, and
George B. McClellan.[24]

Scott, preferring to coerce his enemy into surrender without destroying an
army or terrorizing civilians, moved on to Puebla and to Contreras, and took
Churubusco. He halted without storming Mexico City while an attempt to
negotiate a peace settlement was made. When it failed, the bloody battles of
Molino del Rey and Chapultepec were fought. Both of these, Grant decided
later, were unnecessary; another route into the city should have been chosen.
During the fierce fighting at the gates of the city itself, Grant took the initiative at San Cosme. With a small detachment of men and a howitzer, he
forced his way past a protesting priest with explanations in halting Spanish,
and dragged the gun into a church belfry. There, two or three hundred yards
from the gate into the city, the Americans had the defenders in range. Grant
could not understand why the Mexicans did not drive his tiny firing group
out of the church, but they did not do so, and his effort was so important in
the forcing of entry into the city that he was mentioned, for the only time, in
the dispatches to Washington. Faced with the successful assault by the
American army, General Santa Anna withdrew, and with great pomp and
disregard for possible snipers, Winfield Scott entered the city and took the
"Halls of Montezuma," the great public buildings of the capital. In the peace
settlement, Mexico relinquished all claim to Texas, New Mexico, and California in exchange for fifteen million dollars.[25]

The battles were over. Early on, Grant had confided to a friend, "War
seems much less horrible to persons engaged in it than to those who read of
the battles." By then he had fought at Palo Alto and Resaca de la Palma; after
the exhilarating battle of Monterrey, he told Julia that "fighting is no longer a

pleasure." No longer a pleasure—but it had been. Grant was insulted when his future father-in-law comforted Julia by telling her that he was safe as the quartermaster and commissary of the Fourth Infantry Regiment. In rebuttal, Grant reminded her that he had entered the fighting at Monterrey despite his job. Indeed, he had sought a transfer to a combat assignment, only to be refused because he was too "useful" as a quartermaster. He continued not to let this task keep him out of battle, and he told Julia that what he would like was a leave—to get married—and then a chance to "come back . . . and see the war out."[26]

These and similar hints of Grant's attitude toward fighting lead one to take a close look at the language of the *Memoirs*. The bland words can be deceiving. Take the story of the war's beginning. After describing with low-keyed honesty how he wished he had not enlisted when he woke to the first gunfire of the war back at Point Isabel, he went on to reflect—looking back over a lifetime—on how men feel at such moments: "A great many men, when they smell battle afar off, chafe to get into the fray. When they say so themselves they generally fail to convince their hearers that they are as anxious as they would like to make believe, and as they approach danger they become more subdued. This rule is not universal, for I have known a few men who were always aching for a fight when there was no enemy near, who were as good as their word when the battle did come. But the number of such men is small." At first glance, Grant would seem to be merely the wise old observer of others. A second look makes one wonder if he did not, at least privately, admit to the ache, and number himself in that latter small band.[27]

Virtually unnoticed himself in the Mexican War, Grant watched his fellow warriors carefully. With a sharp eye and neat detail, he caught the essential differences in the command personalities of the generals under whom he served. "General Taylor never wore uniform, but dressed himself entirely for comfort. He moved about the field . . . to see through his own eyes. . . . He was very much given to sit his horse side-ways—with both feet on one side—particularly on the battle field." This was courage; Taylor was poised and relaxed, and took everything in. "General Scott," wrote Grant, "was the reverse in all these particulars." He always wore all the uniform allowed by law. For frequent reviews of troops, he wore his "cocked hat, aiguillettes, sabre and spurs. . . . [He] was precise in language, cultivated a style peculiarly his own; was proud of his rhetoric; not adverse to speaking of himself, often in the third person. . . . Scott saw more through the eyes of his staff officers than through his own." General William J. Worth, though acknowledged to have been a brave man and a bright one when he broke through the walls of houses rather than expose his men to bullets in the streets of Monterrey, was dismissed by Grant: "He was nervous, impatient, and restless on the march [to Veracruz] or when important or responsible duty confronted him." Later, at Puebla, "General Worth had the troops in line, under arms, all day, with three days' cooked rations in their haversacks. He galloped from one command to another proclaiming the near proximity of Santa Anna with an army vastly superior to his own. General Scott arrived . . . and nothing more was heard of Santa Anna and his myriads." Grant had no respect for panic. He said no more about Worth; of Scott and Taylor he wrote, "Both were pleasant to serve under—Taylor was pleasant to serve with." And Grant, the old general of the Civil War looking back on the first generals he had seen in battle, saw himself in both men. But surely in personality he recognized more of himself in Taylor—and never more than when he wrote, "Taylor was not a conversationalist, but on paper he could put his meaning so plainly that there could be no mistaking it."[28]

After the war was won, Ulysses Grant and some army friends went hiking on Popocatepetl. Simon Bolivar Buckner, who had been a year behind Grant at West Point, was the leader of the expedition, which included a goodly number of other future rebels, among them Richard H. Anderson, who was to take Spotsylvania, and George B. Crittenden. They went by horse high up on the mountainside—at one point losing an overladen mule from a cliff-side ledge. The weather on the trip to the base camp was wet and ominous, and they tried unsuccessfully to sleep in a roofless cabin. The next morning they set out to reach the summit in spite of snow and strong winds. They struggled to get above the storm, and as they came out into the sun the clouds behind them broke momentarily and they could see the valley below. The world was beautiful, but everywhere there was snow; late in the day, they agreed they could not reach the top of the mountain, and quickly headed back.[29]

Getting below the snow line, they rode their horses down the treacherous mountain trail and, exhausted, reached the village. They slept on blankets on a dirt floor until "one and then another of our party began to cry out with ex-cruciating pain in the eyes" caused by the preceding day's exposure to the glare of the snow. They were frightened that they had gone blind; the eyes of several of the men were swollen shut, and the next day they had to be led on their horses down to a more comfortable village. There, after another night, all were "entirely well and free from pain."[30]

The weather that morning, wrote Grant, "was clear and Popocatepetl stood out in all its beauty, the top looking as if not a mile away, and inviting us to return. About half the party were anxious to try the ascent again, and concluded to do so. The remainder—I was with the remainder—concluded that we had got all the pleasure there was to be had out of mountain climb-ing." While Buckner and his crew went up to the top of the mountain, Grant and his half of the party explored the villages of the Valley of Mexico. Recalling the experience in the *Memoirs*, he wrote, "I made no notes of this excursion, and have read nothing about it since, but it seems to me that I can see the whole of it as vividly as if it were but yesterday." He could have said the same of the Mexican War or the Civil War, for he had an extraordinary sense of the whole of these far larger and more complex events as well. His memories of the wars came back to him with sequential clarity, the details always illustrating rather than obliterating the total story. When, forty years later, he wrote his excellent history of the Mexican War in the *Memoirs*, he had available to him the letters he had written Julia at the time and the account of his role in Mexico in the biography written by Albert D. Richardson in 1868. But more importantly, he had his own splendid memory. His command of fact was great, and he shaped fact into history with skill. He was impressive in his mastery of chosen episodes of his past.[31]

There was no mistaking the fact that Grant loved Mexico. Perhaps his letters and the *Memoirs* do not elevate him to the fine company of visitors like Fanny Calderón de la Barca, who have richly evoked the beauty of the country, but Grant's observations are keen and sympathetic. The obligatory Protestant contrast between the poverty of the people and the costliness of the rich churches is made, but the churches are dismissed out of hand. Grant took a good many long looks at the fine edifices, so different in their baroque splendor from the buildings he had seen when prowling the streets of Philadelphia and New York. He gave nature its due as well, and the country through which he passed was superb. The mountains, beautiful themselves, made splendid the cities they framed. This was so at Monterrey and perhaps more so in the Valley of Mexico. Writing to Julia in March 1848 he told her, "I generally gallop into town evry day. . . . I wish you could be here to take one of these rides with me and see the beautiful Valley of Mexico. The whole Valley is spread out to the view covered with numerous lakes, green fields, and little Villages and to all appearance it would be a short ride to go around the whole valley in a day, but you would find that it would take a week."[32]

If Grant got to see ordinary people only in crowds on the trips to forty-odd foreign countries that he made after he became famous, he had had, in Mexico in the 1840's, a chance for intimacy. He achieved a bit of Spanish, and as he walked unobtrusively through the streets and talked to the Mexican people, going about their business, he found them tolerant rather than distrustful of the invading soldiers. The poverty troubled him: "I pity poor Mexico. With a soil and climate scarsely equaled in the world she has more poor and starving subjects who are willing and able to work than any country in the world. The rich keep down the poor with a hardness of heart that is incredible." Grant was observant, but he did not offer a comparison between the farmers of Mexico and the people hacking subsistence farms out of the woods of Ohio or working as slaves across the river in Kentucky.[33]

In his realistic look at the Mexican people, Grant sensed their confusion and resignation at being caught in poverty and the events of civil war and foreign invasion, and yet he himself participated in the moral ambiguity of the time and place by taking home with him as a servant a young boy, Gregorio. Grant did not forget that he was an intruder in Mexico and took note of, but could not quite sort out, the contrasts between the warm Mexican welcomes and the cruel treatment by some Yankees of those who were too welcoming. For misguided reasons, presumably of gentility, one or two of Grant's descendants saw to it that when his letters to Julia were published (over a century after they were written), certain of his descriptions of Mexicans were deleted. Too bad. Even if the terms used were pejorative it would have been interesting to see what they were. Grant looked about him clearly and saw the people with sympathy but not sentimentality. His days in Mexico were marked by keen alertness, and his friend Simon Bolivar Buckner was not far wrong when he said, "The Mexican War was our romance."[34]

# IV

# A SOLDIER
# BETWEEN WARS

I have been both indignant and grieved over the statement of pretended
personal acquaintances of Captain Grant at this time to the effect that
he was dejected, low-spirited, badly dressed, and even slovenly. Well,
I am quite sure they did not know *my* Captain Grant, for he was always
perfection.

— *Julia Dent Grant*

. . . *poverty, poverty,* begins to stare me in the face.

— *Ulysses S. Grant*

N O T  L O N G  A F T E R the Mexican War an attractive young woman and a
trim, tanned young veteran were chatting on a stage coming into Bethel,
Ohio. When they reached town, the gentleman helped the lady down with
her luggage. Ulysses Grant's brothers and sisters ran down from their house.
"They all thought as much as could be that it was Julia that I had brought
home." They were wrong. The girl was a stranger who happened to be on
her way to Bethel; Grant would not be married for another month, but his
siblings had the right idea. It would have been eminently logical for the
young bridegroom and his wife, an alert, determined woman, to get off the
stage in a new no-nonsense Ohio town, ready to build a solid life. Grant was
a veteran of a war which was thought to have worked out well, and in which
he had been honorably active. He was twenty-six, healthy, and sufficiently
learned in mathematics to be a teacher; if he aspired to something more lucrative, his experience as a regimental quartermaster could count as preparation
for a career in business.[1]

Grant would have been following standard practice if he had resigned his
commission—West Point graduates who did so outnumbered those who remained in the army—and he would have been re-entering civilian life with

considerable promise. He could have looked forward to time alone with Julia, to children, and to taking over a family business that would command respect and provide the wherewithal for a house and a comfortable life. From West Point and the Mexican War he had obtained a base of prestige that many townspeople in Bethel—or any other American town—could envy. Ulysses and Julia Grant might be said to have had good expectations indeed after their marriage in August 1848.

But the twenty-six-year-old young veteran jumping down from the stage, who looked so ready to be the model man of the mid-nineteenth century, was not sufficiently eager to get into business to be willing to be part of his father's. Instead, he elected to make his way in the peacetime army, until some business he could call his own came along. The day after their wedding, Ulysses and Julia left St. Louis on a lovely, leisurely journey down the Mississippi and up the Ohio River to Louisville. But even on this wonderful trip—Julia's first away from St. Louis and her family—Grant's ceaselessly unsuccessful quest for prosperity intruded. In Louisville, they stopped with his prosperous cousins the Solomon Grants and the James Hewitts. Julia recalled the Hewitt place with admiration—the "house was filled with everything beautiful"—and remembered "too that my dear husband intimated very modestly that if he saw any chance for a business opening he would be glad to resign, and although these gentlemen had large business connections at New Orleans, New York, Liverpool, and, I think Paris, not one of them offered even to introduce him to any businessman."[2]

Julia may have exaggerated the reach of the Louisville connections, but the failure of Solomon Grant and his brother-in-law, Hewitt, to seize the opportunity to link their army cousin to some business enterprise may have resulted less from an oversight than from an appraisal, either quickly made or based on family accounts, of Grant's total lack of business sense. He had none. True, in Mexico, as a quartermaster, he had run a bakery business on the side, but the enterprise was so short-lived that it had no time to fail. His skill as a quartermaster reflected his competence in carrying out the orderly procedures of army affairs, not his possession of either the entrepreneurial urge or the managerial constancy so essential to the businessman.

When they reached Bethel, Julia survived well the ordeal of meeting Ulysses' family. His splendid Simpson grandmother, she wrote, was "tall and robust, quite my ideal of a Revolutionary mother." Julia was more restrained however, in her praise of Jesse Root Grant. "The Captain's father met me cordially, I might say affectionately."* He was, she noted, "much taller than his son." Her recollection of Hannah Grant was forthright as far as physical characteristics went, but her portrayal of her mother-in-law's character was clouded with mists of sentimentality. She found Hannah Grant to be "a

* In her *Memoirs*, Julia referred to Ulysses always as Lieutenant or Captain or General Grant, never as President Grant.

handsome woman, a little below medium height, with soft brown eyes, glossy brown hair, and her cheek . . . like a rose in the snow." Hannah was, Julia insisted, "the most self-sacrificing, sweetest, kindest woman I ever met, except my own dear mother." Her description suggested little of Hannah's elusive personality. Julia liked her husband's sisters and brothers, and concluded, "Altogether, I was well satisfied with my dear husband's family."[3]

Julia was more than a little snobbish; in her *Memoirs* she described the "homes we visited" during the six weeks with Grant's kin and friends in Bethel, Georgetown, and Maysville as "humble, some . . . not." She clearly enjoyed the deference her St. Louis origins and reputation engendered, but the best times were those she and Ulysses spent alone. "Ulys always preferred to take me in a buggy with a fleet little steed to draw us." They saw the world "through magic glasses."[4]

In October 1848 Grant's leave was up and he was ordered to report to Detroit. They had by then returned to St. Louis, and Julia had "to leave my dear home" as well as "parting with papa!" The break was painful: "I could not, could not, think of it without bursting into a flood of tears. . . ." Grant was troubled; he had waited long to have Julia for himself. Luckily, he was helped in achieving their independence of the Dents by the fact that the family's prosperity, which Julia was later to recall with exaggeration, was not sufficient to enable her father to establish Ulysses in a business and thus keep the couple in St. Louis. Indeed, Dent's own sons were off seeking their fortunes—one in California and another, Grant's roommate Frederick, as a career man in the army.[5]

Colonel Dent was dependent entirely on emotional resources in his attempt to hold his daughter: "The week before we were to leave, papa came into the sitting room where Ulys and I were." To his son-in-law he said, "Grant, I can arrange it all for you. You join your regiment and leave Julia with us. You can get a leave of absence once or twice a year, and spend a week or two with us." Julia, he claimed, "could not live in the army." Grant's patience broke. "Ulys's arm was around me," Julia recalled, "and he bent his head and whispered: '. . . Would you like to remain with your father and let me go alone?'" She wept: "No, no, no, Ulys." He told her, "Dry your tears . . . it makes me unhappy." She did, and there was "never again a word said about my staying at home."[6]

Julia and Ulysses left St. Louis and on a cold moonlit night reached Bethel. From there they traveled to Detroit, only to be told that his orders had been changed and they must go to the Madison Barracks, in Sackets Harbor, New York. Demonstrating to Julia that he was an officer to be reckoned with, Grant immediately protested this change in orders. His request for restoration of his assignment to Detroit was granted, but not before the two of them had made the long, cold, difficult, and expensive trip to Sackets Harbor, on the remote but beautiful eastern shore of Lake Ontario. They received permission to delay their return to Detroit, and by the time the spring thaw made it possible to leave, they were sorry to go. Sackets Harbor was the happiest place in which Ulysses and Julia Grant lived.[7]

Caught by winter in the self-contained army post, the two adjusted to each other. They set up housekeeping on their first weekend and Julia planned Sunday dinner after church. Ulysses, on his own, asked some of his bachelor friends to join them. Julia, annoyed at his having stolen her event, made him disinvite them. He did; his old messmates missed dinner that day, and when the cooking proved a success, Julia was sorry they had not been there. Invited for dinner the next day, the young officers, nicely ignoring army-post pettiness, opened the door just far enough to poke their heads in and ask if it was really all right for them to enter. Julia responded well to the good-natured teasing and welcomed them. She and Ulysses were at ease with people at Sackets Harbor.[8]

Julia was an indifferent cook. When asked in 1876 to supply a recipe for a centennial cookbook, she found she had none written down, and had to borrow one from a friend. She took more pride in being able to afford a cook than in cooking. Back in 1848 she was more interested in other matters: "Soon after we were settled . . . I requested my husband to give me a regular allowance—just what he thought he could afford to give me for housekeeping expenses. . . ." This, she asserted, would give her "the privilege of using our *little* to the best advantage." She went on to observe: "I had more than once seen a really loving, good, and devoted wife with her cheeks crimsoned with distress . . . , her usually most generous and kind husband declaring the bills were *too* large. . . . I did not intend to have any such scenes in our dovecote." Ulysses agreed and supplied the allowance regularly. "I never once had to ask for this. I felt . . . I had assumed a very great responsibility. . . ." She got an account book; when there was an error, Ulysses declined to correct it, choosing rather to make up the deficit. Julia kept the family accounts for the rest of her life.[9]

The Grants were careful of their means and pleased with the spontaneous comfortableness of their relations with people. They had trouble learning the unattractive lesson of translating these friendships into vehicles to further an army career. But they tried. Back in Detroit in the spring of 1849 they did all—or most—of the things expected of an ambitious up-and-coming young officer and his wife. Once, when Julia was off on a visit, Ulysses sent her a shawl via Captain Irvin McDowell "whose lady you should have called upon." In addition to keeping alert to army social obligations they met the people of mark of the city. One was Zachariah Chandler, the crude, bright, ambitious businessman and Whig politician who was making his coarse way into power in Michigan. Another was Lewis Cass, titular head of the Democratic party—he had just lost the presidential election to Zachary Taylor— and a powerful man in the nation. Julia claimed Cass as a friend of her father's but Grant could not turn these relationships to his own use.[10]

In her *Memoirs*, Julia defended her clapboard house in Detroit against writers who sought to make a log cabin of every house the Grants lived in until they reached 1600 Pennsylvania Avenue. Actually, Julia considered brick as even more in keeping with her station, but she took comfort in the fact that Lewis Cass's house too was wooden; she saw how far she had to go when she noted that Zachariah Chandler lived imposingly behind bricks. Meanwhile, the young wife had servants to help make up for the clapboards. Julia found, on returning to Detroit, that "some friend had secured a nice house girl for us." And they still had "the boy (Gregorio)" that "Ulys had brought from Mexico as a valet to attend the table and door." Julia reported, however, that "Gregorio did not remain with us quite a year, some meddlesome person prevailing upon him that he could do better for himself. He was a nice, cheerful boy until this was put in his head, and then he became sullen. So the Captain told him he was at liberty to go."[11]

Julia left Detroit for St. Louis to have her first baby at her parents' house. Frederick Dent Grant, named for her father, was born on May 30, 1850. The "little dog," as his father affectionately called him, became a mainstay in Grant's order of things. Fred spent his life in the role of Ulysses S. Grant's oldest son. At twelve, he was at Vicksburg with his father; at twenty-one, he was at West Point; at thirty-five, he was the family spokesman when Grant died. He acquired a rich and pretty wife, and was in the public eye, but when he himself died, at sixty-one, he was still someone else's son more than a man in his own right.[12]

In the summer of 1851, with splendid disregard for climate, Julia and Fred visited her family in St. Louis, while Ulysses, reassigned to Sackets Harbor, spent his time "fishing, sailing and riding about" the cool and beautiful lakeshore country. He also put much time and thought into fixing up their house: "I have had some very nice furnature made in garrison and otherwise our quarters look very nice. All that we want now to go to housekeeping is the table furnature. That I will not buy until you come on lest I should not please you. The furnature made in garrison is nicer than I would buy in Watertown and more substantial. It consists of lounges, chairs, and a center table." The chairs, however, proved so tall that Julia's feet dangled when she sat in them. Footstools were obtained to compensate for the flaw in design.[13]

While her husband enjoyed anticipating domesticity and waited with "an eligant horse and a buggy to take you and Fred. out with evry day," Julia made the long railroad trip to Sackets Harbor. Just because Ulysses was insistent that she travel with someone, she stubbornly came alone, even furloughing her maid in Detroit. In the coach, at night, she and Fred were startled by the sudden screams of a "maniac en route to an asylum," which understandably unnerved her. The journey finally over, she found herself, with the only baby at the barracks, the center of attention in a community in which Ulysses felt confident. Shortly before she arrived he wrote, "Sackets Harbor is as dull a little hole as you ever saw but the people are very clever as you know very well and all together we could not have a more pleasant station." Their winter together was a good one, but in the spring Ulysses was again ordered away from the Madison Barracks and they were separated.[14]

Grant's unit of the Fourth Infantry Regiment was to be transferred to the Pacific Coast. Initially, the transfer order evoked for Julia romantic images of "the Caribbean Sea," with her ship "parting its slashing, phosphorescent waves and sailing under the Southern Cross." But she never made this journey: "When we were almost ready to ship, my dear husband quietly and calmly told me that . . . he had come to the conclusion that it would be impossible for me to go . . . in my condition." She was pregnant. Strong as Julia was, Grant's decision turned out to be a wise one. About a third of the people in his party were to sicken and die during the crossing of the Isthmus of Panama. If Julia had gone along, she would have given birth to her child on the mule trail into the town of Panama.[15]

Before leaving for the West Coast, Grant had an errand to attend to. Since the Mexican War he had been laboring under a cloud. He had been ordered to make good a thousand dollars that had been stolen while he was regimental quartermaster. There was never an allegation that Grant had taken the money; regulations simply made the officer in charge responsible for covering such losses. Grant and his father tried to wield what influence they possessed to have the requirement for repayment set aside. They had written letters, and now, in the spring of 1852, Grant himself made a trip to Washington, his first to the capital. Calls on Senator Cass, on Ohio congressmen and senators, and on a California congressman he had known in Mexico—"I know some ten or twelve members of the two houses of Congress"—did not produce the private bill in Congress that would have relieved him of both the financial obligation and the stigma of involvement in an unsavory bit of business. Grant did not state his case with clarity. He could write clearly, but his documentation of the case was spare to a fault. No picture of the circumstances emerges, nor any sense of personal urgency.[16]

Furthermore, his timing was unlucky; Henry Clay had just died: "Consequently evry house in the city was closed and evrybody at the funeral." Grant, staying at Willard's Hotel, put aside his own errand to watch the capital city in mourning: "Mr. Clay's death produced a feeling of regret that could hardly be felt for any other man." Returning to his own business, Grant did speak to individual members of Congress who might help him, but was put off with the word that he must meet with a full committee; the committee was not scheduled to meet again until after he was due back at Governors Island, in New York Harbor, to sail for the West Coast, so Grant gave up. The young officer calling on the inhabitants of Capitol Hill was eminently forgettable. He left with the obligation still hanging over his head.[17]

The trip on the *Ohio*, on which he sailed from New York, began pleasantly enough for Grant. Delia B. Sheffield, a young woman aboard the same vessel, left an observant account of the thirty-year-old officer. On deck one day Grant pointed out a school of whales. Nonchalantly, she told him she had seen whales before. Surprised that this was not her first time at sea, and flirting a bit, he then asked where her parents were. Asserting her maturity, Mrs. Sheffield claimed a husband, and Grant told her she was too young to be married: "You ought to be under your mother's care, sleeping in your trundle bed." Mrs. Sheffield was intrigued and kept her eye on him: "Captain Grant was . . . an incessant smoker and very taciturn, thoughtful and serious, though affable in manner, and during every day and an early part of each night of the voyage, I would see him pacing the deck and smoking, silent and solitary."[18]

The ship reached the Isthmus on July 13, 1852, in the rainy season, and the passengers contended with slippery puddles and mud in the port towns. They then went by railroad as far as the Chagres River and from there proceeded on flat-bottomed boats poled by "stark naked" black "natives" (who fascinated both Ulysses and Delia), to the town of Cruces, about twenty-five miles from the Bay of Panama, on the Pacific side of the Isthmus. From Cruces the party had to journey on foot or muleback on steep mountain paths. Many of the travelers were ill and dying. Indeed, more would have died if Grant himself had not demonstrated great steadiness. As regimental quartermaster he was in charge of the logistics of the move across the Isthmus, and in discharging what proved to be a difficult assignment, he demonstrated the organizational strength that would later characterize his command in the Civil War, together with a dimension of humanitarian concern that never as fully emerged again. When a contractor failed to deliver mules already arranged for, Grant, faced with extortionate charges from another supplier, sensibly agreed to the demand for "twenty-four dollars American gold for each riding mule" to get his people to the Bay of Panama. (Some earlier-arriving passengers had paid up to fifty dollars a mount.) Captain Grant got reluctant riders on reluctant animals, and single file, led by men with whom they could not converse, the women proceeded to the tattered town of Panama, with its mixture of old dilapidated houses and half-finished new ones built to accommodate people on the way to California. Grant stayed behind in Cruces until the last of his party could be gotten on the road to Panama. By the time he reached the port, cholera had broken out.[19]

Grant established a hospital on a beached ship on the shore a mile from the town and a hospital tent camp on an island in the bay. Delia Sheffield remembered that it was "a common sight to see strong men . . . taken with cramps and die in a short time." She credited the surgeons with "timeless energy" and remarked, "It was not an easy task to control almost seven hundred men during a siege of cholera, for they grew nervous and panic-stricken and Captain Grant had not only the sick ones to contend with but also the well." Grant also had to contend with private grief. Among the 150 people in the Fourth Infantry party who died was John H. Gore, with whom he had spent much of his army life. Grant comforted Gore's widow and arranged for her, along with the other survivors, to sail for San Francisco on the *Golden Gate*.[20]

When Grant himself reached the city, on his way to Vancouver, he wrote

Julia, "We are going to a fine country, and a new one, with a prospect of years of quiet, when one [once?] settled. Chances must arrise merely from the location of land if in no other way, to make something which if it should not benefit us soon will at least be something for our children." It was a muddled, muffled cry of hope, a tentative promise that he would at last make good their expectations. "There is no reason why an active energeti[c] person should not make a fortune evry year." He toyed with all kinds of schemes but never made any of them work. Only four years after the gold rush and with quick riches still in the air, Grant entered partnership with Elijah Camp, a merchant from Sackets Harbor whom he and Julia had known and liked. Camp persuaded Grant to invest all the salary he had earned since leaving New York in a store in San Francisco, and then, arguing that he could run the business better alone, persuaded Grant to leave his money in the venture and take notes totaling $1,500. Next, Camp persuaded Grant to destroy the notes—and trust him to make the business a success—because, said Camp, he could not sleep nights worrying that Grant might come by to collect when there was not sufficient cash on hand. By mail, Julia chided her husband that compared to Grant "the Vicar of Wakefield's Moses was a financier." In her view, the storekeeper's insomnia should have been cured with "something to *make* him sleep: the poker." But Grant went on trusting the man even after the store failed and Camp went back to Sackets Harbor. In 1854, after he resigned from the army and sailed back to New York, Grant took the train all the way to Lake Ontario to try to collect a portion of the funds he had invested. There he learned that Camp had gone out sailing on a new boat. There was always an Elijah Camp in Ulysses Grant's business deals.[21]

Grant saw people like Camp all around him in California and Oregon in the 1850's. He stayed once with his brother-in-law John C. Dent, who ran a ferry and tavern in Knights Ferry, California, and also talked with old Mexican War friends who were sure they could take what they had learned in their service travels and convert that experience into cash—lots of cash. Grant felt compelled to try for the dollars too, but except for eagerness he had no entrepreneurial instincts. At various times he talked of entering all kinds of enterprises—lumbering, storekeeping, farming—but when he made his move, his gullibility was exceeded only by his bad luck. Assigned in 1852 to the remote but busy chief post on the Columbia River, the Columbia Barracks at Fort Vancouver, in what the next year became the Washington Territory, Grant found that the job of keeping the post in stores, as quartermaster, left him with much time on his hands. Magnificent Mount Hood rose just west of Fort Vancouver, and Grant once went with a group which included some who made the ascent. John W. Emerson—a friend, later, in St. Louis—claimed Grant was in the climbing party, but Grant himself never told of having reached the top. He said no, as usual, to hunting and seems to have derived little pleasure from the spectacularly beautiful Columbia River valley. He did try to put some of his time to use in an enterprise of his own.

Seeing immigrants along the river in want of food, he logically set out to raise oats and potatoes as cash crops. In later years, Washingtonians put up a bronze plaque to commemorate his potato patch, but they were saluting a failure. Grant had not anticipated that the river would flood. He lost his crop. Nothing went right.[22]

Among the tales Grant later had to tell about this period was one John Emerson recalled having heard from him at Barnum's Hotel, in St. Louis. It concerned a "solitary miner . . . heating his coffee over a little fire of twigs. . . . He was friendly . . . but his conversations seemed tinged with sadness. . . . After . . . sharing a cup of coffee and a hard biscuit, Grant . . . mounted and bade him goodbye." But the miner called him back and showed him a packet of letters from a woman "pathetically pleading with him" to return to her. The miner, as Emerson recalled Grant's account, "had been genteel and refined, and had dressed like a civilized man before he came to California; but now he was coarse; he knew he had lost his good manner, and had forgotten to talk . . . as he should talk." Grant claimed he told the miner to take his gold to San Francisco, sell it, and go back to the woman who had written him. The miner promised to take his advice, but later Grant met him in the city: "All his money had been lost in one of the gambling palaces . . . and the poor fellow was in utter despair. Two days later his body was taken from the waters of the bay, and the coroner's 'guess' was that it was a suicide." We have only Emerson's word that his friend told this barroom story, but it is a believable parable of Grant's own fears, and Grant did remain steadfastly unromantic about solitary adventurers in the West for the rest of his life.[23]

On the other hand, while still on the Pacific Coast Grant at times talked as if he were a frontiersman, gone west alone to make a fresh start in life. The appeal of this persona was repeatedly evident—for example, in his remarks when in 1864, with awe, he took stock of his responsibilities as lieutenant general, and when, with apprehension, he returned from his trip around the world in 1879, with no responsibilities at all. But if there were a few zestful days at the Columbia Barracks, when Grant saw himself as a new man in the West, there were far more when he saw himself as an exile, separated from his wife and children. He wanted, initially, to combine an army career with business activity, hoping to earn enough from outside investments to bring his wife and children out west, where they could all begin again, away from their Missouri and Ohio families. Business failures kept postponing the reunion, and his army career moved along satisfactorily only as long as he was stationed at the Columbia Barracks, at Fort Vancouver. It collapsed as badly as the business ventures when he was transferred in 1854 to Fort Humboldt, a tiny and bleak post on a bluff on the California coast, where he encountered a malicious superior officer. In that year, he grew so lonely and despondent, and felt so powerless, that he gave up.

Grant's loneliness overrode all the distractions of his attempts to make money. He missed Julia, his son Fred, and his second son, whom he had never seen. Julia had gone, inexplicably, not to her mother and father's but to Grant's family in Bethel for the birth, on July 22, 1852, of Ulysses S. Grant, Jr. Grant had quietly but unequivocally insisted on the name. "If its a girl name it what you like, but if a boy name it after me." Julia resisted the inevitable pressure from other advisers to call the baby Telemachus. He became Ulysses, but for the rest of her life she fought good-naturedly and unsuccessfully to stop people from calling her cheerful Buckeye State son Buck.24

The hardest thing to understand in the story of Grant's intense unhappiness while on the Pacific Coast, which culminated in his resignation from the army, is Julia's seeming unconcern. In her *Memoirs* she told of the pleasant dancing parties at White Haven for her brother and his new bride in 1852, of efforts to begin the education of her older child, Fred, and of getting "our little man" into properly masculine clothes for his third birthday, the next spring. She said nothing about her husband, other than to tell how he had been swindled by Camp, to explain that it was a banker's fault and not Ulysses' that he had to use a quartermaster's pass rather than his own money to get home, and to make clear that Grant stayed respectably with her brother John, at Knights Ferry, while waiting for the pass. (Carefully unmentioned was the rumor she sought to refute: that his money had gone for whiskey and he had spent the time waiting to sail alone and drunk in an attic room on the San Francisco waterfront.)25

She did not mention his great unhappiness, writing only that after "an absence of over two years, Captain Grant, to my great delight, resigned his commission . . . and returned to me, his loving little wife." Her letters from the period do not survive, and the references to them in his few letters suggest that they were not numerous and were greatly delayed in arriving. In September, two months after Buck's birth, he still knew nothing about Julia's delivery. He realized, of course, that the child must have been born, and dreamed one night of coming home and finding Julia, Fred, "and a beautiful little girl all asleep. Fred woke up and we had a long conversation and he spoke as plainly as one of ten years old."26

In October he still had not heard about the baby, but confidently spoke of it as being alive. At last, in December, the steamer "not only brought me a letter from you, but four letters and two more from Clara," his sister. He knew now that both his wife and his five-month-old son were well. His response was joyous, and he tried to take part in the life of both his children by offering a bit of not very serious advice about their upbringing. But when the next steamer came, he was let down: "I had no doubt that I would find letters. I was disappointed." Two weeks later a long letter arrived, and he was relieved. In February he received a letter Julia had sent in early December. In March there were two more cheerful letters, but on March 31, 1853, he wrote, "The Mail has just arrived bringing me a very short and very unsatisfactory letter. You speak of not joining me on this coast in a manner that would indicate that you have been reflecting upon a dream which you say you have had until you really imagine that it is true. Do not write so any more dearest. It is hard enough for us to be separated so far without borrowing imaginary troubles. You know that it was entirely out of the question for you to have come with me at the time I had to come. I am doing all I can to put up a penny not only to enable you and our dear little boys to get here comfortably, but to enable you to be comfortable after you do get here." We do not know what Julia said about the dream that seemed to bar her from her husband, but apparently she reproached him for not having allowed her to accompany him out west in the first place. And it is clear that he wanted them to join him rather than to return himself.[27]

On June 15 three more sustaining letters arrived from Julia, but in response, Ulysses had to give her the news that the Columbia had overflowed its banks, ruining his potato crop and with it, the prospects of obtaining enough money for her to join him. On June 28, 1853, the steamer brought no letters from home: "Where mails come but twice per month it does seem as though I might expect news from you. . . ." He had a bad cold, and in a troubled letter repeated the story of the failed potato crop, but told her as well of his hopes that he would make six hundred dollars selling some pigs he had bought and of speculations he had made in flour futures in San Francisco. In July he was remorseful that he had troubled her with his statement that he had "lost a number of hundreds of dollars which if you had would educate our dear little boys." And he also had to disappoint her with the information that earlier news about an expected promotion had proved premature. He was deeply discouraged: "In a former letter I told you, for the first time, of the *downs* of all I had done. (Before I had never met with a down.)" but he tried to bolster her spirits (and his) with a claim that he was now making money by speculating in food items. He was still at the Columbia Barracks, and still not totally without hope.[28]

Even though Ulysses missed Julia intensely, he found life at the Columbia Barracks bearable because the people with whom he lived formed a kind of family. At Sackets Harbor the Grants had had as servants a splendid couple. In the best tradition of keeping servants in their place, the woman was known only by her first name—Maggy—while her husband, an enlisted man, was known by his last—Getz. Maggy, disheveled but cheerful and affectionate, managed the household and was Frederick's nurse. Getz maintained the house, cut the wood, and tended the garden and the horses. The Getzes went west with the Fourth Infantry Regiment and provided the domestic center without which Grant's world would not hold. From Vancouver, in January 1853, he had written proudly and with seeming security, "The house I am living in is probably the best one in Oregon." He told Julia of the men sharing mess with him—his old West Point roommate Rufus Ingalls, another officer, and their three enlisted men. The tall house had porches upstairs and down on three sides, so little of the splendid view could be missed. And they were comfortable: "Maggy cooks for us and Getz assists

about the house. Everybody says they are the best servants in the whole Territory. With Getz's pay, the sale of his rations, the wages we give and
Maggy's washing, they get about 75 dollars per month." Whenever mail arrived, Maggy asked after Julia and Fred; Ulysses could not quite fathom why
she was not equally curious about Ulysses junior. Once, in a package, he
enclosed a present for Fred from Maggy and Getz. Maggy was the woman
around the house who was so essential to Grant; she was the mother his
mother had never been, the wife—though there is no reason to imagine any
sexual link to Maggy—while his own was two thousand miles away. As long
as Maggy kept the house, Grant was safe.[29]

Apparently Maggy and Getz saved enough of their pay for him to leave the
army, and these two strong people moved out of Grant's life in the summer of
1853. On July 19 Grant wrote a reference: "The bearer, Margaret Getz, has
lived with me over two years. . . . She is a washer, ironer, plain cook and in
evry way qualified to undertake the entire work of a small family." Maggy
was the key member of the couple; he added in her letter that "Getz is sober,
industrious, and capable . . . and no doubt would prove a good porter in a
store." Maggy and Getz were planning to move out of domestic service and
keep a shop.[30]

The next February, Grant was transferred from the Columbia Barracks to
Fort Humboldt, in northern California. There he found no household, no
fraternal community, no surrogate family. No Julia; no Maggy. Grant was
bereft. He shared quarters with Lewis Cass Hunt. This balding young man
was a friend of Julia's brother John, and had known Julia and Ulysses in Detroit and Sackets Harbor days; there seems, however, not to have been sufficient strength in the friendship to sustain Grant. His loneliness yielded to a
profound despair that neither Julia nor the men at Fort Humboldt could have
failed to notice. He despised his superior officer, Lieutenant Colonel Robert
Christie Buchanan, who responded in kind, and now even his army career
seemed in jeopardy. On February 2, 1854, he wrote his wife that he had no
horse of his own and found riding an effort: "I do nothing but set in my room
and read and occasionally take a short ride on one of the public horses." Such
solitude was not natural to Grant, and not safe. Though he was not gregarious in the sense of being an effusive conversationalist, he needed people. He
had to have their company; he had to be able quietly to tell stories and be
with other men. He was an effective people watcher; he literally studied
those around him—as he had studied Scott and Taylor in Mexico. When he
described himself as sitting alone in his room in this letter to Julia, he did not
speak as a man quietly sustaining himself through reading or some other creative solitary occupation. Rather, his behavior was evidence of dangerous
alienation from the world. It was this letter that began, "You do not know
how forsaken I feel here."[31]

Four days later, when the mail boat had again brought no letter from Julia,
he wrote, "I could almost [quit and?] go home 'nolens volens.' " A month

later his whole commitment to an army career began to collapse: "I sometimes get so anxious to see you and our little boys, that I am almost tempted to resign and trust to Providence, and my own exertions, for a living where I can have you and them with me." The desire to resign from the army and embark on a civilian career was natural enough, but in truth Grant did not trust either Providence or his own exertions. He had no hankering for his father's business, he had bungled every try at speculation in the West, no one trusted him to make a dime as a businessman. And he did not trust himself. He went on, "It would only require a moderate competency to make me take the step. Whenever I get to thinking upon the subject however, *poverty, poverty*, begins to stare me in the face. . . ."[32]

Grant had already missed the wonderful exploring years with Fred, when the child was two and three and four; as early as August 1852 he had written, "I am almost crazy sometimes to see Fred," and he had never seen his two-year-old namesake, Ulysses. In this letter he rambled; he could, he claimed, be happy at Fort Humboldt if Julia and the children were there, but, a bit cruelly, he added, "You could not do without a servant and a servant you could not have. This is bad is it not? But you never complain of being lonesome so I infer that you are quite contented." This last thought troubled him. Never before had Grant written reprovingly of Julia's absence; he had missed her, but he had not equated her being away from him with rejection. "I dreamed of you and our little boys the other night the first time for a long time I thought you were at a party when I arrived and before paying any attention to my arrival you said you must go you were engaged for the dance. Fred. and Ulys. did not seem half so large as I expected to see them." He was trying to stop the clock on his children's growing up, and more urgently, he had a sense that he was losing Julia. Seeking reassurance, he asked, "If I should see you it would not be as I dreamed, would it dearest? I know it would not."[33]

But his depression was not dispelled. He continued, "I am getting to be as great a hand for staying in the house now as I used to be to run about. I have not been a hundred yards from my door but once in the last two weeks. I get so tired and out of patience with the lonliness of this place that I feel like volunteering for the first service that offers." But he passed up chances to go on trips along the coast or into the mountains. Neither the exuberance of the days in the Valley of Mexico nor the wildness within him, which he had seen reflected in the gold-rush men, emerged. He suppressed everything and allowed himself to remain trapped at the base. He kept hoping for a transfer order, but it did not come. Grant's frustration mounted not only because his commanding officer, Buchanan, was an irritating martinet, but also because as a lieutenant colonel, Buchanan was the only man who outranked him at Fort Humboldt—the man in whose absence Grant would have been in command. Eventually, Grant's request for transfer was denied. He had been cast upon a beautiful remote coast and was desperate.[34]

Why didn't Julia, after reading the letters he had written in February, get on the next boat for California? To be sure, she had two very small children, she was used to being cared for, and she was somewhat frightened of traveling alone; but she was strong, and the Isthmus crossing was less dangerous in spring than in summer. She did not have the money for such a journey, but she should have been able to coax it from her father or from Jesse Grant. The trip would take perhaps two months. (Indeed, had she set forth in response to his letters, she would have arrived probably too late to stop his resignation and perhaps even too late to find him before he left.) In any case, she did not start out.

Julia's sense of frustration during this period must have been intense. She had gone to her husband's family for the birth of her second child, for reasons we do not know—perhaps there was illness in St. Louis, perhaps either she or Ulysses sought to achieve independence of White Haven—and she was not very articulate. It is possible that what Ulysses took as petulance in two of her letters was a muffled cry of despair. She may have written so seldom because she doubted her ability to conceal from her husband that she too was severely depressed. Of course, another possible explanation for the paucity of letters is that out of sight was out of mind, but Julia did not have a rich source of alternative concern and there is little to suggest she wanted to discard her husband. She did chide him for undertaking pie-in-the-sky ventures and let him know that, in essence, she felt he had abandoned her. And now he felt as if she and the whole world had abandoned him.

Perhaps Julia had given up on the army career before Ulysses did, and wanted him to come back east, but if she had, one would expect to find him responding to suggestions from her that he resign, and no such responses are to be found in his letters. In their respective memoirs Julia and Ulysses were succinct about his days on the West Coast. He wrote with brevity but acumen about the Indians and about life in San Francisco, to which hopeful young men had come and died. In 1852 he had found it a one-wharf new town; in 1853, when he returned, he saw a dissolute city with no reliable foundations, in which murdered gamblers found watery graves beneath the houses built over San Francisco Bay. By the time he left in 1854 it was, he claimed, "staid and orderly." Of himself, he wrote merely, "My family all this while, was at the East. It consisted now of a wife and two children. I saw no chance of supporting them on the Pacific coast out of my pay as an army officer, I concluded therefore to resign. . . ." Julia, for her part wrote briefly and breezily of this period in their lives: "Captain Grant, to my great delight, resigned his commission . . . and returned to me, his loving little wife"; her tone caused Bruce Catton to suggest that the interlude may not have been as important as other students of Grant have thought. This is a cheerful idea, but not a convincing one. In a letter of March 6, 1854, Grant introduced one of his characteristic bits of gallows humor. He juxtaposed a description of the base as "a very healthy place" with the throw-away line "I believe there has been but two deaths. One by accidentally shooting himself and the other by a limb from a tree falling on a man." Such asides can have been no more reassuring to Julia than they are to the modern reader.[35]

When Grant is mentioned, most people respond by asking, in one way or another, "Was he a drunk?" The idea that he drank prodigiously is as fixed in American history as the idea that the Pilgrims ate turkey on Thanksgiving, but the evidence for it is more elusive. All the rivers of alcohol—imagined or real—flow down from the Fort Humboldt days. And Grant's letters do make stories of drinking in this period easy to believe. No eyewitness accounts of his drinking at this time exist, but rumors that he drank were widespread in headquarters in San Francisco then—and ever after. Rufus Ingalls, who was his roommate at West Point, his housemate at Vancouver, and his lifelong friend, believed he was drinking at Fort Humboldt. Hamlin Garland, a careful and thoughtful writer whose excellent biography is favorable to Grant, interviewed a great many people who knew Grant and inquired particularly about the question of alcohol. His conclusion was that Grant did drink.[36]

Whether or not Ingalls and Garland were correct, what surely is more important than estimating the quantity of whiskey consumed or speculating on Grant's favorite brand (we do not know what it was) is understanding the extent of the depression that occasioned the drinking. When a man who has needed the closeness of people with whom he can comfortably talk, who has previously wanted to be alone only to indulge his curiosity about a strange town, and who thoroughly enjoys working with horses, goes to his room during the day, not to read, but simply to be alone, he becomes disconnected from everything outside himself and, finally, even from himself. The watch, if it has not stopped, has run down. In a basic sense, Grant had nothing to do. Without friends, without Julia and the two boys, without any responsibilities on the base, he was at the danger point. The bottle was the signal that it had been reached. Grant did not leave the army because he was a drunk. He drank and left the army because he was profoundly depressed.

On April 11, 1854, while listed on the company roll as "sick," Ulysses Grant wrote two letters. One formally accepted promotion to the permanent rank of captain, a position of considerable prestige in the small peacetime army of 1854, in which there were only fifty captains on active duty. The second letter read, "I very respectfully tender my resignation of my commission as an officer of the Army. . . ." A short while later, in San Francisco, an old army friend, James Elderkin, "was almost ashamed to speak to him on the street, he looked so bad."[37]

It is difficult to measure the response of Julia and others to this action because we do not know how long it took for Grant's letters describing his extreme loneliness to reach them. Grant had asked that the resignation be effective on July 31, 1854. In June, Jesse learned what he had done and moved to stop it. At the last moment, once again trying to reconstruct his son's life, he wrote to Andrew Ellison, an Ohio congressman from Georgetown, asking him to intervene with a fellow Democrat, Secretary of War Jefferson Davis. Ellison, in turn, wrote Davis, "Jesse R. Grant Esq—the father of Captain Ulysses Grant of the Army . . . requests that I would ask to have Capt Grant ordered home on the recruiting service, as a favor, to obtain some rest and see his friends and family[.] If that cannot be permitted, then to allow him a six month leave of absence. . . . It is stated in one of the papers of this city that Capt Grant has resigned, if this be the fact, what I ask is not needed. . . ."[38]

The congressman missed the point. Jesse desperately wanted to keep his son in the army. Ever since Ulysses was a boy managing not to be around the tanyard very much, Jesse had known that he had no sense for business. He had gotten him into the army in the first place because he did not know what else to do with him. Shrewdly, even desperately, he wanted to find a way for his son to keep his commission. When Davis confirmed to Ellison that Grant had indeed resigned, Jesse wrote directly to the secretary of war, citing both his son's Mexican War record (which might have impressed Davis, also a veteran of that war) and the fact that Ulysses had a two-year-old son he had never seen. Jesse sought to have the resignation rescinded and to obtain a leave for Ulysses, during which he could arrange to take his family to the West Coast. Davis replied that as Grant "assigned no reasons why he desired to quit the service, and the motives which influenced him are not known to the Department" he saw no reason to revoke the resignation, and it stood. The secretary of war's refusal was irrevocable. Davis's letter also suggested, with considerable tact, that Grant's motives were not something he wanted to have to face officially. It was not, that is to say, on the record that the young officer was a drunk, but word to that effect was abroad in the gossipy ranks of the army. These stories were more insidious and harder to combat than even a negative official record. They haunted Grant into the Civil War—and into history.[39]

"Poor and forlorn," Grant came back east, but did not immediately make a cleansing new start. The fear of poverty was still stronger than his need to admit to it and hurry home. The slips of paper that pathetically marked inept California speculations still stuck to his fingers. Reaching New York, he borrowed money to pay his bill at the Astor House from Simon Bolivar Buckner, and did not take the first train back to Julia. Instead, borrowing the fare, again from Buckner, he made the long detour to try unsuccessfully to collect $800 of the $1,500 which Elijah Camp had inveigled from him. Grant wanted to get back to his father and his father-in-law with some indication of manly success in affairs to show for his years on the West Coast.[40]

It is not known just how tense Grant's reunion with his family was. Hamlin Garland believed Jesse Grant was exceedingly cool toward Ulysses on his return, and Julia, amid her effusions of joy in the *Memoirs*, let slip one sentence that suggests that Grant was not entirely sure she wanted him back: "Ulys turned to me and said: 'You know I had to wait in New York until I heard from you.' " Grant's last letter to her from the West Coast is the stiffest he ever wrote: "May 2, 1854—Dear Wife; I do not propose writing you but a few lines. I have not yet recieved a letter from you and as I have a 'leave of absence' and will be away from here in a few days do not expect to. . . . You might write directing it to the City of New York." There was no letter from her when he reached the city, and so, futilely, he went on to Sackets Harbor, and then returned to New York to await word from White Haven. He was afraid to return to Missouri without reassurance that he would be welcome. When, at last, she provided the encouragement in a letter, he set out for St. Louis, and by October, Ulysses and Julia were back together. Their third child was conceived in the month he got home; Nellie Grant was born the next year on the Fourth of July.[41]

# V

## GALENA

The foregoing has the ring of biography, without the satisfaction of knowing that the hero, like Grant, lolling in his general store in Galena, is ready to be called to an intricate destiny.

— *F. Scott Fitzgerald*

JULIA AND ULYSSES were together again, but their future in 1854 was unpromising. Ulysses had abandoned the only trade he knew and at thirty-two had to find a way to earn a living. His father had recently moved the family to Covington, Kentucky, and after a few weeks with the Dents, Julia and Ulysses went there to discuss a proposition Jesse was making. Julia put it somewhat poetically: "As we stepped from the boat onto the Kentucky shore, the sun (which had shone most gloriously all morning) was at that instant overcast. . . ." Having disapproved of the resignation from the army, Jesse was in no mood to make things easy for this son who had thrown away a chance to better the family's fortunes. He offered Ulysses a job in the Galena, Illinois, branch of his business, but there was a condition to be met. Julia recalled that her husband was ready to accept the job until "it was suggested and made a necessary part of the agreement that I and my two little boys should remain in Kentucky with them, so as to have the benefit of their school of economy, or go to my father in Missouri." Clearly, Jesse perceived Julia not as a steadying influence on his son, but as a costly appendage, and he was not prepared to underwrite a second family household. Julia could make do in Covington or St. Louis, and Ulysses presumably could board

with his brother in Galena. Julia recorded proudly that "Captain Grant posi-
tively and indignantly refused his father's offer."[1]

This ungenerous reception of the prodigal did nothing to improve Grant's
ties with his father, and it tightened his dependence on his wife. The disastrous separation just ended had taught Julia and Ulysses its lesson; during the
remaining peacetime years they were seldom separated, day or night, and
during the war Julia joined Ulysses at his command headquarters on every
possible occasion, spending more time with her husband than the wives of
other generals did with theirs. While president, Grant rarely went on a political trip without his wife. And after he left the White House they did virtually everything together. Only exceptionally did the general leave her for
holiday excursions with old friends. They needed each other, and if either
needed the other more, it was Ulysses who needed Julia. Theirs was not a
ledgerbook relationship of debits and credits owed by one and collected by
the other. To a remarkable degree these two limited people became one.

Leaving Covington abruptly, the Grants went back to St. Louis and win-
tered with Julia's parents. In the spring of 1855 Ulysses obtained the use of
his brother-in-law Lewis Dent's farm, Wish-ton-Wish, on the family
acreage, and put in a crop. With a certain gallantry, Ulysses and Julia set out
to recreate their lives in a classically American style—as yeoman farmers in
touch with the life of republican virtue. He tilled the good earth, and she
kept busy tending the children, Fred, Buck, and their sister Nellie, and keeping an eye on the barnyard. Julia, in fact, turned out to be a quite good
chicken farmer and dignified the lowly business of gathering eggs and killing
birds by adding ornamental fowl to the flock—she named their Chinese cock
Celeste. Julia intended in her *Memoirs* to present herself as a figure of fragile
gentility, but inadvertently, telling a story about churning a tub of butter in
ten minutes, she revealed how extraordinarily strong she was. Hastily she
added, "I rested here on my laurels. This was my first and only trial at such
work (my dear husband on all occasions furnishing me with the necessary
*help* to do my work)." On the farm, Ulysses once again hoed potatoes. He
also cleared land Julia's father gave them for their own farm, and cut, hauled,
and squared the timbers with which, in 1856, he framed and closed in his
own house, Hardscrabble.[2]

Hardscrabble was a good house, handmade and plain. It was the only
thing Ulysses Grant ever made. The zest with which he (with the help of
hired hands) fashioned the points and raised the building suggests that it had
true creative meaning for him. Unfortunately, Julia hated it. Instead of a
rough, strong, masculine building of hand-hewn timbers, Julia would have
preferred a "neat frame house" which "could have been put up in half the
time and at less expense." Ulysses' house was, she recalled, "so crude and
homely I did not like it at all, but I did not say so." Its timber framed walls
handsomely set off, by contrast, the "pretty covers, baskets, books, etc."
which Julia hurriedly brought in, but these did not overcome the "unattrac-

*Hardscrabble, the house Grant built.* LIBRARY OF CONGRESS

tive" shamefulness of the place in her eyes. To Ulysses, the name Hardscrabble was complimentary; Julia used the term "facetiously." Derisively, she called their home a "cabin"; he described it as the "house" on which he "worked very hard, never losing a day because of bad weather. . . ."[3]

Grant was trying hard to have confidence in his new life. At Christmastime in 1856 he wrote his father, "Evry day I like farming better and I do not doubt but that money is to be made at it." None was. Julia was already uneasy. Soon after she moved into the still unfinished Hardscrabble, she was, she reported, "feeling quite blue (which was rare with me), when a feeling of the deepest despondency like a black cloud fell around me, and I exclaimed (aloud, I think): Is this my destiny?" She hated the "rough surroundings" and the relentless daily routines of the farm. Julia claimed in her *Memoirs* that she rallied herself: "I have never since lost my courage, not even in the dark day of that (what shall I call him?) Ward." She was referring to Ferdinand Ward and another time, a quarter of a century later, when poverty nearly overtook them, with the failure of the Wall Street firm of Grant & Ward. During 1856 there had been only fifty dollars to spend on clothing for the family, and while Julia had determination, she had no inclination to go on being the wife of a dirt farmer. She could not understand why Ulysses had wanted to leave Wish-ton-Wish, and she was more than willing to leave Hardscrabble and go back to White Haven when her mother died in February 1857. She had no awareness that her repudiation of Hardscrabble was a repudiation of Ulysses.[4]

One problem with Hardscrabble was that it presented only an illusion of independence, not the reality. The Grants had not truly set off on their own. They were not settlers on the fertile new lands of Oregon or northern California; they were on her father's land. As much of themselves as they put into building their own house, into caring for their own animals and crops, all was still done under the sponsorship of Julia's father. Indeed, the Grants were financially dependent on him, and to make matters worse, although Colonel Dent had land and slaves, he had little money. Julia's brothers had left to make their living away from White Haven. The "poverty, poverty" which had haunted Grant in the West came east with him.

Grant struggled ineptly, even pathetically, with the economics of farming. In 1855, while at Wish-ton-Wish, he had made a bit of money on his potatoes while the corn and oats fed the animals and, in part, the family. In 1856 his labor was diverted to the building of Hardscrabble. Lacking working capital for the farm, or even "a few dollars to buy any little necessaries, sugar, coffee, etc.," to say nothing of wages for the hired men who did the cutting, Grant tried to obtain cash by selling firewood in St. Louis. Between April 1856 and February 1857 these sales brought in only "a fraction over 48 dollars per month."[5]

In short, the economic situation was desperate. During the winter months Captain Grant, West Point '43, hauled firewood into St. Louis and sold it on street corners. It was a sad business. Legend has it that he stood sullenly next to his cords of wood in his fading blue army overcoat. This activity did, however, get him away from the wretched farm. While in town he was always on the lookout for old army friends—not, in disgrace, avoiding contacts, but actively seeking them. He hunted for them in the hotel lobbies and, though the evidence is flagrantly conflicting, apparently in the barrooms as well. Once his search for someone familiar led to a poignant moment. In the book at the front desk of the Planter's House he saw registered "J.R. Grant, Ky." He wrote to his father, "I made shure it was you and that I should find you when I got home," but Jesse Grant did not arrive, and inquiring again, Ulysses found "J. R. G. had just taking the Pacific R.R. cars." He could scarcely believe that his father had been in town and not visited him. Plaintively, he asked, "Was it you?"[6]

Meanwhile, the farm required cash. In February 1857 Grant wrote his father, "Spring is now approaching when farmers require not only to till the soil, but to have the wherewith to till it, and to seed it." In the past two seasons he had raised only three unprofitable crops—potatoes, oats, and corn—but now he had twenty-five acres planted in wheat and had paid to have three hundred cords of wood cut for sale the following winter. He was in need of money for tools and other necessities for diversifying his crops: "To this end I am going to make the last appeal to you. I do this because, when I was in Ky. you voluntarily offered to give me a Thousand dollars, to commence with, and because there is no one els to whom I could, with the same propriety, apply. It is always usual for parents to give their children assistince in beginning life (and I am only beginning, though thirty five years of age, nearly) and what I ask is not much." Grant asked his father to lend him (or to borrow for him) five hundred dollars "at 10 pr. cent payable annually or semi anually if you choose, and with this if I do not go on prosperously I shall ask no more from you." There is no record of the loan having been made. In the 1857 season, Grant's wheat crop, projected at "four to five hundred bushels" came to only seventy-five, but even as he confessed this disappointment to his sister Mary, he indicated that he hoped for fifteen hundred bushels of potatoes, along with some sweet potatoes, melons, and cabbages which could be marketed. In the end, these crops did not translate into money enough to keep his family in comfort; before Christmas 1857, Ulysses Grant pawned his gold watch for twenty-two dollars.[7]

Farmers suffered in the wake of the severe depression of 1857, and the year that followed it was disastrous for Grant. Reluctantly, he rented Hardscrabble, and when his widowed father-in-law moved to town, he farmed his land. He had no greater luck on these acres than on his own; he began to give up, and talked about selling Hardscrabble and moving either to Covington, where his father might get him a job, or to St. Louis, where Colonel Dent might find him a position.

The men who worked the farm with him were slaves. There had probably been twelve at White Haven, but it is not clear how many moved to town with the colonel and how many remained under Grant's supervision. In 1858 he hired two slaves from their owners and borrowed one, William Jones, from his father-in-law. Jones, whom he subsequently bought, was about thirty-five years old and five feet seven inches tall, resembling Grant in both age and build, and they worked closely together. Though Ulysses owned just this one person, Julia owned four—Eliza, Julia, John, and Dan. The latter two appear to have been young boys, possibly the sons of Eliza and of Julia. Before Julia Grant moved to Galena, Illinois, where these slaves would have been free, she leased them. When the war to free the slaves liberated Julia Grant from Galena, she reclaimed her slave Julia, who thenceforth went along as her maid on her frequent visits to General Grant's headquarters. Julia's Julia was, in fact, almost stolen from her mistress at Holly Springs.

Despite his great need for cash, Grant seems never to have contemplated selling any of his wife's slaves or his own. Julia, who regarded the sale of "dear family servants" as déclassé, denied rumors that her husband used a slave to repay a debt to Judge John F. Long. However, when Grant considered joining his father in Covington in 1858, he did offer to defer to Jesse's judgment as to whether one of the youths owned by Julia should be hired out in St. Louis or brought along to learn to be a blacksmith. The only evidence that Grant disapproved of the institution of slavery is his humane regard for the men—slave and free—who worked with him in the fields and cutting wood. One former slave whom Grant had hired, "Old Uncle Jason," was quoted as saying that Grant was the kindest man he ever worked for: "He used ter pay us several cents more a cord for cuttin' wood than anyone else paid, and some of the white men cussed about it. . . ." One must be wary of aged persons who remember extraordinary early virtue in famous men, but a white Confederate sympathizer, seeking to demonstrate how common Grant was, confirmed the story, sneering about "his fooling away his money paying them —— free niggers ten and fifteen cents a cord too much . . . and a-spoiling them, sir." On one occasion Grant was reported to have stopped the whipping of a slave by a farmer neighbor, and in 1859, when he was leaving the farm to go into business in St. Louis and was severely pressed financially, he did not sell William Jones but instead set him free.[8]

Grant appears to have had close relationships with some of his white neighbors, but these friendships presented greater psychological risk than did his friendships with the black men who worked for and with him. By associating with dirt farmers he risked being looked down on by Julia's friends, the O'Fallons and Longs and others who, like the Dents, had pretentions to the gentry. Once, Grant befriended a farmer about to lose his mule to a bill collector, and in an action demonstrating the best of his nature, lent the man money he could not afford to lose. Such close ties with poverty must have served to suggest to him how near he himself was to begging funds to save a mule. And there is evidence to indicate that Grant was indeed taking small loans from some of these farmers in order to get by. Julia had little patience with such people; she much preferred to see benevolence in terms of *noblesse oblige*, not reciprocity. She proudly told how, in Galena, when her sunny open child Ulysses junior befriended a very poor boy, she generously allowed the child to eat meals in her kitchen. It must have been profoundly disturbing for both Julia and Ulysses to find themselves in the ranks of the have-nots, but on the failing farm outside St. Louis, that is exactly where they were.[9]

The one area of personal relationships where Grant's hold was firm was in his own immediate family. On February 6, 1858, Julia and Ulysses' fourth and last child was born. He was named Jesse, after his grandfather. Jesse was a healthy baby and grew to be an impish child. And Grant himself was a child again, romping with the children. He genuinely enjoyed being with them. There was an affectionate innocence about the roughhousing of the father down on the floor in comfortable physical rapport with his children. The ease of it all was in strong contrast to the austerity of his own childhood, and there was always deep affection between the father and his children. As the years went on, he worried about their education, as well he might; at eight, Fred still could not read, and Jesse when he finally went off to college had had almost no formal education. But such worries never overcame Grant's deep love for and confidence in his children.[10]

In 1858 the Grants at last gave up the farm. The family was not flourishing there, and Ulysses' own health was not good. He had what he believed to be ague, but there can be little doubt that he worried lest the shivering and fever and cough heralded in him the same tuberculosis that was slowly killing his brother Simpson. Illnesses, coupled with their economic plight, meant they had to move. As early as 1857 he had said, "The fact is, without means, it is useless for me to go on farming," and in September 1858 Ulysses wrote his loyal sister Mary that "there was so much sickness in [the] family, and Freddy so desperately ill" that he had been reluctant to alarm her with a letter. For a short time he and Julia planned a move to Covington to join forces with Jesse and his family, but Julia acted determinedly to block that alternative by appealing to a cousin, Harry Boggs, to take her husband into his firm in St. Louis. In the winter of 1858–59, the Grants moved to a small, unstylish house in town, and Ulysses went into the nasty business of rent collecting with Boggs. No one could have been less fit for the aggressive, shameless job of bill collector than Ulysses Grant. He soon found himself disapproving of his partner's jokes about their victims; by summer Boggs and Grant had quarreled and Ulysses was desperate to leave the firm of Boggs & Grant.[11]

In August 1859 some of Grant's friends—he never forgot the people in St. Louis who stood by him in those days, or those who scorned him—tried to secure for him the position of county engineer. For one, Joseph J. Reynolds, a professor of mechanics and engineering at Washington University, wrote a strong letter in his support. In the end, politics, not lack of qualifications, cost Grant the job. One way that Grant had thrown himself into the Dents' world in St. Louis was by voting for a Democrat, James Buchanan, for president in 1856. Now the two Democratic members of the county council voted to appoint Grant as county engineer, but the three Free-Soilers voted against him. His usual luck had held. He stayed on with Boggs, growing increasingly less fond of his partner as their business faltered.[12]

In December 1859, in a letter to his father, Grant outlined, with some confusion, the complex financial transaction which cost him Hardscrabble. He sold it in exchange for a St. Louis house. The former owner was required to discharge a small mortgage on the house; when he failed to do so, Grant sued. The suit was settled with the recovery of Hardscrabble only in 1867. Town life was proving as disastrously unsuccessful as country life had been. The evening he was rejected for the job as engineer, the Grants sat alone in the parlor of their St. Louis house. The children were out playing; the prospects for their parents were bleak. Julia, though it cost her much pride to make the suggestion, told Ulysses he had better go once again and ask his father for help. Jesse, she recalled later, "had always been not only willing but anxious to serve him (in his own way to be sure)." Grant tried to put off going on the ground that the trip would be costly, but Julia countered by suggesting that it would be a chance to get away from his troubles in St. Louis for a few days. Reluctantly, he agreed to go. This was to be the most painful trip of his life.[13]

At thirty-seven Grant had to go back and admit that he was still a failure: the boy who could not bargain for a horse had become a man who could not bring in a crop of potatoes or collect a batch of bills. It was humiliating. The letter he wrote to Julia on March 14, 1860, describing his return to his father's dominion, makes exceedingly distressing reading. (And here Julia's memory surely failed her; she remembered receiving "long and cheerful letters from my husband" while he was on this trip.) Grant arrived at Covington "with a head ache and feeling bad generally." A wreck on the tracks had made him late for his appointment with his father. "As I was walking up the Street home I saw him turn down another street not more than half a square ahead of me. . . ." Grant was so uncomfortable about seeing his father that he did not even run to catch him. He thought he would see him at dinner; instead, he learned that his father was on his way out of town and would be away for the next three days.[14]

At the house he found his arrival was considered an insufficient demonstration of familial loyalty: his mother and sisters wondered where Julia and the children were. "They were quite disappointed," he wrote, "that Fred. & Buck were not along. My head is nearly bursting with pain. . . ." He continued the letter with greetings for the children and with an apology to Julia's father for not writing a promised letter in support of an absurd claim the colonel had brought for land mentioned in an ancient Spanish grant. He signed with an affectionate nickname (Dado), said in a postscript that his brother Simpson had confided that he felt no better, and concluded, "I have not been through the house to see how things look though I have been here three or four hours." He had simply sat down in the dining room, paralyzed by what he had come back to. But back he had come; and this time Grant's father, on his return, said Ulysses could enter the business and bring his family with him.[15]

In the summer of 1860, then, the Grants gave up the St. Louis house, leased the slaves, packed their household goods, and took a river boat, the *Itaska*, north to Galena. The town, a short distance up the Galena River from the Mississippi, was still an important center of river trade. Its wharves were busy in August as Julia carried the baby and herded the other three children ahead of her down the gangway while Ulysses followed with the two kitchen chairs they had used as seats on the boat deck. At thirty-eight a still youthful-looking and thoroughly domesticated American male, he appeared ready for a fresh start.

A strikingly high bluff rises abruptly behind the business streets of Galena. The Grants climbed a steep flight of stairs to Prospect Street, on which half the houses of High Street, a short block below, rudely turned their backs. Although Grant's house down toward the end of High Street was small, it had dignity and charm and like its slightly more important neighbors was made, reassuringly, of brick. A disarmingly comfortable and rambling graveyard lay out back, and Julia and Ulysses could walk easily across the open lots beside it to the small wooden houses of their new neighbors, the Rawlinses and the Rowleys. The people of Galena became the true inhabitants of Grant's world. They did not flood him with friendship when he arrived in the small city; they did not take in the middle-aged clerk in his father's store and make a success of him, but when Grant went to war and to the White House, some of them went with him. Galena people moved to the center of his vision. They made sense to him. Galena people, he discovered, were as anxious as he to get out of town.

When Grant arrived in Galena, he gave no one a signal that he was a man one could profitably befriend. Yet with the High Street house as a secure base he might, given time, have become a respected and dependable burgher in the small midwestern city. Galena was prosperous. There were lead mines nearby. The channel of the Galena River was open and deep and goods came to the docks up the short distance from the Mississippi. Until the railroads enabled its rival, Chicago, to outstrip it, Galena was an important center for commerce with the rest of northwestern Illinois and with Iowa and Wisconsin. Its boom days had been in the 1840's, when Jesse Grant, in partnership with E. A. Collins, opened the store on Main Street. The firm, later styled Grant & Perkins, sold harnesses and other leather goods and purchased hides from farmers in the area. By 1860 the business was Jesse's alone and was run by his sons Orvil and Simpson.[16]

Ulysses made an effort to be a leather merchant, taking trips to Iowa as a salesman and a hide buyer. To prove his commercial respectability, he attended the Methodist church and put in tedious hours in the Main Street store, being solicitous of the customer buying a new strap for an old saddle. He made small talk about the weather or politics and told stories about the Mexican War. But there is no evidence that the men of the town had yet taken him into account. Perhaps given enough time and enough demonstrations of his steadiness they would have. There was no reason why Ulysses could not soon have become a partner, rather than a clerk. He spoke confidently of such a prospect, and the sad fact that his brother Simpson was slowly dying made it likely that the time for promotion was not far off. Orvil Grant, in manner Jesse's true son, was in charge, and as Ulysses could have anticipated, the business was aggressively and prosperously run by this younger brother. Everything was propitious for him to fit in, except for the fact that Ulysses Grant was still Ulysses Grant. Perhaps he could have lived out his days as a solid townsman and successful merchant in Galena. Or perhaps he was lucky not to have to work in the store long enough for the façade to crack.[17]

Julia, making do with an Irish girl in place of her Missouri slaves, was game about being a newcomer in town, rather than the Dent daughter who counted in St. Louis. She was not resentful of having had to move north with Ulysses, but there was a hint of self-consciousness and a sense of superiority in her insistence on dressing two-year-old Jesse in finer clothes than were usual in Galena. Only such minute expressions of differentness were open to her. There was no way for her to play out the energy and determination that she had displayed when she and Ulysses rode horseback vigorously at White Haven or churned butter at Hardscrabble. Nor was there any outlet for him. He no longer even owned a horse. People talked of his vacant expression as he went down the long, long flight of stairs to work and climbed back up them to his house at the end of the day.[18]

# VI

# ESCAPING FROM THE ORDINARY

. . . war, the ordinary man's most convenient means of escaping from the ordinary . . .
— *Philip Caputo*

O N C E  A G A I N Grant was close to silence, a difficult quality to measure in a man, and one which in his case must be read in two ways. There are many men in America who are articulate only to the extent of hinting in clichés at what is locked within them. They talk disparagingly of the weather and of people different from themselves; they joke about sex and theorize solemnly about ways to make money; and as they do so, they work monotonously at something they have no interest in talking about. Their predictable, ritual conversations with one another enable them to endure. Sometimes the talk stops, as it did for Grant at Fort Humboldt; then such a man cannot keep going. The chatter that has been the barrier against nothingness is gone. The void that remains is terrifying. Grant had known that silence as he sought another kind. He wanted a silence born of confidence and command, a time when he could listen to other men's chatter but have no need to add to it himself. This is the silence not of a man deadened to the world, but rather of one come alive to engage it. It is the silence of Ulysses Grant as he appears in the Brady photograph, sitting on a bench hauled out of a church into the sun during the Wilderness campaign (see p. 167). There, as others busily talked, he sat silent and in control.

As a means of getting one's back into life, war can be a bad bargain. It can as often be a boring job at a desk or a wearing slog through rough countryside in the wrong season as something more exhilarating. But it is a way out of a leather store. And for some men it is much more than that—it is the fulfillment that the world will yield in no other manner. For these men, war appears as a refutation of evil, whether it be the evil of Hitler's threat to Marc Bloch's France or of the slaveholders' threat to Thoreau's America, or, less exalted but no less real, the evil of personal hollowness. War, for a man like Ulysses Grant, was the only situation in which he could truly connect to his country and countrymen and be at one with them and with himself. That the price of this connection was killing other men is a fact that many observers quickly note and rightly deplore, but that does not dispose of the matter. The nineteenth-century American world, whether of commerce or wilderness, of politics or sex, of farm or horse, of family or privacy, did not arouse this particular man (and the many others like him) the way war could. Grant did not like the vainglory of victory or the drama of high strategy or the blood of battle, and he did not think all wars worth fighting, yet some essential part of his being was brought into play only in war. He never celebrated this fact, but neither did he deny it; he knew it was true. Only in war—and possibly, at the end of his life, in writing about the war—did he find the completeness of experience that, when engaged in it, was so intensely his.

Grant's war was coming. The politics of war-causing were over and the politics of warmaking about to begin. They began in Galena much as they did in towns and cities all over the North. In Galena, as everywhere else, in both North and South, it was by no means certain where those lines of loyalty would lead. Sympathy for the Confederacy, and for its position on keeping black people in slavery, was considerable in the Illinois town lying close to the Wisconsin border; but unlike those of his townsmen who had such sympathy, Grant had no problem accepting the basic tenets of Lincoln's call to preserve the Union. A private citizen without marked political passions, Grant took the two strands of his political past and made of them an untangled line of commitment to the Union. He was a standard war Democrat, with Whig antecedents as well. In an uncomplicated way he made the two traditions one, and he became a general who knew clearly where he stood throughout the war.

This clarity of view was not achieved through active participation in the politics of the late 1850's, and indeed it may owe something to inactivity in them. Grant, as an alert, stimulated young lieutenant, had been more articulate on the political dimension of the Mexican War than he was to be in the confused and defeating peacetime days that followed. In the 1850's he seemed uninterested in politics, but not ignorant of them. One Missouri friend—John W. Emerson—recalling forty years later the arguments of the 1850's over slavery and its extension into the territories, recorded, "While Grant lived quietly on his farm from 1854 to 1858, no man was better informed than he on every phase of the controversy." Emerson also remembered entering Grant's St. Louis office in 1859 and "on more than one occasion," finding him "sitting alone at his desk with his hand holding a newspaper hanging listlessly by his side, with every evidence of deep thought, suggesting sadness. At first I supposed these were mere studious and reflective 'moods.' But I soon learned from remarks he now and then made in condemnation of some extravagant and vicious sentiments . . . which he had been reading, that. . . . he was deeply pained."[1]

Emerson had come on Grant on yet another occasion in which silence had overtaken him. Only when his friend pressed him did Grant express concern about the divisive issues in the newspapers; until then, political affiliations had been a function of social milieu. When, upon returning from the West Coast, he had tried to mold himself into the kind of farmer-planter his father-in-law was, he had adopted the political outlook of Colonel Dent and other Missouri landowning slaveholders. But Grant had set free the only slave he, personally, owned. To impute moral indifference to this act would be unfair. It was a decent thing to do, the more so because Grant was in financial trouble and the thirty-five-year-old male in good health was worth about $1,500. The freedom William Jones obtained was no less valuable because manumission was effected at a time when Grant was once again shifting his plans for his life. He had given up trying to establish himself as a plantation owner, Missouri fashion, and was moving to town. In the month before he set Jones free he had been trying to ingratiate himself with businessmen and politicians who were Free-Soilers. The ownership of a slave (for whom in any event there was barely room in the house) was not an asset when talking to them.[2]

As Ulysses moved away from the Dents' Democratic world, he was forced back closer to the politics of his father. With the demise of the Whig party, Jesse Grant became a Know-Nothing, and Ulysses joined him briefly in that strange and unattractive political expression of distrust of people unlike oneself. The rhetoric of bigotry that crept into his letters to Jesse in 1859 reflects not only an attempt to accommodate himself, after so many years, to his father's way of looking at things, but also a bitterness born of being beaten by others. The descendant of Matthew Grant of the *Mary and John* saw his job as county engineer go to "a Dutchman. . . . There is," he continued, ". . . but one paying office in the County held by an American unless you except the office of Sheriff which is held by a Frenchman who speaks broken English but was born here."[3]

Later in his life, reminiscing as a Republican, Grant hinted that he had been sympathetic to the Whig candidacies of his Mexican War commanders, Zachary Taylor in 1848 and Winfield Scott in 1852, and saw them as his political forebears. But in fact, he had voted for neither man. He cast his first presidential ballot in the election of 1856, for James Buchanan. Guessing why people vote as they do is risky business; Grant was a Dent in 1856; in 1860, when his Republican brother Orvil said, "You ought to be ashamed of having voted for Buchanan," Ulysses replied, "I didn't, I voted against Frémont."[4]

Fortunately for Ulysses Grant's reputation as a Republican, he had not lived long enough in Illinois to vote in 1860. If he had, he probably would have voted against Abraham Lincoln; Grant was then a Douglas Democrat. Later, when he was a Republican president, he blurred that embarrassing fact by saying nothing of Douglas and stressing, instead, that he had not at all liked the other Democratic candidate, Breckinridge, preferring Lincoln to him. This shift away from Southern planter loyalties again suggests the philosophical aspects of his leaving the Dents and beginning an adjustment to the life of a Northern town, where the concepts of free soil and free enterprise were dominant. And when it came to deciding where he stood on the question of secession and Union, Grant knew exactly where he was. As an observer, he saw it all accurately. By December 1860 Grant regarded his man Buchanan as a "granny of an Executive." He predicted the Fort Sumter crisis with a remarkable sense of the strategy of warmaking, guessing wrongly only which president of the United States would be forced to respond to shots in a way that would create sympathy for the secessionists in the parts of the South that had not yet seceded. On December 10, 1860, Grant wrote from Galena to his St. Louis friend Charles W. Ford, "It is hard to realize that a State or States should commit so suicidal an act as to secede from the Union yet from all the reports I have no doubt but that at least five of them will do it." He was writing just over a week before South Carolina seceded, an act to be followed within two months by six of the states of the deep South, with the consequent formation of the Confederacy. Grant expected in December that, with a weak president in office, "some foolish policy will probably be pursued which will give the seceding States the support and sympathy of the Southern states that do not go out." Unfortunately, neither Grant nor the politicians in power came up with a non-foolish policy. By April a new president was in office, and the warmakers did just what Grant had predicted. Fort Sumter was fired on, Lincoln called for troops, and when the nonslaveholding states of the North immediately indicated they would respond, several of the states of the upper South—including, most critically Virginia—joined the Confederacy.[5]

But when he wrote to Ford, Grant's mind was not exclusively on the secession crisis. He regretted his continued inability to pay off an old debt and wondered how secession talk was affecting the troubled city of St. Louis, noting that in Galena, "the only difficulty experienced as yet is the difficulty of obtaining Eastern exchange." If there is an emphasis on concern for unpaid bills due the firm in this response of Grant's, there is no absence of clarity. His clearheaded detached judgment of the political scene is striking.[6]

The politics of slavery and of the relationship to the body politic of the black people who were slaves were not synonymous with the politics of warmaking, but they were inextricably linked. There is no mass of evidence to indicate a complex involvement by Grant in issues of slavery or relationships with slaves. What we do know suggests a straightforward attitude toward the people and the institution that foreshadowed both the liberality and the limitations of his racial policies during the war and during his administration as president. Jesse Grant claimed that his son was raised in a firmly antislavery home, but there is nothing to show that the issue had any powerful influence on Grant as a child. Someone as observant as he can hardly have missed the local arguments over John Rankin's encouragement of runaway slaves. And yet if he heard the quarrels, Ulysses left no indication of his own views on the Underground Railroad. Of even more interest, given his eight years in the Reconstruction White House, would be Grant's impressions of the black people he saw living in Ohio and Kentucky, both in Maysville and out in the surrounding country through which he traveled, but we have no record of these impressions.

Part of Grant's objection to the Mexican War at the time he fought in it, and more strongly as he looked back, was that it augmented the power of the slaveholding states. But in his sympathetic accounts of the Mexican peasants, exploited not only by those possessing landed and armed power but also by the invading American army, he did not draw analogies to the slaves in the United States. Perhaps because he took the facts for granted, he never wrote similar accounts of the exploitation of black Americans, and by failing to do so he failed fully to confront the parallel. He did not see American Negroes as people to sympathize with. And even Grant's objections to the war in Mexico were based more on the view that it constituted an unfair invasion of a weaker country by a stronger than on a comprehension of the increased sufferings of an already subjugated class.

Like other officers, Grant had servants, and he brought one of them, Gregorio, back from Mexico. The Mexican, far from home, with limited educational resources with which to confront a country with a different language and, no doubt, receiving a very small wage, was in a highly dependent condition. In fact, one of the man's functions was to be an amusing exotic boy, doing great tricks with a lariat. In talking about him, Grant did not show sensitivity to Gregorio's situation, nor did he liken him to a slave. Rather, displaying the same attitude he had toward all of his other servants (save perhaps the last of them, who nursed him as he was dying), he seemed hardly to have noticed him.

Unlike her husband, Julia had always had slaves around her. Her most intimate companions as she acted out childhood fantasies had been the black children at White Haven. The workers in the fields who raised her father's crops were the fathers, mothers, and older brothers and sisters of her playmates. In her fondness for the other children and for several of the older women, particularly Kitty and Rose, there is no suggestion that Julia was in the least troubled by the fact that her family owned people. She held an attitude of undoubted superiority toward slaves, and then former slaves, throughout her life; it is reflected in the tone she used whenever she spoke of slavery. Even in the White House Julia continued to apologize for slavery, and during critical Reconstruction days, her need to define herself as of a su-

perior class caused her to turn facilely to the concept of black people as infe-
riors. Unluckily, Ulysses honored his wife's prejudices. The price of his
doing so proved high for black Americans.

When the nation was at a crisis over secession, Grant, unlike his wife, did
not forget that one result of any decision made, of any course of action embarked on, would be that the relationship of black people to white would
shift. On April 19, 1861, he wrote a letter to his father-in-law that was something of a declaration of independence. Dent emphatically did not support
the use of federal power to prevent secession, and his son-in-law, seizing the
chance to preach a bit to one who had often preached to him, wrote, "The
times are indee[d] startling but now is the time, particularly in the border
Slave states, for men to prove their love of country." Then, after reviewing
the strong Northern response to Lincoln's call for troops and to the secession
of Virginia (Grant thought the state should be made "to bear a heavy portion
of the burthen of the War for her guilt"), he continued, "In all this I can but
see the doom of Slavery. The North do not want, nor will they want, to interfere with the institution. But they will refuse for all time to give it protection unless the South shall return soon to their allegiance, and then too this
disturbance will give such an impetus to the production of their staple, cotton, in other parts of the world that they can never recover the controll of the
market again for that comodity. This will reduce the value of negroes so
much that they will never be worth fighting over again. . . ."[7]

This was sophisticated economics from a failed businessman and evidence
of the intelligence Grant could muster when aroused. Two weeks later he
wrote Julia about the imminent danger of civil war within civil war as Missourians displayed their divided loyalties. Rather blandly, he anticipated that
the ominous martial events in Missouri might retard the state's development:
"Missouri will be a great state ultimately but she is set back now for years. It
will end in more rapid advancement however for she will be left a free state.
Negroes are stampeding already and those who do not will be carried further
South." A black exodus north and west, with any remaining blacks forcibly
moved south, would leave Missouri free—that is, free for development by
white farmers and businessmen, with black labor no longer essential and
black people, no longer present, no longer a burden. Five days later, he wrote
his father that when the Northern forces were properly trained they would
send "the secession army howling. . . ." After that, he predicted, "the states
. . . will . . . be loyal for a generation to come, negroes will depreciate so rapidly in value that no body will want to own them and their masters will be
the loudest in their declaimations against the institution in a political and economic view. The nigger will never disturb this country again."[8]

He was not entirely convinced that serenity was at hand, however, for that
same day he wrote Julia that turmoil might result when the Northern army
caused the leaders of the rebellion to flee and disorder followed: "The worst
to be apprehended is from negro revolts. Such would be deeply deplorable

and I have no doubt but a Northern army would hasten South to suppress anything of the kind." In May 1861 it looked as if Ulysses S. Grant was ready to march not to John Brown's drum, but to that of the men who hanged him.[9]

And yet, earlier that spring, despite the government's call for troops and the massive task of organizing an army and finding commanders for it, the West Point graduate had found no drum to march to at all. On April 16, the day after the news of the fall of Fort Sumter reached Galena, there had been a mass meeting addressed by two townsmen—Elihu B. Washburne, the Republican representing the district in the House of Representatives, and John A. Rawlins, Grant's dark-eyed intense neighbor, a Douglas Democrat. The alliance for war was made in Galena as it was all across the North, and the patriotic fervor at the meeting was strong. Grant was present, as he was two nights later at another meeting, where the subject was the recruitment of troops. By then, the new man in town, the man in the leather store who lived up on High Street, was known to be a graduate of West Point. Grant was, in fact, the only man in town with professional-army training. He was elected to preside over the meeting, and with a quiet sense that what came his way was exactly what he expected, he took the chair.[10]

It was a great moment, and if some in the room saw "evident embarrassment" on his face, the man himself sensed personal vindication. "In this season," recalled his neighbor John Rawlins, "I saw new energies in Grant. . . . He dropped a stoop shouldered way of walking, and set his hat forward on his forehead in a careless fashion." Grant himself spoke succinctly of his new confidence as he put aside the nothingness of his life and embraced the war: "I never went into our leather store after that meeting, to put up a package or do other business."[11]

During the succeeding days he was active in enlisting men for a Galena company of volunteers, and, in civilian clothes, he went off with them to Camp Yates, in Springfield. It is said that Grant modestly stood aside while an ambitious man, Augustus Louis Chetlain, moved in to claim the captaincy of the company, a position that Grant was better suited to hold. What Grant, in fact, told Chetlain was that for him, a former captain in the regular army, to take command of a volunteer company would be a demotion: "I have been educated at West Point, and therefore deserve a colonelcy." In the Mexican War he had been less critical than most West Point men of citizen-soldiers, and later, as a general, he never scorned a citizens' army, but in 1861 Grant was not quick to realize that this huge army would need officers and that the officers would quickly achieve high rank. Instead, petulantly, he claimed he did not want to be "a Capt. under a green Colonel." He had, after all, been called to chair the local meeting designed to pull together one unit of a vast army coming together from towns all across the nation, and he expected word from the War Department calling him back into the national army. He knew that Winfield Scott, the commanding general, was not in favor of integrating West Point officers into state volunteer-army units. Instead, Scott wanted these trained officers to maintain command of elite regular-army units and, in the higher ranks, to assist in the command of the army as a whole—that is, of the combined regular and volunteer segments. Grant expected an expert army to end the war quickly—"My own opinion is that this War will be but of short duration"—and it was to the regular army once more at war that he hoped to return.[12]

At Camp Yates he drilled volunteer units and shared a room and a bed with Chetlain while he waited for the commission that did not arrive. Across the country West Point lieutenants were leapfrogging captains and majors to become colonels, by brevet, of volunteer regiments from the various states.* Grant, however, in his "one suit that he had worn all winter, his short pipe, his grizzled beard and his old slouch hat did not . . . look a very promising candidate for the colonelcy." He worked in the statehouse in an anteroom of the adjutant general's, "at a little square table, of which one leg was gone and which had been shoved into a corner to keep it upright."[13]

Grant's excellent sense of the public political events from the start of the secession crisis, and his elation as he left his store, were not matched by a grasp of the private politics of finding an important place in these events. He might have been shrewd in not taking (or angling to get) the captaincy of the Jo Daviess County volunteer company if that decision had been coupled with a skillful campaign to get a better appointment, but it was not. His strolls through the lobby of Springfield's hotel produced nothing. He had no friends to whom he could appeal, and when he finally made a formal request for such a position he did it so drearily that failure was ensured. True, some of his friends, like Simon Bolivar Buckner, were on the Confederate side and therefore could not help him, but it is poignant that after four years at West Point and eleven in the Fourth Infantry Regiment he knew no one to whom he could simply write, "I'm in good shape; help me get back into the army." The stigma of being thought a drunk was powerful. "I don't know whether I am like other men or not," said Grant, exposing to Chetlain, a hearty Swiss-American, his fear of being different, "but when I have nothing to do I get blue and depressed. . . ." And then, as Chetlain told Hamlin Garland, Grant confessed that he was afraid he would start to drink: "This is the key to Grant's drinking habits. Whenever he was idle and depressed this appetite came upon him."[14]

Grant complained to his father that he "was perfectly sickened at the political wire pulling for all these commissions" and asserted that he "would not engage in it." His diffident ways precluded his use of the more blatant and flamboyant forms of self-advertising practiced by others, but his true distress

---

* A brevet rank was a temporary one authorized for special service or to give an officer prestige. If a man so promoted did not in due course receive a permanent appointment to the higher rank, he was returned to his regular rank when the special circumstances, such as war, came to an end.

lay less in his contempt for those pulling the wires than in his inability to get a hand on them himself. It took him a month to communicate with the army headquarters in Washington, and when he did, he just sent an impersonal and unenthusiastic letter to Lorenzo Thomas, an older officer who was adjutant general. The letter was never answered. He went to Missouri to appeal to two Mexican War veterans, but was rebuffed by both of them—Nathaniel Lyon, the Federal Commander at St. Louis, and Francis P. Blair, Jr., a Unionist politician who was raising Federal troops. He sent hints for a commission to other men in Missouri and Ohio; in Covington, Kentucky, he called on Colonel and Mrs. William Whistler, whom he and Julia had known in Detroit, but the eighty-year-old colonel, old and infirm, had at last yielded the command of the Fourth Infantry Regiment and could not help him. Two days later, he summoned courage, submerged pride, and went to the headquarters of someone nearer his own age, an officer who was already important in the new army, Major General George B. McClellan. During his final year at West Point, Grant had known McClellan, then a plebe, and he had seen him again in Mexico; this was a promising contact. Deferentially, Grant, once McClellan's superior, waited, but did not get to see the general. Checking pride once more, he came back and waited the next day. Again, McClellan did not see him.[15]

"Blue as a whet-stone," Grant was close to giving up. He went back to Galena, but, he wrote his father, "the six days I have been at home I have felt all the time as if a duty was being neglected that was paramount to any other duty I ever owed." He told his father to write him "at Springfield"; he was on his way back to his tasks as a mustering officer. The letter, which expressed Grant's very real patriotic sentiment, would not be unhelpful if Jesse did some lobbying for his son's appointment as colonel. It was recognition, as well, that he could not succumb to his depression and stay at home. To do so would have put an intolerable collar on the energy that the prospect of war had begun to stir. But when he returned to Springfield and the wearisome work of organizing the Illinois recruits, he had no assurance that he could get anyone to rescue him by giving him his own command.[16]

The trip home had proved more than a testing of Grant's despair. He discovered that he had been doing his campaigning in the wrong places. It was fruitless to look up men he had known in his army past, but across the river in a fine house right there in Galena was a man who saw Grant not in the shadow of a tarnished reputation, but in the light of great possibilities. This was Elihu B. Washburne, the congressman for the district. Like many other ambitious politicians, he sought to increase his influence by having an officer beholden to him, for if that officer did well, the politician would have the whole nation in his debt. Washburne took Grant with him to see the governor and was long glad that he had, but his intervention may not have been the key to Grant's finally receiving a commission. (Half of Illinois claimed credit for getting Grant his colonelcy—after he became a commanding general.) There was political jealousy between Washburne and Governor Richard Yates, and when Yates at last gave Grant a place, a nice confusion remained over whether Grant had received the commission because of Washburne's help or simply because the man then in command, an old filibusterer named Simon S. Goode, had proved to be flagrantly and eccentrically incompetent. On June 17 Grant wrote Julia some family news about a visit to Covington, and added, "You have probably seen that I have been appointed to a Colonelcy?"[17]

# VII

# WARRIORS

*I've often longed to see a war, and now I have my wish.*
*— Louisa May Alcott*

S O  S W I F T  was Grant's advance from the leather shop of Galena to the laurels of Vicksburg that one might imagine it completed in a single leap. Actually, however, the late summer and fall of 1861, the whole of 1862, and, indeed, the period of the Vicksburg campaign of 1863 saw the intensive step-by-step education of a frighteningly effective warrior. The quiet man, wearing an old jacket, slouching and watching, was thought by fools to be a no-account and was represented by jealous enemies as a drunk. But at the end of Grant's schooling in war another master at deliberately wearing the wrong clothes, Abraham Lincoln, saw someone very different.

Grant had become a student of war, but never made the mistake of thinking that his subject (or any other involving human behavior) was a science. He knew that even in the immediacy of war people are frightened by their pasts and tend to make odd decisions. He recollected, with skill, what he had experienced in the Mexican War. He forgot little of what he had learned while watching people both in the army and out. He drew on what he had seen people do and on what he knew of his own weaknesses to understand the men he had to fight with and against. As Russell F. Weigley has said, Grant taught us that war is annihilation, and he did so because he brought to the fighting of an American war an indispensable horse sense about American politics. As Adam Badeau put it, Grant "understood that he was engaged in a people's war." Once a moral nation like America fully committed itself to the war, victory had to be total. And total victory against other committed Americans could be achieved only if there were more men available for dying on one side than on the other.[1]

William T. Sherman, not Grant, stated that "in our Country . . . one class of men makes war and leaves another to fight it out," but Grant would not have disagreed. He knew that politics were both silly and potent and that matters of statecraft and matters of life and death bore no reliable relationship to each other. In a profound sense they did not connect. The nation had been unwilling fully to give over the great divisive question of slavery to politicians, and instead turned to war. Now, even in a war of annihilation, it would not yield everything to the warriors. Politics went on, out of phase with the immediate realities of the battlefield. Grant did not expect or seek to impose a balance between sword and ballot box. Unlike countless other generals, Grant always remembered to defer to Washington, D.C., even in times of exultation or desperation. Grant sensed that by doing so he could give the politicians victories.[2]

But the most important part of the student's knowledge was something he carried with him as an almost private joke. He had learned—or had somehow always known—how simple war is. It may have dawned on him as he dozed while sitting erectly at a lecture at West Point, or during the more intense seminar of a Mexican War battle, or at almost any other time. When he learned the lesson does not matter. He knew it. The truth underlying it was uncongenial to American ears, and Grant was too kind and gentle a man ever to come out with it directly. But his whole life was focused on his mastery of the fact and his *Memoirs* was its record: war is an act; to make war is to kill.

Ulysses Grant in his throw-away lines—in his throw-away life—kept trying to get people to see the colossal sick joke. All you do is take the nicest guy on the block—the one who will not be diverted by dreams of vainglory or revenge or by the nonsense of masochism—and knowing he is not good for much else, let him act on the bald fact that war means killing the guy on the other side, or at least scaring him badly enough so that he will quit fighting. Then, all this man has to do is keep the fact in mind all the way to Appomattox. He need not try to convince himself that war is good; he may very well know the opposite. It doesn't matter. In 1861 the war was—it existed—and Colonel Grant, conscious of the fact, went off at the head of a regiment of nice guys from Illinois to fight in Missouri. As he later told Julia, he found in her home state "great fools . . . [who] will never rest until they bring upon themselves all the horrors of war in its worst form. The people are inclined to carry on a guerilla Warfare that must eventuate in retaliation and when it does commence it will be hard to control." In war, people die. That was the one essential, terrible, toweringly simple fact, and guerrilla fighters were, for him, the most frightening of the killers.[3]

Grant was as jaunty as perhaps he was ever to be in his life. At last he was in charge. He expected that before too long his wife would be able to join him; he had his eye out for a horse better than his present one; and in a letter full of these concerns, he gossiped cheerfully. He was respectful of, but bored by, his two senior-officer colleagues: "One is a preacher and the other a member of the Church," said Grant, observing that he could "never have a game of Eucre with them." He reported the other officers to be sober and attentive: "For the Field officers of my regt. . . . one pint of liquor will do to the end of the war." The men were pleased with the new "order in camp" which he had brought about. Bringing Julia into the activities described in his splendidly drawn letter, Grant asked her to hunt about the house for his copy of General McClellan's report on the Crimean War and to send it along; there was more war to be studied. With happy exasperation he closed— "This is a very poor letter but I have not written scarsely a single sentence without interruption"—and signed with a pert selection from the fat assortment of pet names he and Julia had for each other. He was joyously "busy from morning until night." Grant was alive.[4]

Ulysses Grant is not usually pictured as zestful—or as temperamental. One of the most familiar of the solemn tales about his Spartan stolidness concerns the day he took command and the men of his regiment had to decide whether to re-enlist or to go home. Generals John A. McClernand and John A. Logan, both politician-generals (Democrats from Illinois), came to urge the men to stay. Grant was sure the former was loyal but doubtful about the latter. He was concerned about the wrong man. Later, McClernand proved a liability to him in the war effort and Logan an asset, and on this day Logan, who was from rebel country in downstate Illinois, surprised Grant with a persuasive, emotional, patriotic appeal to the men to re-enlist—which they subsequently did—for the fight to come. Grant, called on to follow Logan with a further exhortation, said simply, "Men, go to your quarters!"[5]

This line is often quoted as if it were some sort of elegant understatement exemplifying Grant's mysterious hold over his men. Perhaps it can be regarded in this light, and perhaps not. The truth is that Grant was out of sorts and out of words. "Men, go to your quarters" was in fact, all that, in frustration, he could mutter. Grant had pictured himself that day sitting astride his own horse on a saddle from his family's shop—in other words, at home with his regiment and confident in the presence of the pretentious visiting politician-generals. But things did not work out that way. Grant was on an undistinguished horse, his own having not yet been brought from Galena. As he rode to the mustering-in, an embarrassing and tedious cousin, sent down from Galena, came "dashing into Camp, on horseback with the fine trappings Orvil sent to me, not on Rondy [Grant's horse] but a showey Livery horse hired for the occation." Grant had not spent a dime on transportation for two months, and the cost of the rented steed and of the cousin's journey, which he would have to pay, flashed into his mind: "I was so disgusted that I passed him with but little ceremony." The terse "Men, go to

your quarters" was expression of annoyance with a cousin who had spoiled
his moment of assuming command rather than a stoically simple statement
that assured re-enlistment and was, somehow, appropriate to the great responsibilities that lay ahead. Grant had not yet discovered how he wanted to
look to his men and to himself.[6]

In the early summer of 1861 Colonel Grant rode west to the Mississippi at
the head of the Twenty-first Illinois Regiment. On foot were civilian soldiers
of whom Grant was already proud. One of his officers put it well: "We have
the best of order and every thing mooves off pleasantly." Grant, who insisted on the order, had never been as snobbish as some regular-army officers
with respect to volunteers. He had had his doubts in Mexico, but, a bit
slowly, he had now grasped the fact that the army that would fight the Civil
War, already numbering tens of thousands of men, would not be made up of
professional soldiers. It would be composed of civilians turned into soldiers.
Grant recognized that to a greater degree than any previous conflict, his
would be a people's war. The student of war became the teacher and made
his men students in turn: "My men behaved admirably, and the lesson has
been a good one for them. They can now go into camp after a day's march
with as much promptness as veteran troops; they can strike their tents and be
on the march with equal celerity."[7]

Grant leading the Twenty-first Illinois west from Camp Yates may have
overcome his earlier reservations about taking a volunteer regiment, but his
father had experienced no such change of heart. Jesse, with his unerring instinct for the best way to cut his son down, suggested that in taking the command, Ulysses once again had not done as well as he should have. In a letter,
he not only derided the military accomplishments of his son but also chided
him for not being a better correspondent. In his reply, Ulysses obliquely
tried to fend off his father's scorn for the command he had accepted and his
father's hope that he would return to the professional army: "You ask if I
should not like to go in the regular army. I should not. I want to bring my
children up to useful employment, and in the army the chance is poor."
Limply, he was trying to teach his ineducable father that he was engaged not
in a career, but in a war.[8]

Ulysses S. Grant was well on his way to that war. Julia Dent Grant had
only started out. The idea that women have no taste for war ran deeply at the
time, and women were very rarely allowed to behave in a manner inconsis-
tent with the premise that only men are hunters and fighters. All the social
conventions of the nineteenth century argued that Julia must not participate,
except by allowing herself the emotional indulgence of nobly sending a man
off to war. Such a posture, however, was not what she had in mind. She had
been left behind when Ulysses went to Mexico, but at that point, not yet his
wife, she was still a daughter in her father's family. She had been left behind
again when Ulysses went to the West Coast. For him, the result of that
separation had been disastrous, but whatever Julia might have gained by

joining her husband there would have been obtained at the price of a very unexciting army-post life. Now things looked like much more fun. Her "favorite pet name for the Captain"—Victor—had been chosen, she said, "after he read to me the triumphs of Victor Emmanuel," and she indulged in reveries of romantic glory. Julia craved to be in the middle of Ulysses' adventure and barely remembered that war was regarded solely as a man's world.[9]

At first, she went to war vicariously, trying to assuage her intense wish to be there herself by sending both her husband and a son: "Strange to say, I felt no regret at his [Ulysses'] going and even suggested that our eldest son just then eleven years old, should accompany him." Thus it was thanks in part to his mother that Frederick Grant was with his father at Camp Yates and on the march to Missouri. But Ulysses sent the young boy home when he anticipated that the summer's fun might turn into actual fighting: "Fred. started home yesterday and I did not telegraph you because I thought you would be in a perfect stew until he arrived. He did not want to go at all and I felt loathe at sending him but now we are in the enemies country I thought you would be alarmed if he was with me." Fred, whom his father praised as being "very manly," went by boat up the Mississippi and walked from Dubuque to Galena with an army knapsack on his back.[10]

Before Fred arrived, Julia was indeed "in a perfect stew," but not for the reason her husband expected. In response to Ulysses' letter, she quickly wrote, "Do not send him home; Alexander was not older when he accompanied Philip. Do keep him with you." She was too late; Fred was on his way home. Undaunted, Julia soon recognized that there was no reason why she herself should not be with her Philip on a march of conquest. She might actually get to go to war. The colonel wanted—needed—his family with him. The night that Fred left, Ulysses had written Julia that he had had "one of those terrible headaches which you know I am subject to," and within a week he wrote again, saying, "I should like very much to go into camp some place where you could visit me."[11]

As they moved toward Missouri, Grant was pleased with his men for making "their marches as well as troops ever do." They got good marks for their restraint as well, as he faced a problem that was to become ubiquitous in the wake of marching troops: "There have been a few men who show a disposition not to respect private property such as hen roosts and gardens, but I have kept such a watch on them, and punished offenders so, that I will venture that the same number of troops never marched through a thickly settled country like this committing fewer depridations." During the first week of July, Grant's men marched through beautiful country to Quincy, and crossed the Mississippi into Missouri.[12]

The Missouri campaign—coming, in a sense, before the real war began and involving no great battle—has seldom received the attention it deserves. The year 1861 was the year of the process of disunion. There was no divinely ordained map establishing a Confederacy of eleven Southern states and a

Union of twenty-three Northern states. South Carolina seceded in December 1860. Only six states of the deep South followed before the firing on Fort Sumter, and through the winter it was the hope of the federal government, if not the basis of its policy (for there seemed to be no policy), that no such thing as the solid South existed, or that if it did exist, it consisted only of the southernmost tier of states—from Florida through Georgia and South Carolina west through Alabama, Mississippi, Louisiana, and Texas. The focus of attention for Abraham Lincoln and his advisers in the days of the Sumter crisis was how best to keep other states, particularly Virginia, from joining the Confederacy. The firing on the fort accomplished what the disunionists had hoped for; Lincoln called for troops, and four more states—Arkansas, Tennessee, North Carolina, and Virginia—did join the Confederacy. Lincoln next tried to keep in the Union the slave states bordering those that had seceded. The nation's capital was isolated south of slave-holding Maryland, and troops were harassed by legions of rebel sympathizers as they moved through Baltimore. Lincoln refused to disturb the institution of slavery; he kept Maryland and Delaware in the Union and fought to maintain his hold on the other two slave states, Kentucky and Missouri.

Missouri, rising north of the line defined in the compromise to which the state gave its name, was a psychological and strategic threat to the Unionists. It represented the extension of slavery as well as the thrusting of the Confederacy into the North. If slave-holding Missouri had followed the wishes of its governor, Claiborne Jackson, and joined the Confederacy, there is no reason why its precedent could not have been followed elsewhere. People in southern Illinois sympathetic to the idea of keeping a black population controlled could have followed Missouri out of the Union, and if they had done so, could not Indiana have followed? If Indiana, why not New York City? There was no certain logic to disunion.

Maintaining control of Missouri was essential both for stopping the process of dissolution of the Union and for demonstrating the utility of military force in achieving that goal. It was critical to the control of the Mississippi River. Had Missouri gone with the South, St. Louis, a river port and rail-traffic center, would have been the largest city in the Confederacy. Grant missed the "battle" that initially saved Missouri for the Union. On May 10, 1861, not yet in the army, he was at White Haven visiting his father-in-law, who, he said, "professes to be a Union man yet condemns evry measure for the preservation of the Union." On that day Captain Nathaniel Lyon led Union men into an arsenal and prevented its seizure by a band of zealous St. Louis Confederates. Governor Jackson, the leader of the pro-Confederacy faction in Missouri, bitterly resented Lyon's forcible intrusion of federal power into the affairs of his state. Grant's sympathies were with Lyon, not Jackson, and by July, this one-time Missouri farmer was leading an Illinois regiment into his former home state to assist in the military effort to keep it in the Union.[13]

As he crossed into Missouri, Grant was aware that, for the first time in his life, he was in command of men whom he would have to send into battle. At Palmyra, he found no opposition, but moving to the Salt River he came in sight of an encampment of the Confederate colonel Thomas Harris: "As we approached the brow of the hill from which it was expected we could see Harris' camp, and possibly find his men ready formed to meet us, my heart kept getting higher and higher until it felt to me as though it was in my throat. I would have given anything then to have been back in Illinois, but"—he continued, oddly, in his *Memoirs*—"I had not the moral courage to halt and consider what to do; I kept right on." He found the Confederates had left the camp: "My heart resumed its place. It occurred to me at once that Harris had been as much afraid of me as I had been of him. This was a view . . . I had never taken before; but was one I never forgot afterwards. From that event to the close of the war, I never experienced trepidation upon confronting an enemy, though I always felt more or less anxiety. I never forgot that he had as much reason to fear my forces as I had his. The lesson was valuable."[14]

While stationed at Mexico, Missouri, with orders to keep stable the northeastern corner of the state, Grant learned that he was to become a general. A bit disingenuously he wrote his father on August 3, 1861, "I see from the papers that my name has been sent in for Brigadier Gen.!" And, getting back at his father for having heretofore arranged his life for him, he added, "This is certainly very complimentary . . . particularly as I have never asked a friend to intercede in my behalf." And it was true that Grant's promotion to brigadier general was much more a matter of routine than his awkward attainment of a colonelcy had been. On July 31, 1861, to staff the growing army, Lincoln submitted to Congress the names of twenty-six men for promotion to brigadier general. Most of these were officers with regular-army commissions rather than men who were, or knew, powerful political figures. In the promotions of early August 1861, preference was given first to regular-army officers who had not resigned and then to regular-army officers who, like Grant, had returned to service. Among the latter, Grant ranked sixth. The promotion was what one might have expected for a man who was doing a good job as a regimental colonel.[15]

Ulysses and Julia Grant, however, were not used to being able to count on the expected—certainly not when it was something as desirable as a generalship. The colonel had learned from humiliation. He had played the game wrong once and was determined not to do so again. This time Grant did not beg, but it is unlikely that Julia or his brother Orvil, in Galena, missed a chance to suggest to Congressman Washburne that he remember his townsman when promotions were to be made. Washburne, having sponsored Grant for his colonelcy, had a vested interest in his success. Later on, as Grant became famous, everyone wanted the credit for convincing Lincoln that he should be made a general, and there has been great speculation about just who did so. Washburne probably deserves the honor—at least that part not due to Grant's own satisfactory record—but it would be wrong to see Grant even at this early point as simply a creature of the congressman's. (Soon, in fact, the tail was wagging the dog.) Grant was doing well in his job in Missouri, and the winning posture for him at the time of his promotion to brigadier general—and later—was to eschew the "pulling and hauling for favors" that he denounced so vehemently in letters to his father.[16]

When the appointment came, he wrote Julia a simple, graceful letter (with a wonderful slip in the first line) designed to be shown to any of the people who had helped him achieve the promotion:

> I certainly feel very greatful to the people of Ill. for the interest they seem to have taken in me and unasked too. Whilst I was about Springfield I certainly never blew my own trumpet and was not aware that I attracted any attention but it seems from what I have heard from there the people, who were perfect strangers to me up to the commencement of our present unhappy national difficulties, were very unanimous in recommending me for my present position. I shall do my very best not to disappoint them and shall hope by dilligence to render good account of some of the Ill. Vols. All my old Regt. expressed great regret at my leaving them and applied to be attached to my Brigade.

Shortly thereafter, Grant wrote his congressman in a dignified vein: "Mr. Washburn allow me to thank you for the part you have taken in giving me my present position. I think I see your hand in it. . . ."[17]

Toward the middle of August, he wrote to Julia in a totally different but still triumphant tone. He had been to St. Louis and had hoped to be able to take a few days leave and surprise her. Orders to move a regiment into southern Missouri had spoiled that plan, but he was full of confidence. He had asked one of those friends back in Galena, John A. Rawlins, to join his staff. Grant did not know Rawlins well enough to spell his name correctly— he wrote it "Rollins"—but was so eager to have the aggressive young lawyer with him that he urged Julia to have his brother Orvil press Rawlins to accept quickly. He was feeling fond of the town which had been the agency of his recognition—"Give my love to all the good people of Galena"—and, in a highly private voice, told her of squaring accounts in a bigger town that had mocked him: "I called to see Harry Boggs the other day as I passed through St. Louis. He cursed and went on like a Madman. Told me that I would never be welcom in his hous; that the people of Illinois were a poor misserable set of Black Republicans, Abolition paupers that had to invade their state to get something to eat. Good joke that on something to eat. Harry is such a pittiful insignificant fellow that I could not get mad at him and told him so where upon he set the Army of Flanders far in the shade with his profanity." Grant's successful skirmish with Boggs could be said to have been as important a personal victory as Vicksburg was to be. His account of it was a declaration that at last other people would have to reckon with his strong sense of self. He had learned much about himself. The confidence revealed here was indispensable for all the satisfying and terrifying things that Ulysses S. Grant was to do in the Civil War.[18]

When, with justifiable pride, Grant wrote his father that he was to get his generalship—*not bad, for a failure*, was the unspoken theme of the letter—he took particular joy in the reaction of the officers in his regiment: "Hearing that I was likely to be promoted . . . with great unanimity, [they] have requested to be attached to my Command. This"—he went on, again in the self-deprecatory vein—"I dont want you to read to others for I very much dislike speaking of myself." Jesse still refused to be proud of his son. His exasperating response was to try to use his influence with this new general officer of the army to get a job for the son of a friend (whom he thought capable of reciprocating the favor). Jesse did not succeed. Grant had moved swiftly. "My Staff," he told Julia, "are J. A. Rawlins [correctly spelled now], Clark B. Lagow & W. S. Hillyer, three of the cleverest men . . . anywhere. Father's recommendation came too late." While still a colonel he had fended off other seekers of place, not having many positions to fill in the regiment and not wanting to be saddled with the wrong people. He had told Julia to discourage, gently, a Galena man wanting a job: "You can say to him that as Col. of a Regt. I have no appointments outside of the Regt. and as Brig. Gen. should I get the appointment, none outside the army. In the latter position however it might be possible to secure him a place . . . with the Quarter Master." Grant was already practicing the patronage politics that would so preoccupy him in the White House, and doing so with a decisiveness seldom seen in the presidential years.[19]

That Galena man did not get a job with Grant, but in mid-August, John A. Rawlins accepted his. Rawlins, nine years younger than Grant, was the second eldest of nine children of a failed, and reportedly drunken, lead miner who had left the family to try, with equal unsuccess, to make a fortune in the gold fields of California. Rawlins's mother and her children had lived in poverty on a farm outside Galena which consisted of the house and its garden, cut into two hundred acres of grassland and trees that the Rawlinses acquired in the government land sales of 1847. John, at sixteen, was listed as the owner and was the head of the household. The family's cash income came from the sale of timber for charcoal, used in smelting the lead mined near Galena. His schooling was limited. For eight years, beginning when he was seven, it consisted of a three-month term each winter. The family did manage to acquire enough money to send his sister to the Galena Academy, and John attended the Rock River Seminary in Mount Morris, Illinois, for two years. Unable to afford to return and graduate, he spent the summer of 1853 in the intense labor of cutting wood, firing his own pits, and delivering the charcoal with a team of oxen. The story is that in September, having earned $250, he sold the oxen, gave up the charcoal trade for good, and moved into Galena; how this act affected the family he left is not known. In Galena, he persuaded an attorney, Isaac P. Steven, to let him read law in his office. Rawlins, "at that time blessed with a strong, robust body, a vigorous constitution, and a mind but partly developed, was self-reliant and confident." He was admitted to the bar at age twenty-three, entered Steven's office, and, on the retirement of his partner in 1855, became head of the firm. A Douglas Democrat, he was elected city attorney when he was twenty-six; a year later, in 1858, he entered into partnership with David Sheean. When he met his new neighbor, whose house was close by and whose shop was down Main Street from his law office, the dark, intense, and compelling John A. Rawlins was about as impressive a new success as Ulysses Grant could have hoped to encounter.[20]

Hannah Grant's sister lived next door to Rawlins, who became acquainted with her nephew Ulysses as soon as he moved to Galena. "I got to know Grant slowly and respectfully," he told a reporter eight years later. Rawlins listened as his new friend told fond stories of Mexico, and when disunion came, Grant found Rawlins a fervent advocate of strong prosecution of the new war. Grant may not have known the spelling but he knew the sound of his name when he wrote it as "Rollins" in his letter to Julia. He did not choose Rawlins on someone else's recommendation. The man was Grant's own choice. The general needed strong men around him, but not men he was uncomfortable with. Rawlins's success was not one that had intimidated him; it did not point to Grant's own lack of success.[21]

Rawlins was an attractive man—intelligent and strong, but not so powerful as to make Grant feel in the least weakened. Jacob Dolson Cox, who knew both men in camp, wrote long afterward of the relationship between them:

> [Rawlins's] friendship for his chief was of so sacredly intimate a character that he alone could break through the taciturnity into which Grant settled when he found himself in any way out of accord with the thoughts and opinions of those around him. Rawlins could argue, could expostulate, could condemn, could even upbraid, without interrupting for an hour the fraternal confidence and good will of Grant. He had won the right to this relation by an absolute devotion which dated from Grant's appointment to be a brigadier-general in 1861, and which had made him the good genius of his friend in every crisis of Grant's wonderful career. This was not because of Rawlins' great intellect, for he was of only moderate mental powers. It was rather that he became a living and speaking conscience for his general; as courageous to speak in a time of need as Nathan the prophet, and as absolutely trusted as Jonathan by David.

Cox knew both Grant and Rawlins well. His words carry conviction. Unlike some of Grant's critics, Cox did not see Rawlins as the man who did Grant's military thinking for him, but he did credit Rawlins with carrying on conversations in which conflicting propositions were presented, without accompanying advice, so that having listened, Grant could make his own decisions.[22]

But Rawlins's role involved far more than making military decisions. Rawlins was a man of passion, of absolutes. He could be rude to powerful generals and compassionate with people who were powerless, as he was to be later with the freedmen and with the Cuban insurgents. His friendship with Grant was so intense that he would curse him; so valuable that Grant accepted his rage. Rawlins's father is said to have died an alcoholic, and liquor was the son's deadly enemy. He wanted so much to be loved by Grant that he could test their friendship by admonishing Grant not to drink. Sometimes those warnings were listened to; sometimes they were ignored—the friendship survived these severe tests, for Grant too was a man of passion.

In some ways the human relationship that is the hardest to fix securely when recreating a man's past is friendship. The nature of a relationship to a colleague or even to a spouse seems easier to be sure of than what it means to have been someone's friend. There were few true friends in Grant's life. Yet he needed people around him. He seems to have been a loner and yet to have been terrified of being alone. As a boy, he had liked journeys by himself with his horse, but as a man, he did not trust himself to go that route. The picture of a man sufficient unto himself in the wilds of California was seductive, but that same man might also be the derelict he feared becoming. While commanding thousands during the Civil War, Grant needed a handful of men around him and a friend like Rawlins to keep him in command of himself. Those who were with him in his command posts during the war, and later in the White House, were of immense importance to him.

In these years no one from Georgetown days reappeared, save occasionally and steadfastly Daniel Ammen. Despite the flood of generals who coursed past Grant between 1861 and 1869, few old friends from West Point, from the peacetime barracks, or, more surprisingly, from the Mexican War returned to buttress the general during his second war or his tenure in Washington. Two West Point roommates, Rufus Ingalls and Frederick Dent, in differing ways did, but neither they nor William T. Sherman, who proved so important to Grant in other respects, was as close to Grant as were the men on his immediate staff.

Sherman's brilliant mind was not as comfortable to make camp with as theirs. Charles W. Ford, a fellow officer at Sackets Harbor who left the army to live in St. Louis and remained a civilian, was a friend and business confidant for the remainder of Grant's life. Most other St. Louis people seem to have invoked troubling memories. As they tried to capitalize on their connection to Grant, they brought back to him the unevenness of the Missouri days. Instead of remembering these men comfortably, he was reminded of the time when the search for influence was reversed and he was thought to have been clumsy in using them as assets. An exception was William S. Hillyer, a real-estate man who had rented Boggs & Grant office space and sponsored Grant when he applied to be county engineer; Hillyer joined Grant's staff early in the war.[23]

Joseph D. Webster was close to Grant until he was promoted to a position supervising railroad transportation and left the headquarters staff, and Clark B. Lagow also departed, after being accused by William R. Rowley and others of being an exuberant drinker and, worse, of encouraging Grant to drink. Rowley, like Rawlins, was a back-fence neighbor from Galena. Theodore S. Bowers (also from Illinois) was another of the early staff who remained with Grant throughout the war and beyond. In due time, Ely S. Parker (who succeeded Rowley) and Adam Badeau—opposite in appearance, temperament, and taste—joined the group, as did Horace Porter (who became the staff's most astute chronicler) and Cyrus B. Comstock, whom a New Englander observed was a "Massachusetts man" with "somewhat the air of a Yankee schoolmaster." So too did Orville E. Babcock, who quickly gained an intimate place in the company. Only two of the men were from Galena, but all, somehow, were Galena men: a nondescript lot of ordinary men who provided the utterly essential comradeship in the small cluster of tents of Grant's army headquarters. It was only in the encampments of war that he could find this unassuming but vitally sustaining companionship.[24]

Before any of these allies had joined him, Grant's orders took him to Ironton, in the foothills of the Ozarks. He was therefore not present at the battle of Wilson's Creek, west of Springfield, Missouri. Nathaniel Lyon, a general now, who bravely but rashly attacked the Confederate force there, was killed, and his Union force was routed. It was another Bull Run—the second significant defeat of the Union in a war in which it had yet to achieve a victory. Wilson's Creek was potentially a more dangerous loss than it ultimately proved to be, for as the Union forces retreated, two-thirds of Missouri was in rebel hands. The Union commander in St. Louis was Major General John Charles Frémont, the flamboyant former senator from California who had been, in 1856, the Republican candidate for president. Frémont and his beautiful, powerful Missouri wife, Jessie Benton Frémont, had been in France when he was appointed a general; they came back unhurriedly through New York, and on July 25, 1861, in St. Louis, set up court with a bodyguard company of three hundred men "made up of the very best material Kentucky could afford; average height, 5 feet 11-1/2 inches, and measuring 40-1/2 inches around the breast." The week that this feudal baron moved west, the North had been stunned by the defeat at Bull Run. Gone now was the dream that a big army would scare the South into submission or a quick thrust would defeat it, though few had yet come to realize how long the war would last. In any event, John Frémont would not be the one in command; he lasted only slightly over three months. His fall was due not only to his famous attempt to change the war into a crusade against slavery by declaring Missouri slaves free, but also to his misunderstanding of an army of which, though he chose not to know it, he was but one of many generals. He panicked after the defeat at Wilson's Creek on August 10, and disregarding the authority of both his superior officer, General Winfield Scott, and Secretary of War Simon Cameron, wrote imperiously to Lincoln, demanding his lord's attention: "Will the President read my urgent dispatch to the Secretary of War?" He also sent another, inaccurate, message: "General Grant, commanding at Ironton, attacked yesterday at 6 by a force reported at 13,000." As Kenneth P. Williams has pointed out, no such attack had occurred; Frémont was simply bolstering his case for the immediate need for additional troops. But he had lied—and thereby lost the president's confidence.[25]

Lincoln sent Frémont the reinforcements he wanted, but began looking around for a new general for the Western Department. The replacement was not Ulysses Grant, but an almost unremembered general, David Hunter. Keen students of the Civil War, such as E. B. Long, regard Grant as lucky for not having been discovered too early for such a post. Instead he was able, before he took part in any major battle, to learn how to make an army work, and watching Frémont was one good way to learn how not to make it work.

On September 1, 1861, Grant was ordered to Cape Girardeau. Then on September 2, he moved across the Mississippi and southeastward to Cairo, Illinois. There he was to stand guard over the juncture of the Ohio and Mississippi rivers at the southern tip of Illinois, a point farther south than the Confederate capital at Richmond. Quietly, still more in the manner of the quartermaster of Mexican War days than the fierce warrior of the campaigns ahead, Grant dealt with troop movements and supply problems. He wrote Julia, "I am now in command of all the troops from Ironton to this place." He did not know how long he would be at Cairo, but he told her, "I want you to come here. Get the children clothed so as to be in readiness to start when I write to you." It was, however, two months before she and the children joined him there.[26]

At the river town of Cairo Grant's command truly began. His participation in the Missouri campaign had been critical in his education and had culminated in his promotion to general. But Grant came into his own in Cairo. His general's uniform arrived a month after his promotion, and wearing it, he sat for the worst photograph ever made of him. Perched too far to the back of his head is an out-of-style hat, its right brim rising vertically and a black ostrich plume foppishly flowing along its left side. He holds a sword in a lap full of tassels, and only his hands look real. Behind his regular trimmed beard falls a longer second beard, a Stantonesque squared fringe of frizzled hair. Julia, when she arrived to join the general in his headquarters at Cairo, persuaded him to get rid of these bizarre whiskers, the hat disappeared, and seldom again did he bother with the sword. This silly excursion into self-ornamentation quickly over, Grant put his old jacket back on and settled down to work in Cairo.[27]

# VIII

## BATTLES

And yet, in spite of it, there grew a compelling fascination. I do not
think I exaggerate: for in that fascination lies War's power. Once you
have lain in her arms you can admit no other mistress. You may loathe,
you may execrate, but you cannot deny her. No lover can offer you
defter caresses, more exquisite tortures, such breaking delights. No
wine gives fiercer intoxication, no drug more vivid exaltation. Every
writer of imagination who has set down in honesty his experience has
confessed it. Even those who hate her most are prisoners to her spell.
They rise from her embraces, pillaged, soiled, it may be ashamed; but
they are still hers.

— *Guy Chapman*

AMERICA'S RIVERS, as they flow across a continent, had represented to John Marshall the arteries of the nation's life. The rivers carried the
movement, the growth, and in the full eighteenth-century sense of the term,
the commerce of a people. In view of that splendid conception, a claim could
be made that the strangely beautiful river town of Cairo, Illinois, is better
suited to be the capital of the nation than the sterile federal city lying in a
boggy byway along the Potomac. For Cairo lies where great rivers join. The
Mississippi River, into which the Missouri has already entered from the
west, flows through the nation from north to south. It is met at Cairo by the
Ohio, the west-running river that links the old Northwest Territory with
midland America. And upstream, just a few miles from Cairo, the Tennessee
and Cumberland rivers, which ramble westward through the mountains of
the upper South, cut suddenly northward and flow into the Ohio.

By the fall of 1861, that nation had fallen in two and commerce had been
disrupted. Forts blocked the points where the Tennessee and the Cumberland left the Confederacy and entered Kentucky. The Mississippi was in
the hands of disunionists as far north as Memphis, and new Confederate
thrusts northward threatened St. Louis. Grant, a general as unmajestic as his

capital, was stationed at Cairo with orders to hold back the moves of the Confederacy northward along the rivers into the Midwest. He had probably never read any decision by the great chief justice, but he seems to have grasped the power of Marshall's metaphor. Born far upstream on the Ohio, he had ridden its banks and traveled out into the world against its currents. An unprepossessing general in what others misguidedly thought of as a backwater command, Grant, at Cairo, not only blocked a Confederate move northward but began a southward probing of these rivers that eventually and painfully was to make the nation flow together again.

As he had a sense of the rivers and the people who lived along them, so too did the unintellectual general have a feel for the movement of events. Last year's clerk in the leather shop in Galena had come a very long way from his reluctance to speak out on political matters. While more prominent Union commanders in Washington were focusing on what lay across the Potomac in Virginia, Grant wrote and sent a telegram to the Speaker of the House of Representatives of Kentucky, informing him that "Confederate forces in Considerable numbers" had invaded the state. The message, sent on September 5, 1861, only four days after Grant took command at Cairo, represented a rare overreach of his authority. Less news than warning, it informed the legislators that Grant might find it necessary to take military action in their state. The statement should have come not from him, but from civilians in the federal government in Washington. In any event, its content suggests Grant's early grasp of the political dimension of the war. Unlike most of his military colleagues, he understood the importance to President Lincoln of holding Kentucky in the Union.[1]

The next day Grant gave force to his warning by moving a detachment of men up the Ohio and, without a battle, taking the town of Paducah, Kentucky, at the mouth of the Tennessee River. Similarly, General Charles F. Smith occupied Smithland, at the juncture of the Cumberland and the Ohio. Notice was served that the Confederates were not going to be allowed either to overrun western Kentucky or to move across the Ohio into Illinois. At Paducah, Grant felt at home much as he had when as a boy he visited cousins upriver in Maysville. Ignoring any animosities, the general addressed the citizens of the town: "I have come among you, not as an enemy, but as your friend and fellow-citizen. . . . An enemy, in rebellion against our common Government . . . is moving upon your city. I am here to defend you. . . ." That enemy took the form of the army of Leonidas Polk, the Episcopal bishop turned Confederate general. Polk, coming up the Mississippi, sought to join the Confederate forces active in eastern Kentucky. Rebel and loyal brigades alike were maneuvering in gingerly fashion throughout the state, trying not to alienate their fellow citizens but instead to secure their allegiance. Like the Missourians, the people of Kentucky were deeply unsure of where their loyalties lay. Polk, hoping to enlist them in the Confederacy, had set up headquarters at Columbus, Kentucky, twenty miles south of

Cairo on the Mississippi; his troops were a threat to Missouri, Kentucky, and even Illinois.[2]

With their eyes on that godly warrior, Grant and Captain Henry Walke of the United States Navy set out on November 6, 1861. By chance their action came on the same day that Flag Officer Samuel F. DuPont took Port Royal, South Carolina; the Civil War was moving by water. General Winfield Scott had called his concept of enveloping the Confederacy by exerting pressure on all its perimeters the Anaconda Plan, but the navy had venomous attacks in mind. DuPont's blockade was only one facet of the flexible maneuvers of the navy, whose vessels not only entered ports along the Confederacy's coast but also darted up the rivers of its interior, with small gunboats penetrating its deepest recesses. Grant and Walke's effort was of less social significance than DuPont's; his capture of the coastal fort, with the resulting evacuation of nearby white planters, opened the way for the experiments in farming by the freed people left behind that were to prove so important to Reconstruction. Grant's day was simpler; his object in going out on the river was to get into battle at Belmont, Missouri.[3]

During this action, Grant was careful not to appear insubordinate. The habit was so ingrained that it carried over into his choice of words when he described the episode in his *Memoirs* twenty years later. Frémont had ordered him to make "demonstrations" without, however, "attacking the enemy." Just what a "demonstration" might be, he did not say. Grant never revealed what he had in mind when he left Cairo. He claimed that only after he realized that his men, as they went aboard the boats, were "elated" at the prospect of a battle did he think of fighting. And he would have us believe that only at two the next morning, when he learned that General Polk had sent General Gideon J. Pillow with a relatively large force from Columbus across to the tiny garrison of Belmont, did he decide to fight there. Grant had seen Pillow's ineptness in the Mexican War and was pleased that he would be his opponent. But clearly he had already made the decision to attack when he left Cairo. Why else would he have taken three thousand men out in those boats? The gunboats alone could have made a "demonstration" by shelling Columbus; Grant gave his intent away in an order, sent on November 6, to Colonel R. J. Oglesby, commanding an Illinois regiment nearby in Missouri. Oglesby was told to "communicate with me at Belmont." Grant had set out to fight and to take the fort—not to demonstrate.[4]

Grant had wanted to seize Columbus before Polk did. It was too late for that now, but he could attack across the river at Belmont to prevent the Confederates from augmenting their forces in Missouri. At dawn on November 7 he went ashore three miles north of the fort and led his men through the riverbank thicket of trees. Meanwhile, the gunboats proceeded southward. Learning of Grant's operation, Polk hurried reinforcements across the river, and the two armies engaged in two hours of close, bitter fighting. Grant's men did not yield; finally, Pillow's did, and the Union soldiers overran the Confederate camp.

Polk, assuming Grant's attack at Belmont was designed to mask a second, larger assault on Columbus itself, did not move his whole force across the river, but he did send additional reinforcements to Pillow. These fresh soldiers, despite warnings from fleeing colleagues to go back, moved forward toward the fort, determined to recapture it. Dismayed at the prospect of a new attack, Grant ordered his men—who, in a mood of exultation, had begun looting—to burn the camp and cut their way back through the woods to the river. Grant himself, on his second horse of the day (one had been shot under him), started at a walk, to ensure that the Confederates would not suspect panic and begin a pursuit of his forces. But once he knew he was out of sight, he rode "as fast as my horse could carry me." At one point, through a field of cornstalks, he could see Confederate soldiers not fifty yards away. The horse "seemed to take in the situation," and as Grant stated it, "put his fore feet over the back of the bank without hesitation or urging, and with his hind feet well under him slid down the bank," stepped onto a single plank put out as a gangway and carried Grant, the last man aboard, out of the battle at Belmont.[5]

Terms matter in war. If the action at Belmont was a battle, Grant lost; if a raid, he won. Leonidas Polk declared Belmont to be a battle, which he had won. On November 8 he notified "His Excellency, President Davis" of the "complete rout" of the enemy, in the accomplishment of which his own men were "immortalized by gallant killing in the face of being themselves killed." Best of all, wired Polk, "General Grant is reported killed." Unluckily for His Excellency, the bishop's report was exaggerated; Grant had landed with his men on the riverbank at Belmont and gotten off again, alive.[6]

Grant, in his report to Washington from Cairo, spoke of an "engagement"; the term skirted both the question of insubordination and the question of how to evaluate the day's results. He complimented his soldiers on their valor, commended General McClernand, who had three horses shot from under him while commanding his brigade, and acknowledged his debt to John A. Rawlins, Clark B. Lagow, Joseph D. Webster, and William S. Hillyer of his staff. Grant asserted that his attack on Belmont had halted the Confederates' moves to reinforce their forces in Missouri, but this claim was possible only by luck: Polk retained Belmont and the opportunity to send troops into Missouri, but he failed to begin an offensive, thus draining meaning from his "victory." And Grant's "raid," as his admirers were to call it, was not much to crow about, though it came to be regarded as his first victory. Grant said, grandly and accurately, that Belmont's significance was in the "confidence it inspired in our troops," but the lesson of greater importance for him and his men was that fighting and winning wars has less to do with great "victories" than with messing through days like Belmont and not letting embarrassment over ineptness stop one from setting out again on the morrow.[7]

For Grant himself, Belmont was a critical initiation. To be sure, he had seen men die in battle in Mexico; as a junior officer he had ordered men to cross a stream or seize a building and several of them had died as a result. Similarly, a few of his men had died in skirmishes in Missouri. But now, for the first time he had had the sole responsibility for an attack, in which eighty-five of his men were killed. On the Confederate side, families came to Columbus to take the dead home for burial, and Grant wrote later that "Belmont had caused more mourning than almost any battle up to that time." But he insisted that the effect of the engagement on his men was different. Repeating himself, he affirmed that "the National troops acquired a confidence in themselves . . . that did not desert them through the war." Grant, too, had gained confidence. Shortly after Belmont, when talking to a Confederate officer to arrange a truce to bury the dead, Grant was told exactly what kind of coat he had been wearing during the action. Startled, he asked how the rebel knew and was told by the officer that both he and General Polk had been able to see Grant as he left the battlefield and that Polk had invited a soldier to "try your marksmanship on him if you wish." But, wrote Grant, "nobody fired at me."[8]

Just days after Belmont (but not as a consequence of it) there was a reorganization of commands in the Union army above Grant's level. Henry Wager Halleck was given the Army of the Missouri, replacing David Hunter, who was moved to Kansas. Halleck's headquarters were at St. Louis, and operations in Missouri, western Kentucky, and western Tennessee were under his jurisdiction. At the same time Don Carlos Buell, with headquarters at Louisville, was placed in charge of the Army of the Ohio, with jurisdiction over proposed actions throughout Tennessee. Later in the month there was a change of command at a still higher level. Because of one of those frequent and silly assumptions that age necessarily incapacitates, Winfield Scott, seventy-five years old, was replaced by George B. McClellan as general in command of all Union forces. When McClellan took charge in Washington, he found that there was confusion of authority (as exemplified by Tennessee) among the new commanders in the west. Halleck and Buell were jealous and hence overly respectful of each other's spheres of jurisdiction, and Ulysses Grant, a subordinate of Halleck's, was the one who disturbed the decorum—crossing the western tip of Kentucky, entering Buell's Tennessee, and invading the Confederacy.

But before Grant could conduct an invasion of the enemy's home territory he had had to increase his own authority. At Cairo, he was still very much a local commander and veteran quartermaster, occupied more with problems of supply than with the decisions of field command. He was communicating with his superiors not through personal letters to his commander, but through reports to General Halleck's assistant adjutant general. But at the same time he was doing a bit of standard army politicking. In October, John Rawlins received a letter from their fellow townsman Congressman Elihu Washburne "from which," Ulysses reported to Julia, "it appears that he has been urging me for the place of Major General." After making his usual disavowals of any desire for higher rank, Ulysses asked his wife to "lay aside the rules of society which would require Mrs. W. to pay you the first visit and call upon her and make known the many obligations I feel to her husband."[9]

Grant had a more direct chance to put himself forward with Washburne later in the month. Getting the necessary goods of war had been a problem for every general, and Congress was investigating charges of incompetence and fraud among army suppliers. As luck would have it, Grant's congressman was on the House Select Committee on Government Contracts, and Washburne arrived in Cairo on October 31, 1861, to investigate supply conditions. At the hearing, Grant explained that foreign guns presented problems because they were of a bore for which ammunition was not available in America; the bullets did not fit. Grant did not whine about ineptness in Washington, nor did he overstate the matter, but by the time he had finished, the purchase appeared to have been stupid, while he came through as intelligent. And Secretary of the Treasury Salmon P. Chase, for one, was told so by Washburne.[10]

In November, turning to matters more exciting than materièl, Grant wrote Washburne about a plan for an offensive. The details of the proposal are lost, but not the fact that Grant succeeded in making Washburne aware that if an attack was made, he should lead it. Carefully acknowledging the worth of two other Illinois officers, Colonel W. H. L. Wallace and General McClernand (who, he knew, was also politicking in Washington), Grant began his argument for an offensive: "The battle of Belmont [as he now called it] as time passes, proves to have been a greater success than Gen. McClernand or myself at first thought. The enemies loss proves to be greater and the effect upon the southern mind more saddening." Grant was taking special care not to insult McClernand because the former congressman had received a telegram of praise from President Lincoln after Belmont, while he himself, still the obscure man from Galena, had had not a word. But Grant was beginning to get himself out of the shadow. Washburne forwarded his skillfully written letter to the president, with instructions from one Illinois politician to another: "I want you to take a moment's time to read this letter of Genl Grant."[11]

Meanwhile, in Cairo, Grant was impatient. He displayed both his firmness and his discouragement in a letter to his father, in which he vented some of his anger at the impossible old man by delivering a sermon to him on the purpose of the war. After making his usual little-boy apology for not having written more often, after telling his father that he could not help him get a contract for harness, and taking care to avoid giving any news of his movements because he knew Jesse would leak them to the newspapers, he went on:

> Then too you are disposed to criticise unfavorably from information received through the public press, a portion of which I am sorry to see can

look at nothing favorably that does not look to a war upon slavery. My inclination is to whip the rebellion into submission, preserving all constitutional rights. If it cannot be whipped in any other way than through a war
against slavery, let it come to that legitimately. If it is necessary that slavery should fall that the Republic may continue its existence, let slavery go.
But that portion of the press that advocates the beginning of such a war
now, are as great enemies to their country as if they were open and
avowed secessionists.

These views were entirely consonant with Lincoln's, and here, at the close of
1861, Grant was predicting with precision exactly the way the goals of the
war would change as it evolved into a crusade to end slavery. But Grant's
lofty rhetoric did not hold to the end of the letter. He was depressed: Julia
had gone to visit her father, two of his horses had died, he had forgotten his
good saddle cloth—it was at home—and, finally: "I am somewhat troubled
lest I lose my command here."[12]
  Two months later, in January of the new year, Grant was still uneasy
about his command and bolstered his morale by boasting to his sister that he
had under him at Cairo more men than Winfield Scott had had in Mexico.
He hoped he would "retain so important a command for at least one battle."
The next day, Grant went to St. Louis to persuade his commander that such
a battle should be fought. He had written earlier in the month asking for an
interview, but General Halleck's aide had dismissed the request, apparently
seeing it as an attempt by Grant to find an excuse to visit St. Louis rather
than assuming that he might wish to discuss important ideas about the conduct of the war. Nevertheless, Grant risked leaving Cairo, even though by
doing so he put his rival, General McClernand, in temporary command. As
commanding officer, McClernand seized the chance to send dispatches directly to General Halleck and President Lincoln; when Grant got back four
days later, Rawlins had to inform Halleck formally that "Grant arrived home
this morning, and will again resume command."[13]
  The St. Louis meeting had gone badly. Henry Wager Halleck, heavy-set,
with bulging eyes, was difficult to get close to. Forty-six years old, he had
graduated from West Point the spring before Grant entered and, winning a
coveted spot in the corps of engineers, had gone to California. There, after
resigning from the army, he had become successful in business. It was considered, not least by him, a great gift to the Union cause that he had returned
to the army to manage the war in the west. Grant had known Halleck neither
at West Point nor in Mexico; their paths had crossed only once, when they
met briefly during Grant's difficult days in California. Halleck had heard
(and probably told) some of the virulent stories about Grant's drinking in
California and had heard and believed recent rumors about his consumption
of alcohol at Belmont and Cairo. Indeed, Halleck would not have been surprised by the observation of James Harrison Wilson, gossiping with Samuel

F. DuPont far off on the East Coast, on the flagship *Wabash:* "These generals in the west are not much and Grant drinks all the time." Halleck (whom DuPont thought a "military genius") was exceedingly wary of trusting a general commonly thought to be a drunk. He did not really listen as Grant sought to persuade him to stop rearranging his forces and start an invasion by river. Grant, for his part, had learned that all one could expect from carrying out one of Halleck's pointless cross-country reconnaissance maneuvers was "splashing through the mud, snow and rain." He wanted instead to move not by land but by boat, take Fort Henry, at the Tennessee border, and invade the Tennessee River valley, moving through Tennessee, Mississippi, and Alabama; however, according to Grant, the meeting proceeded with "so little cordiality that I perhaps stated the object of my visit with less clearness than I might have done." Halleck said no.[14]

Grant was profoundly depressed by Halleck's rebuff; he returned to Cairo "very much crestfallen." It was a navy man, Flag Officer Andrew Hull Foote, who restored Grant's confidence. Foote, with a background of New Haven Congregational rectitude, respected Grant and was ready to go into battle with him. Foote either disbelieved the stories of Grant's drinking or didn't care. Instead, he helped the general get on with a sober task. When Grant got back to Cairo, Foote immediately sent Halleck an uncomplicated proposal: "Grant and myself are of opinion that Fort Henry on the Tennessee can be carried with four Iron-clad Gun-boats and troops to be permanent occupied. Have we your authority to move for that purpose?" That same night Grant sent a parallel, succinct telegram: "With permission I will take Fort Henry on the Tennessee and hold & establish a large camp there." With the assurance of Foote's participation in hand, Halleck telegraphed his assent, but in the written order to Grant that followed, pointedly added, "You will furnish . . . Foote with a copy of this letter." Grant was being allowed to go because Foote would be there to keep a fatherly eye on him.[15]

In this first invasion of the Confederacy in the west, Grant's army was an auxiliary of the United States Navy. On February 3, 1862, Foote took seven gunboats, four armored and three unsheathed, upstream on the Tennessee River across the narrow western end of Kentucky toward Fort Henry, poorly sited on low land, where the Confederates had placed fortifications intended to block any Union invasion southward into Tennessee. The Union's unimpressive but effective armada was followed by a fleet of transport ships carrying seventeen thousand of Brigadier General Ulysses S. Grant's men. The river waters were high and carried away Confederate mines laid to defend the fort. On February 6 one contingent of Grant's army, under General McClernand, disembarked and in heavy rain and cold moved toward Fort Henry on close-to-impassable roads along the east bank of the river. General Charles F. Smith led a similar force against the companion fort on the west bank. Foote's gunboats moved to within a mile of Fort Henry and opened fire. For two hours the shelling continued; the returning shot was accurate and deadly. The wooden boats had to hold to the bank; one ironclad was so badly damaged that it drifted back downstream, but the other sheathed boats persevered, despite fierce shelling, and put the fort's cannon out of commission. Recognizing that he could not hold Fort Henry, its Confederate colonel, Lloyd Tilghman, sent 2,500 of his men overland to Fort Donelson, eleven miles away on the Cumberland River, and with the death of but one man, surrendered the remaining seventy. In the words of one authority, James Marshall-Cornwall, "The victory had been won by the U.S. Navy."[16]

In Washington, McClellan was delighted, but his request to General Halleck, "Please thank Grant and Foote and their commands for me," was carried out only with respect to Foote. Halleck could celebrate the success of the naval officer without jealousy; he held back from congratulating his fellow army officer. Meanwhile, Grant and Foote were making people other than Halleck uncomfortable. The Federals were "away down in Dixie," as Grant put it in a letter to his sister, and in the Confederacy, for the first time, there was fear of deep penetration by the Yankees. On February 8 Foote's gunboats pushed all the way across Tennessee and reconnoitered threateningly as far south as Florence, Alabama.[17]

As soon as Fort Henry fell, Grant called his chief officers together to discuss the possibility of attacking Fort Donelson. He once said that he never held a council of war in his life; General Lew Wallace corrected him. There was one such council—in the ladies' cabin of the *Tigress*, the gunboat on which Grant made his headquarters at this time. At the meeting, Wallace found his fellow councilors joined "in icy binding; probably because, like myself, they were mostly new to the business. Our uniforms and swords, worn in compliance with etiquette, may have had to do with the frigidity of the occasion." General Charles F. Smith, a tall, dignified, fifty-five-year-old West Pointer, who had stood in judgment of Grant at the academy as his teacher and was a veteran of a command in the Mexican War, had some sense of the protocol and mores of such gatherings. He contributed a bit of small talk, but "aside from that there was not the slightest pretence of sociability, no introductions, no bowing, no hand-shaking, no conversation."[18]

"After little," Wallace recounted, "General Grant stepped to the table and said, ever so quietly: 'The question for consideration, gentlemen, is whether we shall march against Fort Donelson or wait for reinforcements. I should like to have your views.' " The generals, still standing, spoke in order of seniority. Smith said simply that he was ready to go at once, but McClernand, hammering another nail into his coffin, "drew out a paper and read it." He, like all the others, "was in favor of going at once." However, as Wallace observed, it would have been "better for him . . . had he rested with a word to that effect; as it was he entered into details . . . ; we should do this going and that when we were come. The proceeding smacked of a political caucus, and . . . both Grant and Smith grew restive. . . ." Wallace was aware that while the various officers spoke, Rawlins watched them—taking stock of each of his general's lieutenants. When McClernand was through, Grant immediately gave the order that all were to be ready to leave at a moment's notice, and Wallace thought it "hardly supposable" that "the opinions submitted had any influence" on the decision. "There is evidence that he had already determined upon the movement." Thereafter, Grant dispensed with the charade of appearing to rely on councils of war.[19]

Few Americans have written better about battles than Lew Wallace. February 12 was "a day of summer. River, land, and sky fairly shimmered with warmth," and Wallace, as impatient as his men for the order to move, stupidly allowed them to discard their overcoats. That night the weather changed; two nights later, after they had made the march of thirteen miles to join Smith's and McClernand's forces in the line west of Fort Donelson, Wallace's men were shivering in bleak discomfort and in danger of frostbite. The temperature was twelve degrees.[20]

On February 14, Flag Officer Foote's four gunboats opened fire on Fort Donelson. The exploding shells created a spectacular blaze of fire and the destruction of the fort seemed imminent, but the Confederate defenders, although their best gun was out of commission, poured a hail of artillery and rifle fire down on the gunboats. On one after another the steering mechanism was destroyed, and the once fierce vessels were drawn into the current and swept harmlessly back to the north. This time the navy could not win Grant's fight for him.[21]

The next morning, while Grant was absent for a conference with Foote, the Confederate soldiers—elated by the repulse of the gunboats—attacked the Union armies to the rear of their fort. Smith's men were on the west, Wallace's in the center, and McClernand's on the east, in the path of the rebels trying to fight their way out of the fort and onto the road eastward to Nashville. Fighting well, General Gideon Pillow's men routed McClernand's despite reinforcements which Wallace sent, against Grant's earlier orders. As McClernand's forces—out of cartridges and uneager to replenish their supply from stores in the rear—broke ranks, leaving the road open, Wallace managed to move his force out of the way of the retreat so that they too would not panic and join the rush to the rear. He accomplished little else.

Grant has been criticized for leaving no single general in command while he was away from the front, but perhaps recalling the council of war on the *Tigress,* he had had confidence in none. As he rode back to the battlefield in the afternoon, he noticed "men standing in knots talking in the most excited manner. No officer seemed to be giving any directions." He rode up to McClernand and Wallace, who were also standing and talking, and first proposed that the Union forces back out of range of Confederate fire, but when Wallace told him that a fallback by the right flank of the Union army would allow the entire Confederate force to escape to Clarksville, he changed his mind. Despite the rebel attack, he still thought he could trap the Confederates at Fort Donelson, and he blamed McClernand (and perhaps Wallace) for having relinquished the offensive. Wallace reported that "Grant's face, already congested with cold, reddened perceptibly and his lower jaw set upon the other. Without a word, he looked at McClernand." As that general once more began a long explanation, Grant, fiercely controlling his rage, interrupted him: "Gentlemen," he said, "that road must be recovered before night." Gripping the papers in his hand—Wallace heard them "crinkle"—he continued: "I will go to Smith now. At the sound of your fire, he will support you with an attack on his side." Thereupon Grant turned his horse and rode off at an ordinary trot. Wallace watched him go, "wondering at the simplicity of the words in a matter involving so much."²²

The ground over which Grant rode after he took his leave was the same that Wallace covered when he rode off to follow his new orders, but the two men, both keen observers, saw different wars. They were as unlike as writers as they were as generals. Forty years later, Wallace went squirrel shooting with a gun he had had his orderly take from the body of a Confederate soldier, "its owner looking up at the sky from his sheet of crimson snow," and using the gun reminded him of other corpses of war. He remembered that as he left Grant, his "horse objected to the dead men still lying in the road." Wallace picked his way among them and, working his way through heavy fire, came on "a man sitting against a stump," in homespun and coonskin cap, who was looking mockingly at him. Wallace spoke to his orderly: "Find out what that fellow means by grinning that way. If he answers decently, help him." The orderly dismounted, went over to the man, and reported, "Why he's dead, sir." "That can't be," Wallace replied. "See where he's hit." They then investigated more closely: "The cap when taken off brought away with it a mass that sickened us. A small bullet—from a revolver, probably—had gone through the inner corner of his eye leaving no visible wound, but the whole back of the head was blown off and the skull entirely emptied."²³

Grant, also writing long after the event, recalled different details of his meeting with McClernand and Wallace. It was he who remembered the confused men who stood "in knots talking in the most excited manner," with no orders coming from any officer. Grant did not write of the fury that made him crumple the paper in his hand, and did not choose to mention McClernand or Wallace by name. Rather, he told how with a simple order he rallied the demoralized Union soldiers who had run out of ammunition and retreated in panic. "I directed Colonel Webster to ride with me and call out to the men as we passed: 'Fill your cartridgeboxes, quick, and get into line; the enemy is trying to escape and he must not be permitted to do so.' This acted like a charm. The men only wanted some one to give them a command." Then the general "rode rapidly to Smith's quarters. . . ." Grant somehow erased from his memory the corpses on the road. Or perhaps he did not have to do so; during a battle he did not see them.²⁴

Lew Wallace rode right; Ulysses Grant rode left to where General Smith and his men were facing a fierce Confederate attack from Fort Donelson.

Grant, who knew the qualities of the three generals he opposed, ordered a counterattack that broke the enemy line, closed the road to Nashville, and forced the enemy back into the fort. The three Confederate generals were conscious that they would be the first important rebels to surrender and wondered if they would be charged with treason. They conferred desperately and angrily. General John B. Floyd was particularly apprehensive; he was one of the highest-ranking officials of the United States government to have gone over to the Confederacy. What was more, prior to secession, while President Buchanan's secretary of war, he had been charged with corruption and had been accused of using his authority to move war matériel south. Both Floyd and Gideon Pillow, quarreling with the third general, Simon Bolivar Buckner, refused to surrender, but they also refused to stay at Fort Donelson and try to fight their way out. Instead, they yielded their commands to Buckner, and then Floyd, with four regiments of Virginians (there wasn't room in the boats for his Mississippians) and Pillow, on a commandeered scow, made their escape on the river. These two generals were never again allowed a command by Jefferson Davis. Buckner, left behind and trapped with 11,500 men in the fort, had already decided to surrender to his old friend Ulysses Grant.[25]

How close friends are one to another is almost unknowable, but it can be assumed that Buckner, who had hiked in Mexico with Grant and had lent him money when it was badly needed, was expecting friendship to count for something. Reports of Grant's camaraderie with Belmont captives encouraged Buckner's hopes for leniency, and on February 16, 1862, he sent a formal request for a truce during which conditions of surrender could be discussed. Grant's reply was famous: "Sir: Yours of this date proposing armistice and appointment of Commissioners to settle terms of capitulation, is just received. No terms except an unconditional and immediate surrender can be accepted. I propose to move immediately upon your works." Buckner replied that the overwhelming size of the Union force made it necessary for him "to accept the ungenerous and unchivalrous terms." Grant had given the Civil War a new, grim, and determined character.[26]

After the surrender, Grant rode to the town of Dover, just outside the fort, and was dismayed to find Lew Wallace cheerfully breakfasting with Buckner. (Earlier, a Union naval officer had come to the house to apprehend Buckner for the navy, but had left when he found himself outranked by General Wallace. Credit-gathering was in season.) After Grant's uncompromising demand for surrender, Buckner was worried that as a captured West Point man he would be treated as a traitor rather than a prisoner of war. Wallace, with no sense of how Grant had changed the fundamental terms of the war, had just told Buckner that Lincoln and Grant were decent sorts and he could expect leniency. When Grant arrived, he took over the discussion with Buckner and gave permission only for his men to go out and bury their dead—nothing more. No doubt Grant realized that a few of the burial party might escape, but the rest, including Buckner, were to be sent north as prisoners of war. Then, the war-work of the day done, Grant could be civil with his old friend. Gossiping about Pillow he asked, "Where is he now?" "Gone," replied Buckner, ". . . he thought you'd rather get hold of him than any other man in the Southern Confederacy." "Oh," Grant cut in, "if I had got him I'd let him go again. He will do us more good commanding you fellows." When Buckner told Hamlin Garland of this conversation thirty years later, he added, "This made us both laugh, for we remembered Pillow in the Mexican War."[27]

That night Ulysses sent Julia a hasty note that was not very elegant as historical writing but did, by implicitly comparing Donelson with the actions of the Revolutionary War and of the campaign in Mexico, place his battle in grand perspective: "This is the largest capture I believe ever made on the continent." And his boast was not inappropriate; Donelson was the first important Union victory in the Civil War. In Washington, a week later, Secretary of War Edwin M. Stanton wrote Charles A. Dana, of the *New York Tribune*, "Was it not a funny sight to see a certain military hero [McClellan] in the telegraph office at Washington last Sunday organizing victory and by sublime military combinations capturing Fort Donelson *six hours after* Grant and Smith had taken it sword in hand and had victorious possession! It would be a picture worthy of Punch." Grant was a victorious general, and important people like Stanton knew it.[28]

Grant had a strong sense of history, and he is frequently considered to have been canny in his judgment of the men who were with him in the making of it. Indeed, the question is often asked, If Grant was such a good judge of men during the war, why was he so poor at assessing associates in the White House and in business? The answer emerges from a recognition of the differences between men in war and out of it. Fundamentally, Grant was exceedingly disillusioned about people, including almost all of his generals. He studied them—some had been under his scrutiny since West Point and Mexico—and measured details of personality in terms of expected responses to orders. Except for Sherman and Sheridan—and he had reservations even about them—Grant did not regard his generals as having the capacity for independent judgment.

He expected little and in the war luckily got much. Also, he knew that in the army, in contrast to the civilian world, though orders might be badly carried out, they did have to be obeyed. As long as Grant could sense the movement of battle he could give explicit orders and get from his officers their best. In the White House and on Wall Street that gauge of motion was absent, and he lacked the assurance that his instructions would be listened to and obeyed. During the war he moved swiftly and surely to make men do more than their records might suggest they were capable of. He was, for example, clearly angry with McClernand and probably with Wallace as well when he came upon them out of control of the panicking men. Though he cut off McClernand in mid-excuse, Grant, in command, did not lose his temper and fire him on the spot. Instead, he gave simple unequivocal orders and left. McClernand pulled himself and his men together, and he and Wallace soon found themselves fighting with a sense of direction—and success.[29]

On a battleground like Donelson, and later in vast campaigns, Grant had a remarkable sense of the whole of the event. It was always changing; nothing was ever settled. His perception was not a single snapping of the shutter to give a brilliantly clear image of a battle stopped in full clarity. Instead what he saw always included a dimension of time, an awareness of the unfolding evolving motion of the life of the war. He did not fight crisp, swift, elegant battles. The taking of Fort Henry, executed so clearly that there was but one casualty, and the surrender of Fort Donelson, compelled by the threat of imminent invincible attack, gave the impression of great military style, and there was indeed good generalship on Grant's part in both instances. But it should not be forgotten that in its earlier phases, the fight for Donelson was going so badly that he was close to disaster. Foote could not repeat the kind of naval bombardment that had succeeded at Fort Henry, McClernand's men broke in panic, ammunition was not where it was needed, and the terrible weather could have been allowed to prevent the Union armies from reaching Donelson at all. The outcome might have been for Grant a repetition of peacetime disappointments—but it was not. Now he was at war. He seemed almost to flout adversity and relish snatching success from the desperate edge of failure. He could make his luck hold.

As famous as were Grant's words to Buckner—"I propose to move immediately upon your works"—they were uncharacteristic of his concept of war. The single, splendid, climactic effort was not the reality of war as Grant understood it. He never expected to get caught up with his work, even when a fort was surrendered to him. He knew that each day, and each battle, led to the next. The way to reach ultimate victory was to develop a stronger sense of war's rhythm than that possessed by the enemy. The order perceived by the general was not one of neat battle lines or static confrontations in which opposing forces could be expected to move simultaneously. What he did after Donelson was more characteristic than the battle itself. He moved on, not restlessly or fitfully and not in exuberance, to Clarksville, and continuing eastward, wrote on February 28, "I shall go to Nashville immediately after the arrival of the next Mail, should there be no orders to prevent it."[30]

He had no urge to rest on his laurels, which is not to say that he had no taste for the laurels themselves. He saw Donelson not as a crowning victory, but simply as the important second action in a series that would secure a political entity, the state of Tennessee, for the Union. He had his eye on the rivers as well. Grant reported to an aide of Halleck's on Southern moves in anticipation of a Union attack on Memphis, the largest city on the Mississippi between New Orleans and St. Louis: "Orders have been given [by the enemy] for the evacuation of Columbus [the Confederate stronghold that guarded the city]. . . . The force at Memphis is said to be about 12,000." He was exceedingly eager that Halleck seize the opportunity to take the city and

sent two Memphis newspapers to St. Louis for Halleck to read. "I am growing anxious to know," Grant added, "what the next move is going to be."
The war, and Ulysses Grant, were truly in motion.[31]

Motion mattered to Abraham Lincoln as well. To win at Donelson had
been of critical importance to the president. The day Buckner surrendered to
Grant, Lincoln (not yet knowing the news) wrote Halleck, "You have Fort
Donelson safe, unless Grant shall be overwhelmed from outside, to prevent
which latter will, I think, require all the vigilance, energy, and skill of yourself & Buell, acting in full cooperation." The commander in chief, so anxious
after ten months of war for a victory and so apprehensive that one might
again elude him, could not have been more emphatic: "Our success or failure
at Donelson is vastly important; and I beg you to put your soul in the effort."[32]

Lincoln's letter, with its grasp of essentials, makes it clear that he perceived
Grant as a pivotal figure—as a fighter eager for a fight. Aware of this perception, Halleck wanted Grant pushed aside; once a victor, Grant became a
rival. And so, in the month after Donelson, Grant had to meet and defeat his
fellow Union officer Henry Wager Halleck. It was one of his greatest victories. If he had not won that battle he could have won no others, and the difficulty of the struggle was enormous. To win he had to do what no other general was ever able to do—he had to conquer Ulysses Grant.

Halleck, unlike Grant, was a successful man. He had sacrificed a handsome career to enter the war. A graduate of both Union College and West
Point, he was perhaps the pre-eminent scholar of warfare in the country. His
Lowell lectures were published as *Elements of Military Art and Science,* and he
translated the Swiss expert on war Antoine Henri Jomini. Like Grant, Halleck resigned his captaincy in 1854, but he stayed in California, making
money as a lawyer and a businessman, and writing two lawbooks. He re-
entered the army in 1861, ready to let his book learning work its wondrous
way to a Union victory. Forty-seven, heavy, imperious, with puffy eyes that
were fierce rather than comic, Halleck was a man of authority.

Halleck's aim was to obtain senior command of the whole war in the west
on the strength of the Fort Donelson victory. "Make Buell, Grant and Pope
major-generals . . . and give me command in the west," he suggested to the
commanding general in Washington, George B. McClellan. Don Carlos
Buell and John Pope, who had had nothing to do with the victory, were to
get a free ride to higher rank, at the price of being under Halleck's over-all
western command. Thus Grant would be deprived of being singled out for
promotion. Lincoln frustrated Halleck here; he sent only Grant's promotion, which Donelson had made certain, to the Senate.[33]

Halleck, in St. Louis, might as well have been in Seattle, and he was an
angry man. Grant, while his promotion to major general was being confirmed, continued his move eastward through Tennessee. Partly because of
Confederate interception of telegrams and partly because of Grant's swift
moves to Clarksville and Nashville, Halleck lost contact with Grant—or as

army protocol would have it, Grant lost contact with his commander. Unknown to Halleck, however, he was in communication with Brigadier General George W. Cullum, whom Halleck had sent to monitor him. Meanwhile Buell, still in independent command of the Army of the Ohio, was belatedly moving toward Nashville; should he take that city he might destroy Halleck's hopes for an over-all command. But a greater threat than Buell was the new major general; Grant's aggressive interference in Buell's attack on Nashville seemed to indicate that he was taking command on his own. Buell, at Lincoln's suggestion, had sent a division down the Ohio and up the Cumberland to help Grant at Donelson, and when the men arrived, Grant, not needing them, had sent them on up the river to Nashville. Buell was furious that his men, following Grant's orders, arrived before he himself could reach the city overland. When he finally got to the north side of the river, he could merely join an invasion already launched within what he regarded as his—not Grant's or Halleck's—sphere of command.

Buell, whose exasperation with Grant was never to abate, said later that spring that Grant was either a fool or crazy. But Grant was neither; he wanted the men not needed at Nashville freed for other campaigns. Grant was showing considerable—perhaps insubordinate—independence; he was taking responsibility for the conduct of a major campaign in Tennessee. Indeed, in a letter to Julia he made it clear that although he still regarded Halleck "as one of the greatest men of the age," he wanted his own command: "I do hope that I will be placed in a separate Department so as to be more independent." Implicit was the wish that the department—the command of an army—would be his own. He told Julia not to make his letter public, but not to lose it.[34]

Independence was precisely what General Halleck was determined that Grant not have. By March 3, Halleck had reached the end of his limited patience with his fast-moving subordinate. To Washington he wrote:

I have had no communication with General Grant for more than a week. He left his command without my authority and went to Nashville. His army seems to be as much demoralized by the victory of Fort Donelson as was that of the Potomac by the defeat of Bull Run. It is hard to censure a successful general immediately after a victory, but I think he richly deserves it. I can get no returns, no reports, no information of any kind from him. Satisfied with his victory, he sits down and enjoys it without any regard to the future. I am worn out and tired with this neglect and inefficiency. C. F. Smith is almost the only officer equal to the emergency.

McClellan replied:

The future success of our cause demands that proceedings such as Grant's should at once be checked. Generals must observe discipline as well as private soldiers. Do not hesitate to arrest him at once if the good of the service requires it, and place C. F. Smith in command. You are at liberty to regard this as a positive order if it will smooth your way. I appreciate the difficulties you have to encounter, and will be glad to relieve you from trouble as far as possible.

As Bruce Catton has pointed out, Halleck had more malice to spread. On March 4 he wired McClellan, "A rumor has just reached me that since the taking of Fort Donelson General Grant has resumed his former bad habits. If so, it will account for his neglect of my often-repeated orders. I do not deem it advisable to arrest him at present, but have placed General Smith in command of the expedition up the Tennessee. I think Smith will restore order and discipline." He then sent a wire to Grant: "You will place Major General C. F. Smith in command of expedition and remain yourself at Fort Henry. Why do you not obey my orders to report strength and positions of your command?"[35]

Halleck represented everything that heretofore had defeated Grant. In his mocking query—"Why do you not obey . . . ?"—with which he taunted Grant as being too stupid or stubborn to make the necessary reports, he was Jesse Grant. In his unapproachableness, evident when Grant tried to gain his attention in St. Louis, Halleck matched Hannah Grant's silence. In his role as an intellectual, Halleck the scholar stood for the institutional aspects of West Point and the army that Grant had found unsatisfying. In his civilian career as a lawyer, he had been the successful man of affairs Grant had so long and so unsuccessfully sought to emulate. When Halleck's criticisms and potentially crippling orders arrived, Grant was still sorting out elements of doubt and confidence. In his letter to Julia in Covington telling her that "the Administration have thought well enough of my administration of affairs to make me a Maj. General," he made only one comment on the impressive promotion: "Is father afraid yet that I will not be able to sustain myself?" Was his confidence firm enough to sustain him against Halleck's assault? If elegant little men like Lieutenant Colonel Robert Christie Buchanan had been strong enough to unseat Grant at Fort Humboldt, then surely Henry Wager Halleck, the impressive, powerful man who was Grant's commander in the winter of 1862, should have been able to shatter Grant when he set out to do so.[36]

And Grant was not in the best condition to weather Halleck's attack. A cold that he had had since leaving Cairo was giving him constant discomfort in his chest, and this, as he wrote Foote, was coupled "with a severe head ache, [that] nearly destroys my energy." In addition, his father had come for a visit, hoping to get his hands on some of Grant's handsome new major general's salary of six thousand dollars. Indeed, Grant had to handle both Halleck and his father in one day. Toward his commanding general, he displayed astonishing *sang-froid*. In a dignified letter written on March 5 he denied "having disobeyed any order" and said he had obtained reports on the number of troops from all his generals save General Smith. And here Grant began scoring points on Halleck; the delinquent, Smith, was the man Halleck had named to supersede Grant, and Smith's tardiness, Grant noted, probably was due to his having been ordered by Buell to move (unnecessarily, as one of Halleck's aides had already been told) to reinforce Buell's unopposed force at Nashville. Grant betrayed no trace of complaint in telling Halleck he would turn the Tennessee expedition over to Smith, but then, pointedly, he indicated that Halleck would have to be responsible for the troop withdrawals, and consequent losses of territory, involved in the transfer of authority. Was he, for example, "to abandon Clarkesville entirely or not"? As for the order that he remain in Fort Henry, Grant indicated that following it literally would be a bit difficult: "The water is about six feet deep inside the fort." Halleck was not likely to have missed the suggestion that he was so ignorant of conditions in the area of his command that he did not even know of the flooding of the Tennessee River.[37]

To Julia, that same day, Grant wrote, "Father is just going back and I will take this occation to write you a few lines." He asked her to tell him how much money she had—apparently she was not contributing enough toward expenses at Covington to satisfy Jesse—and added, "You can lend father all you have keeping about $100 for yourself to last until I can send you more. [He had recently sent her seven hundred dollars.] Take a note payable to yourself bearing interest. . . ." Then, reflecting on these astringent familial arrangements, he observed, "I feel myself worse used by my own family than by strangers and although I do not think father, of his own accord, would do me injustice yet I believe he is influanced, and always may be, to my prejudice." Grant did not suggest who might be doing the influencing; perhaps he could not contemplate his father's hostility, unalloyed. He continued, "Kiss the children for me. I am in a very poor humor for writing. I was ordered to command a very important expedition up the Tennessee river and now an order comes directing one of my juniors to take the command whilst I am left behind here with a small garrison. . . . It may be all right but I dont now see it." He signed, simply, "Ulys."[38]

On March 5 and 6, Grant dutifully and efficiently set about turning over the command of the Tennessee River expedition to his old West Point teacher Charles F. Smith. He added gracious congratulations to Smith on his promotion to major general, a promotion Grant had strongly supported. Grant's orders to several of his generals and his attention to the details of the transfer of authority suggest no bitterness or lack of energy, and now he did report the figures on the number of Federal troops directly to Halleck. In doing so he probably guessed that any statistics he supplied would be used by the conservative Halleck to conclude (as indeed he did in a report to McClellan) that a major expedition could not be undertaken without Buell's support—that is, without a reorganization of the western command under Halleck. The momentum generated by Grant's victories at Fort Henry and Fort Donelson had been lost.[39]

On that same day, March 6, 1862, Grant received a second stinging rebuke from the man in St. Louis. After asking again for troop numbers and positions, Halleck added, "Your neglect of repeated orders to report the strength of your command has created great dissatisfaction, & seriously interfered with military plans. Your going to Nashville without authority & when your presence with your troops was of the utmost importance, was a matter of very serious complaint at Washington, so much so that I was advised to arrest you on your return." Receiving this message was of course exceedingly painful for Grant, but he was in strong enough command of himself to read it closely and to strike back.[40]

In a masterful telegram in his own defense, ne stated that he had reported regularly to Halleck's chief staff officer, General Cullum, daily; if Cullum had failed to pass the information along to Halleck, it was not Grant's fault. And, succinctly, he said, "My going to Nashville was strictly intended for the good of the service, and not to gratify any desire of my own." The wire went to Halleck—with a copy to Elihu Washburne. Grant was now putting to use lessons he had learned when he lobbied, awkwardly, for his colonelcy and, skillfully, for his generalship. If there were "enemies between you and myself" as Grant told Halleck in his wire (which closed with a request that he be "relieved from further duty in [pointedly] the Dept."), Grant also had friends. His collaborator Flag Officer Foote had as his guest during these critical days the perceptive Charles A. Dana. Their conversations may have carried to Secretary Stanton, and someone, very likely Rawlins (surely not without Grant's knowledge) got the whole Halleck-Grant controversy before Congressman Washburne, who obviously would not have wanted his star protégé disgraced. The telegrams are in Washburne's papers. Lincoln, who had been anxious for the Donelson victory, was accessible to a Republican congressman from Illinois. What was more, he and Secretary of War Stanton were dissatisfied with the general inactivity of both McClellan and Halleck. Armed with documentation from Grant's headquarters—not too much, exactly enough—Washburne made a strong case for not allowing Halleck to shelve the aggressive and battle-tried Grant.[41]

In Tennessee, Grant had been in the midst of the preparations for an offensive campaign, but he yielded command so that it could go forward. On March 9, he wrote General McClernand, "I did not mean to give any directions about the order of moving. Gen. Smith being in command of the expedition"; he seemed to have capitulated, but he was deeply moved when he found several of his chief officers ready to stand by him. Never before in Grant's life had other men rallied round him as a group. Nothing could have given him more confidence. Nine of his senior officers, including the highly able young officer Colonel W. H. L. Wallace and General John A. McClernand (to his great credit, considering the rebuffs Grant had dealt him), signed a strong letter to Grant deploring his removal from command and placing "this spontaneous tribute at your disposal for such use as you may think proper to make of it." This was not only moral support, but powerful political support as well. At this critical point still another emblem of esteem arrived—by lucky chance at the perfect moment. His officers had ordered a ceremonial sword for him, to commemorate Donelson. Fortunately, it had been a bit slow in coming, for its arrival now was, if ironic, nevertheless of critical importance. His friends were giving him a weapon—not the sword, but their affection—with which to confront discouragement. On board the *Tigress*, his comrades told him they were glad that it had arrived "at this moment when the jealousy caused by your brilliant success has raised up hidden enemies who are endeavoring to strike you in the dark."[42]

When Halleck, writing for the second time on March 6, had accused Grant of "want of order & discipline, and the numerous irregularities in your command"—a thinly veiled hint that he regarded Grant as having been drinking—he had spoken of relieving Grant "unless these things are immediately corrected. . . ." This, of course, made the earlier communication placing General Smith in command more ambiguous than ever—was the point only to give Smith command for a single expedition, or was it something more? Was Grant being examined for psychological sturdiness by Halleck, who believed the stories about his drinking? Whatever Halleck's game was, Grant did not capitulate. He did not show the repentance Halleck seemed to require. Nor was he silent. In earlier personal crises he had been driven to speechlessness. Now he found words. Grant had won an exhilarating battle and had led his men on energetic thrusts into Tennessee. He had felt the lust of war; could assert himself. He did not throw himself on the mercy of Washburne, but saw to it that the congressman had the documentation that would enable him to bring his political force into play to protect a badly exposed flank. He did not retreat into a room, alone. He stepped out and spoke up.[43]

Grant's restrained, dignified words in response to Halleck—not defensive, but suggesting firmly that all he had done since Donelson had been in order—were heeded in Washington. His new reputation had superseded the old. Halleck had gotten support from McClellan for firing Grant, but the War Department and White House were not ready for that, and Halleck received an astringent order: "By direction of the President, the Secretary of War desires you to ascertain and report whether General Grant left his command at any time without proper authority, and, if so, for how long; whether he has made to you proper reports and returns of his force; whether he has committed any acts which are unauthorized or not in accordance with military subordination or propriety, and, if so, what." In short, innuendoes about drinking would not do, and if Grant's actions could be accounted for— and they could—Halleck could only attempt to get rid of him by engaging in a "him or me" argument, which he might lose. The wire came at the "direction of the President"; Lincoln himself had called a halt to the attempt to smear Grant.[44]

Ironically, Grant was also the beneficiary of Halleck's good fortune. The commander in St. Louis had, at last, been given the over-all command of forces in the west. He now had that authority without which any executive feels insecure. He no longer felt threatened by the pulling and tugging of rival generals. In addition, conditions were stable in Missouri and propitious for action in Tennessee. Halleck could now tolerate Grant and, grudgingly, agreed to do so. On March 13, in Tennessee, Grant asked "to be relieved from further duty until I can be placed right in the estimation of those higher in authority." And that same day evidence was received that Lincoln and Stanton had indeed set things right; Halleck telegraphed Grant: "You cannot be relieved from your command. There is no good reason for it. I am certain that all which the authorities at Washington ask, is, that you enforce discipline & punish the disorderly. The power is in your hands; use it, & you will be sustained by all above you. Instead of relieving you, I wish you, as soon as your new army is in the field, to assume the immediate command & lead it on to new victories." Grant had won the fight.[45]

It would be splendid for the Grant story if, after having established personal invincibility, he had moved on immediately to get the war over with. In his *Memoirs*, Grant made a strong case for the possibility that this might have been accomplished if only he had been allowed to press on relentlessly after Donelson. The determination to keep going was the theme of a letter he wrote to Julia after that battle, in which he said he had "no doubt but you have read of Fort Donelson until you have grown tired of the name so I shall write you no more on the subject. Hope to make a new subject soon." He did; two days later he told her about being visited in Clarksville by citizens of Nashville who were fearful that he would attack their city. These frightened people convinced him that the " 'Secesh' is now about on its last legs in Tennessee. I want to push on as rapidly as possible to save hard fighting. These terrible battles are very good things to read about for persons who loose no friends but I am decidedly in favor of having as little of it as possible. The way to avoid it is to push forward as vigorously as possible."[46]

Hindsight argues that Grant was right. We know the quality of the hideous fighting that lay ahead. It is difficult to imagine that anything worse than the terrible indecisive battles of Fredericksburg, Chancellorsville, and Spotsylvania could have resulted had Grant taken the offensive swiftly and massively in Tennessee early in 1862. His sense of urgency reflected a judgment that if the Confederacy was not subdued in the first months of 1862, it would be far more difficult to defeat later. He knew that battles would have to be fought, and friends killed. Other generals could not face such facts; their hesitation about subjecting themselves, their friends, and the men under their command to the hazards of battle is deplored—by experts—as vacillation. Cold-eyed men who can accept the proposition that postponed battles may kill more men than immediate ones consider a hesitating general's sense of humanity in the midst of a war to be misplaced. They think little of reluctant generals, perhaps learned in tactics but unprepared for carnage, who balk at the realities of war. They admire, instead, Ulysses S. Grant's simple logic, which he worked with such messy terror at Shiloh.

# IX

## SHILOH

The war was young. . . . And surely they needed as long notice as possible of an enemy's approach, for they were at that time addicted to the practice of undressing—than which nothing could be more unsoldierly. On the morning of the memorable 6th of April, at Shiloh, many of Grant's men when spitted on Confederate bayonets were as naked as civilians; but it should be allowed that this was not because of any defect in their picket line. Their error was of another sort: they had no pickets.

— Ambrose Bierce

I saw an open field . . . so covered with dead that it would have been possible to walk across the clearing, in any direction, stepping on dead bodies, without a foot touching the ground.

— *Ulysses S. Grant*

Foemen at morn, but friends at eve—
Fame or country least their care:
(What like a bullet can undeceive!)
But now they lie low,
While over them the swallows skim,
And all is hushed at Shiloh.

— *Herman Melville*

"THE POWER is in your hands; use it, & you will be sustained by all above you," wrote Halleck, reinstating Grant and sanctioning an invasion. Grant took a boat upriver, almost due south, to get back to his army. He made his headquarters at Savannah, Tennessee; one division of his army was five miles upriver at Crump's Landing under Lew Wallace, while five more divisions were camped in fields stretching west from a high bluff seven miles farther south, at Pittsburg Landing. There the senior of Grant's generals, William T. Sherman, was in command. A sharp-eyed, red-bearded, nervous, and brilliant man, Sherman too in civilian life had tried and failed to achieve the success that had come to a brother, in his case Senator John Sherman. He too had lost Halleck's confidence—and his own command—and had just been reinstated. He had been in his final year at West Point when Grant entered, but now Grant was his commander, and Sherman had no trouble remembering that fact. When Grant arrived, Sherman assured him that his green army

encamped in clearings stretching to the southwest toward Shiloh meetinghouse was ready for an attack on the Confederate stronghold at Corinth, Mississippi, nineteen miles to the southwest.[1]

At Corinth, other generals had their own attack in mind. Albert Sidney
Johnston and Pierre Gustave Toutant Beauregard had forty thousand men
ready to move; there were roughly the same number of Yankees under Sherman. Huge armies moved slowly on country lanes; rain and the tracks of
wagons and thousands of feet had made a dispiriting mud, and it took four
days for the Confederate army to get into striking position. Johnston, a tall
and confident Kentuckian turned Texan, urged his men toward battle with a
call to be "worthy of your race and lineage; worthy of the women of the
South." He had at his side not only the aggressive Beauregard but also
Leonidas Polk, his West Point roommate; Braxton Bragg, irascible and determined; and William J. Hardee, a veteran career soldier. On Saturday night,
April 5, 1862, the huge force was just south of Sherman's position and so
clamorously noisy that they lost hope that their attack could be a surprise.[2]

They were wrong. But not because none of the Federal soldiers noticed
them—indeed, there was a skirmish on April 5, but Grant, reporting it to
Halleck, commented, "I have scarcely the faintest idea of an attack (general
one) being made upon us." Somehow, Grant had convinced himself that his
was an army just of attackers, not defenders. No protective fortifications had
been built, and as Ambrose Bierce said, there were no organized lines of
pickets to guard the sleeping camp. Unwilling to imagine being on the defensive, Sherman sneered at the cowardice of an officer who gave him a scout's
report that danger was near. And so, naked in their blankets or groggily
standing over campfires cooking breakfast, farm-boy soldiers were borne
down by rebels attacking at dawn.[3]

Grant was at breakfast, too—at Savannah, twelve miles downriver—when
at 6 A.M. he heard gunfire. Leaving his food, he quickly canceled a meeting
with General Don Carlos Buell—who had arrived the evening before, ahead
of his troops—and instead ordered Buell to summon his men (some of whom
were spread back as far as Nashville). Then, on an agonizingly slow river
boat, he started for Pittsburg Landing, pausing at Crump's Landing only
long enough to call across the water to General Lew Wallace to get his men
ready to move. Reassuringly, Wallace replied that he already had. Reaching
Pittsburg Landing about 9 A.M., Grant, who had a sprained ankle, was
helped onto his horse, and with a crutch strapped to his saddle headed up the
high bluff for a conference with Sherman.

The battle had actually begun before any general ordered it to. A nervous
and alert detachment of General Benjamin M. Prentiss's men had gone scouting and encountered what they first took to be a small Confederate raiding
party. The Southerners opened fire and pursued the Northerners. Hearing
the firing, the Confederate commanders, about to order an attack, did so at
once, and it was their raiders who savagely entered the Union camp. Alerted

by the firing, Sherman was instantly up and in the saddle. Although two horses were shot from under him and he sustained a wound in his hand, Sherman spent the whole of that awful Sunday trying to shore up the battered armies. Grant joined Sherman in the morning; his first act on the battlefield was to establish a line to stop the "stragglers," the terrified men who were running away.[4]

The fields and woods between Shiloh meetinghouse and the river were bounded to the south and north by marshy creeks, and Johnston's aim was to drive Grant's men not to the river, across which they might escape, but northward to Owl and Snake creeks, where, trapped in the marsh thicket, they could be cut down. Beauregard was sent to the left, where he took the Shiloh church; Hardee's men, to his right, began the relentless slaughter of Prentiss's men. These Yankees were driven onto low-lying ground adjacent to a twenty-acre peach orchard in splendid full bloom. As the rebel bullets destroyed the trees, the petals—like wedding confetti—fluttered down on dying men. And in the hollow next to the trees, the firing was so intense, so ceaseless, and so lethal that the area earned the name Hornets Nest. Prentiss's men fought there for hours, saving the rest of Grant's men from rout, until finally, Prentiss could last no longer and surrendered the few soldiers still alive to Hardee.

During the day Grant sent men of his own staff to find out what had happened to Lew Wallace. The Indiana general, with no more orders than those he had heard on the riverbank but with the sounds of a desperate battle to summon him, was in fact on the move. The only problem was that he had taken the wrong road. He had also refused to accept spoken instructions from a captain on Grant's staff who found him, and it took Captain William R. Rowley and Lieutenant Colonel James B. McPherson over an hour of hard riding to find Wallace again and force him to confront his error and begin the agonizingly slow business of a countermarch. The operation took hours, and Wallace did not get into the day's battle.[5]

Late in the day, at a desperate hour for the Union forces, General Buell arrived by gunboat, and Grant went aboard to guide him and his men into battle. Grant's story of Buell's reaction to the grim arena into which he was moving suggests powerfully the differences in the perspectives with which the two commanders saw the war.

> As we left the boat together, Buell's attention was attracted by the men lying under cover of the river bank. I saw him berating them and trying to shame them into joining their regiments. He even threatened them with shells from the gun-boats near by. But it was all to no effect. Most of these men afterward proved themselves as gallant as any of those who saved the battle from which they had deserted. I have no doubt that this sight impressed General Buell with the idea that a line of retreat would be a good thing just then. If he had come in by the front instead of through the

stragglers in the rear, he would have thought and felt differently. Could he have come through the Confederate rear, he would have witnessed there a scene similar to that at our own. The distant rear of an army engaged in battle is not the best place from which to judge correctly what is going on in front.

Grant was understanding, even compassionate, in his picture of the stragglers whom his armed guard had not prevented from finding a place to hide, but his calm prose does not explain just what the situation was at the front at the close of the day. Prentiss's men were dead or captured, and everywhere, the Union forces were vulnerable. Why, then, didn't the Confederates finish their destruction of Grant's armies? Why didn't Beauregard fight on into the night and deliver the final blow? How was it that Grant's bewildered, bloodied troops rallied so strongly the next day that they drove the Confederates into retreat to Corinth?[6]

Part of the answer—but only part—lay in the arrival of Buell's and Wallace's reinforcements. Another part of the explanation may be found in the developing recognition of the terrible world of the battlefield as both commanders and men paused to survey it. At the crest of the day, some of Bragg's men, out of ammunition, had charged toward the landing with only bayonets, but such heroics ceased as the almost victorious Confederates looked about them. Like Grant, they could see fields so covered with bodies that one could have crossed them on steppingstones of corpses. They could hear the screams of wounded and dying men. Such terrible carnage, and the inability to face the responsibility for causing more, may have been what later paralyzed the flamboyant commander Joseph Hooker at Chancellorsville. A similar perception may have stopped Beauregard, Bragg, Polk, and even Hardee at Shiloh. Their troops, weary rather than triumphant, wanted not to finish the job, but to sleep—some of them in the tents of the men they had driven out at the start of the day. Their energy was down.

Not so the near-vanquished. Fright had driven some men to shiver beneath the overhang of the bluff, and a similar fear of dying sustained the energy of those who remained in battle. Through an awful night of cold and rain, they knew they would have to fight to survive. Grant was at one with them. His swollen leg aching, he could get no sleep in the rain at the foot of a tree and moved to a log building in use as a hospital. But he found the noise of the surgeons' saws, the smell of flesh, and the agony of the victims "more unendurable than encountering the enemy's fire" and returned to the tree in the rain. Finally, Grant slept, and he woke "feeling a great moral advantage would be gained by becoming the attacking party. . . ." He ordered his men to "advance and recapture our original camps."[7]

Striking early, Grant's armies, including now Buell's and Wallace's troops, fought viciously. Two thousand of Buell's men, fresh to battle, fell wounded or dead. The day was as full of carnage and chaos as the previous one had been, but as Howard C. Westwood has said of Shiloh, "the great thing about Grant was his self-control and stubbornness. He did not panic. He had the genius to meet each contingency, even a contingency produced by his own grave blunder. . . ." And by the end of Monday his men had driven the enemy back onto the road from Corinth on which they had come. But Grant, like George Gordon Meade later at Gettysburg, missed his main chance. He did not pursue and destroy his enemy's armies. Now his energy was gone. "The great fatigue of our men," he wrote Buell, "they having been engaged in two days fight . . . would preclude an advance tonight." The Confederates pulled back to Corinth; when the great battle at Shiloh was over, everything was exactly as it had been before it began, except that a quarter of the men who had fought there had been captured, killed, or wounded. There had been more casualties in two days than had been sustained by Americans in the whole of the Revolutionary War, the War of 1812, and the Mexican War. More than three thousand American men were dead—1,723 from the South and 1,754 from the North. Everything was the same, and nothing was the same. Grant, and slowly the whole nation, learned from Shiloh that the Civil War would not be ended by one side's waiting the other out, or by negotiation, or by some single swift blow, as at Donelson. Johnston had sent his men into the battle—in which he himself was to die—telling them that it must be fought to protect a "fair, broad abounding land." Grant knew after Shiloh that only when he had exhausted the people of that land by annihilating its armies would he break the rebellion.[8]

The Northern newspapers wrote of a great victory, and the people back home, impatient after months of inactivity, had their excitement. Grant was a hero again. And this time he saw what he had wrought. The horror had not stopped him while the battle raged, but on the second day he looked out on a thicket that had been cleared back to a field by bullets that blasted the brush and saw the ground covered with dead bodies. After the battle he reported "another great battle fought between two great armies, one contending for the maintenance of the best government ever devised, the other for its destruction." "It is pleasant," he asserted, "to record the success of the army contending for the former principle." He concluded his report with the statement that the "country will have to mourn the loss of many brave men." There were he thought still more men that Southerners would mourn and, what was more, the "enemy suffered terribly from demoralization and desertion." Grant had won but the failure to pursue the Confederates and destroy their armies diminished Shiloh's value. In his communication to Buell about the possibilities of pursuing Beauregard, Grant hinted that a reluctance to be insubordinate held him back; he told Buell that because of orders "previously received and a dispatch also of to-day from Major Gen. Halleck it will not . . . do to advance beyond . . . some point which we can reach and return in a day." Halleck's attitude led to Lew Wallace's surmise that "after the battle General Grant was as much under General Halleck's order not to do anything as before it." Shiloh had accomplished very little. From the peninsula below Richmond, six hundred miles away on the Atlantic coast—where McClellan was losing battles—young Oliver Wendell Holmes, Jr., wrote home to his parents, "Pittsburgh Landing seems to have been rather an equivocal victory after all . . . [d]oesn't it?"[9]

And for a time it appeared that Shiloh would be equivocal indeed for its victor, Ulysses Grant. Major General Halleck, due to take field command of his forces on April 8, actually arrived at the front on April 11—four days late for Shiloh. Immediately, he set about amassing his enormous armies— General Buell's Army of the Ohio; General John Pope's Army of the Mississippi (which, on the same day as Shiloh was won, had taken Island 10—a critical position on the Mississippi River—and made possible the Union occupation of Memphis); and the Army of the Tennessee, Grant's army. But Grant was no longer to be commander of the Army of the Tennessee. Lincoln, though pleased with the victory, was sobered by the appalling casualty figures. John McClernand, reporting directly to him, spoke of "slaughter" and the president began to wonder if he had placed his trust wisely. On April 23, Stanton wired Halleck, "The President desires to know . . . whether any neglect or misconduct of General Grant or any other officer contributed to the sad casualties. . . ." Halleck, already unimpressed by Grant's performance at Shiloh, did not want him to have a prime field command, and instead raised him to a meaningless position as second in command of all the armies of the west. The Army of the Tennessee was assigned to General George H. Thomas. Lew Wallace recalled that while returning to his own camp one day he "saw a tent out by itself. A man stood in the door. His seemed a familiar figure and, looking a second time, I recognized General Grant, and rode to him. Bringing a campstool, he invited me to sit. The conversation was chiefly remarkable in that he made no allusion to his treatment by Halleck—neither by voice, look, nor manner did he betray any resentment. That very silence on his part touched me the more keenly." Grant had been banished to an island in the midst of his men. "I was," he recalled, "ignored. . . ."[10]

Corinth lies nineteen miles southwest of Shiloh as the crow flies, just south of the Tennessee border in Mississippi. By wagon road it was twenty-two miles away. In Grant's view, long afterward, the Union forces "ought to have seized it immediately after the fall of Donelson and Nashville, when it could have been taken without a battle, but failing then it should have been taken, without delay, on the concentration of troops at Pittsburg Landing after the battle of Shiloh." Grant thought an attack certainly ought not to have awaited the arrival of Pope's thirty thousand men on April 21. But Halleck waited even longer: "On the 30th April the grand army commenced its advance from Shiloh upon Corinth." The absurdity of this ponderous movement of more than 100,000 men toward Corinth—just a little town, albeit the headquarters of the Confederate armies in the west—was not lost on some of the participants. Lew Wallace was subjected to the ludicrous lesson Halleck insisted on teaching his officers for their having been caught without trenches at Shiloh. Halleck "was moving at the rate of a mile a day," wrote Wallace, "throwing up works at every halt. That is, he gained a mile every day to go into besiegement every night. At the end he would have spent a month doing what General Johnston had done in three days."[11]

Lew Wallace had the wit to guess that Grant was ironic when, in his *Memoirs*, he reached for a classical allusion to explain Halleck's Corinth and wrote, "The movement was a siege from the start to the close." Halleck's monstrously large army enveloped itself. It permitted the Confederate armies around it to go free, and as Wallace noted, when the majestic progression was accomplished, "Corinth was not captured; it was abandoned to us. At dawn of May 30th we marched into its deserted works, getting nothing—nothing—not a sick prisoner, not a rusty bayonet, not a bite of bacon—nothing but an empty town and some Quaker guns."[12]

Halleck made much of nothing. He declared the occupation of Corinth a great victory. Five days afterward he wired Washington, "Thousands of the enemy are throwing away their arms. . . . The result is all I could possibly desire." He was right; a month later he would be called to Washington to be given what he most desired, the command not just of all the armies of the west, but of all the armies of the Union. What he did *not* do was to deploy his immense armies immediately against the enemy at Chattanooga and Memphis and Vicksburg. Instead, men were put to work building around Corinth the most impressive complex of earthworks in the world. It was the Confederacy that had won. It had gained time. Grant knew this. "These fortifications were never used," was his bland, damning judgment of the enterprise.[13]

This cool comment was written a quarter of a century after the events; in 1862 Grant could not be so dispassionate. He was disgusted with having been shouldered aside by Halleck and was about to make the blunder of requesting a new assignment, a move which almost surely would have been interpreted as petulance and very likely would have sent him into professional oblivion. Grant needed a friend, and he found one.

William Tecumseh Sherman was the most brilliant man Ulysses Grant knew well. He was not always the wisest, but his surging, savage intelligence was as important in driving Grant ahead in war as it was to be impotent in restraining him in the political world that Grant entered when peace came. Sherman, two years older than Grant, was also born in Ohio. An orphan, he was raised by Thomas Ewing and married his daughter Ellen, with whom he did lifetime battle in astonishingly candid letters—for example, relentlessly taking her to task for subjecting him to double costs in educating their children, school taxes and tuition for Roman Catholic schools. He also conducted a rich political discourse by mail with his brother, Senator John Sherman. He had opinions—almost none of them democratic—on every subject

and might continue the discussion of an idea from conversation to correspondence and back to conversation again. Often a letter seemed to start in
midsentence and press ahead without stopping for a pause of punctuation.
His wit was mordant, his tone exuberant, and his intelligence irrepressible.

He was also almost as much of a failure as Ulysses Grant. He went to West
Point when very young, and served in the Mexican War, of which he saw far
less than Grant did. Like him, he subsequently had a tour of duty on the
Pacific Coast. Resigning from the army, he tried his hand as a lawyer in the
developing state of Kansas, but he did not prosper and brought his wife back
to the Ewings, who had been caring for their eldest child. In 1859, leaving
the family in Ohio, he went to Alexandria, Louisiana, to be the superintendent of a new military school modeled roughly on West Point. With secession, he left Louisiana, and in April 1861 took up employment with a railroad
company in St. Louis, declining a post in Washington which would probably
have led to his being assistant secretary of war; this choice did not enhance
his credentials as a patriot. But his curiosity would not allow him to stay out
of the war. He was horrified when Charles Ewing, his foster brother, wanted
to take his seven-year-old son to watch the tense confrontation between
Nathaniel Lyon and the rebels at the arsenal in St. Louis. But as the day
grew more exciting, he and his son went along to take a look. Suddenly there
was firing in the street: "I heard the balls cutting the leaves above our heads,
and saw several men and women running in all directions, some of whom
were wounded. Of course there was a general stampede. Charles Ewing
threw Willie on the ground and covered him with his body." Like Grant,
Sherman had had no such adventures with his father—indeed, he had had no
father at all—and the two generals filled some deep need within themselves
by bringing their sons into a life that was so intensely theirs. The child, like
the father, was never away from the war from that day on; he grew ill and
died at Vicksburg, and Sherman's letter telling of his death was one of the
most eloquent of the hundreds of thousands of letters of mourning written
between 1861 and 1865.[14]

Sherman had reddish hair, pitted skin, and a scant beard. He was lean and
ceaselessly restless. Genteel observers were apt to describe him as "horrid-
looking"; men who were drawn to him found him exasperating but never
boring. In the early months of the war, he was viewed very skeptically by his
superiors. Sherman joined Grant's command just before Shiloh, and their acquaintance quickly grew into a comfortable friendship based on trust, en-
hanced with easy humor and a sense of private equality, and fostered by
Sherman's never-failing public recognition that Grant was his superior.
O. O. Howard recalled a reunion of the two just before Chattanooga:
"[Sherman came] bounding in after his usual buoyant manner. General
Grant, whose bearing toward Sherman differed from that with all other
officers, being free, affectionate, and good humored, greeted him most cordially. Immediately after the 'How are you, Sherman?' and the reply,

'Thank you, as well as can be expected,' he extended to him the ever welcome cigar. This Sherman proceeded to light, but without stopping his ready flow of hearty words, and not even pausing to sit down." To get Sherman to relax, Grant "arrested his attention by some apt remark, and then said: 'Take the chair of *honor*, Sherman,' indicating a rocker with a high back. 'The chair of honor? Oh, no! that belongs to you, general.' Grant, not a whit abashed by this compliment, said: 'I don't forget, Sherman, to give proper respect to age.'—'Well, then, if you put it on that ground, I must accept.' "[15]

It had been a far less cheerful day when, after Corinth, Sherman heard gossip to the effect that Grant was planning to leave the command. Sherman rode to Grant's exile encampment, which "consisted of four or five tents, with a sapling railing around the front" in a clearing in the woods off the main road.

> As I rode up, Major Rawlins, Lagow, and Hilyer, were in front of the camp, and piled up near them were the usual office and camp chests, all ready for a start in the morning. I inquired for the general, and was shown to his tent, where I found him seated on a camp-stool, with papers on a rude camp-table; he seemed to be employed in assorting letters, and tying them up with red tape into convenient bundles. After passing the usual compliments, I inquired if it were true that he was going away. He said, "Yes." I then inquired the reason, and he said: "Sherman, you know. You know that I am in the way here. I have stood it as long as I can, and can endure it no longer." I inquired where he was going to, and he said, "St. Louis." I then asked if he had any business there, and he said, "Not a bit." I then begged him to stay, illustrating his case by my own.
>
> Before the battle of Shiloh, I had been cast down by a mere newspaper assertion of "crazy;" but that single battle had given me new life, and now I was in high feather; and I argued with him that, if he went away, events would go right along, and he would be left out; whereas, if he remained, some happy accident might restore him to favor and his true place.[16]

Grant had indeed asked for a leave, in order to go to Covington; there he planned to consider whether to seek a transfer within the army or to resign from it. But, he recalled later, "General Sherman happened to call on me as I was about starting and urged me so strongly not to think of going, that I concluded to remain." This seemingly casual conference was a critical turning point in the lives of both men, and perhaps in the Civil War. Grant drew confidence from Sherman's act of friendship. "I . . . am," wrote Sherman, "rejoiced at your conclusion to remain; for you could not be quiet at home for a week when armies were moving, and rest could not relieve your mind of the gnawing sensation that injustice had been done you." Grant did not get lost in the self-defeating politics involved in complaining about commands and attempting to obtain reassignments, but he saw that if Sherman was correct that he must not try to get away from Halleck, there was still a way to get Halleck away from him. A promotion to Washington would do the trick, and when Halleck was called to the capital, Grant took the opportunity, on July 22, 1862, to write to Elihu Washburne. "I do not know the object of calling Gen. H. to Washington but if it is to make him Sec. of War, or Commander-in-Chief, Head Quarters at Washington, a better selection could not be made. He is a man of gigantic intellect and well studied in the profession of arms. He and I have had several little spats but I like and respect him nevertheless." Halleck was named general in chief, and from the nature of their association later in the war, when Grant superseded Halleck in authority while Halleck retained his post as chief of staff, it appears that Grant meant what he said. Only years later did Grant learn of Halleck's underhanded allegations of alcoholism, and lose his respect for the man. In the *Memoirs*, when he made summary evaluations of the important generals, he simply omitted Halleck.[17]

In the summer of 1862 Grant was politic enough never to complain about Halleck in his letters to Washburne; instead, he armed the congressman with politically useful tidbits about how the people of western Tennessee might be made loyal to the Union—notably by the re-establishment of the orderly procedures of civilian life, such as the mail service and trade. He also provided Washburne with texts that would be read by any eyes as evidence that Grant was the model of a loyal general: "It is hard to say what would be the most wise policy to pursue towards these people [the Southerners whom he found to be tiring of the war] but for a soldier his duties are plain. He is to obey the orders of all those placed over him and whip the enemy wherever he meets him." Grant's problem was that he received no such definitive orders. In the summer and fall of 1862 many fierce battles were fought in Tennessee and northern Mississippi—battles in which, as Grant noted, more men were killed than in all the battles of the Mexican War but which in the ultimate history of the Civil War were "dwarfed by the magnitude of the main battles so as to be now almost forgotten except by those engaged in them." Halleck's huge force was allowed to disperse and become scattered, its command divided, and its objectives unfocused; the great concerted drive on the enemy which Grant favored, could not be carried out until someone got the offensive into focus again.[18]

Three months after Shiloh, on the Fourth of July, the Union men in Memphis, whistling in the dark, treated themselves to a great celebration. The city had been taken after Pope destroyed its defenses, and Grant's headquarters were there. At the Independence Day festivities he had as his guest a curious newspaperman whom Edwin M. Stanton had brought into the War Department. Charles A. Dana, who was conducting for Stanton an investigation of quartermastering corruption in Cairo, went downriver to meet the Shiloh general. Dana knew Grant was "under a cloud" because of Shiloh, but received a "pleasant impression . . . of a man of simple manners, straightforward, cordial, and unpretending." He found the general self-possessed and eager to make war.[19]

Stanton and Lincoln listened to Dana, and in the fall of 1862 Grant was restored to the command of the Army of the Tennessee, but his earlier hopes and plans for a swift, merciful victory were gone: "Up to the battle of Shiloh, I, as well as thousands of other citizens, believed that the rebellion against the Government would collapse suddenly and soon, if a decisive victory could be gained over any of its armies." After Shiloh, he knew that the Confederacy was determined in its resolve to fight back and fight back again, and indeed, to go on the offensive and force the Union forces to fight back. Grant could see no indication that vast bloodshed would hasten the end. Neither discouragement at a spectacular defeat, as at Donelson, nor disgust at a spectacle of gross carnage, as at Shiloh, would hasten the rebels into surrender. Not single battles, not the occupation of territories, not the control of rivers on which the commerce of a society moved, would prove decisive. Now it was a war of annihilation, not a game of chasing and beating the other man's army. Now a whole society had to be defeated. Heretofore, Grant and other commanders had exerted much effort to prevent the pillaging of civilian property, but, he reported, on August 2, as he was beginning to reassert himself in the war in the west, "I was ordered from Washington to live upon the country" and "directed to 'handle rebels within our lines without gloves.' "[20]

# X

# VICKSBURG

Off to the west, in Memphis, where the sun's
Mid-morning fire beat on a wider stream,
His purpose headstrong as a river runs,
Grant closed a smoky door on aides and guards
And chewed through scheme on scheme
For toppling Vicksburg like a house of cards.
— *Richard Wilbur*

IN THE FALL of 1862, in western Tennessee, Grant was moving through his slackest days in the war. Halleck's promotion to Washington in July had left no one general clearly in command in the west, and Grant's restoration to the Army of the Tennessee did not guarantee that he would have sufficient authority to act. It was a dispiriting time for him. The only major actions during the period were the inconclusive attacks by Generals E. O. C. Ord and William S. Rosecrans on a vulnerable General Sterling Price at Iuka, Mississippi, in September, and the repelling, at high human cost, of an attack by Generals Earl Van Dorn and Price on Rosecrans at Corinth early in October. Grant, not present at either engagement, was jealous of the good press Rosecrans received, and when, ironically, Halleck prodded him about not aggressively pursuing the enemy after the two battles, his excuses (namely, the insufficiency of supplies and of men) were uncharacteristically lethargic.

It took a rival to wake him up and focus his attention clearly and relentlessly on a single goal: Vicksburg. The rival was John A. McClernand, who without Grant's or Halleck's knowledge had persuaded Lincoln and Stanton to allow him, a volunteer general, to recruit a new army in Illinois—his home state—and in neighboring Indiana, and to begin a campaign to open the Mississippi River to the Union by taking Vicksburg, Mississippi.

That little river town, almost falling off the high bluff on which it is perched, seems an unlikely spot to have given its name to a great martial struggle. But the Confederates had fortified the town impressively in 1862; their guns ruled the Mississippi River. Until Vicksburg was taken it would not be possible to link the Union forces at New Orleans, which had been occupied by Admiral David G. Farragut that spring, with those of General Grant at Memphis, two hundred miles to the north. Until Vicksburg fell, the Union could not challenge the Confederacy's domination of the greatest of America's rivers. Once Vicksburg was captured, the only other important Confederate stronghold that guarded passage on the river, Port Hudson, could be taken easily, and control of the whole river would be secured. The Confederacy would have no dependable link between its western part—Texas, Arkansas, and trans-Mississippi Louisiana—and the remainder. The movement of substantial amounts of foodstuffs or large forces of men to the east to sustain Jefferson Davis's government would be impossible past Union gunboats in the river.

At noon on November 9, 1862, Grant was not contemplating Vicksburg in such grand strategic terms. He was in La Grange, Mississippi, accomplishing little, when he received a communication from one of his generals, Charles S. Hamilton, who reported on local maneuvers and then asked, "Have you heard from Sherman? A letter from Wisconsin advises me that Wisconsin regiments in the State . . . are ordered to McClernand. Is that so?" If this was so, it was confirmation of the rumor that McClernand was raising his own army and would usurp Grant's chances on the Mississippi. This move by a rival general brought both sides of Grant's nature into play. There was a renewal of the suffocating sense of defeat, of once again having someone push past him, and there was a stubborn determination to beat the threat by moving straight on.[1]

That same day Grant, frustrated and immobile, lashed out at the bustling activity of merchants who had rushed in to exploit both his soldiers and the civilians in the region. He sent a telegram to General Stephen A. Hurlbut, in command in Memphis: "Refuse all permits to come south of Jackson for the present. The Isrealites especially should be kept out. . . ." On one level Grant's notorious exclusion of the Jews was simply an expression of the routine anti-Semitism of the day. Grant was fed up with the cotton speculators and the greedy suppliers of goods to his armies, but rather than attack the entire voracious horde, which included an astonishing assortment of entrepreneurs—among them Charles A. Dana and Roscoe Conkling, for example—Grant singled out the Jews. The ancient stereotype of the grasping trader was invoked; once again a frustrated man chose the age-old scapegoat.[2]

There may have been an additional, unconscious reason for the outburst. This is suggested by a comment made in the 1890's by one shrewd, if not always trustworthy, observer of Grant—James Harrison Wilson, himself anti-Semitic. Speaking to Hamlin Garland of Grant's order, Wilson said, "There was a mean nasty streak in old Jesse Grant. He was close and greedy. He came down into Tennessee with a Jew trader that he wanted his son to help, and with whom he was going to share the profits. Grant refused to issue a permit and sent the Jew flying, prohibiting Jews from entering the line." The image of Grant, in high dudgeon, driving a miscreant from the temple does not ring quite true, and yet Wilson may not have been entirely off the mark. Grant, Wilson suggested, could not strike back directly at the "lot of relatives who were always trying to use him" and perhaps struck instead at what he maliciously saw as their counterpart—opportunistic traders who were Jewish.[3]

Jesse Grant was not in La Grange on November 9, 1862, but John McClernand's threat to push Grant out of the way was. That powerful man, close to Lincoln, could not be repulsed at once. Those Israelites could be repulsed, and were. On November 10 Grant told Joseph D. Webster, "Give orders to all the conductors . . . that no Jews are to be permitted to travel on the Rail Road southward from any point." In December, Grant banned all Jews from his department, explaining to Sherman, in great exasperation, that the cotton merchants were so eager to purchase crops that instead of keeping to the rear of the armies they were getting ahead of them. Charles A. Dana, a convert to rectitude, later wrote disparagingly of the "mania for sudden fortunes made in Cotton, raging in a vast population of Jews and Yankees," and Grant, similarly exercised, told Sherman that, "in consequence of the total disregard and evasion of orders by the Jews, my policy is to exclude them so far as practicable from the Dept."[4]

Protests against Grant's anti-Semitism were swift and when they reached Lincoln and Stanton, effective. On December 17, 1862, Rawlins issued an order: ". . . By directions of the Gen in Chief of the army at Washington the Gen Order from these headquarters expelling Jews from the Department is hereby revoked by order of Maj. Gen. U.S. Grant."[5]

If Grant vented his anger at McClernand's raising a new army in ways that suggested he might be retreating into self-defeat, he also gave expression to the steadier side of his character. On November 9, he set in motion a major thrust south to Holly Springs, Mississippi. General McPherson had warned him of a buildup of enemy troops; General Hamilton, of reports that his troops would be diverted to Memphis and McClernand's command. Grant told McPherson to be alert but not yet begin a major engagement; he told Hamilton he was not aware of any order for troops to report to McClernand. In the face of two dangers to his army, he did marshal his forces, and only then, when they were moving, did he, that evening, send an angry telegram to Halleck: "Am I to understand that I lay still here while an Expedition is fitted out from Memphis or do you want me to push as far South as possible?" The next day Halleck's reply came: "You have command of all the troops sent to your Dept, and have permission to fight the enemy when you please." This reply eliminated Grant's immediate worry—that troops on the way to assist him would be diverted to McClernand—though it did not remove the larger question of what would happen if McClernand was given an independent department. In any event, the tone of the telegram did clearly encourage that side of Grant that wanted to act boldly. The offensive, now sanctioned, went forward.[6]

Grant further showed himself in command by issuing an order, on November 11, telling all the officers of new units coming into his army just who on his staff should be "recognized and obeyed." His close aide from Donelson days, Joseph D. Webster, was now promoted to brigadier general and placed in charge of railroads. This move increased the importance of Lieutenant Colonel John A. Rawlins as Grant's chief of staff. Clark B. Lagow left Grant's staff, but William S. Hillyer, William R. Rowley, and Theodore S. Bowers, who were to be with Grant for the balance of the war, were there and now were joined by the outspoken, able, and slightly treacherous James Harrison Wilson, who had left the Sea Islands to come west as chief of topographical engineers. Invited west by McClernand, he became a partisan of Grant's, but one who could be dangerously gossipy about his chief. He also quickly became an intimate friend of John Rawlins's. The ties among the men of Grant's staff were close.[7]

With Sherman on the right, Hamilton on the left, and McPherson in the center, Grant moved south first to Holly Springs and then on to Oxford, while the Confederate general John C. Pemberton fell back to Grenada. Grant was still two hundred miles from Vicksburg, and the dense forests of the river-laced bayou country made the approach to the town by land exceedingly difficult. Therefore, he sent Sherman back to Memphis with a regiment, instructing him to add to his forces two of McClernand's regiments that had arrived there and go south by river, to the point where the Yazoo River enters the Mississippi, twelve miles northwest of Vicksburg. Going up the Yazoo, Sherman was to take the Chickasaw Bluffs just north of Vicksburg, preparatory to an attack on the river town.[8]

Sherman moved quickly; since McClernand outranked him, Sherman had to get off to the Yazoo and Chickasaw Bluffs before McClernand could reach Memphis. McClernand would then arrive to find himself merely a commander of one segment, and Sherman of another, of Grant's Army of the Tennessee. Once he was sure Sherman had left Memphis, Grant sent orders to McClernand, welcoming him to the town and saying, "I hope you will find all the preliminary preparations completed on your arrival and the expedition ready to move." Grant was handling his enemies within his own army with skill, but his Confederate enemies proved more difficult to outmaneuver. On December 20, while Grant was at Oxford, his supply depot at Holly Springs was attacked by General Earl Van Dorn, and huge quantities of supplies, including food, were captured. What was more, the Confederates almost captured Julia Grant. Luckily, with her slave Julia, she had left for Oxford the day before. Meanwhile Nathan Bedford Forrest was attacking Union positions along the Memphis–Jackson railroad and Grant was in grave danger of being trapped deep within rebel territory.[9]

Grant, meeker than he had been at Shiloh or would be in the Wilderness, thought he could no longer keep Pemberton occupied and distracted from Sherman's assault on Vicksburg. Indeed, he did not even know whether Sherman or McClernand was in command on the river. His message to the "Commanding Officer Expedition down Mississippi" told whomever that was that he could no longer keep Vicksburg from being reinforced by Pemberton; he would, in fact, have to give up and go back to Memphis. On December 29, despite aid from David Dixon Porter, who was in command of naval forces on the Mississippi, Sherman was repulsed from the Chickasaw Bluffs; he reported privately to his wife, "Well, we have been to Vicksburg and it was too much for us and we have backed out." On January 3, McClernand arrived down the river, took command from Sherman, and ordered their forces back to winter quarters at Milliken's Bend, on the Louisiana side of the Mississippi. Neither Grant nor McClernand had taken Vicksburg.[10]

The trip back to Memphis was humiliating for Grant; for the refugees who had made themselves dependent on him it was harrowing. Throughout the fall thousands of slaves, finding themselves in the murderous paths of two swiftly moving armies crossing and recrossing the rich cotton lands of southwestern Tennessee and northern Mississippi, had tried to make their way to safety. In many cases their owners had been driven out by the Union armies, leaving the confused slaves to fend for themselves. As Grant, in succinct bewilderment, had put the problem to Halleck, "Citizens south of us are leaving their homes and Negroes coming in by wagon loads. What will I do with them? I am now having all cotton still standing picked by them."[11]

Even before he asked this question, Grant on November 13, 1862, had made an important appointment to bring order to a desperate situation. He had told a reluctant Ohio chaplain, John Eaton (who knew he would be laughed at for taking on so ludicrous a task), that he was "to take charge of Contrabands" who came within Union lines. They were to be organized into work parties in the army camps and "set to work picking, ginning and baling all cotton now out standing in Fields." The indefatigably entrepreneurial traders that had so annoyed (and impeded) Grant in his operations all summer and fall had their eye on that valuable cotton, and Grant now yielded to their pressure and put the contrabands to work harvesting the crop. Under this arrangement the laborers were not free, but they were given protection: "Suitable guards will be detailed by Commanding Officers nearest where the parties are at work to protect them from molestation."[12]

In September a different practical solution to the problems of some of the refugees had suggested itself to General James M. Tuttle, Grant's successor in command at Cairo, Illinois. He told Stanton that Grant was sending "large lots of negro women and children" to Cairo and "directs me to ask you what to do with them." Tuttle had a suggestion: "Parties in Chicago and other cities wish them for servants. Will I be allowed to turn them over to a responsible committee, to be so employed? If so, can I transport at Government expense?" Stanton replied yes, but soon Illinois politicians had second thoughts. David Davis, associate justice of the Supreme Court, told Abraham Lincoln that an influx of blacks from the South into Illinois would "work great harm in the coming Election," and, in John Y. Simon's well-chosen word, a "blockade" was established. Grant would have to care for the refugees within the South.[13]

In late November a camp for these displaced persons was established under Eaton's direction at Grand Junction, Tennessee, under a field order issued by Rawlins on November 14. The baling of cotton was again specified as the work to be done; a detachment of troops was assigned to guard the workers, from attack, but also from escape; and medical assistance and rations were provided.

John Eaton was an able and humane man, and his authority over the black refugees was soon extended to the whole of Grant's department; on December 17, 1862, he was made general superintendent of contrabands. This appointment established the pattern of giving to a chaplain or other man of humanitarian bent within the army the job of caring for people who on January 1, 1863, under the Emancipation Proclamation, would become "freedmen." The role of welfare agent is an odd one for the army, but it was generally agreed by black observers and their friends that, vicious as some army men were, a "do-gooder" chaplain like Eaton was preferable to the Treasury Department agents who were competitors for the job. These officials were so intent on making money by utilizing seized labor that for humanitarian reasons the care of the freedmen could not be trusted to them. Grant's appointment of Eaton was wise. When, in 1865, Secretary of War Stanton was looking for someone within the army to head the Freedmen's Bureau, Grant proposed Eaton, but the post went instead to the then head of the Army of the Tennessee, another Christian soldier, General O. O. Howard.[14]

In 1862 Eaton could keep his charges fairly safe at least as long as marauders stayed away. But when one of these marauders was the cavalry commander Nathan Bedford Forrest, whose cruelty to black soldiers foreshadowed his later leadership of the Ku Klux Klan, the Negroes' fears were well placed. When Grand Junction was ordered abandoned in the wake of the attack on Holly Springs, Grant sent many of his soldiers back to Memphis by railroad and the refugees tried to join them: "Their terror of being left behind made them swarm over the passenger and freight cars, clinging to every available space and even crouching on the roofs. The trains were moved very slowly and with the utmost caution, but even so the exposure of these people—men, women, and children—was indescribable."[15]

Memphis was a crowded river city, and its reputation was not made less lurid by the presence of the army and of those of its followers who speculated in cotton and sex: "Sodom," General Stephen A. Hurlbut called it. Hurlbut, shocked but able, was in command of Memphis during the days when it was the essential supply post for the attack on Vicksburg. Although Eaton strove to provide for them, Memphis proved a strange promised land for the freezing freedmen huddling against the snow around inadequate bonfires in January 1863. Nor was the port a cheerful place for Grant's men, coming back from the aborted attempts to take Vicksburg and to hold the Mississippi lands east and north of it.[16]

Once more Grant's ability was in question. Early in the spring of 1863, Charles A. Dana, the erstwhile newspaperman and cotton dealer, was back in Memphis, ostensibly to audit paymaster accounts of the War Department. Actually, Lincoln and Stanton, seeking to "settle their minds as to Grant, about whom . . . there were many doubts," wanted still another check on the general, and Stanton had sent Dana to spy on him. Dana was delighted. His enthusiasm for the war had cost him his job with a skeptical Horace Greeley on the *New York Tribune*, and poor eyesight had cost him a chance to fight, but this assignment would take him close to the war's center. Grant knew why Dana was back in his department and shrewdly chose not to shun, but to cultivate him. Dana, an intelligent man with an instinct for both news and warriors, had already been drawn to Grant, and soon after getting back to Memphis he moved on to Grant's new headquarters at Milliken's Bend. He stayed first on a steamer, "for though my tent was pitched and ready, I was not able to get a mattress and pillow." This problem did not deter him: "I . . . hunted up Grant and explained my mission." Presumably, by "mission" he meant the auditing, but it is likely that he blurted out his real aims as well. In any case, Grant received him "cordially," and soon he was sharing the general's mess. In the trying spring of 1863, the spy became one of Grant's strongest advocates.[17]

The failed efforts of the late fall and winter of 1862, and the almost impassable terrain between the Mississippi and the Yazoo River, convinced Grant that he could not take Vicksburg from the north. Instead, implausible as it seemed, he would have to attack from below the very town that blocked his passage down the river. And he would have to rely on his own troops, since General Nathaniel P. Banks, in Louisiana, could not be counted on to supply reinforcements from the south or west. So the game of early 1863 was to find, through the morass of islands and near islands formed by the bayous along the Mississippi, a way to get men south of the town. For months the soldiers of the Army of the Tennessee were like children playing in a muddy runoff at the edge of a giant's flooded road, trying to make streams flow where they had not flowed before. Abraham Lincoln, his one trip down the Mississippi on a flatboat in 1828 making him an expert on rivers, was determined that a canal should be dug across a short neck of land at a point at which the river began a fantastic loop up to Vicksburg and then curved back to within five miles of itself. Grant indulged his commander in chief; he thought Lincoln's idea harmless, and it was desirable for the men to be busy rather than idle. The enemy discovered the endeavor and trained deadly guns on the two dredge barges that were at work, and once dug, the canal was not deep enough to become the new channel of the river. Attempts to cut roads along the river or find other passages for boats in the bayous also required herculean labors. If the roads were to be usable, tree stumps could not be left, and at this time of year the roots of the trees being cut began well under the water; similarly, if the new river channels were to carry troop barges, the dense branches of the trees stretching out over the river had to be cut. Finally, when the winter yielded to spring, troops slogged down the western side of the Mississippi to a point twenty-eight miles below Vicksburg, but the ground was so wet and the water formed into streams and pools so frequently that supply wagons could not accompany them. Therefore, on the night of April 16, Rear Admiral David Dixon Porter ran the gantlet, taking a fleet of gunboats and supply barges through, under the spectacular fire of the Confederate guns. Again the navy, as the famous Currier and Ives print attests, did splendidly.

On April 19, Porter's gunboats shelled the Confederate emplacements below Vicksburg at Grand Gulf, on the eastern side of the river, but with no luck; the Confederate guns, raining destructive fire down on the navy boats, were too high to be hit. Grant, told by a local black adviser of an unfortified

Running the Rebel Blockade, *Vicksburg, April 16, 1863. Currier & Ives print.*
THE OLD PRINT SHOP

crossing point nine miles south of Grand Gulf, had McClernand's and Mc-
Pherson's units of his army cross there the next day. They were unopposed,
but McClernand, slow in getting additional men to the crossing, made no
swift inland attack on the town at Grand Gulf, thus allowing Confederate reinforcements from Vicksburg to arrive with the hope of pushing the other
Union force, under McPherson, back across the Mississippi. They did not
succeed; in the battle at Port Gibson on May 1, 1863, McPherson's men held
their ground, and Sherman crossed the Mississippi at Grand Gulf, now
evacuated to the Union.[18]

Vicksburg could be attacked from the south and the rear, along the Big
Black River, but the attacking forces would be dangerously isolated from
supplies and reinforcements. Long before Grant started his assault on the
town, General Sherman, the man over all others whose word Grant took
seriously, had come to his commander and argued that the plan of approaching from the south and rear was imprudent. Grant did not change his mind.
He told his articulate adviser that the country's morale required a quick,
decisive victory. Grant was the politician, and Sherman, resolutely, was not.
Grant had the confidence now to stand alone even against the advice of the
man he most admired. He knew that Halleck would not be reluctant to
dismiss him if his gamble for taking Vicksburg failed. Nor would Lincoln.
Grant, outranking McClernand, had succeeded in assuming the over-all field
command, but having edged past the powerful McClernand he had to prove
the wisdom of taking on all the responsibility himself. Grant knew that Lincoln was watching every move he made with intense curiosity (they had
never met), and he realized that Lincoln would look for still another general if
he faltered. In short, everything was at stake in the Vicksburg campaign.[19]

Grant moved with assurance. On May 5, Stanton had told Dana to let
Grant know that "he has the full confidence of the Government, is expected
to enforce his authority, and will be firmly and heartily supported." He now
had the power to do what he wanted to do, and as always, he had the conviction that everyone was out of step but him. He moved up to the rear—to the
east—of Vicksburg, from the southwest. He did not wait for Banks to bring
his men up from Louisiana to help. Instead, Grant cut his own supply line
and imprudently placed his vast army within a pincers formed by Pemberton
in Vicksburg and the enemy general Grant most admired, Joseph E. Johnston, northeast of Vicksburg above Jackson, Mississippi. Had Grant's plan
failed he would have been pilloried for doing something so stupid, and Johnston was not reluctant to bring on such a punishment. As Grant moved north
to cut the Vicksburg–Jackson railroad, Johnston ordered Pemberton to move
out from Vicksburg to meet him, so that together they could crush Grant.
However, Johnston did not make the rendezvous; instead, McClernand and
McPherson met the Confederate general near Jackson and drove him north to
Canton. There, thirty miles north of Jackson, Johnston remained a threat
to Grant throughout the siege of Vicksburg; it was feared that he could at-

tack the rear of the Federal position at any time. Meanwhile, as ordered, Pemberton had crossed the Big Black and occupied a good position on Champion's Hill. While Sherman moved on Jackson, destroying enemy supplies in Mississippi's capital, Grant attacked at Champion's Hill, ordering McClernand's and McPherson's men forward in a bloody assault on Pemberton. Because McClernand was slow to move, the Confederates were not surrounded; however, their losses were great, and Pemberton was driven back to Vicksburg. Kenneth P. Williams states that some regard Champion's Hill as the most decisive single engagement of the Civil War. Grant won.[20]

As Grant was watching his men drive the Confederates back across the Big Black, he committed the final act of assumption of command: he elected to be insubordinate. Dana's message from Stanton had suggested that not even Halleck could override his decisions now. James Marshall-Cornwall, who has written astutely of Grant as warrior, takes note of the passage in the *Memoirs* in which, with great triumph, Grant told how he broke free:

> . . . an officer from Banks' staff came up and presented me with a letter from General Halleck, dated the 11th of May. It had been sent by the way of New Orleans to Banks to be forwarded to me. It ordered me to return to Grand Gulf and to co-operate from there with Banks against Port Hudson, and then to return with our combined forces to besiege Vicksburg. I told the officer that the order came too late, and that Halleck would not give it now if he knew our position. The bearer of the dispatch insisted that I ought to obey the order, and was giving arguments to support his position when I heard great cheering to the right of our line and, looking in that direction, saw Lawler [a brigade commander] in his shirt sleeves leading a charge upon the enemy. I immediately mounted my horse and rode in the direction of the charge, and saw no more of the officer who delivered the dispatch. . . .

He was in total control. One soldier who had been fighting on the hill watched Grant stand, "cool and calculating," with a cigar in his mouth ordering fresh assaults over bloody ground. Shelby Foote cites the soldier's perception of Grant's "careful and half-cynical" command. When things were going poorly, he acted as if that was exactly how he expected them to go, and sent new men in to make them go better.[21]

After Champion's Hill, Pemberton was trapped in Vicksburg. He had orders from Johnston to move out or even surrender, but he stayed, determined to hold the town and the Mississippi. Grant was equally determined. The whole long, clumsy campaign was reaching its climax, and he wanted to break through the earthworks that Pemberton, an engineer, had skillfully erected. On May 22 Grant stormed them, and for two hours, in a battle without a name, armies only yards apart kept up a blizzard of fire, while assault after assault, with gruesome losses, failed to break the Confederate defenses. All of his commanders—Sherman, McPherson, and McClernand—had been eager for the attack, and so had their men. The Yankees began with the hope of finishing the job.[22]

By noon, however, the eagerness was gone and stymied and frightened men thought they were through for the day. Grant and Sherman, standing together, thought so too, but a message came from McClernand saying he still believed he could break through, if only McPherson and Sherman would order one more attack. Grant was skeptical, but Sherman was aware of how it would look if McClernand could say his boldness had been thwarted, so a new assault was ordered on the well-dug Confederate fortifications, built skillfully into the uneven terrain east of town. Union troops—Sherman's and McPherson's men as well as McClernand's—were forced to rush up steep banks into murderous fire to try to reach the parapets and plunge through the Confederate defenses. Grant, watching intently, saw men agonizingly reach the top of the enemy's earthworks, only to die or be driven back. The dirt was red. Grant later confessed that there were only two days of battle that he regretted: June 3, 1864, at Cold Harbor, and this day in May outside Vicksburg. He lost more men than did his enemy, 3,200 in all. McClernand's second assault did not succeed in breaking through. What was more, there had been no reason to try. The way to take Vicksburg was not by a fierce climactic battle, but by the long, slow starvation of a siege. McClernand, however, did not see victory in such terms. Scurrying to make defeat into victory, on May 30, 1863, he wrote a three-page order to his men exhorting them in spacious rhetoric to aspire to be martyrs equal to those of Monmouth and Bunker Hill and asking, "Shall not our flag float over Vicksburg? Shall not the great Father of Waters be opened to lawful commerce? One thinks the emphatic response to one and all of these is, 'It shall be so.' " One can easily imagine the words the men chose, privately, to respond to this rot, but the big question was how Lincoln and Stanton would react. McClernand had managed to make his domestic political power go a long way in sustaining his military politicking. If, indeed, Grant had faltered again, McClernand was more than willing to become the hero at Vicksburg in his place. McPherson and Sherman, as well as Charles A. Dana, now special commissioner of the War Department, were well aware of McClernand's aspirations even before they finally got wind of this flamboyant publicity ploy in mid-June. Meanwhile, McClernand was counting on impatience in Washington to operate in his favor, for abandoning the senseless frontal assaults, Grant had committed the army to the slow, immobile, nervous business of siege. Vicksburg was to be starved out. And while this ugly logic was being worked, Ulysses Grant got drunk.[23]

He did so on June 6, 1863, and again the next day. Admirers of the general who witnessed his behavior made sure that reports of it neither got into the newspapers to create a scandal that might well have ended with his removal, nor reached Lincoln and Stanton directly to raise fresh doubts in their minds.

Ever since, there has been a loyal conspiracy to protect Grant from the story. Sylvanus Cadwallader, a *Chicago Times* reporter, told it in his memoirs, which he wrote in 1896, in his seventies, when he was a sheep rancher in California. The manuscript was not published until 1955, and when it did appear, both Cadwallader and the historian who arranged for its publication were vilified for violating the gentlemanly silence on the subject. Much fur has flown over the story; John Y. Simon, the careful editor of Grant's *Papers*, citing Charles A. Dana's memory years later, claims Cadwallader was not present for the drinking bout, but does not deny that it took place. He surmises that Cadwallader's story was based on headquarters gossip, of which there was assuredly plenty. The exuberant Dana later acknowledged Grant's drinking in an editorial in the *New York Sun* for January 28, 1887, entitled "Gen. Grant's Occasional Intoxication." This editorial was no doubt the source of much of the story, the most sensible and witty analysis of which is in Shelby Foote's *The Civil War*. No doubt Cadwallader, as an old man, embellished an episode he remembered from long ago. However, he was not likely to have forgotten its essentials, and little about the story, including his claim to have been aboard, fails to make sense, unless one is flatly determined to refuse to believe that Ulysses Grant was ever drunk.[24]

On the evening of June 6, Grant got away from John A. Rawlins, who kept a sharp eye on his chief and was apparently the only person allowed by Grant to speak to him about his drinking. At this time he had been separated from Julia for about six weeks. As Foote put it, "The trouble seemed in part sexual, as in California nine years ago, and it was intensified by periods of boredom, such as now." There had been little fighting in early June, and during the impatient waiting for the siege to do its work, Grant's enormous repressed appetite exploded. Whatever it was that wanted satisfying was released—if only in fraternal talk and good drink—on the steamer *Diligent*, on which Grant was making an inspection tour to Satartia, on the Yazoo River.[25]

Since one of the reasons for war is to have an excuse to do some drinking, it is not surprising that there was an enormous amount of it done during the Civil War. The activities on June 6 and 7, 1863, were made special only by the identity of one of the participants. As Sylvanus Cadwallader tells it, he saw Grant walk drunkenly out of the barroom on the steamer. At this instant the reporter apparently made a decision. He could have sent a sensational story of debauchery to the *Chicago Times*, which might have made him famous as a reporter while perhaps causing Grant irreparable harm. But he knew that if he filed the story he would be thrown out of Grant's command just when the big news of the fall of Vicksburg seemed likely to break. In any event, he chose to do as so many people do, and respected the privacy of a man who had been drinking. Indeed, instead of exposing Grant, he chose to be his protector. When two officers declined to take responsibility for getting Grant to bed, Cadwallader took on the job. He got Grant into his stiflingly hot cabin, insisted on removing the general's coat, vest, and boots, and put him on a bunk. In the suffocating stateroom Grant slept.[26]

Charles A. Dana, another observer who seemed never to miss anything, and who certainly was aboard the *Diligent*, wrote politely, "Grant was ill and went to bed soon after we started." But Dana felt compelled to interrupt the general and did knock on his door when naval officers on a downriver gunboat warned the *Diligent* that it was not safe to proceed. Dana told the officers that Grant was "sick and asleep," but they insisted on knowing the general's wishes. When Dana awakened him, Grant was "too sick to decide" and uncharacteristically told him, "I will leave it with you." But once awake, Grant insisted on putting on the rest of his clothes, and went ashore. Cadwallader coaxed him into returning to the boat and again put him to bed, where he slept while the boat steamed twenty-five miles back down the Yazoo.[27]

The next morning, "fresh as a rose, clean shirt and all," Grant came to breakfast and said, "Well, Mr. Dana, I suppose we are at Satartia now." Dana, always the perfect gentleman, undoubtedly found a way to tell Grant tactfully, without referring to drink at all, that he was at Haynes Bluff, twenty-five miles southwest of Satartia. Untroubled by his mistake, and momentarily refreshed, Grant started drinking again and insisted on moving south past the Chickasaw Bluffs. Cadwallader, apprehensive lest Grant be seen drunk, arranged for a delay, so that they would not reach the Chickasaw Bayou dock at the busy middle of the day. Unfortunately, when they did dock in the evening, they found themselves next to a boat on which a sutler was entertaining a swarm of army officers, and the party soon moved over to the ladies' lounge of the *Diligent*.[28]

Extracting Grant from the party, Cadwallader got him away from the boat (and the bottle) and on shore started back to headquarters. Grant mounted a horse named Kangaroo. It lived up to its name by rearing on its hind legs, but Grant remained in the saddle, and then spurred the beast, which galloped off ahead of the rest of the party. As Foote has it: "The road was crooked, winding among the many slews and bayous, but the general more or less straightened it out. . . ." Grant, in Cadwallader's words, was "heading only for the bridges, and literally tore through and over everything in his way. The air was full of dust, ashes, and embers from camp-fires, and shouts and curses from those he rode down in his race." Kangaroo finally slowed, and Cadwallader caught up with Grant, got him off the horse, and dispatched a man to Rawlins, to have an ambulance sent for the general. When it arrived, Grant was reluctant to admit he needed it and resisted getting in. When the disheveled party finally reached headquarters, Rawlins was waiting. Cadwallader got out first, and then Grant climbed down, straightened his vest, and as if nothing had ever been amiss, said good night and went to bed. Of Rawlins, Cadwallader wrote, "The whole appearance of the man indicated a fierceness that would have torn me into a thousand pieces had he considered me to blame." Luckily for the reporter, Rawlins chose not to resent Cadwallader's having temporarily taken on his own self-appointed role as Grant's protector against liquor; rather, with his fanatic fascination with drink and vice, he asked for every detail. Laconically, James Harrison Wilson noted in his diary on June 7, 1863, "Genl. G. intoxicated."[29]

Rawlins had seen signs that Grant was about to drink: he had found a case of wine outside Grant's tent and a few days earlier had seen the general drinking with a surgeon. On June 6, the very day of Grant's trip up the Yazoo, Rawlins had written his chief a strange, threatening letter that seemed to come directly from a Calvinist conscience. "Tonight," he had stated, "when you should, because of the condition of your health if nothing else, have been in bed, I find you where the wine bottle has just been emptied, in company with those who drink and urge you to do likewise." Rawlins spoke of a promise: "Had you not pledged me the sincerity of your honor early last March that you would drink no more during the war, and kept that pledge during your recent campaign, you would not to-day have stood first in the world's history as a successful military commander." He spoke, too, of the responsibility of a general to "the friends, wives, and children of these brave men whose lives" are "imperilled" by his want of control when he has been drinking. Whether Grant ever read the letter—Rawlins is said to have read it to his friend—and if he did, how he and Rawlins moved past this crisis in their relationship, is not known. Somehow, Rawlins did function as Grant's conscience, or better, as the friend who gave the only orders, other than those from his wife, that Grant willingly obeyed. Furthermore, Rawlins knew he could reach Grant with threats of resignation. The general could not contemplate such an abandonment, and perhaps with no explicit conversation on the point at all, Grant listened, but, on this occasion, did not obey.[30]

Cadwallader, fascinated by his excursion into intimacy with Grant, was nonetheless nervous lest he be ordered out of Grant's department for having been privy to the escapade. Grant's mind worked the other way. He never mentioned the events to the reporter, and the latter, in turn, had the sense never to mention them to Grant. And for the remainder of the war, Cadwallader had privileged access to Grant's headquarters. Dana, also fascinated by Grant and the men around him, particularly the bright and gossipy James Harrison Wilson, sent no account of the incident that could—and would—be interpreted in Washington as indicating alcoholism. He was loyal to his new friends and clearly preferred an occasionally roaring drunk Grant to the pretentious McClernand, who would likely succeed to the command if Grant was dismissed. What Dana did, rather than deny Grant's drinking altogether, was to make light of it in his reports to Stanton; thus he wrote Stanton in July, after the Vicksburg victory, ". . . whenever he commits the folly of tasting liquor, Rawlins can be counted on to stop him."[31]

All of Dana's hopes for that victory depended on the success of the siege. He could only wait and keep his eye on the jealous generals around Grant.

On June 15 General Francis P. Blair, Jr., read in the *Memphis Evening Bulletin* McClernand's exhortation to his men to take Vicksburg. Disgusted, he sent it to Sherman, who exploded over the "effusion of vain-glory" and pronounced it, in a note to Grant, an appeal to Illinois voters at the expense of dead men. To McClernand's accusation that he had not been properly supported on the day of the murderously ineffective assaults in May, Sherman roared "monstrous falsehood," and McPherson agreed. Grant no doubt snorted at McClernand's mawkish prose and, shrewdly, sensed that Lincoln and Stanton had done the same. In the two weeks since the exhortation had been issued, it had not become celebrated in Washington. At last, McClernand had overextended himself.[32]

Grant, by letter, asked McClernand if the newspaper text of the order was accurate, thereby simultaneously reprimanding McClernand for not sending his commanding officer a copy and establishing insubordination. When McClernand replied lamely that his aide had simply neglected to send a copy to headquarters, Grant sent James Harrison Wilson to tell McClernand he was relieved from duty. McClernand was expecting the order; he was awaiting Wilson in full uniform, his sword on the table. Grant had at last moved to get rid of the man who had established himself as something of a sacred cow with the president of the United States. Grant had given McClernand enough rope; Lincoln let him hang. The president, receiving McClernand's protest against his dismissal, said blandly that if events proved that McClernand was right, exoneration would follow. One experienced Illinois politician consigned a second to oblivion, and permitted a third—a novice—to move into a most promising position.[33]

The month of June was spent building trenches through which the attacking units would assault the constantly reinforced earthwork fortifications of the enemy. It was a game of sandbox madness. In the dirt and heat, men dug scooped-out hollows no farther than the other side of a good-sized living room from the scooped-out hollows of other men. So close together physically, and engaged in the same silly, deadly pastimes, they began to talk to one another. Fierce obscenities yielded to friendly ones as boredom made the soldiers forget they were expected to hate those they were shortly to try to kill.

In town, civilians moved uneasily in and out of caves and suffered starvation. The Federals suspected this shortage of food and supposed also that the absence of intense bombardment by Confederate cannon during the time the fortifications were being built was due to a shortage of ammunition. Hence they were surprised, when surrender came, to find that there were large amounts of ammunition as well as nearly 60,000 muskets and rifles and 172 cannon. Realizing the desperation of his people, Pemberton abandoned any prospect of deliverance by Johnston and on July 3, 1863, asked Grant for terms. Hoping, as Grant's old friend Buckner had hoped at Donelson, that prewar friendship would count for something, the Confederates roused from his sickbed John Bowen, who had known Grant in St. Louis and was now dying of dysentery. Painfully, Bowen rode to Grant's headquarters to try to effect a favorable arrangement. Grant would not see him. Instead, Pemberton was told that loss of life could be avoided only by unconditional surrender. But this time Grant did not want the symbol of victory of a surrender of prisoners. He wanted Vicksburg, and Pemberton had to do the surrendering himself. When he and Grant met, the Pennsylvanian rather testily accepted Grant's instructions that his men march out, accept parole (an unenforceable promise not to go back into the Confederate army), and give up their arms— and the town.[34]

"In Vicksburg thank God" began a letter from a Union captain to his wife dated July 4, 1863. The rebels were marching out and stacking their guns; a fellow captain was reading out loud the Declaration of Independence. "We are going to celebrate this Fourth of July in spirit and truth," continued Captain Ira Miltmore, and growing exuberant he declared, "The Stars and Stripes are now waving to our right, and the white flags to our left, as far as we can see. The backbone of the Rebellion is this day broken. The Confederacy is divided—Pemberton is a prisoner. Vicksburg is ours. The Mississippi River is opened, and Gen. Grant is to be our next President."[35]

Success did not pile on success quite as fast as Ira Miltmore had anticipated, but the excitement in Washington and all across the North when the twin Fourth of July victories of Gettysburg and Vicksburg were announced was enormous. General Grant, of Vicksburg, and not General Meade, of Gettysburg, emerged as the hero of the day despite the fact that Gettysburg was the scene of a greater battle than Vicksburg. Indeed, the taking of Vicksburg, the culmination of the campaign to open to the Union a river route through the Confederacy, was not achieved through a battle at all. It was completed not with colors handed gloriously over parapets, but with the ignominious starving out of a small town. The action at Gettysburg, by contrast, had the gory majesty of the storied battles of eighteenth-century and Napoleonic Europe, yet its victor, George Gordon Meade, never caught the eye of the public the way Grant did. It was not so much that the people, along with President Lincoln, were distressed that Meade had not made good his victory by pursuing and destroying Lee's retreating army. It was more the elusive matter of personal appeal. Americans could have found in Meade, as they had found in George Washington, the aristocrat as warrior-hero. Instead, the proper Philadelphian, who would "not even speak to any person connected with the press," exasperated the war correspondents and bored other Americans.[36]

On the other hand, Grant, with simple style, attracted enormous attention. Lee was so maddeningly grand and the generals who had been sent to destroy him so unsuccessful that Americans in the North gave up on grandeur and looked westward to an average man. "Surrounded by the most ordinary set of plebeians you ever saw," himself plain, though not dully so,

Grant might have been too hopelessly colorless to catch attention—even after Vicksburg—had he not had the virtues of his alleged vices. Unlike that monolith of rectitude Robert E. Lee, Grant was vulgar, was thought to drink, and was not known to be a student of anything. In a not uncharacteristic reach for the anti-intellectual and the unknown when problems are greatest, Americans turned their attention toward Vicksburg and took a long look at Ulysses S. Grant.[37]

There are two classes in America: celebrities and commoners. Until July 1863, an eminently forgettable Ulysses Grant was among the commoners, but as the hero of Vicksburg he was irretrievably consigned to celebration. Like other people, Americans are often fickle about their heroes—which, no doubt, is just as well—but in this instance they were not. During the rest of his life, Grant never lost the hold on the people's imagination that in his first forty years had so thoroughly eluded him. Grant had many opportunities to falter after Vicksburg, but in the strange world of public opinion even a bad day on the battlefield, as at Cold Harbor, or scandals such as those which marked his presidential administration could not drive him into obscurity.

# XI

# CHATTANOOGA

. . . the eternal law
That who can saddle Opportunity
Is God's elect, . . .
—*James Russell Lowell,*
*"On a Bust of General Grant"*

IF VICKSBURG made Grant a public hero, his conversion of defeat into victory at Chattanooga proclaimed his military greatness. The Confederate commander in Tennessee, General Braxton Bragg, had outmaneuvered the Union commander, General William S. Rosecrans, and brought the Federal forces into a position where they were almost under siege in the important river and railroad town of Chattanooga, in the southeastern corner of the state. Bragg and Rosecrans had been contending for eastern Tennessee, where Lincoln hoped to stimulate Unionist sentiment in the South by liberating the mountain areas whose occupants had never agreed to secession. And beyond Tennessee lay Georgia. Rosecrans had been slow to move, but when finally in motion he had forced Bragg to retreat after a bloody and indecisive battle at Stones River and then had maneuvered the Confederate general east and south, into southeastern Tennessee. However, Bragg had turned the tables on Rosecrans at Chickamauga and now had him nearly surrounded at Chattanooga. Only one torturous mountain road remained open to Rosecrans. In October he was confronted with the death by starvation of huge numbers of draft and attack animals, and with winter approaching, his men were without warm clothing and on short rations. The situation in Tennessee had deteriorated so severely that Lincoln and Stanton decided on a drastic change in organization and leadership. All the forces west of the Alleghenies (save those of General Nathaniel P. Banks, in Louisiana) were to be united under one command—Grant's. Halleck, though still distrustful of Grant, acquiesced.

In October 1863, Grant was called to Cairo to receive these new orders. As he and Julia traveled by steamboat toward Cairo, he was in great discomfort because of an injury sustained on an earlier celebratory trip. Demonstrating that the Mississippi was indeed his, Grant had traveled down the river after his victory at Vicksburg. At Natchez, high on a beautiful bluff over the water, his fellow Yankees who had preceded him there introduced him to "almost voluptuous luxury" in a house whose walls were hung with Landseers and Sullys and whose ample windows looked out on lavish orchards and richly stocked greenhouses. As he moved still farther down the river toward New Orleans, his steamboat was preceded by another, the *Julia*, and at one point some not quite conquered rebels ungallantly fired on this vessel, wounding three celebrators. At New Orleans, there were hosannas from his army colleagues who had long been in possession of the city and from a surprising number of the local populace as well. (However, some of the permanent residents were sullen, and one officer, Thomas Kilby Smith, found the women "strangely hostile.") Grant was treated to a magnificent dinner and a lavish evening reception, and the next day, ten miles out of town, to a grand review of General Banks's troops.[1]

Riding back to the city with his staff and Banks's, at close to breakneck speed, Grant was thrown by his horse and seriously injured. There were several versions of how the accident occurred. Grant loyalists, for example, blamed a soft spot in the crushed-shell surface of the road, in order to protect, variously, Grant's reputation as a fine horseman, as a prudent man who did not ride at too fast a pace, and as a general who did not get drunk. Nathaniel Banks was enough to encourage the last course in any man, but it is exceedingly hard to be sure just what was the cause of the accident. Alcohol may well have played a role, as a flood of rumors suggested. If these rumors were correct, the fact that neither Julia Grant nor John A. Rawlins was then in New Orleans lends credence to the theory that their presence was crucial in keeping Grant sober.

Grant did ride exceedingly powerful and difficult horses. At Natchez he had lent one of his mounts to the mayor, and as the mayor, on foot, was leading it over difficult terrain, it had reared, its hooves clashing against those of General Thomas Kilby Smith's powerful battle horse, which in response had also reared. Smith had been thrown and was extraordinarily lucky not to have been trampled. Smith was riding behind Grant and Banks at the time of Grant's accident, and his version of the story, which has a ring of truth, is that Grant, riding at an exceedingly strong gallop in traffic, came up so close to a carriage—or a streetcar—that his horse reared. Grant, untypically, was thrown, and the officer behind him was unable to stop his horse before its hooves cut deeply into Grant's leg. In Grant's own account the cause of his horse's panic was not a carriage or a streetcar, but a locomotive. He absolved the horseman riding behind him, blaming the injury instead on his horse, which he said had fallen on top of him.[2]

The doctors treated Grant first at a roadside inn and then, during the next week, at his hotel in town. Still an invalid, he traveled by steamer back to Vicksburg, where Julia, who had gone to St. Louis to put the three older children into school, rejoined him. He had received orders on September 13 to send troops to assist Rosecrans, but uncomfortable in bed, he waited until September 27 to order Sherman to send two divisions to Memphis and on to eastern Tennessee. Before they were ordered out, however, Chickamauga had been fought and lost and Rosecrans driven into the snare of Chattanooga. And so on October 10, 1863, Grant received the telegram—mysteriously, seven days in arriving—that summoned him to Cairo. He knew only that his going involved shoring up Rosecrans, but he elected to read the assignment as more than a temporary diversion. He wasted no time in departing, and as if to ensure that there were no changes of mind, he did not reply that he was coming until he was on the way. Julia came back from riding to find the headquarters a field of snowy tents that had been struck and to face the commotion of hasty packing. She was told to be ready to leave by four; precisely at sundown they got off.[3]

In Ulysses S. Grant's magnificent telling of his own story, this move east takes on far greater drama than the more famous trip five months later to Washington to accept the appointment as lieutenant general from Lincoln. The quick moving of his headquarters from Vicksburg represented the great break forward of his life. In his *Memoirs*, the first volume ends with the telegram which was his matter-of-fact response to a summons to greatness: "Your dispatch . . . of the 3d . . . was received at 11:30 on the 10th. Left the same day. . . ." He had disposed of delay. This was his proclamation that he was on his way and no one would stop him.[4]

Those who might have tried would have had trouble finding him. Grant had a way of being out of touch at critical moments. Officers along the route did not know his precise plans, and he himself only learned at Cairo that he was to go on at once to Louisville. He and Julia took the train to Indianapolis and were just leaving that city to go south to Kentucky when a messenger ran down the track to stop the train. Secretary of War Stanton had arrived by special train and joined the Grants on theirs. It was the first meeting of the secretary and the general. They talked, and the subject was Grant. Stanton gave him orders that, in Grant's words, "created the 'Military Division of the Mississippi,' (giving me the command)." Grant's Army of the Tennessee, Rosecrans's Army of the Cumberland, and the Army of the Ohio, led now by Ambrose E. Burnside, who had lost the command of all the eastern armies after Fredericksburg and had been sent out to the west, were to work together under a unified western command. (The War Department's mysterious loyalty to the concept of the eastern and western phases of the conflict as almost separate and distinct wars still remained.) Stanton gave Grant his orders in two versions, which were "identical in all but one particular." In one version, Rosecrans remained in command of the Army of the Cumberland; in the other, George H. Thomas replaced him. Stanton offered Grant the choice, and he picked Thomas.[5]

When he returned to Julia, she had her Alexander at last. He was no longer directing an action that had been ordered by others. Now he could make decisions and move at his own speed. He was vastly and publicly important—a man to be reckoned with. He might still fall on his face (and the Chattanooga campaign, into which he was moving, would provide plenty of opportunity for him to do so), but he could no longer be ignored. Julia grasped this prominence swiftly, but not swiftly enough to be flattered rather than annoyed when no ferry was waiting to take them across the Ohio to Louisville. Mrs. General Grant did not yet sense just how truly important her husband was. By twentieth-century standards, the security procedures during the Civil War, when an enemy in one's midst was often undetectable, were remarkably casual. Normally, little care was taken to prevent the assassination or capture of key men, but in this instance precautions were deemed necessary: since telegraph messages could be intercepted by the rebels, who were not scarce along the Ohio, it had been decided not to telegraph ahead the precise time that the secretary of war and one of his most valuable generals would be ready to cross the river on a slow-moving and vulnerable ferryboat.[6]

Not all of Julia's concern as they waited in the damp was for the deference due her. Grant was still not fully recovered from his fall, and Stanton was susceptible to illness. Indeed, Stanton himself later believed that his respiratory condition, which killed him six years later, had begun as he stood on that wharf in a cold rain. Once they reached Kentucky the trip was more comfortable, and in Louisville, settled comfortably in the Galt House, Grant and Stanton continued their talk, holding a conference that lasted a whole day. There is no detailed account of what was discussed, but in view of Stanton's probing bluntness it is likely that they were frank about General Halleck. Soon thereafter Grant's communications to Halleck about actions that had been taken or that he wanted taken assumed a tone suggesting that he anticipated no possible rebuff. This may indicate that Stanton had assured Grant that the decisions for the campaigns in the west were his alone, and not subject to Halleck's veto.[7]

That Sunday evening Julia proudly took her husband the general on a triumphant round of calls on the once overbearing Louisville kin whom they had met fifteen years earlier as honeymooners. Just how urgently important her general had become was quickly apparent when a messenger arrived summoning Grant back to the hotel. The assistant secretary of war, Charles A. Dana, had telegraphed Stanton saying that Rosecrans was on the verge of ordering a retreat from Chattanooga. Dana recommended that he be ordered not to do so, and Stanton, his famous temper aroused, was demanding to know where his new commander had gone.[8]

In his unintentionally comic manner, the crinkle-bearded, fiercely intense Stanton had rushed about the hotel asking startled guests if they had seen the Grants. With reasonable promptness, even if it did not seem so to the secretary of war, one of his aides had caught up with the Grants, and the general returned to the hotel to find Stanton, in a dressing gown, pacing nervously around his room. He thrust Dana's message into Grant's hand. The general stated firmly that a retreat from Chattanooga would be "a terrible disaster"; he immediately implemented the order removing Rosecrans and putting Thomas in command of the Army of the Cumberland and told Thomas to hold Chattanooga at any cost. The Rock of Chickamauga sent back his famous reply: "We will hold the town till we starve." It was likely that Bragg would exact the price.[9]

On Tuesday, leaving Julia, now joined by her youngest child, in Louisville with her aunt, Grant set out for Chattanooga. At Nashville he endured the "torture," as he recalled it, of a long speech of welcome by the Federal military governor of Tennessee, Andrew Johnson. His pain came not only from his swollen leg but also from the anticipation of having to reply with a speech of his own. Sensibly, he responded to the effusion of east Tennessee oratory with a simple thank you. The occasion gave him his first chance to size up the strange man who was to be both an ally and adversary on Grant's route to the White House. From Nashville, Grant's train passed through Murfreesboro, Tennessee. One of Rosecrans's men (who was sorry his commander was being replaced) "ran out to the side of the Railroad and as the car passed, was rewarded with the sight of the grim old Chieftain." (Grant was forty-one years old.) Harvey Reid sat down to write a letter home and gave a superb description of the general:

> He was seated entirely alone on the side of the car next to me and I had a fair view of him. He had on an old blue overcoat, and wore a common white wool [hat] drawn down over his eyes, and looked so much like a private soldier, that but for the resemblance to the photographs that can be seen on every corner in this town, it would have been impossible to have recognized him. But that strongly marked Roman nose, the sternly compressed upper lip, and the closely cut brown whiskers and mustache could not be mistaken by anyone who had ever seen his picture. He was either tired with riding all night, or had something on his mind for he appeared almost sad as he looked vacantly without seeming to see anything that he was passing. I do not think that his staff was with him as the car seemed almost empty.

The train took Grant into northern Alabama, where, at Stevenson, he stopped for a conference with Rosecrans. The deposed general had many intelligent suggestions about how the army should proceed, and Grant could only wonder why Rosecrans had not himself put them into effect.[10]

As he drew closer to Chattanooga, Grant met, one by one, the generals who had been fighting in the east and were now under his command. At Stevenson, General O. O. Howard, who had been at Chancellorsville and Gettysburg and now had been detached from Meade to aid in the campaign in the west, made his way through the train to meet Grant. Howard had conceived him to be very large and of rough appearance and was astonished by his small size—"Not larger than McClellan, . . . rather thin in flesh and very pale in complexion, and noticeably self-contained and retiring." As Howard recalled it: "He gave me his hand," and Howard, who had lost his right arm in the Peninsular campaign in 1862, took his new commander's hand with his left. Grant said pleasantly, "I am glad to see you, General." Then, Howard discovered that he "had to do the talking." Filling the silence, he offered to accompany Grant to General Joseph Hooker's headquarters, a quarter of a mile away, in the carriage Hooker had sent. Grant replied, "If General Hooker wishes to see *me* he will find me on this train." Both the answer and the manner in which it was delivered surprised Howard, who quickly grasped that this was "Grant's way of maintaining his ascendancy where a subordinate was likely to question it." Six months earlier, at Chancellorsville, Hooker—whom Howard recalled as "of full build, ruddy, and handsome"—had had a command greater than Grant's, but now "Hooker . . . entered the car and paid his respects in person." Howard "wondered at the contrast between these two men, and pondered upon the manner of their meeting." He concluded: "Grant evidently took this first occasion to assert himself. He never left the necessity for gaining a proper ascendancy over subordinate generals . . . to a second interview. Yet he manifested only a quiet firmness."[11]

As Grant shrewdly outmaneuvered potential McClernands and adroitly established his authority over rival generals, he was equally careful to avoid giving any intimations of excessive ambition. Generals like Hooker and McClellan had created great problems for themselves by seeking high positions and the perquisites that accompanied them, but then not matching loftiness with performance on the battlefield. Grant was determined to keep the horse before the cart; he would perform, and then see that what he had done was celebrated. He thought the wind of recognition was now blowing his way, and he was not going to take any stance that would block it. Howard remembered that as they lay on their cots that night, Grant said, "If I should seek a command higher than that intrusted to me by my Government I should be flying in the face of Providence."[12]

Howard, on his way to his own headquarters at Jasper, Tennessee, traveled by train with Grant to Bridgeport, Alabama, on the Tennessee border. Here, just west of the northwestern corner of Georgia, the railroad line ended; the Confederates had destroyed the bridge that had crossed to the south side of the Tennessee River, which they held. The only Union enclave on the south bank was the town of Chattanooga itself. To reach it required a trip of two or three days by horseback over a poor circuitous mountain road on the north side of the river—the only route into the Union encampment at Chattanooga. At daybreak, outside Howard's tent, Rawlins lifted Grant "as if he had been a child, into the saddle," and in a heavy storm, the small party set off; they covered only ten or twelve miles that day, October 22. As Howard put it: "By this journey he set in motion the entire fall campaign against Bragg." But the grandeur of the situation was not apparent at the time. Their mounts picked their way over Waldron Ridge through the wreckage of discarded wagons and the unfrozen carcasses of starved draft horses, slipping over rocks, roots, and mud. The ride was anguished and difficult for a man with a painfully injured leg.[13]

Miraculously, the motion of the horse eased Grant's pain. The men paused in the rain for the night and then pressed on to Chattanooga. Late in the day, one of the travelers was lifted from his saddle and helped into a small house. "Wet, dirty, and well," as Lincoln learned the next day, Ulysses S. Grant had arrived at the headquarters of General George H. Thomas. Although a Virginian, Thomas was not a cordial host, and an aide had to nudge him and suggest that he offer Grant some dry clothes. Grant, who never warmed to Thomas, declined the offer, pushed his damp jacket open, slumped in an armchair in front of the fire, and lit a cigar. One of the officers in the room, Horace Porter, found him "immovable as a rock and as silent as a sphinx."[14]

Not rising, Grant shook hands with each of Thomas's staff officers and "in a low voice, speaking slowly, [said] 'How do you do.' " Then, somewhat disconcerted, the officers one by one presented their reviews of the precarious military position. Grant's inattentive manner was perplexing, but he was not missing a thing; in particular he was alert for signs that any of them had endorsed the retreat proposed by Rosecrans, of which he so thoroughly disapproved. Porter noticed that when General William F. Smith, the engineer responsible for bridges and roads (whom Grant had known at West Point), began talking, Grant "straightened himself up in his chair, his features assumed an air of animation, and in a tone of voice that manifested a deep interest in the discussion, . . . [he] began to fire whole volleys of questions. . . ." He pursued the matter of establishing a better line of food supply—"opening up the cracker line," he called it— and then asked Porter, in charge of ordnance, if there was sufficient ammunition for an attack. There was only enough for a single day's battle, and immediately the problem of opening a new supply line took on a dimension beyond that of bringing in desperately needed food, shoes, and overcoats.[15]

After listening to each of his subordinates, Grant turned to a table and, ignoring their presence, began to write. They stood by uselessly as he composed orders and telegrams that demonstrated a grasp of the whole of the western theater of the war. From the disjointed reports he had been given, he

put together a coherent picture of the terrain of an area new to him, and of
the vast confused array of men who contended for it. To Halleck, in Washington, he announced, "Have just arrived. I will write to-morrow. Please
approve order placing General Sherman in command of Department and
Army of the Tennessee, with headquarters in the field." Grant was making
doubly sure that his own army would be commanded by his best lieutenant
and would be available wherever he wanted to use it.[16]

The next day he rode with Thomas to the point on the river from which he
was later to push through the new supply route back to Bridgeport. As he
looked along the bank he was in plain view of Confederate pickets on the
other side, but he drew no fire. (Indeed, he recalled, they saluted.) Having
seen for himself one problem, he went back to headquarters, and that evening Porter again watched Grant at work. His writing was the act of an
athlete; it was done with the command of a horseman:

> He soon after began to write despatches, and I arose to go, but resumed
> my seat as he said, "Sit still." My attention was soon attracted to the man-
> ner in which he went to work at his correspondence. At this time, as
> throughout his later career, he wrote nearly all his documents with his
> own hand, and seldom dictated to any one even the most unimportant
> despatch. His work was performed swiftly and uninterruptedly, but with-
> out any marked display of nervous energy. His thoughts flowed as freely
> from his mind as the ink from his pen; he was never at a loss for an expres-
> sion, and seldom interlined a word or made a material correction. He sat
> with his head bent low over the table, and when he had occasion to step to
> another table or desk to get a paper he wanted, he would glide rapidly
> across the room without straightening himself, and return to his seat with
> his body still bent over at about the same angle at which he had been sit-
> ting when he left his chair.[17]

Grant did his own work. Porter was amazed that he simply pushed a finished page off the table onto the floor as he turned to the next, and then,
when finished, picked up the lot and sorted them. The commander of the
armies of the west was his own file clerk. What he readied for distribution
were orders of great precision. Their execution, begun the next morning,
created the campaign that routed Braxton Bragg. Grant squared the corners
of the sheets of paper, handed them to Ely S. Parker, "bid those present a
pleasant good night, and limped off to his bedroom." In the orders, Sherman
and the Army of the Tennessee were directed to move east from Corinth,
Halleck was told (not asked) how the new supply line was to function, and
arrangements were made to reinforce Burnside, besieged at Knoxville, to the
northeast. In fact, Porter noted, "directions . . . were given for the taking of
vigorous and comprehensive steps in every direction throughout the new and
extensive command."[18]

To Sherman, out to the west, Grant had written, "Drop all work on Memphis and Charleston Railroad . . . and hurry eastward with all possible dispatch toward Bridgeport, till you meet further orders from me." Delivery of the message was not easy, and the man who brought it was even wilder with the excitement of war than either the general who sent it or the one who received it. According to Sherman, the messenger's name was Pike, and he came by canoe down the Tennessee, shooting rapids and portaging past rebel guerrillas who occasionally fired at him. Sherman thought him splendid, and liked his response—"Something *bold*"—to the question, "What do you want to do next?" (Later, at the end of the war, Pike told Sherman that he thought he would rather become an Indian than face domestication in the peacetime army in Oregon. Instead, he shot himself.) In November 1863, Sherman was as happy with Pike's message as he was with the man. He abandoned Halleck's orders to complete the boring and slow work of rebuilding a railroad from the west into Chattanooga and hurried his large army eastward to Bridgeport, just to the rear of Grant's position, ready to be called eastward to battle.[19]

Meanwhile, at Chattanooga, Grant was establishing an adequate supply route to the town. A flotilla of scows full of armed men was floated—unnoticed—past Confederate pickets, and the southern bank of the Tennessee, west of Chattanooga, was secured for the Union. General Grenville M. Dodge was put to work restoring railroad service from this point north to Nashville. With haste and skill, bridges were built and tracks laid in the mountainous terrain, and a dependable line of supply was opened. Food came in on Grant's cracker line, and so too did munitions for his attack on Bragg.[20]

Whether Chattanooga was to be regarded as a trap in which Grant was caught, or as a staging area for a splendid offensive, was a matter for the eye of the beholder. Sherman, when he arrived, was as usual a realist: " 'Why,' said I, 'General Grant, you are besieged;' and he said, 'It is too true.' " Grant was once more growing depressed. In two weeks, the vast stimulation that he had felt as he seized the challenge of rescuing the Union army at Chattanooga, and leading it on an offensive against Bragg, had receded. The change in mood recalled in some ways Grant's shift from elation when the war broke out to depression just days later, as he anxiously waited for a commission. Now, as he moved from elation to depression, John Rawlins again indulged his powerful urge to protect his friend Ulysses. "The necessity of my prescence here [is] made almost absolute," he wrote his fiancée, "by the free use of intoxicating liquors at Headquarters, which last night's developments showed me had reached to the General commanding. I am the only one here (his wife not being with him) who can stay it. . . ."[21]

Rawlins sent this letter, but wisely pocketed a second one, a hortatory summons to Grant "to immediately desist from further tasting of liquors." In it, Rawlins states that Grant would earn the "bitterest imprecations of an outraged and deceived people" if he got drunk. He likened Grant to Washington about to cross the Delaware, and declared firmly that "two more nights like the last will find you prostrated on a sick bed unfit for duty." Rawlins did not give the letter to Grant, but he did keep it; it was the written version of all the sermons he had imagined directing at this friend whom he took satisfaction in regarding as dependent on him. The friendship of the two was real, and it was important to both; while Rawlins may have exaggerated the risk to Grant—and the nation—of his drinking, there is no reason to think him an out-and-out liar. Once again, Grant did drink, and once again he sobered up and went back to the other activities of war.[22]

Grant's job was to marshal forces against Braxton Bragg. Thomas's Army of the Cumberland made the first offensive move and was in the center of the line at Chattanooga, and his men were resentful when Grant held them back, in reserve, while entrusting the fighting on the battle line to Sherman, deployed to the northeast, and Hooker, to the southwest. When the attack came, the Confederate response from Missionary Ridge was murderous. Howard observed Grant "looking steadily toward the troops just engaged and beyond. He was slowly smoking a cigar. General Thomas, using his glasses attentively, made no remark." Rawlins rushed up to urge that there be no retreat, "pressing his reasons into the general's seemingly inattentive ear. . . . When General Grant spoke at last, without turning to look at anybody, he said, 'Intrench them and send up support.' " Under the merciless guns of seemingly impregnable Confederate forces in the mountains of Missionary Ridge, all of Grant's troops were needed; it was not Sherman's ill-generaled army but Hooker's men who dramatically (if unnecessarily) took Lookout Mountain on November 24, 1863, and it was Thomas's Chickamauga veterans who, on November 25, in fiercely brave assaults broke the Confederate line. The enemy fled, but Grant, as at Shiloh, did not move in pursuit. It was a great victory, but it had not been accomplished according to Grant's design. Sherman's Army of the Tennessee had not won the fierce battle, and Grant never forgave Thomas for the fact that the men of his Army of the Cumberland, whom Grant held in some contempt, had carried the day. The Union had won—the engagement may even have been the turning point of the war—but the total destruction of Bragg's army was not accomplished and an immediate march southeast into Georgia did not follow. The splendid military victory was not, finally, a complete success. However, Grant's reputation soared.[23]

In his assessment of the battle, Grant gave credit to Confederate president Jefferson Davis for an assist to the Union victory. Davis had come to Missionary Ridge shortly before Grant arrived at Chattanooga to mediate a dispute between two proud commanders, Braxton Bragg and James Longstreet. Grant knew them both from Mexico—Longstreet, in fact, had been at his wedding and Grant had a high opinion of his friend, as he did of Bragg. Together, they would have been a formidable, perhaps invincible, team, but Davis

*Grant, at left, on Lookout Mountain, after the battle, 1863.* NATIONAL ARCHIVES

judged Bragg's temper so sharp as to make co-operation impossible. So the president sent Longstreet to attack Burnside at Knoxville primarily to keep him away from arguments with Bragg. Grant also suspected a second cause for Bragg's being compelled to fight at Chattanooga without Longstreet's forces. He reasoned that Davis, proud of his own skill as a military strategist, may have thought a double victory—at Knoxville and at Chattanooga—was worth trying for. Grant had a very low opinion of Davis's capacity as a military strategist and wrote caustically of the "several occasions during the war" when Davis "came to the relief of the Union army by means of his *superior military genius.*" Had Longstreet stayed with Bragg, wrote Grant, rubbing it in, the Union forces might have lost Chattanooga, and then, he conjectured—leaping rather far—the Confederates would have had no trouble taking Kentucky.[24]

With Chattanooga secured and Bragg routed, Grant immediately sent Sherman to relieve Burnside at Knoxville. That general's telegraph line across the Appalachians had been cut, and he was out of contact with Washington. As a result, Secretary of War Stanton and President Lincoln had one of their most apprehensive periods of the war as they worried about the fate of his forces. Grant too was concerned, though less so than the helpless men in Washington. Unlike them, he could do something about the situation. As

Grant nicely put it, everybody was in a panic about Burnside, except Burnside. Sherman arrived to find that Burnside had enough supplies to hold out for some time longer; with a line across the Tennessee he had been snagging scows loaded with food that were floated down the river past Confederate pickets by loyal Unionists living upstream.[25]

The battles in the eastern mountains won, Grant established his headquarters not at Chattanooga, but at Nashville. He did not set out to take Atlanta, nor did he turn southwest toward a favorite goal that was always to elude him, Mobile. Nashville would be comfortable for Julia, who had been staying in Louisville. She took the train there with Jesse in December and found herself in the same car with General William F. Smith and his wife, who offered her a ride from the station; they were sure, Julia recorded in her *Memoirs*, that the general would be too busy to meet her, but "as the cars slowed up, I heard: 'Is Mrs. Grant aboard?' and saw dear Ulys coming forward on the train greeting each one kindly as he came to meet us."[26]

While he was at Nashville, Grant visited Chattanooga and Knoxville on an inspection trip, and in his description of this trip we may sample a fine bit of the prose of his *Memoirs*, revealing not only his keen awareness of the grassroots sensibilities of the civilians during the war but a fine sense of himself:

> I found a great many people at home along that route, both in Tennessee and Kentucky, and, almost universally, intensely loyal. They would collect in little places where we would stop of evenings, to see me, generally hearing of my approach before we arrived. The people naturally expected to see the commanding general the oldest person in the party. I was then forty-one years of age, while my medical director was grey-haired and probably twelve or more years my senior. The crowds would generally swarm around him, and thus give me an opportunity of quietly dismounting and getting into the house. It also gave me an opportunity of hearing passing remarks from one spectator to another about their general. Those remarks were apt to be more complimentary to the cause than to the appearance of the supposed general, owing to his being muffled up, and also owing to the travel-worn condition we were all in after a hard day's ride. I was back in Nashville by the 13th of January, 1864.

Like Harry before Agincourt, he had his way of disguise. He had found a method of indulging both his capacity for watching people and his intense need for praise.[27]

One of the tragedies of Grant's rise to power was that he divorced himself from direct touch with the people. Something magnificently simple was lost when he could no longer stumble into the reality of an encounter like the one he had along a narrow stream near Chattanooga:

> The most friendly relations seemed to exist between the pickets of the two armies. At one place there was a tree which had fallen across the stream,

and which was used by the soldiers of both armies in drawing water for their camps. General Longstreet's corps was stationed there at the time, and wore blue of a little different shade from our uniform. Seeing a soldier in blue on this log, I rode up to him, commenced conversation with him, and asked whose corps he belonged to. He was very polite, and touching his hat to me, said he belonged to General Longstreet's corps. I asked him a few questions—but not with a view of gaining any particular information—all of which he answered, and I rode off.[28]

With such innocence slipping away, Grant spent the winter of 1864 in Nashville waiting out the efforts of his townsman Elihu Washburne to guide through Congress a bill reviving the rank of lieutenant general. There were now major generals by the score in the Union army, and there were lieutenant generals in the Confederate army, but the latter rank was not then to be found in the Army of the United States. Winfield Scott, the great patriarch of the War of 1812 and the Mexican War, had held the rank of lieutenant general by brevet, but only the Father of his Country had held it in full. There was a sense that a sacred symbol was being re-created as Congress revived the rank George Washington had held, with the expectation that it would be bestowed on Ulysses S. Grant. The son was to perfect the work of the father not only by rebuilding his fallen house but by making it everlasting, and Grant was conscious of the gravity of his responsibility. On March 4, 1864, he wrote to Sherman, "The bill reviving the grade of lieutenant-general in the army has become a law, and my name has been sent to the Senate." He continued, "I now receive orders to report at Washington immediately *in person*, which indicates either a confirmation or a likelihood of confirmation."[29]

# XII

# WASHINGTON AND THE WILDERNESS

It was the bloodiest swath ever cut through this globe.
— *Edwin M. Stanton to Oliver Wendell Holmes*

It is difficult to comprehend the qualities of a man who could be
moved by a narrative of individual suffering, and yet could sleep while
surrounded by the horrors of the battles of the Wilderness.
— *George S. Boutwell*

ULYSSES S. GRANT's entrance into Washington was the most successful in the history of American politics. It was done exactly right. He simply stopped by the White House, paid his call, and left everyone thinking it
would be perfectly natural for him to move right in. He achieved his immediate goal of confirming his military authority, but as he did so he established a
public personality that was unforgettable. Everyone had heard about him as
a military hero. His picture was on patriotic posters; people had read of his
battles and imagined him on battlefields in Tennessee and Mississippi. Now
they saw him at the seat of the civilian government, and he looked just fine.
He was consummately modest and quietly confident; the image held for the
rest of his political career—and beyond, into history.

The only strange thing about the trip to Washington was that Julia was not
with him. His reason for going to the capital was so extraordinary that he certainly had license to bring his wife with him. It would have been unlike him
to refuse to share such an event with Julia, but perhaps when they talked of
the trip the shyness of both argued against her going. For one thing, if Julia
went along it would look as if they were anticipating a triumphant occasion.
Formally, that was not a certainty, as the Senate had still not acted. It was a

primary law with Grant that he should never in the smallest way appear to be pressing for honors.

There were other considerations. Julia, who had visited St. Louis during the winter, had not been well—her eyes were troubling her. Besides, whatever the social activities of the Dents in St. Louis, there was still a layer of awkwardness in Julia Grant. Washington, despite the scorn heaped on it, had an intimidating aura. Together, they would have had to worry over protocol—who should call on whom and in what order. By himself, Grant could be a simple soldier arriving at a new post. So he went without Julia, but with his fourteen-year-old son, Fred. Grant had a wonderfully nice blind spot about his unendearing eldest child. Nothing he had ever done with his own father had been as satisfying as the experience which he, as a father, now shared with his son. And again, Grant's move was sound politically. The soldier who had made his way to the captaincy of the republic was coming simply—a father with his eldest boy—to its capital to claim his rank and responsibilities. He registered at Willard's Hotel simply as "U. S. Grant and son, Galena, Ill."[1]

Grant had never looked better. Theodore Lyman, a young Harvard man on General Meade's staff who was capable of sharply critical assessments, saw the general enter the dining room of the hotel: "He is rather under middle height, of a spare, strong build; light-brown hair, and short, light-brown beard. His eyes of a clear blue; forehead high; nose aquiline; jaw squarely set, but not sensual." Grant came in for dinner accompanied only by Fred. He would have gained nothing from a large retinue of prepossessing staff officers or subordinate field commanders; they might have overshadowed him, and they would have presented even greater protocol problems than a wife. Only two of his staff, Rawlins and Cyrus B. Comstock, had come to the city with him, and at dinner they fended for themselves. Grant and his son Fred were alone at the hotel. This was the right way for the conquest of the capital to begin. It was also an exceedingly effective way to give the lie to any theory that he could not trust himself to stay away from the bottle when in a challenging situation.[2]

Lyman wrote his wife that Grant, as he entered to dine, "was immediately bored by being cheered, and then shaken by the hand by οἱ πολλοί!" What the elegant New Englander took for boredom was an expression of a certain shyness, or that odd disengagement of his. Grant was already past the point where he could be surprised by such a reception in a public place—even a place like the Willard, in blasé Washington. When he had gone to St. Louis in January (on hearing that Fred was desperately ill with dysentery) he had registered at the hotel there simply as "U. S. Grant, Chattanooga"). The word of his arrival had spread quickly, and the news that Fred was out of danger was followed swiftly and incongruously by a series of invitations. The general was asked to put himself on display, and he had assumed his role in a ritual that was to be enacted repeatedly during the rest of his life. A hero was in town and the citizens of St. Louis made haste to claim him as their own. Like a politician at the height of his popularity, Grant was taken on a tour of Washington University and to the theater, and he was given a grand dinner by three hundred admiring noncombatant gentlemen of the city. After the toast to the general, the band burst into "Hail to the Chief." Grant rose, there were cheers, and he spoke—combining his distaste for speaking in public with a magnificent sense of how appealing unexpected brevity could be: "Gentlemen, in response, it will be impossible to do more than thank you."[3]

By March, neither a testimonial dinner nor any other advertisement was needed to bring the once obscure veteran of the Mexican War to the attention of Americans. When he got to Washington, Grant learned that even in a sophisticated hotel he could not move about without people applauding him. Everyone knew why he was in town; Grant was to be a lieutenant general. He would be subordinate only to the commander in chief, the president. Elihu Washburne's bill reviving the rank was signed into law by Abraham Lincoln on February 26, 1864. As expected, Lincoln promptly prepared a nomination for Ulysses S. Grant and submitted it to the Senate; the next day it was confirmed. The formal promotion was to take place on March 9 in the relative privacy of a meeting of the cabinet at the White House.

Grant had arrived in Washington on the eighth, a day on which the Lincolns gave one of their regular evening receptions. Leaving Fred at the hotel, he walked two blocks to the White House, went in with Rawlins and Comstock, and stood near the door. He was a bit late. The crowd, thicker than usual because of the rumor that he might be present, had largely moved into the East Room, but in the front hall, there was a "stir and buzz" when "it was whispered that General Grant had arrived." Gideon Welles, who disliked Grant on sight, thought there was a "hesitation"—an "awkwardness"—in the meeting of the "short, brown, dark-haired man," and the tall president. Others thought not. Lincoln went over to him: "Why, here is General Grant! Well, this is a great pleasure." They shook hands warmly. Then the president chatted in a friendly way. Grant pulled at his lapel and lowered his head shyly, but his eyes met Lincoln's. The two men were off to exactly the right start.[4]

It may not have all been entirely guileless. If Grant had been truly as modest and shy as most accounts of the event suggest, he could have arranged for General Halleck or Secretary of War Stanton to escort him to Lincoln's office quietly during the day. Perhaps because it afforded a kind of anonymity unavailable in an interview in another man's office, he risked the public reception—and the risk paid off. He was not ignored, and he was not gauche. Even Mary Lincoln was pleased. The new general seemed to her not to be a threat to her husband, and he brought no wife. Wives required either being put in their place, if they were attractive, or being made comfortable, if they were shy. Since Grant was alone, Mary Lincoln could skip wifery and pay

full attention to this new and now second most important man in the precari-
ously powerful world at the center of which she lived.

After the Lincolns' greeting, the crush around Grant was intense. Secretary of State William Henry Seward, the major-domo as usual, led Grant
onto the nation's favorite stage-set, the East Room, where decorum gave way
entirely and people began to shove and stare. They wanted to be able to see
and hail the new Caesar, and Grant took the dangerous course of allowing
himself to be talked into stepping up onto a couch. From this wobbly perch
(which could have been a very clumsy point of descent) the general was suddenly and splendidly visible. The assemblage cheered. To Gideon Welles it
was all a bit "rowdy and unseemly," but the Lincolns yielded to the hero,
telling Grant to join them when he could get away. After he had been seen
by all, he climbed down and began shaking hands and accepting congratulations. It was more than an hour before he got back to his hosts (and Welles
could be introduced to him).[5]

Welles found Grant "somewhat embarrassed" again at the formal awarding
of the commission the next morning. Wisely, he had written out ahead of
time his response to the president's charge to him, and what he quietly read
was both appropriate and eloquent: "With the aid of the noble armies that
have fought in so many fields for our common country, it will be my earnest
endeavor not to disappoint your expectations. I feel the full weight of the responsibilities now devolving on me. . . ."[6]

When Grant wanted relief from the realization that great responsibilities
were his (or—late in his life—from the awful sense that he no longer had any
responsibilities at all) he often took refuge in the romantic idea of rusticating
on the Pacific Coast. This appealed to him despite his earlier highly unromantic experiences there. Now, when he got back to Nashville, he told Julia
that his only regret at accepting the promotion to lieutenant general was that
it bound him to Washington; he had been hoping that after the war he might
be given a command on the Pacific slope. Gently, unpretentiously, the remark also served to notify her that they were now committed to a great career
and that its locus was the capital. They had to establish the family and to find
schools for the children in relation not to St. Louis, Galena, or the Pacific
Coast, but to Washington, D.C. The Grant family arrived in the capital on
March 23, 1864.[7]

Before this, before he had even left Nashville to receive his promotion, in
perhaps his most beautiful letter, Grant had written Sherman of the good
news that was coming his way. In the letter, discussing the arrangements of
command, he spoke of Sherman and McPherson as "*the men* to whom, above
all others, I feel indebted for whatever I have had of success." He then continued, "How far your advice and suggestions have been of assistance, you
know. How far your execution of whatever has been given you to do entitles
you to the reward I am receiving, you cannot know as well as I do." With
what for Grant was strong emotion, he added, "I feel all the gratitude this let-

ter would express. . . . ," and he closed, simply, "Your friend." Sherman
responded in kind; he called Grant "Washington's legitimate successor," and
observed, "Until you had won at Donelson, I confess I was cowed by the terrible array of anarchical elements that presented themselves at every point;
but that victory admitted the ray of light which I have followed ever since."
Grant had brought order to Sherman's martial world. Sherman credited
Grant with a "simple faith in success" that he likened to a "faith a Christian
has in his Saviour," a faith which he himself did not possess.[8]

But Sherman also had a warning for Grant. He stated that the promotion
was "an almost dangerous elevation," and urged that Grant "not stay in Washington" and instead "come out West." By west, he meant the Mississippi
Valley, "the seat of the coming empire," away from "the impoverished coast
of the Atlantic." Grant thought of taking this advice, but quickly recognized
that it was wrong. For better or worse, the political focuses of the war were
Washington and Richmond, where the respective presidents were. Jefferson
Davis embodied the rebellion. His capital, Richmond, was the inevitable
magnet of Union attention. However, this political reality did not become
confused in Grant's mind with the question of how that goal should be
reached. He understood that the obstacle to be overcome was not geography,
but the armies that defended the man in the city. "Lee with the capital of the
Confederacy, was the main end to which all were working." Not places, but
men had to be destroyed. Only when men had been killed would their
brothers grow discouraged and yield to the Union. Grant was to lead a campaign of annihilation, and to do so he had to stay east.[9]

Grant knew from his meeting with Lincoln and the members of the president's cabinet that he could not have his headquarters in the west or anywhere else where he could not maintain a basic relationship with Washington. But although he acknowledged the eastern theater as the one most
important in the eyes of those who managed the politics of war, he did not
want to be in the city itself. It was not so much that he wanted to avoid
Halleck (who could have been moved away, as he was after the war when
Grant did transfer his headquarters to Washington) but that he did not want
to have to discuss every move with Stanton and Lincoln. He knew that both
men were not without ideas as to how to fight the war. Both of his superiors
were able and eager to support him, but he could do the job they gave him
better if he was in the field rather than constricted at a desk in the capital city.
Therefore, with Julia established in a house in Georgetown, he set up his
command at Culpeper, fifty miles away in Virginia, at the headquarters of
General Meade and his Army of the Potomac.

Grant now placed Meade, the victor of Gettysburg, in precisely the position he, Grant, had found intolerable at Corinth. There, second in command, with his tent standing apart from Halleck's, he had had no real authority. But Meade chose not to see the awkwardness and observed that Grant's
"object in coming here to the headquarters of the Army of the Potomac is to

avoid Washington and its entourage." At his new headquarters, Grant prepared for the Wilderness campaign.[10]

Grant placed Sherman in charge of the armies of the west and gave General James B. McPherson the now proud command of the Army of the Tennessee. There were, however, no other major shifts of command or reorganizations of troops. Halleck stayed on as chief of staff in Washington, and Meade maintained nominal command of the Army of the Potomac. Indeed Grant made so few changes that he was in danger of repeating other men's earlier errors in the east and getting mired in the almost hopelessly huge task of moving the vast army. Some of his adroitness and decisiveness deserted him; perhaps he was handicapped by the absence of Sherman in his efforts to cut through the cant and overlapping of responsibilities that so befuddled the Union command south of Washington. And yet, if Grant sometimes moved sluggishly, he did move. He never for a moment considered stopping—never dared stop—until Lee was beaten. Lincoln never lost faith in him, and he never lost faith in himself. One day Grant was kidding his old West Point roommate Rufus Ingalls about a bumptious big puppy that Ingalls had brought into camp. When Grant asked if he expected to take the hound into Richmond, Ingalls replied that he thought so, since the breed was long-lived. Grant took the retort in stride. Perseverance would do the job.

Grant's strategy was to make sure more Southerners than Northerners were killed. It was a matter of simple arithmetic, further helped by the fact that the North had a larger population than the South. Demography was a science whose name he did not know, but he understood the importance to his purposes of demographic phenomena. And to take full advantage of them, Grant had to keep all his armies moving—had to keep the killing going—in all theaters of the war. There had been nothing but skirmishes in Virginia for five months, but now, with winter over, Grant discarded his predecessors' habit of building huge armies and then failing to commit them to sustained campaigns. He ordered several simultaneous actions: General Sherman was to move on Atlanta, General Banks on Mobile (even if by now Grant must have had a sardonic sense of how ill-fated this favorite venture was), General Franz Sigel on the Shenandoah Valley, and General Benjamin F. Butler on Richmond from the south side of the James. Everyone was to be in action. Banks, Sigel, and Butler did not get very far, but Sherman arrived at Atlanta in time to help get Lincoln re-elected in the fall of 1864, reached the sea in time to give Savannah to the president for a Christmas present, and then moved north through the Carolinas. And Grant moved through northern Virginia with Meade, who was told, "Wherever Lee goes, there you will go also."[11]

George Gordon Meade was a Philadelphia aristocrat who was frankly contemptuous of the common people, of whom Grant was one. The two men were in joint command of one of the greatest armies in history for a year and never got to know each other. It took Meade that whole year to come close to figuring Grant out. Seven years Grant's senior, Meade too was a West Point graduate and a veteran of the Mexican War. He was a bug-eyed, blunt man whose staff (with a Biddle and a Lyman, they were gentlemen all) called him Pa. They found him less ferocious than did reporters, who loathed him for scathingly attacking them when they lied. Meade was brave, resolute, and unlucky. For a year, he was almost never on his own. When Grant went off for a day, leaving Meade in command, Confederate raiders stole the army's beef cattle and the newspapers carried the story. Earlier, Meade had won at Gettysburg, but he had not captured Lee, and since then he had won no victories. He had not been made a lieutenant general; the victor of Vicksburg and Chattanooga had taken that prize.

As his relationship with Grant began, Meade, a devout patriot, offered to yield the command of the Army of the Potomac to Sherman if Grant needed the latter near at hand. Grant said no in words "complimentary" to Meade, who found his new commander a man "of more capacity and character than I had expected." (Grant, in fact, needed Sherman in the west, but he also may have wanted, as he did later as president, a respite from that brilliant hater of politics who so much liked to give others advice on avoiding anything political. Grant knew that everything was political.) Sherman stayed with his western armies and Meade with the Army of the Potomac. He would command it; Grant would push it. Together, the two might make it go. Although Meade was slow to notice and too loyal to publicly complain that his authority had been diminished, everyone knew that Grant was the boss; Meade would be credited only with the mistakes.[12]

A year later, after both Sherman and Sheridan had been promoted ahead of him, Meade realized that he had been killed with kindness. Grant needed a general he could ignore. He wanted an army that would obediently press the enemy, and Meade was never insubordinate. Grant, with affability and praise of both Meade's organization and his concept of strategy, got the support he needed. He gave Meade no true authority; perhaps wisely, he allowed Meade to make no major decisions. In his official statements Grant backed Meade, but he did not take a brotherly interest in Meade's troubles or help him deal with reporters. By the war's end Meade knew that Grant, who so often said he agreed with his ideas, had merely listened and ignored them: he had not taken Meade seriously as a lieutenant. Indeed, Grant used Meade up. The Philadelphian was shunted aside in favor of both the restless Sherman and the vulgar Sheridan. When, in April 1865, Grant went to Raleigh to countermand Sherman's surrender agreement with Johnston, Meade was "curious to see whether Grant . . . will smother him [Sherman] as he did me." (By then Meade was confessing to his wife, who had had a quicker eye for the situation than he, that she had been right all along: "I . . . now give up Grant.")[13]

Back in April 1864 the war was far from over and Meade was still persuaded of Grant's openness. He found him an "executive man, whose only place is in the field," an "affable" man who was "friendly and confidential" and "agreed so well with me." Grant, he wrote to his wife, "puts me in mind of old Taylor, and sometimes I fancy he models himself on old Zac." Meade said his elegant friends were disappointed in Grant, for he was "not a striking man, is very reticent, has never mixed with the world and has but little manner."[14]

Actually, Grant did have manner, but it was of his own making. His headquarters were always studiously simple, consisting of a few tents. He liked his food simple as well. An old friend from West Coast days, Robert MacFeely, was his commissary officer and casually supplied good meals. Charles A. Dana found him "a jolly, agreeable fellow, who never seems to be at work." The other men of his staff were an odd lot—Rawlins, God-driven, sharp-tongued (even toward Grant); Babcock, the perennial arranger of events and affairs; Wilson, flamboyant, flattering to women and attracted to men. None of their idiosyncrasies threatened Grant. These men were opinionated and verbose; they talked a lot—and Grant listened to all they said, taking it in without commenting. In June 1864, Grant's brother Orvil and five friends arrived to visit the "elephant"—the army—and chanced on the battle of Cold Harbor. One of these superfluous visitors, F. M. Pixley, wrote exuberantly of the physique of General Winfield Scott Hancock, the commander of the Second Corps, and frankly of his own "skedaddle," his headlong rush for the rear when the firing of the rebel cannon began. He also took careful note of his host, who may have been less than delighted that they had picked this day for a visit. His description of Grant is a classic:

> At the evening mess table I met Gen. Grant, and after a very hasty meal, I watched him for an hour as he sat by the camp fire. He is a small man, with a square resolute thinking face. He sat silent among the gentlemen of his staff, and my first impression was that he was moody, dull and unsocial. I afterwards found him pleasant, genial and agreeable. He keeps his own counsel, padlocks his mouth, while his countenance in battle or repose . . . indicates nothing—that is gives no expression of his feelings and no evidence of his intentions. He smokes almost constantly, and, as I then and have since observed, he has a habit of whitling with a small knife. He cuts a small stick into small chips, making nothing. It is evidently a mere occupation of the fingers, his mind all the while intent upon other things. Among men he is nowise noticeable. There is no glitter or parade about him. To me he seems but an earnest business man.

Is this the definitive photograph of Grant? Does it fix him forever as calm and earnest, sensibly keeping his fingers busy as he concentrates, with magnificent simplicity, on the great events of the campaign he is directing? Or is it the picture of a profoundly vacant creature whittling a piece of wood into

nothing and possessing only the "earnest" mind of the most banal of
bourgeois businessmen—unable to conceive of the terrible dimensions of the
martial enterprise in which he is engaged?[15]

What, indeed, was on Grant's mind? It is one of the wonders of the American democracy that in the midst of wars the nation carries on politics as
usual, with enthusiasm. If, as William E. Leuchtenberg has observed, we
carry military rhetoric into our civilian politics, we just as vigorously persist
in taking election talk to the battlefield. Early in June, after the battle of Cold
Harbor, men who had been fighting with sustained viciousness paused
under a truce to bury the dead. As a crowd of rebels and Yankees gathered
around a ten-man grave, one Southerner asked a Northerner who his man for
president was. "Old Abe, I guess," was the reply. "Dirty abolitionist," remarked the man from the South—and the Northerner knocked him out for
the insult. The campaigns of 1864, martial and electoral, were under way.[16]

That every boy has the chance to be president is the official fantasy of the
American republic. There is no evidence but every probability that the boy
Hiram Ulysses Grant indulged the dream. When he had reached forty, the
idea that he, a failed farmer and futureless clerk, could gain the first post of

*Grant and his staff at City Point. John A. Rawlins, without his beard, is at far
left; Ely S. Parker is second from right.* LIBRARY OF CONGRESS

the land was preposterous. Two years later, it was not preposterous at all. Grant grew up with the tradition that access to the White House was not limited to aristocrats like the founding fathers. The first president he could have remembered hearing much about was General Andrew Jackson—the first non-Olympian to gain office, and a westerner. The first election of Grant's young adulthood was that of General William Henry Harrison; Grant was familiar with the hokum of the "Tippecanoe and Tyler too" campaign, with its traveling log cabin, from which Harrison ascended to the White House. Such leaps were possible. And if Harrison could reach back to tidewater Virginia ancestors to give himself secure familial footings, then Ulysses Grant had Matthew Grant of Connecticut.

Ulysses Grant had always known he was someone to be taken into account, even if for forty years no one had done so. From the day he gained his colonelcy and began to confront the war and the officers and politicians who, with him, were waging it, he moved with great inner strength. He seems always, even in his struggles against rebuffs by General Halleck, to have had a sense that he was moving up. He was never vainglorious; his sense of self was too strong for that. It was logical that he should gain—and regain—com-

*Grant at City Point, 1864. Photograph by Timothy H. O'Sullivan.* LIBRARY OF CONGRESS

mand of the Army of the Tennessee, and then go on to command of the armies of the west and finally of all the Union armies. Why was it not just as logical that he should move on to the one equally important post the Republic had to offer—the presidency?

In 1864, the successful, shrewd Illinois lawyer who was in the White House wanted to stay there. No rustic, Abraham Lincoln was a well-established attorney who had put a good many assets between him and his axe. Except when campaigning, he no longer had to think about splitting rails. And in the midst of war, good forearms might not be enough if a competitor had greater strengths; both the rails and the Black Hawk War were, after all, pale in comparison to Vicksburg. Lincoln was far above letting his own political ambitions keep him from giving Grant the full military power and prestige needed to win the war and preserve the Union, but one Illinois politician could size up another. Lincoln wisely obtained from Grant a disclaimer of any hope of a hasty move to the White House. Grant, just as shrewdly, chose to wait his turn.

A person named by a national newspaper as a presidential possibility finds it hard not to savor the idea. Apparently it tastes good. When the victories at Vicksburg and Gettysburg did not lead to a swift defeat of the Confederacy, and the war dragged on, many thought that Lincoln should be replaced. He was attacked from the left by those who waved a radical banner, striped with support for the freedmen. At the other end of the spectrum were those who wanted a more conservative man than he. Still others simply wanted anyone else. Military heroes were highly desirable as political candidates; George Washington, after all, had set a tradition. They were glamorous, and they were thought not to be burdened with too many ideas. The nation had elected five generals to the White House, one of whom was Grant's old hero Zachary Taylor. Some believed the time had come for another. Grant was mentioned as a possibility at least as early as Chattanooga, in the fall of 1863. He immediately adopted the classic attitude toward such talk—the one calculated to make it come true. He denied having any interest in the post.

Rawlins did not discourage talk of his chief for the presidency, although in March 1864 he declared the promotion to lieutenant general to be the greater honor. "I cannot conceive how the use of General Grant's name in connection with Presidency can result in harm to him or our cause," he stated, going on to observe that "if there is a man in the country unambitious of such an honor, it is certainly he." Since there was probably no such man, Rawlins's statement was ambiguous rather than unequivocal; his concern was not whether Grant should speak to the point, but how. He advised against Grant's declaring publicly that he was not a candidate. No nomination had yet been offered by either party: "To write a declaration now, would place him much in the position of the old maid who had never had an offer declaring she would not marry; besides it would be construed by many as a modest way of getting his name before the country in connection with the office."[17]

Grant, claiming regret that talk of his nomination had become public, had sent such a disavowal to some Ohio Democrats on December 17, 1863: "Nothing likely to happen would pain me so much as to see my name used in connection with a political office. I am not a candidate for any office nor for favors from any party. Let us succeed in crushing the rebellion in the shortest possible time, and I will be content with whatever credit may then be given me, feeling assured that a just public will award all that is due." If Grant truly wanted *no* office *ever*, this was exactly the wrong thing to say. If he sensed that his time would come after he had won the war—and after Lincoln had had his turn—he could not have been a better prophet.[18]

Grant was scornful of politicians who misused the war as an approach to the White House. McClernand's hortatory statements had disgusted him. By dismissing McClernand as a commander, Grant had destroyed not only the man's military career but his political aspirations as well. George B. Mc-Clellan—who, of course, did end up a candidate in 1864, on the Democratic ticket—had long been thought to entertain hopes of the White House; so did John Charles Frémont, exiled in West Virginia, Nathaniel P. Banks, still in Louisiana, and Benjamin F. Butler, wherever he was. Grant was shrewd enough to realize that he still had a huge military job to do and was a long way from having sufficient authority to finish it. The source of the authority he needed was President Lincoln—the very man the others sought to replace. Lincoln was remarkably indulgent toward the political urges of his generals. He even indulged Hooker's delusions about the need for a dictator, saying he could live with such an idea if the general could produce a victory. (He had no need to worry.) But Grant, with a keen grasp of the realities of politics, understood that Lincoln would be uneasy with any man who appeared to be trying to unseat him.

Quickest to spot talk of the presidency are those who seek a ride to power on another's coattails. Jesse Grant had already grasped a well-stitched seam and was giving out statements that were highly embarrassing to the general. Exasperated, the son wrote to his father, "From your letter you seem to have taken an active feeling, to say the least, in this matter, that I would like to talk to you about. I could write, but do not want to do so. Why not come down here and see me?" Like Jesse, other people found the rumors fun to play with. Old acquaintances, startled by Grant's eminence but eager to share a bit in his glory, inserted themselves into the game of president-making. J. Russell Jones, formerly of Galena and now a Chicago businessman who was helping Grant invest his six-thousand-dollar salary, told of traveling to Washington, at the president's request, to have a conversation about Grant's desires. Jones claimed he read Lincoln a letter of disavowal by Grant, to which the president replied, "My son, you will never know how gratifying that is to me. No man knows, when that Presidential grub gets to gnawing at him, just how deep it will get until he has tried it; and I didn't know but what there was one gnawing at Grant." However shrewd the observation, its lan-

guage, particularly the "My son," is too folksy even for Lincoln, and it is possible that the two men never had the conversation Jones reported. If they did
indeed talk, it was probably at Jones's or Washburne's instigation rather than
the president's; to achieve longer-range goals they would have wanted to persuade Lincoln—and the nation—of Grant's modest disinterest in the presidency. Julia Grant was another politician who hewed carefully to this line. A
diarist interested in politics noted that when Mrs. Grant was asked in Washington, in May 1864, about "the White House and the next presidency . . .
[she] said most emphatically that her husband would not think for one moment of accepting a nomination." Grant needed Lincoln's support if he was
to have the authority he needed to win the war. When that was done there
would be time enough for rewards. First, he had to meet Lee in the Wilderness.[19]

> For the scheme that was nursed by the Culpepper hearth
>    With the slowly-smoked cigar—
> The scheme that smouldered through winter long
>    Now bursts into act—into war—
> The resolute scheme of a heart as calm
>    As the Cyclone's core.
>
>                    — Herman Melville

*Confederate dead at Spotsylvania, 1864.* LIBRARY OF CONGRESS

In May 1864 Ulysses Grant began a vast campaign that was a hideous disaster in every respect save one—it worked. He led his troops into the Wilderness and there produced a nightmare of inhumanity and inept military strategy that ranks with the worst such episodes in the history of warfare. One participant, for whom the picture was still clear thirty years later, wrote of men "piled upon each other in some places four layers deep, exhibiting every ghastly phase of mutilation. Below the mass of fast-decaying corpses, the convulsive twitching of limbs and the writhing of bodies showed that there were wounded men still alive and struggling to extricate themselves from their horrible entombment." A nation's adulation of the general deserves inspection in the light of this exercise in carnage. When they made Grant a hero, what was it they celebrated?[20]

The spring of 1864 was the worst of times. With ironic beauty, the season arrived in Virginia, and thousands of men marched and died. There was no fool to cry out as their Dmitri moved on to Richmond. The fools had been left at home, with the terrors of loneliness and poverty that other poor men like Grant had put behind them when they joined the army. While the *Northwestern Gazette*, in Galena, told its readers, in stately passages, of Grant on the road to Richmond, it told stories too of other local people. A crippled man—past providing for his family—got himself to the Mississippi, neatly put down his crutches, and let himself into the river. He had tried before; this time he succeeded in drowning himself. And another man, a farmer outside town, back from bleak fields after putting out poisoned corn for the birds, walked into his house and hanged himself. He had to tuck up his legs to prevent his feet from supporting him. No cause for the act was known.[21]

For Ulysses Grant it was a time of no such despair. On May 2, 1864, he wrote Julia, "The train that takes this letter will be the last going to Washington. Before you receive this I will be away from Culpepper and the Army will be in motion. I know the greatest anxiety is now felt in the North for the success of this move, and that anxiety will increase when it is once known that the Army is in motion. I feel well myself. Do not know that this is any criterion from which to judge results because I have never felt otherwise. I believe it has never been my misfortune to be in a place where I lost my presence of mind, unless indeed it has been when thrown in strange company, particularly of ladies." At no other time in his life was Grant as confident. Melville caught it:

> The May-weed springs; and comes a Man
>   And mounts our Signal Hill;
> A quiet Man, and plain in garb—
>   Briefly he looks his fill,
> Then drops his gray eye on the ground,
>   Like a loaded mortar he is still:
> Meekness and grimness meet in him—
>   The silent General.

There were no strangers in his quiet company as he and his men marched into the Wilderness.[22]

In Virginia the verdant richness of spring diminished the visibility in the densely wooded area through which Grant elected to drive 118,000 of his men. He had rejected a move around Lee's left flank (to the west) and chose instead to pass down the east not far from Fredericksburg—indeed, straight through the country around Chancellorsville where Hooker had faltered in his drive against Lee and Jackson just a year before:

> In glades they meet skull after skull
>     Where pine-cones lay—the rusted gun,
> Green shoes full of bones, the mouldering coat
>     And cuddled-up skeleton;
> And scores of such. Some start as in dreams,
>     And comrades lost bemoan:
> By the edge of those wilds Stonewall had charged—
>     But the Year and the Man were gone.

On the night of May 3 the first Union soldiers crossed the Rapidan River at Germanna Ford and Ely Ford and moved down narrow roads past dense walls of second-growth trees. Winfield Scott Hancock, leading the Second Corps, was "the *beau ideal* of a soldier," wrote a dazzled Californian, "blue-eyed, fair-haired Saxon, strong, well-proportioned and manly, broad-chested, full and compact." He was as aggressive as this description required him to be. In contrast was the diffident Gouverneur Kemble Warren, in command of the Fifth Corps, whose hesitancy troubled both Meade and Grant. John Sedgwick, steady (and soon to die), was at the head of the Sixth Corps. The Ninth Corps, the last to move into battle, was under Ambrose E. Burnside, whose finesse at Knoxville was remembered and admired by Grant. Burnside must have had his own memories. He led his men not far west of the town of Fredericksburg, which, as a commanding general long before Grant, he had failed to take in bloody assault in December 1862. Now, following commands, he would try again to get to Richmond.[23]

Had Grant used fewer men on the march, and started a few hours earlier, he might have made it through the Wilderness before Lee could attack. The first delay came on May 4 when two corps, halfway down the road, were halted, and moved to the side, so that the supply train could move up with them. Then, once below the Rapidan, this vast assemblage of men was highly vulnerable to the attack of Lee's smaller quicker army of 64,000. Some of the Confederate soldiers knew their way around in this wood, and all of Lee's corps were ably commanded. In his Army of Northern Virginia the First Corps was under Longstreet, the Second under Richard S. Ewell, and the Third under A. P. Hill. The assaults of the two huge armies as each sought the other out in the maddening forest on May 5, 1864, can be plotted and described, but in truth there was no sense to the battle of the Wilderness.

*Bethesda Church, June 1864. Grant, his generals, and his men in the Wilderness campaign. Grant sits, legs crossed, in front of the two trees.* LIBRARY OF CONGRESS

Grant's supply plans, and his crossing of the river, had been orderly, but when the fighting began it was a blind and murderous stumbling of men unable to see those they smashed through the woods to kill.

If either attack made any sense it was Lee's, and yet his celebrated cavalry let him down. J. E. B. Stuart was colorfully and irrelevantly engaged along the James River, far south of the battle. He had not scouted Grant's army for Lee, and Lee began his major attack on May 5 without knowing how huge the forces were that he sought to destroy. He did not concentrate sufficient troops to annihilate the Second and Fifth corps. But it was not the opposing generals that gave the battle its terrible form in that screaming, shrieking day; it was the lay of the land. Masses of bodies were absorbed into the terrain of tangled roots, mud, and splintered trees. In mercilessly close firing, men were sent in relentlessly to stumble past the dying who had fallen before them.

To say that men replaced men is to suggest more order than existed. There was no front. There was no direction. As the writers of the bland text of *The West Point Atlas of American Wars* put it: "Attackers could only crash noisily and blindly forward through the underbrush, perfect targets for the concealed defenders. In attack or retreat, formations could rarely be maintained. In this near-jungle, the Confederates had the advantage of being, on the whole, better woodsmen than their opponents and of being far more familiar with the terrain. Federal commanders were forced to rely upon maps, which soon proved thoroughly unreliable." Both armies fought savagely, bravely, and futilely throughout May 5 and then again on May 6, by which time all four corps of the Union army were in action. On neither night did Grant yield to any thought of getting his men out and away from the nightmare, despite the screams of soldiers dying slowly in fires that moved through the woods faster than they could crawl.[24]

Grant's campaign in the Wilderness was no more successful than Hooker's had been. Lee's defenses held; his counterattacks were fierce and took a terrible toll of the Union forces. The only difference between the battles of Chancellorsville and of the Wilderness—fought not fifteen miles apart, and with many in the second who had grim memories of the first—was that after Chancellorsville, Hooker cut his losses and, defeated, retreated back across the Rapidan. Grant ignored the losses and—if not victorious, at least undaunted—kept going. On the night of May 7, Grant studied his position and ordered his mauled armies of exhausted men to move. On May 8 they broke out of the ruined wood—only to begin the long, fierce, useless battle of Spotsylvania.[25]

Because fire in the woods prevented him from obeying Lee's orders that he camp along a road, the Confederate general Richard H. Anderson moved to Spotsylvania Court House on the evening of May 8, ahead of the Yankees. The next day, James Harrison Wilson took the crossroads town briefly. But Wilson, unsupported, had to yield it again, and Grant therefore lost his chance to be nearer to Richmond than Lee was. Instead of racing to the capital, Grant would again have to fight the Confederate defenders despite the dismaying terrain, terrain which he simply chose to ignore. One of Meade's staff men wrote that late in one day of heavy fighting, at about "half-past four what should Generals Grant and Meade take it in their heads to do but, with their whole Staffs, ride into a piece of woods close to the front while heavy skirmishing was going on. We could not see a thing except our own men lying down; but there we sat on horseback while the bullets here and there came clicking among trunks and branches and an occasional shell added its discordant tone. I almost fancy Grant felt mad that things did not move faster, and so thought he would go sit in an uncomfortable place. General Meade, not to be bluffed, stayed longer than Grant, but he told me to show the general the way to the new Headquarters. Oh! with what intense politeness did I show the shortest road!"[26]

At dawn on May 10, 1864, the full battle began. Each army had built breastworks to withstand assaults from the other. Lee's forces were in a rough arc, from which there was a protrusion in the shape of a mule's shoe. This exposed area seemed the logical place for the Union attack, and it was here that Emory Upton led his famous brave and futile charge. His men reached the rebel lines and bayoneted their way across them before being killed. They had broken in on Lee, but no other officer had his forces in place to follow them. Two days later, Union soldiers again pressed desperately against excellent fortifications, at a point known with grim accuracy as the Bloody Angle, until the dead and dying lay heaped in piles that survivors could never forget. Only at midnight was that horrible day over—and still with no resolution. And so it was for six more days as Grant, in assault after assault, tried to break Lee's lines. He could not do so. He was beaten at Spotsylvania.

"The ninth day of battle is now closing," Ulysses wrote Julia on May 13. He was near Spotsylvania Court House, and he saw "victory so far on our side. But"—he added—"the enemy are fighting with great desperation. . . . We have lost many thousands of men killed and wounded and the enemy have no doubt lost more." Lieutenant Oliver Wendell Holmes, Jr., speaking of the casualties between May 5 and May 14, wrote in a letter to his parents about how "immense the butchers bill has been." Back in Washington, civilians were watching the general. Walt Whitman wrote his mother, "I steadily believe that Grant is going to succeed, and that we shall have Richmond—but oh what a price to pay for it." Many of the Union wounded, Grant told Julia in the May 13 letter, were "but slightly hurt," but they would not be fit for further duty. Reinforcements would come in shortly, however, and buoy his men's spirits and discourage the enemy. Turning to himself he wrote, "I am very well and full of hope. I see from the papers that the country is also hopeful." After mentioning family matters, he continued: "The world has never seen so bloody and so protracted a battle as the one being fought and I hope never will again." He told her that the Confederates had been "whipped" the day before and that their situation was "desperate beyond anything heretofore known." If they lost this battle, "they lose their cause." They had, he acknowledged, "fought for it with . . . gallantry. . . ." Grant was trying to talk a victory into being, but a Confederate soldier had written in his diary the night before, "Grant was foiled in the purpose he had in mind and sullenly kept up his artillery firing."[27]

The failure to break through Lee's lines at Spotsylvania or later at Cold Harbor made it certain that Grant would have to wait four more years to be elected president. James Ford Rhodes, writing of Grant as he became lieutenant general and moved on Virginia, said flatly, "He was now by all odds the most popular man in the United States." George Templeton Strong wrote in his diary in July that Grant was "*the* great man of the day—perhaps of the age." Abraham Lincoln gained similar accolades only as the martyred hero following his assassination. Very much alive in the spring of 1864, he was not unaware of the adulation of Grant that he, as president, had done much to stimulate. On June 4, the night before the National Union convention was to open in Baltimore, a mass meeting was held in Union Square in New York "to give expression to their gratitude to General Grant, for his signal services in conducting the national armies to victory. . . ." (This, ironically, was the day after the battle of Cold Harbor.) Lincoln, declining an invitation to attend, reminded the gentlemen arranging the salute that Grant had a job at present and would need no other for some time: "My previous high estimate of Gen. Grant has been maintained and heightened by what has occurred in the remarkable campaign he is now conducting; while the magnitude and difficulty of the task before him does not prove less than I expected." It was elegant prose written to bank a fire; Lincoln gave assurance that he too would support Grant—as a soldier fighting under his commander in chief. There is no suggestion that Lincoln suspected Grant of political intrigue, but the president was taking no chances on any sudden wind that might blow south out of New York and reach Baltimore.[28]

Similarly, there is no evidence that Grant thought of stealing the nomination from Lincoln with a blitzkrieg capture of the Confederate capital. And yet, twenty years later, Grant was still imagining the exhilaration of such a rush on Richmond. Writing of Spotsylvania, he remembered the fluke by which Anderson had secured a position that he might otherwise have gained: "By this accident Lee got possession of Spottsylvania. It is impossible to say now what would have been the result if Lee's orders had been obeyed as given; but it is certain that we would have been in Spottsylvania and between him and his capital. My belief is that there would have been a race between the two armies to see which would reach Richmond first and the [Union] Army of the Potomac would have had the shorter line." Legend has it that Lincoln himself said, "If Grant takes Richmond let him have the nomination." And a political convention is a strange box of fireworks, full of sparklers that sometimes ignite runaway fires. It is not impossible that if someone had walked into the convention hall in Baltimore, gotten the attention of the delegates, and announced that Grant had taken Richmond, Ulysses S. Grant would have been the seventeenth rather than the eighteenth president of the United States.[29]

Lee protected Lincoln, permitting Grant no sensational victory. Instead, dead bodies lay in a no man's land between the stalemated armies when the National Union convention renominated Lincoln. The nomination was acclaimed unanimous, but it was made so only after the Missouri delegation changed its vote, having initially cast its twenty-two votes for Grant.[30]

In Virginia, at Cold Harbor, on June 3, 1864, Grant seemed almost not to have been paying attention. East of Richmond and south of Spotsylvania ran a Confederate line through which no passage could be hammered except perhaps at Cold Harbor. There, Grant might assault Lee directly and destroy him. Grant ordered his armies to attack, but when the delays were over and the battle began, at dawn on June 3, 1864, he was not front and center. Meade was. "I had immediate and entire command on the field all day," Meade reported to his wife. The day was a morning of fierce futile charges that resulted in slaughter. Meade went on, "the Lieutenant-General honoring the field with his presence only about one hour in the middle of the day." At one-thirty, after riding to the front to see what was going on and conferring with the corps commanders, but not with Meade, Grant noted that they "were not sanguine of success," and ordered Meade—in a note—to put a stop to the dreadful business. Men in the front lines had to give up the idea that their great effort would carry them through the enemy's defenses—some had reached the top only to be driven back—and, instead, had to dig trenches under the fire of sharpshooters.[31]

Everything had gone wrong. A Confederate attack on June 1 had been repelled, but the Union commanders had failed to follow through by counterattacking immediately. Incorrect orders written by Grant had sent General William F. Smith's army off in the wrong direction, to New Castle instead of Cold Harbor, giving Lee time to fortify skillfully. The Union army's frontal assault had first been ordered for June 2, but as the ponderous armies lurched about, it was delayed until the third. Neither Meade nor Grant had surveyed the enemy's defensive positions or provided artillery support. At the end of the day, official reports suggested that the battle had been a stalemate, with losses about even on both sides. But in fact, the reporting Union generals were covering up carnage of fearful dimensions inflicted by the Confederates on Union soldiers moving straight into their guns. When the first assault had been stopped, another had been ordered. At least one corps commander had been insubordinate, and his men did not move. Those who did had walked straight into bullets. In Bruce Catton's judgment, the Union suffered an "unvarnished repulse." Only at Fredericksburg had Lee inflicted such terrible losses, with so little cost to his own men.[32]

Years later Grant stated that he regretted the assault on June 3 at Cold Harbor, but this admission does not explain away his and Lee's inexcusable behavior in the hours and days following the battle. Union soldiers, who had charged, lay where they had fallen wounded, moaning in the blistering sun. Their brothers watched their torment, unable to retrieve them because of Confederate sharpshooters. Lee, hoping to force Grant to admit a defeat, refused to call off the sharpshooters. After two days, on June 5, Grant sent one of Meade's aides across the lines with a letter suggesting that firing cease while litter bearers went out on the field. Lee insisted that "a flag of truce be sent, as is customary." The next morning, June 6, Grant wrote Lee that at noon men with stretchers and white flags would go out for the wounded, but again Lee insisted that he could "accede with propriety" only to a request

*Grant and Nellie, from a Civil War patriotic album.*
BETSY D. KONTOLEON

made under a flag of truce: "I have directed that any parties you may send out be turned back." Grant, that afternoon, reminded Lee that "wounded men are now suffering from want of attention" and agreed to a formal two-hour truce. Lee replied that it was too late to accomplish this by daylight, but agreed to a break between 8:00 P.M. and 10:00 P.M. that evening. The letter was received by Grant after 10:45 P.M., and it was not until late the next morning, June 7, that Grant wrote and informed Lee of the missed opportunity. Lee then proposed, and Grant accepted, a second truce, which took place that evening. For days, as commanders stupidly corresponded, untended men had lain in agony dying. While they lay there, Grant sat down and wrote the most affectionate of fatherly letters to Nellie. She would soon be nine, and he told her he would get her a buggy for the family pony. He simply shut off the horrors for which he was responsible and retreated into a fantasy of comfortable domesticity.[33]

As Grant understood the war, Cold Harbor was not a defeat. It simply did not contribute to his victory. He did not apologize for it or lie about it in his official report after the war was over; he simply said that it was the one engagement between the Rapidan and the James in which he did not inflict on the enemy losses equal to his own. (The only other such loss in a major battle had been on May 22, 1863, outside Vicksburg.) With the North's greater population, equal losses meant, ultimately, "the complete overthrow of the rebellion." The men who died at Cold Harbor could be replaced. Grant needed only to move on and engage the enemy elsewhere. Cold Harbor, indeed, could prove helpful in this maneuver. The nasty trench fighting that kept up there until June 12 covered the vast movement of forces that Grant ordered as he at last stopped trying to pound his way through Lee's lines and slipped a hundred thousand men east and south, in order to get below his opponent. His aim was to come up under Lee to take Richmond.[34]

Back at Cold Harbor, on a hot June day, a Union staff officer wrote that "after extraordinary delays an armistice was concluded [on June 7]. . . . It was very acceptable for burying the dead; but the wounded were mostly dead too, by this time, having been there since the 3d."[35]

# XIII

## PETERSBURG

*. . . the days we played soldier.*
*— William Tecumseh Sherman*

*All wars are boyish . . .*
*— Herman Melville*

A BRISK YOUNG aide to General Meade rode into headquarters on the night of June 16, 1864, "and found General Grant just going to bed. He sat on the edge of his cot, in shirt and drawers, and listened to my report." Theodore Lyman told Grant that Meade was sending five thousand fresh troops in by moonlight to assist in General Smith's attack on Petersburg. Grant "smiled, like one who had done a clever thing." He had, and the moment of celebration was uncharacteristic both in the breach of bedroom privacy and in the display of self-approval. Grant was buoyed by the realization that his engineers had built a magnificent pontoon bridge, 2,100 feet long, across the James and tens of thousands of men had marched over it "to attack Lee in his rear before he is ready for us." He assumed, climbing into his bed, that he was about to surprise Lee.[1]

Grant had abandoned the terrible and unproductive frontal assaults of Spotsylvania and Cold Harbor to find a new way to get at the enemy. Risking an attack by Lee on his exposed flank, he moved his immense army south, to cross the James River. General Butler had already crossed the river, upstream from the Charles City Court House crossing Grant was planning. Butler engaged General Beauregard on June 9, but failed to dislodge him.

Meanwhile, Grant, leaving one corps facing westward toward Richmond, passed southeast to Butler's rear and accomplished the vast maneuver of crossing the James between June 14 and June 16. The next step was to be a lightning-swift attack on June 16 on the small railroad town of Petersburg, twenty-three miles south of Richmond. The attack was made, but not with brilliant quickness, and once more the Confederate defenses were too strong for him; once again there were "slopes covered with dead and wounded." For the Confederates, Beauregard was adroit, and on the Union side, Smith was timid, but the overarching reason for the failure was the hugeness of the Union army. It could not be moved into battle with the precision with which it had been brought to and over the bridge. And the army's size was matched by the ponderousness of its command structure. Grant did not take Meade into his confidence, and so, all down the line, there was lack of direction. The field commanders did not know what their men were to do. They did not take Petersburg, and as a result Grant's gigantic army was destined to stand in place before that town not only through the summer, but all fall and winter as well.[2]

Grant is famous for not stopping once in motion, and yet he conducted the final nine months of the war immobilized. He stood in place and directed a siege during a war that was being fought over the thousand-mile sweep of a vast segment of a continent. He established his headquarters at City Point, Virginia. This tiny landing town on the south side of the James became in effect the military capital of the United States. Emissaries visited him there, and eventually so did his president. From his tent, later from a small cabin, Grant directed not only the siege of Petersburg, ten miles away, but the whole of the war spread over the entire reach of the Confederacy. As long as Grant kept up the pressure on Petersburg, Lee could do very little without giving up Richmond. Grant stood still so that others—Sherman and Sheridan and, it was to be hoped, Banks and Thomas—could move. But thoughts of moving were not confined to the Union. Despite the constraints, Lee's men broke loose and undertook enterprises of great danger to their opponent.

On July 13, 1864, General Jubal A. Early's skirmishers struck at towns around Washington. The alarm caused the Lincolns to move back to the White House from their summer lodgings at the Soldiers' Home, on the outskirts of town, and Grant sent General Horatio G. Wright with two divisions from City Point to reinforce the capital. Grant also had rebel deserters carefully questioned, and reported to Halleck on July 14 that he "could locate every Division & Longstreet's & Hill's Corps and Beauregard's forces," and was certain that no large force had been moved north to accompany Early on an invasion. And so the Lincolns moved back to their cooler quarters at the Soldiers' Home.[3]

People in the North were on edge not only because of Early's threat to Washington, but also because of the grim casualty figures that had emerged after Grant's Wilderness campaign. Lincoln, as he called for 500,000 volun-

*Ulysses, Jesse, and Julia, City Point, 1864–65.* LIBRARY OF CONGRESS

teers to replace those killed and those leaving the service, showed his awareness of public opinion in the contradictory advice which he offered Grant,
telling him to make a strong attack on Petersburg, but to do so with as little
loss of life as possible. Grant did not reply directly to the president on this
point, but he did volunteer emphatic objections to some of the efforts to
increase the number of men available for war. For one thing, he did not want
the Massachusetts governor, John A. Andrew, to send agents into the South
to recruit black volunteers to fill the man-power quotas of Massachusetts.
Negro men coming across Federal lines, he contended, "are rightfully recruits to the United States Service and should not go to benefit any particular

state." For another, it was a waste of money to pay bounties to recruit men already available free to the army. Even sillier, and dangerous as well, was the practice of recruiting Southern prisoners of war. Grant protested that "each one enlisted robs us of a soldier"—a Union man not returnable through a prisoner exchange—"and adds money to the enemy with a bounty paid in loyal money." He anticipated immediate desertion of any troops obtained in this manner. With such firm statements, Grant was taking strong political positions—against as powerful a war governor as Andrew—and demonstrating no reluctance to speak his voice. He softened the letter's force only by sending it to Stanton rather than directly to Lincoln, as he had originally intended.[4]

Grant was disingenuous in his objection that every rebel prisoner recruited meant a Union soldier was doomed to stay a prisoner in the South, for actually he wanted no prisoner exchanges. The Confederacy's supply of replacement troops was smaller than the Union's; prisoner exchanges would give the Confederates fresh troops just as their stock of men was giving out. Grant knew now that he could win as long as policies were pursued that resulted in using up the South's men. His own supply, when exhausted, could be replenished; there were more men in the North.

A good many Northern men were in Georgia in July 1864. On the twenty-second, Grant's old Army of the Tennessee fought at Decatur, on the outskirts of Atlanta. The troops performed well, and General John Bell Hood, who had replaced Joseph E. Johnston in command in Georgia a week earlier, suffered losses—killed and wounded—of ten thousand men. The Federal losses were somewhat less than four thousand, but one of those killed was the stalwart, popular commander of the Army of the Tennessee, James B. McPherson, whom Grant had coupled with Sherman as one of the two men "above all others" whose "energy, skill, and the harmonious putting forth of that energy and skill" had contributed most to his own success. Now death had destroyed harmony, and Sherman, creating dissension, passed up the swarthy, aggressive Illinois politician-soldier John A. Logan and replaced McPherson with a West Pointer, O. O. Howard. Grant sustained Sherman in this action, and urged Stanton to do so as well: "He [Sherman] has conducted his Campaigns with great skill and success and I would therefore confirm all his recommendations [for promotion]. . . . No one can tell as well as one immediately in command. The disposition thus should be made of the material on hand." "Material on hand" was an odd term for men alongside whom he had fought, but Grant was giving Sherman the support he needed.[5]

Siege was the order of the summer. Atlanta lay before Sherman's forces, and Petersburg, the little Virginia town astride the last railroad into Richmond (from the south and west), had stood barricaded against Grant's huge armies for six hot long weeks, when on July 30 a brilliant but bungled attempt was made to break through its defenses. For a month, a group of Pennsylvania coal miners had been digging a tunnel to a point under a major fort on the Confederate line. When experts said a tunnel longer than four hundred feet could not be ventilated without vertical air shafts, they improvised an air supply, using a wooden duct and a fire that created a draft to suck in fresh oxygen; when proper tools were not supplied, they made their own. Hearing the voices of rebels eighteen feet above their heads as they placed eight thousand pounds of black powder in the tunnel's end, these miners knew they had done their job well. While they dug, another group of workingmen had been preparing to do theirs. It was a new one for them; the soldiers being rehearsed for a quick race through the pass which the explosion would open were black. Although they had fought at Fort Wagner and Fort Pillow, black soldiers were still scorned by most Union officers. Now Burnside, more sympathetic than most generals to his black soldiers, had ordered that his black division, under the command of a white brigadier general, Edward Ferrero, was to rush through the pass, far behind Confederate lines, and open the way for the Union army to enter Petersburg along the Jerusalem Plank Road.[6]

The black men were not to get their chance. Both Meade and Grant were skeptical of the whole tunneling operation, and they anticipated that if the assault failed and it looked as if black men had been deliberately chosen to die futilely, the fury of the abolitionists back home would descend on them. Grant explained this at the later inquiry: "If we put the colored troops in front and [the attack] should prove a failure . . . it would then be said, and very properly that we were shoving these people ahead to get killed because we did not care anything for them." The order of assault was changed; a different and unrehearsed division of soldiers, under General James H. Ledlie, was chosen to go first, while huge contingents were put on the alert to follow.[7]

At headquarters Grant was up and waiting, but when 3:30 A.M., the agreed-on moment of detonation, passed without a sound, he grew restive. At the mouth of the tunnel, the miners and their co-operative lieutenant colonel, Henry Pleasants, sent two very courageous men, Harry Reese and Jacob Douty, into the tunnel to locate the problem: denied a suitable fuse line, the miners had made their own and it had failed at a joint. So the two lit the line on the other side of the joint, and then managed to race back to the entrance as the flame traveled to the black powder. At 4:44 there was perhaps the greatest man-made explosion that had ever occurred: "Without form or shape, full of red flames and carried on a bed of lightning flashes, it mounted to heaven with a detonation of thunder spread out like an immense mushroom whose stem seemed to be of fire and its head of smoke."[8]

Not the least terrified were Ledlie's men, who were expected to charge toward the explosion. The earth was falling back to form a huge crater, sixty by two hundred feet in girth and from ten to thirty feet deep, where the fort had been. Ten minutes were lost as officers forced men to stop fleeing and advance instead. The only obstacle before them was of their own making;

incredibly, Burnside had not arranged for the removal during the night of the tangled wire before his lines, and now, in this moment of intense stress, his troops had to cut their way through it. As they reached the crater Ledlie was not with them; he was hiding and drinking. The leaderless men, instead of racing through the opening and fanning out, huddled within the crater, with some Confederates who had miraculously survived the explosion. They were totally vulnerable.

At first, nearby Confederate soldiers had fled, leaving the open way that Pleasants had anticipated, but soon Beauregard's men, despite a fierce Union artillery barrage, rushed back to the lip of the crater and began sending murderous fire down on the Union soldiers. The black troops had now been sent in, but with no chance of successfully executing the invasion techniques in which they had been drilled. As they tried to move up the sides of the crater, they too were cut down. Confederate soldiers later told without apology of having ferociously reacted not only to what seemed a cheating kind of warfare, represented by the tunnel-bomb, but even more to the insult of being attacked in their Virginia by uniformed Nat Turners. Gunstocks and bayonets bore nappy hair in clogged blood from the heads of the Union assailants, grimly but vainly attacking, and sometimes surrendering.[9]

Grant ordered no further assaults through the crater and sent word that Burnside should pull back those who could still escape. In time, there was a formal inquiry into what Grant called "the saddest affair I have witnessed in this war." Ledlie was cashiered, in disgrace, but when Meade (like Grant, scarcely free of all blame) called for a court-martial for Burnside, Grant blocked it and allowed the general to retire comfortably from the army. Grant was nothing if not frank about the results of this "stupendous failure." To Halleck, he wrote, "The loss in the disaster of Saturday last foots up [to] about 3500 [,] of whom 450 were killed and 2000 wounded. . . . Such opportunity for carrying fortifications I have never seen and do not expect to have." The enemy had been taken "completely by surprise" and "150 yards off, with clear ground intervening, was the crest of the ridge leading into town. . . ." The Confederates had lost only one for every four Union men killed, and they had held their defense lines. Grant told Halleck that Petersburg could have been taken, but did not say who should be blamed for what had happened instead.[10]

Grant had been busy on the day of the explosion getting ready for a conference the next day, July 31, 1864, with President Lincoln. The timing of the meeting must have seemed as disastrous as the explosion had been. But Grant was exceedingly lucky; Lincoln could have seen the episode as evidence of incompetence lunatic enough to put McClellan and all of Grant's other predecessors in Virginia to shame. Instead, the president chose to see Grant as his best bet for ensuring that the war not end in crazy craters. Lincoln was as sure as Grant that Grant was the right man. He saw that the only chance for the Union and for success in the November election was to push the electorate to a commitment to victory at any cost. "I cannot but feel the weal or woe of this great nation will be decided in the approaching canvass" was how he expressed it on August 19. Under pressure to step aside in favor of a candidate who could either win the war or end it, Lincoln could not afford to live patiently through another shift in commanders. He was as firmly desperate to take the crater fiasco in stride—and to keep pushing—as Grant was. Both saw clearly that the general was now to be on the offensive not merely in eastern Virginia but wherever the war was. Their attention extended past battlefields in Georgia and the western theater and into the streets of northern cities, where new protests against the draft were feared, and circled back to the battlefields. Grant and Lincoln both knew that their offensive had to be won. Both saw victory and survival of the Union as synonymous. Grant realized that Lincoln might be defeated for the presidency; if Lincoln went down before a trimmer, all would be lost for both men.[11]

The day after his talk with Lincoln, letting no one think he wasted time on regrets over the failure to take Petersburg, Grant issued one of his most famous offensive orders. Confederate cavalry riding up out of the Shenandoah Valley had burned Chambersburg, Pennsylvania, on July 30 and reminded the North that the town lay along the route Lee had taken to Gettysburg a year earlier. To retaliate, Grant sent the young man whom, after Sherman, and since McPherson's death, he most respected as a soldier, thirty-three-year-old Philip H. Sheridan. Grant told Halleck, "I want Sheridan put in command of all the troops in the field, with instructions to put himself south of the enemy and follow him to the death. Wherever the enemy goes let our troops go also." Lincoln, as savage as Grant—yes the enemy should be followed "to the *death*"—wired from Washington, "This I think is exactly right. . . ." But, he added, "It will neither be done nor attempted unless you watch it every day, and hour, and force it." To start the forcing, Grant took a steamer to Washington and, bypassing the War Department, went to the railroad station to talk to the new commander of the Army of the Shenandoah. Sheridan took to his new command with the ardor of a young lover as he was told by Grant: "Carry off stock . . . and negroes, so as to prevent further planting. If the war is to last another year, we want the Shenandoah Valley to remain a barren waste." Sheridan's was to be warfare on people and property—psychological warfare at its most demoralizing and successful. Furthermore, the action west of Richmond was linked to the whole of Grant's campaign in Virginia: "Give the enemy no rest, and if it is possible to follow to the Virginia Central road, follow that far." This railroad came into Petersburg from the west; Lee was to be ringed round.[12]

To reach out to a still larger ring, Grant on August 7 sent Sherman, outside Atlanta, a message that was a laying on of hands: "Your progress instead of appearing slow has received the universal commendation of all loyal citizens as well as of the President. . . ." To give Sherman a sense of a whole, he quoted his charge to Sheridan "to push the enemy to the very death" and (with considerable exaggeration) sought to encourage Sherman by telling him that he himself had come north from City Point only after "having put all our forces in motion against the enemy."[13]

Grant now saw the war with frightening clarity. Sherman should keep every one of the enemy "constantly employed" in the field: "Every day exhausts the enemy at least a regiment without any further population to draw from to replace it, exclusive of losses in battle." To maintain this pressure on the enemy, Sherman's men would have to be used to the best advantage: "I would suggest the employment of as many negroes as you can as teamsters, Company Cooks, Pioneers etc. to keep the enlisted men in the ranks, and the shipment to Nashville of every unemployed negro, big and little." He wanted the fighting men to have full support, and he wanted them ready to move without the impediment of refugees, white and, in great numbers, black—all victims in the South of this awful war to end slavery.[14]

And his deadly demand for men extended further. "By sending some of your disabled officers you might rake a considerable force from Northern Hospitals," he suggested to Sherman. To Halleck went an order: "Can not troops be got by thinning out about Columbus, Cairo and Paducah. . . . I would like to hear of 1000 a day going by some means." He sent a regiment made up of Confederate deserters and prisoners to Pope, out west, so that a dependably loyal regiment could go to Sherman, and with more men for Georgia in mind asked Halleck, "Have Inspectors or Surgeons gone to the Western Hospitals to clear them out and send the convalescents to the front?"[15]

These last orders were sent from City Point. Grant had spent only four days in Washington, returning in time to come close to being blown up by a bomb smuggled into his headquarters by a rebel on August 9. He had his men keep up the pressure on all the lines before Petersburg and Richmond, and began two thrusts south of Petersburg to prevent Lee from sending any reinforcements to Hood, in Georgia. And he sought to get rid of the one last impediment to his control of the whole of the war effort. Lying, he told Stanton that the Pacific Coast was of great military importance, and went on to say, "I am in favor of Halleck for that Dept." Looking slightly less westward, he warned that the Confederate general Edmund Kirby Smith must not be allowed to come east across the Mississippi to reinforce Hood. As George Frederickson has pointed out, democracy yielded to nation-state Unionism as the war grew older and the supreme commander insisted that, everywhere, the pressure must be intensive; the Northern government, Grant said, must use police as militia if there "is any danger of an uprising in the North to resist the draft." With laconic clarity he added, "If we are to draw troops from the field to keep the loyal states in the harness it will prove difficult to suppress the rebellion in the disloyal states." His attitude toward those disloyal states is reflected in one of his instructions to Sheridan: "If you can possibly spare a Division of Cavalry send them through Loudon County to destroy and carry off the crops, animals[,] negroes, and all men under fifty years of age capable of bearing arms. In this way you will get most of Mosby's men." Here he referred to the able guerrilla cavalry force of General John S. Mosby, which had long harassed the Union. "All male citizens," he continued, "can farely be held as prisoners of war and not as civilian prisoners. If not already soldiers they will be made so the moment the rebel army get hold of them."[16]

Grant was constantly concerned with maintaining the manpower of his huge armies. He backed the draft with urgent messages to Halleck and Stanton and even Lincoln, often giving the officials in Washington statements they could pass on to the newspapers, in the hope that the words of the commander at the front would convince the people of the North of the need for more and more men. Some soldiers were killed; others left when their term of enlistment ran out. Finally, there was the problem of desertion. The war went on and on and would not end, and lonely and unhappy men wanted to get away from it. Grant took as an indication of both the enemy's strength and its morale the number of deserters who came across into his lines, and he was alert to any behavior by his own men suggesting a trend toward increasing desertion. Particularly galling were those who had joined his army for the bounty and then deserted to the Confederacy to pick up another. Sometimes, lonely and confused, these men came back. Three of them, caught as they returned to the Union lines before Petersburg, were sentenced to be hanged, as a warning. With nothing much else going on during the siege, a corporal from Vermont, George H. Mellish, went to have a look. He saw the three led to the scaffold, and could then watch no longer. He went back to his tent and wrote in a letter to his mother, "The youngest was drunk at the time he deserted. He cried all the time he was in the Division Guard House and while he was on the scaffold."[17]

Walt Whitman had heard that particular sound of war a year earlier. In Ward A of a soldiers' hospital he came on "an elderly man weeping bitterly—Joseph Grover—poor man: wretched, wretched father." Whitman made notes on the man's son: "[A] dark haired good looking fellow" of "about 18 or 19," who had been in the army for two years. "[H]e was very fond of his mother & as others had gone off for a while & returned & nothing was done about it he tried to get away. . . ." Whitman then copied into his notebook, without comment, an item from the *New York Herald:* "Wm. Grover & Wm. McKee of Co. A 46 Penn & Christopher Kumbert of Co. H 13 N.J. were shot for desertion at the camp of the 12th Army Corps on Friday last."[18]

By August 1864 little sense of humanity was left. On the sixteenth, furious at the attacks on the Union invaders of central Virginia by the irregular cavalrymen under Mosby, Grant told Sheridan, "The families of most of Mosby's men are known and can be collected. I think they should be taken and kept at Ft. McHenry or some such secure place as hostages for good conduct of Mosby and his men." Only later, when alerted by Washington, did he tell Sheridan to exempt from arrest "the large population of Quakers" in Loudoun County, "who are all favorably disposed to the Union." As for Mosby's raiders themselves: "When any of them are caught with nothing to designate what they are[,] hang them without trial." Once such unequivocal orders had been issued, it was hard to return to civilities, as intermittently suggested by Lincoln. The president urged that Grant and Lee, through emissaries, agree not to burn farms and towns indiscriminately. In firm tones, Grant rejected any arrangement with Lee "for the suppression of insindiaryism." (Grant's command of spelling occasionally deserted him; his grasp of syntax almost never did.) Instead, he urged that department commanders alone have the power to order the firing of a building and then only in retaliation for some publicly specified Confederate act. Grant carefully closed his letter by saying his was only a suggestion, but he had made it clear that he was not afraid to speak his mind frankly to the president. With similar firmness, he wired Stanton to order General John G. Foster to stop exchanging prisoners: "Exchanges simply reinforce the Enemy." The Confederates did not have food enough for their prisoners; they needed their own men back in the line. Grant was willing to sacrifice the former to prevent use of the latter and, in effect, was telling the secretary of war that this was to be governmental policy.[19]

Grant pressed his generals hard as well. On August 18, 1864, he acknowledged to Sherman that Atlanta could probably hold out for another month. This meant that at their convention ten days later the Democrats would be able to point to a stalemate, but perhaps something could be achieved before the November election. Sherman, Grant insisted, must keep trying: "I never would advise going backward even if your roads are cut so as to preclude the possibility of receiving supplies from the North but would recommend the accumulation of ordnance and supplies while you can and if it comes to worst move South as you suggested." Confederate action in Tennessee, to the rear of Sherman, was not to be allowed to stop the march into Georgia. The Army of the Potomac—bottled up though it was—kept Lee's army engaged, so none of it could be detached and sent to stop Sherman. The great campaign of the day was Sherman's, and yet even with a major battle in Georgia in the offing, Grant knew as clearly as ever that the war would never be carried by a single day's battle. He told Sheridan to go on harassing the enemy behind Richmond: "Do all the damage to railroads & crops you can. Carry off stock of all descriptions and negroes so as to prevent further plantings. If the war is to last another year we want the Shenandoah Valley to remain a barren waste."[20]

Lincoln too anticipated no early victory; indeed, perhaps no victory at all. On August 23 he had extracted a pledge from his cabinet that it would cooperate with a new administration in the turnover of power. He expected that he would be defeated in November and that his successor would not press for unconditional surrender. The Democratic convention opened on August 28 and two days later adopted a platform stating that the Lincoln administration had failed to restore the Union with its experiment of war and calling for a convention of men from the North and the South to end hostilities and restore harmony. George B. McClellan was nominated for the presidency; when he formally accepted the nomination a week later, he repudiated the antiwar plank, but clearly, the war was of dubious popularity.

It was General Sherman who turned things around. On September 2 Grant sent a message:

To Commander A[rmy of the] P[otomac] & all Corps Commanders

A dispatch just received from Superintendent of Telegraph in Dept. of Cumberland of this date announces the occupation of Atlanta by our troops. This must be by the 20th Corps which was left by Sherman on the Chattahoocha whilst with the balance of his<sub>∧</sub> he march to the south of the City.

army

U. S. Grant

Lt. [Gen.]

Here was the great news Grant and Lincoln wanted, and in telling it, Grant revealed much about himself as the Civil War commander. As usual, the message was written in pen, in his own hand. His hold on syntax was firm. He wrote so swiftly that for an instant his thought ran ahead of his hand: he omitted the word "army" and then inserted it with a caret, leaving, uncharacteristically, a plural verb—"march"—where the singular form was needed. His salutation brushed past formality—General Meade was not named. Sending a less urgent piece of news, he would have honored protocol; here he wasted no words on deference.[21]

Characteristically, he began with the seemingly unimportant detail of how the news had been sent, along the telegraph wires. His mind worked that way; he saw the way stories worked their way along in the telling. The whole map of the war moved through his head—from Georgia back up to Tennessee, and on to Washington, and finally to himself at City Point. His rhetoric was quiet: "our troops" accomplished the "occupation"; he did not credit Sherman with taking Atlanta, he did not invoke the deity, he used no adjectives. He visualized Sherman's moves although he had never been to Atlanta and had sparse information about them. With his knowledge of Sherman's forces firmly in mind, he guessed that it was the Twentieth Corps that had entered the city while the deadly battle of Jonesboro was being fought below Atlanta. Rivers tell with precision where one is; the creek on Atlanta's north side, the Chattahoochee, was not ignored. And with a kind of unconscious grandeur he anticipated history; Sherman's marching would soon become Sherman's "March to the Sea."

A capital other than Washington (and City Point) also heard the news of Atlanta. On September 3, Grant wrote Stanton that in Richmond a rebel newspaper contained a "rumor" of a battle at Atlanta, but "declines to form an opinion from its rumors." Cautiously, he himself did not send congratulations to his old comrade in Georgia until confirmation of the victory arrived on September 4. When it came, he ordered "a salute to be fired from every battery bearing on the enemy" in celebration. Nicely, in the congratulatory letter, he told how he had been scooped in broadcasting the news; before he had made any announcement, "the fact was known to our picketts. The rebels halloed over to our men that Sherman had whipped Hood—that the latter had lost 40,000 men—and that our troops were in Atlanta." A bit ruefully he added, "All quiet here."[22]

Grant did not rest on Sherman's laurels long. Immediately, his eye was on his old target—Mobile—and he considered having E. R. S. Canby, then in Louisiana, join Sherman at Mobile, or at the least, engage a large enemy force and thus keep it away from Sherman. But military prowess eluded the Federal army commanders in the Department of the Gulf and Grant's attention soon turned to a commander in whom he had already expressed extraordinary confidence, Philip H. Sheridan. On September 15 he again left City Point and again bypassed Washington (after politely telling Halleck that he would stop only if Stanton or Lincoln insisted), going to meet Sheridan at Charles Town, West Virginia. Grant's faith in the fiery commander was firmer than ever. At their meeting, he urged Sheridan to press Jubal Early, and shortly thereafter, he recommended that Sheridan be made a brigadier general in the regular army and, of more immediate significance, head of a new command, midway between the eastern and western commands, to be called, inelegantly, the Middle Division; the Union army would thus be divided into three separate forces. Grant told Halleck that Sheridan did not need new regiments, for he was operating with what would be called today an elite corps. Grant could train raw recruits best in eastern Virginia; he did not want the fast-moving Sheridan held back by green troops, sluggards, or anyone who had ever deserted; all of Sheridan's soldiers had to be fierce professionals. Grant pledged to Halleck that with such men, Sheridan would "wipe out all the stain the Valley of the Shenandoah has been to us heretofore before he gets through." No other region evoked such a streak of revenge in Grant—a fact that is curious in that he had never himself served there, and he had no personal ties to it.[23]

In mid-September, just after their meeting, Sheridan gave his commander justification for his prophecy. In a wild, daring attack, complete with shouts, Sheridan's horsemen under George Crook rode swiftly and skillfully at Fisher's Hill, Virginia. Fifty of Crook's men were killed; Jubal Early found 1,200 men missing at the end of the battle. Whether they had deserted or been killed, they were gone, along with arms the Confederates could no longer afford to lose. Grant had already extravagantly praised Sheridan for his earlier "great victory at Winchester," but concluded that Sheridan had been more than bold enough to suit the dispirited politicians in the White House: "I had reason to believe that the administration was a little afraid to have a decisive battle fought at that time, for fear it might go against us and have a bad effect on the November elections." Lincoln preferred to stick with Atlanta and not risk a defeat. Luckily, Sheridan's succession of raids was a victory. Indeed, in Grant's judgment, "this decisive victory was the most effective campaign argument made in the Canvass."[24]

Jubal Early later revealed that the impact of the engagement was far less great than it might have been; Sheridan could have crushed his whole force if all of his army had pressed on after Winchester. But if Sheridan's men were less than perfect warriors, they still had Grant's admiration. Grant was not the same kind of soldier as Sheridan, but there must have been moments, perhaps as he rode a strong horse, when his imagination went to such bold attacks as the one at Fisher's Hill. Such adventures were a far cry from the sluggish inactivity of his huge forces stalled before Petersburg and Richmond. Stalled they were, but to good over-all purpose. As long as Grant held Lee locked into eastern Virginia, there was no way the rebels could prevent the spectacular successes of Sherman and Sheridan. To the latter he wrote, "May your good work continue is now the prayer of all loyal men." Grant's team was winning its terrible game.[25]

They played it Grant's way. He never mapped strategy, never put pins in charts or moved counters over simulated terrain. Everything was in his head. He heard all that was said around him, he took in every message, he said little. What he wanted people to know he wrote out in his own hand, so there could be no misunderstanding. His crisp, clear orders were almost impossible not to comprehend. Those who did not carry them out either chose not to or lacked any ability to translate words into action.

*To Sheridan in the Shenandoah Valley, September 26, 1864:* "Lee has sent no troops from here . . . except two regiments & one City Battalion. . . . Your victories have created the greatest consternation." With this news, Sheridan knew he was not endangered, and learned also that he was doing his job. *To Sherman at Atlanta, the same day:* "Jeff Davis was in Richmond on last Thursday. This I think is beyond doubt." This spoke to Sherman's worry that the Confederate president would go to Georgia to strengthen his armies there. *To Butler, nearby on the James, September 27:* "Make all your changes of troops at once ready for the execution of orders verbally communicated so as to have troops as fresh as possible." *To Halleck, also on September 27:* "Order all recruits and new regiments from lower Wisconsin, Illinois, Indiana and Ohio, now ready, to be sent at once [to Nashville, and hence to Sherman]." *To Halleck again, on opening railroad lines to Sheridan (there were six telegraph messages to Halleck in one day and four letters as well):* "If he moves as I expected him to Charlottesville, the road to Culpepper would be the one to repair." *To Meade, before Petersburg, again on September 27:* "If troops can be moved tomorrow so as to give the appearance of Massing to our left it would serve to deceive the enemy." He wanted to mask Butler's moves. *Once again to Meade:* "I think also it would be adviseable to send scouts . . . to discover if the enemy are moving Cavalry around towards the James River." Grant's mind and his pen encompassed the whole of the war as it constantly shifted before him. [26]

Grant wrote Sherman that he had ordered recruits sent to him, and he admitted that he had made one wrong call: "I was mistaken about Davis being in Richmond on Thursday last. He was then on his way to Macon." He informed Stanton, in Washington, "Every thing indicates the enemy are going to make a last and spasmodic effort to regain what they have lost and especially against Sherman. Troops should be got to Sherman as rapidly as his lines of communication will carry them." He was explosive on that subject. "If Gen. Rosecrans does not send forward the regiments belonging to Sherman as ordered," he wrote Stanton, "arrest him by my order unless the President will authorize his being relieved from command altogether." He told Halleck what he knew of Sheridan's moves, although his information was less complete than he liked, because the nearby battles at Fort Harrison and Peebles Farm had "prevented getting the Richmond papers." He could see the whole of his war, and he was anxious that nothing be done which would allow the Confederates to impede Sherman. Jefferson Davis was worried about Sherman, and Grant was determined to justify those worries. [27]

Grant was demonstrating great confidence in Sherman, but he showed less for commanders nearer at hand. They had been ordered to make an attack on September 29; the day before, in exasperation, he wrote Surgeon General Joseph Barnes, "I have called on Gen. Butler to know why he wanted the two ocean Hospital Steamers of which you telegraph but have received no reply. Until you hear from me on the subject you need not send them." Butler was moving men and material preparatory to battle; early in the afternoon Grant looked out on the James: "I see a pontoon train being towed up the river. Will it not attract attention and put the enemy on his guard?" On the twenty-ninth his impatience with Butler caused him to go himself to Fort Harrison to observe still another, and final, attempt by the Union army to break through the Confederate lines north of the James in front of Richmond. Instead, he witnessed a desperate effort to halt the savage counterattack by Lee's men. [28]

Along with the large things that had to be watched, there were small ones. If the officers in Arkansas could not keep the railroad lines open from Little Rock to Fort Smith and Port Gibson, Grant declared, they were to "abandon them altogether. The first thing . . . to do is to dismiss . . .[the] Chief Quartermaster and put a line man in his place. The idea that Animals should starve in Arkansas when the enemy can come and supply man and beast is simply ridiculous." He saw it all. He wrote the orders himself. No clerks or counselors interfered. Businessmen, in the guise of inept quartermasters, were an unhealthy intrusion into war. The quartermaster in Grant was not a businessman in army clothes. Grant was an able quartermaster because when he thought of Sherman at Atlanta, he could see all the blankets, and bacon, and bullets that had to be there too. What he did not want to see were the sutlers, the speculators, the in-laws. They brought the weight of the unmastered world of commerce down on Grant, and instinctively he moved to push them away. Before the war, Grant had not dared look at commerce because he could not comprehend it. Business was a requirement of his father's world, not his.[29]

In war, he could meet all the requirements. If there were things he could not do himself, he was remarkably unenvious of those who could do them. The excellent horseman who had never been in the cavalry seems to have been more exhilarated by Sheridan's exploits than by any of his own. He was not possessive about Sheridan or Sherman. He liked it when they cut loose from their bases—when no one (himself included) knew exactly where they were, when no people of business could get to them. He liked having to learn the location of his two favorite commanders from the nervous Richmond press.

They kept moving. Rosecrans, who would not move, he could neither understand nor tolerate. "Anybody. . . . will be better than Rosecrans," he finally said in exasperation. But, paradoxically, he could not move himself. The stalemate at Petersburg dragged on largely because Grant wanted it to; if he kept all of Lee's forces there, they could not go to Georgia to stop Sherman. Still, he yearned for his own victory. On September 30 he was encouraged by the report of a "refugee from Richmond" that "the greatest consternation is felt in the City and citizens generally are anxious that the city not be evacuated by the Military." He told Meade that day, "I can't help believing that the enemy are prepared to leave Petersburg if forced a little." They did not leave for six more months.[30]

Grant may have eliminated business from his war, but he did not try to banish politics. In the account of Sherman's and Sheridan's enterprises in his *Memoirs*, Grant wrote, "The news of Sherman's success reached the North instantaneously, and set the country all aglow. This was the first great political campaign for the Republicans in their canvass of 1864. It was followed later by Sheridan's campaign in the Shenandoah Valley; and these two campaigns probably had more effect in settling the election of the following November than all the speeches, all the bonfires, and all the parading with banners and bands of music in the North." This was sound history—and in 1885 not disinterested; it was natural for the Republican former president, looking back, to see Lincoln's party as having been Republican at that time. And Grant had had an equally strong sense of things political in 1864. Then too he had viewed Sherman's occupation of Atlanta as a "political campaign." (Sherman must have railed at that designation—and Atlantans at the double meaning of "aglow." Nowhere in the *Memoirs* did Grant speak of the burning of Atlanta that November; he mentioned only its occupation.)[31]

Grant was cognizant too of the political implications of a draft call so close to the election, but he needed more men. In a September 13 letter to Stanton he was scornful of "Sec. Seward's Auburn speech when he intimates that volunteers were coming in so rapidly that there would be no necessity for a draft." He was no more impressed, he said, by Stanton's own estimate that "volunteers were coming in at the rate of 5000 per day," and maintained, instead, that "we ought to have the whole number of men called for by the President in the shortest possible time. A draft is soon over and ceases to hurt after it is made. The agony of suspense is worse upon the public than the measure itself." He argued for an immediate draft call also because of the military effect it would have on the South, presenting his views in a way that strongly supported the position of those in the party who opposed a negotiated peace:

> Prompt action in filling our Armies will have more effect upon the enemy than a victory over them. They profess to believe there is such a party North in favor of recognizing Southern independence that the draft can not be enforced. Let them be undeceived. Deserters come into our lines daily who tell us that the men are nearly universally tired of the War and that desertions would be much more frequent but they believe peace will be negotiated after the fall elections. The enforcement of the draft and prompt filling up of our Armies will save the shedding of blood to an immense degree.

The careful editing of this letter suggests that Grant intended it to be made public. Clearly, he thought Lincoln should use this statement by his military commander to bolster his political position as he issued a draft call.[32]

Privately, Grant was once again concerned about desertions from his ranks. On September 20 he scrawled an exasperated note to Meade, telling him that Lee bragged that after one day's work he took "300 prisoners, a large number of horses and some Arms. besides 2500 Cattle." Grant was caustic: "The ease with which our men of late fall into the hands of the enemy would indicate that they are rather willing prisoners." Laxity was his concern that day; Meade was not to relax his discipline in Virginia, and Lincoln, Grant felt, should not permit sloppy civil government in Georgia. Fearing an attempt to establish a Unionist state government of ostensibly loyal Georgians, he started to write directly to the president and then, crossing out Lincoln's name, wrote to Stanton instead:

> Please advise the President not to attempt to doctor up a state government for Georgia by the appointment of citizens in any capacity whatever. leave Sherman to treat on all questions in his own way [,] the President reserving the power to approve or disapprove of his action. Through Treasury Agents on the Mississippi and a very bad civil policy in Louisiana I have no doubt the war has been considerably protracted and the States bordering on that river thrown further from sympathy with the Government than they were before the river was opened to commerce. This is given as my private view.[33]

It was a private view of a public question of great moment, and his expression of it gives the lie to all notions that Grant was a general who stuck purely
to military matters. Lincoln had put much store in the development of a
Unionist government in occupied Louisiana, under the theory that reluctant
Confederates who had been antisecessionists would come back into the
Union by accepting the alternative state government. Similarly, he had allowed agents of the Treasury Department to negotiate the purchase of cotton with civilians in the lower Mississippi Valley. Both policies were aimed
at seducing white Southerners into a return. It was precisely the opposite of
the treatment Grant had urged Sheridan to give the people of Loudoun
County, Virginia. It was not what was in store for Georgians and Carolinians
in Sherman's path. Grant contended that the South would submit only to
fear; the introduction of puppet governments would only stiffen resistance.
He had moved a long way from the day when he tried to win the confidence
of the people—loyal, he hoped—of Paducah.

Grant was waging war with a brutality of which he had been incapable in
1861 and 1862. There was, too, a sense of building toward a climax that kept
eluding him. He knew he would win, and he was eager to accomplish the victory, but his enemy would not let go. He needed a glamorous success, and
Sheridan gave it to him. It started with a defeat. On October 19, 1864, Jubal
Early's raiders, using a hidden path, surprised the Union camp at Cedar
Creek, Virginia, and dislodged two corps of Sheridan's army, seizing prisoners and arms. Sheridan, whose forces were vulnerable, had been in
Washington. Returning by train, he reached Martinsburg, West Virginia, on
the seventeenth, and on horseback, he reached Winchester, Virginia, on the
eighteenth. The next morning, the fierce little general woke to distant
gunfire, ate breakfast, and, with all the splendid urgency portrayed in
Thomas Buchanan Read's vigorous poem "Sheridan's Ride," hurried to
Cedar Creek. There his men, recovering from the surprise attack, were driving off Early's Confederates. This was the last battle in the Shenandoah Valley; the Yankees held it thereafter. Grant was elated: "I had a salute of one
hundred guns from each of the Armies here fired in honor of Sheridan's last
victory. Turning what bid fare to be a disaster into glorious victory stamps
Sheridan . . . one of the ablest Generals."[34]

Sherman, too, was getting ready to move. "The stores to be intended for
Sherman might now [go to] Hilton Head," Grant rather offhandedly told
Halleck on October 21. The Union held Hilton Head Island, off the Carolina
coast just above Savannah, Georgia, and Sherman was about to abandon his
supply line to Nashville and head there. Grant knew Sherman's destination,
and knew it would take him time to arrive: "There will be no necessity for
there going all at once but let them accumulate there gradually." He did not,
however, let other officers know of Sherman's destination until he was safely
away on his march toward the sea.[35]

One sign that the Confederacy might soon crumble came from a foreign quarter. The French government was trying to arrange the evacuation of some of its citizens from Richmond. Grant told Stanton he could inform Secretary of State Seward that there were no objections to having French nationals pass through the lines on their way to safety. But not all the signals from outside the country were encouraging; as the election came closer, Seward notified the mayor of New York that there were rumors in Canada that Confederates would set fire to his city on election day. These stories were not taken idly; Grant had a small contingent of troops hand-picked and sent to New York to be ready in case of trouble.[36]

They were not necessary. The election was peaceful everywhere, and Lincoln's Unionists were victorious almost everywhere. McClellan took only New Jersey (his own state), Lincoln's native Kentucky, and Delaware. In New York the contest was close. On November 10, two days after the election, Grant, having waited with excessive caution to be sure Lincoln had been safely re-elected, sent a brief letter to Stanton: "Enough now seems to be known to say who is to hold the reins of Government for the next four years. Congratulate the President for me for the double victory. The election having passed off quietly, no bloodshed or riots throughout the land, is a victory counting more to the country than a battle won. Rebeldom and Europe will so construe it." The political news did not, however, mean a quick, joyous end to the war. The same day, Grant asked Sheridan, "Do you not think it advisable to notify all citizens living east of the Blue Ridge to move out North of the Potomac all their stock, grain and provisions of every description?" The area was to be made so bare of supplies that it would not be able to harbor Mosby's raiders, and "so long as the war lasts they [the Shenandoah farmers] must be prevented from raising another crop both there and as high up the valley as we can controll."[37]

It appeared that the war might, after all, go another full season, and there was still danger of a rebel offensive in Grant's old western theater of war, Tennessee, where the commander was George H. Thomas. On November 15, Sherman burned Atlanta and headed southeast toward the sea, paced by a vastly outnumbered Confederate force. Grant feared that John Bell Hood, now transferred to Alabama, would also turn his attention to Sherman, and attack him from the rear. This Grant was determined to prevent. Indeed, for months he had been directing the whole war effort with the aim of sustaining Sherman. Keeping Lee's whole army busy at Petersburg, he ordered Thomas to attack Hood vigorously: "If Hood commences falling back it will not do to wait for the full equipment of your cavalry to follow. He should, in that event, be pressed with such force as you can bring to bear." Thomas focused more on what he chose to see as the conditional nature of Grant's order than on its urgency and declined to take the offensive: "I am watching Hood closely and if he should move after Sherman, will follow him with what force I can raise at hand."[38]

Hood, however, had a general other than Sherman in his eye. He had spotted Thomas. In addition, he had thoughts of an invasion of the North across the Ohio River—or so Grant soon came to believe. Hood took the offensive and headed toward Thomas at Nashville. He was stopped about forty miles short of the city, and one army confronted the other in the bitter early winter of 1864. With Hood facing him, Thomas received an oddly incongruous message from Grant, dated November 24. In it, a quotation from a Savannah paper, in which Georgians were exhorted to rise against Sherman, was followed by Grant's exhortation to Thomas: "Do not let Forrest get off without punishment." No more. Thomas must have thought he had enough on his hands in Tennessee without having to look out for Sherman's interests in Georgia. Furthermore, Nathan Bedford Forrest, a dangerous but erratic cavalry officer, was not the Confederate immediately confronting Thomas. That man was Hood.[39]

In his reply Thomas tactfully pointed out that fact: "Hood's entire army is in front of Columbia and so greatly outnumbers mine, I am compelled to act on the defensive." Thomas went on to say that his cavalry lacked mounts, the horses having been sent to Sherman, and he had lost "nearly 15,000 men, discharged by expiration of service and permitted to go home to vote." Finally, seeking to enlist Grant's support but choosing the wrong phrase to repeat, he wrote, "I am compelled for the present to act on the defensive. The moment I can get my cavalry I will march against Hood, and," he added dutifully (and perhaps sarcastically), "if Forrest can be reached he will be punished."[40]

Grant would have done well to tell Thomas more about what he was doing in his support. On November 25, the day after he sent his odd pep talk, Grant had ordered all extra troops in Missouri to report directly to Thomas, thus bypassing the authority of Rosecrans, who was reluctant to release them. On November 27, he urged Thomas to move, but again phrased his instructions conditionally, saying that according to the Savannah newspapers Forrest was on his way to Georgia, and "if this proves true, it will give you a chance to take the offensive against Hood." Thomas replied that there was no evidence that Forrest had left Tennessee, but went on to assure Grant that his own movements would "commence against Hood as soon as possible, whether Forrest leaves Tennessee or not."[41]

On November 30, with Forrest and his cavalrymen now leading the way, Hood's army moved toward Nashville and at Franklin met the Union forces led by John M. Schofield and Jacob Dolson Cox. In fierce fighting in which the Confederate losses—including six generals—were greater than were those sustained by the Union, Schofield and Cox held firm. Grant would have counted the action a victory and taken the offensive. Thomas, instead, told Grant that because he was outnumbered he had "determined to retire to fortifications around Nashville until General [James Harrison] Wilson can get his cavalry equipped." Grant, at City Point, was as close to desperation as he was to come during the war. He immediately told Thomas that for him to stay in Nashville and allow Hood to dig in around him would cost the Union all of southeastern Tennessee—all that had been won at Chattanooga. Grant was anxious for them to fight it out. It would be fine if Hood attacked Thomas, but if the Confederate did not take the initiative, Thomas was to "attack him before he fortifies. Arm and put in the trenches our quartermaster employees, citizens etc." An hour and a half later, still stewing over Thomas's retreat, Grant sent a second message: "After the repulse of Hood at Franklin, it looks to me instead of falling back to Nashville, we should have taken the offensive against the enemy where he was." Allowing that "at this distance . . . I may err as to the best method of dealing with the enemy," he went on to urge that Hood be disposed of: "Should you get him to retreat, give him no peace."[42]

Thomas, claiming that he lacked support troops, said he was not ready to attack. Grant replied, "Time strengthens him . . . as much as it does you." Halleck thought Thomas had so many horses that some would starve unless a few were killed, but Thomas disagreed. He wanted to get more horses—and more men—before moving, and he did not want to start out in the terrible weather that had set in. Thomas did not move, and on December 6, Grant issued an unequivocal order: "Attack Hood at once and wait no longer for a remount of your cavalry. There is great danger of delay resulting in a campaign back to the Ohio River."[43]

The next day Grant told Stanton that if Thomas did not attack "promptly, I would recommend superceding him with Schofield." Halleck replied that if Grant wanted Thomas out he would have to remove him himself, since neither Lincoln nor Stanton was prepared to do so. Initially, Grant demurred; on December 8, instead of sacking Thomas, he sent him a message of encouragement: "Now is one of the finest opportunities ever presented of destroying one of the three armies of the enemy. If destroyed, he can never replace it," and "a rejoicing . . . will resound from one end of the land to another." In contrast to Grant's high road of rhetoric, Halleck took the low. He told Thomas the next day, "General Grant expresses much dissatisfaction at your delay in attacking the enemy. If you wait till General Wilson mounts all his cavalry, you will wait to doomsday."[44]

Thomas could see what was coming. I have "done everything in my power to prepare," he wrote Grant, but the troops "could not have been gotten ready before this." He added that if Grant "should deem it necessary to relieve me I shall submit without a murmur." When Grant, at City Point, got this message, he replied that he had suspended the drafting of an order to replace Thomas. He had, he declared, "as much confidence in your conducting a battle as I have in any officer; but it seemed to me you have been slow." Grant added the hope that the need to issue an order relieving Thomas would not recur and that "the facts will show that you have been right all along."[45]

Grant was being disingenuous. He had no faith that Thomas would move.

When Thomas reported the hills covered with ice and said he would attack as soon as there was a thaw, Grant exploded: "If you delay attack longer the mortifying spectacle will be witnessed of a rebel army moving across the Ohio River, and you will be forced to act, accepting weather as you find." Thomas still was the Rock of Chickamauga—he replied he would not attempt to attack over terrain heavily crusted with ice. Grant's patience gave way, and he made a reckless move that only luck—or rather, George H. Thomas—caused him not to regret.[46]

John A. Logan was a flamboyant horseman, in some ways resembling Sheridan. Grant liked him and privately wished Sherman had chosen him rather than the pious O. O. Howard to command the Army of the Tennessee. Though Logan had been a Democratic congressman, Grant saw him not as a politician, but as an audacious soldier. At this time, Logan was at City Point, and Grant sent him to Nashville, by way of Louisville, with a secret order which was to be presented to Thomas if he had not attacked by the time Logan arrived. The order relieved Thomas of his command and gave it to Logan. Perhaps because he realized, after Logan had left, how dangerous it was to send off a man who lusted for a command with so explosive a piece of paper, or perhaps because Grant too was intensely restless, he set out for Nashville himself. He got as far as Washington—and Logan had reached Louisville—when he learned the news. As Thomas put it privately—he should have said it to Grant, in just these words—"We have whipped the enemy."[47]

On December 15 Thomas attacked, and Hood was defeated in fighting that day and the next. The last major Confederate threat was stopped. Grant got word of the attack at the War Department at 11:00 P.M. on December 15 and immediately responded: "I was just on my way to Nashville but receiving a dispatch . . . detailing your splendid success of today, I shall go no further." Fifteen minutes later Thomas's own modest factual report came in, and Grant sent a more formal wire: "I congratulate you and the army under your command for to-day's operation, and feel a conviction that tomorrow will add more fruits to your victory." It was a cool and contingent acknowledgment of a great success. Thomas was given no greater recognition by Grant during the war or afterward. He received none of the praise or prominence that Grant gave Sherman and Sheridan.[48]

Grant did give Thomas a further assignment. After the victory at Nashville, he urged Thomas to pursue and destroy Hood's army. If Thomas succeeded, he said, there would be "but one army left to the so-called Confederacy capable of doing us harm." Grant himself would "take care of that and try to draw the sting from it, so that in the spring we will have easy sailing." On the last day of the year Grant had Halleck tell Thomas that there must be no relaxation because of the victory: "Lieutenant-General Grant does not intend that your army shall go into winter quarters; it must be ready for active operations in the field."[49]

Grant was correct in his view that relaxing was not possible now, but there was no further need for much in the way of vast actions in the field. The Confederacy was beaten. All that was necessary before the fighting would stop was the passage of time, and the loss of a good many more lives. Thomas's was the last great battle—the decisive one that Sherman, and possibly Grant, had hoped would be his. Grant knew now that the war would be won, but the knowledge gave him no personal peace. In fact, just before Christmas he was deeply depressed. He had had no word from Julia since a brief visit with her earlier in the month in Burlington, New Jersey, a town northeast of Philadelphia where she was living and the children were attending school. It was a time of anticlimax. "I am not very well today though nothing special is the matter," he wrote her. He stayed in bed all day, "eating neither breakfast nor dinner and have not smoked a cigar." He had an intestinal disorder and a headache—"I have taken ten pills and three Sedists Powders with but little effect." (These were undoubtedly Seidlitz powders, a sodium bicarbonate concoction commonly used to fight both upset stomachs and hangovers.) Trying to lift himself from a gloom not made lighter by winter storms, he added, "Better weather and the fall of Richmond may be hoped for however this winter." His mood was leaden, but the next day a letter from Julia "full of ambition of what you expect of me" brought him around, and when Fred arrived on Christmas Day, his depression lifted. Grant was just about to go riding when Fred appeared, so they saddled a second horse and father and son rode together. He arranged for Fred to visit both Meade's headquarters and the front line and promised that he would get him back immediately after New Year's Day so that he would miss no school. Quinine would keep his sickness under control, and the war news had brightened: "All well here now. The good news of the capture of Savannah received from Sherman is worth a great deal. . . . The Confederates are very despondent and say, some of them, their cause is already lost."[50]

On December 18, Grant had written Sherman, who could now receive mail by way of the navy, "I congratulate you and the brave officers and men under your command on the successful termination of your most brilliant campaign. I never had a doubt of the result. When apprehensions for your safety were expressed by the President, I assured him with the army you had, and you in command of it, there was no danger but you would *strike* bottom on salt-water some place." He closed the letter with further congratulations "upon the splendid results of your campaign, the like of which is not read of in past history, I subscribe myself, more than ever, if possible, your friend, U.S. Grant."[51]

Sherman responded with a long letter explaining his plans for an attack northward into the Carolinas and closed: "I do not like to boast, but believe this army has the confidence in itself that makes it almost invincible." Then he turned to more personal matters: "I wish you could run down and see us; it would have a good effect, and show to both armies that they are acting on a common plan. The weather is now cool and pleasant, and the general health very good. Your true friend, W. T. Sherman." Unluckily, Grant could not make the trip, but, on January 1, 1865, he sent Julia a newspaper clipping that he wanted her to save; it must have included a generous statement about him, for Grant commented, "Sherman's letter shows how noble a man he is. How few there are who when rising to popular favor as he now is would stop to say a word in defense of the only one between himself and the highest command." Sherman's letter to Grant as well as one to Halleck had been full of ambitious plans, and he did not resist making suggestions about how the war should be fought to a conclusion. But despite Sherman's ambition, Grant felt sure of his loyalty. In his private letter, he told Julia how glad he was that he had "appreciated Sherman from the first[,] feeling him to be what he has proven to the world he is." There was no mention of Thomas.[52]

Grant had ridden out a time of small despair. The common despondence of Christmas had been alleviated by a visit from his eldest son, by belated but welcome letters from his wife, and finally by a splendid tribute from a friend who was also a trustworthy judge of greatness. "Happy New Year," he wrote Julia. "Fred starts home this morning and will tell you I am quite well."[53]

# XIV

## PEACE

We don't have much to talk of now, but Peace!

— *Corporal George H. Mellish*
*to his father,*
*near Petersburg, Virginia,*
*January 30, 1865*

By quitting when they did, Southerners were able to believe that they
had fought as long as they could, which was true by strictly
conventional standards. Defeat was thus honorable. But they saved
more than honor; they saved the basic elements—with the exception of
slavery itself—of the Southern social, that is to say racial, order. The
social order could not possibly have survived the guerilla warfare which
a continued resistance movement would have required.
— *John Shy*

CITY POINT was not only the command post for the prosecution of the
war but also the center of efforts by soldier-statesmen to bring the war to an
end by negotiation. Ordinary soldiers had already established patches of
peace. In the months of stalemate at Petersburg, men had taunted each other
across the lines for so long that the obscenities bred familiarity and yielded to
conversation. Rebs and Yanks washed clothes together in the streams, and
the kidding that went along with the laundering led first to good-natured
horseplay and then to organized foot races and wrestling matches. Without
waiting for William James to declare athletics the moral equivalent of war,
the soldiers converted it into a field day. But then they had to go back to
killing one another; the slower-witted statesmen and generals in charge of
these games never simply let men leave when they have had enough of the
party.

In January 1865, General E. O. C. Ord was one of the general officers
with ideas similar to those of the privates. On the seventh, Grant assigned
him to replace General Benjamin F. Butler as commander of the Army of the
James. Butler had bungled an attack on Fort Fisher, which protected Wilmington, North Carolina, the last major supply port for the Confederacy,

and with the national election now over, Grant could at last get rid of that outspoken politician. In contrast, Ord proved himself to be the most relaxing of Grant's commanders in the east; the two men enjoyed each other's company, Ord had graduated from West Point the spring before Grant entered. He was a Marylander and, according to romantic legend, the illegitimate grandson of King George IV. Neither vengeful toward the Confederacy nor particularly obsessed with the trappings of victory, he was, both in January 1865 and during Reconstruction, what later political observers would call "soft" on the South.

Another border-state man with similar views was the seventy-four-year-old politician Francis Preston Blair, from Kentucky. After Sherman reached the sea, Lincoln was so confident that the Confederacy could not be sustained as a separate nation that he felt ready to make overtures to Jefferson Davis in the hope of stimulating a negotiated surrender. Blair—whose son Francis was one of Sherman's generals—was the man for the job. A powerful editor in the cause of Jacksonian Democracy, Blair had been close to Andrew Jackson. He was by this time a Republican, and still very much a politician. He had long been a friend of Davis's and proposed now to talk to the Confederate president about ending the war. Blair loved being on the scene of politics and could not resist a chance to play with Abraham Lincoln and Jefferson Davis in the last act of the Civil War. Jubal Early's men, when they threatened the capture of Washington in July 1864, had broken into Blair's country place at Silver Spring, Maryland, and Blair turned the pillage to his advantage; his "cover" as he went to converse with Davis was that he wanted to retrieve some personal papers that had been taken in the looting. Lincoln authorized a pass through the lines for Blair, and he set out for City Point. In time, safe passage was assured by the Confederates, and Blair crossed Grant's and Lee's lines. On January 12, 1865, Blair and Davis sat down in Richmond to talk.[1]

Blair's scheme for achieving a North-South reconciliation was bizarre, but only marginally more so than Seward's idea in 1861 of fostering a foreign war in order to stave off civil war. Both were less insane than the slaughter at Spotsylvania and Cold Harbor. The idea was for Confederate and Union soldiers to stop fighting one another and, with Generals Grant and Lee riding side by side, to march into Mexico to uphold the Monroe Doctrine and drive out Maximilian and the French. What was more, Blair (with confused echoes, from his childhood, of Aaron Burr's scheme) suggested that Jefferson Davis replace Maximilian and become the dictator in Mexico. Davis, who must have recognized this aspect of the proposal as Blair's rather than Lincoln's, listened; what mattered was not the Mexican chimera but the fact that Blair had found a talking point, and Davis responded to his true purpose. It was agreed that Blair would go back to Lincoln and learn whether the president would receive peace commissioners from Richmond. When he reached City Point on his way back to Washington, Blair carried a letter from Davis indicating willingness to have representatives "enter into [a] conference with a view to secure peace to the two countries." Blair was not a restrained talker, and he must have taken advantage of the chance to enlist his host in the cause of his exciting diplomacy; from the time of their long conversation at City Point, Grant missed no opportunity to help bring about peace negotiations.[2]

Lincoln discussed Davis's message with his closest advisers in Washington, and Grant was in the city when the reply was under consideration. It seems unlikely that he was kept completely in the dark about a conference bearing so critically on his military plans. Just the fact that passage across the lines would have to be arranged for those who were to do the negotiating argues that Grant must have been told of Lincoln's decision. The president, balking at Davis's reference to "two countries" but ready to talk, sent Blair back to Richmond with a letter indicating his willingness to receive a representative from Davis "with the view to securing peace to the people of our one common country." Davis, over strenuous objections from some committed Confederates, agreed to a meeting and sent three commissioners, none of them a die-hard and all of them men who had distinguished themselves in both governments: John A. Campbell, assistant secretary of war for the Confederate States of America, had been, as associate justice of the Supreme Court, the highest-ranking member of the United States government to join in the secession; Alexander H. Stephens, the Confederacy's vice-president, had sat in the United States House of Representatives as a congressman from Georgia; Robert M. T. Hunter, once a United States senator, had also served as a senator from Virginia in the Confederate States of America and had for a time been the Confederacy's secretary of state.[3]

Arriving at Petersburg, the three commissioners sent a message requesting permission to cross the Union lines. When it was clear that the officer to whom they were brought did not know of their coming, they asked for Grant and were not buoyed by the reply that he "was on a big drunk." Both Grant and Meade were, in fact, away—Grant with Schofield, planning an attack on Wilmington, and Meade in Philadelphia; Ord, in command in their absence but obviously not alerted to the Confederates' arrival, forwarded to the War Department a telegram from the officer who met the commissioners, which said they had come "in accordance with an understanding claimed to exist with Lt. Gen. Grant. . . ." Stanton replied that "this Department" had no knowledge of any agreement made by Grant for anyone to come across, and ordered the men held at the front lines. The next day he instructed that the Confederate delegation be told only that a messenger would shortly arrive with further word. Grant returned to City Point on the morning of January 31 and, on his own initiative, gave the three commissioners safe-conduct across the lines and invited them to his headquarters. Grant's immediate cooperation suggests that, as the Confederates claimed, he knew they were coming. In his invitation to the three he added encouragingly, "Your letter to me has been telegraphed to Washington for instructions. I have no doubt but that before you arrive at my Headquarters an answer will be received directing me to comply with your request." What they sought was safe passage to Washington, to confer with Lincoln. Grant assured the three that should his optimistic prediction prove wrong, they would be given safe-conduct back to their own lines.[4]

When the commissioners passed across the Union lines, General Meade observed, "soldiers on both sides yelled loudly, 'Peace! peace!' " The cry, he thought, was not in mockery of three appeasers, but came from the heart; similarly, the *Richmond Sentinel* reported that hopes for peace were widely held. Stephens, Hunter, and Campbell were met with no pomp, but were escorted directly to City Point, where Orville E. Babcock, of Grant's staff, told them he would present them to the general. It was evening; they were taken to a very unprepossessing cabin with no guard posted in front of it. Stephens recalled it all: "Upon Colonel Babcock's rapping at the door, the response, 'Come in,' was given in a tone of voice, and with a cadence that I can never forget." They entered to find Grant sitting alone at a table, writing by the light of a kerosene lamp.[5]

The conversation was free and immediately to the point—the making of peace. This inevitably meant that political matters of the greatest moment were under consideration, and Grant cheerfully violated the principle that soldiers should not discuss politics. After a brief, comfortable talk, Grant escorted the three men to a floating hotel—a transferred Hudson River excursion boat, the *Mary Martin*—where they were pleasantly accommodated. Stephens was certain that Grant was "very anxious for the proposed conference to take place." Meanwhile, Lincoln, also anxious to make the conference succeed, sent Secretary of State Seward to Hampton Roads, Virginia, to prepare to meet with the commissioners.[6]

The "detention" of the commissioners that Stanton had ordered proved civilized indeed. Referring to it in his *Memoirs*, Grant said, "They remained several days as guests on board the boat. I saw them quite frequently, though I have no recollection of having had any conversation whatever with them on the subject of their mission." Twenty years afterward, Grant was still trying to demonstrate that he had not exceeded his authority; in point of fact, he had. Both Grant and Meade paid lip service to the concept that generals should be nonpolitical, but the minute they had the chance to enter peacemaking conversations with the distinguished commissioners from the Confederacy, they plunged straight into politics. The talk of the three rebels and Grant and Meade was cordial. Indeed, the initial meeting unconsciously underscored one of the ironic absurdities of the war and, in a sense, foreshadowed the denouement of Reconstruction that followed. Meade wrote his wife that Senator Hunter gave him a letter from Henry A. Wise (the Virginia governor who had hanged John Brown) and "Judge Campbell asked after" her family; the wives of General Meade, U.S.A., and General Wise, C.S.A., were sisters. These enemies were not enemies.[7]

When Grant left the room, Meade "talked very freely with them. I told them very plainly what I thought was the basis on which the people of the North would be glad to have peace, namely, the complete restoration of the Union and such a settlement of the slavery question as should be final, removing it forever as a subject of strife." Stephens urged an armistice, so that matters could be discussed. Meade said that "was entirely out of the question." The Southerners would first have to accede to the two conditions he had put forth. Undaunted by two hundred years of anguish and four years of battle, Stephens said he did not see "the slavery question as so formidable a difficulty." The Georgian was less interested in slavery than in an alteration of the Constitution that would protect states' rights.[8]

Hunter, the Virginian, returned to the matter of slavery; according to Meade, he asked "what we [in the Union] proposed to do with the slaves after freeing them, as it was well known that they would not work unless compelled." Meade, agreeing that this posed a problem, said it was "grave" but not "insurmountable" and suggested that since the people whose interests the commissioners represented "must have labor, and the negroes must have support; between the two necessities . . . some system could be devised accommodating both interests, which would not be so obnoxious as slavery." He was suggesting a system ensuring a subordinate status for the laborers as a substitute for slavery. Flatteringly, they then said, Meade reported, that it was "a pity this matter could not be left to the generals on each side, and taken out of the hands of politicians." Meade agreed, and urged Grant to cooperate fully. While not optimistic, he told his wife that he hoped "Mr. Lincoln will receive them and listen to all they have to say."[9]

Stephens recalled that they all talked quite openly about how the war might be brought to a close, and Grant stated later that "no guard was placed on them" and they were "permitted to leave the boat when they felt like it, and did so, coming up on the bank and visiting me at my headquarters." Howard C. Westwood, in his analysis of the peace conference, considers Grant to have been responsible for its being held, and both Stephens and Campbell indicated that Grant took an important political initiative, both in his own conversations and in seeing to it that no one prevented them from stating their case at the very highest level of government. Grant had had no previous acquaintance with the three men, but found none of them difficult to talk with. He particularly liked Stephens, claiming that he had admired him before the war. Stephens, wizened and strange-looking in a great stiff gray overcoat—he seemed to shrink as soon as it was shed—was a compelling man despite his small size. He was also the one most taken with Blair's Mexican scheme.[10]

The two little men, Grant and Stephens, sat down together. While five miles away, outside Petersburg, two armies wrestled to no resolution, the vice-president of the Confederate States of America and the commanding general of the Army of the United States of America talked easily but with urgency about how to get Abraham Lincoln and Jefferson Davis to discuss peace. All was cordial, and when the other two men joined Grant and his wife for a large dinner, Julia found she also liked the commissioners, and tried to transact some family business. Could they arrange the release from a Confederate jail of her brother John?—"a thorough rebel if there ever was one," she claimed almost proudly. He was not a prisoner of war, she explained, but had gone to Louisiana and been jailed there. The commissioners turned the matter back to her, asking why she had not gotten her husband to arrange his release by exchanging a Confederate soldier for him. She replied that she had asked him to do just that, but Ulysses—who had similarly refused to set up an exchange for his Confederate cousin Richard M. Hewitt, then in a Union prison—had told her that it would "not hurt John to have a good, wholesome lesson." (As a result, Julia noted in her *Memoirs*, "dear brother did not get back until the general exchange of prisoners . . . at the close of the war.") Inadvertently, perhaps, Julia Grant had given the Confederate negotiators a glimpse of the toughness that the general's geniality had disguised.[11]

Hunter reported being told by one of Grant's officers that "Mrs. Grant had expressed her opinion openly that her husband ought to send us on," and observed that the commissioners were "impressed . . . favorably by her frankness and good feelings." However, not everyone was as cordial. Lincoln's messenger, Major Thomas T. Eckert, the chief telegraph officer at the War Department (chosen by Stanton because he was an efficient bureaucrat) arrived with orders that the commissioners were to be sent back unless they accepted the stipulation of "one common country." It looked as if the men would be returned, and "the impatience of the bystanders [in City Point] to bring the parties together grew rapidly." Eckert, a stalwart away-from-the-front-lines patriot, saw himself as preventing appeasement and proved an inflexible barrier to negotiation. He was persuaded that Stanton was afraid "Lincoln's great kindness of heart and his desire to end the war might lead him to make some admission which the astute Southerners could willfully misconstrue," and he was equally worried about Grant. On arrival, he officiously told the lieutenant general that he was not to involve himself, since the mission of communicating with the commissioners had been entrusted solely to him, Eckert. The excuse for keeping Grant away was that if things were bungled, the blame would fall on Eckert, an underling, and not on the commanding general. Grant recognized that this was a pretext and was "vexed" when Eckert insisted on going alone to see the commissioners.[12]

At that meeting on February 1, 1865, Stephens turned on all his considerable Southern charm. He had known Eckert's cousin before the war, when they were members of the same Congress, and had helped Eckert get safe passage out of Atlanta in June 1861 (another Yankee, caught there then, had been hanged). Stephens was determined to win Lincoln's envoy to the idea that their passage to Washington must be arranged, but Eckert would not budge. Having presented the president's message, he left to await formal acceptance of the "one common country" stipulation. Their reply at 6:00 P.M. he found "not satisfactory." The commissioners were in a quandary. Grant, Blair, and Meade had all encouraged them to think Lincoln wanted a peace conference. But now, an underling sent to make arrangements for the meeting was insisting on a legalistic point as a condition for the conference. They were unwilling to break their own instructions and accept the "one common country" provision, but they were also determined to have their conversation with Lincoln.[13]

Luckily, Grant was equally determined that the talks take place. He went himself to the *Mary Martin* and resumed his amicable conversations with the commissioners, during which Hunter spoke frankly to him: "We do not seem to get on very rapidly with Major Eckert. We are anxious to get to Washington and Mr. Lincoln has promised to see us there." Grant's own sense of things agreed with theirs, and he encouraged the commissioners to appeal past Lincoln's emissary; as he prepared to leave the boat about 8:00 P.M. he carried a brief message, addressed formally to him, saying, "We desire to go to Washington City to confer informally with the President personally. . . ." Neatly, the Confederates did not say "President of the United States"; Grant hoped the one country / two country dilemma had been got round. As for the subjects to be discussed, the commissioners referred simply to "matters mentioned" in Lincoln's letter to Blair, and they maintained the position of having made no concessions by adding that they would discuss such matters with Lincoln "without any personal compromise" on any topic in the letter.[14]

Major Eckert, hearing that Grant was aboard the *Mary Martin*, joined him there. Grant had told the commissioners that the message "would or ought to be satisfactory to Major Eckert," but he was wrong; the stubborn telegrapher told Grant that the letter did not meet Lincoln's requirements, and calling the lieutenant general out of the room, but not so far away that the Confederates were unaware of what was being said, reproved him for involving himself in diplomacy. Their conversation was smoldering—Eckert recalled, "Grant was angry with me for years afterward"—but Grant could not flatly override Lincoln's emissary. In fact, the general obeyed the major, and the commissioners were told by Eckert that their request to proceed was disallowed. Eckert did defer to Grant on one crucial matter, however; as he finished his last conversation with the three Confederates he told them that if they "concluded to accept the terms" they should "inform General Grant." Eckert then left the *Mary Martin* and at 10:00 P.M. sent a telegram directly to Lincoln stating that the commissioners had been told, at nine-thirty, that the president's conditions had not been met. The purport of Eckert's message, which quoted the note the Commissioners had addressed to Grant, was that the conference should not be held. But Eckert did hedge on just one point; with no obvious relevance to anything else in his telegram, he added that he did not think it much mattered whether any possible meeting was in Washington: "Fort Monroe would be acceptable." This was the door through which Grant moved to bring about the peace conference.[15]

At ten-thirty that same evening, February 1, Grant with scrupulous attention to protocol sent a telegram not to Lincoln, but to the secretary of war:

Hon. Edwin M. Stanton, Secretary of War:

Now that the interview between Major Eckert, under his written instructions, and Mr. Stephens and party has ended, I will state confiden-
tially, but not officially to become a matter of record, that I am convinced
upon conversation with Messrs. Stephens and Hunter that their intentions are good and their desire sincere to restore peace and union. I have
not felt myself at liberty to express even views of my own or to account for
my reticency. This has placed me in an awkward position, which I could
have avoided by not seeing them in the first instance. I fear now their
going back without any expression from anyone in authority will have a
bad influence. At the same time, I recognize the difficulties in the way of
receiving these informal commissioners at this time, and do not know
what to recommend. I am sorry, however, that Mr. Lincoln can not have
an interview with the two named in this dispatch, if not all three now
within our lines. Their letter to me was all that the President's instructions
contemplated to secure their safe conduct if they had used the same language to Major Eckert.

U. S. Grant, Lieutenant-General.[16]

Then, after the fact, Grant set out to get a document to substantiate the
bold initiative he had taken. He returned to the *Mary Martin* and told the Confederates (with what Stephens recalled as "an anxious disquietude upon his
face") that "Major Eckert was not satisfied," but that he, Grant, had "determined" to send them not to Washington but "to Fortress Monroe the next
day on his own responsibility." He told them that Seward was already there,
and counseled them to be willing to speak to Lincoln's deputy rather than
only to the president. He may well have also said that he had hinted that Lincoln should go to Fortress Monroe to be with Seward for the meeting with
the Confederates. In any case, he told them to be ready in the morning to
leave for Hampton Roads and Fortress Monroe.[17]

When he left the commissioners he carried a letter from them (presumably
written after midnight, since it was dated February 2, 1865); this was carefully addressed not to him, but to Eckert. In it, they again sought to avoid the
one country / two country dilemma by merely referring to Lincoln's letter to
Blair and stating, "It is our earnest wish to ascertain, after, a free interchange
of ideas and information, upon what principles and terms, if any, a just and
honorable peace can be established without the further effusion of blood, and
to contribute our utmost effort to accomplish such a result." Further, they
told Eckert, should they be granted and accept his "passport," they were "not
to be understood to be committing [themselves] to anything." Stephens and

his fellows were protecting themselves from being charged in Richmond with having yielded the concept of Confederate sovereignty, but they also stated that they were "willing to proceed to Fortress Monroe and there to have an informal conference with any person or persons that President Lincoln may appoint. . . ." Grant did not let Eckert have a look at the most important letter ever addressed to him until the next afternoon. By the time Orville Babcock delivered it, at Fortress Monroe, it was too late for Eckert to decide that this letter, too, was unsatisfactory.[18]

The previous evening, at about the same hour that Grant sent his telegram, Eckert, as he left for the coast expecting to join Seward at Hampton Roads and return with him to Washington, also tried to send Stanton a telegram. It was an exceedingly obscure message designed to reconcile the language in the various communications of the commissioners. The telegram would have neither helped nor hindered the cause of the peace conference, but no matter; when Major Eckert tried to send it, the telegraph line mysteriously was out of order. Service had been restored by the following morning. Steam was up on the *Mary Martin*, and the commissioners were anxiously awaiting their departure, when Lieutenant General Ulysses S. Grant, "coming in almost a run down hill," got about twenty or thirty paces from the dock and with "countenance beaming" shouted to the rebels, "Gentlemen, it's all right, I've got the authority." He was waving a telegram, and coming up on deck, he read from it to them: "Say to the gentlemen I will meet them personally at Fortress-Monroe as soon as I can get there." At the White House, during the night, Lincoln had been prepared to act on Eckert's negative report, but at dawn, Stanton had brought him Grant's personal message urging that the conference take place. "This dispatch of General Grant changed my purpose," Lincoln later told Congress. He elected to set aside his own legalistic insistence on the "one common country" stipulation and go himself to meet with the Confederate delegation. Instead of recalling Seward, Lincoln wired, "Induced by a despatch of Gen. Grant, I join you at Fort-Monroe as soon as I can come." Campbell took the same view of Grant's centrality in the matter; he was sure that it was Grant who persuaded the president to make a trip his cabinet disapproved of. Welles and Stanton, in particular, knew how opposed Radicals in Congress could be to anything that would look like appeasement. In this respect the shift from Washington to Hampton Roads proved important on two counts: First, those opposed to having any conversation with the enemy would be mollified by the fact that the meeting took place in a neutral setting aboard ship rather than in the White House; second, Lincoln had more latitude away from Washington. In the capital he would have been exposed to nervous pressures from congressmen, reporters, and cabinet members like Stanton.[19]

When Lincoln's telegram—the one that Grant and the commissioners so cordially celebrated—arrived at City Point, Grant was of course greatly relieved that his initiative had been sanctioned by the president. He was de-

lighted that the conference would be held, and he knew, too, just how powerful his word had become. But much as he may have wanted to, Grant did
not go to the conference. He and one of the commissioners' aides remained at
City Point to discuss prisoner exchanges and the three Confederate commissioners, who knew from their earlier talks with Grant that he took a hard line
on this subject, saw in his willingness to talk about it still another optimistic
sign as with Orville Babcock as escort, they set out for Hampton Roads and
the peace conference on the *River Queen.* [20]

By the accounts of all five participants, it was a civil, even cordial meeting.
After exchanging pleasantries with Lincoln about Whig politics back in 1848,
Stephens asked if good relations could be restored by the acceptance of the
Confederacy's independence. The reply was no. Stephens then explained
that they had been commissioned by Jefferson Davis to propose a joint attack
on Mexico, but were not authorized to talk of the reabsorption of the Confederate States into the Union. It is likely that Lincoln saw the Mexican mission
as a euphemistic expression of Southern desperation. (Hunter, in fact, was
openly scornful of the silly scheme.) What Lincoln failed to see was how
great the pressure on Davis to make peace was; the gentlemanly commissioners did not succeed in making the president of the United States aware of
how hungry the starving people of the South were. Campbell, the most realistic of the three, tried to give a hint of the South's weakness, but Lincoln did
not fully perceive the strength of the North's position. All of the commissioners were surprised—one senses their great disappointment—that Lincoln
did not demand a peace agreement, a surrender. Such a show of strength
might, in turn, have strengthened their hand with Davis when they sought to
persuade him that immediate negotiations would be more fruitful than later
ones. [21]

During the discussion, the Confederates were told that the Thirteenth
Amendment, abolishing slavery, which had already been approved by the
Senate, had now cleared the House and was being sent to the states for ratification. The Confederates knew that both Seward and Chase had been at the
House lobbying for passage (twice previously denied the measure) on the
grounds that such a statement on slavery would strengthen the position of
Lincoln and Seward in any peace negotiations with the Confederacy. It
would persuade the Southerners that there was no turning back on the abolition of slavery. Now, however, on the *River Queen*, Seward toyed with a startling idea. Lincoln stated his position that he would countenance no reenslavement of people freed under the Emancipation Proclamation, but he
listened as the secretary of state suggested that if "the Southern States will return to the Union, . . . with their own strength and the aid of the connections they will form with other States, this amendment will be defeated." In
other words, if the Southern states were to come back into the Union—to
take part in the political process—they could hold off the final end of slavery.
An amendment must be ratified by three-fourths of the states, so the eleven

Confederate states acting together would be able to block approval. It is doubtful whether Seward truly believed the clock could be turned back with respect to the ending of slavery, but he may have wanted the rebels to see that they still had considerable bargaining power and that if slavery could not be salvaged, then some other system of involuntary labor, such as an "apprenticeship" system, might replace it. Thus the loss of a labor supply, and indeed the chaos which, it was feared, would follow when the slaves were quickly freed would be avoided. So, of course, would total emancipation.[22]

Lincoln, at this point, had a different suggestion to make to his old Whig friend Stephens: "If I were in Georgia . . . I would go home and get the Governor . . . to call the Legislature together, and get them to recall all the State troops from the war . . . and ratify this Constitutional Amendment *prospectively*, so as to take effect—say in five years. . . . Slavery is doomed. . . ." The five white Americans then discussed slavery and some "substitute status" for the slaves. When Hunter insisted that the black people, once freed, would no longer be cared for, Lincoln replied with his famous story of the hungry hogs which the farmer had provided for by planting a field of potatoes; when they're hungry enough, said the farmer, they can root. But what, someone asked him, would happen when the ground froze solid? "Let 'em root," the farmer answered stolidly. It was an odd simile for the Great Emancipator to choose, but Lincoln, like Hunter, was not sure the abolitionists had provided for the winter.[23]

Lincoln then introduced one of his favorite ideas, that of compensated emancipation, and Seward got up and paced about the cabin. Undaunted, Lincoln added to his secretary of state's discomfort by saying that Northerners were as culpable as Southern slaveholders and should be willing to share the costs of freedom. Lincoln then reiterated his support of the Emancipation Proclamation and said he would not permit any people freed by it to be re-enslaved. However, when Stephens questioned him he agreed that the Emancipation Proclamation was a war measure and conceded that those who had not been freed by the time peace was established might still be slaves in the eyes of the law. Thus, all five men kept returning to the discomfiting question of what the status would be of four million black people in the South when peace came.

No one seemed aware of the sixth man in the room. It was only to set the scene in his fine account of the conference that Stephens wrote, "During the interview, no person entered the saloon . . . except a colored servant" who brought in "water, cigars and other refreshments."[24]

If they could agree in their insensitive misgivings about the future in freedom of black Americans, the statesmen could come to no agreement on the basic question of sovereignty. Lincoln insisted on the unconditional resumption of federal authority over the whole South, while the commissioners did not have license from Davis even to discuss alterations in the United States Constitution that would have redefined federal authority in ways which might be favorable to the Confederates. The conference ended without agreement, and the commissioners started back toward Richmond.

At City Point, Stephens again saw Grant, who "regretted very much that nothing had been accomplished by the Conference." Julia Grant was equally disappointed. In her *Memoirs*, she recalled with vivid detail a conversation she did not have with Abraham Lincoln, during which she became so frustrated that she upbraided the president of the United States. As she remembered it, she opened the door to the living section of her husband's headquarters the morning after the conference and, seeing Lincoln, could not wait to summon the general before asking the president if there was going to be peace. "Well no," was his reply, as he tried to brush her off. "No!" she blurted out. "Why, Mr. President, are you not going to make terms with them? They are our own people, you know." Taking her seriously now, Lincoln said, "Yes, I do not forget that," and he reached into his pocket and read to her the terms he had offered the commissioners. Then he looked straight at her and she said, "Did they not accept those?" Her account continued: "He smiled wearily and said, 'no.' Whereupon I wrathfully exclaimed: 'Why, what do they want? That paper is most liberal.' He smiled and said: 'I thought when you understood the matter you would agree with us.' "[25]

There is no doubt that Julia Grant would have relished having such a conversation to report, but if she and Abraham Lincoln ever had such an exchange, it was not on the morning after the meeting with the peace commissioners; the president had left for Annapolis and the train for Washington at four the previous afternoon, immediately after the conference ended. In her memory, she may have confused the conversation with one she could conceivably have had with Lincoln when he visited City Point later in the winter; of the fact that her imaginings reflected her sentiments, there can be no doubt. She had pressed her husband hard to see to it that a peace conference was held.

Critics of the peace conference claim it lengthened the war by strengthening the will of Confederates who saw Lincoln, not Davis, as the obdurate force. Why then had Grant, whose job was to win the war, worked so hard to bring the conference about? The answer is that he truly thought the enemy, or at least the saner enemy leaders, ready to stop the fighting, and he believed the peace conference had a chance of succeeding; he believed Lincoln and the three Confederates would find a way to say that enough was enough. If they had done so, Grant would have completed his job in a nonmartial manner. Grant's eagerness to bring the politicians to the table was not, however, entirely born of confidence. By January 1865 Thomas had halted the last threat of a major Confederate offensive and the Confederate armies were locked into place around Richmond, but all was not over. Sherman had yet to complete his circle north through the Carolinas, and he was paced by the still-dangerous Johnston. And even that was not Grant's greatest worry. Rationally, he knew his position was much stronger than Lee's, yet he feared the war would slip out of his grasp. "One of the most anxious periods of my experience during the rebellion was the last few weeks before Petersburg. . . . I was afraid, every morning, that I would awake from my sleep to hear that Lee had gone . . . and the war [had been] prolonged another year." Lee was shrewd, and his small army might prove adroit; Grant feared that the Confederates might slip off not so much to thwart Sherman as to "escape"— to move into the hills and fight as guerrillas. If they did, Grant would lose his personal hold on the war and its destiny. By functioning as a diplomat, working to bring to the bargaining table men from both sides who feared chaos, he remained in command of his war.[26]

Not all observers were totally discouraged by the lack of success at the peace conference. Charles Francis Adams, Jr., about to become the colonel of a black regiment in General Ord's command, saw the meeting as "an indispensable first step which had to be taken." Adams, whose troops had not won his affection, wanted a moderate peace—that is, a peace considerate of the feelings of white gentlemen in the South. (In contrast, his men were inconsiderate of the Massachusetts gentleman; Adams blamed this on the fact that he was a stern disciplinarian: "I no longer wonder slave drivers were cruel. I no longer have any bowels of mercy. . . .") Adams told his father he was glad Lincoln had met with the commissioners: "As for dignity, I do not look to President Lincoln for that. I do look to him for honesty and shrewdness and I see no evidence that in this matter he has been wanting in these respects."[27]

In March, after hearing Lincoln's second inaugural speech, with its talk of malice toward none, young Adams wrote his father, in England, "[The] rail-splitting lawyer is one of the wonders of the day." He saw the speech as setting a tone of peace but observed that "since Hampton Roads, there had been no presidential effort comparable to the conference on the *River Queen*." Others, however, were actively trying to get the two sides to talk again. John A. Campbell, his splendid legal mind searching every corner of the issue for a way to redefine it, tried repeatedly to persuade his government to reopen negotiations; on a less intellectual level, Mrs. General Grant had a similar goal. Perhaps people on both sides who knew how to talk to one another could be brought together to discuss how best to bring an end to the war.[28]

Ulysses had a way of teasing Julia. He would talk to her playfully about something serious and then, abruptly, turn away from the subject when she took it seriously. One day she came out of their bedroom and found Grant and Ord talking. Her husband told her that Ord had been across the lines under a flag of truce and had had a conversation with a mutual friend, the Confederate general James Longstreet. Many years later, Julia recalled her husband's asking her what she would think of "an interchange of social visits between you and Mrs. Longstreet and others when the subject of peace may be discussed, and you ladies may become the mediums of peace." In reply, she at once exclaimed, using the diction of breathless femininity, "Oh! How

enchanting, how thrilling! Oh, Ulys, I may go, may I not?" Grant, Julia reported in her account of the conversation,

> only smiled at my enthusiasm and said: "No, I think not." I then ap-
> proached him, saying, "Yes, I must. Do say yes. I so wish to go. Do let
> me go." But he still said: "No, that would never do." Besides, he did not
> feel sure that he could trust me; with the desire I always had shown for
> having a voice in great affairs, he was afraid I might urge some policy that
> the President would not sanction. I replied to this: "Oh, nonsense. Do not
> talk so, but let me go. I should be so enchanted to have a voice in this great
> matter. I must go. I will. Do say I may go." But General Grant grew very
> earnest now and said: "No, you must not. It is simply absurd. The men
> have fought this war and the men will finish it."
>
> I urged no more, knowing this was final, and I was silent, indignant,
> and disappointed.[29]

No more negotiations were attempted; after the peace conference that
brought no peace, there were eight more weeks of siege at Petersburg. Grant
was not moving, but Sherman was—coming north from Savannah through
the Carolinas. The war was being won, even as the terms for ending it still
eluded the captains of the Union cause. Sherman's advance evoked a "Te
Deum of the nation," recalled Gideon Welles, who nastily added that the
"hosannas to Sherman roused Grant to the necessity of doing something lest
there should be another and greater hero who would eclipse him." Had
Grant sat still and simply kept Lee's men engaged at Petersburg, Sherman
might have walked in from the southwest, taken Richmond, and indeed
become the hero of the hour. Grant foresaw the possibility; when Sherman
wrote that he would decline a rumored promotion—one that would raise him
to Grant's singular place—if it were offered, Grant in his reply was not only
gracious about this prospect but even offered to bow out: "No one would be
more pleased . . . at your advancement than I, and if you should be placed in
my position and I subordinate it would not change our personal relations in
the least."[30]

Grant chose to let that possibility remain hypothetical and began to put
heavy pressure on the Confederates outside Richmond; he did indeed want to
play an active role in his own victory, but Welles was wrong to suggest
that Grant was pigheadedly trying to shove past Sherman. During February,
Grant could see the coming "dissolution" of the Confederate cause on all
fronts. He noted that the number of Confederate deserters was increasing
despite official Richmond attempts to make the "insult" to the Confederate
commissioners at the peace conference a rallying cry for renewed fighting. In
a letter to Elihu Washburne, he wrote generously, "A few days more of success with Sherman will put us where we can crow loud." There already
hung, in the rotunda of the Capitol, in Washington, a painting of Grant
standing with gloved hand on a cannon. He was already in his place as the

war's great military hero, and he wanted to have at his elbow, when the war finally ended, its only greater hero—Abraham Lincoln. On March 20 he wrote Lincoln, "Can you not visit City Point for a day or two? I would like very much to see you and I think the rest would do you good." If Lincoln came, the two men could be together at the war's close, and there would be less risk of Grant's being left out of whatever was going to happen once the war was over.[31]

To the delight of Ulysses and Julia, Lincoln accepted the invitation at once. On March 24, 1865, Abraham and Mary Lincoln and their son Tad reached City Point on board the *River Queen*. The visit proved to be an incongruous mixture of frivolous social skirmishing and the most serious of talk. The men who did the talking were the president of the United States, his two senior generals, Grant and Sherman (who came north by sea), and Admiral David Dixon Porter. The women, frustrated in their impotent rage at a war they could neither affect nor avoid, scarcely knew what to do. City Point, with its tents and cabins, was a strange world which Mary Lincoln's husband enjoyed, but in which she had no place. Had there been no other women around, she might have reigned on foreign ground. Instead, she was confronted with generals' wives who had made City Point theirs, and was out of sorts as she arrived.

Robert Lincoln was already at City Point. His father had asked Grant if his son, who had just graduated from Harvard, might not have a chance to see a bit of the war, and Robert was serving on Grant's staff. He brought the word to the Grants' cabin at City Point that his parents and brother had arrived on the *River Queen*, which stood off the point in the James River. The Grants went at once to call on the Lincolns, and as the men went off together, Julia Grant, feeling ill at ease, was left alone in small quarters with Mary Lincoln. Mrs. Lincoln had gotten up to greet her, and now Julia, as unobtrusively as possible, sat down on the small sofa on which Mrs. Lincoln had been sitting. Only when she looked up and saw the disapproval on Mrs. Lincoln's face did she realize, too late, that she should not have seated herself while the president's wife was standing. She started up with an apology, but was beckoned back with belated graciousness by Mrs. Lincoln, who sat down on the sofa as well. The two women were jammed together in discomfort and silence. After an eternal second or two, Julia rose and "quietly took a chair near her."[32]

The next day things went no better. Mrs. Lincoln, accompained by Julia, was driven to a review of troops in an ambulance that moved slowly and uncomfortably through the mud. The general's wife tried to bring a cheerful note to the tedious trip, but her supply of tact was drawn on heavily. When Mrs. Lincoln grew exasperated with their progress, Julia persuaded her not to get out in the calf-deep mud, but she was totally unable to appease the first lady's wrath when General Ord's wife rode blithely past them on horseback. Mary Lincoln made the day totally miserable, and the memory lingered.[33]

When Grant and Sherman returned the next day from a conference with

Lincoln, in which business of the first importance had been discussed, Julia's first question was whether they had remembered to pay their respects to Mrs. Lincoln. They had not, and Julia scolded them—"Well, you are a pretty pair!" The following day, remembering her chastising words as they went aboard the *River Queen*, they carefully asked for Mrs. Lincoln. The president went to her stateroom but soon returned and asked that she be excused since she was not well.[34]

Julia was tiring of this imperiousness. When, on a social occasion, the topic was, What should be done with Jefferson Davis, if he is captured? Mary Lincoln baited Julia Grant: "Suppose we ask Mrs. Grant. Let her answer this important question." Julia, with good political savvy, caught Lincoln's eye and said she would trust Davis "to the mercy of our always just and most gracious President." Julia had won that round in the eyes of the men but had lost forever so far as the president's wife was concerned. Mary Lincoln hated every woman who played up to her husband, and hated herself for caring. It was particularly galling to be jealous of a dowdy little person like the general's wife. From this moment on at City Point, Mary Lincoln snubbed Julia Grant—refusing, for example, to allow her to go with her party to visit Petersburg after the city finally yielded to the siege. And even in Mary Lincoln's forlorn, unbalanced years after the assassination, Julia never forgave this treatment.[35]

While the women, deprived of any activity save flirtation, yielded to bitchiness, Lincoln, Grant, Sherman, and Porter met for long conversations. The topic was what John A. Campbell had called Reconstruction—that is, they were considering what the relationship of the Southern states to the national government should be when the Union was rebuilt. "Change" was not the key word in the conversations; Reconstruction did not, for those four, involve basic revision of the racial order, enforced by the introduction of a concept of national citizenship. Slavery was dead, but the superiority of white men over black men was not. We have only Sherman's and Porter's accounts of the conference—written when both sought to justify Sherman's later claim that everything he did in making terms with Johnston in April was in accordance with what was said by the four men on the *River Queen* in late March. G. P. A. Healy painted a wonderful picture of the four victors in the stateroom of the boat, but it is a cartoon without a caption. Guessing what was on Abraham Lincoln's mind in the weeks before the death that prevented him from putting any of his thoughts into action has been one of the nation's favorite speculative games ever since the assassination.[36]

We cannot know, but nothing anyone said—certainly, nothing the president himself said—after the talks on the *River Queen* suggests that the commander in chief and his highest military lieutenants wanted anything more than the end of the war and the establishment of a stable civil order. They seem scarcely to have been cognizant of the fact that this order would have no defined place within it for the four million people who would be slaves no

*G. P. A. Healy*, The Peacemakers. *Sherman, Grant, Lincoln, and Porter.*
WHITE HOUSE COLLECTION

more. Porter thought "Mr. Lincoln came down to City Point with the most liberal views toward the rebels. He felt confident that we would be successful, and was willing that the enemy should capitulate on the most favorable terms." Porter was convinced that Lincoln "wanted peace on almost any terms." Conferring with the admiral and the two generals, Lincoln was separated from those in his capital who were desperately anxious lest he give away the victory. Lincoln joked about stern, demanding Stanton; it was a relief to leave behind even for a few days that dogged man and his constant reminders that radicals in Congress, such as Senator Sumner, had in mind dramatic changes in the social order of the South that would give the freedmen power at the expense of the white men who presently directed civil life there.[37]

While the Lincolns were at City Point, Petersburg fell. Lincoln and Grant went into the town that so long, so stubbornly, so valiantly, had resisted Grant's armies. On Market Street, they went up to the pillared house of an old Whig friend of the president's, and Lincoln asked a young gentleman at the door if they could come in. Appalled, the man went back inside and said to his father, "You are not going to let that man come into the house!" "I think it would not do to try to stop a man from coming in who has fifty thousand men at his back," was the reply as he joined Lincoln and Grant on the porch. The callers laughed, and their host, enlarging on his hospitality, invited them into the parlor. As C. C. Carpenter remembered it a quarter of a century later, Grant demurred: "Thank you, sir, but I am smoking." While they stood on the porch, Grant was handed a telegram. He read it, "took the cigar from his mouth, and with the utmost coolness" read it aloud. Richmond too had been occupied.[38]

The army that finally reached the city on April 3, 1865, found that the Confederate government had left for Danville, Virginia. Lee had informed Davis that he could no longer protect the capital and withdrew his army from the defense lines in front of Richmond. A Union officer, Edward H. Ripley, wrote that when his men went over the Confederate defense works they "rushed wildly in every direction," mounting the great iron cylinders "until a howling maniac in blue sat astride every one of the thickly planted guns in reach." The move into Richmond itself became a race, with cavalry units rushing past infantry and competing cavalry—all trying to be first into the city. One infantry unit broke into a run, only to encounter a swamp. Ripley remembered how he had urged his men on through earlier long and agonizing marches by saying, "Close up, boys. Close up." Now the same cry seemed to drive them with an almost sexual energy. As he rode back along the ranks of his advancing infantrymen, he found himself looking down, he said, "into flashing eyes and quivering faces of the men as they glanced up at me in the mute freemasonry of a common joy and glory."[39]

Some of the Union soldiers were black. For them, the fall of Richmond had a special significance. The stories of their entrance into the city have the hollowness of twice-told tales that have been invested with symbolic grandeur, and yet one cannot wholly discount all the accounts of the emotional welcome they got from the black Virginians who came into the streets to greet the day of deliverance. Ripley remembered the freed slaves of the city on their knees, calling out, " 'Glory to God! Glory to God!' . . . while floods of tears poured down their wild faces." Some stories of that day became legends, among them the tale of the black Union soldier who entered one house to liberate his wife, still a slave, only to be bayoneted by the white rebel soldier guarding the white inhabitants. Ripley approved of this action, claiming the Union soldier had been bent not merely on rescue but also on mocking his wife's master and forcing the cook to prepare a meal for him and his wife. Ripley thought it wise when General Godfrey Weitzel ordered his black troops to camp outside the city. In town, "none of the better class of whites were to be seen; blinds on houses were shut."[40]

Saluting the fall of Richmond, Herman Melville wrote, "God is in Heaven, and Grant in the Town," but he was wrong. The general did not enter the enemy's capital—the victorious captain at the head of his troops. He stayed away from Richmond. "Say to the President," Grant wrote in a note to Colonel Theodore S. Bowers, "that an officer and escort will attend but as to myself I start toward the Danville road with the army. I want to cut off as much of Lee's army as possible." Julia did go to Richmond, and was sorry afterward. In perhaps the finest passage in her *Memoirs*, she recorded that there was in the "fallen city" no glory. "When we arrived at the landing, we took a carriage and directed the coachman to drive through the principal streets and past the public buildings. I only saw that the city was deserted; not a single inhabitant visible. Only now and then we would meet one or two carriages with visitors from the North, coming like ourselves to see this sad city, and occasionally an old colored servant would pass alone, looking on us as intruders, as we all felt we were."[41]

Another intruder was Abraham Lincoln, who came into Jefferson Davis's capital and made peace with the highest-ranking member of the Confederate government remaining in Richmond, John A. Campbell. In 1861 Campbell had been one of the last men to try to negotiate a compromise to avoid secession and war. Now he pointed out to Lincoln the distress of the people of Richmond. There had been a great fire and a worse devastation of spirit as the government and army left. "I represented the conditions to him and requested that no requisitions on the inhabitants be made of restraint of any sort save to police and preservation of order; not to exact oaths, interfere with the churches, etc. He assented to this," Campbell claimed. He portrayed Lincoln as wanting his wayward children to come home. If the people of the South would acknowledge the "national authority" he would let them go on about their business with no restraints. Lincoln was apparently ready to jettison Francis Harrison Pierpont's feeble Unionist government in Virginia if the Confederate government "up yonder" in the statehouse would declare, as Lincoln put it to Campbell, that it was ready to change landlords and come back into the Union.[42]

Campbell was delighted with his agreement with Lincoln. It preserved the essentials of the Southern order. Slavery was not mentioned, but the continuance of a government that had so long enforced the racial arrangements of the South boded well for their maintenance. This was a compromise in which Campbell gave nothing and gained much. It was in the tradition of the great American compromises in which white men made agreements at the expense of black men. Pursuing his promising diplomacy, Campbell the next day called on Lincoln, on the gunboat *Malvern*, on the James. Lincoln gave him a document reiterating the need to recognize the national authority and ambiguously saying that "on the slavery question" he would not go back "from the position in the late annual message to Congress and in preceding documents." Using his executive power, he banned further confiscation of property, but he added that this "remission of confiscation has no reference to supposed property in slaves." He ordered General Weitzel, in command of the occupied city, to call the legislature into session. Then, called back to Washington, he left Grant alone to finish the war.[43]

# XV

---

# "ON TO MEXICO"

---

At first every small apprehension is magnified, every anxiety a
pounding terror. Then the pain comes, and I concentrate only on that.
Right there is the usefulness of the migraine, there in that imposed
yoga, the concentration on the pain. For when the pain recedes, ten or
twelve hours later, everything goes with it, all the hidden resentments,
all the vain anxieties. The migraine has acted as a circuit breaker, and
the fuses have emerged intact.

— *Joan Didion*

The pain in my head seemed to leave me the moment I got Lee's letter.

— *Ulysses S. Grant*

THE SURRENDER at Appomattox is enshrined in American history as
the great sacrament of reconciliation. Differences were overcome and dispari-
ties made one in the meeting of two brilliantly different men. One—tall, aristocratic, born at "Stratford," in tidewater Virginia—was dressed in an im-
maculate new gray uniform and wore a ceremonial sword; the other—short,
republican, born in a little house in Point Pleasant, Ohio—was in scruffy
army-blue clothing and carried a cigar. In their disparity, Lee and Grant
were the perfect celebrants of the mass of reunification. Robert E. Lee,
teaching his countrymen the lesson (one they resolutely declined to learn)
that quite a good thing can be made of losing a war, was splendid. Grant, as
the magnanimous victor, was if possible even more so. No matter how much
one might find fault with Grant, one could always look back and be restored
by this hour of his undoubted greatness–his finest hour.

Perhaps so. But there is little to suggest that as the war drew to a close
Grant expected it to end well. By the beginning of April, Lee was trapped.
Grant judged that weakened by casualties and desertions, the Confederate
general was, at last, ready to respond to his call for surrender, which went
out on April 7. That same day, Lee responded, "Though not entertaining the

opinion you express on the hopelessness of further resistance . . . , I recipro-
cate your desire to avoid useless effusion of blood, and therefore, before considering your proposition, ask the terms you will offer on condition of . . .
surrender." The next morning—how early is not clear—Grant replied, "I
would say, that *peace* being my great desire, there is but one condition I
would insist upon—namely, That the men and officers surrendered shall be
disqualified for taking up arms again against the Government of the United
States until properly exchanged." Grant then added that he would assign
men to meet Lee to arrange "definitely the terms upon which the surrender of
the Army of Northern Virginia will be received." He avoided any mention of
the immense political ramifications of such a surrender.[1]

As the note went to Lee, all of Grant's military power was converging on
him. Meade moved ominously north of the Appomattox River; Sheridan's
cavalry pressed westward toward Appomattox Court House itself, with
Ord's army following. April 8 was a day of more fighting and more deaths,
and of great psychic strain on Ulysses Grant. That evening, having still not
heard from Lee, Grant rode on his horse Cincinnati into that night's makeshift headquarters, and uncharacteristically greeted Meade with an affectionate "Old Fellow." Meade, pleased, was gentle in reply, knowing Grant
"had one of his sick headaches, which are rare, but cause him fearful pain,
such as almost overcomes his iron stoicism." The two staffs, Grant's and
Meade's, shared a farmhouse, and one of the officers was pounding the
piano he had discovered there. Music was noise to Grant; he sat bathing his
feet in hot water and mustard, and putting mustard plasters on his wrists and
the back of his neck. His headache was severe. About midnight, when the
farmhouse had at last quieted and Grant rested on a sofa in the front room, a
message from Lee finally arrived. Horace Porter and John Rawlins were
reluctant to disturb Grant, hoping he had managed to fall asleep, but when
Rawlins pushed open the general's door quietly, Grant immediately called to
him to come on in; the headache had kept him awake. He sat up and read
Lee's note by candlelight. "To be frank," wrote the Confederate general, "I
do not think the emergency has arisen to call for the surrender of the army;
but as the restoration of peace should be the sole object of all, I desired to
know whether your proposals would lead to that end." He proposed that
they meet at ten the next morning "on the old stage-road to Richmond."
Grant did not like to be preached to; he wanted one thing and one thing
only—the surrender of Lee's army. He would not talk of terms; he would not
negotiate a peace. He lay down on the sofa again, telling Rawlins and Porter
that he would reply in the morning.[2]

When Porter went to check on Grant at four in the morning, the room was
empty, and going outside, he found Grant pacing back and forth, his hands
pressed against his head. His migraine was excruciating, and Porter and
Rawlins got him some coffee. When the throbbing abated a bit, he wrote
Lee, "I have no authority to treat on the subject of peace; the meeting pro-

posed for 10 A.M. to-day could lead to no good." He did add a plea for a battlefield surrender without any talk of the general political situation: "I will
state however, general, that I am equally anxious for peace with yourself,
and the whole North entertains the same feeling." The eloquence of his statement, but perhaps not its persuasiveness, was diminished by his comment
that the surrender would save not only "thousands of human lives" but also
"hundreds of millions of property not yet destroyed." In all, the message that
went out early in the morning of April 9 had a decidedly urgent tone.[3]

Grant told Horace Porter that morning, at the start of the greatest day of
his life, that the best thing that could happen to him that day would be for
the pain of the headache to clear. It was still torturing him, but he turned
down an ambulance, mounted Cincinnati, and rode off. One would expect
that with hopes so high for an affirmative message from Lee, he would have
alerted officers to his whereabouts at every imaginable point. Instead, finding
one road blocked, he went off with Rawlins, Porter, and Babcock to look for
another, without leaving word of his destination. Perhaps there was a curious
want of confidence at a moment when none but Grant could imagine such a
thing; perhaps he dreaded still another rebuff by Lee. As he had done after
Donelson and again in Louisville (when, shortly after he had been given his
first great command, Stanton could not find him), he now put himself out of
touch with his own generals—and with Lee.[4]

Lee had ridden to the point on the Richmond road where he had expected
to meet Grant at ten, only to receive Grant's note saying he was not coming.
With his military position worsening by the hour, Lee could no longer continue the grim comedy of manners. The time was gone for playing for terms
that did not involve an admission of defeat, and with great sadness, he agreed
to surrender. When this message reached the Union lines, Meade was notified and ordered a truce. Lieutenant Charles E. Pease, sent to find Grant,
had to do considerable hunting. An hour and fifty minutes after Lee wrote
the crucial note, Pease came upon Grant and Rawlins, who were off their
horses, lighting cigars. Pease galloped up, and Rawlins opened the envelope,
read the message, and handed it to Grant, who read it with no noticeable
emotion. Then he sat down on the grass and wrote his reply to Lee. In this
letter he specified with precision the road on which he would be riding, so
that a second message, naming a place to talk, could reach him. He then sent
Orville Babcock galloping off with the letter for Lee, mounted Cincinnati,
and rode toward Appomattox Court House at a trot. The headache was
gone.[5]

He had worn down Lee's great armies and defeated the great patriarch in
war, and now he had managed to beat him in the gentlemanly art of war-end-
ing. From the moment Lee's note arrived, Grant was in perfect command of
himself, and from then on every move of the day was a quiet triumph played
out with consummate skill. There was even an appropriate moment of absurdity; as they rode swiftly westward on the road, intent on reaching Lee,

Grant and his two aides suddenly spotted a swarm of graycoats and it "looked for a moment as if Grant [might] become a prisoner in Lee's lines instead of Lee in his. Such a circumstance," wrote Horace Porter, "would have given rise to an important cross-entry in the system of campaign bookkeeping." Quickly, the Yankees cut across country, found another road, and rode into the village of Appomattox Court House. Sheridan was there with Orville Babcock, who showed Grant the way to a farmhouse.[6]

The passing of the headache was no signal for Grant to step out of character and make a vainglorious entrance at the meeting. But it should not be assumed that he had given no thought to this moment. He had delayed other meetings to suit his plans; he could have rearranged the Appomattox meeting if it were not going to be conducted exactly as he had wanted it to be. Lee, arriving first, "had on the handsomest uniform" his aide had ever seen him wear, and wore a sword in an English-leather scabbard worked in gold. Grant wore no sword at all, his coat was unbuttoned, and "his clothing was somewhat dusty and a little soiled." Later he made a disingenuous apology for his appearance: "I had not expected so soon the result that was then taking place, and consequently was in rough garb." Grant did not wear the unpressed jacket and mud-spattered trousers to insult Lee, or because he had no time to change. He had wanted to be away from headquarters when called to talk to Lee; he had wanted to ride in straight from the field. His attire had been chosen as long ago as the day the little boy mocked the fancy-dress uniform of the West Point graduate; the worn clothing gave him the same sense of confidence that the elegant uniform gave Lee.[7]

Grant walked into the parlor and shook hands with Lee. Grant's personal staff was with him, but except for Sheridan, none of his commanding generals were there; he surrounded himself with men as comfortable as his clothes. He and Lee chatted, and Lee politely tried to suggest that he remembered Grant. He did not; Grant, on the other hand, did remember Lee. They talked about old times in the army in Mexico for so long that Lee had to remind Grant why they were there. Grant then took a pencil and paper and, with his usual directness, wrote that he would accept a surrender if the officers of each of the Confederate's regiments would sign a parole for all of their men, pledging that they would fight no more. He ordered all equipment and supplies turned over to the Union army, except side arms, privately owned horses, and personal baggage. The men who surrendered, he added, would be allowed to go home.[8]

Lee had made no requests for special conditions. Reading Grant's letter accepting his surrender, he commented that the generous provisions for the retention of horses and gear would "have a happy effect upon his army." Trying to make a good thing better, Lee sought to have the animals used by the enlisted cavalrymen and artillerymen treated as private property and asked if men who were not officers might also be allowed to take home the horses they had been using. Grant said his letter, as written, forbade that, but noting that the Southerners would need these animals to get a crop in that spring, he agreed that these animals too could go. Except for this permission to take horses back to the plow, the surrender involved no political terms whatever. Lee asked his aide Charles Marshall to draft a reply, and then, removing some stuffy verbiage, wrote out a simple acceptance. It was not the surrender of one government to another; it was simply—and importantly— the surrender of one army to another. But one of these armies was greatly diminished; Lee's once huge, proud Army of Northern Virginia had only eight thousand men remaining in it.[9]

Grant's letter of acceptance was presented to Lee, and the two men shook hands. When they were about to part, Lee told Grant that his men were des- titute. Grant ascertained from Sheridan that rations for twenty-five thousand men could be supplied and asked Lee if these were enough. They were. As for the horses, it was just as well that Grant had been generous and permitted the disbanding Confederates to take them; there was no forage in the region save the scant early-spring growth on the land. Four years of gore came to this quiet end, and the great day's outcome produced a curious flatness in Grant. He sent the most expressionless of victory messages:

> *Headquarters Appomattox C.H., Va.,*
> *April 9th, 1865, 4.30 P.M.*

Hon. E. M. Stanton, Secretary of War, Washington.

General Lee surrendered the Army of Northern Virginia this afternoon on terms proposed by myself. The accompanying additional corre- spondence will show the conditions fully.

> U. S. Grant,
> Lieut.-General

This was the word the capital was waiting for; it brought huge crowds into the streets in front of the White House to serenade President Lincoln. But in Virginia, Grant silenced the guns that were being fired in a victory salute. He "felt like anything rather than rejoicing. . . ."[10]

The next day, Grant once more met with Lee and tried to persuade him to use his influence to make his fellow commanders elsewhere in the South sur- render. With great political skill, Grant had appeared apolitical at Appomat- tox on the ninth, but on the tenth he was trying to push his former antagonist into the politics of dissolving the Confederacy. Lee once more avoided doing more than surrendering his army; he said he could not urge other surrenders without conferring with his president. Not discouraged, Grant parted amica bly from Lee and "spent an hour pleasantly" with officers of both armies at the McLean farmhouse in Appomattox, where they were enjoying reunions with West Point classmates and looking "very much as if all thought of the war had escaped their minds." Then he rode on Cincinnati to the point to which the railroad had been rebuilt, and began a two-day train journey— punctuated with repeated derailments caused by the hasty, inadequate re- pairs—back to City Point. He arrived at midnight. Julia, exhausted from waiting, had fallen asleep in her clothes, but awakened to greet "her 'Vic- tor.' " The next morning, as Grant walked through his headquarters post and into his cabin, Admiral Porter was having round after round of victory sa- lutes fired in his honor from his flotilla in the James. Annoyed with the noise, Grant sat down and wrote some dispatches, among them a letter to Sherman; when this job was finished, he turned to his office aide and said, "On to Mexico."[11]

Here was Grant's odd low-key humor. It was a dismissal of the bravado of victory, a call to himself and his staff to get back to work, and a recognition that new work must be found. The journey of his mind to Mexico may have been in remembrance of another war that had ended, leaving him with no life to lead. The leap was also a shrewd guess at where the next war might be. In Mexico there was another liberal cause to be fought for, another nationalist struggle under way. The French puppet was a potential ally to whom desper- ate Confederates might be drawn; Maximilian's enemies were Mexico's pa- triots, with whom patriotic Americans might join. Grant's throw-away com- ment was not as bad a joke or as inaccurate a prophecy as it may seem. Grant himself, in 1866, came close to going to the Mexican border before he recog- nized the assignment as the exile that President Johnson intended. Sheridan, the fiery little man in whom so many of Grant's private urges found expres- sion, was on the border within a year—and came close indeed to taking the army into a war in Mexico. And on April 12, 1865, the trip to Mexico that Grant's mind took was a journey of continuance. He himself had concluded a peace, and yet, personally, he could not let the war end. He had to keep his life going. The war was not a discrete event with finite walls of time, separate from something called peace; rather, it was the core of his life. Ulysses Grant was reluctant to let go of war.

Grant did not, however, pursue war into Mexico; he went instead to Washington and straight into Reconstruction politics. Reluctantly, Lincoln had preceded him there. After Richmond, the president had gone back to the capital, to the relief of both congressional radicals and cabinet conservatives. Secretary of the Navy Welles called the president's stay at City Point "an un- usual absence at an important period." Indeed, said Welles, Secretary of State Seward, "who usually attended [Lincoln] on his excursions and was always anxious to do so[,] was taken by surprise" by Lincoln's visit to City Point. The cabinet members had reason to worry. Lincoln had indeed seemed ready to make peace at either Grant's capital or that of the fallen foe, rather than at the nation's. All of the cabinet members, including Welles and Seward, who later were advocates of programs very like those Lincoln ini- tiated at Richmond, thought that the decisions should be made at Washing-

ton—and with their participation. Lincoln was all too much at home with
the generals, who were themselves not immune to thoughts of a brotherly
peace between men who had fought each other for so long. If there was to be
a Reconstruction that was not simply a restoration of amenities and a rebuilding of the old social order of the South, it would have to be engineered in
Washington. However, Lincoln was brought back to Washington before the
surrender of Lee not by any theory about where decision making properly
should be done, but by an accident. Seward was thrown from his carriage
and seriously injured. The president had to give up his chance of being with
Grant for the end of the war in order to visit the secretary of state.[12]

Lincoln returned to the White House on April 9, not yet aware of Lee's
surrender, and Welles found him "looking well and feeling well." Soon the
celebrations began, and when the serenades celebrating Grant's victory were
over, Lincoln met with his cabinet and asked what they thought of his plan to
have the existing Confederate legislature of Virginia take that state out of the
rebellion. Welles, conservative and skeptical, said he had "not great faith in
negotiating with large bodies of men" and was worried lest the legislature
take an action that the federal government would have to repudiate. He also
reminded Lincoln that a wartime Unionist government for Virginia had already been recognized. It did not, of course, speak for the defeated but proud
Confederate Virginians, but simply to pretend that the Unionist government
did not exist was awkward. Stanton was far more adamant in his insistence
that Congress would accept no such lenient program. He persuaded Lincoln
to stop the legislative meeting in Richmond, and a telegram went to General
Godfrey Weitzel, in command in Richmond, telling him that as Lee had now
surrendered, the need for a repudiation session of the legislature was unnecessary and those who had already arrived for this session were to be sent
home.[13]

By Friday, April 14, Grant had arrived in the capital, and he attended a
meeting of Lincoln's cabinet. Gideon Welles's diary makes it clear that
Grant's opinions on a wide range of issues were eagerly sought and readily
given. Welles's unexpectedly favorable assessment of Grant's performance
should be read as recognition that on that particular day the general agreed
with the secretary of the navy, but nonetheless, Grant's performance truly impressed Welles. (In contrast, exactly a week earlier, although crediting Grant
with being "masterly" at war and possessing great "persistency" of character,
Welles had described him as "slow and utterly destitute of genius.") The subject of the meeting was "the relations of the Rebels, the communications, the
trade, etc.," and there is no evidence that Grant showed any reluctance to
discuss these nonmilitary topics. Surely he had no trouble being enthusiastic
about Secretary of the Treasury Hugh McCulloch's suggestion that they get
rid of the Treasury agents who were in charge of trade in all the captured
rebel ports. These men, and the speculators who surrounded them, had exasperated Grant throughout the war and now he "expressed himself very de-

cidedly against them, thought them demoralizing, etc." Welles argued for free trade all along the coast, but Stanton thought this should be permitted only where the Northern army was present and in firm control. Grant said he thought the region in which open trade could be allowed "might embrace all this side of the Mississippi."[14]

Stanton then raised the basic question of Reconstruction. What were to be the relationships of the various people of the South to one another, and to the Union to which they were returning? He had a document for his colleagues to study, and he led the discussion. Lincoln, who had often before achieved his own policy goals by biding his time before announcing them, said little beyond requesting that the gentlemen "deliberate and carefully consider the proposition." Grant had watched as Sherman, on the *River Queen*, advocated lenience toward the white Southerners while Lincoln listened; now he saw the president listening to a contradictory proposal. Lincoln sat impassively, and so did Grant. Men like William T. Sherman and Edwin M. Stanton could mistake Lincoln's waiting game for acquiescence, but Grant did not. He knew how to watch and wait himself. There is no indication that in this part of the meeting the general said a word, or missed a word said by anyone else.[15]

Grant did, however, have the attention of the others when he was anxiously asked how he thought Sherman was doing in his pursuit of Johnston in the Carolinas. Entirely confident of himself, he replied that he was expecting word—and he thought it would be good news—at any moment. At this juncture the meeting took on a mystical note; Lincoln spoke of a dream he had had the night before, a dream that was to turn into legend when it came to be seen as the prophecy of his own death. The president told of being carried "in some singular, indescribable vessel" that moved with "great rapidity towards an indefinite shore." The dream had occurred before every victory during the war, Lincoln claimed, and then spun off a list of these, including Stones River. Grant sourly interrupted the president to say that Rosecrans and Thomas's battle at Stones River "was no victory,—that a few such fights would have ruined us." Lincoln, intrigued by the challenge, "looked at Grant curiously and inquiringly" and said he and Grant might have to "differ on that point, and at all events his dream preceded it." Gideon Welles was fascinated by this intrusion by Grant into Lincoln's personal reverie and saw it as a sign of Grant's envy of other generals. Lincoln appears to have judged it both as an expression of jealousy and as an appealing instance of candor. The two men knew each other well by then; Grant could correct his chief, and Lincoln could challenge the correction. No one leaving that cabinet meeting could have thought that Grant would slide into obscurity simply because the war was almost over.[16]

Earlier that morning, Grant had hoped to have a long private talk with Lincoln, but the president postponed their conference until eleven o'clock, and shortened it, in order to visit with his son Robert. Grant understood;

both men were very used to having familial concerns woven into their days. When Grant did get to the White House, Lincoln asked if he and Mrs. Grant would join him and Mrs. Lincoln at the theater that evening. The general knew better than to accept any invitation without first checking with Julia—even so commanding a one as an opportunity to accompany the president of the United States on his first jubilant outing after the victory. He was right to check; Julia's reaction was an immediate no, thank you. She had had more than enough of Mary Lincoln's imperiousness at City Point. She sent a note to this effect to Ulysses at the White House, and the commanding general was left to make to the president the most classic—and limp—of American excuses: he could not go because of the children. Julia was taking an afternoon train back to Burlington to be with them, and Ulysses was to go with her.[17]

It was Lincoln's turn to understand. Apparently he sensed what he could not allow himself to acknowledge: his wife could be nasty, and his own extreme emotional heights and depths had helped make her that way. These two men, who silently showed a sense of how personal torment could enter public events, were comfortable together. They agreed that the party was off. (Then, the Lincolns seem to have spent the day scouring Washington for anyone who could stand being in a theater box with them. Turned down by the commanding general of the army, the Speaker of the House of Representatives, and who knows who else, they finally went to Ford's Theater in the company of a senator's daughter and the army major who was courting her.)

When Grant, having said good-by to Lincoln, left the White House, there were many people on the sidewalks cheering him—too many to please Mary Lincoln, it was reported. He returned to the Willard, where Julia had had lunch, and late that afternoon, the Grants took a carriage from the Willard to Union Station and left Washington by train. At about midnight, in Philadelphia, a messenger from the telegraph company waited at Bloodgood's Hotel. A carriage "drew up at the door, and inside we saw the light of the General's cigar." Charles E. Bolles, the messenger, waited until the Grants had entered the hotel and then followed them inside; Julia Grant was sitting on a settee in the dining room, taking off her hat, when the general answered his knock and accepted a telegram. Grant read the message and, showing no emotion, handed it to his wife. It was from Major Eckert, still in command of the telegraph office in the War Department, and stated unsensationally but unflinchingly that Lincoln had been shot "and cannot live." Grant was asked, at Stanton's behest, to return to Washington immediately. Julia read the wire and quietly began to cry.[18]

Grant sent a telegram in response saying that he would return immediately, but soon a second wire from Washington, this one from Assistant Secretary of War Charles A. Dana, introduced, cautiously, the subject of security. The shooting of Lincoln was not the act of a single assailant; Seward and his son had also been attacked. Grant was not told to surround himself with bodyguards but was instructed "to keep close watch on all persons who come near you in the cars" and to send "an engine . . . in front of the train to guard against anything being on the track." Julia was frightened, and very likely, so was her husband; although he had telegraphed that he would return immediately, Grant accompanied Julia across the river, by ferry, and together they took the train the short distance to Burlington, with a scapegoat engine running ahead of them on the track. On the train, Grant "silent and in deep thought" turned as Julia asked who he thought had done it. "Oh, I don't know," was his diffident response, but he did not brush Julia off when she asked, "This will make Andy Johnson President, will it not?" "Yes," he replied, "and . . . I dread the change."[19]

When they arrived, people were outside their Burlington house in the starlit night to ask if the news that Lincoln had been shot was true. In Washington the death agony of the president was accompanied by hysteria. The stabbing of the secretary of state was taken as confirmation that the attacks were not the act of one madman, but part of a rebel conspiracy to kill the heads of the government. Word that Grant, by not going to the theater, had had a narrow escape from death began to circulate on the periphery of the feverish talk of the assassination itself. When she paused to recollect the day, Julia Grant told of being rudely watched by a lean mustached man in the dining room of the Willard that afternoon and described the fierce look of that same man as he had galloped past their carriage and then ridden back to stare closely into their faces while she and the general were on the way to the railroad station. The memory of these frightening encounters, real or imagined, underscored the belief that Grant had been one of the intended victims of the conspiracy. It was, in fact, logical that an angry murderer might have pursued an intended victim who was unknowingly making his escape. And Julia's description fitted John Wilkes Booth.[20]

At the time, Grant talked little of this story, but later both he and Julia did tell of receiving a letter from an anonymous and repentant would-be assailant who said he had failed to shoot the general on the train from Washington to Philadelphia only because the porter had locked the door to the Grants' car. This letter may well have been from a crank, but the evidence in the trial of the conspirators does suggest that Grant had been marked for killing. An examination of the evidence, however, reveals—not surprisingly—that the interrogations concerning the preparations for the theater assassination concentrated very largely on Lincoln as Booth's target. The fact that a hole was bored in the door of the box has been regarded by many as an indication that Booth's attention was focused on only one target, but the hole was large— large enough for the scouting of more than one victim—and one conspirator quoted Booth as saying he intended to kill both Lincoln and Grant. Whatever the intention, however, there was just a single victim in Ford's Theater.[21]

When Grant got to Washington the day Lincoln died, he seems, uncharacteristically, to have caught the hysteria of others. Perhaps it was stimulated by Stanton's frantic officiousness, or his own fear of civil disorder, or both. As commanding general, Grant ordered the arrest of the civilian Confederate peace negotiator John A. Campbell, who was on his way to Washington for another conference with Lincoln, to try to restore their previous agreement, from which the president, with Stanton's urging, had begun to retreat. Grant had had most amiable relations with Campbell, but now, it seemed possible that he was a conspirator. With three victims and two assailants there had certainly been a conspiracy, and the secretary of war publicly stated that it was a rebel plot, thus implicating the Confederate government. Campbell went to prison briefly, and was not much surprised that he had been sent there. Philosophically, he viewed his jailing as the result of a misjudgment about who had planned the assassination, rather than as an act of vindictiveness by Grant. But in the immediate context of the assassination, the ordering of such an arrest by a military man seemed to confirm the belief commonly held since the event that an ambitious and dangerous secretary of war had tried to take advantage of the emergency to exercise martial authority over the nation.[22]

If there was ever a real danger of such a usurpation, it had no time to reach fruition before being averted by that marvelously flexible instrument, the Constitution of the United States. Secretary of the Navy Gideon Welles, Attorney General James Speed, and, significantly, Edwin M. Stanton himself turned to that document, and visited Vice-President Andrew Johnson to inform him that he should prepare to accede to the office of president of the United States. At 11:00 A.M. on April 15 he was sworn in. The nation had a president, and the activities of Stanton and Grant that afternoon were those of subordinates. When they issued orders, however impulsively, they did so as officers of the government under constitutional authority. They could be held to account.

Andrew Johnson had met Ulysses Grant only once and scarcely knew the men of the cabinet when, right after being sworn in, he met with them briefly and asked them to continue in office. The next morning, Sunday, at a second meeting, Secretary of War Stanton bustled in an hour late, much to the annoyance of Gideon Welles and, one might imagine, of the new president, though he had himself been half an hour late. Late or not, Stanton seized the day; Lincoln was dead and there was no way to refute the secretary's claim that Lincoln's mind had not been made up on Reconstruction— that the issue was still undecided. Then Stanton produced the document he had introduced at Lincoln's last cabinet meeting and insisted it should be immediately agreed upon, and Welles knew that the secretary of war was making a counterattack against a policy of accommodation of white Southerners by advocating that the federal government make decisions for a defeated South. Stanton was keenly aware that Lincoln, while at the front, had discussed his mild conciliatory policy with Grant and Sherman. According to Grant, this policy, which did not anticipate post-emancipation racism, was based on Lincoln's "desire to have everybody happy, and above all his desire to see all people of the United States enter again upon the full privileges of citizenship with equality among all."[23]

But this formulation left the freedmen's position in grave doubt. Surely, they could not enter *again* upon the privileges of citizenship; only white Southerners—lately rebels—could do that. Stanton recognized that Lincoln's death meant the *River Queen* doctrine could be abrogated; the time was ripe for a fundamentally different approach toward the South. At the meeting, Welles found Johnson "not disposed to treat treason lightly," and Grant judged Johnson's attitude toward white Southerners as one that would "make them unwilling citizens." The assassination provided a chance for a radical leap forward into new social arrangements, but Grant later said of the day that "reconstruction had been set back, no telling how far." To Grant's dismay, Stanton persisted in undoing Lincoln's policy. That evening, with Johnson not present, Stanton called a small meeting of influential people to discuss the direction public affairs should take. At this War Department gathering, he did not hesitate to bring up private cabinet business, and he presented his plan for the reorganization of the Southern state governments to Senator Charles Sumner, Congressmen Schuyler Colfax, Daniel W. Gooch, and Henry L. Dawes, and a former congressman, John Covode. Two "general officers" of the army were also there, but it is unlikely that either was Ulysses Grant. However, Gideon Welles was present—uneasily. It is not clear whether he happened to be at the War Department on business— perhaps checking the telegraph office—got wind of the meeting, and deliberately stayed to find out what Stanton was up to, or whether for some reason, Stanton wanted to have his chief cabinet opponent on hand. In any case, Welles was exceedingly uncomfortable, particularly when "Mr. Sumner declared he would not move a step—not an inch if the right of the colored man to vote was not secured." At this point a messenger providentially arrived with a telegram, and the secretary of the navy, with relief, left "abruptly." Reconstruction was taking an interesting turn indeed. Sumner's black men were a far cry from the white gentlemen Lincoln and Campbell had pictured reassembling in Richmond. They had no place whatever in the thinking of William Tecumseh Sherman, who was still at war in North Carolina.[24]

General Sherman surrendered to the Confederate general Joseph E. Johnston on April 18, 1865, or so a reader of the Radical press in the North would have thought. The two generals were hurrying history. The kind of arrangement envisioned in their surrender agreement came about when other men compromised in 1877. In 1865, however, not all Northerners and few blacks in the South were willing to forgo a try at reconstructing the nation. Papers like the *New York Times* hinted that Sherman was a traitor, and the determined patriot-general fought back, with both grandeur and pettiness, to regain his strong position in the public esteem. All that Johnston had conceded to Sherman in the surrender agreement was that his Confederate

soldiers would fight no more. The civilian governments of the states that had
sent these men off to fight the Union were not required to lay down their
arms. Instead, they were charged with the responsibility of continuing to
govern—of maintaining order—and the guns of Johnston's soldiers were to
go back into the state arsenals, ready for use by state officials to repress any
kind of uprising.[25]

Sherman could never understand why he was criticized for agreeing to
these terms. As he explained in a letter to Grant, it was perfectly logical that
he and Johnston should "not drive a people into anarchy," something far
worse than a state of war. Lincoln had been shot. Sherman was terrified of
popular disorder in the wake of the assassination conspiracy. As another
brilliant conservative, Herman Melville, put it:

> There is sobbing of the strong,
>   And a pall upon the land;
> But the People in their weeping
>   Bare the iron hand:
> Beware the People weeping
>   When they bare the iron hand.

When Sherman had received the telegram, in cipher, informing him of Lincoln's murder, he had told not even the generals in command of his armies,
saving the news for Johnston. And when the Confederate learned of the assassination, sweat stood out on his brow. Like Sherman, Johnston feared that
in the wake of the assassination the soldiers would turn to guerrilla warfare.
Sherman's explanation of his lenient agreement stated the matter clearly: "I
confess I did not desire to drive General Johnston's army into bands of armed
men." Both Grant and Sherman had long ago expressed fear that after the
organized Confederate armies collapsed, the war would continue in the
mountains, and now it was anticipated that the assassination might provoke
widespread wantonness by men of both armies. (Sherman and Johnston
could not have been more wrong. The news of Lincoln's death was numbing
rather than provocative on both sides of the line.)[26]

Quite apart from the fact that the assassination made a quick settlement
desirable, Sherman thought his agreement with Johnston was in line with his
discussion with Lincoln and Grant earlier in the month at City Point. None
of the terms accepted at Raleigh were out of harmony with what Lincoln had
done at Richmond. The trouble was simply that Sherman, as if to confirm
his lifelong disgust with Washington politics, was moving in a direction precisely opposite from that in which the heirs of Lincoln's civil power had embarked on the morning after the murder of the president.

Grant had been as eager as everyone else in Washington to get the word of the end of hostilities between Sherman and Johnston, but when the telegram came on April 21, his response was political. He sent a message to Stanton telling him of the agreement and recommending that the president call the cabinet into session to discuss it. Had Grant wanted to avoid politics, he would have congratulated Sherman on his victory and left to Stanton and others the question of the terms of the surrender. (In his *Memoirs* Grant recorded only that he was "sent for" to attend the meeting, not that he had, in fact, himself instigated it.) As bidden, the cabinet met hastily at eight that evening. Sherman was denounced, and the decision made that his agreement must be repudiated. Grant was present. Welles noted that he avoided denouncing his lieutenant, but did not disagree with the repudiation order he was instructed to transmit. Sherman, of course, had no way of knowing that the wind was blowing so strongly away from City Point, but Grant was well aware of the change and could see that it was essential to bring Sherman into line. Gideon Welles was delighted when Grant decided to take the order to Sherman in person.[27]

The diplomatic mission was a great success. We do not know what Grant and Sherman said to each other, but clearly Grant handled the interview with great skill. The surrender was rescinded, and Sherman, though furious, did not buck. Johnston was informed that the fighting would resume, but at the same time negotiations to end it were invited. When Johnston again agreed to discuss surrender with the Union officers, Grant shrewdly allowed Sherman to go to the meeting without him. Off the record, Sherman could say whatever he liked to Johnston to escape the humiliation of having been sent back to do a better job. This time the terms they agreed to were identical with those made by Grant and Lee at Appomattox.[28]

Sherman had been humbled, and he delivered fiery blasts in damnation of all his tormentors—all, that is, except the person at whom one would have expected him to be angriest, Grant. Sherman, a true conservative, respected and feared power. He took out his wrath on those of whom he dared be contemptuous. He excoriated Halleck and even refused to communicate with him. Halleck, aware that Grant, and not he, had been the instrument of Sherman's humiliation, could only turn the other cheek publicly, while in private he made sardonic remarks about Grant's adroit avoidance of blame.

Although a few units were still officially at war—the surrender of Zachary Taylor's son, General Richard Taylor, came on May 4 and that of General Edmund Kirby Smith's army west of the Mississippi on May 26, 1865—the new agreement between Sherman and Johnston effectively ended the conflict. To celebrate the victory, the armies of the west were called to join the huge armies that had been with Grant in Virginia for a two-day march through Washington, the Grand Review, on May 23 and 24. Sherman came with his men, and those in Washington who knew him wondered whether their fate would be ostracism or a scorching from his blistering tongue. As he approached the capital, he was speaking only to old friends from the Army of

*Ole Peter Hansen Balling*, Grant and His Generals. *Sherman is at Grant's right hand; Sheridan, pushing to the front, is farther along.* NATIONAL PORTRAIT GALLERY, SMITHSONIAN INSTITUTION, WASHINGTON, D.C.

the Tennessee days. On May 22, from across the Potomac, he wrote John A. Rawlins:

> Send me all orders and letters you may have for me, and let some . . . newspaper know that Vandal Sherman is encamped near the Canal Bridge half way between the Long Bridge & Alexandria to the west of the Road, where his friends if any can find him. Though in disgrace he is untamed and unconquered.
>
> As ever your friend
> W. T. Sherman

Two days later he led his men up Pennsylvania Avenue. A band played "Marching through Georgia" as he reached the White House, briskly dismounted, walked up into the reviewing stand, and with all eyes on him, shook the hand of the president of the United States and then, with calculated offense, carefully refused the hand of Secretary of War Stanton, turning instead to greet warmly his good friend Ulysses Grant.[29]

Grant had had a series of days of triumph. First there was Appomattox and the victorious return to Washington; then came the smaller achievement of having overridden Sherman while keeping his friendship with an old comrade intact. Finally, he spent two days reviewing the vast panoply of victorious armies—his armies—marching as the conquerers that they were. At the end of the exhausting celebration, he needed a break of the kind ordinary soldiers gave themselves in the lulls between battles, but when he and Orville Babcock saddled their horses that evening, they did not strike out to the northwest for the escape of a gallop down a back-country road. Instead, Grant rode down to Pennsylvania Avenue and looked at the people who still filled the sidewalks even though the parade was over. They had not expected to see the greatest soldier of the day out by himself—and in a good-natured informal way they cheered him. He nodded and rode on. After the reviewing-stand hosannas he had needed still more accolades; he had needed assurance that the people knew him.[30]

# XVI

# AFTER THE
# WAR

They call this traveling for pleasure. . . .
— *Bronson Howard*, Saratoga, *1870*

IN MAY 1865 rich Philadelphians presented the victor with a splendid house at 2009 Chestnut Street, but Philadelphia was not what the Grants had in mind. Julia found the "closets . . . full of snowy fine linen, the larders and even the coal bins . . . full," and a "quantity of fine silver on the table." Indeed, she claimed she "really felt a pang of disappointment" at not spending the pin money she had been saving to buy fine things for a house of her own. Here were all the makings of a life of sedentary comfort, but it was Washington, not Philadelphia, that was the focus of the general's postwar quest for an occupation.[1]

Julia later reported Nellie's response when she was told that the Philadelphia house was home: " 'No, mamma, no, this is not our home. I have just come from there. Our house is a great, great house (with a struggle to say what it was like) like . . . like . . . the picture in my geography of the . . . the . . . Capitol in Washington.' " For a time Nellie had to make do with Philadelphia, while her father commuted from Washington, but soon Grant found that he could rarely spend twenty-four hours away from the capital, and the family moved from Philadelphia to Georgetown Heights, in Washington.[2]

Although he was living in the East, Grant told Elihu Washburne on May

21 that he would not give up his legal residence in Galena: "It would look egotistical to make a parade in the papers about where I intend to make my home, but I will endeavor to be in Galena at the next election and vote there, and disclose my intention of claiming that as my home, and intention of never casting a vote elsewhere without first giving notice." His political base was thus in Illinois, but, he told Washburne, he must station himself in Washington. He was the commander of the army, and although peace had brought drastic cuts in personnel and budget (of which he approved), his job was not a minor one. But despite Grant's careful reinforcement of his relationships with the president, the secretary of war, and his fellow officers, it did not carry the magnitude that had been his at Appomattox.[3]

The Republic could offer its most famous citizen only one position commensurate with the position he had already held—the presidency. But that post was already occupied. It could not be created for him as that of lieutenant general had been; it would have to be taken from someone else. Grant was conscious of the spirit of unanimity with which the people of the North had rallied behind Johnson when Lincoln was shot—and he joined in it—but the idea of becoming president, which had been sparked in 1863, still smoldered. With the greatest political wisdom, he had said the words that banked the fires as long as Abraham Lincoln lived. Now he needed to say nothing, and the flames leaped. On the reviewing stand with Andrew Johnson, he was the greater man. The crowds knew that, and so did he.

In June 1865, Ulysses and Julia went to New York, to make a ceremonial return to West Point and to attend a rally at Cooper Union in support of Andrew Johnson's presidency. The day of the rally was exhausting; he enjoyed it thoroughly. Crowds gathered early in the morning as the Grants rode from the ferry to the Astor House. The general met first with city officials and businessmen who wanted his support for various projects. At ten o'clock, in accordance with carefully made arrangements—the doors were manned to control the crowd—the people lined up outside his suite were admitted. "Having entered, they stopped. They saw a few young officers in glittering uniforms, but where was the General? Looking for the Lieutenant-General commanding the armies of the United States, they expected to see an imposing figure. . . ." Instead, standing in front of a fireplace was Ulysses S. Grant.[4]

People have an odd way of getting themselves into what they somehow think is modish dress when they come to New York. Ulysses, or possibly Julia, had selected a brown sack coat, light checked trousers, and patent-leather pumps—exactly what a newly successful businessman in Galena or St. Louis might have worn. If Grant did not have a chance to change, he must have looked strange indeed at the end of the day, at the Union League Club. (His new New York friends soon got him to Brooks Brothers, and for the rest of his life Grant dressed correctly, in quiet clothes. Though sometimes thought of as the most unkempt of our presidents, he was, in fact, exceedingly well tailored.) That morning the civilian general received people for two hours, pausing only to light a continuous chain of cigars, for which he apologized to the ladies in the room. He shook hands till his hand reddened and grew swollen, but he did not stop. One old bore, his top hat firmly on his head, planted himself at the general's side for an eternity—and talked. Grant gave him "half-an-ear" while ". . . his entire physicca[l] system was devoted to the crowd." At noon the lines were longer than they had been when he began, and he moved to the balcony over the front door of the hotel and waved to the crowd waiting in the street to greet him.[5]

In the afternoon there was a dinner at which tediously predictable worthies of New York—John A. Dix, Horace Greeley, and a divine or two—gave speeches. At the close of the tributes, Grant rose and, as he had done in St. Louis more than a year earlier, gave the speech which was to become his trademark. The *New York Times* report included the response of his audience: "I rise only to say I do not intend to say anything. [Laughter] I thank you for your kind words and your hearty welcome. [Applause]." From the dinner he went to the meeting which ostensibly was the reason for his being in New York—the meeting in celebration of the new presidency of Andrew Johnson. The *New York Times*, as always, enjoyed being dismayed by the vulgarity of a crowd and reported with relish on the exuberance of the mass of people that jammed Cooper Union. The meeting had been called to order and Daniel S. Dickinson was in midsentence when General Grant came into the hall: there was a roar, and the general learned, perhaps for the first time, how fine a chant his name made. "Grant–Grant–Grant, Grant–Grant–Grant," the crowd insisted. When he sat down on the stage, amid the fulsome attention of Moses Taylor, Moses Grinnell, and a host of others of the elect, people had trouble seeing him. And so Grant "rose and walked to the further end of the platform, while every step was a signal for an outburst of applause—a perfect triumph of enthusiastic hurrahing."[6]

There were calls for a speech, seconded by earnest requests to the general from the presiding officials. Grant at first demurred and then went to the very edge of the platform and "spoke a few brief words of thanks." They included no mention of the man he had come to honor, President Andrew Johnson. "Had the general uttered weighty words of wisdom—had he announced his confirmed intention of giving to each person in the audience a large farm with modern implements, had he told them their sins were forgiven 'on the spot,' the people could not have been more excited. The American vocabulary is inadequate for the occasion," wrote the *Times* reporter, trying to make it do, "the hall was too densely crowded to permit of the turning of summersaults, but from head to foot, from limb to limb, the entranced and bewildered multitude trembled with extraordinary delight . . . with the foregoing 'speech.' "[7]

Grant was conscious of the excitement. Dickinson resumed his speech, but—if the *Times* account is to be believed—no applause followed his references to President Johnson; instead, the speaker was interrupted with the renewed chant "Grant–Grant–Grant" until the general once more rose to be applauded. Finally, pleading a promised appearance at the Union League Club, Grant's escorts led him from the hall. Only when the hero had left could Generals Francis P. Blair, Jr., and John A. Logan, with speeches flowery in their praise of Andrew Johnson, extract from the crowd the cheers for the president that the occasion had been designed to arouse.[8]

After the reception at the club, Grant went back to the Astor House; there, from the balcony, he received a serenade from New York's proud Seventh Regiment. Then the Grants allowed the press, except for the reporter from the *Times*, to think they were taking the night boat to West Point. Instead, they left early the next morning from Castle Garden on a small dispatch boat, the *Henry Burden*—with the *Times* reporter aboard. Flags fluttered and passing boats saluted as the party enjoyed the loveliest of excursions, the trip up the Hudson to West Point. There, at the library, Grant received the officials and later the cadets of the academy. During the day, he borrowed Samuel Sloan's carriage and drove to the Couzzens Hotel to call on splendid old Winfield Scott, who had been born before there were presidents of the United States. Scott, with great grace, had sent Grant a telegram of support "from the oldest general to the ablest," and the meeting was cordial.[9]

That afternoon, too, from across the river in Garrison, came Mrs. Hamilton Fish with Mrs. William Morris Hunt and Mrs. George Templeton Strong. They came to call on the "simple-mannered, plain, quiet woman" who was Mrs. General Grant, and all the years of being unimportant were over. After Julia Kean Fish had called on Julia Dent Grant, there was no going back to Mudville.[10]

"The General was always fond of traveling." So said Julia, with no equivocation, and travel the two did throughout 1865—and, indeed, for the rest of their lives. They were in demand. In New York that fall George Templeton Strong wrote, in his diary, "[Mrs. Strong] slipped in an invitation to dinner and it was cordially accepted. William B. Astor's was declined, but I am verging on snobbery." After visiting West Point, the Grants went to Chicago and then back to Washington. On the way to a Fourth of July celebration in Albany, the general, Horace Porter, and Orville Babcock stopped off in New York City. From there, William Henry Vanderbilt escorted them in his private railroad car to the state capital. At a military review, the crowd seeking to get near Grant overloaded a grandstand and it collapsed; there were, however, no serious injuries. That evening, on the night boat going back down the Hudson, the general found the celebration not yet over. Sitting on deck, he dandled children on his knee, and when he retired to his cabin, he enjoyed overhearing a joyous mockery of the day's patriotic solemnity, in which he had been the chief performer. The celebrants sang a ribald serenade in parody of the music of the glorious Fourth and then gave silent speeches that were greeted with vast applause. When the party subsided, an indefatigable reporter spotted the general back out on deck in his "duster," enjoying a cigar in solitude as the boat moved down the Hudson. This was one of the rare trips on which Julia did not accompany him. Grant was alone at the rail that evening.[11]

After a reception in Boston's Faneuil Hall General O. O. Howard, the head of the Freedmen's Bureau, tried to link Grant to his faltering effort to save the abandoned lands for the freedmen by taking his fellow general and commander with him, on August 4, to the commencement exercises at Bowdoin College. From Maine the Grants moved on to Nova Scotia, Quebec, New Hampshire, and Vermont; then to Union College, in Schenectady, New York, for yet another honorary degree, to Saratoga for a holiday, and finally on August 18, 1865, to Galena. Although Grant had lived in the town for less than a year, a ceremonial return of the native was obligatory. The celebration was a wondrous mixture of hokiness and real enthusiasm. The Grants came to town on a fine railroad car and the line, aware of the commercial importance of its valuable cargo, gave credit where it was due: "The [Chicago and] Northwestern acknowledge the valuable assistance rendered by Messrs. Tobey & Brother, furniture dealers, and Messrs. Hollister and Wilkins, upholsterers." Leaving the splendid car, the Grants rode down Main Street, and the town made good on an answer to a newspaperman's question to Grant about what he would do after the war. He was said to have replied that he would run for mayor of Galena and put in a sidewalk; now across the path of his triumphant entry was stretched a banner: "General, here is your sidewalk." And over the boardwalk, great bowers of flowers and greenery were entwined on makeshift triple arches stretched across the street in front of the DeSoto House.[12]

The townspeople were aware that their claim on the Grants was slim; in truth, few of them knew him. Naturally enough, they wanted to identify the war's greatest hero as their own, but the thrifty burghers had no intention of throwing money away, and one can sense in what they chose to present to him just a trace of the inclination to cut the upstart down to size. They gave him a second-best house, built in the 1850's. If not as grand as Elihu Washburne's or the best of the dwellings up on High and Prospect streets, it was a good house, but when the Grants went inside they found the pleasant furnishings were largely suitable for the summer. It was as if they were being reminded that no one expected them to move in to stay. Indeed, when they left, Grant lent the house to Joe Bascom, his successor as a clerk at Grant & Perkins. Bascom looked around at the furniture and commented, "When I say it is not very rich I do not mean it is poor"; it did seem to him not as fine "as some I have seen in Galena."[13]

While in Galena, Grant acted out the myth of the return of the simple lad who had gone off to war. He visited the old store for the first time since he had happily abandoned it in April 1861. Joe Bascom wrote, "Men rush in while I [am] . . . writing letters or Invoices[,] seize me by the hand (without a particle of warning) and shake and pull it until it seamed as though they wanted to pull it out of the socket to carry home with them as a relic from Grant's store." As Bascom wrote this letter, the general himself, he said, was at the "oposite side of the desk writing and (of course) smoking." The owner of the business had composed an advertisement on the occasion of his son's visit; one of its verses read:

> Since Grant has whipped the Rebel Lee
> And opened trade frome sea to sea
> Our goods in price must soon advance
> Then dont neglect the present chance
> To Call on GRANT and PERKINS.
> J.R.G.[14]

A month later, in September, Grant went on a sentimental journey that was more authentically affectionate; he returned to Georgetown, Ohio, where he had grown up, and visited nearby Ripley, where he had gone to school, and Bethel, where he had happily spent vacations from West Point. But even in Ohio there was no escaping celebrity, no chance to truly go home again, for everything had become elaborate. Mary Louise Williams, the granddaughter of Grant's host in Cincinnati, wrote a fine account of going "to see the great man of our day." She paid a call on the Grants at their hotel and found the general, again in civilian clothes, cordially greeting the leaders of the city's society; she was delighted when she and her mother were invited to join the Grants as they moved on to Columbus. In addition to Ulysses and Julia, the party included all four of the Grant children, and Julia's father. (Conspicuously absent were the general's own relatives, left behind after a visit immediately across the river in Covington, Kentucky.) The railroad car moved at a ceremonial pace: "At all the places along the road," wrote Mary Louise Williams, "the people were collected to get a look at the noble General, but the train only stopped at the largest towns. At Xenia and London the people called so loudly for the Gen. that he went on the platform, they wanted him to speak but he shook his head. Then they wanted to see his children, the two youngest Nellie & Jessie went out."[15]

In a parade in Columbus, the "Generals carriage was drawn by four beautiful black horses," and he rode with the mayor. In the first carriage behind him was David Tod, the wartime governor of Ohio and the son of Judge George Tod, to whom Grant's father had once been apprenticed. There was an immense reception for invited guests, and from the window, Grant bowed to crowds of uninvited Ohioans jammed into the street outside. Porter and Babcock adroitly maneuvered the general through the ceaseless day. When it came time in the evening for the party to go to the Opera House, "Mrs. Grant being very tired did not go." Politely, the other women began to decline as well, but luckily they were rescued: "The gentlemen insisted so we finally consented." They took a streetcar the short distance to the theater. "The play had begun, but when the General entered everything was stopped with prolonged cheers." He and his children took seats in the first row of the parquet; the rest of the party were ranged behind him. "The play was very poor, and as all were tired we were not sorry to see the General start early to go." Getting what must have been the only relaxed breath of fresh air that day, they walked back to the hotel on "a beautiful bright moonlight night." At the hotel, they sat up in the parlor with the Grants "until it was time for them to leave for Pittsburg"—for another reception just as strenuous as those in Cincinnati and Columbus.[16]

After he returned to Washington, Grant had a conference with the banker Jay Cooke, who had accepted the Grants' confidence and "changed our speculation" so that it should yield "about $25.00 [sic]" (presumably $2,500 in annual income). He also wrote Elihu Washburne, "My whole trip has been condusive to health, if one judges from corpulancy. . . . Mrs. Grant and children keep pace with me in enjoyment of travel, if one judges from the dificulty with which they are got up [in the morning]." Grant was anticipating his friend's arrival in Washington, as Congress was about to come back into session after having been adjourned since before the war ended. The congressmen were, at last, to return to work, and in November 1865, just before their reconvening, President Johnson gave General Grant an important assignment as well. He sent him on a fact-finding trip, and it is a mark of the general's stature that this "hasty" excursion, as Charles Sumner scornfully described it on the floor of the Senate, is referred to as Grant's Tour of the South. His observations, based on five days crowded with travel, were heeded as if an oracle had spoken.[17]

The words in Grant's report to Johnson's cabinet on December 15 were measured, and his generalizations, based on his small sampling of evidence, were logical. They were certainly not radical. At both Savannah and Charleston, Grant was just a short boat ride away from the Sea Islands, where black people were engaged in experiments in independent farming, but he did not make the trip to observe them. If he had, he would have arrived during the closing phase of the earliest and strongest attempt by black farmers to establish their economic self-sufficiency. Grant might have been powerful enough to block the return of their land to the former white owners, but he never got into that battle. He never saw the Negroes' independent farms for himself, nor did he listen to reports of the injustices involved in breaking them up. He talked instead to the white men who were getting the land back and forcing independent black farmers into the position of dependent laborers.

Grant was not prepared to place the making of a reconstructed Union even partially in the hands of the freedmen. Instead, he was willing to entrust the black people to the "thinking people of the South." That hoary euphemism for the keepers of a social order, in this instance those committed to white dominion over black, gave Grant no pause. When he used it, he greatly encouraged Andrew Johnson and his allies in the White House who, by December 1865, were seeking to build a new political coalition that included such Southerners. Indeed, after the cabinet meeting, Gideon Welles, the most racially conservative man in Johnson's cabinet, said of Grant (whom he normally did not trust), "His views are sensible, patriotic, and wise." Welles urged the general to put them in writing, and after Johnson made the same request, Grant's famous account of his tour came into being.[18]

The report was as brief as the trip; it took less than a full column in the *New York Times*. Grant, with Babcock, Adam Badeau, and Cyrus B. Comstock as staff, crossed Virginia, visiting Julia's sister and her husband in Richmond. At Cape Fear, a reporter saw him, in plain civilian dress, "buying an apple and calmly surveying the slow motions of a gang of dusky creatures seemingly making an effort to smash the luggage or pile it on a diminutive, snorting tugboat." He spent a day in Raleigh, two in Charleston, and one each in Savannah and Augusta, and said nothing concerning what he saw that was uncongenial to Andrew Johnson. Grant did call for the continuation of the Freedmen's Bureau, having no way of knowing that two months later Johnson would try unsuccessfully to use the veto to end the agency. However, he had no plaudits for those in the Bureau who were seeking to promote black interests. Instead, Grant spoke approvingly of the conservative critics of the Bureau, who sought to drive out agents (of whatever color) who were favorable to the Negroes. Grant credited tales of "abuses" told by enemies of black advancement and recommended that agents perpetuating them be removed. He did not ask if perhaps the sin of these agents was that they favored the freedmen; he simply left the impression that they were corrupt.[19]

Grant would have brought the Bureau more completely within the army— that is, more directly under his own control—and yet he described as "able" its commissioner, General O. O. Howard, who hoped it would develop as an independent liberal welfare agency. Grant's praise contributed to the pressure on Howard to play for more such compliments by having the Bureau abandon efforts to deal with the needs of its freedman clients in favor of a concentration on keeping order. As he read the report, Howard reasoned that he could placate Johnson and Grant and keep his job only if he met Grant's criticism of those agents who were attempting to execute the act of Congress of March 3, 1865, which permitted limited redistribution of Southern lands to the freedmen.[20]

Grant contended that army garrisons were still needed in the South, to ward off foreigners—approaching, perhaps, from Mexico—who might view the South as the nation's Achilles' heel. "The white and the black mutually require the protection of the general government." But none of the troops should be colored; the existence of black soldiers would encourage the freedmen to be assertive. "The presence of black troops, lately slaves, demoralizes labor, both by their advice and by furnishing in their camps a resort for the freedmen for long distances around." He praised the statements made by General Howard on his trip—just prior to Grant's—during which the commissioner had urged the freedmen to acquiesce to the paternal authority of their old masters. If the former slaves were to be returned to their role as a subordinate labor force, the presence of proud gun-bearing black soldiers would be an anomaly. "White troops generally excite no opposition, and therefore a small number of them can maintain order in a given district." On the other hand, Grant shrewdly noted, black troops could invite guerrilla attacks; if there were to be any black troops at all in the South, they would have to "be kept in bodies sufficient to defend themselves." He knew they would be greatly resented by white Southerners.[21]

Those who were sources of potential disorder were all to be found, according to Grant, in the lowest ranks of society: "It is not the thinking men who would use violence toward any class of troops sent among them by the general government, but the ignorant . . . might; and the late slave seems to be imbued with the idea that the property of his late master should, by right, belong to him, or, at least should have no protection from the colored soldier." Grant claimed there was danger of "collision" with the established order in any move toward black solidarity. In areas where there were many freedmen, he insisted, the troops should all be white: "The reasons for this are obvious. . . ."[22]

Grant saw a stable future for his nation if it was protected from any threat by an underclass of disaffected, poor people—white or black. He wrote of the eagerness on the part of citizens of the Southern states to work within the Union, provided there were nothing "humiliating to them as citizens." Speaking in support of President Johnson's hope that unhumiliated, unreconstructed Southerners would be permitted to enter Congress, he ended his report by stating, "It is to be regretted that there cannot be greater commingling at this time between the citizens of the two sections, and particularly of those intrusted with the law-making power."[23]

Grant's report on his Southern trip is a disturbingly good example of his philosophy, if that is not too pretentious a term for his thinking. Now that he had reached the high ground of national eminence, he was going to stay there. Personally, he was terrified of obscurity; publicly, he was frightened by the obscure. Whiggishly, he trusted only the "thinking men"—he used the term twice in his short document—but in truth he was referring less to men of thought than to men of property. Instead of looking around him and understanding those with whom his own early experience should have prepared him to have empathy, he called for a "commingling" of the better people. One of the great and powerful now, Ulysses Grant had forded his river. He was not, if he could help it, going to swim in treacherous common waters again.[24]

Grant's report—his program for Reconstruction—touched the question that everyone was talking about in Washington in December 1865. The freedmen, feared or feared for, were the subject of the day. When the new session of the Congress opened, the first bill introduced in the Senate had to do with the welfare of the former slaves. The *Congressional Globe* was full of speeches on the subject of the mistreatment of Negroes in the South. On December 18, 1865, the Thirteenth Amendment to the Constitution was ratified, but the black people's troubles were far from over. This was the first time the Congress had met since Andrew Johnson had taken office, and the president and the congressional Republicans had not yet taken their positions at opposite poles. The legislators were still trying to line up with the new chief executive. But it was hard to know where he stood. His performance as the wartime governor of Tennessee suggested that he would take a hard line on the rebels and support the freedmen. His pardoning policy, which restored the old leaders of the South to power, suggested the opposite. Many senators and congressmen assumed that they would find a position compatible with that of the president. Grant had already found such a position; the last sentence of his report put him on the side of the president and in opposition to Congress on the first of the major divisions between the two.

Congress refused to seat the representatives from the Southern states; Johnson wanted them seated. Their acceptance would have marked the completion of the Reconstruction program he had been conducting vigorously during the months that Congress had been out of session. It was toward just such a reunion that the final sentence of Grant's report spoke. His call for a "commingling at this time between the citizens of the two sections," to which he added the political coda "particularly of those intrusted with the law-making power," was exactly what Andrew Johnson had in mind. Charles Sumner, on the other hand, in a series of vitriolic speeches denounced Johnson's lack of concern for the freedmen and attacked not only the president but the stupid people advising him. Other senators sought to keep Grant on their side, but Sumner was burning his bridges. Grant was Johnson's most prestigious adviser, and the general did not easily forget taunts like those hurled his way by the senator from Massachusetts.[25]

Charles Sumner may not have known how to protect his own political future, but he did know what was at stake for the freedmen. Black slaves had been emancipated, but Jubilee Day was over. The freedmen were desperately poor, and they were being killed and intimidated by other Southerners, who were frightened that the former slaves, having been released from bondage, could not be contained. Northerners, miles away from the immediacy of such fears, heard of outrages against the freedmen and wanted to prevent their repetition. From afar they sought to prescribe for the region in which these people lived (and they hoped, would continue to live), with the aim of placing the new black citizens in the position of plain ordinary American middle-class citizens. Such a seemingly unrevolutionary goal was, in fact, radical: under the clearly delineated class system of the South, achieving it would have required raising the members of the lowest class not one notch, but two. They would move from slavery past the involuntary servitude of an indentured or apprenticed laborer to the level of the freeholder. In the mythical kingdom of a classless society inhabited by the Republicans, the free black farmer was unthreatening to his fellow Americans; in the realities of the South, the step of the freedmen into the yeomanry would raise them not only above slavery but above the landless white poor.

Superficially, the politics of Reconstruction were not new to America. Andrew Johnson was trying to build one new coalition of partisan supporters, and the Republicans in Congress were trying to build another. The difference in these years was that the makings of class struggle were present, concealed under the flamboyant clothes of race. The opponents of the Radicals were keenly aware of the danger cloaked in the conflict between the president and Congress. Never before had class unrest erupted in so disconcerting a way in America. On the surface, the appearance was of politics as usual. Andrew Johnson was trying to create a new alliance of Democrats and others committed to white supremacy in the nation. Republicans were trying to make their victorious war party permanently dominant. Both factions sought allies in the South and in the North. Their activity seemed to be coalition politics of the kind that had rendered radicalism harmless since colonial days, except that now, in the wake of the war, race and poverty were open issues.

Grant was in the thick of these politics. His personal need was to retain the immense respect in which he was held everywhere in the North and even, he discovered on his trip, in the South. He was aware that he was a symbol of national union. But, as after Donelson and Shiloh and Vicksburg, he knew that he could get nowhere as a stationary hero. He needed to move, to be seen, to have something to do, or he would be forgotten. He was the most popular person in the land—or at least in the North—and enjoyed the confidence both of men in Congress and of the president of the United States. In 1866 Congress voted that Grant should have the rank of general—with no limiting adjective. He was lieutenant to no one. He outranked the Father of his Country. But privately, Grant was not sure he could even measure up to his father—to Jesse Grant's standards. Publicly, he was considered a force that people on all sides had to reckon with. Initially, of course, his power derived from his being the commander of a fearsome army. But when he had won the war, he still held power. People still needed to know that Grant was on their side, that they stood well with the general.

He was, however, never a man on horseback. The great compliment Stanton's biographers Benjamin P. Thomas and Harold M. Hyman paid the secretary of war for maintaining civilian control over things military has less force when one recognizes that the nation's most likely military dictator never for a moment thought of becoming such a despot. Ulysses Grant was not driven to crush a world that had tried to crush him. He wanted something much more simple. He wanted to matter in a world he had been watching closely all his life. A little recognition—a little understanding that he did know what he was doing—was all he required. He needed to be taken into account. And now that he had the eyes—and the ears—of the movers and shakers of the land, he thought he had something to say to them.[26]

What he wanted to say—what he sought to express as he moved about the country—was clearly stated in the conclusion of his *Memoirs*, written at the very end of his life. He sought "such a commingling [he liked the word] of the people that particular idioms and pronunciation are no longer localized. . . ." He wanted the country to be "filled up 'from the centre all around to the sea' " with railroads connecting "the two oceans and all parts of the interior. . . ." Maps "nearly perfect" were his metaphor for a clearly delineated America. He wanted to be done with the terrors of the unknown. Before the war, "an immense majority of the whole people did not feel secure against coming to want should they move among entire strangers." Ulysses Grant had suffered such insecurity. He had only a trace of romantic yearning for the life of the man alone in the wilderness, and yet this was the man Grant was most conscious of, the man he most feared becoming. He told of trappers—what a curious group for the dying general to have thought about—who, long before his own day in St. Louis, were a "class; people who shunned contact with others," and who got for their pelts just enough money for "little articles of luxury . . . two or three pounds of coffee, more of sugar, some playing cards, and if anything was left over of the proceeds of the sale, more whiskey."[27]

As Grant traveled, on the nation's railroads—the first transcontinental connection was completed in 1869—he believed he was "commingling." He saw vast numbers of his countrymen, he shook hands with thousands—and he did not realize how far he had moved from the discarded people of the nation. He seems not to have sensed that the shabby Ulysses Grant of 1860 would not have been invited even to a back table at one of the testimonial dinners of 1866. He was wearing well-cut gentleman's clothes now and forgetting the troubled man they covered. He had been able to put on old clothes for Robert E. Lee; why could he not have put them on again once in a while and talked to some of the people around the country who still spoke in "particular idioms," people who had no clothes fit for a hotel suite in which a great general received? Why could he not have talked to a black dock worker in North Carolina or an out-of-work white man in New York? He had the personality to do so. He was not formidable.

There is a story, probably apocryphal, about a time when Grant, traveling by train, stopped at a midwestern town for a luncheon and found a prepossessing welcoming committee armed with a fine brass band on one side of the tracks and a modest fife-and-drum contingent from the local "Grant" veterans' club on the other. Grant was said to have guessed that the latter group had been excluded from the official welcome because "the municipal dignitaries wanted no vulgar fellows in faded blue jackets at their jollification, at

which toasts were to be proposed and high-flown speeches were to be made."
He listened "grimly" to the welcome of the officials who came into his car,
but when he left the train he crossed on the gravel and ties to shake hands and
visit comfortably with the veterans. When a pretentious official came across
to tell Grant that it was getting late and he should move on to the luncheon,
he allowed that it was indeed late, boarded the train—and left town. "Just
like him," a veteran said, "he believes in common folk and he don't like
frills." Maybe so, but the story suggests what people wanted Grant to be,
rather than what he had become. It would be good to think that there had
been more than one such a moment of intimacy with "vulgar fellows" and
more than one escape from an official luncheon, but unfortunately the record
shows twenty years of almost uninterrupted attention to the fancy folk on the
right side of the tracks. A workingman, in old age, remembered that once, as
a little boy, he had been crossing the narrow footbridge over the river in
Galena and, too late to turn back, looked up to see the great General Grant
approach him. After nearly a century, he recalled that he had been frightened at first and then was put at ease with a quiet greeting from the "little
man about as tall as me." (The workingman, Jacob Gunn, was about five feet
six or five feet seven.) What if Grant had stopped a little longer and talked
with the boy? Or had listened to what was on the mind of the boy's father, a
local lead miner? Why didn't Grant omit just one of those great dinners in his
honor and join the men in a working-class bar instead?[28]

The problem was that he was frightened of intimacy with people on the
other side of the tracks. In such a relationship, their discomfort would have
been momentary, the result of finding themselves in the company of a great
man; they would have relaxed when they found that he was not a man of pre-
tensions. The source of his discomfort, on the other hand, was far more
deeply seated. He did not dare to talk to them, to mingle with them, to
become one with them again. He was afraid of falling back. Seeing groups of
ordinary people brought reminders of the possibility of failure—and failure
frightened him. He could not allow it to return and engulf him. So he kept
his distance and lived with the illusion that he was one with everyone and
that the "commingling" of the great trips was genuine contact with people. A
harmonious, orderly society was the true aim of his famous slogan in 1868,
"Let us have peace." The words evoked Appomattox, but they were more an
injunction to dissident and potentially disorderly workers than a reference to
the days of the past war.

Peacetime brought irony. In March 1866, Grant accompanied Fred to
West Point, where he was a cadet, and Theodore S. Bowers, Grant's aide
since Cairo days, went along. After Fred was settled, the two soldiers crossed
the Hudson to Garrison to take the train back to New York. Grant boarded,
but for some reason Bowers was delayed. The train started and began picking up speed. Bowers jumped; his foot missed the step and was caught in the
coupling. He was killed and dragged 150 feet down the tracks, his face

crushed by the wheels and his arms sliced from his body. The rails were wet with his blood when the train stopped and Grant got off. The *New York Times* reported that he could scarcely recognize the mutilated body of his close friend. Years later James A. Garfield heard a different version of the episode from James G. Blaine, who used it to illustrate Grant's "singularly impassible character." According to Blaine, after the accident, when the train stopped and alarmed passengers moved to the doors, "Grant did not rise from his seat but wrote a telegram, giving orders about the dispo[si]tion of the body, and let the train go on."[29]

Bowers was thirty-four when he died. The small, alert newspaperman from Mount Carmel, Illinois, had joined Grant's staff in 1862. He was an amateur soldier; he brought no professional knowledge of war to the job, but, said the *New York Times*, "he read character and detected motives with great precision." The slender, dark-eyed bachelor was a man of "remarkable self possession." He wrote well and took over much of Rawlins's work, as the latter's duties expanded. But more important than his utility as a clerk was Bowers's membership in the close family formed by Grant's staff. He was one of the men whose talk was so essential to the general. The easy obbligato of their voices reached Grant; he learned what he needed to know of army gossip from them. By being there with him, these men sustained the general. Bowers was the first in Grant's staff family to die. Now, in the most banal of civilian accidents—slipping while rushing for a train—a young friend was lost to him. Grant and the rest of the party went on into the city, and when arrangements for the funeral had been made, he and Comstock and Badeau returned to West Point for the service. Then Grant went back to Washington.[30]

The next month the Grants participated in a very different ceremony. On April 6, 1866, in their new Douglas Row house at 205 "I" Street, N.W., Julia and Ulysses gave a party. A reporter wrote, "Gen. Grant's reception tonight, the closing one of the season, is a grand affair. The capacious drawing rooms and library are literally packed with guests. The President is present and stands between Gen. Grant and Mrs. Grant. . . ." The general and his lady had received regularly since the opening of Congress, but this was their most ambitious attempt at bringing official Washington together, and it succeeded. "It is rumored," wrote the reporter expansively the next day, "that the ladies, are if possible, more elegantly and richly attired this evening than at any reception . . . this season." Gideon Welles, being "somewhat indisposed," planned to send his son as his wife's escort, but when Edgar Welles did not get to town, the secretary of the navy let his curiosity get the best of him and, despite a severe headache, went to have a look at the "numerous but . . . miscellaneous company of contradictions."[31]

That afternoon the Senate had overridden the president's veto of the Civil Rights Bill, and the Radicals, heady with their audacity, had—Welles recorded in his *Diary*—"some pre-understanding . . . to attend and to appro-

priate General Grant, or at least his name and influence to themselves. But,"
continued Welles, "most unexpectedly to them, as I confess it was to me, the
President and his two daughters appeared early. . . ." Lyman Trumbull, the
author of the Civil Rights Bill and hero of the hour for having sustained it
against Johnson's opposition, arrived later with Thaddeus Stevens (who
would shortly steer the bill through the House of Representatives). The triumphant Radicals, were "astonished and amazed" to find at the party not
only Andrew Johnson but another former vice-president, Alexander H. Stephens. Grant's indomitable little friend from the peace-conference days of
the previous year proved, in the reporter's eyes, to be "quite a lion"; he was
soon "surrounded by Senators and Representatives, most of them radicals,
who [gave] him cordial greeting." And turning from the Confederate to his
conqueror, the politicians hovered over Grant, each of them hoping to nudge
the general his way. Ulysses and Julia, no lesser politicians than anyone else
in the room, had achieved a success. The civility, so studiously sought in the
Washington evenings that followed rancorous days, united the whole company; all joined in the common activity of bringing the general to the center
of political life. Amidst discord over Reconstruction, the Grants had created
their own evening of temporary national reunion.[32]

# XVII

# THE RISING
# MAN

It looks to me as if Genl. Grant was to be the rising man. The people
love military glory and renown and love to honor it.
— *David Davis*

President Grant was assured by all about him that he was the delight of
the Radicals, greatest captain of the age, and saviour of the nation's life.
It was inevitable that he should begin by believing some of this, and
end by believing it all.
— *Richard Taylor*

A N D R E W   J O H N S O N did not know what to do with Ulysses Grant.
He was too popular to have around, and too popular to let go. And the president needed allies. The members of the Republican opposition Congress
pulled further and further away from him as Johnson vetoed their Reconstruction bills and they overrode his vetoes. They wanted this legislation enforced, and he very much wanted it to languish. The two antagonists, the
president and Congress, strained against each other, and one focus of that
struggle was Johnson's relationship with the man responsible for enforcing
Reconstruction policies, his secretary of war, Edwin M. Stanton. Except for
the army, there was at this time no federal agency available to carry out the
policies of the national government. To be sure, the Department of the Interior functioned in the territories, and the Treasury and Justice departments,
and of course the Post Office Department, had some staff in the various
states, but the army alone, as a result of the war, provided a presence large
enough and centralized enough to impose federal policy in the South. The civilian at the army's head, the secretary of war, was, therefore, the administrator most critical for Reconstruction. But President Johnson had already
lost confidence in Stanton, who like Grant had tried to walk a compromise

road between the president and the Radical Republicans. Stanton wanted to
hold his job as secretary of war, and his tenacity was great, almost great
enough in the long run to pull down a president through impeachment. And
from the start of the struggle between Johnson and Stanton, which led both
men to politically dangerous extremes, Grant stood in the middle.

When the Radicals achieved passage of the Civil Rights Bill over Johnson's
veto in April 1866, they had done only half the job. That clearly written,
splendidly wide-ranging piece of legislation, miraculously still the law of the
land, would be effective only if enforced. Senator Lyman Trumbull, who
wrote it, knew this, and he anticipated that the Freedmen's Bureau would
become the enforcement agency. But in May a "riot" occurred in Memphis in
which an armed band, composed conspicuously of off-duty policemen, killed
black citizens despite the presence of a Freedmen's Bureau agent. Elihu
Washburne headed a thorough congressional investigation, which showed
that the Bureau was not able to protect its clients' lives, let alone their rights.
More muscle was needed, and that strength would have to come from other
sectors of the War Department. It is doubtful whether Stanton had the mo-
tivation to conduct that enforcement on his own; it is demonstrable that he
could not do so with Andrew Johnson as his president. But in 1866 it looked
as if Stanton might try. The Radicals placed their hopes in him, and the secretary of war, to enhance his own power and importance, held firmly to his
cabinet position.

It was also in General Grant's interest that Stanton retain his office. As
early as the spring of 1866 there were rumors that Sherman would replace
Stanton. General Sherman, with his famous statement in 1884, "If nominated
I will not run; if elected I will not serve," was perhaps that all-but-non-
existent American—the person who genuinely does not want to be president.
But his fascination with the delicious evil of politics made even Sherman
suspect, at least in 1866, a year in which Ulysses Grant took careful measure of his lieutenant. Grant was worried on two counts. First, he was
concerned that the appointment of Sherman, which would make him Grant's
superior, might imperil their very real friendship. Second, he was anxious
lest Sherman, coming in as secretary of war, espouse Johnson's position in
his inimitable, outspoken, unequivocal way and turn the leaders of Congress
against the army—and against Grant.

Johnson had vetoed a bill to strengthen the Freedmen's Bureau. That veto
had been sustained, but the agency limped along under its original grant of
power, and in July 1866 a second bill was passed, over the president's veto.
Meanwhile Johnson turned to other ways of destroying the work of Reconstruction. He headed the executive branch of government; it was his job to
enforce the Civil Rights Act and other laws essential to Reconstruction. He
chose not to enforce them. For example, he used his appointment power to
see that agents in the Freedmen's Bureau favorable to the freedmen were replaced. At the end of July, the police and firemen of New Orleans put down

an interracial demonstration—labeled pejoratively a "riot"—in favor of universal suffrage; clearly, the Freedmen's Bureau still could not even secure the lives of the freedmen. By official count, forty-eight people were killed. One of Grant's favorite generals, Philip Sheridan, was posted at New Orleans but had been out of the city on the day the demonstrating integrationists were suppressed. (His absence had not gone unnoticed as the officials of the Johnsonian city government appraised the limits to which they could go in violently repressing the people, black and white, who demonstrated for equality.) Sheridan, when he got back to New Orleans, called the killings a massacre.

The citizens had gathered in support of a convention, called to amend the state constitution, which they hoped would grant Negro suffrage. Johnson had ordered the head of the Freedmen's Bureau in the city not to bring in troops, though there was a federal army unit a mile outside the city, and this assurance of noninterference invited the attack on black and white demonstrators, and convention delegates, by city police and firemen. The *New York Times* reporter on the scene was unequivocal in blaming the attackers for a premeditated act, but he put the responsibility for provoking the attack on the "Robespierre of New Orleans," a radical dentist named A. P. Dostie. Dostie, one of the injured white men, was dying with stoical bravery, not repenting his prophetic warning, in his rousing speeches, that universal equality was the only proper goal for men of his race to pursue in a world of 300,000,000 white people and 900,000,000 nonwhites.[1]

The New Orleans violence dramatically polarized opinion. On the one hand, Andrew Johnson was pictured as allowing freedmen to be slaughtered. On the other, his adherents said that unless radicals like Dostie in New Orleans and the whole pack of Republicans were curbed, and sensible moderates were charged with handling race relations in the South, there would be more riots. A week later, at the National Union convention called to rally support for the president in the fall elections, Johnson's position was championed. When a delegation of conservative leaders was sent from the convention to the White House to present a declaration of support, Johnson used the occasion for a display of executive unity and power. He summoned his cabinet and his commanding general, Ulysses S. Grant.

They responded, or at least most of them did, but the president wondered where the general was when the appointed hour came. The men of the cabinet (except for Stanton, also absent) stood attentively as Senator Reverdy Johnson began his glowing words of praise for the president. Suddenly he was interrupted. Grant had quietly entered, and applause broke out in the crowded room. The general "walked straight up to the side of the President, who turned and shook hands with him." There was, in Grant's "manner and looks," thought the man from the *New York Times*, something "which all interpreted to mean, 'I am with you gentlemen. I indorse your proceedings.' " As Senator Johnson completed his remarks, "three cheers were enthusiastically given for ANDREW JOHNSON and three more for GEN. GRANT." And then the president and the general "retired arm-in-arm."[2]

The *New York Times* had Grant pegged, or so they thought—he was Johnson's man. Nothing he did in public in August 1866 suggested anything different. However, two days before the visit to the White House for what was taken as his endorsement of Johnson as his leader, the general wrote a letter to Elihu Washburne, another man who had tried playing the uneasy role of patron to Ulysses Grant. In his letter the general demonstrated that he was going to be a lot harder to peg than the *Times* thought. He was seeking a way to get around being Johnson's man or Washburne's man or anyone else's man but his own. Yes, of course he would be coming home for election day, Grant wrote Washburne, who was running for re-election, but he could not endorse Washburne or any other candidate. And then he proceeded to give the congressman a nonendorsement worth six of the genuine article: "I do not think it proper for an army officer . . . to take part in elections. Your friendship for me has been such that I should not hesitate to support you on personal grounds . . . there is no one who cannot recognize great acts of friendship." Arm in arm with his friends, Grant would move across the Reconstruction landscape, getting exactly where he wanted to go.[3]

The journey was not to be without its rough passages. Later in that same month, August 1866, the apolitical general set out as a performer in one of the most famous political circuses in American history. Andrew Johnson, frustrated by Congress, took his case to the American people. Few presidents have been happy that they tried this tactic; Johnson was no exception. The effort was a disaster, but not for want of prior attention to public relations. To decorate the venture with heroes, Johnson took along Admiral David G. Farragut and General Ulysses S. Grant as side-ring attractions.

Nothing went right. At West Point, Grant did not even see his son. Fred had a sore eyelid and was in the infirmary; when Grant went there, the boy had left to look for his father. In the end, everyone in the party visited with Fred except the general. From Albany, Grant complained to his wife of being "pulled and hauled about." Later the same day, in Auburn, Seward's home town, a boy fell under the wheel of a carriage as he pressed forward to shake Grant's hand, and his leg was shattered. Grant visited the injured boy at his house and, that evening, wrote hastily to Julia, "I am getting very tired of this expedition and of hearing political speeches." Duty bound, he added, "I must go through however."[4]

Johnson's speeches were reminiscent of his intensely personal outpouring when he was inaugurated as vice-president; they made his listeners, including Grant, exceedingly uncomfortable. Looking for ways to explain such unrestrained language, slanderous gossips reduced the president and his commanding general to low comics, drunkenly lurching around the northeast. Grant's own opening act had nothing to do with speeches. It was, instead, an elegant turn in Central Park at the reins of William Jerome's superb four-in-hand, but reporters' tales converted the incident into a wild and reckless and just possibly drunken escapade. Almost certainly the drive was exhilarating fun, and few novices could have been more ready to handle the powerful team than Grant, but Julia, having read about it in the papers, remonstrated with Ulysses. In explanation, he said that when they got into the park, Jerome "asked me to drive, which I did. But there was no fast driving to talk of it."[5]

John Rawlins and the other men of Grant's personal staff wished that their chief were appearing before the crowds alone. They believed Grant was wasting political capital in Johnson's company, and as uncomfortable about the trip as Grant, they sought to disassociate him from Johnson. James Harrison Wilson wrote to Orville Babcock, "I hope you and [Horace] Porter will draw your political alliance as close as possible. All good influence which can be exerted should be . . . to keep the General true to his principles. He has been right so far—but you can see what a terrible effort Johnson has been making to commit him to 'my policy.' "[6]

The ambitious and shrewd Wilson continued, "If we can judge from the papers, the President has failed ingloriously—and will doubtless turn his anger against the General when ever it suits his purpose to do so." Wilson urged Babcock to keep Grant's eye on "success" because "*if the General waivers now—it will be as fatal to himself and the country, as hesitation or indecision would have been in the Wilderness!*" Wilson claimed to have "seen the people and know their temper." He was "sure the General knows it too by this time, if [he] ever had any doubt in regard to it." Wilson was convinced that the tour "ought to leave him [Grant] no doubt as to the relative respect entertained for him & the President." And the cavalryman left no doubt as to the hopes he entertained for a latter-day George Washington: "He is the Country's best hope in Peace, as he has been in War!"[7]

Rejoining Johnson's party after a detour to Detroit with Rawlins, Grant approved a skillfully worded statement to a reporter to the effect that he was accompanying Johnson in his role as head of the army, and nothing else. He would take sides with neither the president nor his opponents. On the president's train, being neutral was akin to endorsing the opposition, but officially Grant's stand was that he would not allow the army to "be made a party machine." According to the reporter, a clause declaring that "when he [Grant] becomes partisan he intends immediately to resign his present position" had been deleted from the statement by Grant on the ground that such a declaration "might be taken to imply that at some future time he did intend to become partisan." The conversation on this subject between the general and the reporter took place in the "baggage and refreshment car" of the train outside Chicago, in the presence of Rawlins and of General George Stoneman, one of Johnson's partisans. Grant had taken refuge in this car after refusing to appear before a crowd, on the station platform, that called for him and not for Johnson. Sinking into a chair next to the reporter, Grant spoke

his relief at avoiding an insult to Johnson and said that he "would refuse to receive . . . any . . . demonstrations tendered separately to himself when traveling with the President."[8]

From St. Louis, Ulysses wrote Julia that at last the trip was almost over.
He was starting east and would arrive at home on Saturday, September 15.
"I have never been so tired of anything before as I have been with the political speeches of Mr. Johnson from Washington to this place. I look upon them
as a national disgrace." He cautiously added that Julia must not "shew this
letter to anyone for as long as Mr. Johnson is President. I must respect him as
such, and it is [in] the country's interest that I should also have his confidence." In York, Pennsylvania, Daniel Ammen responded to a telegram
and was at the station to meet Grant and Farragut, as the party moved
eastward. Grant told his boyhood friend that he did not like "swinging
around the circle," and Ammen was startled at how obviously uncomfortable
Grant was: "Perhaps on no other occasion [save this one] have I seen General
Grant discomposed."[9]

Grant had to walk a tightrope. Johnson had put him on display, but now
needed to subordinate him; he was too much of a rival. The president also
needed to find a way to dispose of Stanton. Johnson shrewdly guessed that
public opinion might support the removal of Stanton if the substitute was a
popular general. He had his eye on Sherman, whose Reconstruction credentials were similar to Johnson's own. Johnson, as wartime governor of Tennessee, had been savage in his verbal attacks on the ruling class of the Confederacy; Sherman, in his own inimitable manner, had made himself the
most hated of the Federal invaders of the South. Yet both, since the war, had
favored returning the government of Southern society to white men who
would keep the freedmen in order. Neither encouraged the freedmen in any
aspirations to equality or advancement that would stimulate reprisals from
white supremacists and cause renewed war. Johnson taunted Stanton and
Grant with hints that Sherman was his man. Grant, steady on his feet, kept
Johnson wondering if he dared to push him off the tightrope in favor of
Sherman—or of anyone else.

On October 14, 1866, Johnson asked Grant if Sherman could not be ordered to Washington for a few days. Grant thereupon wrote to Sherman to
come east after they had both attended the Army of the Tennessee reunion in
Cincinnati. In his letter, the commander referred to the time earlier that
year, in February, when Sherman had counseled Johnson against publishing
a letter of Sherman's which was favorable to Johnson, on the ground that military men should stay out of politics. Grant hinted strongly to Sherman that
this advice was still applicable. Speaking frankly of his talk with Johnson,
Grant wrote, "Taking the whole conversation together and what now appears in the papers, I am rather of the opinion that it is the desire to have you
in Washington either as Act[ing] Sec[retary] of War or in some other way."
Grant was trying to warn his friend to steer clear of such a shoal, which

might halt them both. Sherman had achieved his powerful position by always remembering to defer to Grant, while retaining his independence of mind. Grant thought that before Sherman made any commitments, they should talk: "I will not venture in a letter to say all . . . that I would say to you in person." The conversation could be held right at the Grants'. The general invited the Sherman family entourage—however large—to stop with him and Julia at their splendid new house. (There would be no overcrowding or immediate strain on the larder; General Daniel Butterfield, Alexander T. Stewart, and their fellow subscribers had provided $30,000 for the mortgage on this fine house. Even more comfortingly, they had supplied $54,000 in government bonds and $20,000 in cash.)[10]

When Sherman arrived in Washington on October 25, Stanton fully expected him to be made secretary of war *ad interim*. Stanton claimed to be untroubled by his pending removal, which, he told Senator William Pitt Fessenden, "is only the forerunner of the efforts to get Grant out of the way." Grant, however, had a powerful ally in his effort not to be shunted aside. Senator John Sherman, a leading Republican, begged his brother not to "connect your name with this Administration." An endorsement is "just what he [Johnson] wants but what you ought to avoid." John Sherman thought Johnson's swing around the circle had "sunk the Presidential Office to the level of a Grog House." The senator and Grant prevailed; General Sherman, despite long talks in which Johnson tried to persuade him to take the post, steered safely away from the political currents. Grant, however, was very close to them. And there he stayed. His position in the army and in Washington depended on his remaining loyal to the president without antagonizing Republican legislators.[11]

In the early fall of 1866, the Grants made plans to go to Galena for Orville Babcock's wedding to Annie Campbell, a daughter of one of the prominent men of the town. Babcock was immensely proud of his tie to the Grants, and yet for a brief moment that well-organized young man, seeking to provide for his wife in style, talked of leaving Grant's staff. He wrote Annie on October 10, "The Pacific RR people have been at me today again. If they hire me they will have to pay . . . me $10,000 $\frac{00}{100}$ a year, or I will not go." Unluckily for all, including the railroad, which might have made lucrative use of his peculiar talents, Babcock did not get a good enough offer. He was, however, too busy to be regretful; he had another flourishing enterprise at which to succeed—General Grant's career. He saw his place in it as secure. He wrote his fiancée, after a reception at the "I" Street house, that "Mrs. Grant talks now as if nothing would prevent her from going to Galena."[12]

Julia had long been much taken with the attentive younger bachelors of Grant's staff—Comstock, the ill-fated Bowers, Porter, and Babcock, and the bridegroom knew he had a valuable ally in the general's lady. Grant too was fond of Babcock. The general had already asserted publicly that the trip would be purely private, with no political overtones. This was not, however, self-evident, and Elihu Washburne was delighted that Babcock's wedding was to take place shortly before the election, when Grant's appearance in Galena would be politically useful. Meanwhile, Grant was finding time for quieter political chores; he called on Secretary of the Interior Orville H. Browning about a patent that was of concern to a manufacturer in Washburne's (and his own) congressional district. Grant was being so helpful and cordial that the congressman was vastly disappointed when he wrote on October 23, "I will not be able to go to Galena for the wedding. I cannot fully explain to you the reason but it will not do for me to leave Washington before the elections."[13]

Baltimore, not Galena, was getting Grant's attention. The approaching election was the first general canvass since the war's end, and there was considerable expectation of violence. The New Orleans "riot" had been a response to the freedmen's entrance into politics, and the question of their political rights was implicitly present in many of the contests for congressional office in November 1866. The reach of the rank and file of former slaves was greater in the United States than it had been in any other post-emancipation society in history. In the Union state of Maryland (which until 1864 had been a slave-holding state as well) the prospect that black people might make huge gains as a result of the election was causing feelings to run high. And in view of the events in New Orleans, it seemed likely that Grant would have to use the army to maintain order in Baltimore on election day.

Earlier, a Radical Republican had been chosen mayor of Baltimore, in an election in which two police commissioners, Nicolas L. Wood and Samuel Hindes, had the responsibility for voter registration. They were accused of not permitting conservative voters—some of whom had been Confederate sympathizers—to vote. Governor Thomas Swann, a Know-Nothing before the war and now a supporter of Andrew Johnson, was threatening to remove the two for misconduct, right before the election, and to appoint two new police commissioners, James Young and William T. Valiant, to ensure that voters of Conservative leanings could vote.[14]

All this was played out to the tune of impending violence. People of all persuasions had visions of another New Orleans. General Sheridan had asserted firmly that if he had been in New Orleans he and his Union soldiers could have prevented the attack on those demonstrating for the black vote. In Baltimore the particulars and of course the cast of characters were different, but the situation itself was potentially not very different. Federal troops could stop violence, but they could also intimidate certain voters, depending on which politician's drum they marched to. General E. R. S. Canby predicted a repetition in Maryland of the Louisiana killings and in mid-October insisted that Grant meet with him and Governor Swann. After this conference, Grant concluded that there was no likelihood of violence—unless the governor replaced the police commissioners.[15]

But this Swann was determined to do. What was more, he wanted a promise of support by federal troops if his action should produce a violent reaction. He had in mind a comprehensive program for controlling former slaves. (And indeed, once the Conservatives were in full power, they implemented Maryland's notorious apprenticeship program, which substituted for slavery a new system of involuntary servitude. In 1867, Judge Hugh L. Bond, in a decision of great importance in American race relations, found the apprenticeship system unconstitutional under the Thirteenth Amendment.) The Radicals, for their part, were determined to build on their mayoral victory in Baltimore and, in the November 6 election, to win a majority in the state legislature and prevent the passage of anti-Negro legislation.[16]

In the draft of a long letter to President Johnson (which he did not send), Grant showed that he had studied the Baltimore situation with great care and that he was exceedingly reluctant to take troops into Maryland. On October 24 his thinking, as expressed in the draft, was as follows: "The conviction is forced in my mind that no reason now exists for giving or promising the Military aid of the Government to support the laws of Maryland. The tendency of giving such aid or promise would be to produce the very result intended to be averted. So far there seems to be merely a very bitter contest for political ascendancy. . . . Military interference would be interpreted as giving aid to one of the factions no matter how pure the intentions. . . ." Grant was resolute: "I hope never to see arise in this Country whilst I occupy the position of General-in-Chief of the Army [a situation in which I] have to send troops into a state *in full relations with the General Government.* . . ." He was making a distinction between Maryland and the states of the Confederacy. Anticipating the worst, he concluded, "If insurrection does come[,] the law provides the method of calling out forces to suppress it."[17]

Instead of sending troops Grant took a different course. He risked his immense personal power and sought to turn his own posture of political neutrality to the country's advantage. On Thursday, November 1, 1866, five days before the election, Grant and Comstock took a morning train to Baltimore and, at the Eutaw House, on the corner of Eutaw and Baltimore streets, met separately with the Radical police commissioners, whom Swann had removed and with a group of Conservatives. His message was that the registration judges of the rival parties should find a way for their poll watchers to validate voters that would not provoke violence. In a crowded day Grant spoke to the Baltimoreans as a private citizen, but his power to summon the army was implicit in all he said.[18]

He returned to Washington that evening. The next morning, Friday, when the new Conservative commissioners, Young and Valiant, arrived at police headquarters to take charge, they were denied access to the building by Radical police officers. The crowds in the street thickened and were in a dangerous mood by Saturday. In federal district court, Judge Bond issued a writ for the arrest of Swann's two commissioners, and they were put in jail, in the charge of a Radical warden. As arguments in the streets grew more heated, General Canby was authorized to bring in seven hundred federal troops from New York City. Governor Swann, with the memory of the genteel opening of the Peabody Institute a week before all but gone, hurriedly entrained for Washington on Saturday evening. In the capital he had a long conference with President Johnson, Secretary of War Stanton, Attorney General Henry Stanbery, and General Grant. The upshot of this meeting was that when the governor left Washington on Sunday evening he took with him to Baltimore a reluctant Ulysses S. Grant. Once again established at the Eutaw House, the "private citizen" met first with a delegation of Radicals including Judge Bond, Mayor John Lee Chapman, and others. Grant's proposal on Sunday night was, once again, that the election judges for the rival parties in the various precincts agree to disagree and resolve on a case-by-case basis the claims of the would-be voters. The ballots of rejected voters would be kept in separate boxes, for possible later tallying.[19]

During the long Sunday the compromise seemed to be sticking, but by 7:00 P.M. it had collapsed. The next morning Grant tried again with the Conservatives, this time at Governor Swann's house. Once more his message was that he was the mediator; once more the army loomed as a threat. Whom it threatened was not entirely clear, and Grant, no doubt, liked this ambiguity. At 3:00 P.M. on Monday, still determined not to be forced to take sides, Grant left for Washington, "under the delusion," said the *Baltimore Sun* sourly, "that he had been chiefly instrumental in settling the Baltimore political difficulties." But the next day, election day, the spirit if not the details of Grant's compromise was honored. Radical registration judges were in charge, but Conservatives in the city were permitted to vote. And vote they did, electing by a narrow margin the Swann-Johnson candidates for both the state legislature and Congress, with disastrous consequences for black Marylanders. There was no violence beyond the scuffles standard on any election day. The bars were closed.[20]

Governor Swann, responding to a serenade from his triumphant admirers, said that it was with "pain" that he read of his own earlier remarks disparaging Grant and Canby. He proclaimed that he had "never made use of language attributed" to him, and regarded the "distinguished gentlemen" as "honorable peacemakers." Things had worked out fine for him—and for Grant. Emerging from even so short an immersion in Maryland politics unbesmirched was no small feat. But the general had little chance to celebrate.[21]

Back in Washington, despite his contribution to the Johnsonian cause, Grant still had to worry about whether Sherman would become his boss. The Baltimore newspapers, and others across the country, were again full of reports that the long conversations carried on by Sherman and Johnson would result in the general's appointment as secretary of war. After the election, which despite the success in Maryland had been a defeat for Johnson, the president and Secretary of State Seward proposed that Grant accompany Lewis Davis Campbell, the American minister to Mexico, on a mission to that country to negotiate with the liberal government of Benito Pablo Juárez. Johnson was shrewd in picking a Mexican assignment as a way to get Grant out of town. Grant, "zealous on that subject," was an admirer of Juárez, who had fought successfully against the foreign government imposed on his country—a country Grant had learned to love twenty years earlier. But Grant smelled the rat. He did not dare go to Mexico and leave the field at home open for the president to replace Stanton with Sherman. And so he went to a cabinet meeting. He was frequently invited to attend by cabinet members seeking to bolster their positions with his support. This day he ac- companied Secretary of State Seward, but he withheld his support when in- structions were read directing him to go to Mexico. Grant startled everyone—or everyone save Stanton—by saying (as Welles recorded it) that "he did not think it expedient for him to go out of the country." Stanton had expressed his objection to a Grant mission in almost identical language at an earlier meeting, and Welles was suspicious. "The President," he noted, "was surprised and a little disconcerted. He could not fail to see there was an in- trigue. I think something more."[22]

"Grandfather Welles," as Grant called him privately, was always suspect- ing a conspiracy between Stanton and Grant. He was wrong. It was often in the interest of each to agree with the other, but it would have been in no way useful for Grant to be tied conspiratorially with the volatile secretary of war. The general was his own man, and he was not going to be exiled to Mexico. Grant was strong enough not only to refuse an order from his commander in chief, but also to amend that order. He proposed that instead of himself, the president's representative on this important mission should be the man John- son had recently been praising, General Sherman. Sherman was in town amidst new rumors that he would become secretary of war. Instead, he found himself aboard the *Susquehanna* with Minister Campbell on a futile mis- sion to Mexico. Grant had disposed of Sherman, but his own trip past Scylla and Charybdis was not yet complete.[23]

Moderate advisers of the president, such as Senator James R. Doolittle of Wisconsin, had for a long time been urging him to replace Stanton not with Sherman, who was sure to irritate the Radicals, but with Grant, thereby identifying Grant with the administration. Gideon Welles saw the appoint- ment as the only way to prevent Grant from being taken up by the Radicals and made their candidate for president in 1868. Doolittle could not under- stand Johnson's seeming indifference to the possibility that Grant might become his opponent in the next presidential contest, but Welles guessed that Johnson was watching Grant closely and was exceedingly uneasy about en- trusting him with too much power. The president was wary lest Grant become so strong that such a nomination would be inevitable.[24]

At the first meeting of the cabinet in 1867, Grant was present for a discus- sion of Reconstruction in the District of Columbia. The experience of having to consider the position of freedmen in the nation's capital was critical in the education of white Northerners to the Southern white-supremacy position. Supporting civil rights far off in the conquered South was all well and good; to do so in the town in which federal politicians lived for a good portion of every year was quite another thing. Congress had passed a bill disfranchising certain former rebels while giving the vote to black citizens of the District, and white liberals were squirming. The reaction of Secretary of State William Henry Seward beautifully illustrates their dilemma on the question of true black equality. He had voted for Negro suffrage in New York State, where black people were decidedly and safely in the minority. Welles noted, sardonically, in his diary that Seward justified himself by saying that "in the District and in the States where there was a large prepondering negro population it was different." If the black people "were not in a majority[,] they were a large minority" in the capital. The thought of black men governing the governing city of the nation made Seward, and a great many other white men, uneasy.

Seward's imagination rambled toward Egypt, of all places, and he speculated that one day universal suffrage would come to the world. Until it arrived universally, however, he opposed it particularly at home in Washington. He supported the president's futile veto message. So did cabinet members from Connecticut, Ohio, and Maryland—and so did General Grant. Welles noted that Grant did not seem to mind the disfranchisement of the rebels, but "thought it very contemptible business [for members of Congress] whose States excluded the negroes, to give them suffrage in this District."[25]

In distant Arkansas it was a different matter. A delegation was in the city seeking advice on how Arkansas could obtain readmission to Congress, and Welles was disgusted to learn that Grant, privately, had responded by urging that the state ratify the Fourteenth Amendment (with its provisions guaranteeing the rights of citizenship of the freedmen, but not giving them the vote). This was a break from Johnson, but only on the precise point of support of the Fourteenth Amendment. Publicly, Grant was still on the president's side, as witness his view, published in the *New York Times*, that Northerners had better eschew hypocrisy and grant the vote to Negroes in their own states before bestowing it on the black citizens of the capital. The interview in which he insisted on this national standard was given after the president's veto of the District suffrage bill had been overridden. Black citizens of Washington were not as adamant about consistency. They had filled the congressional galleries when the bill was debated and, decorum abandoned, cheered when it cleared the veto. To them this legislation was a step toward equality, and Grant's disapproval of it was a deep disappointment. The general's words, however, were more than acceptable at the White House, and so were he and Julia. They continued to be entertained there, along with the cabinet, as members of the official family.[26]

Early in 1867, the army, the commanding general of the army, and the sec-

retary of war were given an extraordinary role in the governing of the country. Congress passed legislation requiring that in five districts transition governments headed by military governors be established. The intent was not to
send in an army of occupation, but to have senior army men serve as temporary governors general and junior officers act as voter-registration officials
and peace-keepers for state governments under which former slaves would
register to vote and participate as officeholders along with their former masters. It is in this context of social and political Reconstruction, and not that of
the plot of a comic opera, that the tenure-of-office crisis, the removal of Secretary of War Stanton from office, and the subsequent impeachment of the
president should be viewed. Congress, its Republican ranks enlarged by the
election of 1866, set out to enact, and what was more, to enforce its own
Reconstruction program, in opposition to the Conservative policies of the
National Union party president. Johnson had refused to enforce the Civil
Rights Act of 1866, and the governments that Johnson had recognized in the
Southern states had also failed to protect their black citizens.

Republicans in Congress who were concerned with the welfare—the
safety—of the freedmen in the South could see nowhere to turn but to the
army as the agent of enforcement of the law. But there was nothing in the
record, either during the war or after it, that argued that an army man—
simply because he was an army man—could be counted on to be a judicious
defender of the rights of blacks in the South. Quite the contrary, there was
a great deal of evidence to suggest that Old Massa's warnings to his slaves
to beware the Yankee soldiers had been very much in order. As usual, the
question of precisely who did the job was critical, and here the choice was
Grant's. He commanded the army; he would decide which generals were
to be ordered south as governors.

Grant had to be the one in charge of this program. General Howard, the
head of the Freedmen's Bureau, had the confidence of many civilian philanthropists, but he had not proved strong enough to stand up to the president
or to assert his authority over his fellow army commanders, many of whom
sneered in embarrassment at his Christian virtue. No one of smaller stature
than Grant could get the generals to carry out the Radical Republican plan
for a Reconstruction that would guarantee the lives and rights of blacks in the
South. There was much political pressure to accomplish this goal; "I'm afraid
to do anything against the Negro," Sherman had said as early as December
1865, while he nevertheless mustered black regiments out of the army. All
through 1867 Grant was courted by the leaders of Congress, who had given
him the immense responsibility of assigning the generals. His friend Sherman gave evidence that which ones were chosen did indeed matter when he
wrote General Ord, "You and Pope and Reynolds all lean against the
Nigger"; if this statement was correct, the blacks would doubtless be pleased
to have someone else sent to protect them.[27]

It was essential to Johnson that Grant's generals not do Congress's bid-

ding, and he worked assiduously to hold Grant in his camp. Grant, despite his
support of the Fourteenth Amendment, did not seem lost to Johnson. (Indeed, not a few observers have noted that the Johnsonian Southerners might
have been very smart to take the general's advice. If they had accepted the
Fourteenth Amendment and come back into Congress, they would have been
in a splendid position to persuade their white brethren in the North to leave
the establishment of racial mores in the South to those who "knew best."
They would thereby have achieved the Compromise of 1877 and the emascu-
lation of the amendment ahead of historical schedule.) Even those of Johnson's supporters who insisted on opposition to the Fourteenth Amendment as
a test of loyalty to the president were willing to close their eyes in Grant's
case because he was too popular to lose as an ally.

The basic issue became clear in the winter of 1867. General Howard, at
the Freedmen's Bureau, had thousands of carefully documented reports from
his agents of murders and mutilations of freedmen all across the South. He
turned to his commander, General Grant, to try to get someone to pay attention to them. Some Republicans in Congress were also concerned about such
atrocities, and in January, Congress formally requested that the president
explain why he had not prevented them by enforcing the Civil Rights Act.
The War Department response to the request was a long report by Howard,
giving details of killings that the government had not been able to prevent. In
a cabinet meeting on February 15, at which Grant was not present, Secretary
of War Stanton brought in Howard's account, accompanied by a covering
letter from Grant. Gideon Welles, who chose to regard the report as nothing
but an "omnium gatherum of newspaper gossip" and "rumors" that Howard's agents had "picked up" here and there in the South, sought, along with
the president, to find a way to suppress the document.[28]

It soon became apparent that an effort to hide Howard's report by referring it to the attorney general for further investigation would prove futile,
because members of Congress already had copies of both the report and
Grant's letter. Welles, who at this point still loathed Stanton more than he
did Grant, thought that the secretary of war had deliberately leaked the
report, not only to discredit the president but to "help generate difference between the President and the General." Welles, unwilling to believe that anyone truly cared about the freedmen, reasoned that Stanton, like almost everyone else in Washington, was jealous of Grant. Suspicious though the
secretary of the navy was of the general, he knew how important it was that
Johnson not lose Grant's allegiance. The president himself seemed unwilling
to find out exactly where Grant did stand in the virulent division over Negro
policy. He was on the verge of summoning the general from his army headquarters office to come to the cabinet meeting to explain his letter accompanying—or was it, perhaps, endorsing?—Howard's report, when he
stopped himself. He told Welles that "but for the rain," he had been of a
mind to send "for Grant to know how far he really was involved in the matter." Johnson did not quite want to know what Grant was up to.[29]

Grant was magnificently cagey at not tipping his hand. And as long as he did not do so, cards of speculation were sure to fall according to the dealer's political desires. By the summer of 1867, however, it was becoming harder for Grant to avoid declaring himself. In New Orleans, the outspoken Philip H. Sheridan was in charge of one of the five military districts, and he used his soldiers vigorously as voter-registration officials, enrolling black voters. He publicly declared that he would continue to do so regardless of the president's views. In June, Sheridan sent Johnson an insulting letter, and the president, enraged, asked his cabinet to discuss it. This time Grant was present. He blunted a call for Sheridan's immediate removal, supporting a rebuke instead. Sheridan, however, had gotten under Johnson's skin, and the president was determined to get rid of him. Acrimony was in the air; it was an ideal time for the man caught between the two to take a summer vacation.[30]

Long Branch, New Jersey, in the 1860's was a lovely seaside village of small houses—true cottages—with wonderful filigreed porches from which one could look out from high bluffs over the Atlantic. The beaches and the surf were fine, and it was here that the Grants spent their summers from 1867 onward. They took the house next door to that of the publisher George W. Childs and immediately liked it. The general "drove out twice a day," the first time just after breakfast; he often went a good distance, returning at midmorning to read the newspaper and his mail quietly on the porch overlooking

*Winslow Homer,* Long Branch, New Jersey, *1869.* CHARLES HENRY HAYDEN FUND
41.631. COURTESY, MUSEUM OF FINE ARTS, BOSTON

the ocean. He was there, at the shore, away from the Johnson and Sheridan quarrel, when a crisis broke out in Tennessee that required fast stepping if he was not to be required to leave Long Branch. Johnson wanted federal troops sent in to Tennessee on the ground that the Radical Republican governor, William G. Brownlow, was planning to use the state militia to intimidate voters. Grant sent the president a telegram saying that General Thomas had been ordered to the state and that he did not think his own presence there necessary. Johnson was pleased by the dispatch of troops, but noted that Grant was more reluctant to expose himself than he had been in Maryland the previous fall. Grant now appeared unwilling to risk another involvement as a "neutral" in a situation that might result in political defeat for the Radicals.[31]

The president was still not sure of the loyalty of his commanding general, and he still needed it badly. In July he called Grant to Washington for a long talk. Disgusted with both Sheridan and Stanton, Johnson was moving at last to follow Senator Doolittle's advice and tie Grant to himself by making him secretary of war. When the subject was broached he found Grant hesitating. The response proved to be more than hesitation; after the conversation, on August 1, 1867, Grant wrote Johnson a letter which in places shows signs of the guiding hand of a lawyer. It informed the president tactfully but firmly that such an appointment would break the law. The Tenure of Office Act had been passed March 2, 1867, by the Republican Congress, in an effort to hold the gate against defiance of their legislation by the president. Invoking its constitutional right to consent to cabinet nominations, the Senate claimed the right to deny its consent to the removal of men sitting in the cabinet. And there was nothing abstract in these constitutional contortions; the intention was to keep in office Lincoln's wartime secretary of war, Edwin M. Stanton. He and he alone among those in the top reaches of the executive branch seemed likely to do the bidding of Congress. Andrew Johnson regarded the bill as unconstitutional and wanted the Supreme Court to say so, but that court cannot rule on a hypothetical issue. Therefore, the president moved to replace Stanton without congressional consent, appointing in his stead someone he thought the country would not take exception to, General Ulysses S. Grant. If the appointment was challenged, the Court could speak.[32]

Grant's letter declining the appointment stressed not only that the Tenure of Office Act was being repudiated but that the repudiation was being done, unwisely, while Congress was not in session. And then, in a passage that was to make Johnson even more uncomfortable, Grant took the occasion to defend Sheridan, the one general in the South who was actively upholding the Radical Republican plan of Reconstruction: "It is unmistakably the wish of the country that Gen. Sheridan not be removed." Grant did not argue with Johnson in support of Sheridan's pro-freedman policies—the words would have reached deaf ears—but he did remind the president that Sheridan was immensely popular and that his removal would be in defiance of a law passed by Congress. To Johnson, as to Welles, in whom the president confided, the movement of Grant toward the Radicals was clear. "Grant is going over," said Welles. "Yes," responded Johnson.[33]

But the president was not going to allow Grant to get over the fence to the Republicans without making a major effort to keep him corralled. To this end he developed a new plan: he would dismiss Stanton and make Grant secretary of war *ad interim*. A temporary appointment would test the situation. If the president's constitutional position, in combination with Grant's popularity, had the strength to gain public approval of this change, Congress would return in December with Stanton's replacement already accomplished. The time to act, Johnson concluded, in defiance of Grant's advice, was in August, with Congress out of session.

If Grant had truly wanted to remain the simple soldier who simply carried out statesmen's orders, there would have been no insurmountable barrier to his refusing the appointment on the ground that it was inappropriate for him to move to a civilian desk in the War Department. Given Grant's great popularity, a statement to that effect, made public, would have forced Johnson to accept his decision and either name another secretary or keep Stanton. But Grant did not say no. He took this particular administrative post because he was already on an inescapable track toward another. Everyone in Washington talked of the general as the next president. For example, in May 1866, in the House debate on the bill, easily passed, raising Grant's rank to general and giving him a corresponding increase in salary, Thaddeus Stevens had declared—to accompanying laughter and applause—that he was willing to promote "this Marlborough, this Wellington," to "a higher office whenever the happy moment shall arrive." The elevation to the White House had begun a good while ago.[34]

Even those who thought the general a dullard were convinced that he too had his eye on the presidency. Shrewd politics might have argued that his surest way of getting that job was to refuse the office of secretary of war, but there was a risk in refusing. If Johnson appointed a subordinate of Grant's, like Sherman, to the cabinet post, and the new man stole the limelight, he might also steal the nomination. Or the new man might do so good a job as part of the president's team that Johnson himself would look strong enough to win the nomination. If Grant was not to get lost in the shadow of these possibilities, he had to take the job. For the first time since his becoming colonel and his rise out of failure, he had been on the verge of saying no to a new position, and old terrors were at work. Grant did not dare turn down any job, lest he end with none.

He could no longer accept any superior except—temporarily—President Johnson. And he could not step aside into any kind of retirement, even temporarily. He was forty-five. His son Fred's education, at West Point, was costing him no money, but the three younger children needed educating, and he and Julia had no wish to return to second-rate clothes or second-rate living. He could do nothing except stay at the top, and if that icy summit was glazed with an assignment in the cabinet, he must dutifully accept. Grant wrote Stanton an awkward letter, praising the man's long service both to the nation and to him, but indicating that "I have no alternative but to submit, under protest, to the superior force of the President." One observer, John Lothrop Motley, who was no dunce himself, was immensely impressed with how well Grant had succeeded in playing the part of the "dumb, inarticulate man of genius," though he thought the time when the mask should be discarded was "fast approaching."[35]

That genius was about to be sorely tried. On August 5, 1867, Grant wrote Julia, who was in Pennsylvania, that because of "a startling piece of news, which will probably be published in the morning papers," he could not join her but would have to stay in Washington. He was about to become a cabinet member. His acceptance of the post was not a clear-cut leap into a civilian role; he was still a general, his appointment was an interim one, and his portfolio involved military matters. And yet, Ulysses Grant was moving into the administration, into the executive branch of the government. Formally, he was now in politics.[36]

Ironically, this political debut was in defiance of the will of a Republican Congress, as expressed in the Tenure of Office Act. Johnson had appointed Grant secretary of war *ad interim* in order to remove Stanton, the man the Radicals sought to protect. Under the congressional plan for the South, the secretary of war was required by law to administer the military Reconstruction program. During the fall of 1867, Grant increasingly undertook to support the congressional concept that he should interpret and obey the laws of Congress directly, rather than accept instructions from the president. But still he did not break with Johnson.

Ulysses and Julia Grant were determined not to be forgotten, but they worried lest in retaining their grasp on prominence they loosen their almost desperate hold on financial security. In 1867, John W. Forney, the editor of the *Washington Daily Chronicle*, set out to be a president-maker once again. He had the wit to laugh at his own credentials, having helped secure nomination for James Buchanan and Andrew Johnson. Undaunted, he now sought to redeem himself by gaining the White House for Grant. At the outset, he met with a strange rebuke from Grant's man Rawlins. "General Grant does not want to be President," reported Rawlins, going on to state, however, that Grant "thinks the Republican party may need him, and he believes, as their candidate, he can be elected and re-elected." Rawlins then went on to ask, "What is to become of him after his second Presidential term—what, indeed, during his administration?" The problem was money. As general, Grant was sure of receiving "from seventeen to twenty thousand dollars a year"—for life. Rawlins was frank: "To go into the Presidency at twenty-five thousand dollars a year for eight years is, perhaps, to gain more fame; but what is to become of him at the end of his Presidency?" He would have to resign from the army, and there was no pension for ex-presidents. Calculations had been closely made: "Eight years from the 4th March 1869," Grant would not yet be fifty-six. Still relatively young, he would be without a job or an income.[37]

The general, his lady, and his other closest advisers had canvassed the full range of contingencies. "It looks . . . as if Genl Grant was to be the rising man," observed David Davis dourly, "the people love military glory. . . ." Most Americans were more enthusiastic. Not only could Grant be elected, he could be re-elected. And he did not have to look eager for the position, the Republican party needed to have him assume it. Julia was determined that he not be had at too cheap a price, and in his conversation with Forney, Rawlins permitted himself a comparison of the United States to England, which had seen fit to "enrich and ennoble" its Wellingtons and Nelsons. Rawlins suggested that if Forney was powerful enough to create presidents, then surely he could bring Congress to a prior act of financial magnanimity toward the hero of Vicksburg—the substitution of a permanent annual allowance for Grant's army pension, which would lapse if he resigned to run for president. Forney got the hint, but was unable to oblige; Congress refused to authorize such a stipend. "In our country the man who fights for and saves the Republic would be a beggar if he depended upon political office," Forney declared. "Mark it," he continued, "if Grant takes anything from the rich, whose vast fortunes he has saved, after he is President, he will be accused as the willing recipient of gifts."[38]

Julia would have to settle for the White House alone, without the stipend, but to the end of her days she resented the ingratitude of a people unwilling to provide for her Wellington. This is apparent from her reaction on visiting in 1877 the splendidly rich Apsley House of the Iron Duke's son in London. Aware that having left the White House, she and Ulysses had only that raw red-brick box of a house in Galena, she mused, "How would it have been if General Grant had been an Englishman—I wonder, I wonder?" Back in 1867 the chief object was to get at least a four-year lease on 1600 Pennsylvania Avenue. Forney wrote a five-column piece for his and other papers identifying Grant with a willingness to carry Republican ideals into the White House and, "after it was in type," took it to Grant's office. Rawlins was delighted and wanted it in the next day's editions, but Forney was too savvy to print it without Grant's blessing. He told Rawlins that if it appeared "without authority," Grant's opponents would get a reporter to ask the general if he had sanctioned the article. Grant, honestly, would say he had never seen it, thus reinforcing the idea that Forney had simply made up the story. Determined to prevent this from happening, Forney enlisted Rawlins in the task of getting Grant to read the article, warning that if he got off the hook, "all your schemes to make him President will *gang a gley*."[39]

Rawlins took the article into Grant's office and was gone a long time. When he finally emerged, he said, "General Grant is quite pleased with your statement of his political record, and surprised that he proves to be so good a

Republican." Grant had carefully not admitted that he wanted to be president, but Forney was satisfied: "Upon this hint I printed." As predicted, those who hoped Grant would not get the nomination tried, in letters to the newspapers, to suggest that Grant was furious about the piece and also tried to get up a story that Grant and Washburne had broken over the latter's efforts in behalf of Grant's candidacy. Forney categorically denied that Grant was displeased or had broken with Washburne. Grant, save in the matter of money, was exactly where he wanted to be. He could insist in conversation with President Johnson or Secretary Stanton or General Sherman that all the talk about the presidency was the work of columnists and politicians with Potomac fever. But he did not have to deny Forney's skillfully constructed statement that he was leaning the Republican way. From St. Louis, in October 1867, Sherman wrote, "I am just back from Washington, where I left the General and his folks well, & calm as a 'Summer Morn.' "[40]

When Congress reconvened in December 1867, Johnson, complying with the Tenure of Office Act, reported the suspension of Stanton and asked Congress to consent to his removal. The action was considered by the Senate Committee on Military Affairs, which in January 1868, in a report brought to the floor of the Senate by Senator Jacob M. Howard of Michigan, called for the reinstatement of Stanton. The Senate as a whole began debate on the subject on Friday, January 10; on Saturday, with a pledge (not kept) that debate would be continued on Monday, Johnson's supporters conducted a filibuster. This gave Johnson and Grant—and Stanton—a little time to maneuver. And maneuver they did, about as maladroitly as can be imagined.

At issue—quite apart from minor matters like construction of the Constitution and the protection of the lives and rights of four million black Americans—was the question of who would become president in 1868. That damnable lodestar the presidency lured three of the principals in the clumsy drama and perhaps the fourth as well. Andrew Johnson had the job; Edwin M. Stanton wanted it; so did Ulysses S. Grant; and so—just possibly—did William Tecumseh Sherman. Johnson hoped that the Supreme Court would come to his rescue. (With still another hopeful, Salmon P. Chase, sitting as chief justice, one had to worry about motives in that chamber too.) The president's plan was that Grant would retain the office of secretary of war, Stanton would sue to regain it, and the Supreme Court would declare the Tenure of Office Act unconstitutional. Grant promised, so Johnson contended, that he would hold the office until the court acted. Stanton would go, and Johnson would look victorious—and electable. In the state and local elections in 1867 there had been an upsurge of Conservative votes across the North, and Johnson hoped the Stanton crisis could be used to strengthen that trend.

Stanton and the Republicans in Congress were equally committed to stopping it. Grant continued to try to bluff his way through the pass between Johnson and the Republicans in Congress, but his friend Sherman was less sanguine. When he came east in January to stand ready to succeed Grant as commanding general of the army, he was given a temporary office next door to Grant's, and the two men talked every day. On Saturday, January 11, 1868, with a decision by the Senate imminent, Sherman pressed his chief to face the problems before him and decide on a plan of action. "I think I asked you," stated Sherman in a memorandum of that miserable weekend written later in the month at Grant's request, "if you had not promised to give notice to the President and also what course you intended to pursue." "Promised" was the key word; Sherman would scarcely have referred to such a commitment, which had become so sore a point between Grant and Johnson, if he had not indeed heard of such a pledge from the general. Clearly, it was at the center of the conversation the two generals had that Saturday morning. Sherman pointed out that President Johnson's sense of the obligation was that Grant should hold onto the office of secretary of war in defiance of any act of Congress, or, at the very least, should resign so that Johnson could appoint another man, *ad interim*, who would stand up to Congress. Grant recalled that when he had replaced Stanton the previous July, he had given Stanton two days notice; now, he contended, Stanton would surely do the same. With such notice, Grant could take the problem to the president—and avoid involvement in the direct confrontation with Stanton and Congress.[41]

Sherman was not reassured by this logic. Things might not work out as Grant thought—or, rather, hoped (there seemed to have been little thought involved). Discussing the provisions of the Tenure of Office Act, which Grant had belatedly read, Sherman, with his sense of blunt realism, did not let his friend miss the fact that he would be subject to a ten-thousand-dollar fine and even a jail sentence if he broke the law. To be sure, such punishments would scarcely be imposed on the man of Appomattox, but the humiliation of their prospect was not to be ignored. Sherman urged Grant to get to the White House, fast, and tell the president he wanted no further part of the confrontation between Johnson and Congress.

Before Grant could do so, Sherman, characteristically, took his own advice. Accompanying his friend General John Pope, who was in town and obliged to pay his respects to the president, Sherman went to the White House; when Pope left after a friendly few minutes with Johnson, Sherman remained to talk. While he was warming to his subject, Grant walked in. Sherman, glad that Grant had finally decided to talk the matter over with Johnson, and embarrassed (if Sherman can ever be said to have been embarrassed) at having been caught speaking his superior's piece for him, left the two alone. The general and the president then had a long and badly remembered conversation. Johnson talked in constitutional terms of the defense of the power of the executive branch of the government and of the need to defy the Tenure of Office Act, should Congress reinstate Stanton, in order to force the Supreme Court to decide the legislation's constitutionality. Grant realized that he was in the unenviable position of being the sacrificial lamb. Neither popularity nor protestations that he was merely a simple soldier obeying a command would save him in court. When such a decision is handed down, there is no middle ground; one either wins or loses. Grant was no lawyer, but neither was he a fool, and he knew his chances of being the loser were good indeed. Johnson apparently spoke of Grant's great opportunity to serve the interest of the Union; Grant reminded the president that the reward for this lofty service would be a stiff and humiliating fine. Johnson (rather grandly) said that he himself would pay any such fine; it would be a small price for the upholding of constitutional principle. Grant had no trouble sizing up the usefulness of the offer. He wanted out.

What was said in the remainder of the conversation is uncertain. It is clear only that Grant proposed that someone else be given the assignment of defying Congress should Stanton come to take his office back. But either he did not move swiftly or else Johnson parried skillfully, for Grant did not succeed in getting Johnson to replace him right then and there, that Saturday. Instead, the conversation ended inconclusively. Johnson claimed ever afterward that Grant had reaffirmed his obligation to hold the office against Stanton until a court test or until Johnson could replace him with another man—who presumably would do the defying. Grant never categorically denied having accepted such an assignment; he simply suggested that he had made no promise to stay in office and that he expected Johnson to find a replacement before Monday, when Congress would presumably vote on reinstating Stanton. Rumors from the Senate on Saturday made it seem very likely that this reinstatement would be voted, and yet the two men parted with only what Johnson remembered as a promise by Grant that they would talk again on Monday, before any action was taken at the War Department.

While they talked, the Senate, over John Sherman's objections—he wanted his brother to have more time in which to stave off the crisis—went into extraordinary executive session and privately discussed, for better than three hours, the reinstatement of Stanton. As usual in Washington, shop talk did not end when the gentlemen left Capitol Hill. That evening, at a large party, Julia Grant was particularly gracious to Congressman Robert C. Schenck of Ohio, in order to find out what the Radicals were up to. Schenck was happy to pay court to the general's lady and found it not painful; he reported later to his daughter that in a becoming dress Julia "looked a little better" than usual. The Potomac drama was an exciting one, and Schenck, despite a barren temperance dinner earlier in the evening at the Colfaxes', was in good humor. Julia came away alerted, by his eager gossip, to the likelihood of Stanton's reinstatement.[42]

The cuisine was better at the home of Senator Reverdy Johnson. There, over good wine, the Sherman brothers proposed a compromise that appealed to the Conservative Democrat from Maryland. The idea was to appoint Jacob Dolson Cox secretary of war on Monday (the very day his term as governor of Ohio would end). Reverdy Johnson, who was close both to his namesake and to Secretary of State Seward, agreed to go to the White House the next day to urge the president to accept this solution. Then, after a typical Washington, D.C., Saturday evening, the official city went to bed.[43]

On the Sabbath two old warriors sat down again to take counsel together. Ulysses S. Grant and William Tecumseh Sherman would need all they had learned besting General Halleck—and more—to get Grant out the jam he was now in. The best hope, as Sherman saw it, was to make Cox secretary of war. The idea appealed to that side of Grant which was comfortable with any position that pleased everyone as long as it did not please anyone too much. The Cox plan could be counted on to satisfy everyone—except perhaps the nation's black citizens and Edwin Stanton. Cox was popular, but not too popular; he had been a good general during the war, but not too good; and since then had been the governor of his state—and had opposed Negro suffrage. In short Cox was a moderate and was not imposing enough to be a threat to Grant. It was hoped that Johnson would be happy to nominate him and that the Senate would be unable to bring itself to deny him confirmation. Once Cox had been confirmed—so the plan ran—the Senate would lose enthusiasm for reinstating Stanton and instead would be content with monitoring Cox, under the Tenure of Office Act. Grant gave his assent, and Sherman passed the word along to Reverdy Johnson, who was to persuade the president to appoint Cox. But at the end of this critical Sunday, Sherman was dismayed to find no message from the Maryland senator. Apparently, Reverdy Johnson had not seen the president, or if he had, had failed to convince him.[44]

On Monday, January 13, Sherman himself called on President Johnson to urge him to name Cox. Johnson, evasive (or shrewd), left Sherman with the impression that he would make the appointment. The impression was deceptive. In fact, the president seems to have determined on a very different course. He would hold Grant to his promise—and thus force Grant and Stanton into a disagreeable confrontation. Grant, for his part, was getting ready to abandon Johnson—or so Julia Grant's account of that Monday suggests. "And now," she told her readers in her *Memoirs*, "I must not fail to tell of how General Grant happened to be at the President's levee on the evening of January 13, 1868, the night the Senate reinstated Stanton as secretary of war, every circumstance of which I so perfectly remember." She had out-of-town guests who were eager to attend the party, but her husband seemed uncomfortable at the thought of going to the White House that evening: "I would like to gratify you," he said, "but, really, under the circumstances, I do not think I ought to go." (If the "circumstances" had included his loyally standing by Johnson, surely he would have been delighted to go.)[45]

As usual, Julia had her way; she and her friends were all ready for the party, and rather than disappoint them, Ulysses assented. "Just as we were leaving the house," she recalled, "a messenger arrived from the Capitol with a note, which the General read by the gaslight in front of the house." It was the notice that the Senate, after six hours in executive session (but no more

public debate), had voted that Stanton would be reinstated. Again Grant
hesitated about going to the reception—Julia recalled his being afraid that
most senators would view his presence at the White House as an "expression
of sympathy" for Johnson. Again Julia insisted, and Ulysses went to the
White House. On the way home he told her "he really felt embarrassed when
the president grasped his hand so cordially." Grant already knew that he was
going to jettison the president.[46]

On Tuesday morning, Grant walked into the office reserved for the secretary of war, bolted a side door from the inside, left by the main door, which
he locked, gave the key to a War Department functionary, and went to his
old commanding general's headquarters. He had yielded the office; he had
not returned it to the president. An hour later Stanton arrived—the timing
was neat enough to suggest that the two men were not unaware of each
other's exits and entrances. Triumphantly Stanton called for the key, walked
into the office of the secretary of war, wrote a draft for his own back pay, and
dictated a memorandum to Grant and the War Department stating that he,
Stanton, was once again in command. Grant, meanwhile, sent Cyrus B.
Comstock to the White House with a formal letter to the president, of which
he was not the sole author. In it Grant alluded to the "Hon. E. M. Stanton"
and used other uncharacteristic and lawyerly locutions to state that the action
of Congress made it impossible for him to continue as secretary of war *ad interim*.[47]

Tuesday, as it happened, was the day the cabinet met, but the White
House was not totally trusting to habit. Comstock was sent back to Grant
with a reminder that the secretary of war *ad interim* was expected at the meeting. Stanton, of course, was not summoned, and he did not budge from his
departmental chair. Grant set out to attend, but the short walk to the White
House cannot have been a pleasant one. He chose to go to the meeting not as
the secretary of war *ad interim*, but as the invited commanding general of the
army. When he entered the cabinet room, the president politely but
pointedly called for a report from the secretary of war and looked at Grant.
Grant replied that he no longer held that office, and Andrew Johnson, after
two and a half years of wooing Ulysses Grant, tore into him not with a wild
tirade, but much more tellingly, with an icy dressing-down. Cowed and embarrassed, Grant took it. There is no proof that he had lied to the president—
we do not know what had passed between them on Saturday—but Johnson
said he had done so. The fact that Grant took this nasty medicine suggests
that the accusation was true, but what may have discouraged Johnson more
than the lie was the realization that all those months of attempting to placate
the general were for naught. Grant had "gone over."[48]

And Grant's greater deception, a lie more troubling to Johnson than the
matter of the promise to hold onto Stanton's office, was the subtle impression
of disinterested duty that he had fostered. Johnson was enraged by Grant's
presentation of himself as a simple soldier from Galena who would carry out

any orders required of him by the constitutional head of the Republic. Grant wanted to be the president himself, and anticipated that if he defied Congress on the removal of Stanton he might not get to that goal. Openly now, Grant was a creature of private ambition rather than of public service. No longer was he the servant of the public weal, one who stood above selfishness and could always be counted on to do his duty. Grant "felt the few words put to him, and the cold and surprised disdain of the President in all their force," Gideon Welles observed. "Almost abject," he asked to be excused and left the cabinet meeting. The commanding general of the United States had been caught cheating. In punishment, the president treated him as a bad little boy.[49]

The bleak day was not over for Grant. He left the White House and went back to his army headquarters, perhaps expecting some appreciation from the person to whom he had yielded the secretary's office. None was forthcoming. Instead, Stanton pretentiously summoned Grant. The general—more vulnerable to Stanton's imperiousness than usual, with his pride distorted by guilt—obeyed. Sherman, his own vast curiosity past restraint, looked in on the two and saw Grant standing, and Stanton seated, in the once disputed office.[50]

For the moment Stanton appeared to be the winner. Johnson had been thwarted, Grant demoted, and Stanton—with the formal endorsement of the Senate—was the man of the hour. It is possible, even probable, that Stanton had known the night before that Grant would not prevent his return to the office. But there had not been collusion in the conspiratorial sense, as Gideon Welles claimed. Even if Stanton did know Grant's intentions, it is not likely that he had gained that knowledge at first hand. The interests of Stanton and Grant were not synonymous either before the day began or afterward, and once that dreadful Tuesday was finally over, Grant did not intend that Stanton long remain the winner at his expense.

The morning after Grant's humiliation, January 15, the *National Intelligencer* let the public know Johnson's side of the story. Deeply distressed, Grant called formally on the president to deny the newspaper's accusation that he had lied. The general enlisted Sherman as an ally, and in a long letter to the president, Sherman stated that he had seen Grant "after Shiloh when messengers were speeding to and from his army to Washington, bearing slanders, to induce his removal[,] . . . in Chattanooga when the soldiers were stealing the corn of the starving mules, . . . and yet I never saw him more troubled than . . . [now] in Washington . . . compelled to read [of] himself as a sneak and deceiver." The Radical press carried Sherman's defense of Grant, and for two weeks, with much fanfare, the nation's newspapers featured the rival stories, with little documentation to support either. On January 24 (and again on January 25) Grant asked for written instructions from the president to confirm oral ones he had received to the effect that he was not to take instructions from the secretary of war—from Stanton. Johnson wrote coldly (in the third person) on Grant's letters that the general was indeed to take no instructions from the secretary. Upon taking Johnson's reply to Stanton, Grant was told by Stanton that he had received no orders not to issue instructions to Grant, and therefore would continue to do so. Grant, formally informing the president of this response, did not say whether or not he would honor Stanton's instructions.[51]

Stanton sent copies of all correspondence having to do with Johnson and Grant to the Republican Schuyler Colfax, who was Speaker of the House of Representatives. The fact that the file included correspondence between Johnson and Grant indicates that Stanton was acting with Grant's acquiescence. In the House, the general's final letter, a "masterly rejoinder," was brought to the floor, and the "reading of Gen. Grant's letter was several times interrupted by an involuntary applause, and the whole was listened to with most earnest attention." Grant never denied lying; he simply stated that his veracity had been questioned and his honor besmirched. In rejoinder, Johnson had made all of his cabinet members (save an equivocal Seward) certify that Grant had conceded in their hearing that he had promised to return the office to the president before Stanton could get it back. But by then, if the public cared at all, it had come down to a choice between the president's word and the general's. Grant stood for victory and virtue. He received little castigation, while Johnson faced much in the impeachment trial that ensued. Stanton, after enjoying a brief flurry of admiration for his audacity, looked silly barricaded in his office; Johnson looked villainous when, in defiance of Congress, he did at last remove Stanton from office. Grant, somehow, remained unsullied in the eyes of the people. He had won the Johnson-Stanton campaign.[52]

But in that spring of 1868, Grant at last had to accommodate himself to a new secretary of war—one who would serve for the final year of the Johnson administration. William M. Evarts, the president's lawyer, not relying on courtroom rhetoric to win an acquittal, sought someone whose appointment as secretary of war would be acceptable to both Johnson and the Radicals and would win acquittal votes from wavering moderate Republicans. With this end in view, he invited General John M. Schofield to his room in the Willard. Schofield was a respected general in command in Virginia, where he was engaged in the successful politicking that resulted in racially conservative Reconstruction within the framework of the Radical legislation. At the hotel he was explaining that he dared not accept the appointment without General Grant's approval—when Grant was announced. The commanding general was not aloof from matters that affected him.[53]

Later that evening, during a walk with Grant, Schofield gingerly raised the possibility of becoming his superior's superior. Grant did not demur, and reassured, Schofield promptly reported to Evarts. At 11:00 P.M., he called at Grant's house to say he had agreed to have his name submitted. Then he left for Virginia. In truth, Grant wanted no superiors; annoyed with the self-important Schofield, and conscious that a new secretary of war might be just what senators anxious not to remove a president were looking for, he soon advised Schofield, in a private letter, to withdraw. Schofield replied that it was too late, as his name had already been sent to the Senate. After Johnson had been acquitted, at the end of May, the appointment of Schofield was overwhelmingly confirmed. He and Grant maintained correct but distant relations for the rest of Johnson's term. Similarly, Grant had remained publicly distant from the drama of the impeachment trial on Capitol Hill. During the intense excitement of this crisis—when Johnson's highest crime, for some, was his removal of Stanton—Grant stayed close to the ground. Almost everyone else was caught in the cross fire, but the general was perfectly safe.[54]

# XVIII

# THE PRESIDENT AND HIS CABINET

I hope it will not be considered irreverent to say that Washington,
Lincoln and Grant will be regarded as a political trinity.
— *Hamilton Fish, approving*
*the embossing of a medallion*
"pater, liberator, salvator"

I have said to Josiah more'n a hundred times that any man or woman
ought to be President that knew enough not to talk when they hadn't
nothin' to say.
— *Josiah Allen's wife*

G R A N T ' S   P O L I T I C A L   P O S I T I O N   in the spring of 1868 was unassailable. He was hated by few voters and by no close observers powerful
enough to influence the electorate. His dishonorable jettisoning of Andrew
Johnson had won him the lasting disrespect of the president, but almost no
one was listening to Johnson. Gideon Welles was one of the small band that
remained staunchly loyal to the chief, and he too thought Grant despicable,
but the old editor no longer had a newspaper with which to spread the word.
His hatred for Grant found its eloquent way only into his diary.

Grant stood clear of the passionate battles over impeachment. This tactic
was shrewd; when the effort to remove Johnson failed, no one directly involved in the episode was a winner. Edwin M. Stanton was impotent rather
than vindicated, Benjamin F. Wade, who as president *pro tempore* of the
Senate was in line to succeed Johnson, did not achieve his promotion, despite
his own vote for it. The managers of the impeachment, most notably Benjamin F. Butler, were given enormous attention in the newspapers, but to
little positive effect. The trial did not clear the air in Washington. Rather, all
the participants, save perhaps Chief Justice Salmon P. Chase, were left in
sour disrepute. Incumbency was not an asset. Once again purely a general,

Grant stood apart from the vulgar business, and to a great many eyes, he alone appeared clean.

And all eyes should be upon him. James Harrison Wilson was writing a campaign biography that spring; he asked Fred Dent for West Point anecdotes of his roommate: "[I] want all the assistance I can get in telling the people about the *man* as you and I knew him." Meanwhile, the man in question was serene. As Johnson's trial continued, political observers like James Gordon Bennett, who still hoped that somehow Grant could be stopped from reaching the White House, conjectured that he must favor Johnson's acquittal, on the grounds that glory and power might accrue to a victorious Wade (or Stanton) and cost Grant the nomination. Not so. Grant was untroubled by the prospective removal of Johnson. Indeed, he was in as confident a mood as he was ever to enjoy. In a letter to his friend Charles W. Ford in St. Louis, he spoke of the Gravois Creek farm, grumbled about his in-laws ("It is a matter of surprise to me that the Dents retained anything"), and mentioned that he had reluctantly shipped Butcher Boy, his favorite trotter, west. On a dark muddy night, Butcher Boy had stumbled and sprained an ankle; Grant hoped that the horse would regain strength on the farm and that one day, in Missouri, he would again drive him, as well as Legal Tender and the other horses he kept there. Turning from the animals to politics for a moment, Grant asked Ford, "What is thought about impeachment out with you? My impression is that it will give peace to the Country. I will be out to see you as soon as the question is settled."[1]

But although in private Grant was comfortably articulate about the desirability of Johnson's departure, in public he was carefully silent. One reporter planted a story that Grant had bet Stanton a box of cigars that Johnson would resign before the trial was over, but Grant did not rise to such bait. He could not be harassed by newspapermen into making statements or even denying unlikely stories. He kept quiet, while allowing others to put him forward. In March, during the impeachment trial, there had been a congressional election in New Hampshire; as usual, the political eyes of the nation were on the Granite State. The Democrats had done well in elections in 1867, and as Bennett's *New York Herald* observed, the "proposition of universal negro suffrage, upon which . . . [the Republicans] had been so signally defeated in Ohio and New York," weighed against them in New Hampshire. There was, however, another element that could be injected into the contest. General Daniel E. Sickles, splendid as he swung himself forward on crutches (reminding voters of the valor that had cost him a leg at Gettysburg), devoted his campaign to persuading New Hampshiremen that a vote for a Republican was a vote for Grant. He succeeded. "This was, in fact, the initial test of General Grant as a presidential candidate," stated the *New York Herald*, conceding that "the results show that he cannot be beaten."[2]

On the eve of the Senate's vote on Johnson, Grant wrote Ford that a "great deal of anxiety is felt here"; he predicted, accurately, "Impeachment is likely

to fail." Ardent advocates of Johnson's removal, such as Congressman Robert
C. Schenck (who confessed to his daughter that "we are in gloom") privately
concurred. They pressed exceedingly hard to counter the view that expulsion
of the president would weaken the nation. To this end, they persuaded
Grant to issue on the day of the vote a statement that the government was at
present "demoralized," and hence Johnson's removal was desirable.[3]

Johnson was not removed, and the American public quickly turned its attention from his trial to its every-four-year bonanza of ebullience, a national
political convention. The Republicans were scheduled to meet first, on May
20 (not a week after the key vote on Johnson's acquittal), but before they did,
another convention was held that offered encouragement to the Grant people. Civil War veterans met in Chicago in a Soldiers and Sailors Convention
and heard speeches from everyone in sight, including old Jesse Grant, in support of their commander. In fact they "nominated" the general and proposed
to demand ratification of their choice by the Republican convention, whose
delegates were coming into town. Some thought the veterans were excessively martial, but Grant had already moved to dispel any thought that he
was a man on horseback; on May 18 he issued a statesmanlike call for a small
standing army, of only fifty thousand men, to provide "protection" from the
Indians and "to give a feeling of security to the Southern people." Both this
statement and the veterans' demand for his nomination kept Grant's name
front and center in the carefully encouraged furor of the preconvention
hours. One of Julia's brothers was quoted as saying Ulysses would decline
the nomination; Jesse fervently denied any such nonsense. Grant said nothing. Excitement mounted.[4]

On May 20, preceded by Old Glory, General Sickles—once again the
symbol of patriotic sacrifice—led the procession state by state into the
Crosby Opera House. After the delegates had found their seats in the orches-
tra, dignitaries were escorted to the stage, and Jesse Root Grant, "the man
who 'has a boy' " came in surrounded by "sympathizing friends." Grant's
managers, nervous as usual about the old man's marvelously unpredictable
comments to reporters, hovered over him as if he were on the "verge of the
grave." The women who had been admitted to the proceedings sat up in the
family circle, where "gay colors of dusky charmers outshone white sisters."[5]

General Carl Schurz, the temporary chairman, introduced General Joseph
R. Hawley, the governor of Connecticut, who was the permanent chairman.
In Hawley's speech a genuine issue made its unexpected entrance; Hawley,
an advocate of fiscal probity, quickly warned those who favored the expansion of the nation's greenback money supply that they would be shown no
quarter: "Every bond, in letter and in spirit, must be as sacred as a soldier's
grave." As the phalanx of martial gentlemen at the rostrum demonstrated,
not all the soldiers had yet been interred. The next day General John A.
Logan, the same dark, flamboyantly handsome, confident politician who had
ridden into camp to see an awkward colonel take command of his regiment,

rose to make a nomination. Now Logan was calling his commander to a new post. As his oratory reached its climax and Ulysses S. Grant's name was put in nomination, a pigeon painted red, white, and blue was launched from the top gallery. Frantic, the poor bird flew about the hall "in great agitation, not liking the tremendous roaring about him." Jesse Grant stood at the front of the platform in "mute astonishment" while the tumult mounted. Behind him, the curtain rose, exposing a backdrop on which were painted likenesses of the Goddess of Liberty and General Grant.[6]

In Washington, Grant, appropriately, was at his desk at army headquarters when Secretary Stanton, stifling jealousy and unable to resist political excitement—Badeau said he was "panting for breath lest some one else should precede him"—rushed in with the wire announcing the nomination. Grant was completely calm. He had not hovered at the telegraph, nor had he allowed his aides to do so. He and Julia were determined to press on to higher ground, in order not to lose what they had gained, but unlike his father, they had displayed no sign of grasping for power. The news came to Grant in the same way that the nomination came to him: he had not sought it. But neither could he have endured not having it come to him.[7]

On May 29, 1868, two delegations called on the general in Washington. He received the veterans and their "nomination" at his office at Seventeenth and "F" streets in the morning, and in the afternoon, he and Julia met Governor Hawley and his fellow Republican leaders at their "I" Street house. There, Ulysses S. Grant accepted the Republican party's nomination as candidate for president, with Schuyler Colfax as his running mate. He ended his short bland speech by saying, "I shall have no policy of my own to interfere against the will of the people." He had almost said that he would have no policy at all; almost too well he had suggested that he offered the nation a clean slate. More happily, he included in his written statement of acceptance his famous slogan, "Let us have peace," with its echoes not only of his private expression to his friend Ford of the country's need at the time of the impeachment crisis but of Appomattox as well.[8]

In June, the Grants quietly assumed their rightful place. When the diplomat Anson Burlinghame escorted Chih-Kang and Sun Chia-Ku, the first Chinese envoys to the United States, through a series of receptions, the attention to protocol revealed equal concern for political realities; schedules were carefully arranged so that Johnson and Grant need not meet. After a state dinner, according to the *New York Herald*, "the placid Celestials," whose names were not given, "retired to their rooms, lit their opium chiboques, and in dreams revisited the Flowery Land." The next morning they rose to pay short morning calls on all the proper dignitaries: Senator Sumner, senior members of the diplomatic corps, Speaker Colfax, and others, including General Grant. After luncheon, they ended their day with their two most formal calls, one on President Johnson and his family at the White House; the other on Julia Grant.[9]

Modestly, Grant remained at his post as the commanding general until July. Then he and Julia started "home," going first to St. Louis, then out west, and finally to Galena. Julia had worked carefully and successfully at selecting her clothes; for the train, she had a "short suit" (one that cleared the ground) of "handsome black silk," which she wore with an "ash-colored bonnet." While they were on their travels, the capital mourned the death of Thaddeus Stevens and, perhaps unknowingly, marked the end of the deepest of white America's public commitments to black equality in the Reconstruction period. During his last illness, Stevens had listened as General Howard read the Bible to his fellow "nigger lover," and crusty as ever, had been glad each day when the Christian General finished and left his bedside. When death came, black citizens filled the Capitol rotunda for the greatest official tribute to a fallen leader since Lincoln had lain in state, and at Union Station, they saw his body off for Lancaster and its pauper's grave in an integrated cemetery.[10]

As Stevens went to his rest, the Grants were on their way through Illinois with the uneasy accusation of courting black votes hurled at them as they went. At Carlinville, the train stopped in the station, and when Grant opened the window to shake hands with the people crowding the platform, he was struck in the face by a hat. Feeling the sting he pulled back. His supporters kicked his assailant, Bill O'Brien, and pushed him away from the train, but the anti-Grant noise would not let up. The train pulled out of the station without the candidate's having shaken any hands. Reporters claimed matters of race lay at the bottom of O'Brien's act, which momentarily disrupted Ulysses Grant's trip. And racism had spoiled the recent trip of another Republican as well. One of the Texas delegates to the Republican National Convention, on board a steamer out of Galveston, had been denied the cabin he had engaged. He was black. George T. Ruby sued for damages of $5,000 under the Civil Rights Act of 1866 and was awarded $250. The compensation may have been insufficient, but the verdict did indicate that the federal courts were responsive to the infringement of Negroes' rights.[11]

With many black voters already registered in the South, much of the focus of the 1868 presidential campaign was on the issue constantly referred to in a wide segment of the press as the question of enfranchisement. In the presidential election of 1868, black votes counted in sixteen of the thirty-seven states: eight in the former Confederacy; five in New England (the exception was Connecticut); and three others—New York (with a requirement that black men could vote only if they owned property worth $250), Nebraska (which had enfranchised blacks to meet an 1867 congressional requirement for admission as a state), and Wisconsin (where the highest court had ordered a color-blind vote on constitutional grounds). Negroes were registered to vote in Mississippi, Texas, and Virginia, but the electoral vote in these states was not tallied because they had not yet been readmitted to the Union. Blacks gained the vote as a result of the election of 1868 in Iowa and Minnesota. A great many Northerners who were less than fervent for Negro equality could see the glaring irony in "free" states denying a basic act of citizenship to their black citizens, while requiring that it be granted by the former slave-holding secessionist states. Surprisingly, some former Confederates, such as the South Carolinians James and Mary Boykin Chesnut, Joseph B. Kershaw, and Wade Hampton, were willing to acknowledge that they had lost the war and that some black enfranchisement was a logical result of emancipation. With equal logic, they contended that if they had to put up with it, so should the people of the North. In Ohio, where it had recently been refused, the moderate Rutherford B. Hayes would have preferred to see the party take a national position on the issue, to eliminate bitter local contests like those in his own state. The Republican platform, however, spoke only of the need for the vote in the South (where the freedmen were expected to use it to protect themselves) and of its optional desirability in the North. Grant, following a strategy of harmony, said as little as possible on this passionately divisive issue.[12]

As Grant sought to avoid the heat of the suffrage question, so too was he quietly conservative in the matter of monetary policy. There was, in fact, no issue he cared about deeply; no cause in the furtherance of which he sought the presidency. He did not introduce into the campaign any issue of personal concern to him. On the other hand, he had no greed for power for its own sake. There was nothing of the tyrant in Grant. But though he was without lust for cause or might, he still felt that the presidency had to be his. One politician who knew him well, George S. Boutwell, concluded, "It is an error to assume that General Grant enjoyed the exercise of power, but it is true that he enjoyed the possession of power as evidence of the public confidence." As a general, Grant had already felt the sensuous pull of a people who trusted and wanted him. In 1868 he sought, quite literally, evidence from them of his election. He wanted—and would get—their votes.[13]

But they were not his yet. In July the Democrats had held their convention. Meeting in New York, they rejected not only the perpetual candidate, Chief Justice Chase, but George H. Pendleton, who was outspoken as an opponent of the advance of black people and as a proponent of the advance of the nation's poorer white people, which he hoped to achieve through programs that would bring more money into their hands. Pendleton's "Ohio idea" was an outright call for monetary expansion, and by rejecting him, the convention repudiated any move to the left on financial matters. Instead, the Democrats chose Horatio Seymour, former governor of New York, who was a "sound money" man, as their candidate to oppose Grant.[14]

Seymour was an adroit rhetorician, and he made his stand on the money question sufficiently ambiguous to attract voters unsatisfied with what the Republican Congress had done for them. This attraction, however, could not outbalance the stark fact that he had stayed home while Ulysses Grant had gone off to war, and had returned a hero. But Grant took nothing on faith.

When Sherman congratulated him on his nomination (speaking of his "sacrifice" at entering the corrupt world of politics) but said that as an army officer
he would not endorse him publicly, Grant sought to win more active support
from his friend. He borrowed Sherman's prejudices: "I could not back down
without as it seems to me having the contest for power for the next four years
between mere toadying politicians." Grant claimed he understood Sherman's
neutral stance, but shortly General Grenville M. Dodge was imploring Sherman to make the endorsement. And soon Grant saw to it that the endorsement would come into being without Sherman's having to speak a word. He
left St. Louis and took Sherman and Sheridan on a tour of the Indian-war
territory; the three simple soldiers, doing their duty, went west to inspect the
keeping of the peace on the Great Plains.[15]

The *New York Times* took note of the presence in Colorado of "the greatest
Generals of our nation, and the world." The tour focused the attention of the
American electorate on the newest, most promising part of the nation. Publicly there was to be no involvement in politics, but as they crossed Nebraska, Orville Babcock took a private poll of the members of the party. The
ladies, 11 to 4, thought Grant would win; the gentlemen, 44 to 13, agreed.
The unanimity was less complete than one would have expected, but Babcock contentedly wrote his wife, "and so it will go." (Then the sobriety of his
letter trailed off into an exuberantly lecherous anecdote that closed, "P.S.
Genl. Augur has just poured . . . a whisky.") Earlier, at St. Joseph, Missouri, the official military progress had looked a good deal like a whistle-stop
campaign. Bonfires were lit in the streets, and the three generals were called
out onto the balcony of the hotel. Grant, as usual, skillfully avoided saying
anything to the cheering crowd other than "I return my sincere thanks."
Noting that this was his first trip into this part of the West, he then asked to
be excused: "I am fatigued, weary, dusty, and unable to address you."[16]

Sheridan was less restrained, but as he began a speech someone shouted
"Seymour," and disclaiming advocacy of violence, the general said that if he
were a resident of the town, he "would duck that fellow in the Missouri
River." Sherman, characteristically, spoiled the fun by growing testy, saying
to the people that he would not try to speak until they "learned to behave."
The three generals had encountered raw politics. They received still another
reminder that some saw political content in their trip when a fourth general,
Francis Preston Blair, Jr., the Democratic candidate for vice-president, arrived to make his own inspection of the region.[17]

Returning to St. Louis, Grant visited his old farm briefly before going
on to Chicago. There, at his brother Orvil's house, he received a delegation of five thousand tanners. Grant thanked them, but again declined to
make a speech—and went on to Galena, back to heartland America to await a
call to duty. As Lincoln had been and as William McKinley very much was
to be, Grant was perceived as the candidate of middle America. The role
somehow carried a connotation of special genuineness, and he could appear

unbeholden both to the war-creating abolitionist easterners and the war-shunning Democrats like Seymour. The general, who had never stood for any office, was now running for his nation's highest position not from Washington, or Philadelphia, or New York, or even St. Louis, but from the good, honest, American town of Galena. Small matter that when they got there the Grants might just as well have been opening the summer cottage at Long Branch as the house in Illinois. No one had to know that they had to borrow china and linen in order to establish themselves securely at hearth and home. Grant's election headquarters were in two handsome second-floor rooms in the DeSoto House, a good hotel on Main Street, but even there, little politicking was in evidence. Grant stood aside from the effort elsewhere to sell him, or seemed to, but every day he walked downtown and carefully read and appraised the reports that came in from his campaign managers.[18]

In September, Grant wrote Washburne from Galena, "A person would not know there was a stirring canvass going on if it were not for the accounts we read in the papers of great gatherings all over the country." This was exactly the pose of detached concern that he counted on to carry the day for him. While the *New York Times* complimented him on his strategy of silence, a report from Ohio showed how splendidly co-ordinated, if seemingly casual, the Republicans' national campaign was. They conducted a rally in Oxford for Robert C. Schenck, who was campaigning against Clement L. Vallandigham. According to the *Times* reporter, "sofas, rockers, tables, a piano and chairs" were on the carpeted platform, from which he heard "beautiful, happy country lasses singing Grant and Colfax songs." He went on to say that "Bob Schenck never made a better speech," and in the torchlight parade, "fifteen carloads" of fighting boys in blue and Grant tanners marched. To provide "unbounded humor" a mock detachment of the Ku Klux Klan rode in, only to be swiftly dispersed. (In the same issue of the *Times* was the report of an uncomic Klan raid on a Republican rally in Camilla, Georgia, in which several voters were killed.)[19]

In Hartford, Connecticut, one evening a little girl stood at the front door of a downtown house (not far from that of "Aunt Harriet" Beecher Stowe) and watched a torchlit parade of hundreds of uniformed soldiers. The house glowed—"In every one of our tiny window-panes we had stuck a candle"—and there were lamps on either side of her at the doorway. "In the full light of those lamps stood a Goddess of Liberty—eight years old! A white dress, a liberty cap, a liberty pole (which was a new mop-handle with a red-white-and-blue sash tied on it and a cornucopia of the same colors on its top), and a great flag draped around me—there I stood—Living. One crowded hour of glorious life, that was to a motionless, glorified child." When the companies of marching soldiers came to "a specially illuminated house the leader would turn and march backward, keeping time with his sword, and it was: 'ONE! TWO! THREE! U! S! G! HURRAH!' . . ." Charlotte Perkins Gilman, recalling it all decades later, said, "I can hear them now."[20]

The campaign manager, William E. Chandler, in his New York headquarters in the Fifth Avenue Hotel, was worried more about the Midwest
than about Connecticut. In a note to Schenck he said that he had "dropped
in to [Collis P.] Huntington's at the Central Pacific RR (who had already
given us $5000) and upon hearing my fears about you he promptly gave me
$500." Ten days later Chandler wrote Washburne that Alexander T. Stew-
art, Edwards Pierrepont, and others were thinking of buying the *National Intelligencer* in order to use it to assault the Democrats nationwide. "They are a
mercenary and unprincipled set" and "I may be mistaken . . . in dickering
with these scoundrels. 'Can a man touch pitch and not be defiled?' but I am
conscious of the correctness and purity of my own motives, and do not dare
turn away from this opportunity of demoralizing the Democracy. I hope you
will approve; also Gen. Grant, if by any chance he should hear what is being
done."[21]

Grant heard everything that was being done. He had a telegraph line extended across the river to Washburne's house, on the other side of town, and
there, with Washburne, Badeau, Comstock, and a room full of Galenans,
Grant carefully followed the results from the troubling state of Indiana in the
October elections. The vigil ended happily; from New York Chandler reported, "All looks gloriously; but what an escape we have had in Indiana. But
we have got them and they know it. People are already beginning to talk
about the offices." He had been to Alexander Stewart's for dinner and found
contributors, scenting a win, ready with cash and eager for collectorships.
And Chandler, a party man, was already concerned that regular Republicans
might be squeezed out by men loyal only to Grant. From Maine, James G.
Blaine, that most enthusiastic of all campaigners, sent unclouded congratulations:

> Not so deep as well
> Nor so wide as a church Door,
> But tis enough.
> Glory to God and Congratulations
> to the General.[22]

Campaigning in the nineteenth century was blessedly free of the televi-
sion prissiness of the twentieth. Scurrilous charges kept things lively, and of
these, the fathering of illegitimate children was a particular favorite. The
child attributed to Grant had the added charm of being interracial. The candidate was said to have sired an Indian daughter in Vancouver, but the
rumor faltered, not only because quickly assembled facts showed that the
alleged Grant daughter had been born less than nine months after Ulysses arrived there and that her father was probably one Richard Grant, but also
because tomcatting seemed to everyone to be out of character for the general.[23]

Although people did not rise to this sexual bait, the Democrats did not give up trying to find a way to embarrass the general. To the tune of "Captain Jinks of the Horse Marines," backers of Seymour were invited to sing loud and clear the dispraise of his opponent:

> I am Captain Grant of the Black Marines,
> The stupidest man that ever was seen.

Another verse ran:

> I smoke my weed and drink my gin,
> Paying with the people's tin.

The theme of Grant the drunk was familiar enough, but those "Black Marines" provided a newer, lustier chorus. The Democrats sought to damn Grant as a black Republican, as a latter-day abolitionist, as a nigger lover, and they were not entirely off target. Black Americans, needing someone in the White House who would, if not love them, at least act to protect their persons and rights, were anxious indeed to vote for "Captain Grant." One careful observer described the consequences of their eagerness in Savannah on election day:

> A crowd of Negroes had collected early in the morning to exercise the "in-alienable right"—and as soon as the polls were opened, crowded to the main entrance of the Courthouse. . . . Some white people complained that they couldn't get in at the main entrance, and the police (officered of course, by rebel officers) were ordered to make a way through the darkie crowd in the course of which, it is said, some negro resisted, and with other citizens present, they [the police] discharged their revolvers into the dense crowd, killing . . . six to ten and wounding a great many. In the course of the melee two policemen were killed, though who by, I do not suppose any body knows. The Negroes dispersed and did not come near the polls again to vote. If Gen. Meade's dispatch that a riot occurred . . . which was quelled by the police had read that the police and citizens made murderous attack upon the negroes and drove them away from the polls, it would have been more nearly the truth.

It remained to be seen whether Grant, if elected, would accept assignment as captain of a black company.[24]

In Galena, on election day, the great general walked unobtrusively through the rainy streets to his neighbor's house to hear the election returns. The telegraph company had been perfectly willing to carry an extra line to Grant's house, but arranging to await the results in his own parlor would have made him appear too eager. Instead, the telegraph machinery was set up in Washburne's library "in front of the window that looks out on the porch."

Babcock's father-in-law, B. H. Campbell, William R. Rowley, and several other Galena gentlemen were there, as well as Grant's aides Badeau and Comstock and a friend from Quincy, Illinois. Grant arrived just after 6:00 P.M., and the long wait began. One of the men in the room noticed that "the General was very cool, yet anxious." Julia, barred by convention from the masculine activity of receiving returns, had to maintain an excruciating vigil at home with the children. Washburne's "little old library looks like a Committee room of Ward politicians" commented one of the men who crowded into it. Finally, "After success seemed to be assured the Lead Mine Band came over and gave us some music and we felt pretty foxy." Just to be certain, one member of the party stayed up with the telegraph operator. A switch of 29,862 of the 5,717,246 votes cast would have elected Seymour instead of Grant, but that switch did not occur. At 7:00 A.M. Ulysses Grant went home to give Julia the news.[25]

The morning Grant found out where he would be living for the next four years, he wrote in high good humor to his old friend J. Russell Jones, telling him to be ready to join him and Julia when their train paused briefly in Chicago. He could think of no one else that he wanted to accompany them. His object was to get back east as soon as possible, now that his home town had served its campaign purposes. In the middle of the school year, the Grants sold the Galena house and took the children back to Washington. Sold too was the Philadelphia house, leaving them with the "I" Street place, the only house, other than their childhood homes, that Julia or Ulysses had lived in for more than two years. That house had stood the Grants in good stead. After the general had broken with President Johnson in January 1868, each maintained his own court, with aspiring Republicans in attendance. The rivalry between them was not masked. For example, on an evening late in June, the Grants gave a "private" reception, with the general and all his aides in full uniform, for the Chinese dignitaries—private so that the president did not have to be invited. Later in the year the Grant children were kept home from the White House Christmas party.[26]

Grant also still had his army-headquarters office, which was not in the War Department. Secretary of War Schofield (in Johnson's cabinet) and Grant (not speaking to the president) were not a team; instead, with official correctness, they maintained separate offices. Grant's was at Seventeenth and "F" streets in a small two-story private house opposite the Navy Department; his room at the front of the second floor looked more like a parlor than a command post. Grant's standard office desk stood on a bright carpet between two windows: At a side window was a desk for an aide, and on the opposite wall was a six-foot-long table piled high with documents tied with the inevitable red tape. A reporter, coming into the room, rediscovered the often startling fact that famous people may indeed look like their pictures. The pictures of them are not always flattering, as were those of President Johnson, whose lined face showed strain that was missing from his photographs. In contrast, the forty-six-year-old president-elect looked as young and smooth-skinned as he did in his campaign pictures. But the reporter did not see a buoyant man. Instead, Grant was pale, with an "expression of sadness." He wore a plain black suit and moved about the room with a shuffling gait, appearing stooped and "borne down with cares." While the reporter was present, a senator and a Louisiana judge (unnamed in the account) arrived, and Grant did not dismiss the newsman as the newcomers lobbied for his support for government subsidies to rebuild levees on the Mississippi River. They had scarcely begun their plea when Grant said, "I hope the government will not do it." The reporter found this response "not only decisive and final . . . but almost stunning."[27]

Trying once again, the two callers said that all they wanted was a government guaranty for their company's bonds, "so we can sell them without a ruinous discount." Grant replied, "I never knew a government to become responsible for any amount that it did not ultimately have to pay." Grant suggested that private Northern capital be invited in to provide the financing and he added that Negroes should be allowed to provide some of the labor. Told they were too lazy to be counted on, he replied, "They'll work if you pay them for it." The reporter was struck by Grant's "remarkable quietness" of manner and his "positiveness of utterance." But his readers were being misled. Frequently, as president, Grant demonstrated this same immediate firmness and good sense on confronting a situation, only to vacillate later and fail to uphold his own good first judgment.[28]

These callers were typical of the steady stream of visitors who came to Grant's parlor office hoping to plead their cause. Just before the inauguration, a group of black citizens from Nashville came to seek Grant's support of the proposed Fifteenth Amendment, which would enfranchise all of the nation's black men. He listened and they were encouraged, but he was noncommittal. Friends of the proposal hoped, and foes feared, that Grant was leaning toward its support, but neither side could get him to state his position on enfranchisement—or on assuring a whole range of other rights for black people, a question which, in Washington, was proving to be anything but abstract. The freed slaves were emancipating their free-born but severely restricted Northern brethren, and all were taking the business of gaining equality seriously. When Secretary and Mrs. Orville H. Browning planned a reception at their house for all the employees of the Interior Department, somehow none of the black clerks received invitations. Just before the party someone, very likely one of the Brownings' own servants, protested this discrimination, and the next day a messenger was sent to the homes of the excluded employees with a verbal invitation to a party at the Brownings'. The secretary of the interior described the circumstances in his diary: "Very abundant preparation had been made for our entertainment yesterday, and enough was left to furnish . . . another, so we permitted our colored boys, Nat & Henry to give a reception this P.M. . . . to the colored employees in

the Interior Department and the Atto Genls Office. . . . I went into the room
and was introduced to such as I did not know." Browning was rewarded with
a formal address of thanks for his graciousness. Social equality had not yet
come to Washington, but the ball was rolling and the argument that black
people would be uncomfortable in a white man's house did not seem to be
holding as much water as some Washington hosts and hostesses had hoped.
There were black people in at least three cabinet departments, and General
Howard, out at the new Howard University, shamelessly kept pushing new
candidates forward. Black people were moving into the city in large numbers; they were even moving right next door. They were pressing for places
in the city government and on the school board and generally not behaving at
all like the dear old souls Julia chose to remember from her White Haven
childhood. And they were all looking to her Ulysses to do for them what
Andrew Johnson had so disappointingly chosen not to do.[29]

In February Grant gave up the fiction that his job was running the army;
he and Julia began accepting invitations to formal dinners given by the diplomatic corps. These grand occasions heralded his accession to the presidency,
as did speculation about who would be in his cabinet. For example, when the
Grants went to a wedding in Pennsylvania, a fellow guest who had served for
four days in Zachary Taylor's cabinet was proclaimed certain to be appointed secretary of the treasury. In this game Grant played his cards close to
the chest; even the proprietors of Washington boardinghouses did not know
who would be in town. One lady, asked why she wished to speak to the general, told an aide (or perhaps a reporter) that she was calling to learn whom he
had chosen, as she had rooms to rent. While rumors flourished, Grant let it
be known that he would release the names only when he formally submitted
them to the Senate for confirmation. Everyone assumed, unhappily, that
someone else was being consulted; the party leaders in Congress had not yet
realized that none of them was being asked for advice. Once again Grant was
seeking to enter the capital alone.[30]

On the morning of March 4, 1869, at nine-thirty, Ulysses S. Grant and
John A. Rawlins stepped into Julia Grant's fine new phaeton. The general
waved to his wife and children, who were standing at the door, and pulling
on his cigar to keep it lit, stretched a white fox rug over his knees; his black
coachman flicked the reins, and the two fine bays carried Grant off to his inauguration. He and Rawlins stopped first at his office, where Company K of
the Fifth Cavalry, which had guarded him since the war, was on duty.
Grant, in an excellent black suit from Brooks, sat at his desk in his swivel
armchair smoking a cigar (and spoiling his fine kid gloves) and chatting with
his brother-in-law Fred Dent and Schuyler Colfax. At ten-forty he walked
out to the curb past a group of admiring black citizens, and he and Rawlins
set off again in the open carriage, to end a disgraceful charade. Grant had
avoided Johnson's 1869 New Year's Day reception (and underscored the insult by sending three aides, including an Indian, Ely S. Parker, to represent

him), and since then there had been speculation about whether Johnson and Grant would ride together to the inauguration. The day before the ceremony, the *New York Times* reported that Johnson had graciously written a note proposing that they go to the Capitol together. But, noted the *Times*, Grant denied receiving such a note and had announced he would ride alone. Rebuffed, on the morning of the ceremony Johnson called the members of his cabinet to the White House at nine o'clock and, to the surprise of most of them, quietly said, "I think we will finish our work here without going to the Capitol." They then made themselves busy reading and examining bills. Grant and Rawlins, now making their belated bid to be gracious, paused at the gates of the White House, only to be told that the president was too occupied to get away. So, alone save for his old friend, Grant rode to Capitol Hill; while he was being sworn in, Andrew Johnson left the White House for the last time.[31]

When Grant reached the Capitol, there was a huge crowd that, once again, included a strikingly large number of black citizens. He gave them all a "very good natured smile" and climbed the long stairs to the Senate chamber to witness the swearing in of Schuyler Colfax. There Grant sat "calm" and "compact" as the glistening diplomatic corps rattled its way into the room, and a reporter wrote of the contrast between the republican dignity of this inauguration of a vice-president and Andrew Johnson's "plebeian harangue," which had been grist for the anti-republican diplomatic mill four years earlier. As Chief Justice Chase swore in Colfax, and the new vice-president gave his speech, Grant watched with "wonderful coolness and self-possession."[32]

Julia, her children, her father, and her sisters and brothers were all in their place on the portico of the Capitol, waiting to see Grant sworn in. So too was Jesse Grant, but Hannah Grant was not there. Back in February, Jesse had written in a very shaky hand a letter to Julia's brother; the salutation was "Gen. Dent," and it began, "I rec'd a letter from Ulysses, yesterday, in which he says his house will be full." General Grant's father was asking Fred Dent for a favor: to find a room, either in a hotel "or at some respectable private house," for the two women who he hoped would accompany him. They would arrive a day or two before the inauguration. "It is not yet decided whether Mrs. Grant or Jennie will go with me." He then told Dent that if arrangements could not be made for both, he wanted "the Mother to go." The letter closed "Yours most truly" and was signed "J. R. Grant."[33]

Jesse Grant could be a Uriah Heep on occasion, but no degree of irritation with his tiresome ways can excuse Ulysses Grant's callous disregard of his father's search for accommodations for the family. There were not ten houses in Washington that would not have been honored to have the president's mother as a guest. In some still shrouded way, Hannah was too much of an embarrassment to be allowed to spoil Ulysses and Julia's great day. When Jesse arrived without his wife, reporters, understandably, asked where she was. His reply—that she had been invited but declined—prompted the worst fake-rustic copy imaginable; allegedly, Hannah Grant had responded to the invitation by saying, "Pop, do you think I would go to Washington and be stared at by fifty thousand people and every stitch on me printed in fifty thousand newspapers; no, indeed."[34]

At twelve-thirty Grant came forward on the portico of the Capitol, waited "impatiently" for the twenty-two-gun salute to end (he never liked the sound of cannon), and with his hand on the Bible held by a sergeant at arms, was sworn in by Chief Justice Chase as the eighteenth president of the United States. Then he took his speech from his breast pocket and, reading it, told America that he entered his office "without mental reservation. . . . The responsibilities of the position I feel, but accept them without fear." It was pure Grant prose. The word usage was slightly wrong, the effect compellingly right.[35]

He immediately repudiated what he and the Radical Republicans regarded as Johnson's abrogation of acts of Congress lawfully passed over the president's veto. Grant asserted that he would express his views to Congress and veto legislation if need be, "but all laws will be faithfully executed, whether they meet my approval or not." Noting that the country had "just emerged from a great rebellion," he announced that "the greatest good for the greatest number is the object to be attained." In words that all would take as referring to the outlaw disruption of integrated political life in the South, he called for laws to establish the "security of person, property, and free religious and political opinion in every part of our common country." With the phrase "our common country" Grant harked back to his negotiations with Abraham Lincoln and the peace commissioners, but he was now emphatically applying it to the chief issue of Reconstruction.[36]

Grant never knew how to make money. Making monetary policy did not come any easier, but he proved a diligent student of the dreary subject that so profoundly touched so many Americans. Early in the campaign he had written to Elihu Washburne intelligently about the shortage of money in the South and West, which severely hampered farmers in those regions. At the outset of the war, Grant himself had experienced the problems of doing business when one's drafts were heavily discounted because banks in the area were short of cash with which they could be purchased. Since then he had talked to his merchant friends George H. Stuart and Alexander T. Stewart; his monetary views were now conservative, and in his inaugural speech he disavowed an expansive greenback currency when he said, "To protect the national honor, every dollar of Government indebtedness should be paid in gold, unless otherwise expressly stipulated in the contract." He went further: "Let it be understood that no repudiator of one farthing of our public debt will be trusted. . . ." (How many farthings can Grant have seen? This hortatory cry was not characteristic.) He no longer knew exactly what it was he was trying to say, but he predicted prosperity and placed his hope in a higher authority than his banker and merchant friends: "Why, it looks as though

Providence has bestowed upon us a strong box in the precious metals locked up in the sterile mountains of the far West. . . ."[37]

Grant made a general comment about foreign affairs and then moved on to two statements of the greatest importance. He noted that the suffrage question was likely "to agitate the public" as long as the vote was withheld from any citizens and therefore called for the ratification of the Fifteenth Amendment. Even more startling was one still briefer paragraph: "The proper treatment of the original occupants of this land—the Indians—is one deserving of careful study. I will favor any course toward them which tends to their civilization and ultimate citizenship." Humanitarians anxious to halt the terrible decimation of these people took heart.[38]

The ceremony over, the official party was escorted to the White House by a military troop. Behind the soldiers a group of black citizens, in frayed clothes and holding up umbrellas against the rain, joined the march, to the "intense merriment" of the white crowd on the curbs. They had heard what Ulysses Grant said about the Fifteenth Amendment and were as unembarrassed as they were hopeful. At the White House, however, the black appeared in a role more traditionally his in America. The Grants paused at the empty house to meet the staff, and the new president was introduced to the "body servant" whose services would pass now from Andrew Johnson to Ulysses Grant. The *New York Times* reported him to be "a perfect specimen of ornate ebony."[39]

The stop at the White House was brief; then they went home to "I" Street and batches of congratulatory messages; one of the most cordial came from Prussia's Bismarck, who was numbered among the general's warm admirers. That evening the Grants returned to Pennsylvania Avenue for the inaugural ball in the handsome Treasury Building. The new north wing, fine but starkly classical, had been decorated with cedar and spruce under the direction of Fred Dent, Julia's brother, who was in charge of all the inaugural festivities. Some guests almost came to blows in the crush at the men's cloakroom, and the crowds were too dense to permit much dancing, but the ball was pronounced a splendid success. Society reporters, always eager for trouble, could find no fault; Dent had found a single solution for two social dilemmas. The ball was called a private party (though attended by hundreds of people the Grants had never met), so neither Andrew Johnson nor black Republican officeholders had to be invited. Of the latter, the *Times* society reporter felt happier asserting that they had thoughtfully declined to come.[40]

"Nobody knows yet anything about Ulysses the Silent's Cabinet, that is to be," wrote George Templeton Strong in his diary on the last day of Andrew Johnson's administration. That cautious New York Republican did not regret Johnson's departure—"There will be dry eyes at his exodus"—and he had "singular hopes" for the Grant administration. Grant's honesty, Strong wrote, "will stand the ordeal it is to undergo for four years from tomorrow." It was a good sign, thought Strong, that "Odysseus knows how to keep his

own counsel, and shuts up, close as an oyster"; he enjoyed the fact that those
who had tried to pump Grant for information or solicit appointment to a government job had come away without even the raw material for convincing
gossip. Correctly predicting that even Republicans would be "denouncing
him within a month," he went on to note that "a certain pachydermatism
seems to be among his virtues, and he can stand a good deal of newspaper
fire. . . ."[41]

Henry Adams, in Washington, knew no more than Strong in New York.
He lived in the same boardinghouse as Adam Badeau, "General Grant's his-
toriograph," but long talks with that "sociable little man with red face and
spectacles," who claimed to know his master's mind, yielded no correct speculation. Adams's guesses at the end of February were all wrong, but he was
not alone in his ignorance: "The politicians, I am told, are furious at not
being consulted." Not without secret aspirations of his own, Adams "went to
the Capitol" the day after the inauguration "to hear the carefully guarded
secret of Grant's cabinet." He found the gallery jammed and, looking down
on the floor of the Senate, saw General Rawlins, whose presence was assumed to mean that he had brought Grant's list of nominees. There was an
interminable prayer and the painful scene of William G. Brownlow—"Parson" Brownlow, the new senator from Tennessee—being sworn in at his
chair, his once powerful body so broken with palsy that his arm had to be
supported as he took the oath, but when these preliminaries were over,
Rawlins still did not step forward. Then Senators A. H. Cragin and James
W. Grimes (seemingly recovered from his stroke and surely not in disgrace
for having voted to acquit Johnson) were sent to receive the nominations from
the president and in a carriage "sped like lightning to the White House."
There they found doorkeepers turning away, at Grant's direction, "any who
do not have business with me." These constituted a sizable crowd.[42]

The senators "grave and reverend were admitted to the second floor
where, amid the redecorating workmen, they searched for 'the Chief Magis-
trate,' who not being comfortably settled in any particular room was sometimes in one, sometimes in another." He was finally found in the room
Andrew Johnson's secretary had used. Grant, wearing his hat, was "dividing
his time between several officers of his staff and his cigar." After chatting for
about ten minutes, the president thanked the two for their courtesy, but
explained that Rawlins had the list of nominations. Back on the Senate floor
again, Grimes announced to the eager assembly that Grant was indeed ready
to nominate a cabinet, and looked over toward Rawlins, who produced a
message from the president. As he did so, one of the senators, realizing that
none of them had had time to examine the choices before they were made
known to the public, called for an executive session. Adams, disgruntled but
now doubly curious, left the chamber along with everyone else and stood in
the crowded hall outside, waiting for the news. Rawlins would tell them
nothing as he left. Shortly, when the senators emerged and the appointments
were revealed, several people were heard to ask, "Who's Borie?"[43]

*The cabinet, 1869. Paying no attention to the president are, left to right, Cox, Fish, Rawlins, Creswell, Boutwell, Borie, and Hoar.* LIBRARY OF CONGRESS

It was a curious list that the senators had unanimously accepted out of deference to Grant and despite his failure to consult them before making his choices. Elihu B. Washburne was to be secretary of state; Alexander T. Stewart, secretary of the treasury; John M. Schofield was to stay on, temporarily, as secretary of war; Adolph E. Borie had been named secretary of the navy; Jacob Dolson Cox was to be secretary of the interior; Ebenezer Rockwood Hoar, attorney general; and John A. J. Creswell, postmaster general. Washburne, Cox, and Creswell were the only active politicians on the list, and not one of them was party leader. Creswell, from Maryland, representing the old slaveholding region, was the only Radical. The appointment of Washburne was viewed, despite his many years in the House of Representatives, as being simply a reward for his early championship of Grant, and that of Cox was seen as a nod to Ohio and to anti-Radical racial policies. Schofield had been carried over from the previous administration. Borie, giving Pennsylvania a place, was unknown—"Who the mischief is Borie?" asked Joseph Medill of the *Chicago Tribune*. Hoar was from Massachusetts and Harvard. Stewart was from New York and was very rich.[44]

Alexander T. Stewart was, in fact, the centerpiece of the list. His selection spoke eloquently for what Ulysses Grant was trying to accomplish as he moved into the uncertainties of the White House. Stewart was a storekeeper who had not failed. Born in 1803 in Ulster, he was a Protestant who had obtained enough education to know that he could not go as far as he wanted to go if he stayed in Ireland. In 1819 he sailed for New York. There he taught school and eventually opened a small store on Broadway near Chambers Street. From the start he was a careful and shrewd merchant; he purchased at

auctions cheap, unpromising batches of "sample lots" of much-handled salesmen's display goods. He took them home, and in the evenings, "gloves were
redressed[,] laces made to look as if they had never been corrupted." Moving
to a bigger store, he took the risk of keeping his profit margin small, selling
just over his costs. As a result, he held his customers through the panic of
1837 while other merchants, who had operated with higher profits and
higher prices, were forced to dispose of their wares at auction. Stewart was
there to buy what they sold. He also had the wit to hire exceedingly handsome young clerks to lure in the customers, and by 1862 was so successful that
he could open, on Broadway between Ninth and Tenth streets, the largest re-
tail store in the world. When the Civil War came, Stewart, with suppliers beholden to him, could assure government contract agents quick and certain delivery on badly needed uniforms and blankets. And so the rich man grew still
richer. With wonderful disdain for privacy, the newspapers during the Civil
War published the names and amounts of income tax paid by large taxpayers.
The *New York Times* reported Stewart's income to be the largest in New
York, and the *New York Herald* estimated that he was worth forty million
dollars. He had diversified his investments, and owned the Metropolitan
Hotel (where the Grants stopped when they visited New York) and more real
estate in the city than anyone else, except perhaps the Astors and the Goe-
lets. At the time Grant nominated Stewart, his great mansion on Fifth Avenue was nearing completion; less far along were his model housing units for
his clerks, being built at a cost projected at two million dollars: ". . . so far
events seem to have prevented the consummation of a most laudable intention," noted the *Herald*.[45]

Stewart was married, but he had no children; hence his name has not come
down to us as a symbol of great fortune. But great his fortune was. Americans reading about Grant's money man the morning after his nomination saw
Stewart compared to the Rothschilds and read, "His is, without doubt, the
greatest success in a mercantile career that the world has ever known." Stewart's appointment underscored the fact that Grant was the first truly Republican president. Lincoln was a Whig, and his concern was not commerce but
the re-establishment of the Union. Elected as a Republican, he had created
the National Union party to win Democrats to the cause of victory in the
war, and it was this party that re-elected him in 1864. Andrew Johnson was a
Democrat, placed on the ticket to get votes for Lincoln from Southern border
Unionists and Northern war Democrats. Johnson's four years in office were
dedicated to recreating a Democratic alliance, with a new national base. In
time, it would stand powerfully, but it was not yet sturdy enough to sustain
an Andrew Johnson. Instead, Grant, the Republican, was now president.[46]

Many Americans, in voting for him, had affirmed their belief in a world in
which any man, even a black former slave or one of Stewart's notoriously un-
derpaid clerks, could have the opportunity to raise himself from the bog of
insecurity. They hoped that Grant, who had been there himself, would help

them find their way out. Instead, he had found his way to Alexander T. Stewart. The naturalist John Burroughs, who was then a clerk in the Treasury Department, took Grant on his first tour of the offices and money rooms in the Temple; he liked the president's simple manner but observed that "he walked with men of money now."[47]

Grant was not bitter toward those who had succeeded where he had failed; they had simply pulled themselves out onto different safe rocks. Theirs were department stores; his was Vicksburg. Preferring not to dwell on how close they all had come to drowning, the general and the businessmen now forgot the difficulty of the struggle and preached the bland doctrine that any diligent workingman could do what they had done. Over and over as president, and later as the ambassador of American virtue in Great Britain, Ulysses Grant preached this gospel. He saluted the efficiency of Stewart's clerks and drew attention not to the fines they paid when they made errors at the cash register, but to the housing Stewart built for them in Garden City. The idea of the contented, self-respecting workingman, moving up by his own efforts into middle-class respectability and security, had a charm different from Jefferson's pastoral vision of a citizenry, similarly respectable and secure, of yeoman farmers. But this has been the idea—perhaps "notion" is a closer word—that has permeated and defined the Republican party. The party was (and is) turned to by men and women so lacking in self-regard as to crave an institution ready to promise it in fair measure. The maintenance of opportunities to improve one's position (upon which self-regard was based) depended on the strength of the business world, and the counting house was more to be trusted than the farm. There was something slightly dirty, lazy, foreign, or effete about Democrats. Republicans were four square; Grant would look just right on the fifty-dollar bill.

Grant was not troubled by the fact that Stewart, along with virtually all of the stable businessmen in New York City, had supported Andrew Johnson; they had done so because the Radicals, who talked of land confiscation, seemed to promise vague but drastic change in the political economy. Grant did not seem as dangerous, and Stewart, old enough to be his father, had met and liked him, and was happy both to advise and support him. What was more, Julia liked his wife, Cornelia Mitchell Clinch Stewart; both Grants felt sustained by this powerful New York couple. But Grant was able to count on this sustaining force in his cabinet for only a week; then Charles Sumner took him away.

A law, described by the *New York Herald* as "very old fogy" and as having been passed in the days when only those "born with a silver spoon in their mouth" were fit to govern, was unearthed to deprive Grant of the immigrant boy who had made good. Neither Grant nor, at first, anyone in the Senate had been aware of an act of May 28, 1784, that declared that "no person . . . appointed a commissioner of the treasury . . . shall be permitted to be engaged . . . in any trade or commerce." This provision was continued in an act of September 2, 1789, and some bright lawyer in 1869 remembered it and brought it to Charles Sumner's attention. The powerful Massachusetts legislator was not the least aggrieved of the senators at not having been consulted, and he was delighted to have an opportunity to teach the president that he must not be ignored. When Grant was told of this legal barrier, he regarded it as just a technicality and was undaunted. Carl Schurz, the new senator from Missouri, calling on his old commander the morning Grant was confronting the problem, saw that the president was busy "writing something on a half sheet of notepaper" and said, "My business can wait." "Never mind," Grant replied, "I am only writing a message to the Senate."[48]

That afternoon in the Senate, Schurz listened to the reading of Grant's request that the provision disqualifying Stewart be waived. No reasons were given for the request, and no thanks, in advance, were offered. Senator John Sherman was immediately on his feet and "asked unanimous consent to introduce a bill" to accomplish the president's wishes, but Sumner, supported by Roscoe Conkling, a New Yorker of whom Stewart did not approve, demanded instead that the matter go to committee. Such a delaying tactic could easily have produced a prolonged vacancy in what Republicans regarded as the most important post in the cabinet. Several senators, knowing Sumner and fearing a deadlock between him and Grant, conferred hastily in the cloakroom and decided to send Washburne to persuade Grant to replace Stewart. Grant listened to the bearer of bad news, but he did not give up. Instead, he sought the advice of a close friend, George H. Stuart—a Philadelphia merchant, originally from Ulster, who was of the same stripe as Stewart—and then permitted Stuart to go to the Ebbitt House to try to persuade his nominee to sell his business. This Stewart refused to do, but the two shrewd merchants came up with what they regarded as a better idea. When Stuart got back to Grant he had two documents in his pocket. One was a draft of an instrument placing Stewart's vast mercantile interests in trust to William E. Dodge and two other men for as long as he was secretary of the treasury; the other was a letter of resignation. Grant, beginning to wonder if his adroit business friends understood the world of congressional politics and conscious of Washburne's warning that any proposal for getting around the annoying old law could be held up in committee for a long time, reluctantly rejected the concept of a trust. Instead, he accepted Stewart's resignation. When he got home and told Julia what he had done, she was even more unhappy than he.[49]

If the matter of the Stewart nomination deprived the Grant administration of a confident beginning, Elihu Washburne's short tenure as secretary of state gave it a note of confused mystery. One of the few pre-inaugural rumors that later proved correct had been that Washburne would be named minister to France. However, on the way he made a layover as secretary of state, and that route did not make sense. The proposition, often offered, that Washburne was given the senior position in the cabinet in order to enhance his prestige for the Paris post is silly. One does not go downward in a hierarchy to gain prestige. A more likely explanation is that in a moment of exuberance and gratitude on the night he heard the election returns in Washburne's house, Grant made a snap promise. "No other idea presented itself stronger to my mind in the first news of my election . . . than that I should continue to have your advice and assistance" was the way he later put it. However, when Ulysses and Julia got back east and talked things over with some of their newer, grander friends, Grant was persuaded that a country fellow like Washburne would not do as secretary of state. The nation's ambiguous sense of how to present itself to the world resulted in the view that the man chosen as a chief diplomat should be of elegant mold. If true intellectual power was not available, as it had been in Thomas Jefferson and John Quincy Adams, then the diplomat at least had to be able to talk with aplomb to the aristocratic dignitaries of antirepublican Europe. Elihu B. Washburne, with roots in Maine and a truly fine town house in Illinois, was not much more provincial than William Henry Seward of Auburn, New York. But Seward had always seen himself as the titular head of Abraham Lincoln's party, and there was more intellect and much more of the social animal in him than in the "coarse, comparatively illiterate" Washburne.[50]

The real question is not how Grant came to name Washburne, but how, having done so, he got him to relinquish the post. There is, surprisingly, no clue to the way this was accomplished, but the fact that it happened with apparent amicability suggests that Washburne had acquiesced to the change before the inauguration. The two men were on very friendly terms ("There will always be a spare room for you," Grant had written from Washington to Galena in the fall of 1865), but the key to the mystery of Washburne's departure from the cabinet in the spring of 1869 is probably that Grant had outgrown his patron and Washburne knew it. He was an intelligent hard-working congressman, but he was not the kingmaker he had once dreamed of being. He had spotted Grant almost at the outset of the war and had been his champion thereafter, in activities which were climaxed by his steering through Congress the promotion to lieutenant general. But that promotion had had easy passage. Grant's career had its own momentum by then; it no longer needed a congressional engine. Grant knew that Washburne and William E. Chandler had worked energetically and effectively in his 1868 campaign, but he also knew that they recognized how slight the impact of all their efforts was in comparison with what he had accomplished simply by being on the ticket. It was the general for whom the voters voted. Grant, in Washburne's parlor, had been grateful but not beholden. When Washburne came as the bearer of bad news with respect to Stewart and forced on Grant advice he did not want to take, the prospect of his absence seemed more attractive. If Grant could bestow the secretaryship, he could also take it away; Washburne agreed—and went off to France, where he served throughout the period of the Commune, reporting accurately if unsympathetically on the fierce events from which other diplomats fled.[51]

Grant's second choice for secretary of state was much more comforting to the mannerly. He was the man on whom, in the flood of rumors that always attended the selection of a cabinet, the *New York Times* had placed its bet— Hamilton Fish of New York. Save for Washburne's six days, Fish was to serve Grant for the full eight years of his administration. The two men got on splendidly, but in March 1869 they did not know each other well. They had both served as trustees of the Peabody Educational Fund, but there is no record of any extensive private conversation before the appointment of Fish to the cabinet. In his two volumes on Fish's life, subtitled *The Inner History of the Grant Administration*, Allan Nevins never mentions how the two men got to know each other, and it is perfectly possible that when Ulysses Grant chose Hamilton Fish, he had not yet taken much measure of him. But Julia Grant had.

Fish was a large, comfortably ugly man with an impeccable Manhattan and Hudson Valley lineage full of Stuyvesants and Livingstons. He served his single term in the House of Representatives—where he was followed by his namesakes in the next three generations—from 1843 to 1845, and he served as a senator from New York, also for a single term, from 1851 to 1857. When he left the Senate, he seemed also to have left the public world for the aristocratic responsibilities of being, for the rest of his life, president-general of the Society of the Cincinnati. He could have puttered out his years on his lovely Hudson River estate, Glenclyffe, at Garrison or, in town, attended to the excruciatingly dull duties of a leading citizen of New York City, as did his friend George Templeton Strong. Had he done either, he would have had as his mate in boredom Julia Kean Fish.

Julia Fish was consigned to what was called weak health. Whenever her husband needed an excuse for not engaging in an enterprise, he declined, or threatened to do so, on the ground that her infirmity prevented it. Coming from a New Jersey family of founding fathers that was even more financially secure than her husband's, she could do little to free herself from the indolence of privilege, but in 1865 she made one small gesture that enabled her to escape genteel New York and move into the rougher, riskier waters of gauche and exciting Washington. The gesture was not a very dangerous one. Julia Fish, as Anthony Trollope said of an equally highly placed Englishwoman, could "know whom she chooses," and in 1865 she had made a choice when she crossed the Hudson to pay a call on Mrs. General Grant, at West Point. Julia Grant was just coming out of obscurity, and her "ideal of an empress," Julia Fish, "became a true friend." The latter might have intimidated her new acquaintance simply by her stately presence and by being flawlessly, and hence formidably, well bred. Instead, she was kind. Others were obsequious in the presence of the general's wife and scornful behind her back, but Julia Fish had no need to try to hoist herself above another woman by tearing her down. She never mocked Julia Grant for her twitching eye, her poor figure, or what others called her country manners. Julia Fish and her husband could afford to be unequivocally respectful of the general and his lady, and that respect was appreciated. In 1869, Julia Grant saw to it that Julia Fish's husband became secretary of state.[52]

Since New York had voted for Seymour, no favors were due the state. The appointment of Fish was not a political pay-off. His value lay in his quiet dignity and in his not being beholden to any man or faction. Much has been made of the gulf in style—in class—between Grant and Fish, with the assumption that tanner and patrician must have been unable to reach each other. Not so; Grant had never liked tanning, and as long as there was the opportunity to escape to Garrison, Fish enjoyed Washington. Like his wife, Hamilton Fish was kind, and if his style was different from that of Grant's other friends, he nevertheless never exhibited, even inadvertently, any form of social arrogance that would have made Grant ill at ease. The two men liked each other's company. General Grant's walks over to Fish's house to talk with his friend were a comfortable and important aspect of their eight years of association. Repeatedly Fish threatened to resign—only so he could get the response which on one occasion he recorded meticulously in his diary: "Don't think of that—your presence in the cabinet, & the association with you, is to me the greatest possible comfort. I can't think of your quitting." The austere secretary of state was formidable at cabinet meetings, and his advice was not always good, but he was accessible to Grant, who needed companionship. And Julia Fish was steadfastly at Julia Grant's side during eight years of White House pomp and silliness. (The Henry Adamses would have loved the Fishes' assignment. No one offered it to them.)[53]

For his invitation to the New Yorker to enter the cabinet, Grant used what he took to be the rhetoric of Fish's world: "I have thought it might not be unpleasant for you to accept the portfolio of the State Dept. If not will you do me the favor to answer by telegraph tomorrow to the effect that you will be in Washington soon." When the letter arrived, Hamilton Fish had just gotten back from Washington, where he had avoided the vulgarity of the inaugural ball by dining with Charles Sumner and John Lothrop Motley. He declined by telegram, and in the letter that followed gave his wife's health as the reason. Grant, troubled by not having his cabinet settled, had not waited for an acceptance from Fish before sending his name to the Senate. A withdrawal of this public announcement would have been highly embarrassing, so when Fish's telegram arrived, Grant sent Orville Babcock with another letter, in which he urged Fish to change his mind, accept the post, and retain it at least until Congress adjourned. Babcock (who acknowledged Julia Fish as his ally) was persuasive; Hamilton Fish accepted.[54]

Secretary Fish did not like the thought of vulgar people impinging on his world, and he recognized their vague threat to him most easily when they were of an inappropriate color. After a trip to Cuba in 1855, he had written, "We all returned charmed with the climate, the scenery, and the natural productions of the island 'where only man is vile.' With its present population, the island of Cuba will be anything else than a desirable acquisition to the United States, and I can see no means of getting rid of a population of some 450,000 called *white* but really of every shade and mixture of color, who own *all* the land on the island." This attitude accounts for his later resistance to expansionist schemes in the Caribbean far more persuasively than does the theory that he dared not take the side of Cuban insurgents lest he seem to be emulating the British when they sympathized with the Confederates. Such a racial delineation of a class feeling also goes further in explaining Fish's distaste for the strong Freedmen's Bureau Bill early in 1866 than does the cant with which he extolled constitutional principles when he celebrated Andrew Johnson's veto of the bill. Fish did not want a portion of America governed by landowners with whom he would be uncomfortable dining, and this objection went not only for Cuba but for Mississippi. He closed his eyes to atrocities against nonwhites in both places because he refused to face the prospect of the success which such people were likely to have if they were protected and supported.[55]

Reversing the course he took in finally selecting his secretary of state, Grant chose as his new secretary of the treasury a congressman, George S. Boutwell of Massachusetts. An underestimated politician, Boutwell showed himself capable of supporting idealistic positions within the Republican party from the 1860's, when he championed the rights of black freedmen, to 1898, when he broke with his party to become president of the Anti-Imperialist League. Boutwell had led the first, unsuccessful, effort to bring a bill of impeachment against Andrew Johnson, on grounds more germane than those involving the quarrel with Stanton: Boutwell's thorough hearings on conditions in the South established the degree to which Johnson had willfully refused to execute the Reconstruction laws passed by Congress. He too had worked as a clerk in a store as a young man, but he was not known for a strong interest in fiscal matters. Henry Adams, conservative about money (because his mother had so much) and patrician where Boutwell was plebeian, complained that "Boutwell is not a Wells man." David Ames Wells, an economist, was the man that Adams and others who advocated free trade and noninflationary money hoped would be appointed to the Treasury post. Boutwell was not the intellectual that Wells was, but his appointment was swiftly confirmed. Just as quickly, he set about liquidating the debt of the United States. He did so good a job that the shrinkage of currency resulting from the retirement of government bonds and the release into the market of gold with which the bonds were bought almost ruined the nation's farmers and, incongruously, such risk-taking entrepreneurs as James Fisk, Jr.[56]

Along with Boutwell's appointment, the Senate confirmed that of John A. Rawlins as secretary of war, replacing Schofield. Rawlins was dying of tuberculosis, but had lost none of his dark and passionate zeal. His fellow cabinet member Jacob Dolson Cox, secretary of the interior, was fascinated by the relationship between Grant and Rawlins and regarded Rawlins's death, in September 1869, as "an irreparable loss" to Grant and his administration.

"Other men might fill the office of Secretary of War," wrote Cox, "but no other man could be found who could be the successful intermediary between General Grant and his associates in public duty. His friendship for his chief was of so sacredly intimate a character that he alone could break through the taciturnity into which Grant settled when he found himself in any way out of accord with the thoughts and opinions of those around him. Rawlins could argue, could expostulate, could condemn, could even upbraid, without inter-rupting for an hour the fraternal confidence and good will of Grant." Cox considered that Rawlins "had won the right to this relation by an absolute devotion" which ran back to the first year of the war and which had made Rawlins "the good genius of his friend in every crisis of Grant's wonderful career." In Cox's judgment, this power came not because of Rawlins's "great intellect, for he was of only moderate mental powers. It was rather that he had become a living and speaking conscience for his general; as courageous to speak in a time of need as Nathan the prophet, and as absolutely trusted as Jonathan by David."[57]

Rawlins had undertaken to be the conscience of Grant's personal life in 1863 when he remonstrated so firmly against alcohol, and in the cabinet he became the president's moral mentor in the public realm as well. Quick to react with anger to what he saw as injustices perpetrated on him, Rawlins was equally sensitive to injustices done to people who had not the power to protect themselves. With the possible exception of Boutwell and Creswell, he was the only member of the original cabinet who could identify with the suf-fering and bitter disappointment of the freed slaves, who were being intimi-dated and driven back into a state of dependency, and he was the leading ex-ponent of intervention on the side of the oppressed people of Cuba, who were in revolt against their Spanish masters. Even those, like Fish and Cox, who opposed these and other policies that Rawlins espoused, admired his "openness of character" and contrasted him in this respect to Babcock, to the latter's distinct disfavor. Cox also compared Rawlins to the secretary of state and reflected on his rectitude: "Rawlins might have differed from Mr. Fish as to the foreign policy of the government, especially in regard to Cuba, but he would have seen to it that no kitchen cabinet committed the President to schemes of which his responsible advisers were ignorant. Indeed," concluded his cabinet colleague, "there was no danger that a kitchen cabinet could exist till Rawlins was dead." Rawlins might have protected Grant from the dubi-ous informal advice he was to receive.[58]

No doubt there were army officers who were uncomfortable to have as sec-retary of war the sharp-tongued lawyer who had sometimes made their calls at Grant's wartime headquarters less than pleasant. Furthermore, Rawlins was firm in keeping in check those officers who were most cruel to the In-dians whom they encountered on duty in the West. He was equally alert to oppose people whom he regarded as leading his president away from the straight and the true: "He had blunt, wrathful words of objurgation for those who put in Grant's way temptations that he knew to be dangerous." As Cox put it: "A moral monitor and guide not hesitating at big oaths and camp expletives seems a strange type of man, but no one could deny that Rawlins's heart was as true and his perception of the thing demanded by the honor and welfare of his chief was as clear as his manners and words often were rough." Rawlins was the one cabinet member who could alter the direction of a conversation until it engaged Grant's attention, who would insist that information be obtained and analyzed before the president made up his mind, and who could be counted on to know what the Dents and Babcock and Porter were saying to Grant in all those hours between cabinet meetings.[59]

Jacob Dolson Cox of Ohio, the secretary of the interior, had been born in Montreal. His family was from New York—"Cox" had originally been "Koch," and the Dolsons too had been Dutch. He had attended Oberlin College, where he not only studied with Charles Grandison Finney but married his daughter, Helen. A lawyer, a Whig, and an early Republican, Cox became a Civil War general. He had no protracted close contact with Grant during the war, but in what contact they had Grant was sufficiently at ease for it to make sense early in 1868 for Sherman to propose Cox as Grant's superior during the crisis with Andrew Johnson over the position of secretary of war. Cox had by then served a term as governor of Ohio. None of Grant's cabinet appointments can have been more dismaying for the freedmen than that of Cox. Not only had he opposed Negro suffrage in postwar Ohio, but, in a message to his abolitionist alma mater, Oberlin, he had advocated forcible segregation of the races, with the black people to be placed on a reservation deep in the South. Those Republicans whom he would have thus discarded could perhaps persuade themselves that Cox's Department of the Interior had nothing to do with the racial issues of Reconstruction—the faint hope that the federal government would aid the blacks of the South to move onto homestead lands in the West was already dim to the point of extinction—but they knew that his negative voice would be heard at the cabinet table.

Cox was convinced that had Rawlins lived, Grant's administration would have remained admirable. As it was, Cox early became associated with men who became critics of the president. Grant, for his part, came to dislike Cox's moralistic tone. Along with Attorney General Hoar, Cox opposed the effort to annex Santo Domingo in 1869–70 and, further alienating Grant, sneered at advisers like Orville Babcock, calling them a "kitchen cabinet," while he pleaded for civil-service reform. Grant did, in fact, implement a merit-related personnel policy in the government, but he did not like those who, like Cox, espoused that cause in a way he took to be critical of men he had appointed and, therefore, of himself. After Hoar had departed, Cox, on October 5, 1870, was next to go. Grant was not sorry: "General Cox thought the Interior Department was the whole government, and that Cox was the Interior Department. I had to point out to him that there were three controlling branches of the Government, and that I was the head of one of these and would so like to be considered by the Secretary of the Interior." Cox went off to the Liberal Republican movement—which was just the fate that Grant thought he deserved—and to become dean of the Cincinnati Law School, a writer, and student of Gothic cathedrals.[60]

Adolph E. Borie, the secretary of the navy, was a rich Philadelphia merchant, but unlike Grant's other Philadelphia friends—George H. Stuart and George W. Childs—he seems not to have felt obliged to exemplify the Protestant ethic. His mother was a Huguenot. His father had been a tradesman first in Santo Domingo and then, with great success, in Philadelphia. Borie was born in 1809, graduated from the collegiate department at what is now the University of Pennsylvania at sixteen, studied in Paris, and by 1869 was exceedingly happily situated at his "country seat" some dozen miles outside Philadelphia. Grant liked to visit there, partially because he could admire his own oil painting, of the Indian family and the trader, which he had given to Borie and of which he was justifiably proud. Borie was shrewd, affable, and lazy. He wasted little time on church and philanthropic activities. He liked to play cards, and he did so interminably with Grant on the trip around the world which the former president took in 1877. Borie had rested well for the contest. He served in the cabinet only until June 1869, when he retired to private money making. He was replaced by George M. Robeson, a New Jersey lawyer, who served till the end of Grant's incumbency. To both Borie and Robeson, ships were things that carried goods; neither man conceived of the navy in terms of martial function, and it declined from its Civil War level of efficiency.[61]

To ensure high moral tone in the cabinet, a Massachusetts man was chosen as attorney general; to be certain that local vote-getting patronage was sensibly dispensed, a Maryland man was chosen as postmaster general. The appointment of Ebenezer Rockwood Hoar as attorney general "promised friendship" to Henry Adams, but most of his fellow cabinet members found little friendship in Judge Hoar's less-than-wholehearted participation in the Grant administration. Hoar was named both to reward the Republicans of Massachusetts and to please that state's powerful senior senator, Charles Sumner. Fish thought him supercilious and could not stand him. Hoar had made still other Whigs uncomfortable when, before the war, he spoke approvingly of himself as a Conscience Whig. He later joined the Free-Soil party, and then the Republican party, and for ten years had been on the Massachusetts Supreme Judiciary Court.[62]

Hoar's father, Samuel, was a hero to black Americans. In 1844 he had been sent to Charleston, South Carolina, to protest the jailing there of black Massachusetts seamen while their ships were in port. A resolution of the South Carolina legislature and a mob outside his hotel made his departure mandatory, but his slow, firm step as he walked past the many who wanted to drag him out of town made him a proud symbol of defiant opposition to slaveholding. His son had graduated to a more abstract opposition to the "oligarchy of color," as the press put it, but nothing except his friendship with Charles Sumner gave a clue as to his precise position on racial matters. When he was nominated by Grant, the *New York Herald* noted that "his taste and habits, especially of late years have led him to more conservative ways." Spectacled, slightly stooped, Hoar was a pillar of the American Unitarian Association and the perfect Harvard gentleman: "He is," insisted the New York press, "the man of most wit and of most humor" in the Saturday Club, in company with Oliver Wendell Holmes and James Russell Lowell. That wit was not to save him from an early and severe clash with Grant.[63]

John A. J. Creswell was a Whig in 1850, but by 1856 he was a Democrat. Subsequently becoming Republican, he was a congressman from Maryland during the war, a senator from 1865 to 1867, and a Grant delegate at the Chicago convention in 1868. To the surprise of many who expected little but partisanship from a man who loved the shifts of politics, he proved an efficient administrator; he both improved the mail service and made it less expensive. He remained in the cabinet until July 1874 and served as counsel in the Alabama-claims negotiations before returning to private practice as a lawyer. After a temporary replacement, Creswell was succeeded by Marshall Jewell, a manufacturer of leather belting from Hartford, Connecticut, where he was also active in insurance, banking, and railroading. He had already served under Grant as minister to Russia. Once in the cabinet he sided with critics of the president, and he was replaced in the summer of 1876 by James N. Tyner, a former congressman who had specialized in postal matters.

There were three generals at Grant's cabinet table—Cox, Rawlins, and Grant himself. Given the temper of the times and the huge supply of military men, the presence of more generals in the Grant administration would not have been surprising. There was no army "take-over." Washburne, Fish, Boutwell, Creswell, Hoar, Borie, and Vice-President Colfax were all civilians. Except for Boutwell, whose appointment the Radicals pushed when a place opened in the cabinet, none could be called a party regular, let alone a party leader. Gideon Welles, totally hostile to Grant, wrote, "The Radicals are astounded, thunderstruck, mad, but . . . try to reconcile themselves . . . that things are no worse—that Grant has not, besides kicking them one side, selected Democrats."[64]

"The Stewart fiasco has given a dreadful shock to the prestige of the new administration," wrote Horace White of the *Chicago Tribune* to Elihu Washburne. "The bad start we have got has almost made me sick. . . ." He was troubled not so much because Boutwell had replaced Stewart, or because rumor had it that Boutwell's entrance would require Hoar's exit (since both were from Massachusetts), "but because it is such boys' play." Herman Melville, who regarded all soldiers as boys, could not have been surprised that Grant should gather as his presidential staff those who had played with him during the war. Horace Porter, Fred Dent, and Orville Babcock were all announced as aides to the president, as Grant began to assemble his official household.[65]

Julia was not entirely happy about where that household was to be. She disliked the White House, which she thought of as the Johnsons' home, and after the inauguration made only a ceremonial stop there before going home to "I" Street. Aware that she would have to take up official residence in the Executive Mansion, she did visit it the next day, and while Ulysses tried to make himself at home in the offices, she prowled the house, finding it "in utter confusion." With an assistant, she took measurements and made drawings of every room, and set workmen to the task of completely redecorating the place; Mary Lincoln's notoriously costly curtains were banished; fresh paint was brushed on everywhere.[66]

Meanwhile, the "I" Street house was still full of relatives and other house guests who had come for the inauguration, and she used them as her excuse to put off moving. Ulysses was less hesitant; one day soon after he took office, he told Julia he had sold the house. Startled and angry, she asked who the buyer was, and how much he was to pay. Grant replied that Sayles J. Bowen would pay him forty thousand dollars, over ten years. She then asked why they had to sell at all; if they rented the house, they would have it after Grant left office. When he answered that he did not want to rent the house, she proposed that they close it:

> To this, he only replied: "I have already sold it, I told you, and the matter is settled." "Then have I nothing to say in this matter?" I had enjoyed my independence too long to submit quietly to this, and like a flash it occurred to me that whenever papa had bought a piece of land, he was obliged to make his wife a handsome present to induce her to sign the deed or else the deed would be imperfect. With exasperating coolness, I said: "You have sold the house?" "Yes," he repeated. "But," I calmly asked, "if I decline to sign the deed, what will the consequences be?"
>
> The General looked up with an incredulous laugh and said: "Oh, nothing. It would make no difference except it would be a little embarrassing to me; that is all." "Oh, is that so! Well," I answered, "I will not sign it."
>
> At this, the General looked over his paper and said: "Very well, I will send word to Mr. Bowen that my *wife* will not *let me* sell the house." The dear General thought this shaft would annihilate me, but it did not. I said, as I left the room quite indignant, "Very well, you may do so."[67]

It was Alexander Stewart who settled this family quarrel. Bowen, the mayor of Washington, did not get the "I" Street house (and in the midst of the 1872 campaign threatened to sue Grant for breach of contract), but Stewart led still another subscription committee composed of Grant's admirers, and raised the money to purchase the house at a price more acceptable to Julia Grant. It was then presented to General Sherman (who grumbled for years about the cost of its upkeep).[68]

With renovation of the White House only begun, the Grants took up residence there two weeks after the inauguration. Horace Porter and Orville Babcock moved in with the family, and so too did Grant's father-in-law, that unlovable old unreconstructed rebel Colonel Dent, who happily invaded enemy headquarters at 1600 Pennsylvania Avenue. There he insulted phalanxes of Yankee guests; his presence stood as Julia's reminder to Ulysses that he was not quite the master of his own White House.

But the White House was the first house of the nation. Julia and Ulysses Grant were, in the spring of 1869, at the top of the street. Whatever they had been previously denied could be denied them no more, and yet they still searched for evidence that this was so. On the Sunday after the inauguration the first family set off for church. Many visitors were still in town; the Metropolitan Methodist Church was crowded and the service well under way when the Grants arrived. Ulysses started down the center aisle toward the front pew that he had been told would be kept vacant for him. But the pew was occupied; the people in it, startled, stared at him, and he at them. He turned, Julia caught his eye, and gathering her children and sisters, she started for the rear door. Ushers, realizing what was happening, scurried for chairs, while one of them raced down the aisle and whispered to Julia that seats would be found. But embarrassed and indignant, Julia kept on toward the door and left the church. Ulysses followed her out and on to the First Presbyterian Church, where a black sexton showed them to their rented, and empty, pew.[69]

# XIX

---

# ORIGINAL OCCUPANTS

# OF THIS LAND

---

... and even this poor remnant of a once powerful tribe is fast wasting
away before those blessings of civilization "whisky and Small pox."
— *Ulysses S. Grant, Washington Territory, 1853*

... a finer set of men would be difficult to find. All were full chested,
and with features decidedly those of the American Indian.
— New York Herald, *Washington, D.C., 1870*

ULYSSES GRANT had allowed a personal concern to be visible in his
inaugural address at only one point. The great formality of the occasion had
not permitted him to say that when he himself was near despair in the Pacific
northwest, he had seen Indians living in still greater misery and hopelessness. Instead, he promised to "favor any course . . . which tends to . . . [the]
civilization and ultimate citizenship" of the "original occupants of this land."
Unsaid but understood was a commitment to prevent the extermination of
the native Americans. This was the only issue, the only cause, mentioned in
the speech in which Grant had a deep personal interest, and he followed his
startling and heartening statement by making the most interesting of his appointments. He named an Indian commissioner of Indian affairs. On all
other counts, the selection of Ely S. Parker was a most typical Grant appointment; Parker was a crony from army days. But that was exactly what made
his appointment fascinating and encouraging. The president perceived this
man, to whom he was giving charge of the enormously important relations
between the federal government and "the original occupants of this land,"
not as a symbol of a cause or as an exotic figure, but rather as a person he was
used to having around during a working day. Parker was a reliable staff man;

he also happened to be a Seneca Indian. Here was a chance for a breach in the racial barricade that had long stood between most red and white Americans.[1]

Not all Indians were as comprehensible to white Americans as Parker was to Grant. One of the brightest and in many ways the most attractive of the white Americans was Clarence King, who published his great book *Mountaineering in the Sierra Nevada* in 1872. In it he wrote powerfully of the funeral of an Indian woman, Sally the Old. Buck, her husband, "watched with wet eyes that slow-consuming fire burn the ashes of his wife," and as King watched the man, he knew he was seeing "not a stoical savage, but a despairing husband." Leaving the scene, King's mountain-man friend Jerry said to him, " 'Didn't I tell you Injuns has feelings inside of 'em?' I answered promptly [wrote King] that I was convinced; and long after, as I lay awake through many night-hours listening to that shrill death-wail, I felt as if any policy toward the Indians based upon the assumption of their being brutes or devils was nothing short of a blot on this Christian century." But the next morning, when King asked where Buck was, another Indian, Revenue Stamp, pointed to a hut and replied with an affable smile, " 'He whiskey drunk.' 'And who,' I inquired, 'is that fat girl with him.' 'Last night he take her; new squaw,' was the answer."[2]

A twentieth-century observer might venture the thought that Buck's quick and full expunging of grief was true mourning. His return to the ordinary business of living may have done quite as much honor to the woman who had been his wife and the mother of many of his children as that which Clarence King's friend Henry Adams paid his dead wife with a Saint-Gaudens statue. However, King, in 1872, could not see it that way. He banished Buck forever into membership in an inscrutable group. King resolved that hereafter he would "guardedly avoid all discussion of the 'Indian question.' When interrogated, I dodge, or protest ignorance; when pressed, I have been known to turn the subject; or, if driven to the wall, I usually confess my opinion that the Quakers will have to work a great reformation in the Indian before he is really fit to be exterminated." If this is where a lover of the West as enlightened as Clarence King found himself on the "Indian question," it is clear that anyone, including Ulysses Grant, would find arguing for a humane relationship with the Indians a huge and difficult job. Old warriors such as William Tecumseh Sherman—never mindful of his middle name—and George A. Custer simply sneered at the belated sentimentality of the man who had fought at Cold Harbor. But Grant told a Philadelphia friend that "as a young lieutenant, he had been much thrown among the Indians, and had seen the unjust treatment they had received at the hands of the white men."[3]

This treatment was part of the process by which Americans were making the lands of the continent their own. White America had no thought of leaving the West in a state of permanent wilderness—in which wild Indians could roam and their wise men dream of a good life. A few rare spirits such as Clarence King dreamed of letting nature reclaim the beautiful country of the

West from the ravages of all men, red or white. King was comforted to find that where there are "rude scars of mining and disordered heaps cumber the ground, time, with friendly rain, and wind and flood, slowly, surely, levels all, and a compassionate cover of innocent verdure weaves fresh and cool from mile to mile." In reverie he delighted in an Eden empty of people and their imprint, and yet his job was to map the land so it could be used. Francis Parkman, well before the Civil War, wrote his elegies for the native American. He understood Pontiac and his people, and he admired them, yet he could see no fate for the Indian other than to bow before the flow of progress that surged over the great stretches of forest and plains of the continent. The land would have to yield to those civilized men who would take axe and plow to it and prosper. The land was too good to be left to savage nomads. With the end of the Civil War the job of populating the West went forward with relentless fervor. Immigrants were carried out onto the plains and to the Far West on the great transcontinental railroads that were built. At any moment, Indians who had previously chosen or been driven to a particular location might find that settlers wanted to farm or mine their land or to build another railroad on it. In addition, the slaughter of the vast buffalo herds in the 1870's killed the food source of hunting tribes. It destroyed the Indian economy.[4]

The United States Army had the job of protecting the white settlers against the Indians, who were sorely provoked by the invaders of the West. Not all white people in the nation were comfortable about the savagery with which the army sometimes disciplined the savages of the vast region, but Denver newspapers had applauded in 1864 when word came that Colonel John M. Chivington had tracked down a band of Cheyenne Indians who had made peace and turned in their guns, and, at Sand Creek, killed almost all of them. Black Kettle escaped, and when details of the vicious slaughter—of children and women as well as men—reached the East, there was a cry from the heart against the sadism of the Methodist minister turned soldier and his murderous troops.[5]

After the war, Senator James R. Doolittle of Wisconsin, committed to Andrew Johnson's views with respect to the Negroes of the South and blind to the terrible attacks on the freedmen, opened his eyes to the inhumanity of the treatment of the Indians in the West. He brought about a congressional investigation and the establishment in 1867 of a peace commission that investigated the broad question of the settlement of the West and the future of the Indians who would be displaced. Nathaniel G. Taylor, commissioner of Indian affairs, chaired that panel, which included three other civilians and at first three and later four army generals, of whom William Tecumseh Sherman was the most forceful. The commissioners toured the territories, conducted hearings, and compiled their findings; these were released in January 1868. In Taylor's words: "Nobody pays any attention to Indian matters. This is a deplorable fact. Members of Congress understand the negro question, and talk learnedly of finance, and other problems of political economy, but when the progress of settlement reaches the Indian's home, the only question is, 'how best to get his lands.' " Sherman had long argued that the cause of all the Indian attacks on white men was the injustices done the Indian, but he went on to draw conclusions in which he parted company with Taylor and other humanitarians. There was, this chilling thinker contended, no stopping the movement of civilization; unjust though it assuredly was, stone-age man would have to yield before the inevitable thrust of civilized man. He saw little point in putting off the grim day of extermination with ameliorative measures, but neither did he have any patience with the corrupt Indian agents that the commission found in such abundance. Reluctantly, Sherman did sign the report, because it called for replacement of dishonest agents with honest ones. Taylor and Doolittle's work was the foundation of what was to become in 1869 the Grant Peace Policy. In 1868 treaties were signed with most of the Indians of the northern plains; three army posts in Indian territory were to be razed, and the Indians agreed to stay on reservations and accept the schools and other ministrations that the white men would bring to civilize them. Grant, as commanding general, ordered Sherman to carry out the destruction of the army bases "and to make all the capital with the Indians that can be made out of the change." Peace in the West seemed a possibility.[6]

This hope was destroyed in August 1868 when fighting broke out between white settlers and the Cheyenne, Arapaho, and Sioux. Now Sherman moved with force. He placed Philip H. Sheridan in command of the Army of the Missouri and ordered a fall and winter campaign that would harass the Indians back onto reservations. When another army man was elected president that fall, the reformers were increasingly nervous; there might be no harnessing the soldiers once Grant reached the White House. Therefore, in the winter of 1869, prior to Grant's inauguration, the reformers worked diligently and successfully to persuade him to protect the Indians. Two plans emerged, both with that goal. One proposal, called derisively at first, and later appreciatively, the Quaker Policy, was designed to replace entrepreneurs with missionaries as Indian agents. The men of God would not only look after the welfare of their flocks but bring them into the Christian fold. "Quaker Policy" was to a large degree a misnomer; the plan was indeed urged on Grant by members of the Society of Friends, but it was also sponsored with jealous zeal by the mainstream Protestant evangelical sects. Each tribe was assigned, for protection and proselytizing, to missionaries of a given denomination. One reservation—and hence one complete group of native Americans—was designated Episcopalian, the next Dutch Reformed, and so on; Grant, although not a church man, agreed.

The second plan for the Indians was embodied in Grant's Peace Policy. This called for (1) the end of the treaty system that presupposed that each tribe was a sovereign nation, (2) the treatment of Indians as individuals, responsible for their own welfare, rather than as members of a tribe, dependent on a community, (3) the containment of the tribes on reservations—a concept obviously incongruous with that of individual treatment—and (4) the use of education to compensate for all the economic and cultural lacunae in the policy, and to produce American citizens. Such a process had produced Grant's aide Ely Parker, and the president-elect could see no reason why it would not work for all of Parker's fellows. Grant never wrote explicitly on the subject of his famous Peace Policy, which emerged from his experiences and conversations prior to taking office. By the same logic that says it takes a thief to catch a thief, military men often are more capable of catching out other military men than are civilians. Grant had a good idea what Sherman and Sheridan thought about the Indians, and he did not subscribe to the view that the only good Indian is a dead Indian.[7]

One Indian who was very much alive was Ely S. Parker. The heavy-set copper-hued general was one of the members of the staff who had been so essential to Grant during the war. The president had every intention of keeping these men on the job when he moved into the White House. With a bit of simple logic that has escaped a great many other presidents when making appointments, Grant placed Parker in a post where one—though not all—of his concerns lay. It occurred to neither man to think of Parker exclusively in what we would call "ethnic" terms. Grant had talked to Parker about the Indians' hopes for themselves just as he had talked to many white reformers about their prescriptions for the future of the people who were natives of the land and not yet part of the white man's America.

The name "Parker" is said to have been that of a British captive who had lived with Ely's forebears; already moving from one culture into another, they adopted it for use in tandem with Seneca names. Ely himself was known also as Ha Sa No An Da and Donehogawa. His father, William Parker, a Seneca chief, fought the British in the War of 1812, farmed, and married Elizabeth, also a Seneca, about 1820. They had six children: Levi, Nicholson, Caroline, Ely (born in 1828), Spencer, and Isaac Newton. Clearly, the Parkers' ways of saying things were being anglicized; the Seneca culture was being overwhelmed and the language silenced, while the arts of basketry and beadwork became commercialized. The Senecas, once part of the proud but defeated Iroquois league of Five Nations, no longer farmed on a large scale, and white settlers were rapidly displacing them on their lands. As a boy, Ely responded to these changes by running away from home and finding work caring for horses at a Canadian military post. Then, taunted by white boys for being Indian, he came back determined to beat his tormentors at their own game by gaining an education. At the Tonawanda mission school, he was motivated not by desire for revenge, but by the urge to excel in order to be able to demand recognition.

He next studied at Cayuga Academy, where the pioneer anthropologist Lewis Henry Morgan—ten years his senior—had also been educated. "During his schooldays," wrote Parker's biographer, "Ely had already met many of the distinguished men of New York, and he had dined at the White House as a guest of President Polk." How Parker leaped from his academy desk to President Polk's dinner table is not explained; it would appear that the quick-witted adolescent accompanied lawyers and chiefs on their frequent trips to Washington in the ultimately futile efforts to hold their lands. On these trips, Parker was taken up by white hostesses charmed by a just-a-bit civilized—and handsome—young Indian. But Parker had a far greater role than this to play as a bridge between two cultures. Lewis Henry Morgan, outraged not only by the defrauding of the Indians but by the destruction of their culture, began to interview his native American neighbors, and three of his most important sources of information were Parker's parents and Ely himself, whose biographer did not greatly exaggerate when he wrote, "The Parker house was in a measure the spot where a new American Science was born." Morgan's book *League of the HO-DÉ-NO-SAU-NEE, Iroquois*, one of the landmarks of anthropology and American intellectual history, is dedicated "to HÄ-SA-NO-AŃ-DA, (Ely S. Parker,) a Seneca Indian."[8]

Parker next moved into another white man's enterprise—commerce—supervising work details at the western terminus of the Erie Canal and in a freight office in Rochester. Next, on assignments for the army, he worked at building lighthouses along the Great Lakes and later on the construction of the Chesapeake and Albemarle Canal. In 1857 Parker superintended the construction of a customhouse in Galena. Always a joiner, Parker was a Mason; he helped form Miners Lodge No. 273 in the lead-mining town of Galena, and in September 1858 became its Worshipful Master. He knew his new townsmen well, and legend has made much of Parker's friendship with Galena's most famous harness-shop clerk. The chances are that he knew Grant only slightly, but the connection was made. When the war came, Parker went back to New York State, won his father's reluctant approval to enlist, and, never one to aim low, went to Washington to discuss an appointment with the secretary of state, his western New York neighbor William Henry Seward. Seward is reported to have said that the war "was an affair between white men and one in which the Indian was not called to act," and for the moment, Parker went back to farming in New York, but by 1863 his lobbying for a commission had been successful. He was appointed captain of volunteers and joined Grant's staff in the Vicksburg campaign. He served with the intimate band of staff men for the balance of the war and went along to Grant's headquarters in Washington after its close. Even before the members of the cabinet had been selected, he knew he would be appointed commissioner of Indian affairs, and in February 1869, in anticipation of his new job and a change in governmental policy, he wrote to the Quakers and asked them to recommend agents for two tribal reservations.[9]

The new policy that Grant and Parker created was designed to encourage precisely the kind of transformation that Parker embodied. The Indians were to be helped to enter the mainstream of American life. They were to do what other Americans did; they were to become Christians and wear neckties. That was almost what had happened to Grant; it had happened to Parker. Grant had settled in his own mind that the great result of the Civil War was that America was one nation, with a national norm, a single idiom. What the president-to-be, with a nice naiveté, did not see was that Parker was an exception that proved a racist rule. Parker not only had been willing to try to be assimilated into the American culture but had succeeded in the attempt. A white man's Indian, his detractors would call him, but having said that they had to concede that he was a general in the army. Only later, when the positions he was given were more minor than they would have been if he were white, did Parker learn that being an agreeable fellow who had served on General Grant's staff did not make him immune to American racism.[10]

In March 1869 Parker still had a great opportunity. President Grant was listening—and at his inauguration, speaking. Americans in 1869 who thought the elimination of the Indians desirable could not miss the fact that Grant, by calling them "occupants of this land," was giving the Indians a proprietary claim to an existence on it. By calling for their "civilization and ultimate citizenship," Grant was categorically rejecting the twin notions that the Indians were evil savages incapable of change and that the course of civilization would inevitably carry past them. He was asserting that the Indians were capable of change and that the American society was capable of accepting them within it. He had laid the foundation stone of his Peace Policy. If it had worked as well as he and Parker hoped, it might have proved a monument worth as much as Appomattox. It still stands as an honorable milestone on a road strewn with markers of national disgrace.

From the perspective of the twentieth century—and decades of gross mismanagement of the Peace Policy—it is easy to condemn Grant's approach as lacking in feeling for the deep cultural heritage of the Sioux, the Arapaho, the Navaho. In March 1869 it promised something better than Sand Creek or, to look ahead to American race relations during Grant's second term, Little Bighorn. Grant's words gave great hope to Americans who wanted the Indians alive rather than dead. Champions of the reform of American Indian policy were elated by the inaugural speech.

Shortly after inauguration day, on March 24, 1869, President Grant and Secretary of the Interior Cox were visited by a delegation of well-placed Pennsylvanians which included William Welsh, a rich Philadelphian and an Episcopalian; George H. Stuart, also a Philadelphian and a Presbyterian; and Judge William Strong, of the Pennsylvania Supreme Court. These men urged that an autonomous commission be established to ensure that the provisions of a recent treaty with the Sioux were carried out fairly. Welsh told Cox that although he was a fine gentleman, a private commission was necessary. Without such a commission, Stuart told Grant and Cox, no reform was possible because no one trusted the Interior Department to prevent corruption. Cox was enough of a reformer himself to acknowledge the accuracy of the accusation, and disguised his feelings about the self-righteous Philadelphian because he knew that the gross mismanagement of Indian affairs in the past did indeed argue for the kind of supervision of a private Board of Indian Commissioners that Welsh proposed. He probably guessed, from this first meeting, that what lay ahead was a clash between the elite members of a private board of overseers on the one hand and a governmental employee, the commissioner of Indian affairs, on the other. (The very confusion in terms—the Board of Indian Commissioners, upon which the commissioner of Indian affairs did not sit—suggested the clash to come.) Grant and Cox agreed that a board was needed—but not for the Sioux (or the Episcopalians) alone. It should supervise the whole of the government's Indian policy.[11]

Indian matters got priority in Congress during the first month of the Grant administration, and on April 10, legislation was passed creating the Board of Indian Commissioners. Grant called on one of his Philadelphia friends: "Stuart, you and Welsh have got me in difficulty with this bill." Now Grant wanted Stuart to get him out of trouble by naming "some leading men from different sections of the country, who will be willing to serve the cause of the Indians without compensation." Stuart was an excellent man to ask; earlier, General O. O. Howard, seeking money for freedmen's schools, had found the Philadelphia philanthropists—and Stuart in particular—more forthcoming with cash and organizing energy than their brethren in New York and Boston, and now Stuart's suggestions produced a board of ten, including Felix R. Brunot, a steel man and an Episcopalian from Pittsburgh, and William E. Dodge of New York, immensely rich as a result of shrewdly investing his wife's vast inheritance and a dedicated Presbyterian. Not surprisingly, there was no one from the South. Significantly, there was no one from west of St. Louis and Chicago; no attempt was made to enlist western support by the appointment of a popular westerner. Similarly, no effort was made to coerce military co-operation by the inclusion of some generals, as had been done in the selection of the peace commission in the Johnson administration. There were no Quakers, nor were there any representatives of the government's other foray into the world of welfare administration, the Freedmen's Bureau. People like Stuart and Dodge had contributed to private schools established with Bureau assistance, but General Howard and other Freedmen's Bureau men were conspicuously absent in the administration of Grant's Indian policy.[12]

In accordance with the Peace Policy which the board was to oversee, under Welsh's direction, the Indians were to be held on the reservations, so that they would be protected from white incursions while the incoming white settlers were protected from Indian attack. On the reservations, the members of each tribe were to be educated to the ways of social and economic life in civilized American society. Critical in this process was the Indian agent, who was a combination governor, teacher, supplier, and—in theory, at least—

representative of the interests of the Indian in transactions with those who, for whatever reason, wanted to have dealings with him. Since the agent was paid only $1,500 a year, the opportunity for graft was enormous. The Indians, often destitute because they had been removed from good hunting lands to poor farming lands, were dependent on the government for food, clothing and blankets, and tools. The supplier who paid the agent the most got the government contract. One keen observer, the Episcopalian bishop Henry B. Whipple, noted that it was "a tradition that an agent" paid $1,500 a year could "retire upon an ample fortune in three years." The bishop did not greatly exaggerate; the cost to the government in overcharges easily exceeded that of all the agents' salaries. The cost to the Indians of disgustingly inferior supplies was harder to calculate.[13]

Not all of the agents were crooked, but many were. Not all of those who made a profit were cruel in their treatment of the Indians, but many were. Therefore, obtaining honest and humane agents was the immediate goal of the reformers, including Grant. He retained his contempt for the sutlers he had encountered during the war, and recognizing the Indian agents as kin to them, he trusted instead the missionaries who—assigned by denomination to the various tribal groups—were willing to live on the $1,500 salary in exchange for the opportunity to convert the Indians. He also trusted his own kind, army men, who could be expected to accept the responsibility of serving as Indian agents as a standard army assignment. This attitude resulted in the odd pairing of missionaries and soldiers as Indian agents in the Grant era.

The missionaries, exemplified by Lawrie Tatum (whose famous account tells us much about the work of the agents), were often sympathetic if demanding guardians of the Indians. The best of them were resourceful men— and women, for the wives of many of the agents clearly performed a function as large as that of their husbands. Less is known about the quality of the governing done by the army men, but surely the behavior of the individual army agents was distinct from that of their fellows in army units with a totally different assignment, keeping the peace. These units were the source of danger to the Indians. Even a rumor of Indian discontent might cause an army officer in the field, without first discussing the complaint with the agent in charge, to move directly against the Indians—often with savagely fatal results.[14]

In January 1870 one such attack, which gravely undercut the trust the Indians had in Grant's nascent Peace Policy, was made by Colonel E. M. Baker, with General Sheridan's enthusiastic approval, on a settlement of Piegan Indians. Once again there was indiscriminate slaughter. The details were sickening—and well publicized by Vincent Colyer, an outspoken member of the board. Such occurrences pricked the conscience of many Americans and put the reformers in a strong position. With so much to work toward from that position it is extremely odd that William Welsh spent so much of his energy trying to get rid of the one Indian involved in making decisions about Indian affairs. Welsh hated Parker and would brook no competition from him in his determination to be the spokesman for the Indian cause. When government-employee Parker refused to consult private-gentleman Welsh, and when a budget, which is to say power, was not given Welsh's Board of Indian Commissioners, the Philadelphian resigned. His early resignation, however, did not end his vendetta with Parker. His successor, Felix R. Brunot, was a close friend, and Welsh stayed in sufficient contact with the board to be able to harass Parker.[15]

Parker and Welsh were at an extraordinary and illuminating standoff. Welsh's determination to protect the Indians from extermination and from being cheated was genuine, and even after his resignation, he was indefatigable in pursuit of these aims. However, when he traveled in the West to visit his Indians on their native ground 'he chose to see them as a remote people, attractive both for their seductively different ways and for the splendid challenge that their culture afforded those who would have the joy of cleansing it with Christianity. In Red Cloud of the Oglala Sioux, Welsh saw a majestic and exotic chief, and he vastly preferred this picture of an Indian spokesman to the spectacle of Ely Parker, who sat slouched on a camp chair or a White House couch swapping bureaucratic lore with the likes of Orville Babcock and Ulysses Grant. The Episcopalian gentleman regarded the Indians as a people to be brought into godliness, rather than into the Republican party. He hated corruption. He did not want civilization to mean for the Indians the opportunity to do all the things (including cheat) that white Americans could do. Paradoxically, the savages, in Welsh's view, were cut out to be something nobler than ordinary Americans. But Grant had said his goal was to civilize and ultimately make citizens of the Indians, and Ely Parker was exactly the kind of citizen Grant wanted in his administration. There was less hypocrisy or fantasy in Grant's vision of what the Peace Policy would provide than there was in Welsh's.

In Welsh's conception, the Indian was purer than pure. When Parker proved to be mortal instead, Welsh made him more the target of his disgust than the white suppliers of goods who were cheating the Indians. In arranging purchases, Parker's new method was the ostensibly fair one of advertising the need for supplies and giving the contract to the lowest bidder. The problems were two. First was the matter of quality; the lowest bidder might supply goods of a low grade. Second, the contract system was corrupt. A "low" bidder might agree to sell six hundred blankets at a low price and a hundred hoes at a very high price, with the total bid being the lowest offered. Then he would supply fifty blankets and a thousand hoes, and the agents, perhaps bribed, would accept a shipment that was highly lucrative to the contractor.

To prevent such abuses, men far above the battle came down to the accountant's desk and dutifully sought to prevent disreputable entrepreneurs from cheating defenseless Indians. William E. Dodge and George H. Stuart, committed to Christian benevolent enterprises and now so rich that they no longer had to touch the rust of day-to-day commerce, sat down like two Dickensian clerks and diligently audited stacks of vouchers passed for Indian supplies. Their eye was acute, but Stuart could never quite understand why, after he had disallowed contracts that flagrantly wasted the government's money on bad beef and inferior goods, there was criticism when large new contracts were awarded to his good friend the exemplary Christian business-man John Wanamaker. Earlier, the auditors' work had produced more severe criticism of Ely Parker. Welsh leaped at every bit of evidence of graft, and at his insistence, the House of Representatives in December 1870 began an investigation into Parker's acquiescence in violations of the government requirement that contracts be advertised. Welsh and others testified and, by implication only, linked Parker to abuses of the Indians carrying far beyond the matter of contracts at hand. The congressmen exonerated Parker, but Welsh won nonetheless. The reformers had succeeded in shaking public confidence in the commissioner, and in July 1871, Grant yielded and Parker resigned. Parker was replaced temporarily by H. R. Clum and then by Francis Amasa Walker, who needed a salary to continue his demographic work, based on the 1870 census. Walker, however great his intellectual talents, was astonishingly cold-blooded about his Indian clients; he was succeeded as commissioner in 1873 by E. P. Smith, a Congregational minister, and he, in turn, was followed in 1876 by J. Q. Smith, an Ohio politician. When he set out to replace Parker, Grant assured Stuart that the man he chose not only would have "the full confidence" of the Board of Indian Commissioners, but would be "fully in sympathy with a humane policy towards the Indians." All of Parker's successors named by Grant, however, were white, and none was a truly powerful champion of his clients.[16]

Parker moved to New York and, in the manner of the age, sought to prove his worth by succeeding on Wall Street. He did well enough to have a house in town and a country place in Fairfield, Connecticut, but the prosperity did not last. When his business career failed, he sought another government position, but no official post commensurate with his past eminence was open to him. He resurrected his skills as an engineer and became the architect of the New York City Police Department. Later he was its supply clerk. The "last grand sachem of the Iroquois" died in 1895 in Fairfield. Donehogawa was given an Episcopalian funeral and buried in Connecticut, but later his body was moved to an upstate New York cemetery on ground where the Seneca once counseled together.[17]

The attacks on Parker in 1870 and 1871 were reminiscent of those relentless demands for purity with which any black politician who had even looked smilingly on a contractor was tracked down in the later days of Reconstruction. Often the demands were made by fellow politicians who were themselves not above friendly commerce. In the attacks on Parker, it was almost as if the William Welshes, in a perversion of their fascination with the noble in full regalia on the plains, needed to prove the innate depravity of those whom they hoped to conduct into Christianity and capitalism. And so Welsh branded Parker—and by implication all Indians—as "but a remove from barbarism" and not capable of honesty. Welsh got rid of Parker, but his position on the Board of Indian Commissioners did not give him enough power to become the Christianizing czar of the Indians; over the years he became embittered, and was by 1876 an advocate of transferring jurisdiction over Indian affairs from the Department of the Interior to the War Department. Welsh's successor, Felix R. Brunot, led the fight to block the repeated attempts to achieve this transfer, which would have destroyed the Peace Policy.[18]

The reformers were right in viewing their cause as difficult. Their efforts at amelioration of the Indian's lot were, after all, carried out in the context of the unremitting Indian wars. During the years of Grant's presidency, over two hundred battles were fought. The cause of reform suffered terrible setbacks—a great many in the years of the Grant administration and beyond—but repeatedly there occurred a new massacre or other outrage by white Americans that was sufficiently disgraceful to convince other white Americans that the Peace Policy was at least better than annihilation. What the reformers had wrought, with Grant's indispensable help, withstood even the demand after the defeat of Custer at Little Bighorn in 1876 that the army be allowed to finish the job on the Indians. The attempt to transfer jurisdiction over Indian affairs to the War Department failed once again then, even amid the cries that Custer's martyrdom had to be avenged. The Peace Policy lived on after Grant was gone.[19]

There were, however, two fundamental issues that Grant and the men who with him formulated the Peace Policy did not address. Francis Paul Prucha recently observed, "These friends of the Indian had little acquaintance with Indian character; they did not appreciate the human nature of the people. They did not know that their minds were already occupied by a multitude of notions and beliefs that were firmly fixed there—rooted and grounded by an inheritance of a thousand years." In a word, the Indians did not want President Grant's civilization. Second, there was no recognition of the basic political economy of the people. The relationship to the land of Indians remanded to a reservation was completely different from the relationship to the land of free hunters. Even in "civilized" Lockean terms the Indians were given nothing that could ensure their liberty. Transplanted from good hunting territory, they were expected to undertake farming on desolate land from which they might be evicted at any time if white men found on it anything valuable. Individual Indians were not exterminated; they struggle still to prove that Sherman was wrong, that they are not doomed to extinction by the inevitable wave of someone else's civilization, but they struggle from a position of poverty that would more than justify a Helen Hunt Jackson's writing now of a second century of dishonor.[20]

Much had changed, and yet not so very much, since Ulysses had written

Julia in 1853, "You charge me to be cautious about riding out alone lest the Indians should get me. Those about here are the most harmless people you ever saw. It really is my opinin that the whole race would be harmless and peaceable if they were not put upon by the whites." In 1869 President Grant made a sensible beginning by calling for civilization of the Indians and, more, by saying no to their extermination. Ely Parker was his friend, and he had reason to believe an Indian as commissioner would be a protector and friend of the Indians. Grant's eight years in the presidency were years of savage warfare with the Indians, but they were also the years of his Peace Policy, which never fully lost out.[21]

In May 1870, Spotted Tail and a delegation of Oglala Sioux arrived in Washington and crowded into a suite in a hotel. A reporter found them sitting cross-legged on beds, cots, and the floor. There was more naked flesh than the *Herald*'s man in Washington often saw in his encounters with distinguished visitors to the capital, and he was impressed: "Physically a finer set of men would be difficult to find. All were tall, full chested, and with features decidedly those of the American Indian." Red Cloud, the Oglala chief who most assiduously pursued an accommodation with the United States government, was "like a statue"; Big Bear, who arrived to join Spotted Tail's contingent, seemed "fierce." Putting on splendid beaded shirts and leggings, as well as buffalo robes, the delegation asked Secretary of the Interior Cox and Commissioner Parker for protection of their treaty rights. The reporter, who could see that Red Cloud was "no innocent," detected Cox talking to him and the other Sioux as if they were babies. The conversation reached the usual conditional conclusion: if you keep the peace, you will not be disturbed. Even under Parker, the onus always fell on the Sioux. Then, their business transacted, they climbed into carriages to make a formal call on President Grant.[22]

It was seven-thirty in the evening and the light in the East Room was dim as they stood with Cox and Parker and watched official Washington perform its tribal dances. President Grant entered with Mrs. Grant on his arm, accompanied, according to strict protocol, by the cabinet and the diplomatic corps. After brief formal greetings, the curious white people tried to find ways to chat with these men who seemed so strange to them. Edward Thornton, the British minister, spoke to Red Cloud in his impeccable English and had no more luck at being understood than did the Russian ambassador, who tried French. The light grew weaker, the chiefs more silent and ominous, and Grant, at last, moved to revive the doomed occasion. He led the party of Sioux into the brightly lit dining room, where the buffets were heaped with bowls of strawberries and pitchers of cream. This friendliest of white American gestures only confused the red men more. With the berries uneaten, Parker escorted the chiefs through the grave ceremony of shaking hands with the president and his entourage, and they departed.[23]

When in 1871, splashed with the paint of corruption, Parker resigned as commissioner of Indian affairs, Grant lost a friend who, by chance, was an Indian. Parker's removal somehow discredited Grant's concern for the native Americans. The president did not turn on them, but thereafter he was only a brake on the excesses of their exterminators. His contacts with the Indians were not those of a sympathetic young captain who knows some troubles himself; instead, Grant was the Great White Father receiving delegations of Indians, who spoke of their lost world in words that, in the White House, no one understood.

# XX

# A FRIDAY AND
# A FRIEND

Our eight years in the Executive Mansion were delightful, but there
were some dark clouds in the bright sky. There was that dreadful Black
Friday.

— *Julia Dent Grant*

Friendship is evanescent in every man's experience, and remembered
like heat lightning in past summers.

— *Henry David Thoreau*

IN MARCH 1869, when the Grants moved into the White House, both
Julia's and Ulysses' families proved vulnerable to attentions that were at once
innocent and dangerous. Jesse Grant, to the delight of reporters, who could
count on him for outlandish comments, had become embarrassingly prolix
on the subject of his son. Julia's widowed father, old Colonel Dent, in the
White House with his daughter's family, provided a Confederate chorus in
the temple of Republicanism. He did not keep silent any more than did Ulysses' father. Both old men liked attention and responded to it. Hannah Grant,
in her strange silence, was the only member of the family (other than her eldest son) who was able to ward off those who came to collect gossip. And
some came with more compelling and dangerous intentions.

Grant's three sisters had been unmarried and living at home when he went
off to war. While he was away, his eldest sister, Clara, and his eldest brother,
Simpson, both died. His youngest sister, Mary Frances, was married in 1863
to the Reverend Michael John Cramer, leaving Virginia at home alone with
her mother and father. In March 1869, Virginia, or Jennie, a spinster at
thirty-seven, was not even sure that she would get to go to Washington for
her brother's inauguration. By June she was in great demand for dinner par-

ties in New York City—when her brother was her house guest. She had been discovered to be a valuable commodity by a sixty-one-year-old financier from New York, Abel Rathbone Corbin. Theirs was not a blind and rapturous romance; unquestionably, she was exploited for her connection to her brother. However, it should not therefore be assumed that she had a bitterly unhappy marriage, like the one her niece later endured. In any case, as Virginia Corbin she saw a good deal more happening than she had as Virginia Grant.

Her marriage to Corbin was part of the chain of events that resulted in Black Friday, September 24, 1869. It all began the previous spring, on a day when Jay Gould joined Ulysses Grant at the Corbins'. Gould and his partner, James Fisk, Jr., were two of the most brilliant young men on Wall Street. Gould, thirty-three and so slight as to seem fragile, had strange energies. He was a historian and a gardener—"a rather peculiar man," Fisk thought—as well as a financier bold enough to take on and best Cornelius and William Henry Vanderbilt in the "Erie War" for the control of that railroad in 1868. Fisk, probably not equally bright but surely as bold, was at thirty-four a celebrator of the joys of being rich. A brassy dresser, a forthright storyteller, a flamboyant gambler, and a vulgar (that is, successful) womanizer, he was killed in 1872 for having overextended himself in the last of these enterprises. Jealous of Fisk's success with the beautiful Josie Mansfield, Edward Stokes entered the fashionable Grand Central Hotel and shot Fisk dead. During his lifetime, Fisk was apt to tell the truth if he could not think of any good reason not to, and in his view one good reason for doing so was that he despised hypocrisy in others. He liked being rich and assumed other people had a similar hankering; he enjoyed talking about money.[1]

Monetary policy is the dullest of subjects. And yet its manipulation, by which men and nations become rich or poor, has provided some of the most exciting times in modern history. The season of one such exciting time was splendidly launched by a dinner that Gould gave for Julia and Ulysses Grant on June 15, 1869, the day of their visit to the Corbins'. It culminated in Black Friday, when brokers who had contracted to buy gold for their customers at $160 an ounce found, after the price collapsed, that payment for the purchases had to be obtained by selling the gold at only $135 an ounce. What was worse, in many cases the original purchase had been made with a loan supported by collateral worth far less than the total of the loan. When payment was called for, the collateral, whether gold or other assets, had to be sold in a rapidly falling market. Scores of Wall Street speculators were ruined; hundreds more lost vast sums.[2]

Fisk later told a congressional investigating committee that in his years on Wall Street he never saw anything to match Black Friday. There was the "deathlike silence" of intense concentration, as gold was traded up from $143 to $162 an ounce. (Fisk had let out the word that one had better buy at $160 that day; it would cost $200 on the next.) As buying continued, the speculators were held in "dream-like terror" that the swift, unnatural rise could not continue. Then, suddenly, selling began, and there was "the wildest confusion and the most unearthly screaming of men, always excitable, now driven to the verge of temporary insanity by the consciousness of ruin, or the delusive dream of immense wealth." Noting that they were in "bedlam" and that one of their former associates was now "crazy as a loon," Gould and Fisk, "not desiring to stay there any longer . . . went out by a side door" and drove uptown to Fisk's office over the opera house. When the day was over, it was "each man drag out his own corpse."[3]

The Gold Room, in which this scene was played out, and the opportunity for such speculation, were bizarre outgrowths of the government's successful attempt to pay its bills during the Civil War. The cost of supplies had been enormous, and legislation had been passed empowering the federal government to greatly increase the volume of money in circulation by issuing greenbacks. These were bills of exchange, ordinary dollar bills, that were not backed dollar for dollar by gold—hence the establishment of the market in gold, for use in foreign commerce, that was institutionalized in the Gold Room. The greenbacks were backed by the pledge of the Lincoln government, which, through a confident appeal to patriotism and profit, was able to sell huge bond issues to a well-employed citizenry that had available for their purchase plenty of greenbacks earned by supplying the army. After the war, Andrew Johnson's secretary of the treasury, Hugh McCulloch, who was conservative, began a policy of severe monetary retrenchment in an effort to return the dollar to a point where it would once again be redeemable in specie. The volume of business also dropped, and the economy was in a mild recession.

This is not to say that the country was in a depression—that was yet to come. But some regions suffered more severely than others from the reduction in the money supply. Hardest hit were the South, still desperately poor in the aftermath of the war, and the other great rural part of the nation, the West. Conservative businessmen in New York applauded the retrenchment program, with its promise of a stable currency that would benefit existing businesses. But western wheat growers, with huge crops and little money, were eager to sell their crops overseas, and the program could be expected to discourage foreign purchases by raising the cost of the dollar in terms of other currencies. Gold had held at a relatively stable level from the end of the war until the start of the Grant administration and was selling at a low point of $130 an ounce in March 1869, as Grant and Secretary of the Treasury Boutwell undertook to continue McCulloch's retrenchment program. The greenbacks, which no longer commanded confidence, were to be turned in (at a discount) and removed from circulation, in exchange for currency redeemable in gold and, hence, expected to appreciate in value. The problem, as the citizens of the West and the South recognized, was that fewer people would hold those fewer dollars.

Prosperity was, of course, the goal of the new administration, and people kept their eye on the president as he went, briefly, among the money-changers in New York. On Thursday, June 15, 1869, Julia and Ulysses, after visiting Fred at West Point, arrived at the Corbins' for an afternoon visit before going on to Boston. One of those who called on the president there, and was welcomed cordially by Corbin, was Jay Gould. Grant had already accepted a sumptuous invitation from Gould, and after the visit with Corbin, Gould escorted the president and his lady to the most splendid of his steamships, which carried passengers by way of Long Island Sound to Fall River, Massachusetts. There, they would take the train to Boston. At the dinner party on board were several men active in the financial world who were more than willing to go out of their way to learn Grant's thoughts on monetary policy. The president was on his own; no one else connected with the government was present. He did not have Secretary of the Treasury Boutwell there to advise him.[4]

James Fisk recalled the occasion in his testimony before a congressional investigation committee seven months later:

> . . . on our passage over to Boston with General Grant, we endeavored to ascertain what his position in regard to the finances was. We went down to supper about nine o'clock, intending while we were there to have this thing pretty thoroughly talked up, and, if possible, to relieve him from any idea of putting the price of gold down. . . . We talked there until about half-past twelve. When we first commenced to talk, I could see that he was for returning to a specie basis. I remember the remark that he made that we might as well tap the bubble at once as at any other time, saying that it had got to come to that.

The president, like the more conservative of the gentlemen with whom he was dining, expected the economy to shrink. Jay Gould, who did not want it to, recalled at the congressional investigation that Grant "thought there was a certain amount of fictitiousness about the prosperity of the country." Gould advised the president that the way to combat this was not with further contraction of the currency. Instead, he believed, Boutwell should increase the supply of money in order to stimulate the economy. More stringency, he argued (with a bit of exaggeration that must not have appealed to Grant) could "almost lead to civil war." Gould went on to assert that "strikes among the workmen, and . . . the manufactories would have to stop." Grant, according to Fisk's recollection, entered into the conversation with a good deal of spirit: "I [Fisk] made up my mind that he was individually paying a good deal of attention to the finances, which he would to a certain extent control. . . . I know that when we got to Boston, Mr. Gould and myself made up our minds that the prospects [for keeping the government from selling gold and diminishing the money supply still more] did not look promising." Gould said succinctly that he "supposed from that conversation that the President was a contractionist."[5]

Clearly, Fisk and Gould had a job cut out for them. But neither of them was afraid of this particular kind of work. Their ally was to be Abel Corbin, "a very shrewd old gentleman," said Gould at the investigation, who was "much more far-seeing than the newspapers give him credit for." Corbin later denied ever having arranged to bring Gould and the president together, but the fact is that after June 15 and prior to September 24 Gould met Grant at Corbin's house three times. In addition, it was assumed by Gould and Fisk that when alone with the president, Corbin was assiduously pressing their case against the government's sale of gold. Later, in great distress before the investigating congressmen, Corbin took out of his pocket his daybook and recited all the times his brother-in-law had stopped on his way through town—to Newport, to Saratoga—but he denied arranging any interview for Jay Gould or, emphatically, for James Fisk, Jr.[6]

Gould, for his part, described for the investigators his three meetings with the president. No occasion was too sacred; when Grant was traveling south to see Rawlins, who was dying, Gould called and found that the "President had changed his views. . . . he was satisfied that the country had had a very bountiful harvest; that there would be a large surplus; that unless we could find a market abroad for that surplus it would put down prices here. . . ." Gold, dear against the dollar, would be cheap against foreign currencies, and gold was accessible to foreign buyers who needed it to buy American wheat. Gould gained the impression from Grant that he would make sure his administration would "facilitate the movement of breadstuffs." Gould was impressed by the fact that this international trade "seemed to have been a matter of study with him"; the astute trader was "surprised at the clearness with which he seemed to comprehend the whole question." Things seemed to Gould to be well in hand.[7]

Gould's discussions with Grant left him confident that no gold would be sold by the government. Fisk was reassured on less intellectual grounds. He had arranged an early-warning system. Fisk knew that Corbin had tried to get his first wife's son-in-law, Robert B. Catherwood, the job of assistant treasurer of the United States. In this capacity he would have handled the sale of gold on the Wall Street market. Catherwood had backed out when he learned that he would be expected to co-operate in the use of a code system to ensure that Corbin and Gould would be informed before public announcement was made of any prospective government gold sales. Failing to get Catherwood into the job, Corbin lobbied successfully for the appointment of General Daniel Butterfield, the man who had headed Alexander T. Stewart's subscription committee that financed the purchase of Grant's "I" Street house. The appointment of Butterfield had the reassuring support of Stewart as well as Corbin, and Grant agreed to it. General Butterfield, it turned out, had a particular interest in his work; Gould had arranged a margin account for him, and Butterfield played the market he was supposed to be regulating.[8]

Still stronger assurance that Grant would support gold appeared in the form of a rumor that Corbin, in addition to carrying an account in gold of $2,000,000 for himself, was carrying speculative accounts of $500,000 each for Julia Grant and Horace Porter. Orville Babcock was also said to have been charmed into accepting such an account. Seven years later, in a congressional investigation of other activities of Babcock's, evidence was presented to the effect that he had indeed carried a gold account, with Harris C. Fahnestock of Jay Cooke & Company, and had lost $40,000. Fahnestock's later testimony tends to confirm Porter's involvement, but there is only the word of James Fisk and a possibly doctored record of the shipment of cash by the Adams Express Company to Mrs. Grant in October to suggest that the first lady too was a speculator. Fisk told the congressmen, "Mr. Gould . . . sold $500,000 of gold belonging to Mrs. Grant, which cost 33 [$133], for 37 [$137], or something in the neighborhood, leaving a balance in her favor of about $27,000, and . . . a check for $25,000 had been sent." It is possible that Corbin and Gould had lied to Fisk in order to induce their ebullient colleague to get Mrs. Grant's name out on the grapevine, but Fisk's manner when talking to the congressional investigators suggested that he had long known and accepted with equanimity the fact that she was a fellow speculator.[9]

In the middle of September, soon after the third conversation with Grant, Gould once again became nervous, not about Grant this time, but about Boutwell. He knew that his Wall Street enemies the contractionists were working hard to persuade the secretary of the treasury to adopt a policy of selling gold and buying and retiring greenbacks, and that they had planned a dinner party for Boutwell. Wondering if it was possible that the president might change his mind and agree to the government's sale of gold, or that Boutwell might do so on his own authority, and drive the price of gold down, he looked to Corbin for reassurance. "I went to see Mr. Corbin about it," Gould testified at the congressional investigation, and "he said he did not think it possible, the President had so thoroughly made up his mind. . . ." Corbin, because "he knew the man so well" was confident that his brother-in-law, who had "arrived at his conclusions after a good deal of deliberation and examination," would not change them.[10]

Gould, who did not want this important matter left to chance, persuaded Corbin to write a long letter to the president, which proved to be a hortatory lecture on the benefit to the nation of not depressing the market by the sale of government gold holdings. The Grants were then visiting relatives of Julia's in Washington, Pennsylvania, and Fisk provided a trusted messenger, W. O. Chapin, to make sure the brotherly letter reached its destination. Later, no one seemed clear on whether Chapin reached the western Pennsylvania city on September 18, 19, or 20; the nineteenth is most likely. Grant and Porter were playing croquet when Chapin arrived—a proper, well-dressed Wall Street messenger, appearing important, but in fact simply a dutiful employee unaware of the significance of the letter he carried. Not spoiling the president's shot, a servant told Porter that a gentleman was waiting, and Porter replied that they would be in as soon as the game was finished. As they entered the house, Porter went into the parlor to receive Chapin, while Grant remained on the porch. Porter then asked Grant to come into the parlor; the president took the letter from the messenger, and walked back out on the porch to read it. Porter, exceedingly curious, followed him, but later he pointedly said that he had walked out "in another direction"—that is, he did not sneak a look. Grant did not read the letter to him, and Porter went back into the parlor and chatted with Chapin about the weather. Grant presently returned, and the messenger, anxious to be of service, asked if there was any reply. Grant said that everything was all right, that there was no answer, and the man left the house, went to town in his buggy, and sent a telegram to New York: "Delivered. All right."[11]

Back at the house, his curiosity aroused, Porter asked the president who the man was. Grant had assumed he was simply an accommodating local postman, but Porter told him that he had come with a letter of introduction from Corbin. It was clear to Porter, as it now was to Grant, that Corbin had gone to the great trouble of sending a specially chosen messenger equipped with credentials that would ensure his letter's being put straight into Grant's hands. Corbin's urgency was approaching desperation, and now, at last, Ulysses Grant smelled a rat. The letter from Abel was not a selfless treatise on the wisdom of one economic measure in contrast to another.[12]

Julia was in the library, reading and answering a second letter brought by the messenger—one written to her by Jennie Corbin. Ulysses walked in and asked her to whom she was writing. Julia, in her *Memoirs*, recorded this less than blissful moment in her marriage: "I answered, 'your sister.' He said: 'Write this.' Then he dictated. . . ." Now, Ulysses Grant did not dictate to his wife; if he did so in that instance—and the word is hers—it was because she was in a compromising position. Around the household, she was in charge; she did not silently defer to her lord and master, particularly on money matters, unless she was in a very tight spot. She later recalled that in the "delightful" eight years in the White House, "there were some dark clouds in the bright sky." She was referring to this day when one very dark cloud indeed fell over Washington, Pennsylvania—just before "that dreadful Black Friday."[13]

According to Corbin and Gould, the only two men known to have read Julia's letter to Jennie Corbin, she wrote her sister-in-law, "Tell your husband that my husband is very much annoyed by your speculations. You must close them as quick as you can!" This would have been understood by Jennie as a warning that the president was not prepared to be duped any further and would instead size up the market without reference to possible harm to his sister and her husband. The possibility that gold might be sold by the government was not stated. It did not need to be. The letter was signed "Sis." There are not a great many of Julia Grant's letters extant, and it is impossible to know how frequently she used such a term; there were certainly some occasions on which she and her relatives did use the affectionate nickname "Sis." In any event, its adoption in this instance strikes one as a highly convenient way to avoid having "Julia Grant" attached to a very sensitive and authoritative document.[14]

Meanwhile, in New York, the telegram saying everything was all right had been received, and Fisk, Gould, and Corbin took it to mean not that the message had been delivered, but that Grant had acquiesced to the logic of Corbin's letter and would not sell gold. On the evening of September 22 Fisk talked with Mr. and Mrs. Corbin at their house:

> Mrs. Corbin came into the room. I had been introduced to Mrs. Corbin before. The thing had gone beyond . . . mere courtesy. . . . That was the first time I had seen her in reference to this transaction. We sat down and talked the matter over quite fully. I did not cover any matters up. I took it for granted that they had bought gold, and . . . had as much interest in the matter as I had. She made this remark: "I know there will be no gold sold by the government; I am quite positive there will be no gold sold; for this is a chance of a lifetime for us; you need not have any uneasiness whatever."[15]

On September 23 the Corbins opened their mail and were terrified by the letter from dear "Sis." The jig was up; Ulysses was on to what they were doing. When in the later investigation Congressman Norman B. Judd asked repeatedly, "What do you mean by 'Sis'?" Corbin replied, "I mean just what I say. That was the signature to the letter. I am so agitated. . . . I am a little excited, very weak, and very nervous. I am perfectly broken down, and there is but a wreck left." But the questioner did not relent, and Corbin had to resume his testimony and state that he was sure the letter was from his wife's sister-in-law. He also described how he had reacted when shown the letter: "I was very much excited, and my wife still more so—such rumors were so disgraceful. . . . Engaged in buying and selling gold; what a terrible thing! . . . I never did have a more unhappy day than I had when witnessing the distress which that letter inflicted upon my wife. I must get out instantly— instantly!"[16]

It was not until evening that Corbin got Gould to call at his house and showed him the letter. Barely credulous, one of the investigating congressmen asked, "Did you put it into his hands?" Corbin replied, "No, sir. The correspondence was between two ladies. . . . We were in my library, sitting under one of the chandeliers, in front of the table, so that he might possibly have looked over my shoulder and seen it; but I think [he was] too much of a gentleman to do that." Gould recalled no such delicate indiscretion: "I took the letter in my hands, and of course I had to glance at the whole of it. He [Corbin] called my attention to the particular parts." Gould could see, as Corbin had, that there was no longer any assurance that the government would not sell gold. Indeed, the opposite was likely.[17]

Now the question for both of them was how to get out of the market without starting a panic that would depreciate their holdings before they could sell them. Corbin tried to get Gould to buy his account, so he could say to his brother-in-law that he owned no speculative gold. Gould refused to bail Corbin out. Instead he maneuvered to lock him in and proposed giving him a check for $100,000 to feed out to parties of interest. Gould did not dare permit the sale of Corbin's gold for fear it would trigger a collapse in the market, and he still wanted to hold Corbin hostage against Grant's actions. On the night of September 23, talking to Gould, Corbin still hoped to use his supposed influence over Grant to save the speculators' day. He wanted Gould to agree to buy his gold; then he would write the president that "he had not a dollar of interest in gold or governments," and would urge the president, as a disinterested observer, not to allow Boutwell to sell any gold. Said Gould, "I did not bite. . . ."[18]

Gould had to keep Corbin in the deal: "Mr. Corbin, I am undone if that letter gets out." Perhaps $100,000 would ensure that it would not, and that Corbin would stay in the market. Gould urged Corbin to think about it overnight. Returning to the Corbins' on Friday morning, September 24, Gould was admitted to the hall of the house, and standing at the foot of the stairs, said to the old man on the landing, "If you will remain in and take the chances of the market I will give you my check for $100,000." Jennie Corbin joined her husband at the railing and pleaded with him to give up the speculation. Corbin turned to his caller: "Mr. Gould[,] my wife says, 'No; Ulysses thinks it wrong, and that it ought to end.' " Gould's reaction was later described by Corbin to the investigators: "Mr. Gould stood there for a little while looking very thoughtful—exceedingly thoughtful. He then left—about 10 o'clock—and went into Wall Street. . . ." There Gould forced the price of gold still higher on the basis of the fact that Corbin was still in the market, which, he implied, meant that Mrs. Grant too was still in the market. Then Gould began, anonymously, selling from his own gold account; he knew what was apt to be coming from the Treasury.[19]

Meanwhile, the Grants had had enough of croquet and left Washington, Pennsylvania, for the District of Columbia. Secretary Boutwell also arrived in the capital on Thursday, September 23, and that evening he and the president had a conference at the White House. The belief was that a price of about $145 an ounce would encourage the sale of wheat abroad. But now the price of gold was expected to go still higher. The gold market no longer reflected foreign trade; runaway speculation had begun. The president and the secretary of the treasury, recalling the panic of 1857, agreed that if the

price went up again on Friday they would sell government gold to drive the
price down. The next morning, with the price still climbing, the only question remaining was how much gold to sell. The two men, meeting alone, discussed the amount. Boutwell proposed $3,000,000; Grant—with the convic-
tion of a convert—suggested $5,000,000; finally, they settled on $4,000,000.
The sell order was sent over two telegraph lines, to ensure its arrival and to
deprive Butterfield, whom they may already have suspected of collusion, of
the opportunity to get advance notice to anyone. They did take the risk that
some telegraph-company employees might have been paid to tip off a broker,
who could then act seconds before the news became public. In any event, regardless of whether any other traders sneaked out whole, as Gould did, there
was no stopping the impact of the government's sale of gold. The telegram
reached New York at 11:57 A.M. The price of gold had passed $160 at 11:53
but perhaps because of Gould's gold sales, had begun to fall by 11:54, before
the arrival of the telegram. The result of the government's sale was a rout. By
12:07 the price was down to $140. It was a day of hysterical trading in the
Gold Room. Some men were ruined. Others, who had gambled that the
price would fall, became rich. Because of the collapse, Corbin could not realize enough on the sale of his gold to cover the loan he had taken out to buy it.
Although not altogether ruined, he did find himself in greatly diminished circumstances. The Corbins moved to Jersey City.[20]

Black Friday caused severe panic in the gold-buying community and in the
financial world that supplied the credit for its speculations. One bank, the
Tenth National Bank of New York, failed, but a general recession like the
one that was to be triggered by the failure of Jay Cooke in 1873 did not occur.
Had the government in the preceding months not tried to be neutral but instead participated actively—buying or selling gold as necessary to keep the
market stable—the game would not have been the speculators' alone. It
would then have been possible to execute either an expansionist or a contractionist policy without causing the kind of panic that broke out when, after no
activity for so long a period, the government sold gold worth $4,000,000. (It
is interesting that so small a sum could have so large an effect. The total
amount of money in 1869 was very limited indeed.)

The Congress that voted to investigate the circumstances of the panic was
in the control of Grant's own party, but the committee nevertheless subjected the administration to close scrutiny. As a result of its findings, General
Butterfield was forced to resign; Grant had suffered his first experience of the
exposure of a corrupt official in his administration. The chairman of the committee, Congressman James A. Garfield of Ohio, worked hard to convert the
taking of testimony into a seminar on monetary questions. A champion of
"sound money," he wanted the events in the Gold Room on Black Friday
turned into a metaphor for the horrors of an expansionist monetary policy.
The committee Democrats, on the other hand, doggedly focused their attention on matters less exalted than economic theory. They wanted to question

Mrs. Corbin and Mrs. Grant about whether the Corbins' account was also, in fact, Julia Dent Grant's speculative account. The Republican majority blocked the summons of the two women to appear as witnesses, but did not prevent a limited inquiry into a mysterious shipment that had arrived that fall at the White House for Julia. Rumors that the first lady had received a package that did not contain clothes or curtains led to a check of the records of the Adams Express Company. Suspicious congressmen wondered if the amount of money—apparently in cash—delivered to Mrs. Grant was $2,500, even though a clerk at Adams's insisted that there had always been a decimal point in the figure listed in the record book and that Mrs. Grant had received only $25.00.

No firm proof exists that the packet of money was connected with a speculation by Julia Grant, but why would she have received cash in the mail unless someone could not write her a check? And why had Ulysses been so uncharacteristically stern with her when he discovered her writing the letter to his sister on that "dreadful" day? Julia was both naive and shrewd. She knew little of the ways of the New York financial world, but she knew everything about being deprived of money. She believed fervently that her Ulysses—and she—deserved well of the Republic, and she lived in a world that, in large part, saw rewards in terms of money. They had been able to accept gratefully railroad passes and houses with closets full of fine linen, financed by subscription; why could there not be a small loan permitting her to make a perfectly legal investment? But if Grant's wife as well as his sister had been involved in the speculation, did he now fear that he was in danger of exposure as having been a party to Julia's attempt to add to their not very stable fortune? We do not know. We do know that here, in the fall of his first year as president, the greed for money of people at least as close as his sister had left its touch on his administration.

There was still another dimension of ugliness to the frantic money grubbing of September 1869; this was the fact that it coincided with the death of Ulysses Grant's closest friend. John A. Rawlins had consumption, the "dreaded dark disease." In August, while with his young wife and three infant children at her family place in Danbury, Connecticut, Rawlins had an attack, but when he received notice of a cabinet meeting he set off for Washington. His wife, possibly afraid the children would catch the disease, stayed behind. In New York he had another hemorrhage but, on a hot dusty day, insisted on making the trip to the capital. In Washington he again hemorrhaged, and Grant and Hamilton Fish, who had come down from New York for the meeting, were surprised to see Rawlins at his customary place at the cabinet table, next to the president.[21]

Grant had watched his brother Simpson die of tuberculosis; there had been lapses and recoveries and then the long final process of the disease. Now Rawlins had the same affliction, and Grant must have known his friend would die. The day after the cabinet meeting, Rawlins sought out Grant at the White House; after a long visit, Grant said good-by to his closest friend and resumed his restless summer travels, going north in a private railroad car to rejoin Julia at Saratoga. There the Grants prepared for a side trip to Utica with Senator Roscoe Conkling. But on Sunday, September 5, while on his way back from church with Horace Porter, Grant was handed a message saying that Rawlins was not expected to survive the day. At the hotel he wrote Conkling a note, asking to be excused from the Utica trip because he wanted to get back to Rawlins, although, Conkling reported him as saying, "[I] scarcely . . . [have] a hope I may see him alive."[22]

Rawlins, alone in Washington without his wife or best friend, was tended by another of the band of men who had been so close during the war, Ely Parker. That Sunday, Tecumseh Sherman was also at his bedside, as was Jacob Cox, who had known neither Grant nor Rawlins intimately during the war, but had come to visit his cabinet colleague. As Rawlins talked—or struggled to—Cox became intensely aware of how powerful was the pull of friendship between Rawlins and Grant. At one point, when they expected him to die at any moment, Rawlins said to Sherman, "What time is it?" And as Sherman looked at his watch, Rawlins said, "When will he get here?" Sherman gently lied: "In about ten minutes."[23]

Grant had not yet left Saratoga. He did not know if he had too little time or plenty with which to reach Rawlins, he disliked disrupting Julia's plans, and, with little taste for melodrama, he wished to avoid summoning a special train on a Sunday afternoon. At 4:45 a telegram arrived from Sherman, saying that Rawlins was calling for Grant, and the president realized he must go at once. Julia, possibly fearing for her own children and, consciously or unconsciously, resentful of Rawlins, did not want to go to Washington. So Ulysses set out without her, on the 5:50 train. (Julia followed the next day, as far as the Corbins', in New York; the White House, being redecorated, was still "uninhabitable," was the excuse given the press for her staying away from Washington.) On the train a private area had been screened off in a dining car for the president, but he had to endure the company of Roscoe Conkling and Judge Ward Hunt, who had come to escort him to Utica. When he got off the train, Conkling told reporters that Grant was "melancholy" and "talked of little else but the close relationship that had long been held between himself and General Rawlins."[24]

Reaching Albany a little after 7:00, Grant was dismayed not to find the special train he thought had been arranged for. Rather than wait until 2:00 A.M. for the next regular train to come through from Chicago, he took the night boat to New York and spent much of the maddeningly placid trip south on the Hudson sitting alone on deck, talking to no one. The boat docked early in the morning; he took a taxi to the Astor House for breakfast and a conference with Jay Gould, then another taxi and a ferry to Jersey City, where, again, a promised special train was not waiting. On the regular train, at Wilmington, he was given a message that Rawlins was sinking. At Baltimore, the special locomotive and car at last appeared, and he sped the last lap of the trip into Washington. Sherman and Cox were on the platform and, his face immobile in sorrow, "the President almost buried himself in the carriage," during the drive from the station. Ulysses Grant walked into John Rawlins's room at 5:15 P.M.; his friend had died at 4:12.[25]

When the doctor told the president how his patient had repeatedly called for him, Grant could only mutter that he had wanted to be there. Flooded with frustration, he "explained to Dr. Bliss the obstacles that lay in the way of his reaching here sooner." Then, as if he had been there on time, he sat down and wrote a message of condolence to Mrs. Rawlins: "Your beloved husband expired at twelve minutes after four this afternoon. . . ."[26]

The meaning of the death of John Rawlins to Ulysses Grant lay not in the removal of an honest voice of humanitarian conscience, great though that loss was. Grant had never seen Rawlins as a mere adviser; he was a friend. He was the friend Grant had been deprived of as a boy and as a young man. He had been powerfully present during the intense years of the war; they had been through it together. No one could replace John Rawlins. Now in the first year of the frightening business of the presidency, Rawlins was stolen from Grant, and he had not even been on hand to protest the theft.

# XXI

# ENGLAND AND
# SANTO DOMINGO

The hostility of England to the United States during our rebellion was
not so much real as it was apparent.
— *Ulysses S. Grant*

Santo Domingo was freely offered to us, not only by the
administration, but by all the people, almost without price.
— *Ulysses S. Grant*

GENERAL GRANT'S CIVIL WAR was, of course, the great event
of Abraham Lincoln's presidency; the absence of civil and international war
was the greatest of Ulysses Grant's. With the major exception of the warfare
against the Indian peoples on the plains, no military conflict occurred during
Grant's administration, and most historians would consider the settlement of
a major controversy with Great Britain without resort to arms as the prime
accomplishment of his presidency. In point of fact, however, he scarcely
gave the settlement with England the time of day, but complained bitterly
for the rest of his life that he had been unable to annex the Dominican
Republic and thereby consummate an energetic effort in Caribbean imperialism.

Grant's two major international diplomatic enterprises differed strikingly
in style. One resulted in an exemplary resolution of a family quarrel by the
most gentlemanly means; it has served as a beacon of enlightened diplomacy
ever since. The other is customarily pictured as a cheap effort to buy a bit of
Caribbean real estate. What was more, the purchase seemed to have been attempted without the slightest regard for the wishes of the people who lived
on the island, but with intense regard for the pocketbooks of the brokers of

the deal, one of whom lived in the White House. The first of these diplomatic enterprises was the successful settlement of the Alabama claims against Great Britain. The second was the unsuccessful attempt to annex the Dominican Republic—or Santo Domingo, as Grant called it.

As in the matter of Black Friday, one needs to consider style critically. It is easy to be swept along by a cast headed by Sir Edward this, Sir John that, and an Adams or two, through three acts of a comedy of mild irascibility and impeccable good manners, culminating in an uncritical burst of Anglo-American self-applause. What of the substance of the agreement? Some very rich bankers got richer because of the settlement of the Alabama claims without a war. (Once, in a cabinet meeting, on being advised that the position of the United States government would be strengthened by employment of the house of Morton & Rose as disbursing agent in London, Grant sardonically asked Secretary of State Hamilton Fish if Morton's firm might perhaps be strong because of the government's patronage rather than the other way around.) The bankers deserve praise for helping avoid war—they were not the only beneficiaries of peace—but are they to be seen as selfless men of virtue, while the men, no more and no less acquisitive, who failed to take over Santo Domingo are castigated? Is the Santo Domingo matter fairly understood as an aging, steamy, little out-of-date production, peopled with Sidney Greenstreets and Peter Lorres and individuals carrying not very clearly remembered Latin American names?

After all, Charles Sumner tried to wreck both deals, and that alone makes one want to take a close look at both. President Grant himself could never appear interested in the Alabama-claims matter—except to tell Fish to get it settled before the next election—and yet it is called the greatest feather in his peacetime cap. On the other hand, he cared greatly about the annexation of Santo Domingo, and he made his claim for this annexation on the grounds of the highest of policy. He saw it as a vital part of the solution of the nation's race problem. One can doubt not only the practicality but also the wisdom of establishing an all-black American state to which discontented former slaves would be invited to migrate; but one cannot, in the face of Grant's definition of the annexation in such terms, dismiss the effort to achieve it simply as corrupt money grubbing.

To take handsome matters first, the Alabama claims covered a host of disputes between Great Britain and the United States. There was the eternal question of fishing rights on the banks off the coast of New England, the question of the unfixed boundary in the coastal bays between the United States and British Columbia, and the problem of Great Britain's unwillingness to recognize as American citizens those former subjects who had emigrated and been naturalized (including people of Irish ancestry who, on returning to the old sod, might find useful the protection of their American citizenship). But the focus of the controversy was the damage done American shipping and the American cause during the Civil War by five ships—the

*Florida*, the *Georgia*, the *Rappahannock*, the *Shenandoah*, and most famously, the *Alabama*—that had been built in British dockyards and used by the Confederacy. These vessels destroyed Union ships, disrupted the blockade, and terrorized Northern commercial shippers. Insurance rates went up, and 750 American ships were transferred to foreign flags.

Charles Francis Adams, the wartime minister to London, had tried unsuccessfully to persuade the British government to make retribution with a monetary settlement. After Adams was recalled in 1868, Andrew Johnson's next minister, Reverdy Johnson, worked out a moderate compromise with Lord Clarendon, the British foreign secretary. But Reverdy Johnson was out of favor with the Republicans in the Senate. They detested him for his cordiality to Confederate sympathizers in England and saw him as the discredited envoy of a discredited president. Shortly after Grant's inauguration, on April 13, 1869, the Johnson-Clarendon Convention was rejected by the Senate.

Things were going from bad to worse, and it was Charles Sumner who was carrying them there. The magnificent defender of the equality of humankind in general and of black Americans in particular was, nonetheless, a man of unpredictable enthusiasms. Ulysses Grant got along less well with that handsome, vain, lonely, and ambitious man than with any other person he encountered in his entire life. As the conscience of the party and the chairman of the Senate Foreign Relations Committee, Sumner expected the new president to defer to him. Or rather, he expected to be asked to be secretary of state. Grant had learned to dislike Sumner long before he chose a cabinet. He not only passed him by for the post but did not ask his advice about whom he should appoint. It was bad enough for Sumner when Grant appointed Washburne, a bumpkin whom the Harvard man could scorn (and could anticipate dominating); it was still worse when Grant beat Sumner at his own game by naming Hamilton Fish, an aristocratic gentleman from New York. Before Grant could do so, Sumner had sought to define the lines of American international policy. He made the Alabama-claims issue his own in the Senate debate over the Johnson-Clarendon Convention and gave expression to his odd, vitriolic anglophobia in a demand for a huge payment— amounting to $2,500,000,000—for the "indirect" damage done the American cause by the ships built in Great Britain, instead of payment for direct losses, which Hamilton Fish calculated at $48,000,000. The smaller amount—subject to compromise—was not too large a price for peace. Insistence on the larger sum would mean war. Sumner did not seem to mind that this was where he was leading the nation. Charles Francis Adams thought his difficult friend took this bellicose position out of a perverse want of "virility." It was a kind of wild will to self-destruction. Sumner was asking for enough money to obstruct any peaceful settlement, and he was doing so in a way that would undermine everyone's confidence in his ability to provide the leadership for the attainment of that settlement, or any other policy objective of the Grant administration.[1]

Like William Henry Seward and Hamilton Fish, Sumner had in mind that Canada would be a convenient substitute for the money sought for wartime damages to the United States. In addition, Sumner was determined that England admit its guilt. Massachusetts people like to get other people to do this. To Sumner, a tidy commercial sum would not express sufficient contrition. Only a huge payment—a vast settlement—would fully signify acceptance of a "moral debt." Sumner's way of speaking was so extreme that it made moderates who were demanding some recompense sound like apologists for England. It foreclosed useful public debate on the issue and forced Fish and Edward Thornton, the British minister in Washington, to negotiate in private.

Those negotiations would have made a fine Trollope novel. In January, in order to improve Anglo-American relations, Thornton—he became Sir Edward in 1870—urged Fish to get Grant to attend a dinner in honor of Prince Arthur, Queen Victoria's nineteen-year-old son, then visiting the United States. The president could not understand why a grown man should be respectful of a boy; he was as unenthusiastic as he was to be nine years later when he refused to demean himself before the boy emperor of China. He was not going to any dinners for visiting children. In London, one of the male old ladies in the American minister's office approved of Grant's refusal, remembering that the queen had been willing to receive former President Fillmore only after President Buchanan had insisted. In Washington, Baron Gerolt of Prussia called on Fish to protest Grant's discourtesy. Would the queen call on Grant's twenty-year-old son? asked Fish, when the ambassador complained of Grant's rudeness. Teacups were rattling, but a resolution was reached that did not require unwilling men and boys to sit down together. Grant and Fish, standing, received the prince in the Blue Room of the White House; Julia and her father were in the Red Room, where "the Prince and suite were presented." At Thornton's dinner for the cabinet and the vice-president, the prince gratefully toasted the secretary of state for his tactful and safe handling of the Fenians—the Irish-Americans who had threatened an invasion of Canada and a return to Ireland to gain its independence. Fish replied with fitting modesty. The Grants agreed to appear at the ball for the prince, once again standing, and old protocolist Benjamin Brown French, ever alert to his social duties, waited till he saw the president's carriage, then hurried up the stairs to bring the prince down to greet the head of state.[2]

"I could have wished the President had been more courteous," complained Thornton to Clarendon: "But the President is naturally the most uncouth man I have ever met with, and has on this occasion intentionally endeavored to show by his conduct to the Prince that the people of the U.S. consider themselves aggrieved by us." More negotiations were clearly needed, and with His Royal Highness still in Washington, Fish and Thornton proceeded. The secretary of state, now with his own version of claims for "indirect" damages, asked when Britain would pay its $200,000,000. Thornton responded by talking of $25,000,000, and said, "You would not expect us to pay more than you would yourselves." "Certainly we do—we expect liberality from you," retorted Fish playfully. Thornton replied, "What of that oppressed, tax-ridden, down-trodden monarchy." Fish recorded this exchange in his diary, including the fact that he and his friend were soon laughing. Thornton ended the conversation by saying that America's debt was its own protective wealth because the instruments of that debt, American bonds, were in many a London portfolio: "What would an Englishman think himself worth, without a large bundle of 'Consols'."[3]

It was all good clubmen's talk. And many other commercial gentlemen—commercial, but decidedly gentlemen—joined in. The international bankers did not want a war, instead they wanted an easy flow of commerce, the trading in securities that represented British investment in American and Canadian economic development. Rising quickly in that immense investment field were Levi P. Morton of New York and John Rose, a Scotsman who had made a fortune in Canada and returned to London to enjoy it. The firm of Morton & Rose replaced Baring Brothers as disbursing agent for the United States government in Great Britain, and both Morton (who, not incidentally, had contributed liberally to the Grant campaign) and Rose worked tirelessly and effectively to get the claims issue settled peaceably, and for a sensible sum.

The negotiations needed to be pressed. From London, on January 29, 1870, Benjamin Moran, an official in the American ministry, wrote his intimate friend Adam Badeau that "John Bull is getting into a bad temper with us." The radical politician John Bright, a consistent friend of the North during the war, was ill, and Moran worried about the effect of his absence from public affairs on America's chances for a peaceful settlement. On the other hand, Moran found that the reminiscences of the aged Earl Russell contained admissions helpful to the American cause. Russell, whom Moran thought "as sapless as Charles Francis Adams," had been foreign secretary at the time the ships were fitted out, and now he acknowledged the British government's complicity. Fish, heartened by this admission, went right on, in his courtly way, talking to Thornton. His hope was that the English would prove careless about Canada and agree to let it become independent or perhaps join the United States, as many Americans assumed it inevitably would. The independence or annexation of Canada would settle differences with America; it would be in the natural order of things. Moran said that "we should get Canada while Gladstone is in power." He had the Bahamas in mind, as well. The territorial grabbing that was in the air was distinctly disconcerting to the English.[4]

While the gentlemanly negotiations of the Alabama claims were slowly proceeding, Grant was occupied with another undertaking—the effort to annex Santo Domingo. The president never saw the two matters in contrast. He was a man of simple logic. If it made sense to settle a quarrel with the English to avoid war, encourage commerce, and further the economic development of the American empire, then it made sense to annex Santo Domingo to encourage commerce in the Caribbean. There America would find a new frontier region with mineral resources as well as space into which troubled black people, harassed by the Klan, could move. They would then be among fellow blacks, but would still be Americans.

For the rest of his life, Grant did not waver from this belief. He did not take a racist view of foreign affairs, but others did. In its account of Grant's New Year's Day reception in 1870, the *New York Herald*, under the heading "A Gorgeous Nigger," told of the arrival of the Haitian minister, General Alexander Tate, in a swallow-tailed coat with elaborate gold braid on its collar and lapels. Grant was cordial as he shook his hand, but other diplomats snubbed Tate; Postmaster General Creswell, noticing this, went over and had an amiable conversation with him. (United States citizens fared less well; the *Herald* reported that in the line of people waiting to be received, the blacks had been sent to the rear. This was done, the paper explained, "on account of the odor that might have troubled . . . the white ladies and gentlemen. . . .") Buenaventura Báez, the president of the Dominican Republic, at the other end of Tate's island, was a mulatto—in North American terms black, because his mother was black—but this made little difference in Grant's thinking about annexation. Others, then and now, have made a distinction between the character of the negotiations with white gentlemen over the Alabama claims and those with black opportunists about the Dominican annexation. Grant did not; to him both John Rose, in the former case, and Báez, in the latter, were perfectly respectable speculators out to make themselves richer. To be sure, Báez was shameless in his pursuit of the goal of relinquishing his country's independence in favor of its merger with a great power, but the subsequent unhappy history of his nation does not argue that his logic was totally flawed. Americans who eschew separatism do not like the image of black Americans going off to a black state in the Caribbean which they prefer to the unsatisfactory black-and-white world of other states. One wishes that Grant had solved the racial problems within the continental United States instead of espousing a latter-day colonizationist scheme. As things stood, some black Americans, disappointed by the failure of Reconstruction in their own South, went north and west into Kansas and Oklahoma. Migration is, after all, the classic American way of trying to solve a problem, and whatever one thinks of a segregated settlement, the proposal to annex Santo Domingo is not evidence that Grant was applying unrealistic logic to the harsh situation that the freedmen faced.[5]

The Santo Domingo story began before Grant became president. William Henry Seward, secretary of state under Lincoln and Johnson, was an ardent expansionist; he thought he had found the ideal peaceful route to achieve America's manifest destiny: in the Age of Capital he would buy that which he would possess. He purchased Alaska, tried to buy the Danish West Indies, and had negotiated for the Dominican Republic during the Johnson administration. These negotiations were reopened early in the Grant administration by Colonel J. W. Fabens and General William Cazneau (ranks courtesy of the Republic of Texas). These two cagey operators enlisted as an ally Orville E. Babcock, who, living in the White House, could easily communicate his enthusiasms to the president. And Babcock was soon immensely enthusiastic about Santo Domingo.

Orville Babcock was another of those totally unexceptional men whom Grant trusted. Born in 1835 in a small town in northern Vermont, he graduated from West Point in 1861 and was assigned to the corps of engineers and sent to the front, where he served ably in various commands. During the Chattanooga campaign, he was placed in charge of building bridges critical to the defense of Knoxville. It was there that Grant met the slight, dark-eyed, forthright officer. Grant brought him onto his staff in 1864, and Babcock was soon given assignments that involved the general's intimate concerns. It was Babcock who was sent by Grant to see how Sherman fared in Georgia in 1864, and who on several occasions was sent to convey Grant's wishes to Stanton. After the death of John Rawlins in 1869, Babcock was Grant's closest friend. Except for Daniel Ammen, with whom he maintained a rather remote relationship, Grant had no lifelong friends. One by one he separated from all of his wartime associates; he let go of Babcock not because he was the crook that the whole country believed the man to be, but because he had lied to Grant. Only as Babcock was banished from the White House did he, too, drift out of Grant's life.

Babcock had none of the fire and moral force of Rawlins. Rather, he was an agreeable man, friendly, convivial, and shrewd. He had a knack for knowing when and where Grant's attention was focused and an ability to articulate Grant's enthusiasms. Babcock's was a voice in the White House saying yes in language that was neither obsequious nor condescending. That he was never threatening to Grant was not the least of the reasons why he commanded a loyalty from his chief that no other man achieved.

Babcock early took hold of the Santo Domingo negotiations; he and Grant were at one in their eagerness to annex that beautiful but troubled island. Despite his anti-imperialist reactions to the American invasion of Mexico, Grant began his presidency with expansionist enthusiasms. His friend John Rawlins had wanted to help the Cubans in their bitter struggle with Spain, and Babcock's eager reports from Santo Domingo were to strike a similar note, though never with the humanitarian reverberations that Rawlins added.

Hamilton Fish wanted to hear nothing of either Caribbean adventure. As early as April 1869, in a cabinet meeting, he tried to stay Grant's eagerness with the comment that Congress would not have time to get to the matter of Santo Domingo. Babcock, on the other hand, had every intention of getting to it. In July, carrying a letter of credence signed by Grant and a passport signed reluctantly by Fish, identifying him as a "special agent" of the United

States, Babcock went off on his steamy pursuit of empire. At the end of the month, he wrote his bride, more comfortably situated in East Hampton, Long Island, that he had declined an invitation from President Báez to stay in the presidential palace but was not totally wanting for comfort—he had brought his own bathing tub on the *Tybee*. He thought Santo Domingo a "dull country," rather like an army post. He had done a bit of exploring and had attended a "performance" of mass in the cathedral. The young man found the seventy-year-old American consul in the city of Santo Domingo "perfectly unfit for the place," and he did not think any more of those whom he intended to make his countrymen: "The people are indolent and ignorant. The best class of people are the American Negroes who have come here from time to time."[6]

In August, still in Santo Domingo, he gave orders to a navy ship, the *Tuscora*, to move in to deflect a "pirate" ship, the *Telegrafo*, that was harassing President Báez. The *Telegrafo* was in the service of a rebel citizen of the Dominican Republic, Gregorio Luperon, who was quite likely the most trustworthy exponent of the wishes of the Dominicans. A black man, he identified himself not with the exploiting upper classes on the island, but with the people. Later, two other navy ships were sent by Secretary of the Navy George M. Robeson, to protect Báez's government from invaders from Haiti and to intimidate dissidents led by Luperon in the republic itself. The American navy kept Grant's Dominican allies in power while the annexation negotiations progressed.[7]

Back in the United States in September 1869, Babcock wrote Cazneau that he had given Grant his report recommending annexation, and asked Cazneau to see Báez and make sure that he did not obtain a loan from the British. Babcock did not want any other power to beat him to the draw. There was, however, one major problem, which he discussed in the letter: "The question of 'State' as used in the confidential communication caused some consternation. I assured the President that we had discussed the question and that President Baez . . . understood St. Domingo *could not* be *admitted* as a state, but that she would have to be treated as a territory until she had conformed to the requirements of the *United States* for admission as a state."[8]

Those like Benjamin Moran who dreamed of "an American front, representing the two continents from Cape Prince of Wales to Cape Horn" welcomed the negotiations with men like Báez. Moran, in London, tired of English snobbery—at least some of it—wrote his friend Adam Badeau, "I notice with unfeigned pleasure what you say about the President's feeling towards the South American and Central American Republics." The people who came from them were not universally welcome in England: "The representatives here complain much and justly of the cold treatment they receive . . . here, none of them ever having been invited to Marlborough House, and not one to Windsor for years." Moran was not afraid of including some Spanish-speaking cousins in an American hemispheric family. Other observers, how-

ever, saw only black, black, black, when they thought of the possible inclusion of Santo Domingo among the United States. Orville Babcock was one of
the band of Reconstruction men who were nicely color-blind—who saw the
postwar world as fresh and new and were eager to seize its opportunities.
Unfortunately, this spirit often became clouded with an opportunism that ignored ethical values in the pursuit of personal gain, as Babcock demonstrated
in his eager efforts to obtain the annexation of Santo Domingo. In the fall of
1869 he returned to the republic's capital city, this time accompanied by
another of Grant's old friends, General Rufus Ingalls.⁹

   While they negotiated in Santo Domingo, the president attempted to do
the cause some good in Washington. On Sunday, January 2, 1870, Ulysses
Grant set out to pay a call. It was early evening, and he walked out of the
White House and across Lafayette Square to the home of Senator Charles
Sumner. The butler was undaunted at seeing the president of the United
States and was about to refuse the caller, because the senator was at a meal,
when Sumner heard Grant's voice and went to the door. Flattered but not
flustered, he invited Grant to join him at the table, where he was dining with
two newspapermen, John W. Forney and Ben Perley Poole, and Grant
kindly obliged.

   Protocol had been shattered. Grant had done, in Bancroft Davis's words,
"what probably no President ever did before under the same circumstances."
He had come hat in hand to ask the powerful senator to support the annexation of Santo Domingo. Sumner himself said, "Never before have I known a
President to take any such interest in a treaty." Grant had left a conference
with Vice-President Colfax and Secretary Fish, at which he had allowed
himself, not for the first time, to vent his rage at Sumner by storming about
the senator's friend John Lothrop Motley, whom Grant had been cajoled into
sending to Great Britain as minister. Then, coolly, he had set out to seek
Sumner's support for his annexation treaty. Grant assumed that Sumner
would give this support once the worth of Santo Domingo to black Americans had been made clear to him. But Sumner, wanting black men treated as
equals within the United States, did not want to besmirch the republic by
making strange foreign territories part of it. In places such as Santo Domingo
black men were not schooled in Anglo-American values. To Sumner, the
proper man of color was represented by his colleague in the present session of
Congress, Hiram R. Revels, the dignified new senator from Mississippi—not
by Buenaventura Báez. Sumner did not like Grant's Santo Domingo scheme,
but he did not miss the fact that Grant knew he needed help and had come
seeking it. Grant did not like Sumner, but he was willing to pay court to him
to get Santo Domingo.¹⁰

   Instead of being asked what he had on his mind, Grant, sitting at Sumner's
table, had to hear the others discuss the woes of James M. Ashley, a pro-im-
peachment man, who had been fired as governor of the Montana Territory
and whom Sumner wanted reinstated. Grant was not very polite about Ash-

ley or any other subject not related to the purpose of his call, and he doggedly brought the talk around to Santo Domingo as, dinner over, the party moved into the library. In the years that followed, Grant insisted that Sumner agreed that evening to support annexation, and went back on his word when he vehemently opposed it. Admirers of Sumner claimed he turned the conversation to Montana and Ashley in a cunning move to avoid discussing Santo Domingo. But Grant recalled the talk of Ashley as a bid by Sumner for a patronage *quid pro quo*—an offer to support annexation in return for Ashley's restoration as governor. Some individuals, fascinated by the thought of a president calling on a senator, said, predictably, that he was drunk. Without doubt, Grant was determined to make Santo Domingo part of the United States. As commanding general he had been able to stroll over to the tent of another general, give his instructions, and, regardless of cordiality or lack of it, assume that he would be obeyed. Now he was doing more than he had been willing to do when General Joseph Hooker had expected him to call on him on the way to Chattanooga. On that occasion, Grant had said that Hooker could do the calling, and Hooker did. Sumner had been lofty since preinaugural days but had never demonstrated disobedience to Grant. Now Grant had gone to the extraordinary length of asking a Republican captain for support; it did not occur to him that the officer might prove directly insubordinate.

Five months later, when Sumner flatly defied Grant, John W. Forney told Orville Babcock that he distinctly remembered hearing Sumner say he was for annexation. Grant left the house assuming that Sumner's grand parting words signified support. Sumner had said, "Mr. President, I am an Administration man, and whatever you do will always find in me the most careful and candid consideration." The misunderstanding on the occasion of Grant's call was "destined to be," in David Herbert Donald's judgment, "the turning point in Grant's administration and in Sumner's career as well." But Grant did not know this as he walked back to the White House. He thought he had Sumner's vote.[11]

The time for annexation was now. One of Babcock's men, still in the republic, wrote in January 1870 that an invasion by Haiti was expected and emphatically urged Babcock to rush the treaty through. The informant also attempted to draw on State Department funds to pay those who had given him this information, but Bancroft Davis, the assistant secretary of state, starchily forwarded the informant's expense voucher to Babcock, at the White House. "My dear General," he wrote, "I believe that this budget belongs to you"; and he added, "I fear there is no hope that the treaty will make its way through the Senate. If there ever was a ghost of a chance the Davis Hatch case will kill it."[12]

Davis Hatch was probably no less a buccaneer than any of the other Captain Hooks who were interested in Santo Domingo. He was an American citizen and a businessman; he favored annexation, but he did not want it to come about to the benefit of Buenaventura Báez. Indeed, his opposition to Báez landed him in jail, and the opponents to annexation made excellent use of his plight, pointing out that by holding Hatch without trial and threatening him with execution, Báez made a mockery of the claims of Babcock and other supporters of the treaty that they were bringing into the Union a territory, ultimately to become a state, with the finest of governors. The Dominican Senate changed Hatch's sentence from death to banishment, but President Báez held him in jail nevertheless, because, it was alleged, his return to the United States would work against Báez and the pending treaty. Once he was released, Hatch brought formal charges against the United States government for not protecting him.[13]

In Washington, the maneuvering was considerable. On March 10, Charles Sumner, in his imperial manner, wrote Babcock that he hoped it would "be convenient for you to meet [tomorrow] the Committee on Foreign Relations . . . with regard to Dominica." The hearings were brief, and the next week Sumner permitted the treaty to come to the floor of the Senate, but five of the committee members disapproved of annexation, and only two, Oliver P. Morton and James Harland, sustained Grant's position. Edward Thornton, the British minister, writing to Lord Clarendon, reported that "Genl Badeau, who is very intimate with Grant," had stated that the president was "much disappointed and a good deal amazed at the prospect of the Santo Domingo Treaty." Grant was particularly "angry with Sumner, because when he first spoke with him, he promised to support it." Santo Domingo, or San Domingo (it was never granted an appellation that was comfortable within the American language) was not much wanted. Babcock, however, would not let the president give up, and in early April, Grant walked over to the Fishes' to talk about the endangered treaty with the secretary of state. He was troubled that Senator Lot M. Morrill of Maine had, that morning, urged him not to press for the annexation and certainly not for statehood. He judged correctly that he needed better support from the State Department if he was to convince enough senators to agree to annexation. To gain that support he went twice to Capitol Hill.[14]

One of Babcock's cohorts on the island had told him that if the consul then in Santo Domingo, John Somers Smith, could be promised a lucrative job at home, he could be counted on to break with the anti-Báez party—and to cease giving the State Department ammunition against annexation. Hamilton Fish probably never knew about this proposed bit of bribery, but he did know that Babcock was arranging for Colonel Fabens to see Grant directly. In the cabinet he suggested that such aggressive deportment by the annexationists would "down" the proposal in the Senate. Others in Washington were also curious about the aggressive lobbying. Edward Thornton reported to Lord Clarendon, "I cannot discover if Grant has any personal interest in the matter, tho' it is strange that he should be so tenacious with regard to its acceptance."[15]

On May 6, 1870, Fish loyally conferred with Senators Morton and William E. Chandler to ensure their enthusiastic support, but a week later Senator Carl Schurz called on the secretary to show him the results of a canvass he had made of 72 senators: with 32 opposed to annexation, the administration appeared far short of the required two-thirds vote. Grant was on a cruise on the Potomac; Fish, both impressed by the canvass and in agreement with Schurz's conclusion, could not get to the president. He told Bancroft Davis to see if the question of statehood could not be left moot. If annexation was to be gotten through the Senate, it would have to be with as few commitments as possible about the future of the island and its people.[16]

On June 1, with the cause of annexation in great trouble in the Senate, the State Department, which had its own sources of news, got a report from Santo Domingo denouncing Colonel Fabens as corrupt and calling Babcock a "damed rascal." That rascality was soon made a matter of public record; in June 1870, the Senate held public hearings into the Davis Hatch case. It was a wonderfully colorful proceeding complete with the details of a lurid shipboard murder. One of the witnesses at the hearing was Raymond H. Perry, the consul who had succeeded John Somers Smith. Perry, who was related to Commodore Oliver H. Perry, had been acquitted of repeated charges of being a mule thief during the war; his credentials for diplomacy had been established on the Texas frontier with General Philip H. Sheridan. His testimony at the committee meeting began with the following exchange with the chairman:

Q. Are you armed now?
A. Always.
Q. With what?
A. A revolver.

When the investigation had been completed, the majority report, by Republican loyalists, dismissed Hatch's claim for damages and exonerated Grant's men, but Carl Schurz's relentless and revealing interrogation of Generals Babcock and Ingalls, as well as of Davis Hatch and the two American consuls, Smith and Perry, suggested that Babcock and Ingalls had been given land on the Bay of Samaná which would greatly appreciate in value if either the whole Dominican Republic or just the bay area was acquired by the United States. And what was worse, as Schurz and two colleagues revealed in a damning report, Babcock had worked actively to keep Báez in power in order to accomplish the annexation, ordering the dispatch of navy vessels that prevented Luperon from carrying out a revolt, and acquiescing in the imprisonment of Hatch, under sentence of death, because he was a partisan of one of Báez's rivals. Carl Schurz, the nineteenth-century liberal par excellence, exposed Babcock's activities with respect to Santo Domingo in a way that was humiliating to Ulysses Grant. And Grant did not forget that he had done so. Schurz, claiming he had to stay within the mandate of the Senate to investigate only matters relating to Hatch, obviously did not stay there at all. He presented clear and conclusive evidence that Báez, Cazneau, Fabens, and Babcock were, from the time of Babcock's first visit in July 1869, so committed to annexation as to have no regard for any opponents, whether Dominican citizens or American citizens. However, Grant accepted the exoneration of Babcock by loyal senators, ignoring Schurz's allegations about him. Indeed, Grant regarded as directed at himself the attack Schurz seemed to him to be making on Babcock. As if to say he would take no such treatment from anyone, he set Babcock immovably in place. The damaging inquiry resulted not in Babcock's removal, but in his becoming entrenched more powerfully than ever as Grant's trusted aide who decided who would be admitted to the president's private office.[17]

Ulysses Grant was being made a fool of. "I never saw father so grimly angry" Jesse recalled, "as at that time." Intellectuals and polished gentlemen would not listen to his reasons for wanting to annex Santo Domingo and, instead, insisted on connecting disreputable men to the idea. They were, it seemed to him, trying to make him out to be one of those disreputable men. Taking their advice to abandon both annexation and Orville Babcock would have been an admission that they were right—and he refused to make that admission. Quite the contrary, his loyalty to his man Babcock was a statement of faith in himself. Underlying Grant's "extraordinary" and, to the British minister, "unaccountable" interest in annexation were his doubts about his ability to succeed in the world of negotiations. He stuck doggedly to both annexation and Babcock, hoping that determination would bring the treaty home and vindicate not so much Babcock's judgment as his own.[18]

Meanwhile, his assistant secretary of state, Bancroft Davis, was secretly undercutting the president by feeding Senator Sumner information on the corruption of the negotiators of the annexation and on details of the Davis Hatch case. Davis's immediate chief, Hamilton Fish, was not much more enthusiastic than Davis and Sumner about Santo Domingo, but "vexed" with his old friend Sumner, Fish stayed loyal, publicly, to Grant. Determined to keep the country out of a war with Spain over Cuba, the secretary of state paid the price for Grant's reluctant support of a neutrality proclamation; he agreed to support annexation of Santo Domingo. On June 13, the day Grant issued the proclamation on Cuba, Fish and Grant had a long talk about Santo Domingo. Grant was distressed that his party was divided over annexation— not only in the Senate but in his cabinet, which, he said, "is not sustaining me." Boutwell was explicitly opposed; Hoar, Grant declared, "sneers" at the treaty; and Cox did "not open his mouth—not a word in favor of it."[19]

General Grant was being beaten in the first major campaign of his presidency, and he resented it profoundly. A man he thought effeminate, Charles Sumner, was outmaneuvering him, and unable to remove this very real opponent, Grant was reduced to impotent rage. He saw or thought he saw disloyalty within his own cabinet. One morning, Hamilton Fish asked Grant if he included him among the enemy. Grant paused for a long time before saying no. As they were talking, Rockwood Hoar came in; Grant looked at him and left for breakfast. Hoar felt the chill and remarked to Fish that the Santo Domingo question was in the way of all other matters before the nation, and was dividing the men in Grant's cabinet.[20]

Not in the cabinet room, but in his office in the White House, Babcock sat with Raymond H. Perry and urged him not to defend Hatch and spoil the prospects for annexation, but Perry was determined to tell the president all that had been going on in Santo Domingo. Perry, who had originally been in league with Babcock, was biased and brash, but he was also the kind of man who can sometimes blurt out the truth. When he went to the president's office, Grant was too busy to see him, but, persisting, he said he would return the next day. It was not an interview Grant enjoyed: "I wanted the President to understand the whole matter. . . . I did not think the President liked to hear these things, and he got up and told me he had to go out to dinner, and he went out of the room." One more enemy was trying to brand Babcock and sabotage Grant's advance on Santo Domingo.[21]

Jesse Grant recalled later how deeply troubled his father had been during the "strangely tense days" when the annexation was being debated. The only time he remembered being barred from his father's office was when Fish and Daniel Ammen came to confer urgently with the president on the matter. Grant's pressure on loyal senators was intense. On June 28, Senator Adelbert Ames of Mississippi was sick in bed, so sick that his friends were worried about him. At 10:00 A.M. he received a note from Babcock saying that an attempt would be made at noon to vote an executive session, in order to move to a vote on annexing Santo Domingo, and asking Ames to be there for the vote. "I would have been here," Ames wrote, "had it even been necessary to get out of my coffin." But he was Lazarus to no avail: "At about one we voted ourselves into Executive Session. . . . In a quarter of an hour we were voted out again and my work being over I came back to bed again." There was, Ames concluded, "not a very flattering prospect for ratification of the treaty."[22]

Charles Sumner could not be pushed out of his obdurate place, but Grant could at least rid himself of those he saw as Sumner's friends. He told Orville Babcock that he wanted to dismiss John Lothrop Motley as minister to Great Britain. Babcock quickly leaked a rumor of the resignation to the press, so that, having become public, it would be difficult to revoke, and so that senators whose votes or influence were essential to the ratification of the treaty would know that a major patronage plum was available. When the *New York Tribune* carried a story that Fish would be sent to London to replace Motley, Grant quickly called the secretary of state to the White House "to explain to you precisely what may have . . . given rise to [the story]." Grant's Santo Domingo allies in the Senate, Oliver P. Morton, Zachariah Chandler, and

Matthew H. Carpenter had been in, complaining of a dearth of patronage. (Chandler, "a man of very rough manners and with a great love of Whisky," or so the British foreign office was told, had a particular ax to grind. When in London, Motley had refused him introductions the senator felt he deserved.) The senators were irritated that they, Grant loyalists, had had no post to offer equal to that which Grant's enemy Sumner had bestowed on Motley. It had chafed that Sumner, the chief opponent of annexation, had his man Motley in London. If that fact troubled the senators, it irritated Grant still more, and he cheerfully joined them in toying with other possibilities. First he proposed Edwards Pierrepont for London, but Chandler had a still better idea; Grant could make Pierrepont secretary of state and get rid of cautious, conservative Hamilton Fish by sending him to London. In reporting this conversation to Fish, Grant said he did not want Pierrepont as secretary of state, but Fish added, "Whether he . . . made this remark to Chandler or [only] to me, I was not sure."[23]

In his diary, Fish took a lofty tone about the opposition of those "who could not use me," and he wondered if Grant was, indeed, going to dismiss him. At one point the president did ask the secretary of state if he yearned for London, and Fish replied that he did not. More reassuring was Grant's request, as the two went through one of their regular minuets over resignation, that Fish stay on at least until fall and that he promise not to schedule any cabinet meetings that summer, as he had the previous year. Fish consented readily. He preferred the Hudson Valley to the Potomac in August, and thought there was no need to govern in the summer; after all, "President [Jackson] was absent for months at a time and this before telegraphy." Grant, for his part, would "come in occasionally from Long Branch, more for appearance . . . than for any necessity." Returning to the struggle over Santo Domingo, Fish urged Grant not to "hit Motley for Sumner's sin." The advice was not heeded. The Senate rejected the annexation treaty on June 30; on July 1, in a cabinet meeting a sullen Ulysses Grant talked not of Santo Domingo, but of the historian serving as minister in London. "I will not allow Mr. Sumner to ride over me," he growled. "But," said Fish, "it is not Mr. Sumner, but Mr. Motley, whom you are striking." "It is the same thing," said Grant, with finality.[24]

When Hamilton Fish was again mentioned as a possible replacement for Motley, he went to Grant to find out whether or not to pack his bags. The president, who was testing Fish's loyalty, explained that he had let the rumor circulate in order to avoid having to talk about the numerous other claimants. Fish himself had an interesting candidate for the post—Charles Sumner. But Grant, however eager he was to remove Sumner from Washington, was unwilling to reward him in any way, and Fish might well have wondered if sending the outspoken critic of England to London would foster a settlement of the claims questions.

On July 14, 1870, Grant sent Fish a note asking him to draw up papers naming a former senator from New Jersey, Frederick T. Frelinghuysen, minister to London. Although he did not have any particular objection to his wife's "unexceptional" cousin, Fish was unenthusiastic. So was the British minister. He wrote the foreign secretary that "Frelinghuysen looks just like a Methodist parson, is rigid in matters of religion and dry; I don't think you will get much out of him"; however, for an American, he was not "bad hearted." Fish pointed out to Grant that the state of New Jersey was small and Democratic. Furthermore, a New Jersey man—Joseph P. Bradley—had just been appointed to the Supreme Court. Grant, usually sensitive to the necessity for state-balancing and for rewarding of Republican constituencies, did not this time listen to his secretary of state. When he returned to the capital for the annual ceremony of signing bills as Congress adjourned for the summer, he signed the nomination of Frelinghuysen. But Frelinghuysen declined the offer. Meanwhile, Motley was refusing to resign. The secretary of state, on vacation at Garrison, was in an embarrassing position. He tried to persuade Senator Lyman Trumbull of Illinois to take the post: "I do not know that we are on the eve of a settlement of great questions with Great Britain but there are reasons to justify the hope that very important questions may be adjusted [during the term of the next minister]." But a diplomatic mission, however important, had no attraction for the able senator, and he declined.[25]

Back in Washington in September, Fish was without a minister to Britain at a critical point in his Alabama-claims negotiations, and he was not in any way sanguine about the progress of these talks. When he and Thornton chatted one Sunday after church—both went to St. John's—the secretary of state did "not find much in the tone . . . of his conversation today to encourage the idea of . . . a settlement." Fish could not get agreement on the claims, and he could not even get a minister to send to London. After Trumbull declined the appointment, Senators Lot M. Morrill and George F. Edmunds also did so. Senator Oliver P. Morton of Indiana accepted, but then withdrew when the state's voters elected a legislature that would have sent a Democrat to the Senate in his place. Fish recorded that after a cabinet meeting in October, Grant suggested Senator George H. Williams of Oregon, "saying at the same time 'he is hardly big enough for the Place.' " To this view Fish added his "assent." Fish's Garrison neighbor Edwards Pierrepont thought himself of sufficient stature for the ministry or any other good post Grant might offer and, from his town address, wrote a most charming note to Mrs. Grant telling her he was sure Grant would be re-elected two years hence and inviting her and the general to stop with them when next in the city.[26]

Grant too had that election in mind. He was exasperated with the whole English business, and casually, but with great point, he told Fish in November 1870 that he wanted it settled before the next presidential election. Furthermore, he told Fish to abandon hope of getting Canada joined to the United States through the negotiations. This critical decision was, perhaps, the turning point that led to the settlement. Grant thought no more now of the expansionism directed at Canada than he had in 1846 of the expansionism threatening Mexico. His silence amid the heady public talk of annexation did much to awaken a great number of Americans from the dream that Canada would, one day, inevitably be made part of a continental American union. And, privately, his lack of jingoism could be cited by Fish to help allay the fears of the British. Now they could negotiate without thinking that a grab for Canada lay behind every American move.

Meanwhile, the question of who would be minister to London was at last on its way to an inelegant solution. Robert C. Schenck, a Civil War general and past master at poker who as a congressman from Ohio had been a leader of the attack on Andrew Johnson, had not been re-elected to his seat in the House. Schenck needed work, and he got it; indeed, although some have come close to him in this respect, there has never been a man more unabashed in his ability to exploit familiarity with government circles in his quest for a private dollar. His behavior was so outrageous as to take on a certain charm. As a former congressman, he was able to lobby effectively. His services were anxiously sought, and he was eager to provide them. One entrepreneur, Max Woodhull, asked him to represent the Northern Pacific Railway in Washington, suggesting that his efforts would result in "Congressional grants" that would quickly allow Schenck to "earn from $200,000 to $500,000." Schenck could then advantageously invest these earnings in land along the railroad that should be worth four million dollars in ten years. Woodhull, urging Schenck to join him in Philadelphia for a conference with Jay Cooke, engagingly asked, "Will you take the tide of the flood?"[27]

The waters carried the good general from New York, through Philadelphia, to Washington. There Schenck tried the old maneuver of trying to make two men critical to his appointment each think the other favored it. He called promptly on President Grant to ask if Fish had mentioned him for the post of minister to Great Britain. Grant was noncommittal. Schenck then called on Fish, who took a while to get the point; it "appeared" Fish reported in his diary, "when we parted, he called expecting me to 'pump him' on the subject of the British Mission. He said the President requested him to call." On checking with the president, Fish found that Grant did indeed like the idea of sending Schenck to London. The next day, Woodhull enthusiastically wrote in a note to Schenck that the "papers say you had yesterday a two hour interview with the President." Able to add two and two, Woodhull told Schenck that the deal with Cooke and the Northern Pacific was all set, and that he could do his work as representative of the interests of the railroad with his former colleagues in Congress before leaving for Great Britain. Woodhull closed his little note, "aff. yrs. Max W."[28]

Dining with Fish the next evening, Schenck told him that he was "anxious to go to England," but hesitated because he was "offered the confidential counsel-ship of the Northern Pacific RR (Jay Cooke's) at a salary of $20,000" and "other compensations are available also with other businessmen." Fish called him to his country's cause. "Perhaps these can be held open till after [your] service in London is up," he murmured as they left the fine table. Schenck, for his part, wanted to be sure that the Alabama-claims negotiations would be entrusted to him. Fish told him they would be "if [the] Pres. so desired." Grant, wanting no more embarrassment, told Fish that the appointment was not to be made public until it was certain that Schenck would accept. The news went out on the wires on December 10.[29]

On December 20, on his way home from a dinner at Postmaster General Creswell's, Fish took advantage of a private moment with Grant to ask if Schenck was truly to be entrusted with the Alabama-claims negotiations. He anticipated that British officials in London would try, in their early conversations with Schenck, to learn what the change in envoys meant to them. Grant said that Schenck's instructions should be the same as Motley's had been. But Fish pointed out that Motley had been told to stall if pushed to state a position, and that since the United States had rejected the Johnson-Clarendon Convention it was, perhaps, now up to the United States to start a new phase in the negotiations. Grant agreed that Schenck should do so.[30]

Schenck did not leave the country hungry. New York gentlemen raced to give dinners in honor of his departure. That tireless lawyer Edwards Pierrepont got there first; he was followed quickly by the banker—now collector of the port—Moses Grinnell, who submerged his own hopes for the appointment in his generosity toward the man from Ohio. On January 13, Harris C. Fahnestock, whose family had forsaken the communal life of Ephrata, Pennsylvania, for the worldlier ways of Gotham, wrote, "I can give you an intensely respectable bankers dinner, or make it 'cheerful' as you may prefer." Fahnestock's more devout partner, Jay Cooke, had already provided for Schenck in another way. On December 27, Schenck deposited in Cooke's bank a check for $25,000—the proceeds of a note secured by a $25,000 bond of none other than the Northern Pacific Railroad. In February, Benjamin F. Wade very graciously agreed to act for Mr. Cooke until Mr. Schenck returned from London.[31]

Meanwhile, John Lothrop Motley had been loath to leave London. When he finally agreed to go, he issued an "End of Mission" statement. The dignity of its tone and protestations of accomplishment evoked the idea that Grant had removed him simply out of anger with Sumner for denying him Santo Domingo. On January 2, 1871, Grant called his cabinet to the White House to hear Fish's draft of a reply to Motley. The secretary of state was now furious with both his old friends, Sumner and Motley, and Schuyler Colfax had to urge him to delete a reference to the date of Motley's removal, the day after the defeat of the Santo Domingo treaty. Colfax, who presided in the Senate, had been tactfully trying to mollify Sumner, and he knew Fish's remarks to Motley would infuriate Sumner. Grant knew this too; he told Fish to leave the rebuke to Motley (and Sumner) exactly as it was.[32]

Grant had already resumed his campaign for Santo Domingo. In his second State of the Union address, on December 5, 1870, he had stated his case powerfully. Santo Domingo, he said, was a "weak power, numbering probably less than 120,000 souls, and yet possessing one of the richest territories under the sun, capable of supporting a population of 10,000,000 people in luxury." (A hundred years later, 5,300,000 people live there in poverty.) Grant, like Sumner, expected these people to be black, but the president saw the future in terms not of independent black republics, but of a vast new black American frontier. He anticipated Frederick Jackson Turner's view of the frontier as a safety valve that allowed conflict to escape, harmlessly, away from older settled areas. "San Domingo, with a stable government, under which her immense resources can be developed, will give remunerative wages to tens of thousands of laborers not now upon the island." Annexation would solve immense problems. Santo Domingo would "become a large consumer of the products of Northern farms and manufactories," and "Porto Rico and Cuba [would] have to abolish slavery, as a measure of self-preservation, to retain their laborers." He predicted that even Brazil would have to eliminate slavery and that somehow the annexation would force an end to the "exterminating" war in Cuba. Grant was cautious about recommending the emigration of laborers from his own country, but the idea that among the 10,000,000 might soon be some of the more seriously disillusioned of the 4,000,000 freedmen of the South was implicit in his message. He concluded that bringing Santo Domingo into the United States would be "a rapid stride toward that greatness [to] which the intelligence, industry, and enterprise of the citizens of the United States" entitles them.[33]

Grant sent an investigating commission of distinguished citizens to Santo Domingo to bring him an objective report. It was hoped that these men would recommend annexation and that the Senate would then concur. This more dignified procedure was coupled with efforts by Senator Lyman Trumbull, one of the wisest men in Washington, to effect a reconciliation between Grant and Senators Sumner and Carl Schurz (whom Sumner had now placed on the Foreign Relations Committee). Trumbull thought his chances were better with Schurz and approached him first. Schurz knew that his opposition to Babcock had made him unwelcome at the White House and was reluctant to call there, but Trumbull insisted that paying a call upon returning to the capital was a "matter of respect to the office, and it has been the practice of even members of the opposition to call on their arrival here." With some trepidation, Schurz went to the White House, but to no avail. "I think it was unfortunate that Grant should have been unable to see Schurz when he called," wrote Trumbull to an astute political friend. "Wrong inferences will be drawn from it."[34]

Inferences, wrong or right, were indeed being drawn about Grant; the president, it appeared, was no longer willing to court his senatorial enemies. As George S. Boutwell and Hamilton Fish walked downstairs after a cabinet meeting on December 23, 1870, they talked of Charles Sumner's vitriolic insinuations in the Senate two days earlier. Sumner, responding furiously to newspaper accounts that he had been insulting to Grant—so insulting that, one paper said, "[General Babcock] is reported to have gone so far as to declare that if he were not officially connected with the Executive he would subject Senator Sumner to personal violence"—had called on his old friends the secretaries of the treasury and of state to be witnesses to the fact that he had never been other than courteous. Boutwell and Fish were not prepared to accommodate him. During their conversation on December 23, Boutwell told Sumner's old friend Fish that on several occasions the senator had made "charges against the President so outrageous and violent" that he was unwilling to repeat them. Fish responded, "Sumner is 'crazy,' a monomaniac upon all matters relating to his own importance and his relations toward the President." Boutwell told Fish that the senator "more than once, in speaking of the President's interview with him last winter at Sumner's house, about San Domingo, had said that Grant was drunk." According to Boutwell, Sumner cited as proof of Grant's condition the fact that the president "called [him] Chairman of the Judiciary Committee." Boutwell (who Fish thought had been present at the interview) went on to remark, "He was no more drunk, or excited than he was when we left him upstairs five minutes since—no more than Sumner himself."[35]

While Grant defended annexation on the ground of the usefulness of the "island of San Domingo" to black citizens of the United States, Charles Sumner attacked it because it would mean the dissolution of the Dominican Republic—one of the world's two black republics. Grant, calling for the purchase of the Bay of Samaná area, predicted that "a great commercial city [would] spring up" and argued that it would be "folly" to reject such "a prize." To Sumner, America's embarking on such an "imperial system" would be a "dance of blood." He drew a contrast: "There you have it . . . President Grant, speaking with the voice of forty million, and this other president who has only eight hundred thousand people, all black." Sumner regarded such behavior as bullying, and Ulysses Grant never forgave the insinuation that he was a bully.[36]

Grant's break with Sumner was complete. The senator had protested loudly and publicly about the abominable treatment of Motley. Grant, for his part, began insisting that Sumner be replaced as chairman of the Foreign Relations Committee. This he accomplished, but at no gain to the cause of annexing Santo Domingo. Sumner, in reviewing his disagreement with Grant over Santo Domingo, told the *New York Tribune* that "when he came to the serious consideration of the project, he was most concerned as to its relations to the future of the African race. He thought it all important to that race that a republic created by it should be maintained in this hemisphere as an example and inspiration and that the extinction of Santo Domingo was sure to involve at the next step the extinction of the other black republic [Haiti] occupying a part of the same island." To Sumner, the image of Toussaint L'Ouverture still stood for the rights of man. For the last senator of the enlightenment there was "injustice" in "impairing the predominance of the colored race in the West Indies." He was quoted as having said in secret Senate debate, "To the African belongs the equatorial belt."[37]

In his speech in the Senate on December 21, Sumner had likened the an-nexation agreement to the Lecompton Constitution in Kansas, "which was sought to subject a distant Territory to slavery"; he mocked the diplomacy of "young" Orville Babcock, an "aide-de-camp of his Excellency General Ulysses S. Grant, President of the United States"; and he called Buenaven-tura Báez a "political jackal." He implied that Grant did not know what was in the documents he had submitted. Name calling aside, there were no inac-curacies in his denunciation of the annexation proposal. But Sumner could not stop the approval of Grant's plan to send a commission to the island to weigh the merits of annexation, and he lamented the willingness of Frederick Douglass to accompany the mission as a consultant. The presence of the great editor would do much to counter the suggestion that Grant's plan was not in the best interest of people of African descent in the hemisphere. There was consolation for Sumner in a letter of support from William Lloyd Garri-son, but it was scarcely enough to compensate for the concerted effort under-taken by Grant's men, led by Senators Morton and Conkling, to remove Sumner from his post as chairman of the Foreign Relations Committee. That effort can be dated from this speech of Sumner's; its goal was achieved when the Forty-second Congress was organized in March 1871.[38]

Grant had won his battle with a rival captain, but this time at the cost of the war. Sumner was gone, but so was the possibility of annexing Santo Domingo. A favorable report by the investigating commissioners was not enough to counteract the powerful arguments that Sumner had presented. In the spring of 1871, Grant's men could not get the two-thirds majority in the Senate needed to approve an annexation treaty. Neither would Congress pass a joint resolution which would permit Ulysses Grant to have his island in the sun. He never forgot that it had been denied him.

Matters were more businesslike in the negotiations with the British. Sir John Rose—he had recently been knighted—arrived in Washington, ostensi-bly to see the secretary of the treasury about the marketing in London of a new United States bond issue by Morton & Rose, but also to discuss the related matter of the Alabama claims with Secretary of State Fish. Rose had the blessing of Lord Granville (the new foreign secretary) and of Prime Min-ister William E. Gladstone, as well as that of the British minister in Washing-ton, for his effort to see what settlement might be effected. At the home of Bancroft Davis for dinner, Rose and Fish reached in private an accord that eighteen months later was completed in public. The United States would drop attempts to link the annexation of Canada to the settlement and would drop as well the determination to force England to acknowledge its guilt by paying for huge "indirect" damages—costs of the prolonged war. A commission would meet in Washington to settle the issues unrelated to the war: the border dispute in the northwest, the question of British fishing rights in the waters off New England, and the matter of British recognition of the United States citizenship of former subjects who had emigrated to this country and been naturalized. The issues related to the war would then be submitted to an international board of arbitration.[39]

In a cabinet meeting on January 17, 1871, Grant himself took a critical part in the establishment of a diplomatic strategy. It was suggested that the United States set as one of the conditions for going ahead with negotiations a demand that Great Britain promise not to press claims for the value of any Confederate bonds purchased by British subjects. Grant rejected this proposal because, in his view, it would suggest that Americans were not confident enough to hold firm once the negotiations actually began. And so, without strings, the trading began. Thornton, the British minister, was optimistic: "The President, Mr. Fish, and Mr. Boutwell are extremely anxious to come to a settlement; the first because he thinks it will help his re-election; Fish, because he wishes the honour before he leaves office which he is anxious to do; and Boutwell because he believes it will help if not be indispensable to the placing of his new 5 per cent Bonds, of which Rose's bank and the Barings are to be principal agents."[40]

There now were intense confidential discussions in the cabinet and among leaders in Congress. For public consumption, many politicians went on record as supporting a tough stand with England, and initially Grant hoped that Schenck could make a deal better than the one Rose proposed. Fish, consulting Schenck, found that the new minister had plunged enthusiastically into peace-making efforts and that he agreed with the Rose proposals, including the one calling for the negotiation of certain issues in Washington. At home, most congressional leaders were privately relieved that the matter was on its way to resolution, but once again, Charles Sumner was a possible stumbling block. Feeling exceedingly uncomfortable, Hamilton Fish called on his former friend; to his surprise, he found Sumner frosty but not antagonistic. Sumner "declaimed" against England but in the end was noncommittal. Sir John also called on Senator Sumner, and was treated to a lesson on the Monroe Doctrine and manifest destiny. If the British would "haul down the flag"—the flag of their empire—everywhere in the Western Hemisphere, all would be well. Rose passed a report of this outburst along to Lord Granville, the foreign secretary, as documentation for the need to get the negotiations going. (When Fish heard of Sumner's strong words, he caustically remarked on the senator's advocacy that America take up British holdings in North America and the Caribbean, "but not Santo Domingo.") Sumner's desire for Canada was very real, but the British negotiator Sir Stafford Northcote found him "distinctly friendly," and Prime Minister Gladstone was happy that his "red hot" anti-English rhetoric did not impair negotiations.[41]

The British commissioners who had arrived in Washington in March for the negotiations discovered that their business was not separate from American domestic politics. The critical question was whether Grant would be re-elected. Northcote, one of the ablest of the diplomats, thought that "the Presidential election was the mainspring of the whole machine of the Commission." From the start, the British were determined that Hamilton Fish not press claims for "indirect" losses—those connected to, but not directly a result of, the ships' activities. On April 10, the Americans accepted the British "expression of regret" for their "misdeeds," and by May 6 the long bargaining sessions had produced an agreement in accordance with Rose's and Fish's discussions. Northcote was fascinated by the five red and blue ribbons pulled through each copy of the treaty as it was prepared for signing and sealing: "Something like the mode for assigning partners in the cotillion."[42]

The morning of May 8, 1871, was "brilliant." At ten, the British and American commissioners met at the State Department. All of the department staff were present, in a room full of flowers, as the seals were fixed on the treaty—"a slow process," one signatory noted, "as the unfortunate clerk who prepared them was awkward and nervous." One of the British commissioners, Lord Tenterden, "did not help to put him at ease by dropping quantities of burning sealing-wax on his fingers," and "the poor man . . . burst into tears at the conclusion of the affair." Reconciliation came with the serving of an abundance of strawberries and ice cream.[43]

It was a great day for Hamilton Fish. He reported in his diary that Lord de Grey, the most able of the British diplomats, had said to him, "This is the proudest day of my life, I congratulate you, & myself, & our two Countries." On a lighter note, Fish wrote, "When Sir John MacDonald was about to sign, while having the pen in his hand, he said to me (in a half whisper) 'well here go the fisheries!' " Fish noted that "Thornton . . . was much moved & holding my hand said 'this is a great result, you & I have worked hard for this, & have done what those [other] gentlemen do not know to bring it about; we have worked for two years.' " After the photographs were taken and the ceremony ended, Fish, alone, was reminded of the feeling of anticlimax in his college days when, after "a laborious preparation for Examination, when striking for the Honors of the College," he had taken the test but did not yet know its result. There was a "feeling of want of something to do, & of the absence of the excitement under which the labor has been sustained."[44]

The ratification of the treaty by the Senate and its acceptance in Parliament was not an easy achievement, but in both countries heads of state were a help. Queen Victoria, in a succinct and unequivocal message, which was seen as carrying her personal commitment, called for acquiescence to certain qualifications the Senate had made in the treaty. Toward the same goal, Grant had Fish send a cable to Schenck telling him that the United States would not enter "indirect" claims at Geneva. The minister quickly took the message to Westminster, where it was given to the aged Earl Russell. After reading it, he made his way into the House of Lords and withdrew a motion he had made that would have blocked the arbitration plan. The Treaty of Washington was accepted in London, while in Washington, strenuous and successful efforts were made by Grant and Fish to bring the necessary two-thirds of the senators to vote for ratification.

Under the treaty, the war-related claims were submitted to an international board of arbitration. The American member was Charles Francis Adams, whom Grant accepted with much reluctance—he disliked all Adamses. The British representative was Sir Alexander Cockburn. The other arbitrators were a Swiss statesman, an Italian count, and a Brazilian baron. Internationalists all, they bargained at Geneva, but American politics were not totally remote. Sir Edward Thornton, in Washington, worried for a time lest Grant, in the "fever" of the election campaign, resurrect the claims for "indirect" damages under a patriotic banner. But eventually Thornton was able to inform the foreign office that Grant had put out "feelers" to see if obstinacy would help renomination and had decided that it would not. He was heartened when, at a party, Mrs. George M. Robeson, the wife of the secretary of the navy, told a member of his legation that she was "happy to hear we are not going to scratch each others' eyes out." Grant and his cabinet had decided not to press the matter of "indirect" damages, and Thornton welcomed the president's probable re-election: "Grant has the best chance, and miserable as he is, I believe he is not so bad, as far as we are concerned, as many others might be." As the campaign proceeded, Adams quietly dropped, for good, the business of "indirect" damages, and England agreed to pay for direct losses to the tune of $15,000,000.[45]

The great schoolmasters of nineteenth-century liberalism, Great Britain and the United States, taught by example. Two major powers could resolve serious differences without going to war. Critics of their pedagogy have made light of the accomplishment: "Twentieth-century power politics showed up the vague and rose-spectacled visions of nineteenth-century liberalism for what they were. Arbitration can only be employed to settle a dispute where nations genuinely want a just solution." Fair enough. Sir John Rose, Levi P. Morton, and a host of other bankers in both countries did indeed want not war, but a chance to exploit the great opportunities for growth investment in North America. Not selfless, of course, the agreement was nevertheless a great accomplishment. Both countries have gone to war over smaller matters, and with the future of Canada in the balance, the questions at issue were not trivial. Arbitration has come to seem a quaint relic of nineteenth-century thinking, but the accomplishment of Adams and his fellow negotiators was not minor. The accord was signed in September 1872. The Grant administration had kept the peace, and had done so in time for the election of 1872.[46]

# XXII

# DEMOCRACY

. . . there's gret risk they'll blunder on,
Ef they ain't stopped, to real Democ'cy.
— *James Russell Lowell,*
The Biglow Papers

WHILE GRANT'S ADMINISTRATION made peace with white men in England and lost a bid to make a peaceful sanctuary for black expatriates in the Caribbean, black Americans in the South and, of all places, at Grant's West Point, sought to make America wholly theirs. They were trying to reconstruct the nation, and the white Americans who were their political allies were baffled by it all. In February 1870, at a dinner party in Washington given by Attorney General Rockwood Hoar, James Russell Lowell looked at Ulysses Grant's troubled face and saw "a puzzled pathos, as of a man with a problem before him of which he does not understand the terms." Part of Grant's puzzlement at that time may have come from failing to appreciate how august the attorney general's Saturday Club house guest was, but the next day Grant came to know Lowell in the way an author likes best— through his work. After another dinner party, the president heard the last of *The Biglow Papers* spoken by a monologist, and Hoar reported to Lowell, "Our friend Ulysses (or 'Ulyss' as Mrs. G. calls him sometimes) had a revelation the day after you left." Lowell in these political essays in dialect verse (the second series of which was dedicated to Hoar) escaped from some of his own personal cautiousness, and in the one to which Grant listened,

"Mr. Hosea Biglow's Speech in March Meeting," dated April 5, 1866, he allowed his Yankee character to give what Grant pronounced "the most perfect statement of the whole doctrine of reconstruction" that he "had ever met with."[1]

Hosea Biglow, a not-so-simple Yankee, began with a good swipe at Andrew Johnson. In his "Argymunt," describing the content of the "speach" to follow, he said, "Gits into Johnson's hair. No use tryin' to git into his head." From this point on, Hosea had at least one member of his audience with him; Grant no doubt found familiar and congenial all of the four-year-old indictment of Johnson's and Seward's policy of giving away the victory won in the war. But Hosea did not follow that accusation with a call for severe retribution. Instead Grant heard him say:

> My frien's, you never gethered from my mouth,
> No, nut one word ag'in the South ez South,
> Nor th' ain't a livin' man, white, brown, nor black,
> Gladder'n wut I should be to take 'em back;
> But all I ask of Uncle Sam is fust
> To write up on his door, "No goods on trust";
>                              [Cries o' "Thet's the ticket!"]
> Give us cash down in ekle laws for all,
> An' they'll be snug inside afore nex' fall.
> Give wut they ask, an' we shell hev Jamaker,
> Wuth minus some consid'able an acre;
> Give wut they need, an' we shell git 'fore long
> A nation all one piece, rich, peacefle, strong;
> Make 'em Amerikin, an' they'll begin
> To love their country ez they loved their sin;
> Let 'em stay Southun, an' you've kep' a sore
> Ready to fester ez it done afore.[2]

In this passage, Hosea said no to vindictiveness, but yes to the South's need to accept a cash-on-the-barrelhead deal. Lowell's metaphor for a good nation was commercial trustworthiness, and the coin of the realm was newly minted law. As Grant sat listening to Hosea's words, the Fifteenth Amendment—the quintessence of "ekle laws for all"—was about to be ratified. The amendment would establish the right to vote regardless "of race, color, or previous condition of servitude." Attorney General Hoar, his abolitionist friend James Russell Lowell, and President Grant were all counting on that equal law to do a huge job; it would make Southerners "Amerikin." It would signal the advent of national citizenship. The United States would be one nation, and laws applicable to all would save the South from being simply a black-ridden colony, as was Jamaica in the British Empire. Instead, under equal laws, black people would simply be so many more law-abiding citizens living in the South, at one with all other citizens. Surely all reasonable Southerners would recognize the sense of what Hosea Biglow had to say.

The Yankee went on to appeal further to their sensibilities:

> Ef treason is a crime, ez *some* folks say,
> How could we punish it in a milder way
> Than sayin' to 'em, "Brethren, lookee here,
> We'll jes' divide things with ye, sheer an' sheer,
> An sence both come o' pooty strong-backed daddies,
> You take the Darkies, ez we've took the Paddies;
> Ign'ant an' poor we took 'em by the hand,
> An' they're the bones an' sinners o' the land."
> I ain't o' them thet fancy there's a loss on
> Every inves'ment thet don't start from Bos'on;
> But I know this: our money's safest trusted
> In sunthin', come wut will, thet *can't* be busted,
> An' thet's the old Amerikin idee,
> To make a man a Man an' let him be.
>
> [Gret applause.]

In a hickory-nut shell, the argument was as follows: If we can put up with the Irish in Boston, you can put up with the Negroes in your Southland. We in New England know that we don't have all the problems—or all the answers—but, as usual, we have a good many of the latter. Just as we trust in sound money, so we are certain of the principle that all that Americans need do "to make a man a Man [is] let him be."[3]

A black man in a cabin in South Carolina might have agreed with the ladies and gentlemen sitting in the Washington parlor and nodding in approval at this reading—if only he could have been assured that he would, indeed, be "let be." The problem was that Hoar and Lowell and Grant, by supporting the Fifteenth Amendment, were encouraging an advancement of the freedmen that many whites had no intention of permitting. The black Carolinian, for his part, already had a pretty good idea that, unenforced by the power of that America which Lowell and Grant revered, the voting amendment was not going to ensure that he would be "let be" any more than had any of the other "ekle laws" that had come out of Washington since the act creating the Freedmen's Bureau in March 1865.

Because he was not ready to accept it himself, Lowell should have recognized why some white Southerners were not going to buy his simple solution. Like Hosea, they were aware that if Yankees did not stop passing laws designed to achieve racial justice there was "gret resk" that folks ". . . 'll blunder on . . . to real Democ'cy." And they did not want that. Hosea, getting a second wind (and beginning to say things that Lowell—in his own person—did not dare say) blundered into irony to suggest what Reconstruction might have been:

Ef we're to hev our ekle rights,
't wun't du to 'low no competition;
Th' ole debt doo us for bein' whites
Ain't safe onless we stop th' emission
O' these noo notes, whose specie base
Is human natur', 'thout no trace
O' shape, nor color, nor condition.

Despite his observation that "we've took the Paddies," Hosea did not quite realize that he would have to share his America with them. By the same token, it was not long before James Russell Lowell was not only counseling Englishmen not to let all other Englishmen vote but also advising Americans that civil-service reform was more important than the enforcement of the rights of black people. And Ulysses Grant, too, after the intoxication of the evening's poetry cleared, learned to avoid the dangerous currency of equality. Once the men who sought to enforce the Civil Rights Acts had been blocked, the president allowed himself to be persuaded by Ku Klux Klan violence and the blandishment of sound bankers of human conduct not to settle for any racial greenbacks "whose specie base / Is human natur', 'thout no trace / O' shape, nor color, nor condition." But on that night in February 1870, Grant had, over brandy and cigars, heard the sound of democracy.[4]

Others heard it too at the end of the Civil War—people who thought the war had truly changed things in America. In the course of the struggle over the annexation of Santo Domingo in the spring of 1870, an eager young senator from Mississippi, caught up in that drama, revealed much of what was best and most hopeful in Reconstruction. But at the same time, he exposed exactly what it was that would spoil that great experiment in a biracial rearrangement of things in America. His name was Adelbert Ames, and he was a carpetbagger—"My carpet-bag is upstairs . . . ," he once said aptly, although, as it happens, with reference to his desire to visit his fiancée. "If I only had it where my eye could constantly rest on it, I would be perfectly at home." Not yet thirty-five years old, he was lithe, attractive, boyish, and, when not concerned with matters of state (and not wrestling and pillow fighting with his brother in their bedroom in a Washington boardinghouse), he sat at his desk in the Senate chamber writing charming letters to the lovely young Blanche Butler, the daughter of General Benjamin F. Butler.[5]

Ames's fascination with politics in the Senate chamber and with the thought of his absent fiancée got wonderfully tangled in one letter to Blanche Butler:

Last night I had rather an unpleasant dream—nothing ominous dear. It was simply this—I know you will smile. I dreamt that someone in the Senate was presenting bills for Railroads and other corporations in which your name appeared as one of the corporators! I resented in my own mind that you should be looked upon as trying to gain money in such a way so I strove to defeat the bill at least to get your name removed. I succeeded, but no sooner was the bill disposed of to my satisfaction than somebody would offer another at the head of which was your name—for your sake I kept fighting [and] winning a thousand battles to find I had them to fight over again.

Ames was courting a beautiful woman, and her father and his fortune as well; he was a senator charged with acting in the public interest, but he knew how other lawmakers, like his distant cousin Oakes Ames, looked after their railroad and other financially rewarding interests first. He was an ardent young man determined to get ahead in this world of conflicting values.[6]

Just where in this world the Mississippi senator resided was not entirely clear. He urged on Blanche that they be married in July rather than in September so that (among other reasons) they could spend a month or two with his family in Minnesota, and then several more weeks with his constituents in Mississippi, before returning to Washington in the fall. However, on another day he considered living in her town of Lowell, Massachusetts—"all I care for is to visit my parents and be long enough in Mississippi to establish a name or get the name of going there as my home." Three weeks later he was giving Mississippi a bit more consideration: "I think I ought to give that state nearer two months than one inasmuch as this will be our first visit there after our election and that I desire to become more intimately connected with it."[7]

Adelbert "Del" Ames was born in the prosperous Maine seacoast town of Rockland, and as the first of many tries to find a direction for his ninety-eight years of life, he obtained an appointment to West Point. He graduated in 1861; in 1865, not yet thirty, he was a brigadier general, having received a congressional Medal of Honor for gallantry at Bull Run and a battlefield promotion at Gettysburg. After the demise of the Johnsonian white-supremacy government of Mississippi, Ames, under the provisions of the Republican congressional Reconstruction legislation, was named provisional governor of the state. In March 1869 Grant made him the military commander of the Department of the Mississippi. When the state reconstituted itself, with provisions for black participation in politics, scalawag James Lusk Alcorn, a Confederate soldier and delta planter, was elected governor and Adelbert Ames was chosen senator by the black and white members of the Mississippi legislature. He was not the first man to sit in a Senate seat from Mississippi since the Civil War. That honor belonged to Hiram R. Revels, also a carpetbagger, who in February 1870 took his seat as the first black man to enter the United States Senate. Ames went to Washington and entered the Senate chamber on April 1, 1870.[8]

No one in town had more fun that spring. In the passage between the Senate and House chambers, Ames came upon a vendor selling souvenir paperweights made of globes of glass in which photographs of the great were magnified, and was delighted to see himself in one of them. He bought it and sent it to his fiancée who was in New York, shopping (at Tiffany's) for an engagement ring. As he thought of her putting the ring over her finger, he wrote, from his Senate desk, a mock admonishment not to be "beautiful and fascinating and have a great man for a father." Then, in full admiration, he continued: "What a grand space you're . . . occupying in the world—how completely you fill *my* world." Suddenly the letter ended: "I have just been interrupted by Genl Porter who brought a message from the President. We dine together."[9]

*Grant in a photographer's studio.* LIBRARY OF CONGRESS

The "we" was not Grant and Ames; instead, the senator had dinner with Horace Porter and Orville Babcock, two other young men of Washington with whom he grew friendly. They teased him about his "secret" engagement—common knowledge as far away as Europe, though not yet announced—and talked politics. The subject was the development of a Southern strategy, Reconstruction style. Ames was one of that first generation—and it was a brief generation—of post–Civil War Americans who truly thought there was in the wind a permanent evolution of the position of former slaves in the American world. The freedmen were on the move into, if not social equality, then surely some integral and prosperous part of the social and economic life of the South. Their position would be far above the one allotted them in any system of involuntary servitude or of other, less formal, dependence on a white master class. Immediately after the war, Ames—like Alcorn, the native white man, and Revels, the out-of-state black man—took this new political reality as given. Black people and white people would have to work together whether they liked it or not—and not one of these gentlemen wasted much time worrying about whether they did. They thought they could build good careers for themselves and lives for their families in this new racial context.[10]

Certainly Ames was determined to build a good—indeed, great—career for himself and for Blanche. One evening in the spring of 1870, while playing billiards, Ames and his future father-in-law discussed Reconstruction in general and the dismissal of Attorney General Hoar in particular and "decided exactly what should be done." Ames and Butler (at this time a congressman) agreed that the senator would go to the White House and "have a talk with the President and tell him what the situation is." Ames was a bit nervous about actually doing so, but his reveries were bold indeed: "Am I not getting rapidly into the political circle when at this early day I go to the Executive to point out his errors and to indicate the proper path for him to pursue? Whatever I may do Grant will know it will be in his interest and not mine that I work." Growing still more confident, he wrote, "I am as strong as I want to be . . . and now *if* I can bring over the Southern senators to his support and be a bond of union between him and your father all for the good of the party I will have accomplished something and be in reality a power which I am not now and which I had never dreamed of." The young man was reaching high, and the idea of driving the administration into a coherent policy with respect to the South made a great deal of sense.[11]

Coherence, as usual, was hard to come by. In its path was the memory of the war and of the men who had died in it—as Ames and Butler had not. Many of the Union dead were buried in Southern soil. Partisans of the Union cause, mostly black, honored these dead and celebrated their own freedom by decorating the graves—to the intense consternation of adherents of the Confederate cause who were uneasy about that freedom. Ames and Butler would have liked to see Decoration Day made a national holiday. They did not succeed in 1870, but Ames enjoyed the informal celebration on May 30 in Washington—Fourth of July without noise—and took note of how important it was to the black citizens of the capital. And two days later he set out on another errand of concern to them. The senator went, for the first time, to the "White House—comfortable place—and saw the President about the colored boy appointed to the Military Academy . . ."[12]

Ames may have known the issues that were of emotional concern to Grant's black supporters, but he still had to face the problem of getting the white Southern Republicans into line if his solid South was to be constructed. In the midst of the Santo Domingo fight he wrote Blanche that, like her father, "I feel that the President *must* fight." He had gone to the White House to say so, to Porter and Babcock, and did some talking in his own domain as well: "Yesterday I was talking to two Southern Senators to get them to support the President—I saw they would if a few changes could be made—today they had increased the price necessary to buy them!" They were after patronage; specifically, one of them had an office in New Orleans in mind.[13]

However, with the Santo Domingo treaty of such critical importance to the president, the patronage channels were clogged, even in the South. Grant's own family had things blocked. Julia's brother-in-law, James F. Casey, had control of posts the president might have used to ensure Louisiana votes, and when Ames entered the White House on June 15 he "met or *saw* my old enemy Judge Dent of Miss." This was Julia's brother Lewis, whom Grant had not supported in his white-supremacist bid for the governorship of Mississippi, but to whom he had not closed the familial door. "It is not pleasant," the Republican senator continued, "to have to confront one you dislike as [much as] I do him. We are not acquainted but he pretends to look very grand and muttered something between his teeth. I was ready for a fight even in his own brother's house."[14]

There was, perhaps, a means other than putting a fist to Lewis Dent's jaw to get to Grant and urge a change in his approach to the South. Ames's immediate strategy for this was to work with his ambitious father-in-law, the "great man" who for the moment was merely the congressman from Lowell. Benjamin Butler, a rich man who had made his own money, championed the down-and-out members of society in order that, in perfectly logical political fashion, he himself might reach higher personal goals. Together the senator from Mississippi and the congressman from Massachusetts would work against another great man, Charles Sumner, to build a coalition of congressional Republicans firmly committed to Grant. The point of attack in early June 1870 was the office of attorney general, held, as noted, by a Sumner man, Rockwood Hoar.

Which of his Southern colleagues in the Senate joined Ames in his overtures to Grant for a Southern attorney general is not known. There were eleven senators (including Hiram Revels) who could be described as carpetbaggers. Ten of these had served in the Union army, four as generals and one as a chaplain. Their martial service, of course, said nothing about a concern for the welfare of their black constituents, but at least two of them had some demonstrated interest in protection of the freedmen. An additional two Southern senators, who were scalawags—native Southerners—urged on Grant the need to appoint a strong prosecutor to protect their black constituents. The line of argument was that once assured of their safety, the black and Unionist white voters could be counted on to stay in the Republican column and, in turn, Southern Republicans in Congress could give Grant their full support. They would demonstrate this commitment in their support of the annexation of Santo Domingo and then, with huge credit established in the political ledgers, draw on Grant for support of their efforts to secure a Republican grasp on the South. Ames wanted a Southern attorney general who would sustain the civil rights of black Republicans and ensure Grant's future and his own.

During the spring of 1870, Ames and Butler reminded Grant that Attorney General Hoar was not supporting him on Santo Domingo, that he was Sumner's man, and that, despite his closeness to Sumner, he had done little to assert aggressively the rights of black men. (Later, in Congress—in 1874—Hoar opposed a bill to enforce civil-rights laws.) Butler, with his eye on Sumner's Senate seat, suggested to Grant (as had Hamilton Fish) that the senior senator be gotten out of town with an appointment as minister to Great Britain. (If he accepted, Butler observed, Grant could send a special envoy whenever he could not trust Sumner to carry out his wishes.) If Sumner declined the appointment, he could no longer claim that the president had ignored him. Nothing came of this particular scheme to get rid of Sumner, but Butler and Ames still had a chance to outflank Sumner with respect to his black constituents. A firm Southern advocate of black rights in the cabinet would achieve that end. The brilliant lawyer Thomas Jefferson Durant of Louisiana would fit the bill, but he had not lived in his adopted state since being driven from it by an anti-integrationist mob in 1866; however, there were other able Republican lawyers in residence in the South. Ames and Butler pressed their case.

Secretary of the Interior Jacob Dolson Cox, a proud man who took his job seriously, was immensely surprised when, on the evening of June 16, 1870, he read in the *New York Times* that his fellow member of the cabinet Judge Hoar had resigned. There in the paper was a very terse letter of resignation from Hoar, followed by Grant's only slightly less terse reply of acceptance, but no details were given. Cox immediately left his Capitol Hill house and hurried to take the Pennsylvania Avenue horsecar to Hoar's lodgings on "F" Street, to find out what had happened. On his way, the secretary was embarrassed to run into the junior senator from Massachusetts, Henry Wilson, who also had just heard the news, and wanted to know its cause. "Nonplussed how to answer, and shrinking from revealing the fact that I was more ignorant than he," wrote Cox many years later, "I took refuge in commonplaces about the natural result of there being two Cabinet officers from one State. . . ." "I know all that," said Wilson, who did indeed remember that Boutwell and Hoar were both from his state, "but what do you think of the new man whose name has been sent in this afternoon?" "Worse cornered than ever," wrote Cox, "as I could not even guess who had been nominated . . . I could only mumble, 'Oh, I think you'll find he's all right.' " Just then the horsecar came and Cox escaped, mumbling to himself, "With how little wisdom the world is governed."[15]

When Cox got to Judge Hoar's he discovered that he was not the only member of the cabinet who had been surprised by the president. The attorney general had been in his office the day before when a very abrupt note, with no mention of cause, had come from Grant asking for his resignation. Hoar told Cox that at first he was afraid that "the President had been imposed upon by some grave charge against me" and his "impulse was to go at once and ask the reasons for the demand." The proud Harvard man, however, could not do so—"self-respect would not permit this"—and instead took his pen and began drafting a reply. At first he played with the conventional phrases of such letters—referring to the press of family business and the like—but then he again looked at Grant's note and decided that "since no reasons are given . . . for the demand, it is hardly honest to invent them in the reply." So he wrote his terse note, carefully locked its only copy in his desk, and sent the original next door to the White House.[16]

That afternoon Hoar took some pardon cases to the president and found Grant not unfriendly. All fear of charges evaporated, and now Hoar felt confident enough to ask his chief what had caused the dismissal. He knew that it was linked somehow to his ties to Charles Sumner and to the fact that he, Hoar, had never given the Santo Domingo treaty the support Grant wanted from him. What he had not reckoned with was the complexity of Grant's bid for treaty votes in the Senate. Speaking to Hoar, Grant "frankly connected his own action with the exigency in which he found himself, and the necessity, to carry out his purposes, of securing support in the Senate from Southern Republicans, who demanded that the Cabinet place should be filled from the South."[17]

Now the conservative attorney general realized that Reconstruction was involved, as well as the fate of the Santo Domingo treaty. And if a powerful Reconstruction program was to emerge, Republican vanity, as Hoar phrased it, was in jeopardy. In the party spectrum on racial policy, Hoar stood in the middle, Cox was on the right, and Wilson, a supporter of Radical Reconstruction legislation, was on the left, but all had been a part of a group that had sought to hold Grant and the various factions of the Republican party to a unified position on Reconstruction. Grant's report to Johnson in the fall of 1865, which was antithetical to the Radical program of Reconstruction, was still remembered. In contrast, these Republican leaders accepted—indeed in Wilson's case championed—the Radical Reconstruction program designed to protect the freedmen and contain them in the South; but none of these men were willing to face the consequences of their acts and continue the federal government's commitment to a responsibility of prosecuting terrorists actively in the federal courts.

Gentlemen count on gentlemen, and Hoar thought "responsible" Southerners would, somehow, find a way to protect the freedmen. By 1870, however, Grant seemed to have lost the faith in the "thinking people of the South" that he had held in the fall of 1865, and was listening to carpetbaggers. The carpetbagger senators, heartily encouraged by the future father-in-law of one of them, had asked Grant for an attorney general who would vigorously prosecute those who were terrorizing their constituents. Hoar's prejudices argued against so strong an identification with black people; what was more, he despised Butler, whom he did not consider to be a gentleman—a judgment he underscored by blocking Butler's honorary degree from Harvard a decade later—and with quiet force he warned Grant against being "subjected to a pressure in favor of unfit men." Grant, trimming, responded by suggesting that perhaps they both ought to keep the whole matter of the resignation confidential until he could think it over.[18]

Reprieved, Hoar was at work at his office in the Treasury Building on the morning of June 16 when a reporter from the *New York Tribune* asked to see him. Cautiously, the attorney general declined to do so, but the reporter persisted with a note: perhaps the attorney general would speak to him about the news of his resignation that he had read in the *Times*. Sending a surprised and troubled clerk to "give the gentleman any information you are possessed of," Hoar stormed to the White House, walked in on Grant, and said, "Mr. President, I have come to tell you that somebody about you betrays you." Grant, "deeply stirred" by the release of his correspondence with Hoar, got up from his desk and went into the adjacent office, where Babcock and Porter worked, determined to "severely punish the breach of confidence." Soon he came back "mollified," explaining to Hoar that his secretaries "could account for the leak only by supposing that some unauthorised person must have got access in the outer office" to the copy of Grant's acceptance of the resignation. The explanation was too thin for Hoar to believe, but he could not call the president a liar and so settled for diffidence.[19]

Nothing was said about how Hoar's letter was copied and came to be known to the reporter from the *Times*, for Grant, with bland authority, had already begun asking Hoar what he thought of Amos Akerman of Georgia. Akerman had been appointed United States district attorney for Georgia during Hoar's regime, and the attorney general had recommended him for a federal judgeship, but Hoar found it awkward to comment on Akerman's qualifications to be his own successor: "It would hardly be proper for me, Mr. President, to say what should be the standard of fitness for the attorney-generalship of the United States." With this, Ebenezer Rockwood Hoar left the White House. Nominations required the great seal affixed by the secretary of state, and thus, that afternoon, Hamilton Fish learned that he was to have a new colleague in the cabinet.[20]

Amos T. Akerman (both *a*'s are long in Cartersville, Georgia) was a lean and balding man with a thicket of eyebrows over penetrating eyes, a large nose, and a richly curled lower lip. Reporters saw a "face of learning and disposition to deep meditation" when the firm-minded Yankee turned Georgian arrived in the capital. A year older than Grant, Akerman was born in Portsmouth, New Hampshire, in 1821, studied at the Phillips Exeter Academy, and attended Dartmouth College, where he was president of one of its two literary and debating societies, a member of Phi Beta Kappa, and the editor of the literary magazine; his commencement address was entitled "The English Poets as Advocates of Liberty." After graduating in 1842 he moved to the South to make a living as a schoolteacher. In Savannah, he served as a tutor to the children of Senator John Macpherson Berrien, another Northerner who had moved to Georgia, and while teaching, read law under Berrien, who had been Andrew Jackson's attorney general. Admitted to the bar, he practiced in Elberton, Georgia, northeast of Atlanta. There is astonishingly little biographical information on Akerman, considering that he was a cabinet member; the conspiracy of historical silence that came down on Reconstructionist integrationists dealt severely with the attorney general.[21]

Akerman went with his adopted state when Georgia seceded, and served as quartermaster of a home-guard brigade that saw action when the state was invaded. He was married the day before leaving for the front. After the war he came to political prominence as a member of the Georgia constitutional convention of 1867–68, which resulted in black participation in the governing of the state; he was not a party to the resurgence of white supremacy in Georgia that resulted in the removal, in 1868, of the Negro members of the state legislature. When the right of blacks to hold office was restored, Akerman went to Washington to lobby for the readmission of Georgia. It was then that he met influential Radical Republican senators, who had assumed that the grant of political rights to the freedmen would secure their safety. However, as the participation of black citizens increased in the South, so too did the determination of white supremacists to stop them from achieving equality. When legal maneuvers failed, the white supremacists moved outside the law, and the Ku Klux Klan, founded in 1867 in Tennessee, grew strong in areas where black people were politically active. By 1869 the secret organization was using terrorist techniques to frighten voters into subservience. It soon became clear that local law-enforcement officers, within the state court systems, would not prosecute the Klansmen, and witnesses to crimes who were brave enough to report what they had seen often found that their reports were turned over to the Klan, and they themselves then became the victims of terrorist attacks. As law-abiding Southerners like Akerman sought some protection for the black Republicans, they began looking not to the state courts, but to the federal courts. For a man with young children to combat the Klan took courage, which Akerman did not lack. At first his efforts were not effective, despite his skill as a lawyer and his powerful position as United States district attorney. In this position, Akerman was charged with the duty of enforcing the federal rights of his neighbors, but neither in Georgia nor anywhere else in the South, save Kentucky, did a rigorous program of prosecuting terrorists exist in 1870.

The Civil Rights Act of 1866, designed to enforce the Thirteenth Amendment, was on the books, and shortly after the ratification of the Fifteenth Amendment, the enforcement bill of May 31, 1870, designed to end the intimidation of black voters, was passed by Congress. But none of this body of law meant that President Grant and Attorney General Hoar were insisting that United States district attorneys in the Southern districts aggressively prosecute the people terrorizing and murdering black citizens who exercised their rights. Some excellent federal judges, such as Hugh L. Bond, attempted to bring justice to the South, but neither in Akerman's days as United States district attorney in Georgia nor during his first year as the nation's attorney general was the prosecution of the Klan aggressive enough to be effective.

Akerman had, however, become attorney general at an auspicious time for enlarging the responsibilities of that office. Largely to eliminate the expensive practice by which cabinet departments hired lawyers for specific cases involving the government's interest, Congress in June 1870 created the Justice Department. In the new department, the attorney general was responsible for all litigation involving the federal government; to help him carry out these added duties, a new position—solicitor general—was created. The solicitor general was to argue cases in the Supreme Court, and the attorney general supervised his work as well as that of the United States district attorneys, who argued cases before the federal circuit courts. Litigation before these courts was growing to major proportions as the pressure to protect black citizens in the South through the use of federal law and federal courts increased.

"Outrages," as the Freedmen's Bureau termed the murders, cruel beatings, and terrifying threats of both that were intended to relegate black people in the South to a dependent position, had been going on since slavery ended. The records of the Bureau were full of documented cases of brutal mistreatment. Yet not until the December 1870 term did Congress finally move to stop the criminal activities in the South. In April 1871 the nation's legislators established a joint committee which began a massive investigation of the activities of the Ku Klux Klan. The committee members' thorough interrogations (recorded in thirteen volumes of testimony, along with balanced conclusions) began when Congress, anticipating their findings, passed a bill to enforce the Fourteenth Amendment. Initially, there had been difficulty getting Grant's support of this bill. It called for the president to press for protection of the black people in the South through the courts; if compliance could not be obtained through the co-operation of the state and federal judicial systems, Grant would be empowered to use the army to enforce court decisions and to suspend the writ of habeas corpus to make prosecutions effective. Moderate Republicans like James A. Garfield and James G. Blaine balked at this, and Grant, skeptical of the usefulness of the army in enforcing racial justice, and wary of charges that he wanted to make himself a military dictator, was reluctant to support the legislation. An earlier bill, which had had Grant's sanction but not enthusiastic support, had been defeated, and the managers of the legislation, Congressman Benjamin Butler prominent among them, concluded that they could not put through any legislation without a strong call for it by the president.

This Grant was reluctant to give. On March 23, 1871, he told George Boutwell, the only member of the cabinet besides Akerman who firmly supported the bill, that he was going to Capitol Hill to explain to those he had previously encouraged that he could not endorse legislation that might result in the use of troops for its enforcement. Dismayed, Boutwell climbed into the carriage with his chief and tried to dissuade him. At the Capitol, Boutwell's argument was reinforced by the citation of atrocities documented in their investigation by the managers of the bill. Grant there and then agreed to issue a public endorsement; conservatives Hamilton Fish and George Robeson were able only to modify the tone slightly, and Grant's written message of March 23, 1871, established the basis for federal jurisdiction in the cases by stating that the collection of taxes and the passage of the mail were endangered. With this somewhat tepid but indispensable call for action, Congress on April 20 passed a strong measure, called the Ku Klux Klan Act, designed to enforce the Fourteenth Amendment.[22]

Armed with this legislation, Amos Akerman moved forcefully to protect his own—the people of the South, both black and white, who believed the Civil War had really changed things and who were willing to work together within a lawful society. He identified his party—the Republican party—with this cause. In the summer of 1871, Akerman wrote a fellow Southerner about the great power of the Ku Klux Klan and "the necessity of protecting the Republican citizens of the South against outrages." He went on to say, "In my opinion we make nothing by concession to the Democracy. I am for a strict adhesion to our doctrine, as not only right in principle, but expedient in policy." He looked forward to Grant's renomination because he believed it would ensure the continued enforcement of antiterrorist measures—no one, he told a friend, was "better" or "stronger" than Grant—and he sought to instill confidence in the Georgian so he would dare to testify publicly before the congressional committee that was in the South investigating terrorism.[23]

In August 1871, Akerman was much troubled by the threat of still more radical violence, in Louisiana. "The New Orleans trouble is serious," he stated at the beginning of a letter to Grant on August 5, but as he explained in conversation with Babcock, the Negroes had not formally tried to obtain protection under state law, and therefore, under federal law—duly cited in his letter to the president—he could not act. In North Carolina, on the other hand, he encouraged the bringing of indictments against terrorists. Akerman reported to Benjamin Butler—whom he did not permit to bully him into an appointment of which he did not approve, or to deflect him from concentrating on the South—that from "one of the worst counties" of North Carolina a request had come that prosecution be eased "lest there be starvation, because so many of the outlaw class are hiding in the woods for fear of arrest." Akerman doubted that there was actual starvation, and he would not accept the concept that one ceases to protect an injured party because such protection is inconvenient for the injurer. To Akerman, the complaint from North Carolina demonstrated that his United States district attorneys were indeed having an effect in the South. He acknowledged, however, that in "other states we have not yet made much impression."[24]

Concerned, Grant came to Washington from Long Branch in August and conferred with Senator John Scott of Pennsylvania, chairman of the joint committee that was investigating the Klan. It was clear from the discussion that if all known violators were arrested, the jails would be filled and the court calendars taxed. To permit men who had tormented blacks to go free on their own recognizance was to invite them to continue assaults on the already victimized Negroes. On the other hand, the only constitutional ground, other than invasion, for suspending habeas corpus was to declare an area to be in rebellion; for the president to do this and direct that those arrested be held in military detention centers until they could be brought to trial was to invite the charge that martial law was in effect. Grant was never happy with the image of himself as a military despot grinding the South under his heel, but the evidence of brutality presented by Scott was overwhelming. Therefore, he sent Akerman to North Carolina with instructions to encourage the judges to move the trials speedily. The attorney general was able to press prosecutions in that state, but when he moved to South Carolina, he found in the early fall that the terrorists were out of control. On October 12, 1871, a warning was given; it went unheeded, and on October 17, Grant issued a proclamation suspending habeas corpus in nine counties. Cooperating with United States marshals, army officers led detachments of soldiers out into the countryside to arrest suspects, who were then held for trial before the federal district court for violation of the act of April 20, 1871. Akerman remained in South Carolina during October, taking personal charge of this campaign against the Klan.[25]

He could see the debilitating effect on the black citizens of the savage attacks on them, but he found it difficult to make that savagery comprehensible to his countrymen in the North. To many it was literally incomprehensible. One Northerner, trying to understand the virulence of the hatred in the South, asked Akerman if relief from the whiskey tax would dispel it. Akerman was afraid more than that would be necessary:

A portion of our southern population hate the government of the United States, because they understand it emphatically to represent northern sentiment, and hate the negro because he has ceased to be a slave and has been promoted to be a citizen and voter, and hate those of the southern whites who are looked upon as in political friendship with the north, with the United States Government and with the negro. These persons commit the violence that disturbs many parts of the south. Undoubtedly the judgement of the great body of our people condemns this behavior, but they take no active measures to suppress it.

There, baldly, was the problem. Grant could not have asked for a clearer analysis of Reconstruction than that offered by his attorney general. The question was what it would take to make the popular president lead the country into sustained "active measures."[26]

Akerman could see no point in conciliation. To E. P. Jackson, the United States district attorney in Jackson, Mississippi, who could get nowhere with the federal district judge before whom he argued his cases, Akerman wrote that he thought either impeachment or congressional action reassigning the district court were the only cures, and he expected neither. The judge, he concluded, was typical: "It is my individual opinion that nothing is more idle than to attempt to conciliate by kindness that portion of the southern people who are still malevolent. They take all kindness on the part of the Government as evidence of humility and hence are emboldened to lawlessness by it." Akerman was not growing gentle on the job: "It is the business of a judge to terrify evil doers not to coax them."[27]

Akerman was willing to perform even symbolic acts to indicate where he stood. He took rooms for his new department in the handsome new headquarters of the Freedman's Savings Bank, across the street from the Treasury, in August 1871. He applauded thrift and education among the freedmen, but he did not subscribe to the idea that emancipation had automatically cured all the deficiencies from which blacks suffered as a result of having been slaves. He defended barring Negroes from juries because they were "uneducated," and he vigorously argued that Republican acquiescence to this position in New Jersey would not drive the black voters into the Democratic camp. In a letter marked "unofficial," written to William E. Walker, a New Jersey Republican and a black man, he was as tough as he had been about the white Mississippi judge. Outspokenly and without condescension, he rejected Walker's threat to take his followers into the Democratic camp: "You do not, on that matter, represent . . . your colored fellow citizens. I cannot believe that they are capable of such meanness." The blunt attorney general pressed his allies hard. To a beleaguered Mississippi official he observed that "six years of leniency" had not "melted" disrespect for the law, which would "only disappear before an energetic, but at the same time, strictly just and lawful exercise of power."[28]

By November 1871, Akerman began to see the enormity of the problem of bringing racial justice to the South. To a friend in Brooklyn he confided, "A judge of one of the State courts, who is very kindly disposed to his Ku-Klux neighbors, writes to me a remonstrance against the action of the United States Government, and unwittingly lets out the fact that from fifteen hundred to two thousand of his neighbors have absconded." Akerman observed that "none but the guilty would flee," and the number of potential defendants disturbed him. He reasoned that local courts would not act and the federal courts would only be able to handle a fraction of the cases. "Really these combinations," he concluded, "amount to war."[29]

Akerman was stern, but he had some sense of humor about himself. He admitted to a friend that he was "chronically garrulous on the Ku-Klux"— but he was not so tired of hearing himself on the subject as to yield in his determination to break the Klan. Having witnessed at first hand the extreme difficulty of enforcing the Ku Klux Klan Act in South Carolina, he had only praise for the courage and tenacity of Major Lewis W. Merrill of the United States Army, stationed in Yorkville, South Carolina, who was trying to do so. Merrill, described in the *New York Tribune* as having "the head, face, and spectacles of a German professor, and the frame of an athlete," did, in the judgment of Allen W. Trelease, as much as any man in America to combat the Ku Klux Klan. Akerman would have agreed. He wrote a discerning and elegant evaluation of Merrill that suggests a public servant of the highest order. He told Merrill's commanding officer that the young man was precisely the person for the job because he was "resolute, collected, bold and prudent, with a good legal head, very discriminating between truth and falsehood, very indignant at wrong, and yet master of his indignation; the safer because incredulous at the outset, and, therefore, disposed to scrutinize reports the more keenly. . . ."[30]

There were nowhere near enough Merrills. Akerman was dismayed that the public thought Tammany frauds in New York more interesting than the murder of black people in the South. In a speech in Brooklyn he tried to bring Northerners to a different order of priorities with a "simple narration" of the murders in South Carolina that Merrill had documented for him. He also took Merrill's report and his own observations to Grant and urged the president to support firm prosecution of the Ku Klux Klan cases. Black people and their friends registered their approval of Akerman's efforts with an invitation to him to serve on the visiting committee of Howard University.[31]

As late as the second week in December, there is no hint in Akerman's correspondence that he was about to be fired. Early in November, however, he had called on his predecessor, Rockwood Hoar, in Arlington and when Hoar was "not in" to him had set down in writing, with characteristic and fatal directness, "concisely the point of objection" to Hoar's contention that the railroad he represented had completed its road and hence was eligible for land grants from the federal government. Akerman was exceedingly stern with Hoar. ("Your road is not *completed* until it is finished . . . to a site legally fixed for a junction.") Hoar was no doubt annoyed by the attorney general's summary rejection of his claim. He himself may not have been in a position to extract a reversal of Akerman's decision from President Grant, but his clients were.[32]

Meanwhile Akerman continued to work to build a strong Republican party in Georgia and across the South as the only means of supporting, locally, the federal effort to enforce the laws protecting the freedmen. And he wanted through politics to achieve a very high goal—to prevent the black voters from becoming so discouraged that they would embrace racial separation. To the Reverend Henry McNeal Turner, a brilliant black minister and political leader whom Grant had named postmaster at Macon, Georgia, and who used that post to become an important figure in the state Republican party, Akerman wrote, "Those who think of organizing to vote for colored men exclusively fall into the Democratic [error?] of making politics a matter of race. A black man's party is just as wrong as a white man's party. The best man of the soundest politics should have your votes, without regard to his color."[33]

The man who wrote this was dismissed by President Grant a month later. Hamilton Fish, long annoyed with what he regarded as Akerman's obsession with the Klan, counseled against stern prosecution of that organization. Instead of insisting, as Akerman did, on persevering in the protection of a national citizenry by action in the federal courts, the secretary of state preferred to let the victims pay the price; he hoped to achieve abatement of Klan violence through lenience toward the murderers. Grant knew that under the Constitution habeas corpus could be suspended only in cases of invasion and rebellion, and he did not want to conceive of the Klan's activities as a reopening of the Civil War; he was uneasy about Akerman's zeal. This uneasiness, coupled with pressure from Secretary of the Interior Columbus Delano in behalf of Collis P. Huntington and Jay Gould, whom Akerman had thwarted with strict rulings unfavorable to their railroads, led Grant to remove the attorney general. On December 12 and 13, 1871, Akerman and Grant exchanged brief polite notes of resignation and the acceptance thereof, and in a personal covering letter Akerman wished the president the continued success of his administration. Then the finest champion of human rights in the Grant administration went home to Cartersville, Georgia, where he practiced law privately for only eight more years. He had given up on his native North and on Northerners. In a letter free of bitterness over his resignation, he wrote his governor, Benjamin Conley (who was also being forced out of the battle), "Even such atrocities as Ku-Kluxery do not hold their attention . . . the Northern mind being active and full of what is called progress runs away from the past."[34]

Akerman's judgment on the Grant administration, as he left it, remained positive. It was, he said, the best in forty years—since that of John Quincy

Adams—for "its merits are in primary things, its faults in trivial things." He did not elaborate on his optimism. In a more intimate and affectionate letter, he wrote Major Merrill, whose judiciousness and concern for the freedmen he so admired, "Perhaps I should violate confidence, and possibly should make mistakes if I now were to state what I suppose to be the true causes of the state of things which make that step [resignation] proper on my part." Stoically (but inaccurately) he added, "My successor is an able and experienced man, and in administering the office will be free from some of the hostilities that have obstructed me." Grant did not stand by Akerman, and politicians with interests different from and more powerful than the Georgian's drove him out. Shortly before he left Washington, he indignantly denied that the cause of his going was his disagreement with the "Secretary of Interior," as he icily referred to Columbus Delano (who had less trouble agreeing with Hoar and Huntington), but he did achieve a dignified exit. With Akerman's departure on January 10, 1872, went any hope that the Republican party would develop as a national party of true racial equality.[35]

Akerman was one of an exceedingly small group of white Republicans who were not embarrassed by what they had wrought in the way of such equality. Washington opened the eyes of others. In the capital city, integration was progressing with alarming success. Black Americans were taking the concept of equality seriously. They were becoming more than servants. Black people moving into the city—moving next door and attaining power in the local government—made Northern congressmen suddenly ready to listen to those who purported to know how to keep them in their place. An awkward moment in the life of Senator Adelbert Ames illustrates the problem well. In the spring of 1871 a petite young woman in a good street dress and hat came into the senator's office and asked him to recommend her for a government job. He said that he could not do so as he did not know her. "You ought to," she said as she left; "I was in the house long enough." Only after she was gone did he recall that she was "the colored girl who was our chambermaid" a few months before.[36]

All of Adelbert Ames's efforts to protect the black citizens of his adopted Mississippi after he became governor in 1874 are diminished by this brief encounter between a young man and a young woman of Reconstruction America. For all his efforts, Ames could not see the woman as a person, through the cloud of class and race. "I felt very cheap," he wrote his wife, "and would willingly give the letter of recommendation to regain what was lost—to avoid even the appearance of being neglectful or unduly forgetful towards one so lowly." What Ames had lost, however, was past regaining. Amos Akerman had had his troubles with paternalism too, but he never forgot the names of the black politicians in Georgia or New Jersey with whom he argued and whom he cajoled and saluted in their mutual fight to achieve racial justice. He apparently was not afraid that he might have blundered on "to real Democ'cy."[37]

The United States Military Academy was perhaps the last place to look for democracy, but black people sought to find it even there. They had the idea that Reconstruction should be a national accomplishment; they saw nothing incongruous in seeking equal treatment in an army that had fought the war that ended their slavery. The man who took on this small but significant effort in reconstructing the North was James Webster Smith of South Carolina. He was the "colored boy appointed to the Military Academy" about whom Senator Adelbert Ames had called on President Ulysses Grant on June 1, 1870.

Smith had been spotted in Columbia by a northern philanthropist, David Clark, as "a remarkable scholar" of "excellent character," and had been brought by Clark to Hartford, where he did superior work in high school before going on to Howard University. In 1870, Congressman Solomon L. Hoge of South Carolina, a former Union army officer raised in Ohio, nominated Smith for a cadetship at the military academy. Smith had been carefully picked to achieve this "first." A black man sat in the Senate of the United States, another had argued a case before the Supreme Court; now Smith took on the risky assignment of making the black man's way into another bastion of the establishment, the regular United States army. Martin Delany and a few other black men had served as officers of some of the 200,000 black volunteers during the Civil War, but no black officers had been trained at West Point.[38]

In the same year that Smith was appointed, two other young black men who were appointed were refused admission on medical grounds, and a third, Michael Howard, was excluded when he failed to pass his entrance examination. Smith was too well prepared to be kept out for reasons like these. His passage, however, was anything but smooth. From home, young Smith got strong encouragement. Israel Smith, in Columbia, knowing the "rebels will devil you so much you can't stay," nevertheless urged James to be strong: "You must not resign on any account, for that is what the democrats want." For James Smith, alone at West Point, this was a demanding assignment. Both officers and other cadets had been angered by his entrance into the academy, and the harassment of the young man was relentless. At first the public could only be suspicious of racism; as word of the persecution began appearing in the press, editorials suggested that the treatment of Smith—for example a pail of slops thrown over him one night as he slept—was just normal hazing, and the writers spoke in the vein of "boys will be boys." One of those boys was Frederick Dent Grant. As the president's son, he was in a unique position to be of great assistance to Smith and indeed to the whole process of integration of the United States Army. Unfortunately, Fred Grant—a member of the first, or senior, class in 1870–71—used his peculiar authority in precisely the opposite direction.[39]

Smith's opponents, determined to drive him from the academy, extricated from all members of the first class pledges that no display of support for

Smith—not even the exchange of a word—would come from any of them. He was to be "silenced." Fred Grant later denied that he had been an organizer of this conspiracy, but he never denied having joined it, and to the dismay of some of his father's admirers, there was considerable evidence to suggest that he was an active participant in the ceaseless harassment of James Smith. The black cadet had not been at the Point for an hour before he was reminded that he was "nothing but a damn nigger"; he had to take his meals cold because he "should not touch anything on that table until the white cadets were served"; he drilled alone: "Stand off one side from the line, you d——d black. You are too near that white man." In June, Smith wrote to Clark that he was lonely and that "these fellows appear to be trying their utmost to run me off, and I fear they will succeed if they continue as they have begun." The harassment was so severe that Smith lodged charges with Emory Upton, the commandant of cadets. In response Upton, knowing that no cadet would testify on Smith's behalf, told him he "must prove the charges." Clark, furious when he heard of Upton's answer, made Smith testify in his own behalf by releasing one of the cadet's letters on the subject to the press.[40]

Clark also had an interview with President Grant and urged him to champion Smith as a model for the advancement of black people everywhere in the society. Clark pointed out how good Smith's academic record was, and Grant acknowledged it, saying, "Don't take him away; the battle may as well be fought now as any time." However, according to Clark's version of the conversation, Fred Grant was in the room and "*in the presence of his father*" said that "the time had not come to send colored boys to West Point." Clark pointed out that if black men were in the Senate, surely they should be at the military academy, to which (reported Clark) Fred replied, "Well, no damned nigger will ever graduate from West Point."[41]

If Ulysses Grant had had all the wit and wisdom in the world, it might not have been enough to bring eleven rebel states into line on Reconstruction, but one word from him could have reconstructed West Point enough for James Smith to emerge, relatively unscathed, as a second lieutenant. It was not that the academy was easy to reform. As the president knew from his own years there, the place was impregnable to thought of any kind; his word would have penetrated neither mind nor heart, but it would have struck in whatever part of the body the responsiveness to promotional possibilities resides. The president of the United States—this one a former general of the army—knew how powerful a weapon the promotions list was. With this stick President Grant could have forced the officers in charge of West Point to keep the tormentors off James Smith's back.

The stick was not used. Fred Grant had done his work well; the absence of any admonition from the White House made the persecutors of Smith sure they were safe. Despite Fred's outburst with Clark, the president chose to ignore the patently racist core of the problem and see it as one created by the wronged party rather than by those perpetrating the wrongs. Writing at the height of the controversy to Secretary of War William Worth Belknap, who was well known for his own disinclination to assist black causes, Grant said, "I received two or three letters from my son Fred who informs me that the cadet is very objectionable there. . . ." The publicity in the newspapers did stir other consciences, and the outcry resulted in a court of inquiry in the summer of 1870. The cadets who did the harassing, among them General Quincy Adams Gilmore's son and Secretary Belknap's nephew, were reprimanded but not punished, and the pressure on Smith continued. It culminated, significantly, in September, the month when the traditional ball was held at which plebes are first allowed to entertain women guests. The ball was not a minor social event in the life of West Point. Julia Grant attended, as did Senator Ames and his bride and Secretary of State Fish's son.[42]

That Smith might exercise his privilege and attend the ball—share a sexual pageant—with white men and women was the greatest threat he posed to the other cadets. Smith himself told of another such occasion, when his brother and sister came to visit him, stayed with "Mrs. Simpson in Highland Falls, and brought Mrs. Simpson's two daughters to a parade." As Smith pointed out a good tree under which to sit while watching the parade, in which, proudly, he was expecting to march, a cadet officer ordered him out of the parade and told him to stake down a tent. Meanwhile other cadets and their young lady friends, "on the *qui vive* to get a glimpse of 'nigger Jim' and the nigger wenches who are going to the hops," pointed to the Smiths and the Simpsons and said, in voices that could clearly be heard, "See the mokes, come to attend the hops." "Moke" was nineteenth-century slang for "ass," and in the United States, was one of the almost endless list of synonyms for "nigger." Smith was learning the ugly power of that word and of other derogatory terms as well. The previous fall, in the episode that brought matters to a head, Smith had been arrested for striking a fellow cadet and court-martialed for "conduct unbecoming a gentleman"; his weapon was a coconut dipper which he had wrested from a tormentor when taunted with a remark about monkeys in trees.[43]

Smith had been subjected to a series of hearings and courts-martial conducted by officials at West Point during the summer of 1870, and now, in the fall, his defenders demanded that the War Department involve itself in his case. In October 1870, General Howard, head of the now feeble Freedmen's Bureau but still regarded as the spokesman for Negro rights in the government, was sent to preside over still another of Smith's trials. This was recognition of the gravity of the situation, for Howard, one of the highest-ranking generals in the army, outranked the West Point superintendent, Thomas G. Pitcher, and Commandant of Cadets Upton. Howard's court heard full testimony, including that of Cadet Smith himself, who appeared without counsel. Patronizing white newspapers, favorably disposed to Smith, cited this acceptance of full responsibility for himself as evidence of his surprising intellectual equality. The account of the trial itself stands as a monument to his dignity and courage.[44]

The transcript of the proceedings confirms that Smith was not a man anyone pushed around. "I," testified Cadet Wilson (with whom Smith had fought over the dipper), "said to him, 'let me go by.' He did not move but said to me *'God damn you.'* " Wilson went on to say that Smith then hit him with the coconut shell. Howard and his colleagues on the court were not impressed by young Wilson's claim of being severely wronged; they cleared Smith of one charge and on the other, the sin of fighting, gave him a light punishment. Many of Howard's fellow army officers, who wanted Smith expelled, were affronted by the lenient sentence, and on November 20, 1870, the Bureau of Military Justice formally protested to Secretary Belknap that it would be better to have no sentence than one which, by making light of the crime, was an insult to the academy. Grant was said to agree with this reasoning, and posting of the decision of the Howard court was delayed. The finding, clearly a triumph for Smith, was posted only on January 5, 1871. The wait for vindication had been long, but any satisfaction in the victory was denied Smith. The harassment immediately redoubled, and before the day closed he was again arrested, this time for refusing to hold up his head when marching. It is hard to cry, unseen, and hold your head up. Again Smith was tried by a West Point court and convicted, and his case was again appealed to Secretary Belknap. While it was pending, the first-year examinations were held; despite the strain he was under, James Smith finished with a high rank in his class. If this was an embarrassment for his fellow cadets, who so forcefully suggested that he was not worthy to be among them, they betrayed no sign of it. Outside West Point, Smith's white admirers pressed Belknap and President Grant to ensure that the conviction would be overruled. No word came from the secretary of war, however, because Belknap did not want to announce any decision that would spoil the Grant family graduation celebration. The presence of the president of the United States and his lady made commencement day 1871 on the Plain, with its magnificent late-spring view of the Hudson, particularly festive. Ulysses and Julia were the proud parents on hand for the graduation of Frederick Dent Grant, who was forty-first in a class of forty-one in discipline; thirty-seventh in academic standing.[45]

Graduation over, Secretary Belknap issued his finding in the Smith case. The cadet was pardoned and permitted to return to West Point—but required to begin again as a plebe, despite his excellent academic record. Before the blurred vindication came, the old abolitionist Lewis Tappan had counseled that Smith should accept exoneration and transfer to Amherst or Williams, where Tappan would pick up the bill. In Hartford, Smith's sponsor, David Clark, was furious with the equivocal ruling. "I feel that Cadet Smith has been outraged by the Secy of War and the President. Fred Grant a low miserable scamp has been the cause of much of his trouble," he wrote.

"If Grant is renominated for the presidency—God sparing my life & strength," Clark continued, "I will prevent this state from giving her electorate vote for him. He is unworthy of his position. [In my] opinion Smith ought to resign and leave the rotten institution. I may publish a history of the whole affair including the conduct of Grant's son." Unfortunately, Clark did not write his book; he put his charges, instead, in a fiery letter to General Howard.[46]

Smith did stick it out. But the graduation of the class of 1871 did not end his harassment or that of the three black cadets who entered that fall. All of them were driven from the academy. The agent of Smith's going was neither a cabal of cruel fellow cadets nor the equally unsympathetic officers of the army, but a professor of philosophy. Professor Peter S. Michie, asserting that "neither caste nor aristocracy" existed at West Point and that the black cadets "all displayed a marked deficiency in deductive reasoning," gave Smith his examination in private—in defiance of custom. Smith failed. A request for retesting, customarily granted, was denied. He left West Point; two years later, while teaching school, he died of tuberculosis. With unintended irony, Secretary Belknap summed up the government's treatment of James Smith when he said that he did for the cadet "what has never been done for a white boy in like circumstances!"[47]

The black cadets kept the faith. Despite Smith's fate, they struggled to make the academy—the nation—theirs, but the academy did not yield. General Howard wrote, "No barbarian could torture a captive so as to wound him in spirit more keenly than other young fellows have done to Napier [another black cadet, who had joined Smith at West Point in the fall of 1871] simply because it is in their power." Howard admired the courage of the black cadets, but he could not match it with effective action in their behalf. When Smith was required to repeat his first year, an enraged David Clark quite simply ordered General Howard to move into action: "I wish you to see the Sec'y of War—and the President if possible and learn what they propose to do." But soon after Clark issued his order, Smith and Napier were being arrested to prevent black men and women from going to a party together with white men and women. And unlike the black cadets, who kept trying until, at last, Henry O. Flipper graduated in 1877, their white liberal friends were picking up their marbles and going home. When (to no avail) Clark, in July 1871 issued his marching orders to Howard, he also wrote, "The time has now come when the question must be settled by those in authority whether colored cadets have equal rights at West Point with others or not. I have been watching events one year. It is plain to me they have not. The declaration that they have is a sham—a cheat—a catch for votes—If this is true—then all I have given ($60,000 since the close of the year) and done to elevate the Colored race is foolishly squandered—and the time has come for me to stop." David Clark stopped; all of white America stopped blundering on toward democracy.[48]

# XXIII

---

# GREATNESS

---

He was sincere and devoted in his friendships, but when he discovered
that his confidence had been misplaced, a reconciliation became
impossible. With him there could be no genuine forgiveness. . . .
— *George S. Boutwell*

The President . . . is as stubborn as ever, and seems determined to risk
his all upon that one card. He seems to have a genius for suicide.
— *Carl Schurz*

ULYSSES GRANT had a genius for survival. To Carl Schurz he
seemed bent on his own destruction in his inflexible and relentless insistence
on obtaining Santo Domingo, but Schurz did not understand his adversary.
Once Grant had decided to ford the stream and get Santo Domingo, he
would not be turned back, and he would not forgive those who, however rationally, thwarted his will. To be sure, he did lose Santo Domingo in a vain
and costly pursuit of a dubious cause. But just as he had outmaneuvered all
the generals who might have stepped in front of him during the war, so
would he best the politicians who had denied him Santo Domingo. He would
never give up contending that annexation was desirable, and, more immediately, he would present evidence of his vindication. He would win reelection.

No Republican had dared oppose him in 1868, but by 1872 many were
ready to do so. Some were men on whom he had once counted, such as Alexander T. Stewart, Jacob Dolson Cox, and Carl Schurz. As a junior senator
Schurz had enlisted loyally in 1869, but he had become insubordinate in his
opposition to the Ku Klux Klan Bill as well as the Santo Domingo annexation. Grant scorned the intellectuality of the men who formed the Liberal

Republican movement. To him they appeared ungrateful and disloyal. In April 1871, Schurz wrote Cox that he considered "the Administration with its train of officers and officemongers" to be the "great incubus pressing upon the party," and he predicted optimistically that "the superstition that Grant is *the* necessary man is rapidly giving way. The spell is broken, and we have only to push through the breach."[1]

Schurz may not have been entirely wrong about the aura of unassailability having lifted from Grant by 1871, but he could not have been more in error in his assessment of his foe. It was not a policy—monetary, diplomatic, constitutional—with which Schurz was contending, nor was it an administration conducted by Babcocks and Porters; it was Grant himself. In the lost campaign for Santo Domingo, the general and president had learned on whom he could count—and, almost more importantly, on whom he could not count—in his war of survival. He was not going to be driven from the White House by anyone, least of all the likes of Charles Sumner and Carl Schurz, to say nothing of effete creatures like Henry Adams and Edwin L. Godkin.

These two journalists were spokesmen for many well-informed people who were protesting Grant's brand of Republicanism. Liberal Republicans wanted government not of the rich and the well born, but of the intellectually well endowed and the well bred. They favored civil-service reform, free trade, hard currency, and civility. They held in disfavor political patronage, inflationary monetary policies, and the militarism they associated with a national constabulary necessary to police a national citizenry. Theirs was a liberal conception of a limited government existing to encourage private virtue, rather than a nationalistic approach that recognized the existence of inequities in the society and sought to redress them through equal application of federal law enforced by the federal government. Except for Sumner, most of their leaders had opposed the Ku Klux Klan Bill. They also had lost most of their affection for General Grant; they had never been particularly fond of the soiled people who still liked the president very much indeed.

"The Tanner" and "the Cobbler" were the good workingman names on campaign posters in 1872. Ulysses Grant was running for re-election, with Henry Wilson of Massachusetts as the vice-presidential candidate in place of Schuyler Colfax, discredited for having accepted a very few dollars' worth of stock from Oakes Ames in the notorious Crédit Mobilier scandal. The choice of Wilson was intended to mend part of the tear in the Republican fabric caused by Grant's bitter fight with Wilson's senatorial colleague from Massachusetts, Charles Sumner. An orphan apprenticed to a farmer, whose name he was given, Wilson had learned to be a shoemaker and subsequently operated a shoe factory. Entering politics in 1840, he reached the Senate in 1855, and served with distinction as chairman of the Committee on Military Affairs during the Civil War. He was an able and honest man, but despite a long life in politics he thought his only claim to lasting fame was as a scholar; he wrote a fascinating work of history that placed the blame for the Civil War

on a conspiracy of great slaveholding families in the South. He repudiated
these oligarchs as undemocratic in a republic that honored good hard work.
But he himself did not, in fact, make very many shoes anymore. And the
cobbler's running mate had always loathed the tannery.

As one biography later put it, the road had led *From Tannery to the White
House*, and Ulysses Grant had no interest whatever in going back down that
road. He was determined to keep his position at the top, and he would do so
by the very simple appeal of an ordinary man to all the other ordinary men
who were still stuck in the tannery or shoe factory. Justice David Davis was
the candidate chosen at the National Labor convention, which hoped to win
support for a workingmen's party. The appeal was in vain; Grant's supporters claimed him as a man of the people, and he got the votes. Grant was
untroubled by Davis and had nothing but scorn for those extraordinary "better" people who were so disgusted with the corruption that had emerged in
his Washington. The Charles Francis Adamses and Carl Schurzes could ful-
minate and call the electorate to move to higher ground all they wanted to.

*The Republican ticket, 1872.* LIBRARY OF CONGRESS

Grant could hold the vote of midwestern farmers even when his monetary policies meant they were acting against their own interests; he could hold the vote of the freedmen because the Democratic party was committed to denying black people equal opportunities; and he could hold the vote of the soldiers he had led into battle.[2]

The re-election campaign did not spring from some spontaneous urge to keep the general on his horse for another four years. He had had his cautious, careful eye on keeping his job—his self-esteem—for a second term all the time he was serving his first. The warrior stood for peace and for order. He had told Hamilton Fish to get the Alabama claims business out of the way before the second election, and his lieutenant had done so. He could also point to a semblance of order in the reconstructed South. The nation was not at war or on the brink of war. Grant was safe and dependable. He seemed oblivious to the corruption within his administration, although it was reminiscent of the activities of army suppliers which had so disgusted him during the war. He stood apart from it, and the voters made the corrupt men in Washington almost an asset to Grant. In contrast to their venality, he seemed all the purer. It bothered many loyalists that the besmirchers should bring ugliness so near their revered hero.

It was an odd election. Grant's challengers were men of undoubted intellectual strength and considerable political experience. The president had firm control of the regular party, so his opponents proposed a new one—designed to appeal to a wide range of Democrats as well as disaffected Republicans—that would borrow unevenly from the spirit of Abraham Lincoln's "malice toward none" and, forgetting the freedmen, grant amnesty to proscribed white Southerners. They planned well and came to their separate convention in Cincinnati in late April with a firm set of principles, ready to search for a leader to carry them into battle. Though their choice of Horace Greeley, a proponent of tariffs, was strange for a group so heavily committed to free trade, the crusade was politically remarkable. It even captured the Democratic party momentarily. The Democrats, not stifled during the Civil War and with no cause for excessive embarrassment over their loss in 1868, nonetheless abandoned their independence and adopted the Liberal Republican candidate as their own. Editor Greeley, though lacking the conventional exuberance of a professional politician, canvassed vigorously from the rear of a campaign train, bringing the call for reform and change to the people. In midsummer many thought the people were listening.

The Grants were on display as well, but this time they did not return to Galena; instead, come fall, they were at their post of duty, the White House. One foreign observer—Sir Edward Thornton, who was not overly acute—thought Greeley had an advantage "for he can speak & Grant cannot deliver himself of even the simplest sentence." He could not explain why Greeley was slipping back. Silently, Grant looked superior, and after early victories in Maine and Pennsylvania there seemed to be nothing to worry about.

*The opposition view, 1872.* LIBRARY OF CONGRESS

Previously, Henry Wilson had been concerned. He made a campaign trip and reported to George Childs that he and Grant were likely to lose the election. Childs went to Grant with the dour prediction: "The general said nothing, but sent for a map of the United States. He laid the map on the table, went over it with a pencil, and said, 'We will carry this State, that State, and that State.' . . . When the election came, the result was that Grant carried every State that he had said he would. . . ." The Liberal Republicans won only where a Democrat would have: in parts of the redeemed South— states where opponents of the Radicals were back in power—and in the border states, where white-supremacist majorities disliked the pro-Negro legislation of the Republicans. Crowds of people called at the Executive Mansion to congratulate the president. Grant told Congressman James A. Garfield that the Liberal Republicans were like "the deceptive noise made in the West by prairie wolves." He had once estimated that he was listening to a hundred only to discover all the howling came from but two animals. (Garfield noted this as the "first story" told by way of illustration he had ever heard from Grant.) According to the *New York Herald*, the president thanked all his callers and added that "apart from the political issues involved, he was gratified that the people had vindicated his private character, which had been assailed during the campaign."[3]

For Greeley there was no consolation. He had lost not only the election but control of his beloved *Tribune*. His wife, long ill, died a week before the election, and suffering both mentally and physically, Greeley himself was dead three weeks later. Grant, correctly and generously, attended the funeral. His doing so was just a simple tribute to an honorable opponent, but there could have been no better symbol of the totality of his victory than his trip to New York for the service.

With the election behind him, Grant had to get on with governing, and he needed good men to talk to about that task. Henry Wilson, his new vice-president, might have been a help in the second term, but in May 1873 he was stricken with paralysis. He continued to preside over the Senate, but after his attack he was not strong, and in November 1875 he died—in the Capitol. With no powerful new advisers finding their way into his confidence, Grant relied on Hamilton Fish more heavily than ever. When the Fishes closed their Washington house in 1872, it was widely believed that the secretary of state would be replaced, but a new house was soon found, and Fish remained. Fish was honest, and Grant trusted him, but he was a man of very narrow vision. Perhaps he should not be faulted for sticking to his own job and being more interested in foreign matters than domestic ones, but unfortunately the president did count on him for advice on domestic questions. Fish's lack of concern for Americans with less financial security than his own led Grant away from actions that his administration should have taken to aid the freedmen and the workingclass victims of economic stress during his second term.

There was hardly anyone else in the cabinet worth talking to, and Grant felt deserted. He had found Jacob Cox more interested in rectitude than policy, but his voice had been more helpful in the cabinet than was that of his dim successor as secretary of the interior, Columbus Delano. Secretary of the Navy George Robeson contributed very little; Amos Akerman was gone, and the new attorney general, George H. Williams, was neither learned nor concerned with much of anything except his career and his exceedingly costly wife. Orville Babcock was Babcock. Rawlins's successor, Secretary of War William Belknap, was a bluff, hypocritical, unimaginative man. Yet there were men Grant could have talked to, men who might have made a difference in the second administration if Grant had trusted them and paid attention to their advice. He himself had a spacious concept of the new nation that had been born out of the Civil War. He saw a continental colossus that spoke with one voice; it was to be a great nation-state. But Grant, its leader, had no sense of statecraft. He spent an inordinate amount of time on appointments to petty offices, in an endless attempt to balance state representation and placate party factions. Except perhaps (rather surprisingly) in international politics, there was no grand design. There was no sense that the Republican president was building a party and a government with a coherent and wide-ranging philosophy. Instead, he was capricious and fitfully personal in his appointments. Nowhere was this tendency more apparent than in his handling of the opportunity to reconstruct the Supreme Court. Andrew Johnson

did not appoint a single justice; Grant named four, one of them a chief justice. Each time, there was enormous conjecture over whom he would choose,
with highly interesting men mentioned as possibilities. Not all of the four he
actually appointed were totally wanting in intellectual power, but in the end,
he chose them with about the same discernment that went into his selection
of consuls and postmasters.

There were those not totally self-serving who hoped he would do better. "I
came over in a sleeping car with the President last night," wrote Benjamin
Helm Bristow to his law partner on December 4, 1872. He described a rich
conversation with Grant, who "was on his way to Mr. Greeley's funeral." It
was a long talk, and Bristow was happy to report that Grant's "state of mind
is just about what I think you and I would like to have it. My opinion [is]
that he means to avail himself of the grand opportunity that now lies before
him to make a great name for himself and to do great good for the country.
Among other things that I do not care to write, I said to the President that I
sincerely hope that he would recognize the original Union men in the South
in his next appointment to the Supreme bench and I still more ardently
hoped that when he came to look for the man, he would light on you."[4]

Bristow's judgment was sound. The partner to whom he wrote, John
Marshall Harlan, was to be one of the greatest justices of the Supreme Court,
but Grant did not place him there. Bristow's call to Grant to rise to this
height in choosing a justice masked personal disappointment. He had already
held the most distinguished new post created in the Grant administration,
that of solicitor general, from 1870 until November 1872. The solicitor general was the government's lawyer in cases before the Supreme Court, and
Bristow could quite naturally imagine rising to the bench himself. For a time,
it looked as if he would do so. Judge Samuel Nelson, who had been on the
Court since 1845, was retiring, and the remaining justices (except for Chief
Justice Salmon P. Chase) went to the White House on December 2, 1872, accompanied by Bristow, to discuss Nelson's departure. Bristow reported that
they "gathered around me and expressed their individual desires that I
should be appointed Judge Nelson's successor." Reporters who were present
overheard this, and when Grant came back into the room and invited Bristow
to take dinner with the family later in the day, the newspapermen put two
and two together.[5]

Grant had done different arithmetic. The story went out on the wires, and
Bristow even sent a telegram to his wife telling her the good news, but when
next he talked with the president he learned that Judge Ward Hunt of New
York had been selected, and that the president had been committed to him
for some weeks. Gamely, Bristow prepared to return to private practice; he
reported to Harlan that the appointment, "though not a brilliant one is entirely reputable, and will reflect no discredit on General Grant." (Later
Susan B. Anthony thought otherwise. Hunt had not valued the First
Amendment highly when he upheld her conviction for picketing a Rochester

polling place on election day in 1872, and in her judgment, Hunt's attitude toward women exposed in the case was "the greatest outrage History ever witnessed.")[6]

Hunt's appointment, which was confirmed, brought no more greatness to the Court than had the seating of the two men Grant had earlier chosen for the bench. The appointment process had begun, with some promise, in 1869 with the selection of two men of considerable public prominence, but ultimately neither of these was seated. When the aged and ill Robert C. Grier was persuaded to resign in December 1869 and when Congress restored a ninth seat to the court, Grant had named two men with whom he had had difficult dealings—his old chief, Edwin M. Stanton, and his attorney general, Rockwood Hoar. He knew both to be skillful lawyers with impressive national reputations; he may also have felt a need to make amends to Stanton. Besides, once they were on the Court he would not have to contend with the overly energetic bustle of Stanton and the supercilious wit of Hoar.

However, the appointment of Hoar soon ran into trouble. As attorney general he had not deferred to senators from the states from which he chose federal judges, and he was resented on Capitol Hill. In addition, he was forced once again to be a whipping boy. Hoar was the victim of the animosity toward his friend Charles Sumner that some senators did not have the courage to express directly. In what was an exceedingly embarrassing rebuke to the distinguished Harvard lawyer as well as to President Grant, Hoar's nomination was tabled in January. Stanton's nomination had been approved quickly, but on Christmas Eve 1869, before he could take his seat, he died. Grant once more had two appointments to make.

In the meantime, the Court had handed down its decision in *Hepburn* v. *Griswold*, holding that the greenbacks issued during the war were not constitutionally valid forms of money. The two men Grant now appointed, Joseph P. Bradley of New Jersey and William Strong of Pennsylvania, had been railroad lawyers. The railroads were not anxious to pay interest on their bonds in gold-backed currency, and to no one's surprise, the new justices joined those who had been the minority in the *Hepburn* case, and in two new cases, overturned the earlier decision. Greenbacks were once again acceptable legal tender, so the supply of money necessary for the development of the nation's railroads was not diminished. Controversy has raged ever since as to whether Grant knew how the two men would decide the second *Hepburn* case and chose them on that account. Predicting how one's appointees will vote in Supreme Court decisions is not an art at which presidents have been talented, and Grant probably had no guarantee from the men concerning their vote. Nevertheless, he was widely criticized for packing the Court to achieve a specific decision.

With Bradley, Strong, and now Hunt, Grant had not given the Supreme Court true distinction; his last and greatest chance to do so came when on May 7, 1873, death finally ended Chief Justice Salmon P. Chase's voracious political appetite. Julia and Ulysses Grant rode to Chase's funeral at the Capitol with Senator Roscoe Conkling of New York. Julia loved a funeral as well as the next person, and Chase's in the Senate chamber was suitably grand, but her thoughts were not entirely on the dead: "When the officiating minister alluded to the mantle of the Chief Justice and invoked divine instruction as upon whose shoulder it should fall, I looked around and my choice, without hesitation, was Roscoe Conkling. He was so talented and so honorable, and I must say that woman-like I thought the flowing black robes would be becoming to Mr. Conkling." Riding back to the White House alone with her candidate, she said, "Senator, if it were with me, I should know exactly where to place the robes of justice." That evening she mentioned her idea to the general, and he told his wife that he had anticipated her; he was going to nominate Conkling. But the New York senator disappointed his champion and declined the offer, as did Senator Timothy Howe of Wisconsin. The Supreme Court was not the loser.[7]

Rebuffed, Grant had no other grand choice in mind. Instead, personal matters crowded in on him. Old Jesse Grant died in Covington at seventy-nine. He had been born in the same year as Justice Grier; ancient ties to the eighteenth century were breaking. We can only speculate about the sense of relief, mingled with guilt, that Grant must have felt at being at last not beholden to a father. Grant went to the funeral and then to Long Branch; meanwhile, all spring and summer and into the fall, rumors spread about whom he would name as chief justice. But if the president was dormant, some others were active indeed. The myth that justices of the Supreme Court, once raised to the high bench, have elevated themselves above place-seeking is quickly destroyed by a look at the frantic efforts of Justice Noah H. Swayne to gain promotion. He was convinced that Benjamin Bristow was the key to the post of chief justice; his scheme was that Bristow should convince Grant that he, Bristow, should be made an associate justice, to fill the post to be vacated by Swayne, who would make a splendid chief justice.[8]

Swayne, a Virginian who had moved to Ohio after his Quaker wife freed her slaves and whose son, Wager Swayne, headed the Freedmen's Bureau in Alabama, had been appointed to the Court by President Lincoln in 1862. Now, in September 1873, he spent a desperate day in New York City sending Bristow telegrams and, as he changed hotels, rushing from one to another in search of answers to the telegrams in the hope that Bristow would take up his cause with the president. Swayne's hopes were raised when he heard from Bristow, who was in Maine, that Grant had him under consideration. "Your letter," he replied, "relieved me from all suspense and I became at once very jubilant." In addition, Swayne wrote, another of his friends had seen Grant the previous Saturday and reported that "no one ever appeared more frank & candid than did the P. [the President] throughout the conversation." Grant was reported to have said that if he appointed a chief justice from the bench, he would "certainly" appoint Swayne. But Swayne, to prod

Bristow, mentioned his fear that the president had doubts that Bristow would accept the appointment as associate justice, and his fear that the president was concerned lest Swayne, then sixty-nine, might soon retire or die, making it necessary to repeat the distressing process of finding a chief justice. Bristow's job was to reassure Grant on both points.[9]

Grant could quickly have ended the pressure by naming his chief justice. As long as he did not, he had to listen not only to Congressman James Garfield and other Ohio advocates of Swayne but to the Iowa partisans of Justice Samuel F. Miller and the New Jersey supporters of Justice Bradley. There were also great efforts to resurrect the cause of former Attorney General Hoar, while Julia and others had not entirely given up on the not very judicious senator from New York, Roscoe Conkling.

Hoar would not do. Grant had never liked him, and in the months following his rejection by the Senate, while he was still attorney general, he saw in Hoar a reminder of the power of Congress. He feared a repeat of the earlier humiliation, even though it appeared that changes in the membership of the Senate meant that Hoar would, this time, get through. As one keen observer put it, "If the President were very firm about it, he could carry the confirmation," but Grant was not firm about Hoar or about any man. William M. Evarts was suggested, and the president fretted over that idea and discarded it. He had never liked the man; Evarts was much too sure of himself and had defended Andrew Johnson too well in the impeachment trial. Another obvious candidate, simply because of the office he held, was Attorney General Williams, but most of the lawyers of the day did not mention his name in their conjectures—lest someone hear it. And if the attorney general was vying for the place, he demonstrated it in odd ways; leaving the White House on Tuesday, September 30, 1873, Hamilton Fish ran into Williams, "who had forgotten that there was a cabinet meeting."[10]

Later in the fall, Fish recorded that at another cabinet meeting Grant offered the appointment as chief justice to him, but that he told the president he had been twenty years away from the law and was not competent for the post. Grant replied, wrote Fish, that "he would be the judge of that, and he thought I was." Again Fish demurred, urging a younger man, whereupon Grant—or perhaps Fish—came up with an appalling *non sequitur*, proposing Caleb Cushing. That seventy-three-year-old accomplished scholar and Democratic party hack, with an unimpressive record of antiabolitionism and advocacy of manifest destiny, had recently done the Grant administration a good turn as the counsel to the Alabama-claims arbitration commission in Geneva. He was put forward, in Fish's phrase, "to bridge over the embarrassment of making a selection." Reversing Swayne's logic, Fish thought it desirable for Cushing to serve briefly and then resign so that Grant, at that later date, could appoint the right man. Perversely, Benjamin Butler also urged Cushing and offered Grant an odd analogy: the British counsel at the Geneva arbitration of the Alabama claims had been made lord chancellor;

America should do the same for Cushing. Grant's cabinet, except for Fish, was highly hesitant about Cushing, and used his advanced age as an excuse to push him out the door.[11]

The man who then belatedly walked in through it was the uninspiring attorney general of the United States, George H. Williams of Oregon. Grant nominated him as chief justice, and Benjamin Bristow, who had returned to private law practice, was notified that he was to be the next attorney general. On hearing the news, Edwards Pierrepont, who himself very much wanted one post or the other and suspected that the appointment as attorney general would eventually lead Bristow to the Court, sent Bristow congratulations: "The place of Atty Genl is good while it lasts but the bench is better as it lasts for life and always for long life, except to those who pine for the Presidency." Unfortunately, Bristow never got a chance to test Pierrepont's hypothesis.[12]

"There is a screw loose in W[illiams]'s nomination," wrote a Washington friend to Benjamin Bristow on December 12. "I do not know what it is—He will be either withdrawn or confirmed early next week." This observer told Bristow that he, on the other hand, could rely on his quiet and strong reputation to carry his nomination: "You are *all* O.K. Do not come to Washington. Say not a word to anybody! All commend and applaud you!! I will keep you posted." Bristow did as he was told, but unfortunately for Williams, Mrs. Williams had come to Washington, had had a great many words said about her, and had pushed—much too hard—for her husband's elevation. "Mrs. W. is not a favorite with her own sex however much she is with ours," noted one Justice Department official. And in assuming her position in Washington society, she had equipped herself too well. She had bought the finest carriage in Washington, far grander than the Grants', and equipped it with a coachman and liveried footman—all paid for by the Justice Department.[13]

With the delicious allegations about Mrs. Williams delighting the early holiday gatherings in the capital, the Williams nomination came apart, but not before Ulysses Grant angrily and doggedly supported the choice that he had finally sent to the Senate. "The pressure from the White House is tremendous and it is distinctly understood that the President makes it a matter of party fealty," wrote an assistant attorney general, C. H. Hill of Massachusetts. Grant had Conkling's support, but he had trouble getting that of chairman of the Judiciary Committee, Senator George F. Edmunds of Vermont. Angry with the Senate—"Senators complain that the President resents all attempts at remonstrance or criticism"—Grant was also once more angry with its symbol, Charles Sumner. "I fear . . . that an effort will be made . . . to defeat Sumner [in the Senate] which is madness," wrote C. H. Hill. "The President needs advisers badly and if he does not get them soon, Heaven only knows how this session will end."[14]

In the midst of the battle, on December 15, 1873, old Colonel Dent died. Julia's father was eighty-seven, and she recalled his death somewhat distantly: "My dear father passed away without suffering." She also saw to it that he got the honor due him as the great man of the family: "The General and the gentlemen of our immediate household accompanied his remains to St. Louis." Back in Washington, Grant had to try to focus again on the Williams nomination. The situation became even more blurred when John Marshall Harlan arrived at the White House with a letter from Bristow in which he declined to serve as attorney general. Associate Justice David Davis looked ahead to a seat on the court for Bristow, and advised his friend (who had just reported to Davis on research he had done to disprove charges of Lincoln's illegitimacy) to "stay close to Grant and he will appoint you." Refusing the lower post was, however, an odd way for Bristow to get the higher one. The nomination of Bristow along with Williams had given the appointments their only luster. Now it was gone. Grant was being repudiated. Benjamin Bristow, the man who had called the president to greatness, had decided not to take the trip with him. On December 30, Hamilton Fish called on the president and found him sitting alone in the cabinet room, dejected. Grant wanted to know if Fish had been called on by Senators Conkling and Frelinghuysen, as he had been. They had come to the White House to tell the president that Williams would not be confirmed. Williams's use of Justice Department funds to pay for his carriage was not "illegal" in the senators' eyes, but it was surely "indiscreet." What was worse, during the panic of 1873, when several banks suspended payment on checks, the Williamses had drawn on departmental funds (which they later replaced) for household expenses.[15]

Mrs. Williams, meanwhile, pressed her husband's case in her own fashion. She sought to keep Hamilton Fish and Roscoe Conkling from defecting from her husband's cause by telling Julia Fish that she knew about the use of secret-service funds to secure the re-election of Senator Conkling. Grant, when he heard from Hamilton Fish of this bit of attempted blackmail, pronounced Mrs. Williams's story "untrue." Grant, who himself made liberal use of the secret service, had indeed heard of the matter and now stated that "the only use made of that fund was to pay . . . . for the registration of voters in New York City." This, the president insisted to his secretary of state, "was perfectly legitimate, and I stand ready to defend it." Mrs. Williams's effort had not worked. Williams fought to mend his tattered reputation, but on January 9, 1874, Grant withdrew his name. For the second time in his administration the Senate had been unwilling to accept the man he named to the high court. As in the matter of Santo Domingo, Grant had been rejected.[16]

"The old man got mad," said a writer for the *Nation*, but he did not stop fumbling; Grant's next scheme was to resurrect the candidacy of Caleb Cushing, who, meanwhile, had been rewarded with the ministry to Spain. Cushing would be made chief justice; Bristow—or so his partisans hoped—would again be asked to serve as attorney general; and Williams, who according to

Bristow's friend J. W. Stevenson would "prefer to walk and talk Spanish rather than remain in the Attorney General's office," would go to Spain, despite the fact that "Mrs. W. prefers Washington!" Stevenson, who was Kentucky's Democratic senator, predicted that Cushing would be confirmed, "but not without a *grunt* from some of the Republican leaders." The Massachusetts Republican C. H. Hill reported that the appointment of Cushing, "a septuagenarian intriguer . . . whose moral character is the very worst possible," was urged by "Fish and Butler (two of his only three partizans, Sumner completing the extraordinary group)." Conkling was sent to sound out the Senate, and found that except for Sumner, only the Democrats there were happy with the choice. Commenting on the mess that the nomination had become, Hill wrote, "What a sad pity it is that our poor President has not some one to guide him. Heaven only knows where he will land the party."[17]

Somehow Grant landed it on its feet but not without another tumble. Grant nominated Cushing in January, and the fur flew. David Davis wrote his friend Bristow, "I know that one of the judiciary committee told the President that if he had nominated you for Chief Justice you would have been confirmed. I wish to God he had & then the country would have been saved the disgrace of nominating a common prostitute for Chief Justice." Rescue actually came in another way; on January 13, in the White House, Grant, Babcock, and Porter labored over a rough draft, in Grant's hand, of a message withdrawing the nomination of Cushing. The men in the cabinet knew Cushing was the wrong man and were encouraged when the president was willing to consider three new possibilities: two obscure circuit judges—and Morrison Remick Waite.[18]

Waite, who had served as arbitrating counsel in Geneva with Cushing, was an honest, competent, but little-known Republican from Ohio who had been minimally active in politics but was admired by many party politicians. An able practitioner of the law, Waite was nominated as chief justice on January 18, 1874. On the twentieth, one of those disappointed wrote another: Noah Swayne informed Benjamin Bristow "that the nomination of Mr. Waite will be confirmed to day."[19]

While the desultory business of choosing a chief justice wound its way through Grant's mind, the most important event of his administration took place. This was the financial crisis of 1873, which resulted in the longest depression the United States had ever experienced. In accounts of the period, the depression of 1873–79 is often dismissed with the telling of the dramatic story of the collapse on September 18, 1873, of Jay Cooke & Company, as a result of the sanctimonious banker's inability to sell the securities of his Northern Pacific Railway. Wall Street did indeed treat the nation to one of its inimitable emotional orgies of feverish faces and failed fortunes, but as usual the gentlemen regained their composure—and much of their money—and left the working people of the nation in severe straits. The depression is usually said to have lasted six years; according to some reckonings, which join it to the economic troubles of the nineties, it continued for the balance of the century. Between 1873 and 1876, the daily wages of city workers fell 25 percent while the cost of food dropped only 5 percent. Even that drop in food costs meant a loss of income for the farmers as well. Estimates vary on the number of unemployed—it was almost certainly in excess of a million out of a total population of forty million—and these people suffered great deprivation. This percentage of unemployment is not large by later standards, but there was no governmental welfare system, and the reduction in wage levels resulted in gravely reduced circumstances that were grim indeed for those still employed. Private relief organizations like the Overseers of the Poor in Boston reported long lines at soup kitchens and doubling up in overcrowded city tenements. Americans who were even more desperate than the slum dwellers took to the roads in search of subsistence.

The depression began with a crisis not unlike the one Grant had experienced on Black Friday four years earlier. This time, however, he had to face the absurd but highly dangerous hysteria of Wall Street without George S. Boutwell. One of the most underrated of the Radical Republicans, Boutwell had no genius for financial matters, and therein lay one of his strengths. He was not doctrinaire and not a believer in cure-alls. One cannot reasonably conjecture that all would have been well economically had he still been secretary of the treasury in the fall of 1873, but Ulysses Grant surely could have used his counsel. Boutwell had left the cabinet to take the Senate seat that Wilson vacated when he became vice-president. He was only as far away as Capitol Hill, but that can be a great distance from a president. The friendship between Grant and Boutwell held for the rest of Grant's life, but Boutwell was not available in the cabinet to work with the president in the attempt to stabilize the economy.

On September 20, two days after Jay Cooke failed, the stock exchange had suspended trading; President Grant went to New York with his new secretary of the treasury, William A. Richardson. Richardson was a learned and able lawyer who had come from Massachusetts to be Boutwell's assistant secretary. His promotion was recognition of genuine ability, but to Wall Street he remained an underling. The distraught but proud bankers did not go to Washington to discuss the panic; the president went to them, and in their eyes, he came with a weaker ally as secretary of the treasury than he had had on Black Friday. That earlier crisis had not brought on a depression; Grant went to New York in the hope that the nation's good luck would hold. That evening at the Fifth Avenue Hotel, and the next day, the two men met with a series of New York bankers and other exponents of orthodox finance, such as William E. Dodge. Some conservatives insisted that the government must hold to a policy of returning to a specie-based currency, risking deflation in a reach for a secure dollar with which to conduct foreign trade. Others feared the unemployment and hardship that would result from deflation, and urged

Grant not to fear the already considerable inflation in taking measures to revive the economy. They urged him to have the Treasury redeem government bonds, thus releasing into the diminished money supply of Wall Street funds that could be lent to faltering brokerage firms and other businesses. Grant agreed to the bond purchases but wavered on more extreme measures, probably because he did not understand any better in 1873 than he had in 1869 what the results of his monetary actions would be. When he got back to Washington, Hamilton Fish counseled against any inflationary measures, and Grant moved toward easy money only to the extent of permitting Richardson to reissue greenbacks amounting to $26 million that had been retired. This helped get Wall Street past its crisis but did little to affect the depression that was setting in across the nation.

At the same time that he was allowing the reissuing of currency not backed by specie—gold and silver—he sent to Congress his 1873 annual message, which seemed to claim that just the contrary was being done. He discussed the "general panic now prevailing" only after a good many international matters had been covered. Grant wondered if the panic would not prove a "blessing in disguise"; and added, "My own judgment is that however much individuals may suffer, one long step has been taken toward specie payments"; in some way, not clearly put, the crisis had moved the nation toward resumption of specie payment. He expounded on its virtues at some length, but said nothing about the effect of the economic crisis on the people of the country.[20]

It would be anachronistic to expect Ulysses Grant to have become the spiritual cheerleader that Franklin Roosevelt made of himself in a similar period sixty years later. Still, it is curious that Grant could not stretch his imagination past the economic thinking of the reformers whom he had so roundly trounced in the election a year earlier and, instead, put himself in the position of the failed businessman and of the worker with his wages slashed. Grant and Wilson had campaigned and been elected as two workingmen, and had received the endorsement of many labor organizations. But now Grant made no effort to lead a fight for better conditions. A fight with Congress must have been tempting, since Carl Schurz and Charles Sumner were the exemplars of rectitude and enemies of all efforts to inflate the currency. Grant, however, declined the battle. Similarly, he made no effort to identify himself with the efforts of workers' organizations which sought government actions that would restore jobs and refill pay envelopes. Indeed, one of the chief casualties of the 1873–79 depression was the union movement, which lost membership as the owners of mills, plants, and railroads put pressure on their workers in the worsening conditions of 1874 and 1875. Grant himself never succumbed to the nation's red scare, as did Carl Schurz, in his hard-money speeches, and Thomas Nast, with his cartoons that viciously evoked images of the Paris Commune. The president did, however, revive his 1868 theme—"Let us have peace"—to suggest that he would not allow labor organizations to provoke the wrath of the employers. He had never liked using troops to keep civil order, and was spared setting the precedent established by his successor in calling out the army against organized labor. But in England in 1877, although he was given a hero's welcome by the working people, he spoke approvingly of the suppression of the major railroad strike of 1877, the most dramatic result of the depression.

In December 1874, after twelve months of hard times, Grant began his annual message to Congress with a discussion of the "prostration in business and industries," and there was no more talk of a "blessing in disguise." "It seems to me," the president stated, "that nothing is clearer than that the greater part of the burden of existing prostration, for the want of a sound financial system, falls upon the working man, who must after all produce the wealth, and the salaried man, who superintends and conducts business." But relief was to come only from putting the currency on a gold and silver standard—from resuming specie payments. Congress had not been so limited in its conception of possible cures, and the long debate that had taken place the previous spring in both houses gives the lie to the idea that in the late nineteenth century the federal government was not regarded as having a legitimate role in the economic life of the citizenry.[21]

The result of all the talk and bill drafting had been a relatively underrated piece of legislation that was completely in keeping with the more comprehensive radical program that the Populists would espouse in the nineties. Known pejoratively, but not inaccurately, as the "Inflation Bill," it called not for the redemption of greenbacks and the restoration of a currency based on specie, as advocated by both the Johnson and Grant administrations, but for the reverse. Additional greenback and specie-based currency would be issued together. The amount would be a mere $64 million, but both proponents and opponents saw in the bill the start of the practice of determining the supply of currency by the fluctuating needs of the economy. The bill, which had the backing of western congressmen, ambitious eastern businessmen who had not yet made their money, a growing number of farmers, and most of the nation's factory workers, reached Grant's desk early in April 1874.

Historians and economists who presumably understand money castigate presidents who do not. They should not be astonished by the presidents' failure; the problem lies in the language. The mechanism of the economy can be learned—if this goes up, that goes down—but it all becomes something other than a machine when ethical words like "value" and "trustworthy" or emotionally weighted terms like "soft" and "hard" are introduced. A man like Ulysses Grant, who knew what it was to have a business fail, to lack money to pay bills, to be out of work, could not evaluate the machines built for him by contending economists and others who claimed to know. The "more money" machine seemed to work when it was demonstrated, but the "less money" machine looked just as good when its mechanic turned it on. The problem, which Grant could never fully articulate but which is evident in his

grapplings with the subject in his state papers, is that he could not connect
metaphor to reality. What would it mean to the bill collector in St. Louis if
President Grant told Secretary of the Treasury Richardson to sell government bonds, or to buy them; to "create" more money, or to do the opposite
(presumably to "destroy" money)?

He could see that times were bad, that businesses were failing, that people
had lost their jobs or—more characteristic of the depression of the seventies—were working for reduced wages. The president was under intense
pressure during 1874 to come to the rescue of conflicting Ulysses Grants.
One was the out-of-a-job, lonely, restless Ulysses Grant who wanted a new
start. The other was the man hanging on desperately to a job, trying to keep a
family secure, holding fast to an image of responsibility, who did not dare
budge lest it all be lost.

To go the way of the first Ulysses Grant was to go with the inflationists,
who wanted to combat the depression by creating more money that people
could spend, as individual consumers or as speculative investors. The advocates of this course were the working people and speculative entrepreneurs
like James Fisk, Jr. The Grant who applauded the growth and expansion of
the nation was comfortable with the idea of creating more money.

But the other Ulysses Grant was drawn to the opposite view. The conservatives urged him to hold tight. They warned that the newly created dollars
would not be honored by those in the East and England who already had
their money. They appealed to morality and decorum. The advocates of
creating more money, a policy which had as its base great expectations rather
than accomplished achievement, were rude men like Benjamin Butler and
vulgar men like James Fisk. Dirty farmers and dangerous workers, as clean
and orderly people thought of them, wanted more money too. If President
Grant joined with the farmers and workers, would there truly be an America
of equality and opportunity—would his pursuit of happiness get him to his
goal? Or would he simply go west and go wild, becoming the drunken tramp
he had so nearly become? Irwin Unger, in one of the finest passages of *The
Greenback Era*, describes Grant's chilly reception of William Gray, a Boston
banker, who came to Washington at the end of March to urge a veto of the
"Inflation Bill." The president had been insulted by critical things said about
his management of financial affairs, and he refused to be lectured to by the
Bostonian. The next day, a group of sound-money men from New York arrived at the White House and were dismayed to find that Grant had but-
tressed himself with Senators Logan, Carpenter, and Thomas W. Ferry—all
easy-money men. While the New Yorkers were stating their case, Benjamin
Butler "shouldered his way into the room and took the President off to a corner, leaving the New Yorkers cooling their heels." Unger regards Grant as
having been "deliberately insulting" to the bankers because they were "repeating the inconvenient . . . promptings of his own conscience."[22]

The sound-money advocates did not expect a veto, but a veto came. As
Hamilton Fish recalled the discussion in the cabinet, Grant "earnestly de-

sire[d] to give his approval," but Fish led him from one machine to the other and got his chief to see that the arguments for the bill were "fallacious and untenable" and, instead, Grant and his cabinet wrote a veto message. "In the end," concludes Unger, "the conservatives had gotten through to the President. His truculent behavior toward the merchants probably betrayed a painfully tender conscience rather than a firm commitment to soft money." Or, to disagree and put it another way, Grant wanted to tell the good sound patriarchs to go to hell, but in the end did not dare. He was suffering not from a "tender conscience" but from a sense of rage at having to do the respectable safe thing in order to hold on to what he and Julia had won—the deference of the "better" people. He did not trust himself—or his fellow countrymen—not to become dispossessed if he defied the possessors. "Ultimately, even the obtuse and insensitive old soldier," says Unger, "could not deny the impelling conservative image of soft money as the 'sum of all iniquity'; specie as 'philosophy, morality and religion.' "[23]

Individual Republicans argued vehemently for years longer about the merits of a monetary policy that would help men who had failed in business or struggled as farmers or wage earners as against those of a policy that brought still greater profit to the successful, but Grant's veto made the stand of the Republican party official. From this date it was the party not of the working class but of those who were or aspired to be the capitalists. The latter were overjoyed. Grant's "heroic" espousal of hard money raised him "100 per cent" in George Templeton Strong's estimation. He and other orthodox men of finance moved to capitalize on the wisdom of one they had called "Ulysses the unwise" by achieving a return to specie-backed money in the wake of the veto. Seeing Secretary of the Treasury William Richardson, like his predecessor, George Boutwell, as a friend of the expansionists, Boston reformers moved to get rid of him. The club they used was that one that was all too available in the Grant administration—corruption. John D. Sanborn, an ally of another easy-money man, Benjamin Butler, had obtained a contract to inform on persons who were delinquent in paying taxes; in return for the information, Sanborn would obtain a percentage of the money collected. This practice had been ended by legislation in 1872, but Congressman Butler had managed to attach to the bill a rider making an exception for Sanborn and two other informers. William Richardson, then assistant secretary of the treasury, had signed a contract with Sanborn, and therefore came to be regarded as sanctioning this unsavory method of doing business. Sanborn simply went to the Boston office of internal revenue, and using Richardson's authorization as leverage, obtained an already compiled list of tax delinquents, whom he then ordered to pay up, claiming for himself 50 percent of what they owed. Sanborn subsequently admitted to the congressional investigators that he was paid $213,500 for collecting taxes that would have been paid even if he had done nothing.[24]

The investigation, which continued from February to May, was highly publicized and deeply damaging to the Grant administration. On June 2,

1874, to the delight of the reformers, who had no problem connecting softness on money with flaccidity in the conduct of official business, Secretary of the Treasury Richardson was shunted aside into a judgeship, and the department passed into the impeccably clean hands of Benjamin Bristow, a sound-money man. Grant had been warned that if he did not appoint a reformer, the corruption issue could result in Democratic victories in 1874 and 1876. Reluctantly, he agreed to give Bristow the post.

Faced with a Democratic victory in November and the opposition's organization of the House that would come in March 1875, the hard-money Republicans pressed for a bill to resume specie payments. This time the administration did give leadership. As noted, Grant's 1874 message to Congress called for resumption, and Bristow lobbied strongly for the bill. What passed was a moderate compromise measure, but its result, due in large measure to Bristow's active contractionist policies, was an acceptance of the international gold standard. In 1875 the Democrats did organize the House, but without a majority in the Senate they were unable to stop the hard-money policy. The greenback movement, which seemed to have such promise for working-class America in 1874, had been successfully contained by the reforming conservatives by 1875.

During the depression years Grant turned to the task of shoring up his own economic future. Beginning before the crash, and continuing serenely through the troubled fall of 1873 and on into 1874, he tried once again to forget his troubled Grant past and make himself a country gentleman, in the not very convincing mold of the Dents. He and Julia still owned the farm in St. Louis, and after her father's death her holdings increased. The farm had been neglected, but earlier that year Grant had begun to give it attention with the ardor of an absent squire eager to return. He discharged one manager and hired another, Nathaniel Carlin. In a forceful way, he told Carlin that he would personally give him instructions and that reports should come directly to him; should matters arise that Grant could not oversee himself, Carlin could look to the man who handled his business affairs in St. Louis, Judge John F. Long. In addition, Carlin's former employer, Charles W. Ford, an old friend of the president's, would look in from time to time. Grant's instructions in October were specific; Carlin was to "sell all the calves you can at good prices"—he wanted to be out of cattle entirely by spring— and take in as many horses to board "as you can attend."[25]

The president had big plans and wanted no tenants—they had been nothing but a bother in the past. Turning to farming, he told Carlin in November that he favored top dressing when it came to spreading the manure, and he hoped the fields could all be gotten into grass as soon as possible. Carlin was to straighten the road that had been dislocated when the railroad line was put across the land, down at the creek, and he was to restore some damaged fences. Grant then moved to the subject of his horses, which had been mistreated by the former manager.[26]

The president was surprised "that Young Hamiltonian is still alive now with the care—or lack of care—that he has gone through with." The horse was from the finest line of trotters in the land. Grant gave instructions that all of his horses on the farm should either be trained to be driven or bred to produce fillies which could be driven. Trotters were the horses Grant most enjoyed, and they would bring a profit when sold to other enthusiasts. He explained Young Hamiltonian's line to Carlin. The horse was "sired by Iron Duke, now owned and always owned in Orange Co. N.Y." (Goshen was a great trotting town.) His "dam was a very fast and stylish mare—Addie— that I got in 1865. She was full sister of one of the best stallions in Massachusetts." On and on the horseman went, with full recall of the qualities of the several horses he thought should be mated. No affairs of men and nations commanded so thoroughly the attention of President Grant.[27]

In the summer of 1874, Grant asked Judge Long to ship east one of his favorite horses, Butcher Boy, "if he is not too decrepit from old age." Then he added, "If I get him here I will keep him as long as he and I live." There is a nice sense of continuance in this—the tie of man to horse that might have added small, but rich, value to Grant's life. It stumbled away from him. Butcher Boy was moved, not east for the president to enjoy, but rather to Chicago, where J. Russell Jones, late of Galena, could impress his new and affluent friends by driving out behind General Grant's horse.[28]

Things did not work out for Butcher Boy—or for Grant; the farm was not going as smoothly as he wished. In November 1874, on time borrowed from the writing of his message to Congress, Grant wrote Judge Long that it must not be considered a criticism of Carlin that there were bills to be paid which could not be met from receipts. He was sending a thousand dollars to pay the taxes. In December, in a letter to Carlin, he praised his manager for his good work with the horses but had to say no to a request for equipment: "I have already paid out this year some $12,000 on the farm and have not got the means to go further." Grant had made a major investment in his estate and hoped he could go out in the spring "to put the place on a good footing."[29]

That footing was never gained. The Grants, with the Bories and Orville Babcock, visited the farm during a western trip in April 1875, but their time in St. Louis was short and largely consumed by the social comings and goings of a president; Grant's attention had strayed from the idea of a country seat. That fall, Carlin received formal notification from Judge Long that all of Grant's personal property on the farm—which meant the horses— was to be sold, and the farm was to be rented. The dream of a fine country holding with splendid horses was dead. Once they left the Executive Mansion, Ulysses and Julia would not go back to where they had ridden together, courted, and built the only house they were ever to build. The attempt between 1873 and 1875 to create a secure domestic economy for themselves and their children was no more a success than were Grant's confused efforts to establish greatness in the government with a distinguished appointment to the Supreme Court or to restore the prosperity of the nation.[30]

# XXIV

# WEDDING
# AND WHISKEY

And helpless governors wake
To resume their compulsory game . . .
— *W. H. Auden*

N ELLIE  G RANT  was one of the most appealing and most unhappy of
the long line of disconcerted White House children. She was only thirteen
when she moved into the Executive Mansion and into the grasp of the society
that haunts it. At eighteen she was the bride at a wedding in the East Room.
It was not so much that she was young when she married, but that she was
handed over from one empty world to another. She was the daughter of two
people so dangerously innocent that they could not fully comprehend their
own vulnerability, or that of their children. Julia and Ulysses were the
owners of an unusual property; Nellie was sold at a low price—it took only a
dashing young man with an English name and imaginings of a splendid life to
fetch her. The young girl was barely allowed to have any life at all. It was as
if Henry James, who after all kept a close eye on Grant's America, had had
her in mind when he created Daisy Miller.

Nellie was an only daughter; she carried (but did not use) the name of her
beautiful grandmother, Ellen Wrenshall, and she was expected to find, somewhere, that bower her mother had left behind in memory. She was seen as
the president's princess daughter, while she was, in fact, a nice teen-age girl.
Her father doted on her in exactly the way a nineteenth-century father was

expected to. He fluffed up her femininity, as when he wrote to her about her pony, which her younger brother rode and then harnessed to a cart for her. She was not even allowed the freedom that had once been her mother's to get up on a horse's back and ride.

There had been no young girl in a presidential family since the Tylers moved out of the White House a quarter of a century earlier, and Nellie Grant was good copy for reporters out to please a sentimental America. They had had her on display since 1864 when, at a sanitary-commission fair in St. Louis, she was photographed in spectacles as the old woman living in a papier-maché shoe. In 1869, an engaging Brady portrait showed her in a tartan and cloak; Queen Victoria had covered Balmoral and half of America—including Nellie—in plaid. Nellie had a bit of charm, and if she had had the fortitude that Alice Roosevelt displayed so strenuously thirty years later, she might have found the White House fun for a teen-age girl. However, she was not that strong; Nellie seems not so much to have asserted herself as to have been pushed ahead. Her mother, while fussing about the critics who did not approve of a fifteen-year-old girl's dancing all night at a cotillion, secretly delighted in all the attention that was paid the first young lady of the land. In 1872, at sixteen, Nellie was sent to Europe with the Bories and taken up by the American minister in London, Robert C. Schenck, and his social daughters. She was presented to the queen and, to complete the storybook romance, on shipboard on the way back to America, she fell in love—with Algernon Sartoris.

The name is too good to be true, but true it was. And what's more, Algernon was a cad and a bounder. His family, of the minor gentry, was of not very ancient lineage and limited distinction, but had an eye for acquisition. The Sartorises already owned one of the great ornaments of nineteenth-century England—Adelaide Kemble, Algernon's mother. Adelaide Kemble is remembered today as Fanny Kemble's sister or as the daughter of the great actor Charles Kemble, but she herself was an opera singer of impressive accomplishment. If the reviews are to be believed, she may have been the more talented of the two stunning Kemble women. She sang what must have been a very grand *Norma*, as well as a good number of other splendid soprano roles, and was at the top of a great career when she married and left the operatic stage.

Adelaide Kemble Sartoris (pronounced *Sar-tress*) was a hostess known as "one of the best leaders of talk"; at her house on Park Place, London, she entertained writers—Charles Dickens, Henry James, and Matthew Arnold—as well as singers from her world of opera. "Her dinners were perfection," reported a fashionable friend. But when Algernon's older brother was killed in 1873, she withdrew to the country. Mrs. Sartoris was a woman of substance, but her husband and younger son were of another cut. Though comments on both men are exceedingly guarded, the suggestions are that her husband was a philanderer and so was their son. When Nellie met Algernon, however, he

*Nellie's wedding, 1874.* **LIBRARY OF CONGRESS**

seemed simply a charming young Englishman, which is to say the most desirable of suitors for an American princess. Apparently she fell in love. Perhaps he did as well. Their wedding was on May 21, 1874, and Ulysses Grant gave his daughter away. In letters to Nellie when she was a little girl and he was off at war—and again much later in his life—Grant revealed that he loved his daughter very much indeed, but whatever thoughts he or her mother had in 1874 about her happiness were smothered in talk about the clothes and presents and arrangements for the wedding. Nellie entered the East Room on the arm of her "stolid father"; her mother, who "looked sad," followed with Jesse and Buck on either arm. Under a bell of white camelias, accompanied by his groomsman Fred Grant, in military dress, Algy stood rigidly, as if his "life depended on the exactness with which the duty is discharged." During the ceremony, the president "looked stead-fastly at the floor" and wept. After the White House wedding, Nellie went off to live in southern England with her young prince.[1]

Accountants of such matters might reckon that Algernon Sartoris had done well in marrying the daughter of the president of the United States. In fact, the Grants acted as if Nellie had gotten the better of the bargain. Julia, still relishing her fantasies of White Haven, created new dreams of her daughter living in splendor and happiness with the best of people. As Mrs. Sartoris, Nellie could, it was true, call a countess cousin, but she was nevertheless miserable. The newspapers are short on details—family legend has it that Algernon drank—but in any event there was soon frank, if guarded, talk of her unhappy marriage. However, it was not too unhappy to produce four children. Nellie came home in the summer of 1875 and, while staying with her parents at Long Branch, gave birth to their first grandchild. She took Grant Greville home to England; he lived only till the next spring. Almost immediately she was again pregnant. She was visiting her parents when the Grants left the White House in March 1877, and went with them to stay at the home of Julia and Hamilton Fish; there Algernon Edward Urban was born on March 17. He was followed by Vivian May in 1879, and Rosemary Alice in 1880.[2]

Except for the children, Nellie's life seems to have had little center. Very early, discreet references in the press and in letters suggested that hers was a dead marriage. In the summer of 1875 Adelbert Ames found proud grandparents when he visited Long Branch, but noticed "sorrow" when they spoke of Algernon's unwillingness to live in America. He was unpersuaded when Julia talked to him about Nellie's life in England: "I could see she would have me, as all the world believe and know, that she had a good, happy home there." One of the saddest aspects of it all was that Julia and Ulysses Grant, who had made so sturdy a building of their own marriage, seemed unable to impart strength to Nellie. Henry James, after visiting the Sartorises in the country, described Adelaide's brilliant conversation and wrote, "Meanwhile poor little Nellie Grant sits speechless on the sofa, understanding neither head nor tail of such high discourse and exciting one's compassion for her incongruous lot in life. She is as sweet and amiable (and almost as pretty) as she is uncultivated—which is saying an immense deal. Mrs. Sartoris who appears (*sick* with fastidiousness as she is) to do her [Nellie] perfect justice, thinks very highly indeed òf her natural aptitudes of every kind, and cannot sufficiently deplore the barbarous conduct of her mother leaving such excellent soil so perfectly untilled."[3]

Nellie proved to be of small value to her husband, for Algernon Sartoris gained little stature in English society from his marriage to her. When the Grants were in England in 1877—and stayed at Windsor and Apsley House and a score of the other finest houses—the opera singer's son and his wife were not with them. Julia and Ulysses spent only one week with their daughter and grandson and the Sartorises at their pleasant house on the south coast. Perhaps the Grants were not welcome; perhaps they were too preoccupied with their own public lives. In any case, they saw little of Nellie. She did travel with them in Italy in 1878, but then she was joining them for a holiday rather than for a real re-establishment of the family. Nellie was committed by her marriage to the Sartoris world, and she could not easily escape from it. Perhaps the most poignant footnote to her story came in the item of a society writer at the time of her father's funeral. Nellie had been over from England to be with Grant when he was dying; now, reported the *New York World*, "Mrs. Sartoris is in correspondence with her family in England to have her children brought over here. If they consent . . . she will remain this winter with her mother, if not, she will go back about Oct. 1." She went back. At thirty, the daughter of a president of the United States, she—with her children—was still the property of a hated husband. She went back to England, and five more years were to pass before she was permitted to come back across the Atlantic with her children and get a divorce.[4]

Nellie's wedding marked the encasing of Julia and Ulysses Grant in the heavy-bordered middle-class grandeur of the American presidency. Grant never abandoned his simplicity of style, but he never again had a simple place in which to indulge it. It was all great houses, world's fairs, testimonial dinners, and those ceaseless republican progressions—the endless trips that proclaimed that they had nowhere that was home, nowhere that they were any longer allowed to be Julia and Ulysses. Nowhere, except the White House.

And there in that house their private love affair flourished. When Julia suddenly needed to break into her husband's public day, she would—as she did on May 22, 1875—take a sheet of note paper, fold it in three, into an impromptu unsealed envelope, and mark it "The President, immediate." The note on the reverse that day read:

> Dear Ulys
> How many years ago to day is [it] that we were engaged:
> Just such a day as this too was it not?
>
> Julia

As quickly and affectionately as it went, the query came back with its answer:

> Thirty-one years ago. I was so frightened however that I do not remember whether it was warm or snowing.
>
> Ulys[5]

The White House was their home and their bastion against a world in which they had never learned to be comfortable. It was one of the great ironies of the Grant story that the man who had had the honesty to tell Congress in a formal address that he was not prepared for the presidency could grasp at that office—even covet a third term—because there was nothing else he was prepared for either. The White House offered security and so did a seemingly loyal staff, but over the eight years of the presidency some of these people failed him. And one of the worst demonstrations of that failure came in the tawdry business of swindling the government out of taxes due on, of all things, whiskey.

*Julia Dent Grant. From John Russell Young,* Around the
World with General Grant.

Strangely, it was from within the family, the cabinet, that the exposure of
the whiskey frauds came. The investigation was initiated by Benjamin Helm
Bristow, the upright Kentuckian who had been solicitor general, had expected to be named attorney general, and had at last, in June 1874, been
brought into the cabinet as secretary of the treasury when Richardson was
forced out. From within the administration, Bristow exposed the worst of the
scandals of Grant's presidency. As a result, he became both the unforgiven
enemy of his chief and the hero of the anti-Grant wing of the party. Benjamin Bristow possessed that sticky double commodity, principle and ambition, and he was in the uncommon position of being able to rise to the first
while advancing to the second. Ulysses Grant found the man and his cause
cloying; he never fully owned up to how crooked the things were that Bristow discovered.

Distillers and distributors made an almost routine practice of bribing tax
agents to ignore the mismeasurement of bottled whiskey or to supply tax
stamps in excess of the amount paid for them. On Bristow's desk when he
took office was ample evidence that Treasury employees administering the
tax had been involved in such practices since the Lincoln administration.
Certainly it could be established that each year since 1870 from twelve to fifteen million gallons escaped the tax. The crime was known, but not the criminal, and such corruption within the Grant administration severely discred-

ited the president. In January 1875, Vice-President Wilson told James Garfield that "Grant is now more unpopular than Andrew Johnson was in his darkest days; that Grant's appointments had been getting worse and worse; that he is still struggling for a third term; in short that he is the millstone around the neck of our party that would sink it out of sight." Bristow was one man whose appointment was applauded by those otherwise dismayed by Grant's choices, and he took it to be his job to rid the president of the corruption around him. In the late fall of 1874 Bristow obtained from Congress an appropriation of $125,000 to conduct a full investigation, but it was a bold and thorough newspaper reporter who cracked the story. On February 11, 1875, George Fishback, the editor of the *St. Louis Democrat*, wrote Bristow, "If the Secretary wants to break up the powerful ring which exists here, I can give him the name of a man who, if he receives the necessary authority and is assured of absolute secrecy about the matter, will undertake to do it, and I will guarantee success." That man was Myron Colony.[6]

An archetypal investigative reporter, Colony was nosy, shrewd, and not overly scrupulous. After he was hired by Bristow and the solicitor of the Treasury Department, Bluford Wilson, he used extraordinary ingenuity to accumulate massive evidence that a conspiracy did indeed exist and that it involved people close to Grant. General John McDonald of St. Louis had been appointed by Grant to be collector of internal revenue for the district, embracing seven states, that had its center at St. Louis. He and the president were old acquaintances, and McDonald had the endorsement of several of Julia's family friends. Now in the spring of 1875, all of Colony and Wilson's evidence pointed to McDonald as the central figure of the whiskey-fraud conspiracy in St. Louis.[7]

In April 1875, McDonald, who was aware that the investigators had his scent, was called to Bristow's Washington office. There Bristow confronted him with massive evidence against him. McDonald broke down and confessed. But after he left the secretary's office—conscious that an indictment loomed—he tried to move around his problem. He called on Bluford Wilson and asked for indemnity against being prosecuted, in return for a promise to collect the money owed by the delinquent distillers. According to Wilson, McDonald urged that the distilleries not be seized, as was planned, because in a full-scale prosecution "the party interests in his State and his district would be greatly damaged. . . ." McDonald, Wilson claimed, tried to impress him with his power in the Republican party, presumably not only with those close to the head of the party, but with Grant himself. Wilson reported that if he had had the authority to do so he would have fired McDonald right then and there.[8]

McDonald, in his account, mentioned no conversation with Wilson, stressing instead his talk with Bristow. He claimed that the secretary, "with some anxiety . . . in his face, . . . inquired if I intended talking with the President." McDonald said that he did indeed see Grant and urged that the evidence be burned, but that Grant recommended that it be sealed instead. There is no corroborating evidence of this alleged conversation; Wilson's version of the next step in the story is that he and Bristow called on the president on May 7, 1875, and revealed the scope of the frauds and the need for swift prosecution. At this point Bristow and Wilson detected nothing but cooperation in Grant's attitude toward the task of finding honest replacements for McDonald and the similarly crooked supervisor in Chicago. Wilson recalled, when later he testified before the congressional committee of inquiry, that Grant that day told him and Bristow that "McDonald had been a friend of his, and had grievously betrayed, not only that friendship, but the public." Wilson claimed Grant was entirely sympathetic to the prosecutions at that point. When a congressman asked whether and when there was "any change in the demeanor of the President of the United States in reference to these prosecutions," Wilson replied in the affirmative and said, "It began in August, 1875." He then explained, "It was not until we struck Babcock in what seemed to be strong suspicious evidence of his complicity that we began to grow apart." From that point on, "the relations of the President to the Secretary of the Treasury and myself were not as they had been."[9]

Bristow, when he testified, declined to comment on Grant's attitude toward the investigation or on any aspect of his own conversations with the president. As the president's "constitutional adviser" he regarded all communications between the president and his cabinet members, and between various cabinet members, as "of the highest privilege," and he repeatedly declined to answer the congressmen's probing questions. By the time of the testimony, early in July 1876, Bristow had left the cabinet and his estrangement from Grant was well known, but the manner of his testimony sheltered Grant. Rather than leave the impression that Grant had done such improper things that he did not dare talk about them, the dignified former secretary of the treasury used a concept of executive privilege to lift "the President" above any action a man named Ulysses Grant might have taken in connection with the investigation of the whiskey frauds. (In a very different context, Marc Bloch once said caustically, "No doubt the argument runs that only by drawing a decent veil over the more glaring indiscretions of our public men can the morale of the country be kept at a high level.")[10]

Wilson, acknowledging Bristow's claim of constitutional privilege for the president, did not comment on what Bristow and Grant had said to each other, but he did not feel bound to refuse to talk about what Grant had said to him. He claimed that the president had, in effect, acknowledged McDonald's guilt and acquiesced to his prosecution. Asked by a congressman if Bristow said explicitly at the May 7 meeting that McDonald had confessed his guilt, Wilson replied, ". . . he did not, for the reason that it appeared at that interview that the President and the Secretary had previously been in conference touching that subject, and that the President understood that branch of the case quite as well as General Bristow did." Except for Wilson's recollection that Grant spoke of McDonald as a betraying friend, there is no firm evidence that Bristow and Grant, at this juncture, had mentioned McDonald's name. Wilson claimed that Grant gave his blessing that day to relentless prosecution of anyone who was culpable.[11]

On May 13, 1875, the special investigators moved, and some 350 men in the government and the distilling industry were arrested, but by then, mysteriously, Grant would no longer acknowledge McDonald's guilt. On May 22, Benjamin Bristow told Hamilton Fish that Grant had said (speaking of McDonald) that "there was one honest man upon whom they could rely, as he was an intimate acquaintance and confidential friend of Babcock's." In response, the exasperated Bristow had told (or reminded) the president that Babcock's friend McDonald "was the head centre of the frauds; that he was at this time in New York with $160,000 of money fraudulently obtained, ready to take a steamer on the first indication of any effort to arrest him."[12]

As for McDonald's (and Grant's) friend Babcock, Bristow was still at a loss as to how to make the president see that his most trusted aide not only was lying about McDonald's innocence but was himself party to the frauds. To persuade Grant, he sent General James Harrison Wilson, Bluford Wilson's brother and Grant's former cavalry commander, to see him. Grant had had confidence in Harry Wilson back in the days of the war, and now Bristow gave the general his assignment: "Wilson you've got to go to Grant and state to him what your brother and I know [about Horace Porter and Orville Babcock]." In recalling the conversation, James Harrison Wilson said, "Well, that was a hell of a contract for me." When he responded to this effect at the time, Bristow and Bluford Wilson laughed and went on trying to persuade him. "Grant is about to dissolve this cabinet," Bristow insisted. "I am to be dismissed, and your brother Bluford will go with me and the whole country will be scandalized."[13]

General Wilson was reluctant, but he finally concluded that it would be in order for him to go to Grant for the sake of his brother's career. As he told Hamlin Garland years later, he "went over to the White House" only to be told that the president could not see him; he was out for a walk with Alexander R. Shepherd, the chief Republican politician of the District of Columbia and a friend of Babcock's. Wilson returned later in the morning and was directed to the library. He walked in and saw not only the president but "Boss Shepherd walking back and forth." Nothing could have been more dismaying to a reformer than to see Grant and the archetype of the corrupt party politician engaged in intense private conversation. To Wilson it was now clear: "Shepherd had been to St. Louis, intervening in the investigation going on there of the Whiskey Ring and he was reporting to Grant." General Wilson left, but returned with a note urging Grant to see him privately.[14]

That evening Grant and Harry Wilson had their talk—and it ended their friendship. Grant could not suffer the bearer of bad news; years later Grant said that the Wilsons "disappointed me more than any persons I ever reposed confidence in." As Wilson recalled his conversation with Grant: "I told him . . . that Porter and Babcock were concerned in the Whiskey Ring and that they were making use of the White House, and imperiling his good name." Grant was "profoundly" troubled by the accusation, and asked Wilson who his authority for the allegation was. Wilson, seeking a source Grant would trust, replied that it was Dr. Alexander Sharp, Julia's brother-in-law, and Grant asked Wilson to send Sharp to him. It is not clear how Sharp knew of Porter's and Babcock's complicity, but in time, he did pay his call and corroborated Wilson's charges. He reported that Grant was so disturbed at the attack on his two friends that he wept—and called for Wilson to come back from New York so they could talk further about the ugly business. Wilson, returning, told the president more about the case, "but he refused to believe that Porter was guilty and I don't think he admitted to anyone that Babcock was guilty. He shielded Babcock all he could." Wilson, a flamboyant and demonstrative man himself, but different in temperament from Grant, said of the president, "He was a deeply affectionate man, and was surrounded by mean, low hangers-on."[15]

The most damaging evidence against Babcock consisted of the telegrams he had exchanged with McDonald and an ally, William Joyce, alerting them to the progress of the investigation that might catch them all. The most telling and famous of these was dated February 3, 1875, and read, "We have official information that the enemy weakens. Push things. (Signed) Sylph." Wilson, who had had a copy of the telegram in his possession since spring, had confronted Babcock and Porter with it. In their effort to dissuade Wilson from trying to figure out the meaning of the message that bore this code signature, they retreated to the outlook of the locker room. As Porter explained it privately to Bluford Wilson:

"Sylph" was a lewd woman with whom the President of the United States had been in intimate association, and . . . she had bothered and annoyed the President until at one time it chanced that McDonald's attention was called to her . . . in the vicinage of the President, and he said, "Why, that is Sylph." General Babcock said, "Do you know that woman, Mc-Donald?" And Mac. said, "Yes; I know her well." General Babcock said . . . "She has been giving the President a great deal of trouble; I wish you could relieve him of her in some way." And McDonald said, "Certainly; that is easy. I can manage her." And he did manage her, and so important was the service which McDonald thus rendered the President that the term "Sylph" became a common matter of joke between General Babcock and McDonald, so that they were in the habit, as occasion might require, of addressing one another under that name.

Obviously the allegation that Grant had had an extramarital sexual relationship was designed to persuade Wilson to drop any further investigation of the "Sylph" matter, lest it lead embarrassingly to the presidential bed. Wilson refused to be bluffed and proceeded on the assumption that the telegram had to do with the whiskey frauds, and nothing else. In the spring of 1876, when Porter was asked about the "Sylph" telegram by inquiring congressmen, he categorically denied the sexual dimension of the story. Even if there was a private joke of some kind, the text of the telegram did not suggest anything very amusing.[16]

The Grants went to Long Branch for the 1875 summer season, and there awaited the birth of their first grandchild in July. During that month Edwards Pierrepont, who was now attorney general, and Hamilton Fish traveled down from New York and confronted the president with damning evidence that Babcock was guilty. (Porter's role in the whole affair has never been made clear—no one other than Wilson seems to have thought him as centrally involved as Babcock. Porter had left the White House in 1872 and lived privately in New York. He still visited the Grants when in Washington.) Grant did not repudiate Babcock; instead he wrote instructions to Pierrepont to go forward with legal actions in the many cases, adding, "Let no guilty man escape. . . ." As he frequently did, he then weakened his own taut prose, this time with the clause "if it can be avoided."[17]

In August, Bristow confronted Babcock with the telling evidence of the order for the "Sylph" telegram to McDonald, written in what clearly was Babcock's hand. This message, and others, cryptically suggested that the sender had deflected investigations, and generally referred to efforts to forestall arrests and thereby protect McDonald. Babcock faced Bristow down; though he admitted he had sent the "Sylph" telegram, he claimed it referred not to the whiskey investigation but rather (inexplicably) to bridge building. Grant chose to believe him; Bristow did not. Grant began to feel that Bristow and Bluford Wilson were hounding him. Somehow they had picked his closest friend in the White House as a victim, and Grant felt that he was the real target of their probing.

Babcock and others who were guilty in the whiskey frauds sought to foster this feeling in the president in the hope that he would call off Bristow and Wilson. On September 26, 1875, Wilson wrote a letter to former Senator John B. Henderson, director of the investigation in St. Louis, introducing a new agent and stressing how important it was that they "reach the very bottom or *top* of the conspiracy and its ramifications." McDonald (or an associate) gained access to the letter and interpolated "W. H." (for "White House") after the word "top," to support the charge of Grant loyalists that Wilson had put spies on the president himself. Luckily for Wilson, he had his letter-press copy and could prove that the addition was a forgery. His contention was that he could not have an agent follow Babcock when he was visiting St. Louis without having it appear that he was checking on the Grant family, since Babcock was traveling with the president's party.[18]

By midfall 1875, David P. Dyer, the United States district attorney in St.

Louis, had sufficient evidence against Babcock to bring him before a grand jury. To persuade Grant not only of his friend's complicity in the frauds but also of the need for him to face the jury, Secretary Bristow and Attorney General Pierrepont stayed behind after a cabinet meeting (thereby avoiding the necessity of making an appointment through Babcock) and showed him the "Sylph" telegram, together with several other telegrams from William Joyce to Babcock. The messages were so cryptic that they invited all sorts of conjectures: Did "Poor Ford is dead" mean Grant's St. Louis friend Charles W. Ford was dead, or that some other Ford had died; or was "dead" a euphemism for "useless to the conspiracy"? Was the name indeed "Ford," or was it—as it appeared in Bristow's notes—"Fred," and therefore possibly a reference to Grant's brother-in-law or his son? Whatever the precise and correct interpretation, the telegrams, studded with names of men under surveillance, did seem to be confirming evidence that Babcock was in league with them. It appeared that before the investigation began he had been asked to ensure that Grant see to it that men friendly to the conspirators be appointed, and in the fall of 1875 he had been asked to keep associates in St. Louis informed about Bristow and Wilson's plans for their prosecution. Having read the telegrams, Grant called in Babcock and asked, in the presence of the two cabinet members, what they meant. Coolly, Babcock spoke of some matter to which he and Grant were privy but which was unintelligible to Bristow and Pierrepont. The president seemed entirely satisfied with Babcock's interpretation of these messages, but the cabinet officers insisted that Babcock send a telegram to his telegraphic correspondent, ordering him east to give his version of the matter.[19]

Babcock left the room to carry out his assignment. He was gone so long that Pierrepont, anxious about whether he had gone farther than his office next door, went to check on him. Babcock was trying to write a complex message to Joyce, in St. Louis, that would convey without actually saying it the idea that he should be on guard. Pierrepont, furious, grabbed a pen, spilled ink over Babcock's efforts in the process of editing them, and shouted at him, "You don't want to send your argument; send the fact, and go there and make your explanation. *I* do not understand it." Life in the White House was growing less pacific.[20]

On December 2, 1875, when he realized that Dyer and Bristow had sufficient evidence to indict him, Babcock asked for a military court of inquiry. Reluctantly, Grant's cabinet acquiesced, and Grant saw to it that three generals not unfavorable to Babcock were appointed to it. The judge advocate general—the prosecutor—was Asa Bird Gardner, a lawyer teaching at West Point, who had performed legal services for Babcock in a real-estate transaction and in dealings with Harris C. Fahnestock of Jay Cooke & Company. It is possible that Grant did not know of Gardner's conflict of interest, and it is likely that he did not, at this point, know that Gardner had been involved in a Black Friday transaction; yet in structuring the trial he certainly was not stacking the deck against Babcock. He ordered Attorney General Pierrepont to direct Dyer to deliver to the court of inquiry the findings of the grand jury, which had been hearing evidence that would lead to the indictment of Babcock. Dyer's defiant response on December 9 was to obtain from the grand jury a true bill against Babcock, which brought him to a civilian trial after his acquittal by the army panel.

Dyer was Bristow's man, and Grant felt that his own secretary of the treasury was conspiring against him. He suspected that he was being spied on and reciprocated by enlisting the services of a slippery man named Charles S. Bell. A native of Mississippi, Bell had been (until fired) an investigator of mail frauds. He had subsequently gone to St. Louis, walked into Dyer's astonishingly accessible office, and stolen some documents critical to the whiskey-frauds prosecution. Perhaps he was a member of the secret service (which Grant had used before), but it is more likely that he was fishing in fascinating ponds in the hope of gaining notoriety or of obtaining money from someone who sought to avoid notoriety. Then he came to Washington, where Colonel Levi P. Luckey, one of Babcock's cronies and probably a fellow conspirator, obtained an appointment for him with Grant. Bell called at the White House at 3:00 P.M. on December 13, went into the president's office, where the two men could talk privately,. and opened his conversation with Grant with the congenial thesis "that there was an attempt on foot to injure him" through General Babcock. After a discussion of this alleged conspiracy, Grant instructed Zachariah Chandler, his current secretary of the interior, to make Bell a special pension agent in his department, with an assignment in St. Louis. There he was to find evidence that would exonerate Babcock.[21]

Chandler was not the only loyalist in the cabinet; on December 21, during a regular meeting, Secretary of War Belknap read a letter from Gardner, the prosecutor in Babcock's military trial, that was highly critical of Dyer. As intended, this reading made Secretary of the Treasury Bristow uncomfortable, and, at Grant's elbow, Secretary of State Fish stiffened. He said nothing at the moment, but later, in his diary, he wrote, "The statement was throughout that of a partisan and seemed to evince the loss of opportunity for some purpose which I do not wish to speculate upon."[22]

In Washington early in January, while out for a walk, Grant encountered Elias W. Fox, editor of the *St. Louis Evening Dispatch*. The two men had known each other since 1861, and, of more immediate moment, Fox had served on the grand jury that indicted Babcock. Charles Bell claimed credit for the fact that the editor and the president chanced to meet. (He further claimed that Grant called on Fox "at Willard's Hotel, room No. 124," the Ebbitt House, and several times at Babcock's house. The president was indeed being spied on, by his own agent.) Fox subsequently denied before the congressional committee of inquiry that he had revealed grand-jury secrets to Grant, but he did not deny that Babcock was the topic of their conversation. He left a strong impression in the hearing room that he had sug-

gested what some of the evidence against Babcock was, with a view to aiding
Grant to refute it.[23]

There were other ways to counterattack as well. The president was repelled by Bluford Wilson's practice of granting immunity to guilty men who
had been arrested, provided they would turn on their fellows. He knew it
was likely that one of them might turn on Orville Babcock. Fred Grant had
told a reporter for the friendly *New York Herald* that Babcock's indictment
was the result of a conspiracy between Wilson and Grant's enemy Senator
Carl Schurz, and on January 27, 1876, Grant summoned Wilson to the
White House to insist that plea bargaining stop. Wilson knew that Zachariah
Chandler, who was present, was alert to the political cost to the Grant wing
of the party of the investigation, but it was on the ground of fairness, not of
political expediency, that the president took his stand: "Major, when I said
let no guilty man escape, I meant it, and not that nine men should escape,
and one be convicted." Wilson replied, "Pardon me, Mr. President, we are
not in this battle counting heads." He wanted to get to the center of the ring
and contended that he could do so only by plea bargaining, letting lesser men
off in order to get evidence against the heads of the conspiracy. Grant's position sounded more honorable and unequivocal; it also meant that perhaps no
one would have the incentive to point a damning finger at Babcock. In January 1876, on Grant's orders, Attorney General Edwards Pierrepont
directed that no more grants of immunity be made.[24]

Grant was fighting back, but the winds were strong around the White
House. In the newspapers in January, in addition to stories about Babcock,
there were rumors that not only Grant's brother Orvil and his brother-in-law
Lewis Dent (who had died in 1874) but also his oldest son, Fred, had been
gaining money from the whiskey frauds. Grant was besieged. On February
8, 1876, he confided to his cabinet his feelings about those who were pursuing him. According to Fish, he "manifested a great deal of excitement and
complained that they had taken from him his Secretaries and Clerks, his
Messengers and Doorkeepers; that the prosecution was aimed at himself, and
they were putting him on trial; that he was as confident as he lived of Babcock's innocence. . . ."[25]

No one else was confident. Pension-agent Bell had been busy in Missouri,
doing more occasional reading in attorney Dyer's office, but by Christmas he
had become convinced that Babcock could not be cleared. He knew that
Grant would not like the news, but apparently hoped that the president
would nevertheless accept conclusive word on the case. He later reported
how he proceeded back in Washington in February: "I took measures to inform him (meaning the President) that I believed he (Babcock) was guilty. I
did it, because the President himself told me that if General Babcock was
guilty he wished to know it, and he wished him punished. I took the President at his word, . . . I got my dismissal in three days afterward." Chandler's
letter dismissing Bell was dated February 16, 1876.[26]

Grant had not wanted to know whether Babcock was guilty or innocent;

he just wanted to know that he was innocent. Somehow, to lose Babcock would be to lose everything, and he was determined to go to St. Louis as a witness in Babcock's trial to save him. For a president of the United States to take the witness chair in a criminal court to try to protect a man arrested for a crime would have been an unprecedented act. Fish, in particular, counseled as strongly as he could that Grant must not go on this errand of loyalty. Instead, on February 12, Lucien Eaton, an attorney for the prosecution, came to the White House to question the president. Babcock's lawyer was present and was allowed to cross-examine. Also on hand were Secretary Bristow, Attorney General Pierrepont, and Morrison Remick Waite, the chief justice of the United States Supreme Court, who signed the deposition that Grant gave proclaiming Babcock's innocence. It was read into the record at Babcock's trial, and there can be little doubt that it achieved Babcock's acquittal, which came on February 28, 1876.

To Ulysses Grant an acquittal was an acquittal; innocence was innocence. When Orville Babcock came back to Washington, walked into the White House, and sat down at his desk as usual, Grant was undisturbed. But Hamilton Fish, when he arrived for a cabinet meeting and saw Babcock back at work, was appalled. Being a man of principle, Fish was interested in appearances. He insisted that Babcock had to go. Grant finally agreed, but only after he was forced to look again at that first debacle of his administration, Black Friday. Fish showed Grant evidence that Babcock, like Daniel Butterfield, had been speculating in gold while privy to decisions about governmental monetary policy. Butterfield had been discharged; now Fish insisted that Babcock be discharged. At last, Grant could see that even Babcock had kept things from him—had failed him. Still, the moment of separation was difficult. Finally, on March 1, Grant walked over to see Fish and told him he'd been waiting for half an hour for a letter of resignation from Babcock. Icily, Fish said there was nothing to resign, and Grant after "a moment's pause . . . smiled and said, 'that's true, he's only got to stay away.' " Grant's son Buck took Babcock's place.[27]

The facts surrounding Babcock's guilt are curious. There is no getting round the evidence tying him to McDonald's activities in St. Louis—activities for which McDonald went to jail. While there, McDonald wrote a fascinating book (with illuminating details on prison life) in which he made no bones about the fact that Babcock ought to have been there with him. And surprisingly, Babcock carefully preserved material, including the order for the "Sylph" telegram, that fully corroborates his guilt. Why did he keep such documents? Was he somehow unable to divorce even incriminating material from the other intriguing letters that showed him to have been so very close to the nation's seat of power? Or did he keep them so that he could try using them to blackmail the president into pardoning him, should he actually be sent to jail? The cryptic messages do not appear to implicate members of the Grant family, but perhaps if he had explicated them accurately for the president, Babcock might have been able to persuade Grant that the evidence was there.

Another possibility, of course, is that Ulysses or Julia Grant too was banking the proceeds of some of the frauds and Babcock could prove it. McDonald came right out and said that the president was doing just that. However, he did not offer any concrete evidence for the allegation, though one would have thought that having made the sensational charge he would bring forward as much evidence as possible to corroborate it. Both Orvil Grant and Lewis Dent were capable of dubious dealings, and Grant may have been protecting them; if Fred Grant was involved, his father would certainly have shielded him. But what seems most likely is that Grant was troubled by Babcock's plight not so much because he or his relatives might be implicated, but because he felt threatened by some frightening "they."

Ulysses Grant knew that Orville Babcock was guilty and yet went so far as to perjure himself before the chief justice of the United States to keep his aide out of jail. No talk of his being duped by knaves will explain his refusal to look at the clear evidence presented by Bristow and Wilson. And that evidence was irrefutable. After hours of damning testimony, Bluford Wilson was asked by the Democratic congressman Alexander G. Cochran, "If the President of the United States was acting in good faith in this matter, how do you account for his action in reference to that 'Sylph' dispatch?" Babcock's bridge building and Porter's sexual explications were silly, as Cochran, Wilson, and even Grant must have known. Wilson could not answer the congressman without saying that Grant was a perjurer, and so he said, "Let the facts speak for themselves." As usual, they don't, but both the congressman and Wilson left the matter in that ambiguous place. There was no evidence that Grant received illegal money, and a thorough reading of the report of the congressional inquiry does not suggest that he did. It does, however, prove that he knew Babcock was guilty (while being unable to accept the consequences of the fact) and that he believed that upright men like Bristow and Wilson, who claimed they wanted to disassociate him from crooked men, were plotting to get him. Grant was sure that he, not Babcock, was the target. He covered for Babcock, and both Fish and Bristow knew that he did. With devious as well as open use of power he kept Babcock out of jail. His were the actions not of a duped innocent but of a man fighting back with desperate effectiveness. He had struggled for too long to allow himself to be called a fool for letting someone steal a few dollars in tax stamps.[28]

Orville Babcock, an odd, restless, ambitious man, was curiously affectionate. During his courtship of Annie Campbell he had been shameless in suggesting how his closeness to Ulysses and Julia Grant would bring him success, which she would share. He wrote candidly and often charmingly to his wife, and he tended his fine dahlias and shared them with neighbors like the Frederick Douglasses. A great many politicians in Washington hated him for his imperious ways as he blocked their access to Grant, but none accused him of using his position to grow rich. Annie Campbell Babcock did not ride about the city in a carriage, like Mrs. Williams; it is one of the mysteries of the Whiskey Ring that after five years of alleged activity in the frauds, Babcock had not made more money. He lived very simply. And when he had to leave the White House, his friend who was still there found him a job that would keep the family going. Orville Babcock became an inspector of lighthouses, and in 1884, while on a trip as part of his job, he drowned, at Mosquito Inlet, Florida.

The sorry business of the whiskey frauds carried down to the final year of Grant's tenure in the White House, and it helped deflect the president's attention during his last two years in office from matters of far greater moment. In 1875 Grant was faced with insurrection in the South. He had thought he had finished with that phenomenon a decade earlier, but he was wrong. This time, however, he was determined that he would not fight a war to subdue the rebels. The rebellion was designed to dismantle the racially integrated political structure of the South.

The national government, which had won a colossal war, proved powerless to maintain the peace. Because it could not keep its new citizens alive, it gave that task to state governments consisting of Southern whites who were not intimidated by the new status of their black neighbors and of the newly enfranchised blacks themselves. Thus Reconstruction, in its most radical phase, had to rely on a reactionary doctrine: states' rights were invoked to protect not the slaveholder but the former slave, in order to absolve the federal government from that responsibility. At first, of course, it was an exciting business, with black men, not three years away from slavery, writing constitutions, voting, and participating in precinct politics. However, if the doctrine of states' rights was now imposed on the South to protect its freedmen, it took only the turning of the table to utilize the same political theory to ensure their subservience. The table turners were not slow to set to the task. Conservative white domination was achieved before 1871 in Tennessee, Virginia, and North Carolina; in Georgia they pressed in too clumsy a fashion, expelling the Negro members of the legislature. This action was reversed, and methods less obviously unconstitutional, but still effective, were sought—and found.

As the counterrevolution moved ahead in state after state, there was still the lingering thought that somehow the federal government did have an obligation to sustain these state experiments in Reconstruction—to protect the black people who had been encouraged to risk partaking fully of their freedom. Grant sensed this. Just as he had known in Memphis during the war that he had to do something to keep the black refugees alive and safe from the worst of exploitation, so in Washington in 1874 he heard cries for protection against "outrages"—murders—and felt an obligation to do something. When the counterrevolutionary white-supremacist Democrats, using violent intimidation, took elections in Texas and Arkansas, Grant, ignoring the means employed, recognized the administrations that resulted. However, when Arkansas began repealing parts of the constitution by which it had come back into the Union, and when Grant was told, with graphic details, that the election had not been peaceful—that the black people had been systematically terrorized—he reversed course and asked Congress to act.

He had already taken action in Louisiana. At the urging of Julia's brother-in-law, James F. Casey, who was the collector of customs in New Orleans and a power in Louisiana's Republican party, he had tried in 1874 to sustain the Republicans against the terrorists (and Democrats). Even the most cynical interpretation of his support of his relatives and his party cannot dispose of the fact that Grant acted also to save the lives of citizens who were powerless to save their own. He ordered General Philip H. Sheridan to use army troops to prevent killings.

It is difficult to know how Grant could have made his point more clearly. In his message to Congress in January 1875, justifying the orders that he had given General Sheridan, he quoted verbatim the statement of facts made by the judge in *United States* v. *Cruikshank*, during the trial of white men accused of violently interrupting a political meeting of black Louisianians. According to Judge William B. Woods: "In the case . . . there are many facts not in controversy. I proceed to state some of them in the presence and hearing of counsel on both sides: and if I state as a conceded fact any matter that is disputed, they can correct me." Unchallenged, the judge continued: "Most of those who were not killed were taken prisoners. Fifteen or sixteen of the blacks had lifted the boards and taken refuge under the floor of the court-house. They were all captured. About thirty-seven men were taken prisoners. The number is not definitely fixed. They were kept under guard until dark. They were led out, two by two, and shot." The president then went on to quote the descriptions of the "pistol-shot wounds, the great majority in the head, and most of them in the back of the head."[29]

Here were facts. This was what was happening to citizens of the United States. Grant had been bitterly criticized for sending Sheridan to Louisiana and permitting the general to use the army to prevent such attacks. He had taken this action not so much in the name of enforcing the Fifteenth Amendment-right to vote, and the concomitant right to engage in political activity, as in the name of section 4 of article IV of the Constitution, which expressly required: "The United States shall guarantee to every State in this Union a Republican Form of Government, and shall protect each of them . . . on Application of the Legislature, or of the Executive (when the Legislature cannot be convened) against domestic Violence."

There was domestic violence in Louisiana. The incident that Judge Woods had described in such calm prose was not isolated. Citizens were being killed if they exercised their right to assemble or to take part in politics. "To hold the people of Louisiana . . . responsible for these atrocities would not be just," Grant said, "but it is a lamentable fact that insuperable obstructions were thrown in the way of punishing these murderers." The president seemed to ask, What am I to do? as he pursued his thought in a sentence that he allowed, for emphasis, to stand as a separate paragraph: "I have no desire to have United States troops interfere in the domestic concerns of Louisiana or any other State." But how else, how other than by using General Sheridan, was he going to prevent domestic violence? Grant cordially disliked William Pitt Kellogg, the Republican governor of Louisiana, but he could not refute his logic in calling on the president of the United States as the only one who could prevent the violence that was raging in the state.[30]

Congress, with Thaddeus Stevens dead in 1868 and no leader—black or white—strong enough to replace him, declined to make Reconstruction truly national again. The Civil Rights Act of 1875 did not speak to the emergency. It carried no new prescription for enforcement—no demand for any increase in the authority of the federal attorney general to prosecute, as Amos T. Akerman had done, those who denied the civil rights of black citizens. Akerman had been sent home to Georgia long ago; Edwards Pierrepont, who had followed George H. Williams as attorney general, was not disposed to lead a major effort to bring civil-rights offenders into court. His brother lawyers on the Supreme Court (with whom he very much hoped one day to sit) had a similar disinclination. Two years earlier, in December 1872, they had interrupted the progress of the Fourteenth Amendment on the track toward a true national citizenship. In the Slaughter-House Cases the justices had upheld the right of state legislators to decide where in a city citizens could slaughter their animals, and by inelegant extension, this decision was soon construed to mean that the states had the power to define the rights or lack of them of their citizens, including their black citizens—without those citizens having recourse to federal protection. The Fourteenth Amendment, ratified to serve only the needs of "that race and that emergency," as Justice Miller had stated in this decision, was being directed toward a very different future. Fewer and fewer white Americans, north or south, were caring about the people of that race and their very real emergencies.

Grant was said to be "plucky and serene" that December as he prepared to send this message to Congress on January 13, 1875. Marshall Jewell, who had become postmaster general in 1874, thought him determined "to protect the colored voter in his rights to the extent of his power under the law, and if we cannot protect them we shall lose most of the fruits of this terrible war." But neither pluck nor plain words did the job. Despite Grant's message to Congress describing how black Americans were murdered if they tried to rise to assert themselves in meeting their emergency, Congress did not take adequate action. Nor did the president. In Mississippi, the would-be redeemers were so confident that they could bring a white-supremacist government back to their state in 1875 that they challenged General Ulysses S. Grant either to marshal all of his power to stop them or to acquiesce to the ending of an interracial political society. The president was under enormous pressure to do the latter not only from white-supremacist Southerners but from white-supremacist Northerners, some of whom were in his cabinet.[31]

The blacks of Mississippi had made enormous strides since the end of slavery. Only ten years after the war, people who had been chattel workers, under total domination of a master class, were moving everywhere in the body politic. Even more ominously, to some of their former masters, they were also entering new economic realms, thereby endangering the class domination of the whites. The overturned Black Code of 1865 had forbidden freedmen to own land outside of towns; their success as commercial farmers had been feared then, and it was feared still in 1875. Black men were prospering, and not only had they been represented in the Senate by Hiram R. Revels and in the House by John R. Lynch, but, more importantly, they were gaining the kind of local political positions—as sheriffs and probate officers, for example—that produce true community power. But great as were their gains, their power was still strictly limited. They still had to defer to white partners—who got most of the best jobs—to achieve their goals. Specifically, they had to rely on their carpetbagger governor, Adelbert Ames.

The young Yankee had left the Senate in 1874 and run successfully for governor. As his bride did not like Mississippi, and with their three babies stayed much of the time with her family in Lowell, Massachusetts, Ames was almost immune to destruction by social ostracism. Wives were the best target of that tactic. When the black and white legislators and other politicians gathered for parties—in hotels rather than private homes—few women attended and, thought Ames, all in attendance felt awkward. Had Mrs. Ames been present she would have had to realize that the next day the proper white women in town might well snub her. Her long stays in Massachusetts also caused him to write his excellent letters, which chronicle the defeat of one of America's finest efforts at democracy.

Vernon Lane Wharton, in the excellent essay "The Revolution of 1875" (in *The Negro in Mississippi, 1865–1890*) records how the Democratic party systematically, and with great skill, organized the state-wide intimidation of black Republicans. In Yazoo City in September, Colonel A. T. Morgan, the Republican sheriff, was addressing an integrated rally when men broke into the meeting, killing at least one Negro and wounding several others. The assailants then moved out into the town and the surrounding country, killing black people. No force to stop them was available. Republican leaders had urged Ames not to organize a black militia company, lest it arouse anti-Negro sentiment among white people. Such reasoning was irrelevant by September; Ames wrote, "So far has this intimidation gone that I can not organize a single company of militia." He knew he was doomed: "The old rebel armies are too much for our party and the colored men do not dare to organize even when they know their liberty is at stake."[32]

The "only hope is through the U. S. enforcement laws," Ames wrote in the same letter. Ten years after the war, Grant, who had always been exceedingly wary of using army men as civilian police, had to decide whether to support Ames and his party. Attempts in the courts to enforce the Civil Rights Acts of 1866 and 1875, and other legislation supposed to implement the three Reconstruction amendments to the Constitution, had been totally unsuccessful. Ordinary civil order would not protect black lives, as the terrifying attack in Yazoo City demonstrated.[33]

A few days after the attack, a woman—the only person among the victims who had a chance to leave Yazoo City to seek help, and who dared to try— came before dawn to the door of the governor's mansion. This was Colonel Morgan's sister-in-law. She pleaded with Ames to disperse the armed men holding Yazoo City. All he could do was issue a proclamation, knowing it would be laughed at, in the hope that it would "pave the way for national interference."[34]

The next day, violence reached nearer to Jackson. A man broke into Ames's office, exhausted after a ten-mile ride from Clinton, to tell the governor of an attack there. At a large Republican barbecue, a band of "white men fully prepared" had fired into the crowd; two women and four children were among those killed. The attackers then moved on through the town and the country killing Negroes—including "one old man nearly one hundred years old—defenseless and helpless." Telling Ames of his escape, the messenger described carriages and carts abandoned along the Jackson road by black people whom the horsemen had caught up with and pursued into the woods. Ames pronounced the attacks cold-blooded murder by the "white liners"— those planning to vote the line on the ballot of candidates favoring white supremacy—but he did not know what to do: "I have not been able to find anyone . . . willing to take military appointments." He turned the governor's mansion into a shelter for the refugees, and went off to an upstairs corner to write his wife.[35]

He thought the white liners would prevail in the coming election. Such severe intimidation was bound to succeed unless he could get federal troops, which he knew would be a difficult thing to do. And, indeed, he did not yet try; he waited. Only on September 6, when reports of assaults like that at Clinton came from all over the state, did he say he might "find it necessary to call on the president" for troops "tomorrow."[36]

He worried over burdening his wife with these troubles; he himself, he said, "tired of hearing of them long before the day closes." On September 7, he issued his proclamation calling on armed bands to disperse, and, by telegram, asked Grant to send an investigating committee which could confirm the need for troops. His appeal to Grant was on the grounds that the United States Constitution required him, as governor, to protect his constituents. It had been reported to Ames that General Christopher Columbus Augur would send troops but "he requires authority from the President." Augur, Ames had been told, thought a "militia of colored men [might] precipitate a war of races to be felt over the entire South," for the general had been informed that "thousands in Louisiana are ready to come here to fight the Negro."[37]

The members of Grant's cabinet, enduring fierce September heat in Washington and with no Rawlins and no Akerman among them, were annoyed by these flamboyant happenings in Mississippi. Ames, not waiting for the previously requested investigation, soon asked for an immediate dispatch of troops. He tried to be confident of a positive reply while he awaited an answer. But Democrats wrote that no troops were needed, and to the delight of the cabinet, one Mississippi sheriff wired that troops were not needed in his county. Ames's request was denied. The governor was furious, first with Grant and then, when he learned of the telegram, with the sheriff. He composed a long, angry wire of his own to Attorney General Pierrepont—but did not send it, choosing to wait out "the development of events." When, the next day, Pierrepont wired him, asking if he had "exhausted all . . . powers to protect," the governor did send his telegram, and Pierrepont took it to Grant on September 13. On the seventeenth, Pierrepont sent a telegram that was, Ames wrote, "severe" in its criticism of Ames and his associates for taking "no action to protect ourselves." The governor replied that he had tried to raise a militia, and failed. Already "disgusted" with Pierrepont, he now was "quite exasperated."[38]

On September 21, he decided to call for volunteers, black and white, for a militia company, and placed orders for muskets. Army men warned him against this move, saying that the use of federal troops was preferable, but Grant was exceedingly reluctant to send such troops. The attempt to muster a militia company failed: "I have not been able to find even *one* man to cooperate with me" the governor complained. He could not call the legislature into special session as there were sufficient Democrats in the Senate to prevent a quorum, so he determined to "fight it out . . . alone." Ames began to take a tragic view of himself—". . . of course, all the blame comes on me"—and his worried wife sought to join him in Jackson. He thought this too dangerous; his telegram to Blanche said, simply, "No." Once again he tried to raise a militia company, this time going specifically to the blacks for recruits.[39]

The white liners were shrewd. Having mightily scared their enemy early in September, they decided, as Ames reported, "to remain passive till two or three days . . . [before] the election." Ames, too, grew passive. He did not campaign for the Republicans seeking seats in the legislature; he waited for their defeat and anticipated his own impeachment. Augur, who was in Jackson, told Ames that he could act swiftly, but only if ordered to do so by Washington. Ames was afraid "that my Negro militia has not the courage or nerve—whatever it may be called—to act the part of soldiers." Disheartened by the prospects of violence, he turned to reading (a good deal of English history) and gossiping with Blanche about the trial for adultery of Henry Ward Beecher—the great event of 1875, which vastly overwhelmed Mississippi's revolution in the national press. (Ames, it might be noted, believed the preacher was guilty.)[40]

On October 9, Ames was enormously relieved when his company of black militia escorted a shipment of arms for forty miles without being attacked, but he guessed, correctly, that the white liners were simply biding their time until the election. The Democrats feared that an attack on the blacks would bring in federal troops. White Republicans, "intimidated by the white liners," would not join their black brothers in the militia, and most of "the Negroes are no less intimidated. Election day may find our voters fleeing before rebel bullets rather than balloting for their rights."[41]

In mid-October, Benjamin Butler went to Washington to try to persuade Grant to order troops in to sustain his son-in-law. He knew that the Republicans had feared they would lose Ohio, where election day was in October, if Grant sent troops into Mississippi (the white line ran well north of the Ohio River). But he hoped that with the election over, Grant would dispatch a force to Ames's support. Blanche Ames, a shrewd political observer—if overly confident in her menfolk—suspected that the white liners were desperate. Their extreme abuse of Ames suggested to her that they were "frightened" that he and his black allies would win on election day.[42]

Ames was far less sanguine, but he was, once more, aroused. He had been told that a request for troops must be made in writing, not by telegram; a letter would take four days to arrive, then Grant would have to make a decision, and finally it might take five days for troops to move to Mississippi. It was, Ames thought, "too late." The "terror" had done its work: "Yes, a *revolution* has taken place—and a race are disfranchised—they are to be returned to a country of serfdom—an era of second slavery." And he added, "It is their fault (not mine, personally). . . . They refuse to prepare for war . . . in time of peace." With resigned fury, he wrote of his request to Grant and Pierrepont for help. The president did not respond, but the attorney general did, in a way that Ames knew was final. Said the governor, "The nation should have acted but *it* was"—and here Ames quoted Pierrepont's telegram—" '*tired* of the[se] autumnal outbursts in the South.' " Ames concluded, in tragic exasperation, "The political death of the Negro will forever release the nation from such 'political outbursts.' "[43]

Grant would have none of the war Ames wanted black Mississippians to fight. He knew that in a racial battle, white Americans would support their white brethren, across regional lines. He was doing so himself. He was willing to allow the revolution—to end black liberties and aspirations, and to accept the resultant bloodshed and the terror of intimidation—in order to prevent the greater bloodshed of a race war. He was not ready to use his authority or his troops to persuade white Mississippi that the federal government would refuse to acquiesce to the demise of black rights or to racial massacres.

As the election approached, the white liners worked out their strategy. A committee asked Ames to disarm the militia, promising a peaceful election in return. Reluctantly, he agreed, and sent two companies of the militia home. The sheriff of Yazoo County had already refused to go back to Yazoo City as the head of a militia company because he feared "assassination." State Senator Charles Caldwell disbanded his militia company and bravely returned to Clinton, where his enemies waited until after the election to murder him. Other black militiamen, however, declined to be dismissed and turn their guns in to the army. The white liners then claimed Ames had broken his promise to disband the black forces, thus legitimizing, from their point of view, any violence that might occur. Ames thereupon revoked the commissions of the militiamen. The brave black men who would not bow to the white liners now gave up on their white Yankee governor. Dreading that "somebody will think I have 'sold out,' " Ames rationalized in time-honored fashion: "By and by they will thank me for it." As he lapsed into this not very accurate sense of the future, Ames worried that his letters might be tampered with: ". . . I am making important history and everybody knows it. . . ."[44]

Out-of-state campaigners were busy in Mississippi. One of the most effective was the popular Confederate general John B. Gordon, who came from Georgia; another effective speaker was L. Q. C. Lamar, who taught and practiced law in Mississippi. They were shrewd; in their powerful speeches to the white liners they never explicitly called for violence, but when they were through, aroused men and women among their listeners did. The two gentlemen were also effective outside Mississippi. They and entrepreneurs like them were fast persuading their counterparts in the North that their particular Southern way with the Negroes should prevail, since otherwise there would be either violence or a lot of pushy black people in the country. A spendid example of the latter, in their eyes, was the black Louisiana Republican P. B. S. Pinchback, who also campaigned in Mississippi—for the other side. Ames attended a supper given for Pinchback when he came to Jackson, but made only a lackluster speech in honor of the visitor. Ames had given up. He played croquet and expected a peaceful but fruitless election, which for himself would be a humiliating failure.

The white liners were so sure of victory they had not felt the need to attack the black militia, and they seemed certain that nothing would cause the federal government to send in the troops that would restore the confidence of the integrationist voters. In truth, Pierrepont was exceedingly eager to see that Ames did not break the calm and sent George K. Chase, a former Maine man then living in New York, to see Ames in Jackson. Chase arrived in mid-October, got on well with Ames, stayed with him in the mansion, took two days' holiday in New Orleans with him, and confided to the governor that Attorney General Pierrepont, who, as a member of Grant's Republican administration, should have been sympathetic to his party in Mississippi, had instead been explicitly critical of Ames and the Mississippi Republicans. Ames was feeling abandoned in his adopted state and his attention began to turn elsewhere. Chase, a "good liver" who enjoyed croquet, talked enticingly of the high life of New York and urged Ames to abandon Mississippi and politics and go into business.[45]

Chase also, at Pierrepont's direction, met with the leaders of the Mississippi Democratic party, the white liners, to hold them to their peace pledge, and at the eleventh hour, Grant and the attorney general responded to Ames's request, saying that troops could be sent in if the pledge was broken. Ames, for his part, thought their response too late. "Our side is so thoroughly demoralized that I doubt if they can be rallied," he wrote. And he gave some thought also to the long-term outcome. "The republican candidate for presidency next year may want this state," he mused, "but he as well might want the moon for a toy."[46]

November 1, election eve, found some Republican leaders either lying low or away from home. The intimidation had had impressive results, and the white liners were confident. Ames had orders ready to give to army troops— but could issue them only if actual bloodshed had taken place. The troops were stationed only in three towns, and Ames was sure that in any election-day violence, those towns would be carefully spared, though others all over the state might erupt. But there was no violence. When the election returns came in, with their story of a complete Republican rout, Ames quietly went out to the lawn for another game of croquet.

Grant received a dressing down from Benjamin Butler for failing to support the party—and Butler's son-in-law—in Mississippi. The president replied that he had sent troops and Ames had no cause for complaint. Ames countered—but only in a letter to his wife—that Grant's handling of the troops had been useless, except to the white liners. Blanche Butler Ames had urged everyone she knew in Washington to press the president to support the black and white Republicans in Mississippi, but Grant had not done so. "Grant's professed order that troops should be at my disposal . . . was," Ames lamented, "a sham and the election a fraud." He added, "The democracy has been denouncing me for years—the republicans say I have 'sold them out.' Grant will probably say 'it was Ames' fault. I gave him . . . troops. . . .' " Ames had established his "character," even among his enemies; now his own party had destroyed it. His jeremiad went on: "While Grant may this day try to shield himself . . . and Pierrepont repeat what he knows to be false and the newspapers hound [me,] I am convinced that I am a better man than any of the whole crowd."[47]

What if one looks beyond the men involved to the law they had made? During Reconstruction, Republicans built a formidable constitutional machine designed to protect, equally, the rights of a national citizenry. The three postwar amendments to the Constitution, the civil-rights legislation of 1866, 1870, 1871, and 1875, and the creation of the Justice Department were monumental achievements. Grant contributed to all that was accomplished during his administration, most notably by his trip to Capitol Hill to win passage of the Ku Klux Klan Act of April 20, 1871, and by his great message to Congress on January 13, 1875. But what was the value of the machine if it could not be made to move in behalf of the citizens? When skillful racists organized opposition to blacks, Grant did not find a way to make the laws effective. He could have sent scores of government lawyers south as United States district attorneys under the direction of the Justice Department, as Amos T. Akerman had done in 1871. He could have established a vastly strengthened constabulary of United States marshals; instead, as in Louisiana, he did nothing until he was forced to send troops because local violence had reached crisis proportions. Time and time again, Grant was described as angered at cabinet meetings by a report of some cruel murder in the South; time and again, by the next meeting, the arguments of Fish and Pierrepont and his own lassitude had dissuaded him from any action. Understandably and honorably, President Grant, remembering that he had been a general, was reluctant to see armies once again marching across the South; less commendably, he could devise no sustained federal program of law enforcement. He asked Congress to act and was frustrated when it did little to implement its own legislation and referred the responsibility back to him. It has been contended that the racism existent in the post-Emancipation period was so strong he could not have done more. Some think he did enough; conservative historians, looking at the splendid constitutional structure and accompanying federal action, pronounce that Reconstruction was not a failure. One wonders what would have been the judgment of the black people at that political picnic in Clinton, Mississippi, in September 1875.

The picnickers' man was soon gone; the once hopeful governor of an uneasily integrated state of Mississippi left the South. Ames resigned, knowing impeachment was the alternative. The gallant optimist of post–Civil War America left politics. He lived to be old and rich and cultivated, but a villa on Lake Como and golf with John D. Rockefeller, half a century after the revolution of 1875, never quite compensated for the loss of a glorious chance, which he had shared with Ulysses Grant, to make history in Yazoo City and Clinton.

# XXV

# WAIFS

We are told that it is a bitter moment with the Lord Mayor when he
leaves the Mansion House and becomes once more Alderman Jones, of
No. 75 Bucklersbury. Lord Chancellors going out of office have a great
fall, though they take pensions with them for their consolation. And
the President of the United States when he leaves the glory of the
White House and once more becomes a simple citizen must feel the
change severely.

— *Anthony Trollope*

ATTENDING New Year's Day receptions in Washington was an
Olympian sport. One old gentleman, Benjamin Brown French, recorded in
his diary, not long before he died, a day begun in Georgetown that continued
on a labyrinthine course through Washington, skirted the White House,
where the crowd was so great it would have taken him an hour to get in, and
ended on Capitol Hill, where he helped his wife receive 140 guests at his own
house. He was not, however, too tired at the end of the day to record, caustically, the fare at thirteen of his stops. Younger, but not fitter, Congressman
James A. Garfield recorded in his diary for January 2, 1876, simply that he
had made "about 65 calls." The hostesses too were competitive. Julia Grant,
in the White House, was of course ahead in the game, and her enthusiasm
contributed to the success that was assured by her position. "She enjoyed her
presidential life," reported one of her guests, "and good naturedly said so.
. . ." People-watching flourished at these wonderfully wearing occasions.
Clumsy wives of rustic congressmen could be made invisible, and newcomers of greater splendor appraised and perhaps nodded to. In the flow of
stunning people the eye was always out for the extraordinary. At Julia
Grant's 1876 reception, few were more fascinating to the crowd than the

great editor Frederick Douglass, a leonine figure, his white and wiry hair rising from his huge handsome head as he moved confidently through the White House parlors. His elegance mocked the curiosity that his presence at white America's social events always provoked.[1]

One of Julia's friendly rivals in the matter of New Year's Day parties was Mrs. William Worth Belknap, of whose "charming grace and manner" one guest spoke admiringly. Unfortunately, Amanda Belknap's 1876 reception was her last. Three months later, the guest who had been so taken with her charm—Rebecca Latimer Felton—had other news of Mrs. Belknap to send to her home-town newspaper in Cartersville, Georgia. On the night of March 2, 1876, rumors about Secretary of War Belknap "ran through the city like a prairie on fire." Mrs. Felton, being a woman as well as a highly combative politician, had to exercise her love of politics in the congressional galleries (save for the two days in 1922, when, at eighty-eight, she was to serve as the nation's first female senator), and during the spring and summer of 1876 she looked down from the gallery and took in every detail of the impeachment proceedings of General Belknap, who for seven years had been Grant's secretary of war.[2]

Mrs. Belknap, called "Puss" both by her intimates and by mocking reporters, was not in the gallery. She remained in seclusion while the impeachment order was debated, awaiting any sympathy that might come her way. The newspaper reporters who camped outside her house on the lookout for the general, rumored to have committed suicide or to be about to escape to Bermuda, one day saw her invite a police officer inside. They also caught a glimpse of Belknap, who was alive and had not fled, but looked a "perfect wreck." Mrs. Belknap was in need of sympathy—and more. Seclusion had not been her style prior to her husband's resignation, and Mrs. Felton had been right in regarding her as the one hostess who was in every eye, for Mrs. Belknap was gorgeous. Her marvelous figure was set off by good dresses from Worth and splendid diamonds and pearls; it could have been calculated by anyone who stopped to do so that their cost placed a strain on her husband's salary of eight thousand dollars a year.[3]

Amanda Tomlinson Bower Belknap had married her sister's widower in 1873, reigned voluptuously as his hostess until the dark days of 1876, disappeared from society, and in time, irrepressibly, regained her stride. In 1889 she was the center of a momentary scandal when she was seen at Coney Island in a red-and-white-striped bathing costume that revealed more of her fine arms and legs, excellent in silk, than was thought respectable. In October 1890 she did not quite make it to the bedside of her dying husband, the cause of whose death was variously described; one dependable source said he was a suicide.[4]

William Worth Belknap was born in Newburgh, New York, on September 22, 1829. He attended Princeton while his father served in the Mexican War. Later he studied law at Georgetown University, and he was admitted to the bar in Keokuk, Iowa, in 1851. A Douglas Democrat, he volunteered for military service in the Civil War, entered the army as a major, and was cited for "always being at the right place at the right time" in the thick of the battle of Shiloh. He rose under General Sherman's patronage, and commanded a division in the "March to the Sea" and the Carolina campaign. After the war, he went back to Iowa, was named collector of internal revenue in the region, and again with the blessing of General Sherman was promoted, on Rawlins's death in 1869, from obscurity to the much-controverted post of secretary of war. Both Julia and Ulysses Grant found him agreeable to have around. As secretary, he distinguished himself only by not getting at loggerheads with Sherman, his proud and difficult former commanding officer, who was now commanding general of the army. To General O. O. Howard's dismay, Belknap was unsympathetic to the cause of the freedmen to the point of deliberately undercutting the small efforts being made on behalf of black citizens. Belknap also won the raging hatred of General George A. Custer, who, in a manner not untypical of many army officers, saw nothing incongruous in being at once ruthlessly lethal in fighting the Indians and outspokenly critical of those who swindled them.[5]

Belknap, a big man, weighed two hundred pounds and stood six feet tall; he was handsome—in a fleshy way—and genial. In cabinet meetings he was noticeably reticent, but on March 2, 1876, he went to the White House and, in tears, made a confession to Ulysses Grant.

Washington entertaining is costly. The Belknaps were not people of means, but when money was needed, money was found. The handsome Mrs. Belknap was the secretary's third wife, and the arrangement that in good part paid for her fine clothes and fine parlor had been made by her predecessor, her sister Carrie Tomlinson, who died in 1870. It was a simple, businesslike transaction. Soon after Belknap succeeded Rawlins as secretary of war, Carrie Belknap undertook to arrange for a New York friend, Caleb P. Marsh, to have the lucrative trading post at Fort Sill, in the Oklahoma Territory. In return, he would pay her $6,000 a year. Here the first hitch arose; the present holder of the tradership, John S. Evans, had come to Washington to be sure he was not forced to give it up. But this complication was soon disposed of. Marsh and Evans made a contract, duly drawn by Marsh's lawyer, that Evans would keep his tradership but pay Marsh $15,000—amended to $12,000—a year. Marsh would pass on to Mrs. Belknap half of these proceeds, in convenient quarterly payments.

Carrie Belknap lived to enjoy but one payment; she died of tuberculosis in December 1870, a month after her son was born. When Marsh called on her sister, then Mrs. Bower, to pay condolences, he assured her that the infant child would be the continuing beneficiary of the arrangement. Amanda agreed, saying that Carrie "gave the child to me and told me that the money coming from you I must take and keep for it." Unluckily, the child also died, in June 1871, but payments continued to be made, to Belknap, while the aunt traveled in Europe and the genuinely bereft father performed his cabinet duties. When General Belknap married his sister-in-law on December 11, 1873, the payments from Marsh were still continuing although their amount had been reduced because deteriorated economic conditions had made the Fort Sill trading post less lucrative. At Belknap's trial it was established that the Belknaps had benefited to the probable total of $20,000.[6]

When Carrie had entered into her agreement with Marsh, she reportedly told him, "If I prevail upon the Secretary of War to award you a post you must be careful to say nothing to him about presents, for a man once offered him $10,000 for a tradership of this kind and he told him that if he did not leave the office he would kick him down the stairs." Perhaps that offer had been rejected because it was below the market price for trading posts, or perhaps Belknap learned to suppress such violent urges, for Marsh testified that the payments he made to the widowed secretary were pacifically received. Said Marsh, "The money was sent according to the instructions of the Secretary of War; sometimes in bank notes . . . I think on one or more occasions by certificate of deposit on the National Bank of America in New York. Sometimes I paid him in New York in person."[7]

These details of the Belknaps' finances emerged in a congressional investigation that was part of a searching scrutiny of the Grant administration conducted in 1876. As a result of the elections of 1874, the Forty-fourth Congress, which met for its first session on December 6, 1875, had a Democratic majority in the House of Representatives. The Democrats elected Michael C. Kerr of Indiana as Speaker, and promptly and with zest began vigorous investigations into the corruption in the Republican administration. They credited their election to claims that such corruption existed, and they were determined to demonstrate the reality of their claims. The task was not excessively difficult.

Before they were through, every one of Grant's cabinet departments had been investigated, including that of the seemingly unassailable Mr. Fish. In his realm of foreign affairs, Robert C. Schenck, Grant's second minister to Great Britain, was exceedingly ambitious socially (and, in private letters, condescending about the naiveté of Mrs. Grant and her daughter Nellie, whom he had had the pleasure of presenting to Queen Victoria in 1872). Schenck was not shy about obtaining the wherewithal to support his social life. While still in Congress and chairman of the Ways and Means Committee, he wrote his daughter, "Yesterday I got down town to meet Mr. Jay Cooke. I am gradually willowing the ground and personally putting in the seed for profitable enterprises." His appointment as minister to Great Britain, it will be recalled, was welcomed by Cooke and many other men of business who saw in the changing of the guard new opportunities for support of their interests.[8]

Once in London, which was still the center of capital investment not only for the whole British Empire but for the United States as well, Schenck lost no time in championing American enterprises, including one in which he was personally involved. The Emma Silver Mining Company, with mines in Utah, was held to have great promise, and advertisements suggesting that Britons buy shares included the enthusiastic endorsement of Schenck. Strong criticism of Schenck resulted, and on November 27, 1871, Hamilton Fish, with Grant's concurrence, wrote Schenck, advising him to withdraw his name from the management of the company. Schenck did so on December 6, but delayed announcing this severance of his ties with Emma Mine until January 12, 1872, to give himself and his friends time to sell their holdings before his announcement depressed the market value of shares in the company.[9]

Emma Mine failed, along with Jay Cooke's other ventures, in the crash of 1873, but Schenck's relationship with the company was still alive in the minds of congressmen in 1876. Abram S. Hewitt of New York headed an investigation which, while clearing Schenck of fraud, did not remove the strong suggestion that he had used his public position for private gain. And Schenck's troubles were not merely with the Democratic congressmen; he was under threat of legal action in England. He resigned in May 1876 and came home.

Another man from Ohio who was in grave trouble was the secretary of the interior, Columbus Delano. Early in the previous year, Secretary of the Treasury Benjamin Bristow had received a letter, dated March 24, 1875, from one L. C. Stevens of Cheyenne, Wyoming. Enclosed with the letter were canceled checks, an endorsed bank draft, and other documents suggesting that John Delano, Columbus Delano's son, was being given partnerships in surveying contracts that surveyors would not otherwise have received. Stevens's letter also claimed that Columbus Delano had written to thank Surveyor General Silas Reed, who awarded the contracts, for favors rendered his son.[10]

Stevens had discovered the documents while a clerk in Reed's office in Cheyenne, and seeking to expose his employer and John Delano, he sent them to the cabinet member best known for rectitude. Bristow, already immersed in the task of exposing Orville Babcock's involvement in the whiskey frauds, rather enjoyed being placed in an awkward spot by "an entire stranger." A year later he told investigating congressmen, "There were peculiar circumstances surrounding me at the time which embarrassed me very much by having the papers come into my possession." Stevens, he claimed, insisted that he put them into Grant's hands, and to the president's great discomfort, Bristow did just that. Stevens knew when he wrote Bristow that the president's brother Orvil too was the holder of a contract which brought him payment for which no cartographical service was rendered; during the 1876 investigation, a congressman asked, "Did you ever know Orvil Grant to do any surveying in that territory?" Stevens replied, "No, sir; I do not think he was ever in the territory."[11]

On April 29, 1875, Surveyor General Reed called on the president and "had a long talk with him about this affair. . . ." Confronted with the documents, Reed claimed Stevens was a thief and asked Grant to give the papers to him. Grant refused, but, according to Reed, pronounced them unimportant and, as they appeared to him to belong to John Delano, proposed returning them to him. Without the papers (and therefore still vulnerable), but aware that Grant was not anxious to pursue the matter, Reed left the White House and sent a telegram firing Stevens. (He subsequently gave the job to Charles J. Reed, his nephew.) That evening Grant and Hamilton Fish discussed the accusations against Columbus Delano that were appearing in the same newspapers that had attacked the president during the 1872 presidential campaign. Whether they discussed Reed's visit is not clear, but it is likely that Bristow had told the secretary of state about Stevens's charges. Both cabinet members thought Delano should be asked to resign, but Grant told Fish that such a request would be "retreating under fire" and would be regarded as admission of the truth of the charges. Grant was under siege. Despite Stevens's evidence against Delano, he sided with the attacked against the attackers.[12]

As in the investigation of Babcock and the whiskey frauds, Bristow led the attack, but when he realized that Grant was doing nothing with the evidence, he retrieved the documents from the White House and, on July 2, returned them to Stevens. He excused this action on the grounds that he had done his duty by informing Grant and was responsible for no more than that since this matter, unlike the whiskey frauds, did not involve his department. Why Grant yielded the documents is not clear except that, all along, he had wanted to wash his hands of the affair. Technically, there was no law to stop a firm under contract to survey parts of a territory from paying for the services of a cabinet officer's son or a president's brother (although legislation of May 18, 1796 did specify that skillful surveyors should be employed), but the evidence that John Delano was shaking down trained surveyors was strong and there was no good reason to suppose Orvil Grant was incapable of doing the same.

Grant was not close to his younger brother (who had been his boss in Galena) and had more than once remonstrated with him for capitalizing on their relationship; just after the war Orvil advertised his services in the notorious business of collecting bounties due servicemen for enlisting in the war, and Ulysses had urged him to stop. Like his father, Orvil was unable to resist petty enterprises, shady or otherwise. He was unembarrassed by the fact that his brother largely ignored him, and his staying power proved great; after Ulysses left the White House and Washington, Orvil remained in town, trying to ingratiate himself with any Republican with official money to spend. (During Hayes's administration, for example, he was happy to lend his buggy to Congressman James Garfield, who was serving on the Appropriations Committee of the House.) Exasperating as Orvil was, he was part of the family, and Ulysses tried to prevent the exposure of his unethical and possibly illegal acts by retaining Columbus Delano and thereby suggesting that no such improprieties had occurred within the purview of the secretary of the interior. Unfortunately, pressure in the opposition newspapers mounted, and Grant was forced to act. On August 7, 1875, he wrote Silas Reed, "In accepting your resignation, allow me to say that I know of no reason to be dissatisfied with your administration of the office of surveyor-general." At the same time he accepted Columbus Delano's resignation, but still reluctant to face the publicity, he did not make it public until the fall, when Bristow himself threatened to resign unless Delano was required to leave. In October 1875, Grant's old friend from Detroit days, Zachariah Chandler, took Delano's place as secretary of the interior.[13]

Moving around the cabinet table, one came to George M. Robeson, who had succeeded the amiable Adolph E. Borie as secretary of the navy in 1869. Robeson had served in an almost totally unnoticeable fashion ever since. When he was appointed, he had what was regarded as a slender law practice, and his net worth was $20,000. Soon after he took office, the Philadelphia firm of A. G. Cattell & Company, grain merchants, began receiving contracts with the United States government to supply foodstuffs. The firm flourished, and so did Robeson. When allegations that he was receiving bribes from the firm were investigated in 1876, Robeson released his bankbook to the congressmen; it showed that during his years in the Navy Department, when his salary was $8,000 a year, he made deposits totaling $320,000. In addition, one of the Cattell family was said to have given a cottage in Long Branch to Robeson. A great deal of circumstantial evidence supported the widely held view that Robeson had indeed received both the money and the house from the Cattells, but when the congressional investigators, in a massive inquiry, went through the books of the firm, they found them in disorder, and there was no evidence of payments to Robeson.[14]

The report made by the committee in July 1876 accused the secretary of the navy of gross misconduct and claimed that a system of corruption had grown up which, "from the peculiarity of its character and the cunning of its contrivance, must hereafter be known as 'Cattellism.' " There was talk of impeaching Robeson (which even one Democratic member of the committee thought shrilly partisan) but that action was never undertaken, perhaps because another such action already dominated congressional attention. On a bill of impeachment voted by the House of Representatives, the Senate of the United States was conducting its trial of Grant's former secretary of war, William Worth Belknap.[15]

Belknap's form of corruption, it will be recalled, had been receiving bribes from men who grew rich as the Indians became impoverished. The *New York Tribune* estimated that a $15,000 initial investment in a trading post brought an annual profit of $40,000—at the expense of the Indians. The newspaper, admittedly more than willing to be critical of the Grant administration, claimed that since 1874 not "a single important tradership had been secured without the payment of large sums" of money. Congressman Hiester Clymer of Pennsylvania had been seeking firm documentation of such payments, and with careful work he got it. At 11:00 A.M. on Tuesday, February 29, 1876, the House of Representatives Special Committee on Expenditures in the War Department heard Caleb Marsh's damning testimony. That afternoon, Secretary Belknap himself was the witness. When he and his lawyer perceived the hopelessness of his position, Belknap withdrew, leaving his counsel, who made a "verbal proposition" with respect to the report the committee was determined to make to the full House the next day. The proposition was, in all likelihood, an offer to have Belknap resign in return for the abandonment of impeachment proceedings. The committee members made no response and, that evening and the next day, met privately in the rooms of one of their number to discuss Marsh's testimony. Without question, Clymer told them to say nothing, so that nothing would dull the thrust of his request to the House to impeach Belknap. However, Lyman K. Bass, a Republican member of the committee, trying to make some hay with the administration, took the news of Belknap's crookedness to the leading foe of corruption in the cabinet, Secretary of the Treasury Bristow.[16]

Bass saw Bristow early on the morning of Thursday, March 2, and the secretary immediately grasped the seriousness of the charges. The Belknaps and the Bristows attended the same Bible class, and the chore of warning Grant cannot have been a cheerful one, but Bristow knew the accusations against their friend were irrefutable. At the White House, Grant, due at Henry Ulke's studio to sit for his portrait, was at the breakfast table when Bristow came in. The secretary told the president that there were unanswerable charges of bribery against Belknap and urged him to meet with Bass immediately, so that he would know all the particulars before the full committee called on him in the afternoon. After Bristow left, the president sent a note to Congressman Bass, asking him to call at noon. Then he finished his breakfast and prepared to leave for the artist's studio. At the door he encountered Belknap, "nearly suffocated with excitement." Zachariah Chandler, who accompanied Belknap, was trying to calm him, but the man broke down on seeing Grant. Weeping, he confessed, and begged his chief to accept his one-sentence letter of resignation. Grant read it, sent upstairs for someone to bring him a draft of an acceptance, studied it, but then as usual chose to write his own letter; standing at a mantelpiece at 10:20 A.M., the president wrote, "Your tender of resignation as Secretary of War, with the request to have it accepted immediately, is received and the same is hereby accepted with great regret." Still distressed, but greatly relieved, Belknap left with Chandler. Grant again started for the door but again was interrupted, this time by Senators Lot M. Morrill and Oliver P. Morton, who talked earnestly about the "Belknap horror" for fifteen minutes. "When they left," wrote James Garfield, to whom Grant described these events in a private conversation the next day, "he walked leisurely to Ulke's and sat for an hour and ten minutes. He did not know the shocking details which Bass was to tell him; but he did know that his favorite minister and his wife were disgraced." Garfield recorded that he asked Grant "if he supposed the artist saw anything unusual in his face," and Grant replied, "I think not." Garfield then asked if he was "himself conscious of any unusual agitation which was changing his ordinary expression." Grant—said Garfield—"answered, 'Oh no,' as if surprised at my question. I told him I did not believe there was another man on the continent who could have said the same under such circumstances." And in the privacy of his diary, Garfield added, "His imperturbability is amazing. I am in doubt whether to call it greatness or stupidity."[17]

Whether this response showed greatness or stupidity, Grant's old instinct for survival had unquestionably been at work, and his quick action was effective. At 11 A.M. the letters of resignation and acceptance were presented to the House committee; its members were furious with Grant for having anticipated them. Garfield, coming onto the floor of the House, "found great excitement." He listened as the committee "reported the strange and pathe[t]ic story of his [Belknap's] course, which found his accomplices in both his dead and his living wife. Rumors abounded that he had committed suicide, and for . . . [a]while, I almost wished they were true. A resolution for his impeachment was reported unanimously and adopted by the House without a division, though he resigned at ten 20 this morning. Since the death of Mr. Lincoln, I have never seen more sadness in the House."[18]

Grant, sitting for his portrait, thought he had found his response to the Belknap scandal. Rather than face the music, he would simply not hear it. But the next day he found he could not escape it entirely. To the earnest James Garfield—whom Grant saw as almost as eager as Bristow to weed moral gardens—he showed a face of remarkably cool unconcern, but in private with Hamilton Fish, he claimed that it had been the emotions of the moment that caused him to accept Belknap's resignation instantly. Garfield, in his diary, saw in Grant an awesome calm; Fish, in his, recorded the emotional response of one friend to another. Both observers missed the fact that Grant's swift action had achieved a highly rational purpose. It enabled Belknap to resign before formal charges were made. If the charges had been made first, the president would have been forced either to require Belknap to stand trial while in office or to accept a resignation that could only be regarded as an admission of guilt. In the next cabinet meeting, twenty-four hours after the strange transaction in the front hall of the White House, Grant could see that not only Bristow but also Fish was dismayed by what could be termed his obstruction of justice, but Grant told his cabinet officers that Bristow's call at breakfast was the first he had heard of Belknap's misdoings. The president, Fish reported, said "that he had accepted the resignation on its being tendered, and under the wrong impression, as he did not fully understand the statements of Belknap, who was very much overcome and

could scarcely speak." Grant, according to Fish, "did not know that acceptance was not a matter of course." Belatedly, the president ordered Attorney
General Pierrepont to consider whether criminal charges should be made
against Belknap. Meanwhile, Congress proceeded toward an impeachment
trial, despite the resignation. In the weeks before the trial Grant was short-
tempered with reporters who pressed him on the matter. He could not keep
the discord away totally.[19]

Grant truly found it hard to imagine that the activities of his comfortable
close associates caused people who did not know them to condemn them. So
it is possible that he had never conjectured about the source of the Belknaps'
obvious affluence and that Bristow's alarmed report that Thursday morning
was indeed the first he had heard of the secretary of war's profit from the
"sale" of traderships. It is also possible that once the exposure of unethical
acts in that realm was mentioned, Grant immediately realized that the heat
might reach even closer to him than the cabinet table. He knew other men
who dealt in traderships: the newspapers soon revealed that Orville Babcock's brother had obtained one, which he "rented" at a good profit; Julia's
brother John C. Dent had one, which his brother-in-law had explicitly
requested for him in a letter dated September 15, 1867, to General C. C.
Augur. Orvil Grant later denied "owning" three, claiming that he only held a
partial interest in two trading-post stores. How the profits from these arrangements were distributed was never shown with the unmistakable clarity
provided by Marsh's testimony about the Belknaps, but Grant surely must
have been wary of anything that would lead to full scrutiny of the affairs of
these members of the family. If the light stayed on the Belknaps, it might be
kept off the Dents and the Grants, and the president and his wife, paradoxically, would have reason to be grateful to the Belknaps. Julia, perhaps feeling guilty that her family had escaped the disgrace that had befallen Amanda
Belknap's—and because she was genuinely fond of her fun-loving friend—
wrote notes to all the cabinet members and then, in tears, pleaded with them
in person to call on Mrs. Belknap; she had to be allowed to appear as the wife
of a respected colleague who had resigned, not of a common criminal. When
Amanda Belknap was received at the White House, Julia Grant's pardon had
been bestowed.[20]

In the twentieth century, a hasty resignation (followed by a hastily granted
pardon) prevented history from repeating itself and staging an impeachment
trial for the nation's bicentennial; in July 1876, there was no such deprivation. The capital enjoyed the gaudy spectacle of the Belknap trial, and despite the heat, seats in the Senate gallery were at a premium. It was not as
dramatic a show as the one eight years earlier, when a president had been on
trial, but Grant's Democratic opponents gave a powerful performance.
There was much for them to work with. On August 1 the Senate voted, and
Belknap was acquitted of having committed high crimes and misdemeanors.
The managers of the impeachment had failed to obtain the necessary two-

thirds vote; twenty-three senators who thought him guilty had nevertheless voted for acquittal on the ground that the Senate did not have jurisdiction over an individual who was no longer in office. Grant's quick acceptance of the resignation was the adroit act that saved Belknap.[21]

The sordid Belknap affair boiled down to the business of cheating the Indians. The very first efforts of the Grant administration had been directed at ending that destructive exploitation of native Americans and achieving a program for the peaceable coexistence of the two races that were competing for the western plains. The Belknap trial was evidence that the reformers had not ended the crookedness at the trading posts; the relentless moves across the plains by white America, in the face of Indian opposition, demonstrated how deeply Grant's Peace Policy had been eroded.

In November 1872, the Modoc Indians in eastern Oregon had begun a series of attacks in an effort to secure lands they were contesting with white settlers. There was strong support in Sherman's army for a ruthless attack on the Modoc leader, Captain Jack, and his people, but Grant insisted that peace commissioners be allowed to try to work out a nonviolent solution. Negotiations were still under way in April when, at a meeting of the two groups, the angry and suspicious Indians turned on their white counterparts and shot and killed General E. R. S. Canby and a Methodist minister, Eleazar Thomas. An agent of the Bureau of Indian Affairs, A. B. Meacham, though close to death, survived to tell his story of the killings. General Sherman, who had had little patience with Grant's missionaries but had followed his commander's orders, now instructed Canby's successor, General A. C. Gillem, to make total war on the Modocs: "You will be fully justified in their utter extermination." Sherman sent this order without consulting Grant, who never used that term, but after they discussed the murders, he told his commanders that the "President now sanctions the most severe punishment of the Moducs." Steadfast adherents of the Peace Policy, like Alfred H. Love and Lucretia C. Mott, urged Grant to recall that the Modocs were still members of the "human family"; the government, they contended, should not overreact. But the newspapers in the West were full of bloodthirsty calls for revenge. Just a month before, in his second inaugural address, Grant had said, "Wars of extermination, engaged in by people pursuing commerce and all industrial pursuits, are expensive against the weakest people, and are demoralizing and wicked. Our superiority of strength and advantage of civilization should make us lenient toward the Indian." But this time Grant did not stay Sherman's hand. By October, Captain Jack and three other Modocs had been captured, tried, and hanged. Their people were driven to the alien ground of an Indian reservation and forced to stay there.[22]

On the northern plains, the Northern Pacific Railway was pressing its relentless imperialistic way through the lands that the Sioux had been persuaded, with such perseverance, to agree to take as their own. As the railroad opened new areas for settlement, the incoming whites demanded that the army protect them from the displaced and angrily despairing Indians. Sherman, who expected great trouble as the railroad pushed west of the Missouri River, was given a momentary reprieve from an unlikely source; the panic of 1873 forced the Northern Pacific into bankruptcy. But the delay was only temporary, and the railroad, reorganized, soon pressed forward against the Indians again.

Civilization was threatening another Sioux area as well. Banishing Indians to the Black Hills, land no white man would want, had made sense until gold was discovered there. Sherman, who had assured Red Cloud that he would honor promises to sustain Indian boundary claims, warned would-be miners that they had no right to invade property that was not theirs. Meanwhile, the Indians made it clear that they would use force if necessary to protect their lands. And soon, in the contact areas, white settlers began the familiar practice of committing provocative acts with the expectation that Indian reprisals would force the army to move in against the Indians.[23]

To counter this, Red Cloud, Spotted Tail, and Little Wound went to Washington in June 1875. Grant tried to persuade the Indians to take $25,000 in return for the rights to hunt along the Platte. Red Cloud refused, and the threat of war continued to hang over the Dakota Territory through the rest of that year and into 1876. That spring, Sitting Bull, an Indian leader independent of Red Cloud and distrustful of his negotiations, began urging the Sioux to stand up against the white men. The army, sensing a strengthening of the Indians' position, wanted to move into action, and no army man was more eager to do so than George Armstrong Custer. This flamboyant West Point graduate, who at twenty-six had been a major general in the Civil War, had made himself *persona non grata* at the White House with his outspoken and detailed accusations not merely of the Belknaps but also of President Grant's brother Orvil and of Julia's brother John. Like Sherman, he was ruthless when he thought the Indians had broken their word, and regarded them as savages likely to do so, but he was far more contemptuous of white men who degraded themselves by cheating the Indians. When he urged Sherman to give him a command in the Dakota Territory in order to fight against the Sioux, Sherman denied his request, on orders from Grant. Furious, Custer went to Chicago to plead his case publicly and with General Sheridan. Grant, in turn, was furious with Custer, but allowed Sherman to give Custer his command.[24]

On November 3, 1875, Grant and his wartime friend Philip Sheridan sat down in Washington with Secretary of War Belknap and Secretary of the Interior Chandler to discuss the almost frantic urge of gold miners to enter the Black Hills. Sheridan was not sure the army could continue to restrain them, and Grant, as Sheridan reported it, "decided that while the orders heretofore issued forbidding the occupation of the Black Hills country, by miners, should not be rescinded, still no further resistance by the military should be made to the miners going in. . . ." Grant, disgruntled, believed "such resistance only increased their desire and complicated the troubles." As a result of this conference, Sheridan ordered his commander in the field, General Alfred H. Terry, to "quietly cause the troops . . . to assume such attitude as will meet the views of the President." With Grant's promise to the Indian leaders broken, the miners rushed in, but as Grant and Sheridan should have anticipated, the Sioux did not take the invasion lying down. War broke out.[25]

Just after the Fourth of July holiday in 1876, the newspapers (which received the news before the War Department did) reported the defeat and death of Custer and his men at Little Bighorn. The military men were more restrained about the loss of their brother officer than were many of the western newspapers. Sheridan knew that Custer had badly misjudged his enemy, and reported that the defeat was "due to misapprehension and superabundance of courage, the latter being extraordinarily developed in Custer." Politicians were more bellicose. Senator A. S. Paddock of Nebraska introduced a bill calling for a volunteer army to proceed with the extermination of the Indians. Sherman, who had used the unequivocal word "extermination" often, proved once again that in his relations with the Indians he talked a more murderous game than he chose to play. He fended off the threat of having to command another volunteer army, as, unpopularly, he had once done in Georgia. Nevertheless, the campaigns that he did sanction, while not assignments in total extermination, were vicious. General Nelson A. Miles moved against the Sioux in eastern Montana with savage effect. Farther west, General O. O. Howard, the exponent of interracial co-operation, who had allowed himself to be banished to the Far West by his old comrades Grant and Sherman to escape the accusations of improper conduct in the Freedmen's Bureau brought to embarrass him by Secretary of War Belknap and other anti-black men in the army, now found himself forced to participate in an attack on people of still another race. In the winter of 1877 he was ordered out against Chief Joseph and the Nez Percé. When Chief Joseph was finally captured, many months after Grant left office, Howard made him promises of land not dissimilar to those he had made the freedmen—and once more he proved too weak to force his government to keep them. But even the promises indicated that Grant's badly battered Peace Policy, not extermination, was still the government's official policy.[26]

If Grant was depressed by the fact that his Indian policy had come down to Little Bighorn and the pursuit of an able and honorable Indian chief by an old wartime comrade known as the Christian General, if he reflected on the fact that the destitute, frightened Indians he had once seen at army posts were no better off in Howard's Department of the Columbia a quarter of a century later, he should have been equally disheartened about the plight of black people in the South, still threatened with the desolation he had seen them endure as refugees in Memphis during the war. As the election of 1876 drew near, black citizens—Republicans, for the most part—were being subjected to violent intimidation. It had all happened before in Louisiana and

Mississippi; now South Carolina, still governed by an integrated Republican administration, was the center of white-supremacist activities. On July 8, 1876, there was a murderous attack on blacks—labeled a "riot"—in Hamburg, South Carolina. Republican Governor Daniel H. Chamberlain called on Grant to assert the authority of the "General Government" to protect the people of South Carolina and ". . . restore confidence to the poor people of both races. . . ." As the fall election approached, he feared the grisly events at Hamburg would be repeated, along the pattern experienced a year earlier in Mississippi. Grant was not in town when Chamberlain's telegram (preced· ing a formal letter) reached Washington, and Secretary of State Fish and Attorney General Alphonso B. Taft (who had succeeded Pierrepont in May) deemed the request not "in pursuance of the Constitution" and turned it down without even consulting the president. When Grant got to Washington and read Chamberlain's letter of July 22, he did not override his cabinet officers but instead reiterated the claim that he was constitutionally powerless to act, even though he could see that what was happening in South Carolina in 1876 was what had happened in Mississippi in 1875. Grant's letter of reply was a hortatory call for perseverance; what was needed, he said, was a "fair trial and punishment of all offenders without distinction of race, color, or previous condition of servitude, and," he added flatly, "without aid from the Federal Government." Grant then sent to the Senate all the documents relating to the Hamburg murders, including explicit details of how they had occurred and copies of Chamberlain's letter and his reply. The Senate, in turn, published the documents but took no other action. When, later in the fall, Grant did send soldiers to guard the polling places and protect voters, it was too late. The black voters had been intimidated; the Republicans lost the election, and the abandonment by Northerners of efforts to keep black people in some semblance of parity with white people—to save Reconstruction—was all but complete.[27]

By the summer of 1876 there was no one around the White House who gave a damn about the black people. John A. Rawlins was long dead; Amos T. Akerman had been fired five years before; they had made Grant send Orville Babcock off to look at lighthouses. Hamilton Fish had never been able to get the freedmen into his line of vision; Benjamin Bristow had, briefly and dimly, but Grant now hated him more than any other man in America. Edwards Pierrepont, the attorney general who had cared least about the need of blacks for help from the Justice Department, was gone—to London to replace Robert Schenck as minister—but Alphonso Taft cared only marginally more. (When Taft moved to the Justice Department in May 1876, he was succeeded as secretary of war by J. D. Cameron.) Julia still thought of black people as her father's slaves; Fred had demonstrated the quality of his concern at West Point; Buck and Jesse weren't interested; and Nellie, in England, was too far away for Grant to talk to about anything. No one in the White House—and fewer and fewer in white America—cared about the former slaves anymore. It was too late for Grant to bring about Reconstruction, even if he had had the will.

The year 1876 was troubling and frustrating for Grant. The pendulum would not hang still. He had been deprived of Babcock, and he had been showered with glamorous attention at the Centennial Exposition in Philadelphia. His first grandchild—Nellie's son, Grant—died in May; his first granddaughter—splendidly healthy—was born in June. And, amid all the contrasts, he had the private woe of facing replacement. His term would be up in a year, and he saw no signs that the pendulum would carry him up from the abandonment in which politicians, concentrating on his successor, would leave him.

Both Julia and Ulysses Grant were so attached to the White House that people who desired a repudiation of "Grantism"—the corruption exemplified by the misdeeds of Babcock and Belknap—feared they would try for a third term. But the scandals were strong enough to preclude a sustained effort to achieve renomination for the president. Grant found it galling that Republicans felt a need to repudiate his record rather than build the next victory on it. And what was worse, Benjamin Helm Bristow was a most likely candidate to replace his chief. He had become the hero of reformers who, unlike the

*No third term.* LIBRARY OF CONGRESS

# TRYING IT ON.

Liberal Republicans of 1872, sought to achieve reform within the regular Republican party. To Grant, any other Republican was preferable to Bristow, and he watched sardonically as Bristow and his former law partner John Marshall Harlan, who was managing his campaign, strained their great friendship at the Republican convention in June in Cincinnati. Bristow's chief opponent was James G. Blaine of Maine, a far more glamorous and less honest politician than he. Blaine, with better than a hundred more convention delegates than Bristow, was short of a majority, and Bristow supporters thought they were building to a victory over Blaine when a curious accident blighted both their chances. Blaine suffered a stroke (from which he recovered well), and Bristow, hearing the news, rushed to Blaine's house. At the door, Bristow saw Blaine on the floor with "a number of persons rubbing his limbs." He started to enter, only to hear Mrs. Blaine say, "Mr. Bristow you have got your will; don't come in here." Thereafter, Blaine's questionable health and Bristow's appearance as one rushing to advantage over a fallen foe made neither fully attractive to the convention. Two other contenders, Senator Oliver P. Morton and Senator Roscoe Conkling (Grant's choice) lacked the strength to win, and in the face of a stalemate, the well-crafted campaign of Governor Rutherford B. Hayes of Ohio gained force. Finally, when it appeared that only Hayes could block Blaine if Bristow faltered, Harlan—with more swiftness than some Bristow supporters thought seemly—released Bristow's delegates to Hayes, who won the nomination. It was rumored that night that Harlan would be rewarded with an appointment to the Supreme Court, and he did indeed later receive this appointment. Bristow, who had long wanted to reach the Court himself, instead retired to private practice, and the friendship of the two men, whose careers had been too parallel for the sake of either, was never as strong again.[28]

It was clear that whether nominated or not, Bristow would leave Grant's cabinet, and on June 21, 1876, he was replaced by Lot M. Morrill of Maine. As he resigned, Bristow drafted a long bitter letter to Grant, complaining that he had been blocked from doing his duty; then, thinking better of it, he wrote a shorter formal letter of resignation. When he arrived at the White House with this letter, Grant was just leaving for a drive. Silently, the president took the letter, got into his carriage and drove off. At his last cabinet meeting, on June 20, Bristow stayed only long enough to exchange formal pleasantries with Grant and his colleagues. Then the reformer withdrew, leaving the Grants with the prospect of being replaced in the White House either by a Democrat who had not fought in the war or a pious nonentity of a minor Republican general.[29]

It was after the election in November 1876, and in a mood of resignation and retrospection, that Ulysses Grant wrote his astonishing final State of the Union message, under the dateline, "Executive Mansion December 5, 1876." He began that remarkable document with the fact that this message was his last, and then presented an apology: "It was my fortune, or misfortune, to be called to the office of Chief Executive without any previous political training. From the age of 17 I had never even witnessed the excitement attending a Presidential campaign but twice antecedent to my own candidacy, and at but one of them was I eligible as a voter." In this formal and normally most impersonal of government documents, he took his countrymen back to his boyhood and tried to make them see why things had gone wrong. As a little boy he had witnessed political campaigns in Georgetown, he had heard his father argue politics, and it had all been real. Then that reality had been taken away; his boyhood had ended when he was seventeen, and during the campaigns of 1840, 1844, 1848, 1852, and 1864, he was somewhere with the army. In 1860 he had not lived in Galena long enough to vote. His only ballot had been that inglorious one cast in Missouri for James Buchanan in 1856. Now, in his self-pity, Grant chose to forget how intense had been his consciousness of politics in 1864, and during every day of his life since then.[30]

Because he was cursed with this political innocence, "it is but reasonable to suppose that errors of judgement must have occurred." He did not, however, shoulder all the responsibility: "It is not necessarily evidence of blunder on the part of the Executive because there are these differences of views. Mistakes have been made, as all can see and I admit. . . ." He went on to place the blame only indirectly on himself; it seemed to him that the mistakes were "oftener in the selections made of the assistants appointed to aid in carrying out the various duties of administering the Government" than in his own actions.[31]

The problem in the selection of assistants, as Grant saw it, was not cronyism, but the opposite. He was troubled that "in nearly every case" the officials for whose acts he was apologizing were "selected without a personal acquaintance." It was not Orville Babcock who was on his mind, as he sought to explain how things had gone wrong. Furthermore, he wanted it understood that he was not the first president to make errors: "History shows that no Administration from the time of Washington to the present has been free from these mistakes. But I leave comparisons to history, claiming only that I have acted in every instance from a conscientious desire to do what was right, constitutional, within the law, and for the very best interests of the whole people. Failures have been errors of judgement, not of intent." People had failed him, and the times had been against him as well: "My civil career commenced . . . at a most critical and difficult time. Less than four years before, the country had emerged from a conflict such as no other nation had ever survived. Nearly one-half of the States had revolted against the government, and of those remaining faithful to the Union a large percentage of the population sympathized with the rebellion and made an 'enemy in the rear' almost as dangerous as the more honorable enemy in the front." In these comments Grant was more fearful than he had ever been during the war, when the activities of the Peace Democrats were of justifiable concern to a military commander. The comments were bound—designed—to rankle the present-day

Democrats, now a majority in the House of Representatives, to whom the message was addressed.[32]

In his recapitulation of the events of his eight years, Grant turned first to Reconstruction, which "to speak plainly" was a matter of "whether the control of the Government should be thrown immediately into the hands of those who had so recently and persistently tried to destroy it, or whether the victors should continue to have an equal voice with them in this control." No one could claim this was not plain speaking, and Grant spoke proudly of standing behind congressional Reconstruction measures and of his "heartily" given support for the Fifteenth Amendment. He had counted on the "late slave," once enfranchised, to "increase" the "Union-loving and Union-supporting votes." The freedmen too had let him down, but he had an idea why: "If *free* in the full sense of the word, they would not disappoint this expectation." But he pursued this line of thought no further; after the reference to his enthusiastic support of the Fifteenth Amendment, he plunged, in midparagraph, into talk of debt and taxes, before moving on to another group of troubled people.[33]

If black Americans were not truly "free," neither were red Americans safe from the "avarice of the white man," who had "violated our treaty stipulations in his search for gold." Grant was unequivocal in his condemnation of the treaty breakers who had invaded lands that he had promised the Sioux. He then posed an obvious question: "The question might be asked why the Government has not enforced obedience to the terms of the treaty." The answer, he quickly added, was "simple"; it lay in numbers and greed. The first people going into the Black Hills had been evicted by the troops, but then gold had been "found in paying quantity, and an effort to remove the miners would only result in the desertion of the bulk of the troops that might be sent there to remove them."[34]

This was about as hard-hitting and succinct a lecture on the history of the West as one could hope for, but Grant spoiled it all with his bland codicil: "All difficulty in this matter has, however, been removed—subject to the approval of Congress—by a treaty ceding the Black Hills and approaches to settlement by citizens." If he allowed himself to think about it, Grant cannot possibly have believed that this surrender to the miners with a new treaty could be counted on to meet the continuing needs of the Sioux any more than the compromises in the South met those of the black citizens of South Carolina and Mississippi.[35]

Having prodded the Senate to ratify the Indian treaty, the president proceeded to chastise both the House and the Senate for reducing appropriations for the consular service. There would be no consul in Bolivia, Ecuador, and Colombia, he told them, and ministers were to be replaced with mere chargés d'affaires in Portugal, Denmark, Greece, Switzerland, and Paraguay. (He may have felt the projected change of representation in Denmark was a rebuke to his sister Mary and her husband, who was the minister in Copenhagen.) Now Grant asked Congress to reconsider its action. The money saved was not, he argued, "adequate consideration for the loss of influence and importance" that would result from downgrading the foreign service. Grant looked to the growth of America's power in the world arena rather than to its diminishment.[36]

The balance of the message dutifully informed Congress that each cabinet department was doing its job; the routine prose of these sections was a metaphor for the tedium of so much of Grant's last eight years. But he allowed himself two exceedingly interesting digressions, two signals about matters of interest and concern that lay ahead for the American government. He called attention, in a way that suggests he had not read it, to the report of the commissioner of agriculture (not yet a cabinet secretary). This included, said Grant, a summary of findings in "chemistry, botany, entomology, etc." which constituted a good argument for the development of more scientific agriculture. And he pointed to the practical information in the report about which crops were overproduced in the world and which were not and hence could be profitable for the nation's farmers.[37]

Second, he urged Congress, as a step toward the goal of scientific and profitable farming, and toward the development of the economy in general, to build permanent halls in the capital to house the fine exhibits assembled for the Centennial Exposition in Philadelphia. In the hope that Congress would respond to his plea (and that of the director of the Smithsonian Institution) that such halls be swiftly built, he requested that the Philadelphia exhibits not be dismantled. It was an interesting and hopeful sign of the interest of a president in the work being done by Americans in science and the arts.[38]

After these two looks into the future, Grant turned back to what clearly was the greatest disappointment of his years in the White House, the failure of the Senate to allow him to annex Santo Domingo. His odd tenacious affection for his and Babcock's enterprise in the Caribbean was revealed again, with a chamber-of-commerce salute to the productive promise of the island, which would be realized once the soil was in "the hands of United States capitalists." He seemed to be saying that he had not wanted the island simply to satisfy his whim or Orville Babcock's ego and pocketbook:

> The emancipated race of the South would have found there a congenial home, where their civil rights would not be disputed and where their labor would be so much sought after that the poorest among them could have found the means to go. Thus in cases of great oppression and cruelty, such as has been practiced upon them in many places within the last eleven years, whole communities would have sought refuge in Santo Domingo. I do not suppose the whole race would have gone, nor is it desirable that they should go. Their labor is desirable—indispensable almost—where they now are. But the possession of this territory would have left the negro "master of the situation," by enabling him to demand his rights at home on pain of finding them elsewhere.[39]

Despite his affection for it, Grant now did not really have his heart in his dubious Santo Domingo plan. He told Congress he was going into the matter not to reopen the annexation question, but to "vindicate any previous action in regard to it." Vindication was what the message was about, and in ending that message, he circled back to himself: "With the present term of Congress my official life terminates. It is not probable that public affairs will ever again receive attention from me further than as a citizen of the Republic. . . ." Grant's choice of words was almost ominous; he had once said that getting out of the White House would be better than anything else except possibly getting out of West Point, but now he did not say that with the end of his term he would go happily into private life. What he said was ". . . my official life terminates." Was he glad to go, or terrified of the void into which he was heading? The message is often regarded as an embarrassing episode in Grant's career—a whimper from a strong man become weak and admitting his failure, a somewhat petulant request to be excused for his mistakes because he was forced against his will to take a job outside his competence. But the opposite is true. This was one of the rare moments when Grant revealed himself as he truly was, and one of those even rarer moments when a president of the United States, in an official document, dared show himself as a normal mortal struggling to make sense of his situation. If the ordinary people of the land had not been so accustomed to seeing their leaders try to lift themselves above human worries, they might have heard—and indeed some did—the sound of the human being that they had sensed to be there but that Grant, until then, had kept hidden.[40]

Ulysses and Julia did not leave their house just yet. There was still one more season in which they were at the center. There was still one more New Year's reception, and the president's lady was not afraid to make a grand occasion grander. She alone decided how to do so. At her New Year's Day reception in 1877, as throngs of callers came to the White House through a heavy snowfall, she presented her youngest guest—another Julia Grant, Fred and Ida's daughter, born in the White House on June 7, 1876. And once started, this young lady was not to be stopped; nearly a century later, as Princess Cantacuzene, living in her lovely Connecticut Avenue apartment, she still received party invitations that took her back to the White House.[41]

Nineteen other men had lived in her grandfather's house by the time Princess Cantacuzene died in 1975, but in the winter of 1877 it was still his. And it was not at all clear who would live in it when he left. Grant had not been in Galena or in Washington, D.C., when the returns of the election of 1876 came in. He was in Philadelphia, at the home of his friend George W. Childs, and he went to bed convinced that in the morning he would issue a congratulatory statement conceding the election to the Democrat candidate, Samuel J. Tilden. Such a statement might have altered the delicate balance of the famous maneuvers that followed; it would surely have comforted Tilden as much as it would have dismayed Hayes. Luckily for the latter, the next morning, before Grant spoke to any reporters, "an eminent Republican senator and one or two other leading Republicans walked in, and they went over the returns."[42]

In New York, during the night, the chairman of the Republican party, William E. Chandler, had been busy. The defeat of Rutherford B. Hayes, which had seemed a judgment on the Grant administration, was, perhaps, not a defeat after all. If the count of votes in Florida, South Carolina, and Louisiana (three states which still had Radical governments) could be challenged, Hayes might still be elected. William Chandler, moving quickly, wakened Grant's old friend Zachariah Chandler; by dawn, they had been in touch with Republican officials in the three states and the delegation had left to call on President Grant. As Childs recalled it: "One of these leaders, notwithstanding the returns, said, 'Hayes is elected.' . . . General Grant listened to them, but said nothing. After they had settled things in their own minds, he said: 'Gentlemen, it looks to me as if Mr. Tilden is elected.' "[43]

Despite this sardonic assessment, Grant did not issue his congratulatory statement, and he did nothing to cripple the energetic efforts of the two Chandlers and their allies to mount a challenge. He did, however, make them exceedingly nervous. Grant had no affection for Hayes, and the party leaders could glean only that his goal was a resolution of the impending crisis, which now threatened to result in civil disorder similar to that which he had experienced in 1861 and feared in the spring of 1865. Conjectures of how chaos might occur were many. If the electoral votes of the three Southern states in which the count was disputed went to Hayes, he would win; if, at the same time, an Oregon elector (who, illegally, was a government employee) was replaced by a Democratic appointee, there would be a tie. The Constitution calls for the electoral votes to be opened in the presence of both houses of Congress, but it does not say who should do the counting. If the Republican Senate majority decided the count went one way, the Democratic majority of the House of Representatives might decide it went the other. Another possibility was a Senate filibuster, begun before the count could be made, that might extend past Grant's last day in office, leaving the United States without a president. And the disastrous interregnum between the election of 1860 and the inauguration of 1861 was not so far in the past as to make worries about disorder groundless.

Even more recently, impeachment proceedings against a president had been instituted, and Grant did not like the strident calls for such action against him for using troops to guard the polls in South Carolina in November 1876. He did not want to take any step that could result in his being called a dictator, and he was no more sanguine about having the Republicans in the Senate make a decision to accept the returns of the Republican electors in the disputed states. Such a resolution would, he feared, be "stigmatized as a fraud." Even Tilden would be better than such a victory, and he asked his friend Childs if there was not some other way out of the impasse.[44]

Meanwhile, eager politicians were courting Grant, hoping to ensure that whatever procedure was adopted, the result would be a Republican president. Early in January 1877, Hayes's supporters were afraid Grant would follow the lead of his friend Roscoe Conkling. Conkling, powerful in the Senate, piqued that he had not been the nominee, and genuinely troubled by Hayes's lack of concern for the stalwart black and white Republicans who were desperately fighting to stay alive in Southern politics, was believed to favor a compromise that would yield the presidency to Tilden. If Grant agreed, the struggle would probably be lost. Therefore, Hayes sent one of his closest friends, James M. Comly, to call on the president. Comly's approach to Grant was skillful; it only involved sacrificing one reformer. As Comly reported to Hayes, once Grant was assured that "there was not one chance in a million that you would appoint Bristow to a Cabinet position in view of the fact that he had made himself so personally obnoxious to the President . . . ," all was well. Grant responded with "strong emotion" to this assurance and *"drew the friendly cigars from his pocket,"* a gesture which Comly took as highly propitious.[45]

When a Tilden rally was scheduled for Ford's Theater, Grant engaged in some alarmist rhetoric, declaring the District of Columbia was as safe as a "garrisoned fortress, and any demonstrations or warlike concentration of men threatening the peace of the city or endangering the security of public property or treasure of the Government would be summarily dealt with, should the public safety demand, by a declaration of marshal law." Privately, he was on a quieter course. He invited several Republican senators and his friend Childs to the White House to hear arguments in favor of an independent electoral commission to decide the issue. The dinner party was not a success; as Grant said to Childs, "You see the feeling here. I find them almost universally opposed to anything like an Electoral Commission."[46]

Childs's response was to work all the harder to achieve this elite solution to the dilemma, and he persuaded Grant to do something he had not done before—use Democrats as the agents to carry out a policy. He arranged for Grant to meet with Samuel J. Randall, Speaker of the House of Representatives, and General Robert Patterson, an eighty-five-year-old Pennsylvanian who had been a friend of Andrew Jackson's. Grant had fought with him at Cerro Gordo, and since the Mexican War he had been an investor in the Pennsylvania Railroad and the owner of extensive sugar properties in Louisiana. Patterson represented well the commercial values underlying the compromise that eventually emerged. Childs told Grant that Patterson had "a great deal of influence with the Democrats, and particularly the Southern Democrats." Knowing he could find support in the opposition party, Grant next turned to his fellow Republicans. He called in Roscoe Conkling, who told him that he was not alone in opposing an electoral commission; Senator Oliver P. Morton, powerful among Republicans, disliked the idea as well. Despite the opposition of these loyal supporters, Grant replied, "I wish it done."[47]

How much weight the president's command carried is hard to measure. As a lame-duck president, with little remaining patronage, he obviously had severely limited means of exerting direct pressure. Even so, and despite the scandals of his administration, General Grant was still a powerful force. The commission idea carried with it an aura of fairness, and it won overwhelming support in Congress. In the Senate, twenty-six Democrats voted for it, and one against, while only twenty-one Republicans supported the commission. Sixteen Republican senators defied Grant. In the House, the Democratic majority ensured a victory, but twice as many Republicans went against the president's advice as were willing to accede to it.[48]

After the vote was taken, strong advocates of a Republican victory at any price hoped that Grant would reverse himself and veto the bill. It was true that Grant's attention to the matter of the electoral commission was not total; as Childs recalled it: "After the bill had passed and was waiting for signature, General Grant went to a State fair in Maryland the day it should have been signed, and there was much perturbation about it." Frantic telegrams were sent, but Childs, feeling confident that he knew where the president stood, reassured the backers of the commission that Grant would sign the bill. And he did so, though not without a sense that he was probably handing the White House over to a Democrat. Later that spring, when no such horror had occurred, Grant told Childs "with rare candor" that "from the beginning" he had thought the Louisiana votes would go to Tilden. But the electoral commission found for Hayes; Congress accepted the decision, and Hayes arrived in Washington on Friday, March 2. The carriages of the Hayes party rushed to the White House, and ushers announced the president-elect. Hayes, "grasping President Grant's hand in both of his, and looking in the President's eyes, seemed for a moment too overcome for expression." Grant, a good deal less overcome, said simply, "Governor Hayes, I am glad to welcome you. . . ." The next day he and Buck returned Hayes's call, and then Grant went to Capitol Hill to sign bills. That evening Julia gave her last White House reception—for two thousand people. At midnight Hayes was sworn in, privately (because Grant's term ended on a Sunday). The public inaugural went forward on Monday, March 5, 1877.[49]

Leaving the White House was torture for Julia. Once the new president moved in, and she had had to go, she and Ulysses traveled west for "dinners, receptions, and serenades . . . many and charming" in Cincinnati, St. Louis, Galena, and Chicago, and then in Harrisburg, and finally back in Washington, where in a hotel "our parlors were thronged all day long. And at night, it was like the President's levees." She was trying to continue the wonderful eight years she had spent as first lady. (Ulysses got away from all of this briefly when he and Daniel Ammen, leaving Julia in Cincinnati, took a carriage up muddy roads for a sentimental journey back to Georgetown.)[50]

Julia's final day in the White House had been made to last as long as possible. Nervous people in the Hayes party began to wonder if she would ever go. She declined an invitation to attend the inaugural, on Capitol Hill, and rejected her husband's suggestion that they leave quietly before the Hayeses reached the White House after the ceremony. Instead, as if it were her house still, she welcomed President Hayes and gave a fine luncheon. The guests were relieved to be back from the Capitol and inside the White House: one of them, Congressman Garfield, spoke of the "indications of relief and joy that no accident had occurred on the route for there were apprehensions of assassination." Julia's luncheon was a success, and when it was over, the Grants said good-by to the servants and stepped into their four-in-hand. The Hayeses, and all of the party, came out under the portico to say good-by. As they drove off, Garfield silently made his assessment: "No American has carried greater fame out of the White House than this silent man who leaves it today." Near him, "Mrs. Secretary Robeson stood crying . . . saying this is my place to stand on the steps and see my King go."[51]

The Grants and Nellie stayed with Julia and Hamilton Fish until Nellie's baby was born, on March 17. A week later they set out for Ohio. They were escorted to the train by Zachariah Chandler, who thanked Julia for the "propriety and dignity" with which she had "presided over the Executive Mansion during these eight years past." She and Ulysses waved to the party on the platform as the train pulled out of the station, and then Julia went to her compartment and wept. The general heard her crying and went in, asking what the trouble was. "Oh, Ulys," she answered, "I feel like a waif." "Is that all?" he replied. "I thought something had happened. You must not forget that I too am a waif."[52]

# XXVI

# AROUND
# THE WORLD

*. . . all the world's my way.*
*—William Shakespeare*

O N  M A Y  17, 1877, Julia and Ulysses Grant left Philadelphia, sailing
on the *Indiana* for a vacation in England. Two years later, after having
been nodded to by almost every crowned head in Europe, after touring fiords
in Norway and ruins in Pompeii, after riding donkeys into a city in upper
Egypt, and the afternoon train from Paddington Station to spend the night as
Queen Victoria's guests at Windsor, after conversing with Prince Bismarck
and Disraeli during the Congress of Berlin, and with Gorchakov in St.
Petersburg, after visiting Russia, India, Siam, and China, and receiving a
handshake from the emperor of Japan, they came home. Julia and Ulysses
had looked at the whole wide world. Theirs was perhaps the grandest tour an
American couple had ever made.

The two tourists were themselves on display. The unpretentious man in
the dark suit was his country's greatest warrior-hero, and the world wanted
to have a look at him. The general and his lady were ambassadors of both
American simplicity and American power. They exemplified their strange
democracy, which had uneasily made itself into a nation-state and was to
become a great power. The military strength was not yet there. Or rather, it
was gone. With Grant's help, the Civil War army had been shrunk to minus-

*At a pyramid in Egypt, 1878. The Grants are in the front row, third and fourth from left.* LIBRARY OF CONGRESS

cule dimensions, matching those of the exceedingly modest navy. But the world had read about the ferocity of the armies that had swollen into huge size and done such terrible battle in Grant's Civil War. General Grant, coming among them, was a reminder to people around the world that such might could well up in America again.

Ulysses and Julia Grant stood for a stolid American strength that was not to be repudiated for a century. Poking about the world, peering at the sights, they looked through almost every door that America later entered as a world power. A hundred years after, American leaders, more hurried, moved around the world on trips considered mandatory by politicians committed to the idea that the United States must be not merely a strong nation, but the strongest of them all. Lincoln and Grant had reunited this nation; in doing so, they had created a country very different from the one into which they had been born.

Displaying the visible signs of greatness was a business that English settlers had been about since they had come to the new land and made it theirs and themselves Americans. Assertions of superiority were made by seventeenth-century Englishmen—turned Americans—in their anguished and devout definition of themselves as people of a new and better world. By the

*A cartoonist's view of Grant as a traveler.* LIBRARY OF CONGRESS

time Benjamin Franklin went to Paris there was a new republic to proclaim, and his coonskin cap somehow gave it authenticity. Franklin's particular salesmanship had something to do with getting venture capital for an exciting new enterprise and for winning a war. But despite his practical urgency, Franklin—and John Adams, and Thomas Jefferson, and other American travelers—spoke for a nation that asserted that its leadership in the world was in the realm of the moral.

Styles changed—Grant carried a tall, black silk hat—but the techniques of a particular brand of American diplomacy did not. Grant was true to American form in the manner he displayed when he called on the most powerful man in Europe. Dispensing with a carriage, the general "saunters in a kind of nonchalant way into the court-yard" of Bismarck's palace and "throws away a half-smoked cigar" in order to return the salute of the startled guards. Then "before he has time to ring, two liveried servants throw wide open the door, and the Ex-President passes into a spacious marble hall." Grant had made exactly the entrance he wanted to make. Jefferson, who walked to his inaugural, would have approved. It was American. The difference was that the America that entered by those wide-open doors of world politics was a nation that had lost its republican innocence. American superiority was no longer primarily moral. And the man who embodied both that loss and the material and martial strength that replaced it was the simplest of Americans, Ulysses Grant.[1]

The trip began as a personal adventure. The Grants had had eight years in the White House, and they had come under a crescendo of criticism for the corruption of the administration. Since they had nowhere to go and nothing to do, it was natural for them to take a vacation, one that would get them away from all the hectoring. England, where their daughter lived, was the most logical possible destination. It was to be a family visit. And yet from the moment they arrived in Liverpool, or rather, from the time they prepared to leave from Philadelphia, the trip was not private at all. In all the months in England, they spent but a few days with Nellie and her new baby, and these visits seemed almost afterthoughts next to the great republican progression of public occasions on which Julia and Ulysses embarked. The tour was celebrated in two handsome lavender-bound volumes with beautiful illustrations, entitled *Around the World with General Grant*, that lay on hundreds of fine marble table tops in the 1880's. The book was written by John Russell Young, a reporter for the *New York Herald* who was part of the entourage. The trip was anything but simple.

It all began at the Philadelphia home of the Grants' friend George W. Childs. Grant wrote his youngest son, Jesse, kidding and mildly chastising him: "You young worthless[.] I expected to see you at Grandmas. You will not now get to see her before sailing for Europe." (The Grants had been visiting the Corbins, with whom Hannah Grant now lived.) "You know we sail on the 17th and if you should not get here you will be left without visible means of support." Before the seventeenth arrived, there was a luncheon with the banker A. J. Drexel, whose correspondents around the world were to handle Grant's finances on the trip; a reception at the handsome brick Union League Club on Broad Street; another reception at Independence Hall, at which "2500 people an hour in a steady stream" came to view the former president; fireworks in the city's handsome Fairmount Park; and yet another banquet. On the day before they left, "a very pretty ceremony took place, when the soldiers' orphans—wards of the state—marched in procession past Mr. Childs' residence." With perfect deportment, the children walked past the man who as much as any was responsible for their dependent status. Grant stood on the steps "extending to each little one . . . a pleasant word." On the morning of the seventeenth, Grant breakfasted with his chief lieutenants from the war and from the presidential years—General Sherman and Hamilton Fish—along with Governor John F. Hartranft and old Senator Simon Cameron. Jesse had caught up with his parents by then, and it was time to go.[2]

So many people escorted the Grants to their ship that two cutters were needed to carry them. Buck Grant and Colonel Fred Grant were there, but Horace Porter was the only one of the old army staff present to say farewell to the general. On Julia's boat was a man with an eye for grandeur, the artist Albert Bierstadt. Small boats decorated with bunting filled the river and nervously avoided each other as their passengers cheered the general. The party transferred to a third boat for a bon voyage luncheon; then, after seven toasts, with accompanying short speeches, and the general's reply, they all set off on still more escort boats. Finally, the Grants boarded the *Indiana*, to sail across the ocean.

Julia was seasick. Ulysses, smoking cigars constantly, was just fine; the first morning at sea, as legend has it, he said "that he felt better than he had for sixteen years." The general was said to recall later, ". . . from the 4th of March till the 17th of May I dined formally . . . every day . . . and sometimes took two lunches the same day [and therefore] I thought I was a good subject for seasickness, and expected the motion of the ship would turn me inside out. As a matter of fact, I was disappointed." After ten days they reached Ireland and, the next morning, May 28, 1877, Liverpool. There they encountered an enormous cheering crowd on the dock—as well as Adam Badeau—and, the following evening, a banquet. All these Englishmen, as ardent as any Americans who had ever greeted him, fascinated Grant. Badeau, now consul general in London, was more fascinated by the barrage of invitations to visit other cities. Officiously, he took charge of Grant's tour of England, but what happened was that England took charge of Grant.[3]

The Grants spent two days in Liverpool, where "the party minutely inspected the new dock works in progress," the town hall, and the "free library." Next, they went to Manchester for "a round of visits among the celebrated manufactories." In his response to the mayor's address of welcome,

Grant said, "I was very well aware during the war of the sentiments of the great mass of the people of Manchester"; they had favored the North and the antislavery cause even though, being in the cotton trade, they invited hardship by doing so. "There exists," the general said, "a feeling of friendship toward Manchester distinct and separate from that which my countrymen feel towards all other parts of England." At Bedford, the mayor likened Grant, the conqueror, to Hannibal. Then the party took the Midland Railway to London. On May 31, Julia and Ulysses Grant arrived at St. Pancras Station, Sir George Gilbert Scott's new and glamorous medieval castle in brick.[4]

The next morning, the Prince of Wales and the general met at the running of the Oaks at Epsom; the next night, Julia and Ulysses walked up the curved staircase around the body of Canova's naked marble Napoleon to enter the magnificent dining room of Apsley House, the home of the duke of Wellington. There Julia saw how the British honored their warrior-heroes; Apsley House was splendidly appointed. The Iron Duke's son greeted a general who was as flattered by comparisons to the victor of Waterloo as he was dismayed by those which likened him to Napoleon. Looking into the eyes of Lawrence's fine portrait of Wellington, Grant commented on how much the other warrior had accomplished with fewer men and arms than he had commanded. His host, eager to find brashness in his American guest, took the remark as Grant's boasting that he was the mightier general. The anecdote, embellished to illustrate American gaucherie, made its rounds in Tory society, but Grant heard nothing of such *sotto voce* sneers. The next day, Sunday, in Westminster Abbey, the Grants listened as the dean worked a "graceful allusion to the . . . Ex-President" into his sermon.[5]

On June 5, Edwards Pierrepont got his reward in his particular heaven. At his fine house on Cavendish Square, that particular gentleman gave a reception for the Grants that drew everyone he could have desired, including the Prince of Wales. At dinner, the Prince sat next to Grant and directly across the table from Julia. Afterward, the Grants received a "small and early party" of celebrities, including most of England's leading politicians. These were present in numbers rivaled only by the society reporters. "Mr. & Mrs. Gladstone," presumably chatting about something other than the former prime minister's partisanship of the South during the war, "remained . . . with General Grant until the arrival of Lord Derby, when . . . [they] moved loftily away." The foreign secretary, reported Kate Field, in the next day's *Morning Post*, beamed radiantly as he approached the general; a bit later, Grant was cordial as the staunch old Quaker John Bright, "with a wealth of snowy hair which surmounts the massive, cheery face" came up and greeted him heartily.[6]

Outside, a vast awning covered the walk from the street to the door of the minister's house, the roadway was carpeted, and servants in scarlet opened carriage doors and held lanterns and torches, "so that no tiny foot in satin

shoon shall make a false step." On the opposite curb, the London policemen
stood in front of "massed . . . detachments of England's poor and hungry,"
who had come to "get a glimpse of the fairy land wherein abide riches. . . ."
Riches, and Ulysses Grant of Point Pleasant, Ohio. Amid yards of marchio-
nesses and duchesses, the earl of Caithness walked up to Grant: "On his arm
was the Countess, whose bosom was," alarmingly, "literally ablaze with
diamonds." Julia in claret stamped velvet and cream-colored satin, with a
high collar and long sleeves—in June—was talking with the "stately and even
beautiful Mrs. Gladstone," who wore soft "blue and white, with a cluster of
fine diamonds setting off the long blue plume in her hair." All the notable
Americans in town were present, among them the Junius Spencer Morgans,
Julia Ward Howe, and Moncure D. Conway. Robert Browning was there,
and so was Arthur Sullivan. The great ladies of London appraised Grant and
pronounced him fit. "He looks like a soldier," said a viscountess.[7]

And on it went. Society reporters outdid themselves: the general and his
lady, they said, sat down to dine with fifty peers at the duke of Devonshire's
table and with royalty at Princess Louise's Kensington Palace. Recalling
Grant's presidency, the marquess of Ripon, who had been in America six
years earlier to negotiate the treaty of Washington, gave a dinner, and Sir
Edward Thornton was present. The general called on ancient Earl Russell at
Pembroke Lodge, and talked, one might guess, more happily of grandchildren than of wartime politics. At the breakfast table of the *New York
Tribune* reporter George Smalley were men of letters: Matthew Arnold,
Frank Hill, Robert Browning (again), and Sir Frederick Pollock, but Anthony Trollope, though he hurried to the reception, missed meeting Grant.
Benjamin Disraeli gave "my colossal American dinner," with forty male
guests—and Julia. "I sate," reported the host, "next to the General, more
honorable than pleasant." At the Reform Club there were distinguished Liberals, magnificent cuisine, and a long rambling speech by Lord Granville
that, inappropriately, wound up being a tribute to President Hayes's reunification policy; at Marlborough House, there was dinner with the Prince of
Wales and two splendid Tories, Disraeli and Lord Derby, who were most
grateful to Granville for having made such an ass of himself with his ignorance of American politics. At midnight, the dinner over, Grant and Badeau
went to Printing House Square and saw the presses running off accounts of
their activities in the next day's *Times*.[8]

The general was treated to the splendor of the Guildhall, where the lord
mayor, attended by the aldermen in scarlet, and wearing his own splendid
robe, handed the black-clad guest the freedom of the city. After the luncheon
for a thousand, Grant rode in the lord mayor's coach to the Crystal Palace,
around which thirty thousand people were said to have gathered. A band
played "Hail Columbia" as he entered; in the evening there were thunderous
fireworks. Grant sat silently with his cigar and endured them: "After a flight
of fiery pigeons to and fro from their cots, there was displayed a portrait in

fire of a distinguished man, in whose honour the fête was designed. 'Do you recognize it?' said a lady to the ex-President. 'It is very good,' he replied."[9]

The London *Times*, in a long tribute to Grant on June 4, left it to Americans to judge whether he had "culpably wasted the lives of his men during the war," and pronounced that during Reconstruction "he failed, as all save one or two men in a generation would have failed," but nonetheless concluded that "after WASHINGTON, General GRANT is the President who will occupy the largest place in the history of the United States." Grant, in a private letter to George Childs written in the midst of all this vast and exhausting attention, spoke as if the people crowded on the inelegant docks of Liverpool mattered more to him than all the personages in London. He also indulged in some understandable chauvinism; having mentioned the dinner at Apsley House, he was moved by his American pride to say that he doubted if there were a private house anywhere more tastefully decorated than the Pierreponts'. He was proud of his welcome in England but insisted that "the attentions are more for our country than for me." He added that it "has always been my desire to see all jealousy between England and the United States abated, and every sore healed," going on to assert that "together they are more powerful for the spread of commerce and civilization than all others combined, and can do more to remove causes of wars by creating moral interests that would be so much endangered by war."[10]

The London *Times*, sounding a different note, did not agree with Grant's vision of the two countries in harmony: ". . . there is a great, and perhaps growing, difference between [the] two peoples; and nobody could represent it better than the distinguished man to whom the City did honour yesterday." Speaking of the Guildhall ceremony, the *Times* continued, "There is a difference in the type of national character, in the manner of the people, in the collective drift of their thought, in their political aspirations, and in that literature which is the best expression of their individuality." Anticipating Frederick Jackson Turner, the *Times* concluded, ". . . the great cause of the difference lies, after all, in the physical peculiarities of the two nations." And yet, it was not all a matter of America's having a continent's worth of land. The *Times* cited Disraeli's remark "that if America were to suffer some great political convulsion she could 'begin again.' " England, the prime minister asserted, could "not begin again."[11]

But what had Grant and America begun after the Civil War? They had, indeed, kept going, but motion to the sound of applause was all that the new beginning amounted to. Grant thought there was more. The world now paid tribute to America for having fought the war and survived. He wrote George Childs, "I love to see our country honored and respected . . . and I am proud to believe that it is by most all nations, and by some even loved." He knew something of what does and does not accompany power.[12]

Late in June there was a brief visit with Nellie, who was on the south coast of England with her baby. It was only two summers ago that Julia had

spoken so plaintively to Governor Ames about Nellie's having moved to England—and had tried so hard to persuade Ames, and herself, that Nellie was
happy there. Nellie was trying to persuade herself of the same thing. Algernon Sartoris had not turned out to be the splendid figure that the naive young
girl on shipboard had thought him. (Henry James, an admirer of his mother,
Adelaide Kemble, found him "blowsy.") He was not grand enough to be
brought to London for the great receptions for her parents. The matter was
not simply a question of rank—though there was not very much of that—but
rather of reputation. He was considered dissolute. All was not well in her
marriage, and yet Nellie could not leave her husband. Her own stubborn
pride said she must show her parents she had done the right thing, but in
June 1877 the Grants could fit into their public world only a few brief days of
awkward visits and drives and picnics with Nellie's English family.[13]

The Grants soon returned to London, and the royal family having circled
the Grant flame, and the nation having pronounced the general's light to be
true, the time came at last for England's queen to stir herself slightly for the
American cousin. The honor of all honors arrived—an invitation to Windsor.
This visit proved to be a terrifying triumph. The party took the five o'clock
train from Paddington Station on June 26, and arrived early. What was
worse, like any good American family, which would surely bring the kids
along, the Grants brought Jesse—"our pet," as Julia described him to the
queen—though he had not been invited. (There was a minor diplomatic *crise*,
as duchesses mediated, and an *ex post facto* invitation was begrudgingly
achieved.) The court circular said the queen greeted the Grants as they arrived. Actually, and perhaps not entirely by accident, the queen was out riding with her own youngest child when Jesse and his parents reached the
castle.[14]

Someone did answer the door, arrange a hasty tour of the paintings in the
vast halls, and show the Grants to their rooms. There they huddled, not yet
knowing how they were to be introduced to Victoria. Adam Badeau, fuming
because he and Jesse were to eat with the household, not at the queen's table,
fluttered officiously about, keeping Julia in a state of agitation. Jesse, nearly
twenty, but acting ten, took up Badeau's cry and said he would not eat with
"the servants" and wanted to go back to town. No doubt that was what everyone wanted. Victoria's first response to Jesse's threat was, "Well, let him
go," but two ladies and two lords in waiting negotiated this second crisis, and
Jesse was duly invited to Her Majesty's table, at which three of the queen's
children were also to sit. Julia was greatly relieved when, at seven-thirty, the
earl and countess of Derby, with whom she was now acquainted, joined
them to ease the introductions. Half an hour later, there was a decorous commotion outside as the queen arrived back at the castle; half an hour after that,
in mourning black but bright with diamonds, Victoria received the Americans in the vast corridor outside her private apartment. Edwards Pierrepont
introduced General Grant; Lord Derby escorted Julia past formidably gracious ladies in waiting; and two uncomfortable women—about the same age

*Meeting Queen Victoria at Windsor, 1877. From John Russell Young,* Around the World with General Grant.

and with equally excellent capacity for childbearing, but with not much else in common—shook hands. Victoria found Julia "civil & complimentary in her funny American way."[15]

The Grants were given not a state banquet but the greater compliment of a supper at the queen's private table, at which sixteen sat. Her Majesty was safely abutted by her son Prince Leopold and her son-in-law Prince Christian of Denmark. The general was flanked by one of Victoria's daughters and a duchess; farther down the table Jesse sat not next to Princess Beatrice, but between Lady Derby (who had been assigned to take on the scamp) and his mother. Although the band of the Grenadier Guards played outside in the quadrangle, the supper was not jolly, but luckily it did not last long. All the accounts make it clear that after the meal the queen spoke most graciously to each of her guests—not even Jesse was neglected, though afterward she pronounced him "a very ill-mannered young Yankee." As Victoria was taking her leave, at ten, she complained of her fatiguing duties, and Julia is said to have mustered strength and replied, "Yes, I can imagine them: I too have been the wife of a great ruler." The queen withdrew. The Grants never saw her again. Early the next morning the general received a telegram: "Your comrades in national encampment in Providence, Rhode Island, send heartiest greetings to their old comrades, and desire, through England's Queen, to thank England for Grant's reception." The folks back home had not forgotten him; comforted, the Grants were driven through Windsor Great Park along lovely fields, under beautiful oaks, and around the equestrian statue of George III, pointing off to nowhere; then they made their escape to London on the ten o'clock train.[16]

Julia and Ulysses were as healthy as horses: indeed, they had the stamina of Percherons. The routine of luncheon, followed by an afternoon reception, followed by dinner, followed by another reception, followed by the same the next day, seemed never to tire them. They thrived on it. Much has been said about how Grant, the simple fellow, manfully endured adulation because it was his duty to do so. This is nonsense. He and Julia had come to need this noise. They could not get enough of it. On June 9 Ulysses wrote contentedly to Elihu Washburne that he was engaged every day through the twenty-sixth. He was a private citizen, and the English people were genuinely fond of him; if he had said that he and Mrs. Grant, though grateful, would like to be allowed to be by themselves in a quiet hotel or at their daughter's house, their wish would have been honored. But he said no such thing. Grant's private world had been almost totally captured by the public one. In July he wrote his son Buck, "I have not written more frequently because the papers have kept you fully advised of our every movement." And so, with no exercise other than an occasional walk after one of the stupendous dinners, with food and wine in enormous quantity and richness, followed by brandy which the general countered with countless cigars, the Grants plunged onward from England to Europe.[17]

There, every royal and republican capital took its cue from London, and the restless pattern continued. In Belgium the Grants attended another, and easier, royal dinner; then they went on to Germany—to Cologne, Frankfurt, and Hamburg; and then on to Switzerland—to the Lake of Lucerne, Berne, and Geneva. Next they visited the Italian lakes, where they were joined by Ulysses' sister and her husband, the Reverend M. J. Cramer, whom Grant had named minister to Denmark. Together, they went to Copenhagen. From there, the Grants went to Antwerp, thence back to London, from which they left by train for Edinburgh, where much was made of Grant's Scottish ancestry.

It was during the Edinburgh visit that reporters began to wonder what Grant was up to. He almost seemed to be running for president—but of what, was not clear. Why did he not abandon the campaigning and go home? He acknowledged that the handshaking was "a great nuisance, and it should be abolished. . . . It demoralizes the entire nervous and muscular system." But shake thousands of hands he did. With his mind firmly on politics—as T. S. Eliot has said, one needs something to protest if one is to be a protestant—he declared he had no political ambitions and was staying away from home to keep out of President Hayes's way. This absence would, he might have added, also keep him disassociated with anything unpopular that his successor might do. And during the months in Britain he found out how enormously popular he still was, wherever he went.[18]

In September, Grant experienced that extraordinary triumph in Newcastle. In an amalgamation of the burning energies of working-class and of middle-class England, Englishmen came to cheer him. At first, the visit seemed routine. When his train pulled in from Edinburgh, the station was jammed with people, just as others had been all up and down the island. There was the obligatory excursion to a castle, a demonstration of seaside life-preserving techniques, and the inevitable luncheon given by the chamber of commerce—with speeches. But then, on September 22, came one of the most remarkable days in Ulysses Grant's life. People poured into Newcastle from all over the North Country by train, by wagon, and on foot to see this man who personified the bourgeois virtues they so greatly honored. In the procession in his honor they claimed the silent, powerful man from America as one of their own and as the champion of each of a myriad of causes:

Then came the Durham Miners' Association, carrying a blue silk banner, bearing a design which represented the change in the condition of pit-boys, by the introduction of short hours of labor; the Hepworth and Ravensworth colliers, carrying a blue silk banner, representing the union of capital and labor, a coal owner and workman in friendly conversation, with the legend, "Reason, Truth, and Friendship"; the Blaydon Colliery, with the inscription, "The Workman is the Pride and Stay of the Country"; the Pelaw Union Wardley Colliery; the Urpeth Colliery; the Kingston Union of Odd Fellows. Then came the Northumberland miners, sixteen different collieries, represented by their banners and designs, under marshals and captains, each colliery with its own band of music. Some of these banners had significant emblems. The Seaton Burn Collieries had the following lines on their banner:

> "No gloss or coloring will avail,
> But truth and justice here prevail:
> 'Tis education forms the youthful mind,
> Just as the twig is bent the tree's inclined."

Another showed a figure representing emancipation, and the tree of union in full bloom. Another banner, of blue silk with yellow border, contained the words, "We claim manhood suffrage."

After the miners came the Newcastle dock laborers and trimmers, carrying a new banner of blue silk with crimson border, bearing this motto:

> "A golden era bursts upon the world:
> The principle of right shall soon prevail:
> Meek truth and justice soon shall lift their heads,
> And wrong shall sink to everlasting night."

Then came the Hammermen's Society, the Plumbers, the House Furnishers, and the Tanners of Elswick. The latter carried a banner bearing these words: "Welcome back, General Grant, from Arms to Arts," "Let us have Peace," "Nothing like Leather." The Masons, the Independent Order of Mechanics, the Newcastle Brass Moulders and Finishers, the Tyne District Carpenters and Joiners, and the Mill Sawyers and Machinists followed. The Sawyers carried a banner with these words: "Welcome, General Grant, to Newcastle. Tyneside rejoices to see thee. Welcome, Hero of Freedom." The United Chainmakers' Association finished the procession. These workmen marched in good order like battalions of soldiers. There was no disturbance of the peace, and a few policemen only kept the line. It was a moving stream of red and blue banners, and badges, and insignia.

After the procession, Grant rode in a carriage into an open area jammed with thousands of expectant people; "the cheers . . . could be heard at St. Thomas's Church, nearly a mile distant," as he walked out onto the platform.[19]

Thomas Burt, the great North Country workingmen's Liberal leader, with a long career ahead of him and already a past master at getting out a crowd, had organized the meeting, but not even he could have made his people respond with the affection they displayed for Grant. Burt was delighted with the demonstration. In his address of welcome, he began, "General: in the name of the working classes of Northumberland and Durham, we welcome you to Tyneside . . . ," and he ended, "General! we beg your acceptance of this address as a testimony of the . . . admiration in which you are held among the working people. . . ." It was then that Grant replied with his splendid statement of solidarity with the workingmen; he talked of how wars, when they come, "fall upon the many, the producing class, who are the sufferers," the ones who must furnish the means for those engaged "in destroying and not in producing." It was a speech that Karl Marx could have made. Then, after a few polite words about English and American friendship, Grant drew to a close: "I do not know, Mr. Burt, that there is anything more for me to say, except that I would like to communicate to the people whom I see assembled before me here this day how greatly I feel the honor which they have conferred upon me."[20]

Only a few of the thousands of people watching Grant could hear him, but he had communicated with them all. Caught up in the mood of the day, a newspaper reporter present described Grant as

delivering, for him, an unusually long speech, and speaking with an evident feeling which shows that the crowd, as is nearly always the case with men who have handled large bodies of men, has touched his sympathies. The vast concourse, still rushing up from the turnpike, and which now musters at least eighty to a hundred thousand, estimate the unheard speech after their own thoughts. . . . Hats are waved with a self-sacrificing obliviousness to the affection subsisting between crown and brim which is beautiful to witness. And right in the center of the crowd, little shining rivulets glistening on his ebony cheeks, and his face glowing with intense excitement, the whole soul within him shining out through his sable skin like a red-hot furnace seen through a dark curtain, stands a negro, devouring Grant with a gaze of such fervid admiration and respect and gratitude that it flashes out the secret of the great liberator's popularity.[21]

Purple prose of a reporter with a good story, of course, but the writer was onto something. Grant had a gift given to few men; he could reach ordinary people without condescending to them. He was, they sensed, one of them. They saw themselves in him. They loved him for both his failures and his successes. They saw in them their own aspirations. And he, at Newcastle, looking down, saw all of this in their faces. Why couldn't he reach the same

*Newcastle upon Tyne, September 22, 1877. From John Russell Young,*
Around the World with General Grant.

kind of people—or rather, sustain their embrace, once reached—back home in Pittsburgh or Milwaukee or Lowell? Why did this gift of Grant's dissipate into Black Fridays, banquets, and all the other colossal wastes of this greatest of his talents?

In October, the Grants spent ten days with Nellie in Southampton and then went on to Paris. They had planned earlier to be there for the Fourth of July, but had been persuaded not to go, to avoid political embarrassment. While president, Grant had congratulated the Prussians on their victory in the war with France, and Victor Hugo's cry of outrage had been vigorous. It was not at all clear that the Grants would be as popular in Paris as they had been in London. Now, in October, the Grants were received at the Elysée Palace by Marshal MacMahon (whom John Russell Young, in the privacy of his diary, said looked like a "stupid Irishman") and were guests at superb dinners, but they were also left to their own devices as tourists. (They were not, however, totally outside notice; the inimitable Paris police had Grant under surveillance, and every time he walked out to buy cigars the details of his coming and going were recorded.) The Grants visited the studio of G. P. A. Healy, who had painted one of the finest portraits of Grant, and there met the republican hero Léon Gambetta, whom Grant regarded as one of the two greatest men he met on his trip, the other being Bismarck. Young's call on Georges Clemenceau, who had been in America as a reporter, did not produce any hope that France's greatest writer would receive the general. "Hugo is an old man," Young noted in his diary, "and great enough to do what he pleases."[22]

Young saw to it that Grant was photographed reading the paper in the *Herald*'s Paris office. Julia went to Worth's. Young himself went to the Jardin Mabille and pretended to be "disgusted" by the cancan. While the Grants were on their second trip to Paris a year later, police were told of a party of four Americans who entered the Bal Valentino by *"une porte secrète"* one evening and went upstairs to a private box from which to watch the spectacular dancers. The shadows were deep, but the informant was sure that one of the party, the one with the ordinary build, gray beard, and fresh complexion, was the *"ancien Président de la République des Etats-Unis d'Amérique."* Paris was perplexing to everyone in the Grant party. Reporter Young was, in general, not much taken with the French—"monkeys and barbers" a friend of his called them—and found the American colony in the city "regarded very much by Paris . . . as New York would regard a German colony in Hoboken. . . ."[23]

Young was not unhappy when, after a month, the party headed for the Mediterranean and boarded the *Vandalia*, a United States Navy ship. They cruised to Naples, where Young was appalled to find a wine named Lachrymae Christi ("horrible irreverence"). The general wanted to go to the top of Vesuvius, and an early start was planned, "but many high people in uniforms, commanding one thing or another, had to come on board" and the party was delayed. Once under way, the carriage moved slowly up the mountain and at the end of the road stopped. The passengers picnicked in a gloomy building that Young was sure had been a dungeon. They got a fire started and had their luncheon "in good homely American fashion, for we were as far from the amenities of civilization as though we were in Montana." By then it was cold and getting late, so they decided to turn back; once more, Ulysses Grant did not get quite to the top.[24]

At Pompeii they indulged in the romance of imagining the life of the city that had been stopped in time, were bored by a laboriously arranged "dig"—"nothing came of any startling import"—and carefully avoided the "house of unspeakable shame which the guide, with glistening eyes" pointed out to the general as the special object of interest to tourists—"but our General had no interest in scenes of shame and vice. . . ." Grant did comment on a flaw in the pavement of one of the roads, and someone made a joke about Boss Tweed and municipal contracts. The inscriptions on the walls of the rooms suggested to Young that "there was a great deal of human nature—of Massachusetts and Brooklyn human nature—in the Pompeiians. In those days people wrote on the walls, as home idiots do now, their names and inscriptions, verses from a poem. . . ." If the innocents abroad did not themselves turn toward home, their allusions always did.[25]

Julia and Ulysses and Jesse spent Christmas 1877 on the *Vandalia*, lying in the harbor at Palermo. On shore, Grant went for a walk in the rain while some of the officers went to the Episcopalian chapel. Julia, at the holiday table with naval officers, Young, Ulysses, and Jesse, was the only woman in the party (except for her maid)—and she was entirely happy about it. The *Vandalia* was Julia's idea of home, and the illustration that accompanies the story of their Christmas Day in Young's book provides perhaps the most honest and most attractive picture of Julia Grant that survives.

The Grants had now been traveling so long that newspapers at home, seeking to poke up a fire where there were no embers, conjectured that the former president was in a kind of exile, that he was spending vast amounts of money, and that the money was not his own. Young maintained that the money was Grant's own, its source being the income from the gifts the general had received at the end of the war—invested, presumably, by A. J. Drexel. The ship was, he allowed, paid for by the nation, but it would have been cruising the Mediterranean even if the Grants were not aboard. The Grants did not take pretentious and costly quarters in the fine hotels at which they stayed in the various cities, and their party was never large. On this part of the trip, their only companion was Young; their only servants were a maid and a valet-secretary-translator named Jacques Herzog, whom they called "the Marquis." He took on the role of buffoon, adopting an attitude of obsequiousness, and he was endlessly and flatteringly curious about his famous master.

Grant was not noticeably masterful. Tanned and relaxed, he went on deck

*"Entering Siout," Upper Egypt,*
*1878. From John Russell*
*Young,* Around the World
with General Grant.

in the morning, lit a cigar, and read a newspaper if there was one, or else Artemus Ward, Mark Twain's *Innocents Abroad*, or the *Nasby Papers*. He also talked a great deal. "His manner is clear and terse," wrote Young. "He narrates a story as clearly as he would demonstrate a problem in geometry" (he would have made a good mathematics teacher, after all). He spoke easily and unresentfully about the war and the men who had fought it with him. Young gained "the impression . . . that he has immense resources in reserve," and "has in eminent degree the 'two o'clock in the morning courage' which Napoleon said he alone possessed among his marshals and generals." The war—the time when these traits were needed—was relived there on shipboard as Grant told about it. Some of Grant's most revealing comments about his campaigns came out under the gentle shipboard prodding of the *Herald* reporter.[26]

The party steamed into Alexandria on January 5, 1878, moved on to Cairo, and then set off up the Nile. This ageless journey was the quintessence of the nineteenth-century Westerner's examination of his history. For the Grants, it was a marvelous jumble of quiet movement along riverbanks that had been inhabited for longer than anyone in the party could comprehend, and the noisy welcomes of the "King of America" by village people confused by the European-style receptions arranged for Grant by the Syrian traders who served as consuls for the United States. On several wonderful days, in the immense clothes of 1878 and with her head swathed in scarves against the desert dust, Julia Grant rode sidesaddle on a donkey past "fields parched, and brown, and cracked," and dry irrigation ditches, into remote villages. The drought was severe (it was a year of a "bad Nile") and "with the exception of a few clusters of the castor bean and some weary, drooping date palms, the earth gives forth no fruit. A gust of sand blows over the plain and adds to the somberness of the scene." There were ancient farm villages, and there was Luxor and Karnak and Thebes. The Grants missed scarcely anything that was in the guidebooks.[27]

Next on the trip was the Holy Land, where the list of places that had to be seen was even more numbing. Reaching for appropriately reverent rhetoric, Young wrote, "Of course to feel Jerusalem one must come with faith"—which rather left Ulysses and Julia unprepared. He acknowledged "heathen questionings" among the party, but claimed that both in Egypt and in the Holy Land—this was for him its only name—the past carried one out of any unbelief. The general trudged, and rode on donkeys, and took it all in. Mark Twain helped.[28]

Leaving the Holy Land, the party seemed to have been biblically blessed. It was as if a nineteenth-century Red Sea parted for the great American: "General Grant's arrival in Constantinople had been fairly well timed, as it occurred but a few days after the treaty of San Stefano." Even wars yielded for him. The Turks and the Russians stopped theirs, and he could visit Saint Sophia and shop in the bazaars. Next they sailed to Greece, but surprisingly, Ulysses did not indulge any urge to trace the route of his namesake; instead, they went straight to Piraeus and, in Athens, to the Acropolis—and still another royal reception. "The General is gradually getting over the idea that it is possible for him to travel as a private citizen," Young noted. After Greece, there was Rome and a call on the new pope, Leo XIII. For the sake of his solidly Protestant readers, Young hastily added that the "interview . . . of a most agreeable character . . . was not to be considered as partaking of anything of a religious character." But Julia's cross was blessed by the Holy Father. Then King Humbert fed them.[29]

In April they moved on to Florence, and in that lovely city visited the Uffizi and the Pitti Palace in pursuit of their "usual [and thorough] programme for sight-seeing." Young recorded the party's tribute to great European masters, but saved some applause for an American, the sculptor and teacher Hiram Powers, who had lived in Florence until his death in 1873, and for students from home: "As for Americans engaged in art studies, we hardly ever visited a gallery of any distinction without finding some one from the United States busy with brush and palette, diligently working away, and studying the grand old masters."[30]

After Florence, there was Venice, where Grant is said to have made his famous statement that it would be a fine city if they drained it. Edmund Wilson, less romantic than some about the odorous canals, has speculated that Grant was being a sanitarian. As astute historians have observed, Victorians cared greatly about their drains, Americans not less than Englishmen, and Wilson is correct in stating that more than one American has thought draining, cleansing, and refilling the canals would not be the worst of ideas.[31]

Nellie was spending the spring in Italy with her husband and his parents, and as a fellow tourist, joined her own father and mother for sight-seeing in Rome and Florence and went with them to Paris, where the Grants visited the Paris exposition. The nineteenth century measured everything, and one of the objects on display was a magnificent scale. Ulysses and Julia weighed themselves and kept the evidence. In Holland they visited their first zoo and a model farm where, Julia was pleased to notice, a McCormick reaper was in use. And later that year they went on to Denmark and Norway, to St. Petersburg (for a formal call on Czar Alexander II and "hours spent chatting and smoking" with Gorchakov), Moscow, Warsaw, and Vienna, and finally to Spain.[32]

In Madrid, the United States minister was the affable poet James Russell Lowell, whom Grant had met in 1870. The arrival of the general and his lady meant arduous duty for the Lowells in the intricately formal Spanish court, but the Grants were as the Bostonians remembered them—"simple-minded and natural people"—and Lowell admired the way the general confronted the receptions with "a dogged imperturbability." Grant balked only at one constant threat, the opera. After five minutes he claimed that the only noise he could distinguish from any other was the bugle call and asked Mrs. Lowell, "Haven't we had enough of this?" The Lowells felt sympathy both with Grant at the opera and for Julia at a splendid dinner when, with serene naiveté, she simply disregarded the fact that neither of her dinner partners spoke English—and spoke English. Her "confidence in the language of Shakespeare & Milton as something universally applicable that had triumphed over Babel was sublime."[33]

That was Madrid, but nothing was as memorable as Bismarck's Berlin. The Congress of Berlin was meeting and the powerful were balancing their world—Europe and the parts of Asia that abutted it. The United States was not participating—neither President Hayes nor Secretary of State Evarts was there—but an ex-president and ex-general named Ulysses Grant, a private citizen, was present. He was a tourist in a hotel, yet Prince Bismarck sent in his card, and General Grant set out to return the call. A few minutes before four, the time set for the appointment, he left his hotel, lit a cigar, walked the short distance to the gates of Radziwill Palace, entered the courtyard, and to the astonishment of the erect, lavishly uniformed guards, walked up to the door, tossed away the stump of his cigar, and for all the world looked as if he were going to knock and see if anyone was home, when alert servants opened the door to General Grant. There had been no fine carriage, let alone a splendid military escort, to accomplish the entrance. Grant had done it much better. The simple, good American had come on foot.

Bismarck, in uniform, greeted Grant and in slow careful English began a conversation in which the two men proved to be extraordinarily compatible. Bismarck commented on how young Grant was, and at fifty-six the general, only a bit thick in the waist despite the vast quantities of food that had confronted him on the trip, was indeed in fine shape. They chatted about a man they both admired, Philip Sheridan, who in Europe recently had observed with outspoken admiration the success of the Prussian army in the Franco-Prussian War. Grant pronounced Sheridan as great a general as had ever lived; Bismarck paid tribute to his guest's wonderfully quick eye.

This common ground established, they turned not to matters of state, but to questions of the philosophy of statehood. They were men of power who spoke of order and disorder. Grant approved of Bismarck's having convened the congress, although ostensibly Germany had no stake in the settlement of the recent war between Russia and Turkey that was the occasion for the meeting of the great powers. That meeting pointed toward order in Europe, and Grant asked how it was progressing. Wearily, Bismarck replied that it was hot in Berlin and he was glad that he and the other old men at the congress were about through, for he wanted to get to the country. Nevertheless, he was clearly pleased that Grant could appreciate what was being accomplished in the way of redefinition of power, redefinition which in no way diminished the strong position of Germany. He was pleased that a man like Grant noticed.

There was another kind of disorder on the minds of the two men. Emperor Wilhelm was in seclusion following an assassination attempt by a socialist with a Ph.D. ("So much for philosophy," said Queen Victoria.) Cautiously, and hopefully, Bismarck said he expected his master to recover. In praise of the emperor's character, Bismarck insisted that he was "so republican in all things that even the most extreme republican if he did his character justice would admire him." He could not understand the attempted murder: "Here is an old man—one of the kindest old gentlemen in the world—and yet they must try and shoot him!" Grant (according to Young's report, based on Grant's account to him of the conversation) "answered that the influence which aimed at the Emperor's life was an influence that would destroy all government, all order, all society, republics and empires." It would lead to the same chaos and disorder that he and Sherman had feared when Lincoln was assassinated. The American advocated the "severest punishment" for the unsuccessful assassin, saying that "although at home there is a strong sentiment against the death penalty, and it is a sentiment that one naturally respects, I am not sure but it should be made more severe rather than less severe." (Presumably he meant it should be more widely applied.)[34]

Bismarck leaped to agreement, recalling how he had "resigned the government of Alsace because I was required to commute sentences of capital nature." According to Young, he stated that " 'as the French say, . . . something was due to justice, and if crimes like these are rampant they must be severely punished.' 'All you can do with such people,' said the General quietly, 'is to kill them.' 'Precisely so,' answered the Prince."[35]

After this chilling exchange they passed on to an even more sanguinary topic, the American Civil War, and Grant, as he had not done elsewhere on his trip, agreed to review a detachment of troops, with Crown Prince Frederick the next day—not, however, before protesting that he was "more of a farmer than a soldier" and that although he had fought in two wars, he "never went into the army without regret and never retired without pleasure." This standard observation of Grant's was followed by Bismarck's equally familiar European observation: "You are so happily placed . . . in America that you need fear no wars." But then Bismarck turned to consider one of them, and this exchange followed:

> "What always seemed so sad to me about your last great war was that you were fighting your own people. That is always so terrible in wars, so very hard."
> "But it had to be done," said the General.
> "Yes," said the prince, "you had to save the Union just as we had to save Germany."
> "Not only save the Union, but destroy slavery," answered the General.
> "I suppose, however, the Union was the real sentiment, the dominant sentiment," said the prince.
> "In the beginning, yes," said the General; "but as soon as slavery fired upon the flag it was felt, we all felt, even those who did not object to slaves, that slavery must be destroyed. We felt that it was a stain to the Union that men should be bought and sold like cattle."

The conversation continued:

> "I suppose if you had had a large army at the beginning of the war it would have ended in a much shorter time."
> "We might have had no war at all," said the General; "but we cannot tell. Our war had many strange features—there were many things which seemed odd enough at the time, but which now seem Providential. If we had had a large regular army, as it was then constituted, it might have gone with the South. In fact, the Southern feeling in the army among high officers was so strong that when the war broke out the army dissolved. We had no army—then we had to organize one. A great commander like Sherman or Sheridan even then might have organized an army and put down the rebellion in six months or a year, or, at the farthest, two years. But that would have saved slavery, perhaps, and slavery meant the germs of new rebellion. There had to be an end of slavery. Then we were fighting an enemy with whom we could not make a peace. We had to destroy him. No convention, no treaty was possible—only destruction."
> "It was a long war," said the prince, "and a great work well done—and I suppose it means a long peace."
> "I believe so," said the General.[36]

The conversation, if Young had reconstructed it accurately—and neither Grant nor Bismarck denied that he had—was a remarkable one. Grant was never more articulate about the war that he had won. Too brief a war, Grant suggested, would not have ended slavery, would not have produced the order Grant had maintained as president—and, though this thought remained unspoken—would not have given Grant his personal chance to do what Bismarck called his "great work." Save for his unequivocal position in opposition to slavery, the Grant sitting in Bismarck's library was in vivid contrast to the one the workingmen had cheered at Newcastle. Bismarck accompanied his guest to the door, and they parted. Outside, Grant lit a cigar and walked back to the hotel.

Julia had liked the cheers for the general in the city on the Tyne, and had pronounced it a great day, but there was no day like the one in Berlin when Bismarck, with his daughter, came to call on Julia. Later there was a reception at the British legation with Disraeli, a dinner one evening with Crown Prince Frederick and Princess Victoria—Julia was getting expert at carrying homey bits of family news from court to court—and another dinner, given by Bismarck at Radziwill Palace. "Nothing," she pronounced, "could exceed the cordiality of our reception by this great and most distinguished man." The chancellor showed them the room where the Congress of Berlin was meeting, and in response to Julia's coquettish request to know what the meeting was all about, he is reported (one hopes inaccurately) to have said that Russia had swallowed too much turkey and they were trying to get her to relieve herself. Julia remembered that as they left, Bismarck's daughter "took my wrap from the attendant and wrapped it affectionately around my shoulders. When I gave my hand to Prince Bismarck to say farewell, he bent low over my hand and kissed it. I said, laughing, 'If that were known in America, Prince Bismarck, every German there would want to be kissing *my* hand.' The Prince, still holding my hand in his great palm, looked down admiringly upon it and said: 'I would not wonder at all at them.' I was, of course, enchanted with Prince Bismarck." This passage from Julia's *Memoirs* conveys the character of her prose and suggests too why the trip went on and on and on. The memory books were balanced in Berlin. Humiliations—being laughed at for her uncontrollable eye, being regarded as married to a failure, being cut down by Mary Lincoln—all were made up for at Prince Bismarck's palace. She was at last the princess of childhood fantasies at White Haven. Julia could not get too many princely attentions.[37]

Leaving the Continent, they went again to England, where Julia visited Nellie while Ulysses went on to a string of ceremonial visits in Ireland. No sensible American politician skips Ireland, but that duty done, the Grants concluded that they had had enough of the restless crisscrossing of Europe. Wanderlust truly had hold of them, and from Marseilles, a reconstituted party, with James Gordon Bennett of the *New York Herald* paying the bills, set out for Asia. Jesse, who had been practicing writing, had gone home to make a try at life in California. His brother Fred now joined his parents; so did amiable and querulous old Adolph Borie, along with his nephew, a doctor. Young, the lavender-bound Boswell, continued his duties as the *Herald's* reporter of the great adventure. Once again Julia and her maid were the only women on a long, long journey.

They rode a train down the length of the Suez Canal and, the only Americans aboard, sailed south on the Red Sea on a commercial ship. They took for their own an awning-covered space in the stern, atop a grating through which they could watch the sea churning. There, Julia "sits back in a sea chair, wearing a wide-brimmed Indian hat, swathed in a blue silk veil," for there was "the sun to fight." Grant too had "fallen into Indian ways enough to wear a helmet"; his was "girded with a white silk scarf." Borie read old copies of the *Philadelphia Ledger*, while Fred, with uncharacteristic verve, read *Vanity Fair* and was sure that Becky Sharp was modeled on a woman he knew in Washington. He was getting "a fine bronzed mahogany tint, and it is suggested that he will soon be as brown as Sitting Bull." The general sat, smoked, and listened as Young read to them from travel books on India. In anticipation, Colonel Fred "laid out a campaign of tiger shooting," while his father, hearing a different part of the Indian story, recalled the cholera epidemic with which he had coped twenty-five years ago in Panama.[38]

In India they first visited Bombay and emulated the life of their English hosts on Malabar Point: "The General strolled over a few minutes ago with some letters for the post . . . a scarlet servant running ahead to announce him, other scarlet servants in train." Each of the party hired a servant, for a rupee a day. In describing this part of the journey, Young babbled on about problems with the servants—they were lazy and worthless—in a manner calculated to amuse his readers. But to do him justice, this chatter abated as he moved into his second volume, with its important accounts of Grant's view of the Civil War and of politics, as well as voluptuous tales of Asian splendor. There was a gorgeous visit to the maharajah of Jeypore and then tours of Delhi and Lucknow. British imperialism was in full flower, and the entertainment was splendid. But no matter how sumptuous the arrangements, it all added up to one stuporous dinner after another on an endless trip, and one looks for evidence that Grant sometimes beat the boredom. He deserved to get drunk, and apparently he sometimes did. The most spectacular occasion came while the Grants were the guests of the viceroy, Lord Lytton. As the host recounted it:

> On this occasion "our distinguished guest" the double Ex-President of the "Great Western Republic", who got as drunk as a fiddle, showed that he could also be as profligate as a lord. He fumbled Mrs A., kissed the shrieking Miss B.—pinched the plump Mrs C. black and blue—and ran at Miss D. with intent to ravish her. Finally, after throwing all the . . . female guests into hysterics by generally behaving like a mûst elephant, the noble beast was captured by main force and carried (quatre pattes dans l'air) by six sailors . . . which relieved India of his distinguished presence. The marine officer . . . reports that, when deposited in the public saloon

cabin, where Mrs G. was awaiting him . . . this remarkable man satiated there and then his baffled lust on the unresisting body of his legitimate spouse, and copiously vomited during the operation. If you have seen Mrs Grant you will not think this incredible.

To be clinical, if Grant had consumed as much liquor as Lytton (and the vomiting) suggests, it is unlikely that he could have achieved an erection. And if he had, it is inconceivable that Julia would have allowed him to have sex in the presence of half the British navy. She was, after all, at least as strong as her husband and quite capable of pushing aside sexual advances made in front of others. With respect to her comeliness, or lack of it, the less said about Lytton's gallantry the better.[39]

John Russell Young's account of a state dinner, a cruise on a steamer, a "merry pleasant feast" under a banyan tree, and a vast reception for Indian nobility, mentions nothing of the incident, and Lytton, who knew how to carouse himself, surely took more than a little poetic license as he wrote his letter recounting the event. There is, however, no reason to assume the tale is all a lie. There is a certain locker-room admiration in its brisk telling, and this salacious gossip affords an untrustworthy but not uninteresting glimpse of a force in Grant more elemental, perhaps, than the one which so beguiled Henry Adams. That it took six fit British sailors to subdue a short middle-aged American is not the least of the compliments paid Ulysses Grant.[40]

In the markets of Benares, things had been tamer as the Grants went shopping. Ulysses, in a messily scrawled note to Young, who had not gone along, told of the experience in the blandest of tourist language: "Met many merchants who accosted us on the streets, and more beggars. Purchased from the former—at their prices—and contributed to the latter." Teasingly he suggested that they might be ruined by this economy: "But we will try to get through to Calcutta, even if we have to leave a hostage. I should fear to leave Mr. Borie because he would contract such obligations." Next, they moved on to Burma and to Singapore, and they visited the exquisite court of young King Chulalongkorn of Siam, whose father had opened his nation to the West and had had his son educated by the British teacher Anna Leonowens.[41]

In Cochin China, they found Saigon as decidedly French as India and Singapore had been British. Aware of being in a part of the world few Americans had seen, Grant wrote Washburne about the people of southeast Asia and the "Governments that have been forced upon them." He had arrived in Singapore thinking "English rule" was "purely selfish," with "pampered sons sent here to execute laws enacted at home, and nothing for the benefit of the governed"; now this opinion had altered. "I will not," he continued, "say that I was all wrong, but I do say that Englishmen are wise enough to know that the more prosperous they can make the subject the greater consumer he will become, and the greater will be the commerce and trade between the home government and the colony and greater the contentment of the governed." It was his view that if the English were to leave they would "scarcely get off the soil before the work of rapine and murder and wars between native chiefs would begin." From Saigon the Grants moved on to Hong Kong, and then to Canton, where their hosts were not Europeans or Americans but Chinese. In a procession half a mile long the Grant party was borne by sweating coolies in sweltering heat to the palace of Liu K'un-i, the governor general. Bamboo poles rested on red welts on their shoulders, as they carried the brilliantly painted boxes in which sat, awkwardly, the Americans in evening clothes. A "Chinese crowd, densely packed, silent, staring" lined the route. Young studied "the strange faces . . . so unlike the faces at home, with nothing of the varying expressions of home faces—smooth, tawny, with shaven head and dark, inquiring eyes." As Grant passed, some of the more elegant of the young men "looked upon the barbarian with a supercilious air, contempt in their expression, very much as our young men in New York would regard Sitting Bull or Red Cloud from a club window as the Indian chiefs went in procession along Fifth Avenue."[42]

From Canton, they went to Shanghai and then up the Yangtze, apparently oblivious to the drought north of the river that was affecting millions of people and causing death by starvation for tens of thousands. Later, in Tientsin, flags and bunting covered hundreds of junks as the Grants went ashore. The disagreeable noise of guns firing salutes was mingled with the strange and beautiful reverberations from gongs. General Li Hung Chang—"tall and gorgeous to behold," as the Grants' granddaughter found him years later when he planted a tree near Grant's grave in New York—greeted his guest with the simple statement: "You and I, General Grant, are the greatest men in the world." Li, perhaps the most powerful person in China, was regarded by the American party as "the Bismarck of the East," and he was indeed thinking of himself as a builder of national union when he said, in his welcoming speech, "General Grant and I have suppressed the two greatest rebellions known in history." He was referring to the bloody repression of the Tai Ping rebellion in the same years that Grant had put down the American rebels. Li was so impressed with Grant that he asked the general to carry a message to the Japanese government with respect to a territorial quarrel between China and Japan. This Grant agreed to do and, subsequently, negotiations between the two countries were opened.[43]

In Peking, Grant was urged by fellow Westerners to help hammer away at the exclusivity of the Chinese by requesting an interview with the seven-year-old emperor, Kuang Hsü, but he declined. He found calls on dignitaries who were children to be demeaning. Instead, he visited at length with the sophisticated head of the government, Prince Kung. After this conversation and similar talks in Japan, Grant, in long, intelligent letters, predicted the power China would attain in the twentieth century and compared China's prospects to the bright commercial future he saw for Japan.

In Japan, which Grant found "beautiful beyond description," the ceremonies were, if possible, even more opulent than anywhere else the Grants had been. They were taken into a forbidden world, the imperial palace, to meet Emperor Mutsuhito and Empress Haruko. The emperor was another of the nineteenth-century rulers who had put down a major rebellion. In September 1877 his army had suppressed an uprising by the Satsuma samurai; like his guest, he had greatly consolidated his nation's power. The general, in evening dress, escorted by the American minister, naval officers, and the heads of the Japanese government and members of the royal household, moved from chamber to chamber and "entered another room, at the farther end of which were standing the Emperor and the Empress. . . . Our party slowly advanced, the Japanese making a profound obeisance, bending the head almost to a right angle with the body. . . . The Emperor stood quite motionless, apparently unobservant or unconscious of the homage that was paid him." The emperor looked young and slim, and "but for the dark, glowing eye, which was bent full upon the General, you might have taken the imperial group for statues." The empress, "at his side, wore the Japanese costume, rich and plain. Her face was very white, and her form slender and almost childlike." Young found the "solemn etiquette that pervaded the audience chamber . . . peculiar," but reminded his readers that the Emperor was so sacred that even to be received at all "might be called a revolution." When the group was formed, "His Imperial Majesty . . . advanced and shook hands with General Grant. . . . This seems a trivial thing to write down, but such a thing was never before known in the history of Japanese majesty. . . .

*Hiroshige III*, General and Mrs. Grant with Japanese Emperor. *Julia is second and Ulysses fifth from left in main reviewing stand.* NATIONAL PORTRAIT GALLERY, SMITHSONIAN INSTITUTION, WASHINGTON, D.C.

The manner of the Emperor was constrained, almost awkward, the manner of a man doing a thing for the first time, and trying to do it as well as possible." Calmly, even cordially, Ulysses Grant had made another conquest and achieved another notable surrender.[44]

At last the restless roaming around the world was ending. The previous winter they had talked of getting back in June; in April, from Singapore, Grant had written Washburne, "It looks now as if we would reach San Francisco as early as August. I am both homesick and dread going home. I have no home but must establish one when I get back; I do not know where." But, finally, the return could not be avoided, and the *City of Tokyo* brought the commoner-king and his party home across the Pacific. In San Francisco they were greeted as royally as they had been in Copenhagen or Karnak or the "ancient city of Philadelphia," from which they had sailed twenty-six months earlier. They were welcomed to a "young city," which the mayor compared favorably to all the others the Grants had visited. If California lacked anything, it was surely not buoyancy. As they moved through the streets on one of their processions, they were startled by an explosion of sound and looked up to a balcony; there an Italian diva and, as the press had it, a chorus of five hundred sang an ode of welcome. The Grants kept right on with their royal progression, scarcely noticing that this was not still another foreign port.[45]

On November 1, 1879, they were taken out to see the natural wonders of Yosemite Valley, in the national park which had been created during Grant's presidency, and from there, after a quarter of a century, Grant revisited Oregon. General O. O. Howard was in command at Vancouver, and he

*Buck, Julia, and Ulysses Grant (standing, center), Virginia City, Nevada, 1879.*
LIBRARY OF CONGRESS

walked with the Grants past the house where, without Julia, Ulysses had lived. "After looking at the house for some moments, he turned to the right in the evening twilight—we could see quite a distance up the river—and said: 'Julia, that is the field where I planted my potatoes.' " Slowly he was beginning to get back into things American. From Oregon he traveled to Sacramento, the California capital, to speak to twenty thousand people (a good many of whom could vote), review a military procession, and watch a sham battle. Young wrote in his diary, "The General is as severe a traveler as he was in the East; fierce, hard, merciless to himself." Back in San Francisco at the Palace Hotel—a long way from the attic room in which Grant had spent his final defeated night in the city after resigning from the army—Senator William Sharon, rich in silver, gave him an entertainment as splendid as any he had received from an Eastern potentate. Two hundred and fifty gentlemen took home their menus as souvenirs of the dinner; theirs were engraved in silver, General Grant's was worked in gold. Later, in Virginia City, Nevada, the "center of our El Dorado," as Julia put it, the party was invited to inspect a deep mine. Ulysses lost a wager that Julia would decide against joining the men, and donning dusters and floppy hats and clutching lanterns, they were all lowered down a shaft. Up in the light once more, she reflected on what "cruel, hard work this mining is" and concluded that "it is pleasanter far to 'wear the gem than delve the mine.' "[46]

The Grants completed the circle on December 16, 1879, with their return to the place where it had all started, Philadelphia. "The procession took four hours passing a given point" on Chestnut Street, and was "decorated with exquisite taste." Grant's open carriage passed under one arch draped with flags and bunting that said, noncommittally, "Philadelphia's welcome to his her representative citizen" and then under another, above Eighth Street, described as "far outshining the former in beauty and massiveness. Upon this arch were five hundred ladies." Unfortunately, none of them could vote.[47]

# XXVII

# GRANT
# & WARD

I suppose there is no man in this Vanity Fair of ours so little
observant as not to think sometimes about the worldly affairs of
his acquaintances, or so extremely charitable as not to wonder how his
neighbour Jones, or his neighbour Smith, can make both ends meet
at the end of the year.

— *William Makepeace Thackeray*

THE STRATEGY for winning a third term was brilliant; the timing was
dismal. The trip around the world was the strategy; it was a two-and-a-half-
year campaign tour unlike that of any previous candidate for the presidency.
John Russell Young's rich accounts in the *New York Herald* of the Grants'
stunning receptions, copied in newspapers all across the country, were calculated to say to Americans that they should receive their hero with an equally
warm greeting and carry him once more to the republic's seat of highest
honor. Cleansed of the odor of corruption by the exhilarating air of travel,
Grant should once more be put in command of the nation's fortunes. His return to the presidency would seem as irresistible as it was desirable. The victor returned would dazzle with his simplicity and put out of sight all competitors who had spent the time he had been away doing humdrum business.

It might have worked; the trouble was that Grant returned too soon. As
nearly endless as the trip had been, he had wanted to go on to Australia to
spend some more months away from home, but no steamship service was
available from Tokyo. As William B. Hesseltine states in his account of the
try for a third term (the finest section of his biography), if Grant had "delayed his return for six months he might have received the Republican nom-

ination in 1880." Instead, the Grants came home nine months before the convention in June 1880, and before the delegates met, the strenuous attempts to keep the home-coming party going had become visible. Starting east from San Francisco, coming home to Galena, a swing through the East and, later, the South—entering all the regions of the country—the welcomes became labored.[1]

In Europe, he had put everyone off the scent. Back in the summer of 1878 Young had been deceived—almost. In his diary he wrote of Grant as "the most admirably poised man I ever knew. All this talk of the Presidency never disturbs him, he never alludes to it. On one occasion when some over-kind Americans were pressing him, he answered in an impatient way that he knew what the Presidency was, and had had all he wanted." Young thought the "bill to add his name to the retired list with any reasonable pay would put an end to the whole business—Still 'there are more things in Heaven and Earth etc.' " Of earthly matters Grant had written Washburne in October 1878 that "it is bliss to be out of the United States . . . at a time when every bad element in the country is carrying everything before them. It is to be hoped, and I think confidantly to be relied on, that all the isms will have run their course before /80." And after the November elections, which resulted in Democratic majorities in both Senate and House, he had written that paradoxically, he was pleased: "It seems to me to put the republican party right for /80. Providence seems to direct that something should be done just in time to save the party of progress and internal unity & equality." But in 1879 he jumped the gun on that critical moment. Now Grant's protests that "I am not a candidate for any office, nor would I hold one that required any manoeuvring or sacrifice to obtain" were contradicted by the intense conversations he held with party leaders at every stop on his American trip. These talks were read by all but the most guileless as studied attempts to lock up delegate votes. Grant's skill at appearing never to seek the success he so desperately sought failed him.[2]

He had anticipated that failure. He had known in Japan that he would have to come home to still another attempt to prove himself. In August he wrote Badeau, "At the end of twenty-six months I dread going back, and would not if there was a line of steamers between here and Australia. But I shall go to my quiet little home in Galena and remain there until the cold drives me away. Then I will probably go south—possibly to Havana & Mexico—to remain until April." The stay in Galena actually lasted only six weeks. Had he been willing to go straight there and settle down, that town might have worked for him in 1880 as it had in 1868. Instead, there were the trips all across the continent, and, finally, there was just one too many of the magnificent banquets.[3]

The occasion was a vast reunion dinner in Chicago, on November 13, 1879, of the Army of the Tennessee, but the man who brought it all down was not a member of the army, but a Confederate veteran—of a few days service—Samuel L. Clemens. The night before the dinner, Grant had been on the stage of Haverley's Theater, where, "through all the patriotic rant, the bombardments of praise and adoration, the unfurling of a shredded battle flag and the roar of a thousand men singing 'Marching through Georgia,' Grant sat slouching in his chair, his right leg crossed over his left, not moving a muscle, an iron man." Clemens was fascinated by Grant. He liked other celebrities, but there was more that was intriguing about this man, and a friendship began that eventually took Julia and Ulysses to Hartford and Clemens's whimsical and beautiful house. Here in Chicago, however, Clemens saw the sphinx as a challenge, and was delighted with the challenge. What Grant was thinking up there on that stage no one knew, but Adam Badeau guessed: ". . . though he had the faculty of receiving adulation with a greater appearance of equanimity than any other human being I have known, he was not indifferent to the recognition of the world or the praises of his friends. He who never betrayed on that imperturbable countenance that he relished the plaudits of the multitude has told me often with delicious frankness afterward of the compliments he had received. . . ."[4]

The next evening at the Palmer House, after oysters and beef and buffalo steaks, there was brandy and whiskey—and six hours of oratory. Justin Kaplan, in one of the finest passages of *Mr. Clemens and Mark Twain*, describes what happened:

> Somewhat after two in the morning, Clemens, the fifteenth and final speaker . . . responded to the toast he himself had devised for the occasion: "The babies—as they comfort us in our sorrows, let us not forget them in our festivities." By the end of his third sentence—"When the toast works down to the babies, we stand on common ground"—he knew he had mastered his audience, and, all the while watching Grant, who was no longer impassive now but laughing like the others, he marched through an elaborately double-edged tribute to the man of war, majestic on the battlefield but ridiculous in the nursery. . . . Relentlessly, with an apparent unawareness of the reverence in which these veterans held Grant, he described the future commander in chief of the American armies lying in his cradle and occupied with "trying to find some way of getting his big toe in his mouth." . . . This goal, Clemens went on, "the illustrious guest of this evening turned his entire attention to some fifty-six years ago." Here he remembered that the laughter ceased, there was only "a sort of shuddering silence," . . . and then he sprang his masterful and breathtaking surprise: "And if the child is but a prophecy of the man, there are mighty few who will doubt that he *succeeded*."

"Tornadoes of applause" rang in Clemens's ears. And laughter—the veterans loved the story and demonstrated that fact, once they had made sure that the one who had received the brunt of it was laughing too. He was. As

Clemens put it, ". . . my truths had wracked all the bones of his body apart."
Kaplan is brilliant in suggesting that "by making this iron man laugh and
cheer with all the others he had, in a sense, destroyed him." "I knew I could
lick him," Clemens boasted; "I shook him up like dynamite."[5]

Clemens's victory was, of course, psychological, but there was a hint of
political destruction as well, for his story carried overtones of another tale,
that of the emperor's new clothes. The image of Grant in the cradle, naked,
exposed the nakedness of the attempt to regain the presidency. There was no
substance to clothe his campaign. It had developed no idea or issue. There
was no reason at all why he should be elected president again. Grant had
become nothing but a symbol—a mighty one perhaps, but with no more currency than an old battle flag. If the symbol of the nation's power was reduced
to a ridiculous helpless baby, there was not much reason to vote for him. He
was simply trying to put his foot in his mouth, and this time he was going to
succeed.

He did not know that yet. From Chicago, the Grants went east. One observer there wrote Elihu Washburne, "If he really wants to be President he
came home too soon, and having come, he lingered in Philadelphia too long."
The pageant of receiving honors from the citizenry seemed to be degenerat-
ing into mere vote-seeking. The former president and his lady spent
Christmas 1879 in Washington, D.C.; they went to Florida in January, to
Cuba in February, and then to Mexico, to enjoy again the undiluted deference that now was theirs in foreign countries. And perhaps there could be
another triumphant return, another burst of enthusiasm, that would carry
him to victory in the Chicago convention in June. In Houston, after their
visit to Mexico, it seemed that it might happen. The welcome was warm and
there was a poignant reminder of what had been a genuine issue indeed. It
was the black people of Houston who gave Grant their blessing. An Illinois
farmer, T. L. Crowder, who had known Grant at Camp Yates, was there: "I
pushed my way through the dense mass of people who packed every available space for blocks around the Hotel, 'niggers' by the hundreds[,] thousands, acres of them big and little[,] old and young, good looking and [two
words obliterated] well dressed and ragged, . . . a perfect medley of 'd----d
niggers.' "[6]

Later, inside, Crowder climbed up on a sofa with a friend to watch the
reception for Grant. The black citizens crowded into the room and stood
"sandwiched between beautiful ladies in silks and satins." The general,
Crowder continued, "stood calm and serene while the 'coton fiel' patriarch
with white head, bowed frame, clad in a 'spiketailed' coat of the eighteenth
century (which his old 'Master' gave him) spread out his long bony hand and
pronounced his blessing upon him. Those touching scenes would doubtless
have brought tears to our eyes . . . but for the little streak of meanness that
my friend and I inherited which led us to enjoy the chagrin and discomfiture
of the 'Colonel Suh' or the beautiful southern lady who must simply stand

and wait until this royal devotion of the liberated man had spent its force."⁷

The devotion was real, and so were the problems these Republicans faced in Texas. What was truly spent was the force that had once been Ulysses Grant's to move these people into the stream of progress he had so confidently made flow for the citizens of the nation. As long as men like Crowder saw only the discomfort of defeated rebels in the earnest reach of the black people of the South toward Grant, there was no hope that this politician or any other would reach back to them, with a program addressed to their problems. Grant would have their votes if he won the nomination, but during his second administration he had allowed the power to be drained from an integrated Republican party in the South. There was little these black Southerners could do to give him a victory this time.

The Grants re-established themselves in Galena, in good proximity to Chicago, where the Republican convention was to be held. "It was now only a few weeks before the convention," Badeau wrote later, "and Grant manifested as much anxiety as I ever saw him display on his own account." Julia concurred: ". . . how can I describe that week of suspense for me!" Badeau recalled that Grant "calculated the chances, he counted the delegates, considered how every movement would affect the result, and was pleased or indignant at the conversion of enemies or the defection of friends. . . ." Julia was particularly conscious of the latter; she did not trust her old friend Roscoe Conkling, whom Grant counted on to rally support among the stalwarts. No doubt Julia wondered if Conkling wanted to rally them in such a way that they would swing from Grant to himself. Within Conkling's own New York delegation, William Henry Robertson led a group of dissidents who fought the unit rule that would have allowed Conkling to give all the votes of the largest bloc of delegates to a single candidate, and Julia was not persuaded that Conkling was demonstrating sufficient fervor to carry the day for her husband. Soon, in fact, she was sounding like the campaign manager he should have had if he truly wanted to win.⁸

Grant's position was strong, but so was that of his chief rival, handsome, compelling James G. Blaine of Maine. On the first ballot, with 370 votes needed for the nomination, Grant had 304 and Blaine 284. John Sherman of Ohio (nominated by James A. Garfield) had 93, George F. Edmunds of Vermont 34, and Elihu B. Washburne, trying now for the presidency on his own, had 30. (Grant never forgave his old sponsor for drawing these votes from him.) The convention deadlocked, and the balloting went on for days.

As the strain of the stalemate persisted, there was much jockeying to see who should yield. At a conference in Galena a letter of withdrawal was drafted; it was to be used by the most trusted of the leaders of the Grant forces, the Pennsylvania senator J. D. Cameron, with the concurrence of Senators Conkling and John A. Logan, only if Grant's position grew hopeless. The politicos wanted to be sure they were in a position to shape the ticket even if their man went down. Grant signed, but when Julia heard of it she let Don Cameron know that he was "*not* to use that letter. If General Grant were not nominated, then let it be so, but he must not withdraw his name—no, never." For Julia it was all or nothing.[9]

The Grants were due to pass through Chicago on Monday, on their way to Milwaukee for a Grand Army of the Republic reunion. "How I entreated him," wrote Julia, "to go on Sunday night and appear on the floor of the convention on Monday morning." She knew how he could ignite a crowd; she was desperate for him to try. It might well have worked, but he refused to go: "He said he would rather cut off his right hand. I said: 'Do you not desire success?' 'Well, yes, of course,' he said, 'since my name is up, I would rather be nominated, but I will do nothing to further that end.' 'Oh, Ulys,' I said, 'how unwise, what mistaken chivalry. For heaven's sake, go—and go tonight. I know they are all making cabals against you. Go, go tonight.' "

Ulysses wanted the nomination, but he would not beg for it. He looked at his wife and said, "Julia, I am amazed at you," and walked away. Frustrated and embittered, Julia went with her husband not to the convention in Chicago, but to the veterans' reunion in Milwaukee; in Galena the *Gazette* of June 8, 1880, stated, "Suspense Over," and noted, "No Deserters Among the Grant Forces." But "Ulysses S. Grant" was missing from its masthead, which now read, "For President of the United States, James A. Garfield of Ohio."[10]

Grant took it all with a certain equanimity. On June 27, in a long letter to Nellie, he said kiddingly, "If little Algie is such a bother to his pa send him over to us and we will bring him up '*and* away he will go.' " He would pass his ambitions along to his grandson; he was more interested than ever in the family, now that he had been deprived of something major to do with his life. The letter was full of news of Nellie's brothers. Fred was stationed on the Rio Grande, and Ida and their daughter, Julia, were there with him. Jesse, back from dabbling in mining ventures in Arizona, would soon leave for New York City, where he was "in business"—Grant did not specify just what the business was, probably because he was not sure. As for the third term: "I felt no disappointment at the result of the Chicago Convention. In fact I felt much relieved. The most unscrupulous means had been resorted to by the friends of other candidates—no doubt by their advice—and even then a good majority of the delegates chosen were for me. But means were resorted to to displace them and give a small majority for all other candidates combined." If he had control of his disappointment, he had not mastered his bitterness, and neither had Julia mastered hers: "I had been with him on his triumphant journey . . . and knew the people wanted him. They all told me so, but *I knew* of the disaffection of more than one of his trusted friends. The General would not believe me, but I saw it plainly." Neighbor Washburne was one of the friends whom Julia crossed off their list.[11]

In August the Grants went to Colorado to inspect mines in which he hoped, somehow, to invest. On August 5, stopping at Gunnison, he found a letter from James A. Garfield proposing that they campaign together. He replied immediately, saying that he would be happy to do so. He told Garfield that he would be at the state fair in Madison, Wisconsin, on September 6 and 7, and would also visit two fairs in Illinois, at Rockford and Sterling. Then after a stop at Galena, he would start east for New York and Boston on the twentieth. If Garfield could not fit country fairs into his schedule, "could you not join me some place in Ohio, or further west, and go east with me as far as might be convenient to you?" He added, "I feel a very deep interest in the success of the republican ticket, and have never failed to say a word in favor of the party, and its candidates, where I felt I could do any good." He was being precise in his choice of words; he spoke unequivocally of his support to the party—without mentioning Garfield's name. He closed with "my most hearty best wishes for your success in the coming campaign."[12]

When Grant reached Galena he found an invitation from Garfield to spend the night under his roof at Mentor on September 27. He wrote saying that he and Julia would be in Chicago that day meeting Jesse and his bride, Elizabeth Chapman, who were arriving from their wedding in San Francisco. The four Grants were then to go on to New York, where the young couple would sail for Europe on a wedding trip. Julia and Ulysses had not been at the wedding, and the brief trip to New York was to be their private celebration. But Ulysses could not stay out of the public world even for this occasion. Julia did not like James Garfield any better than she liked anyone else who had stolen the White House from her: "The General and I were invited to go to Mentor. The General went but I would not go." The two men actually met in Warren, Ohio, at a large Republican rally, and Grant was the center of a great deal of welcome attention. In October he campaigned in upstate New York, particularly in Utica, to demonstrate his reconciliation—or the absence of any need for one—with Roscoe Conkling.[13]

Grant, watching the campaign carefully for signs of success, urged a surprisingly dour Garfield to cheer up. "The news from Maine seems to have improved since your letter was written," he observed in his response to Garfield's invitation, and he added, "He laughs best who laughs last." When that laugh had been had, he wrote Garfield a long, rather formal, and even fulsome letter of congratulations. The victory over Winfield Scott Hancock, who had fought with Grant in Virginia, seemed so sound that he thought it would drive the "unfair and unholy" Democratic party into "dissolution." Grant was relieved that the Republicans no longer had to rely on Hayes's "small majority, and the necessity of having to carry three southern states to obtain that majority. The party knew . . . [it] could not get another electoral vote from the south." Instead, the party now had a solid Northern base: "I predict for you the least vexation any Executive has had since /60." Taking note that "papers not heretofore particularly friendly to me, are mentioning my name in connection with a Cabinet position, a foreign mission, or other reward for my supposed services in the campaign," Grant declared that there was "no position within the gift of the President that I would accept." He added, "I have great hopes of being able to do [service to the country] by advice in relation to our affairs in Mexico and the East, especially China & Japan. There is a great future for the commerce of this country by a proper understanding with these countries."[14]

Generously, Grant had taken the initiative, making it unnecessary for Garfield to offer him a post, but leaving the door ajar for a special assignment in the Far East (and not entirely slamming shut the possibility of becoming secretary of state). Garfield was grateful and gracious. In reply, he told his former commander and former president that his counsel would always be welcome. And Grant did give counsel, not always from the lofty perch of the elder statesman. Sympathizing with Garfield as the newspapers busied themselves "making and unmaking" his cabinet, he wrote candidly about the man both had fought at the convention, James G. Blaine: "I do not like the man, have no confidence in his friendship nor in his reliability." He nevertheless told the president-elect, "I do not think you ought to ignore him because I do not like him," and indeed he advised Garfield that he ought to choose no man for his cabinet who was obnoxious to Blaine. But, obsessed with the allotment of patronage by states, as he had been when he was president, he urged Garfield to choose for the cabinet not Blaine, but instead someone from New York. Presumably he was thinking of his ally Roscoe Conkling, and whatever his disclaimers, the point of the letter was to block Blaine, just as Blaine's candidacy had blocked his. Garfield did not take Grant's advice, nor did he accept a more cryptic (and bizarre) suggestion a week later that John Jacob Astor be made secretary of the treasury.[15]

Garfield was grateful to Grant, and gracious, but also wary of accepting him as a mentor. When Garfield named William Henry Robertson collector at the port of New York, Grant wrote a long letter about the appointment, addressed to "Gen J. A. Garfield, President of the U. States." He had never liked the sanctimonious Rutherford B. Hayes and had had high hopes for Garfield when a first "batch of appointment" of party regulars corrected "a grievous mistake of your immediate predecessor," who had pandered to "disgruntled Sections" in the party. But he objected when Garfield, without consulting the senators from New York (he meant Roscoe Conkling) appointed "to the most influential position within the gift of the President in this state" a man who "did not support the nominee at the Republican party in 1872." Robertson, Grant reminded Garfield, "gave indications at the convention which nominated you that if the nominee of 1872 were nominated in '80 he would not support the ticket." He continued, "I am disposed to ignore, if I cannot forget, all wrongs perpetrated against me personally, for the general good. But insults and wrongs against others for the crime of having supported me I do feel and will resent with all my power to resent." Warming in his anger, Grant went on to say, "I gave you a hearty and strong support in the presence of an assembled crowd the moment your nomination was sent

over the wires. I claim no credit for this for it was my duty," for, he acknowledged, he "had been honored as no other man had by the republican party
and by the nation. . . . But I do claim that I ought not be humiliated by
seeing my personal friends punished for no other offense than their friendship."[16]

Grant was so eager to reach straight to Garfield and to be felt on this matter that he sent the letter by hand, with Senator John Percival Jones of
Nevada as courier, "to insure its reaching your hands without going through
the hands of a secretary." But the president sent a long, judicious and firm
reply (not written in his own hand, as Grant's letter had been) in which he
rejected Grant's position. He had "selected one of your warm supporters
[Robert Todd Lincoln] for a very important cabinet position"; he had named
ten Grant men to posts in New York State; and, he claimed, he had not
known when he selected Robertson that he was obnoxious to Conkling. But
if he had known, he still would have named him: "I feel bound as you did
when President to see to it that local quarrels for leadership shall not exclude
from recognition men who represent any valuable element in the Republican
party." He thus rejected Grant's view that disgruntled elements should not
be included in his administration, and, preaching a bit in a way that irritated
Grant, he added, "While I am incapable of discriminating against any Republican because he supported you, I am sure you will agree I ought not to
permit anyone to be proscribed because he did not support you."[17]

Grant did not entirely agree, and he had to learn this very hard way that an
ex-president, even one named Ulysses S. Grant, could not direct the White
House on appointments, or on any other matter. Indeed, he had already
turned to other business; Grant's letter had been sent from the "City of Mexico." When he had accepted the fact that the third term was not to be, he had
still felt a need to be president of something. As it had for so many of his
fellow veteran generals, this something turned out to be a railroad, and
despite his earlier dismay about a United States invasion of Mexico, it was a
Mexican railroad. Through his friendship with Matías Romero, whom he
had first met at City Point in 1865, when Romero was Mexico's minister to
the United States, he became president of the Mexican Southern Railroad,
with a New York office at 2 Wall Street, at the corner of Broadway.[18]

In a fine essay on Grant as one of a series of American promoters in late-
nineteenth-century Mexico, David M. Pletcher has traced the course of
Grant's interest in the nation's neighbor to the south. The young lieutenant
had been sensitive to the oppressive poverty cruelly enforced by rich landowners, when, as part of the American invading army, he had been in Mexico in the 1840's. He was a partisan of the reformers who sought to oust Maximilian and, as our Civil War ended, even contemplated leading an army into
Mexico in support of Juárez. Pletcher, looking at Grant's urge to annex Santo
Domingo, his championship of an American Isthmian canal, and his encouragement of trade with the Far East, sees Grant as "an expansionist" who was

"a little ahead of his age." He does not, however, accuse the general of having had annexationist urges toward Mexico during his presidency, and he claims that Grant scrupulously insisted, to both American and Mexican audiences, that his new railroad was planned not as a prelude to a land grab, but rather was intended to foster the free trade he had advocated all around the world on his tour. [19]

Grant's love affair with Mexico stretched back to his Monterrey days, but Whitelaw Reid of the *New York Tribune* knew that the real reason for his interest in the Mexican Southern Railroad was that he was "exceedingly eager to make money." This unfriendly critic accurately predicted that the "dazed" general was "sure to be used in these [Mexican] schemes until he is only a squeezed orange." But Grant's partner in the undertaking, Matías Romero, remained a close friend for the rest of Grant's life. When Julia and Ulysses had visited Mexico early in 1880, as part of the buildup of Grant as a world leader, the people had saluted their one-time foe with the same glorious tumult that had become the routine of the Grant travels. There were great banquets and musical tributes, and Grant took it all in his usual stride, all save the bullfight. This was too reminiscent of the tannery for him to stomach, and he left the stadium before the slaughter was completed. At the other, happier, events given in the Grants' honor, Romero was one of the chief celebrants, and when his friend failed to get the nomination for the American presidency in 1880, he saw a fine opportunity to obtain the services of the ideal promoter for his dream of a railroad in southern Mexico. The idea was to open the southern state of Oaxaca to commerce with a railroad running from Mexico City and then connect the line to United States railroads by means of a branch running north across the Rio Grande. [20]

Carrying a concession from the governor of Oaxaca to build the railroad, Romero came to New York in the fall of 1880 and on November 11 gave a dinner at Delmonico's that would have satisfied the most demanding enthusiast for robber-baronry. Collis P. Huntington was there, Jay Gould was there, and the guest of honor was Ulysses S. Grant. Over excellent food and wine the gentlemen disingenuously agreed to act in consort in the further development of railroads in Mexico, in general, and in support of the new Mexican Southern Railroad, in particular. They planned to meet again in January, but never did; the dinner, however, provided enough impetus to launch the enterprise. On March 23, 1881, after the New York State legislature had responded to a request from Gould and Grant for a special law enabling that state to sanction corporate enterprise slightly outside its jurisdiction, the Mexican Southern Railroad was incorporated. Ulysses S. Grant was president, Grenville M. Dodge (a Gould ally), vice-president, and Russell Sage, treasurer. Three days later, Grant and Romero left for Mexico City. There Grant found that hopeful businessmen were somewhat less celebrated than visiting Caesars, but he put some Mexican critics at ease with a speech assuring potential investors that he sought commerce and not annexa-

tion. Nonetheless, it took two months for Grant and Romero to overcome
anxieties in the Mexican government and gain from it the concession they
sought. That goal achieved, Grant came home, and he and the family went to
Long Branch for the summer.[21]

For Grant, the most immediate result of not being re-elected president of
the United States was that he did not go back on the payroll. Therefore, the
former president was assiduously trying to effect a major improvement in his
finances. The investments that had been made with the subscription funds
given him produced an income of only six thousand dollars a year. Julia described their position by saying, "General Grant was poor"; she did not say,
"We were poor." When the Grants came east in the fall, after a short stay in
Galena, they moved into the Fifth Avenue Hotel, but even with the "very
liberal terms" established by the hotel, they were hard pressed. They
counted on the Mexican Southern Railroad, and once again, on George W.
Childs. The Philadelphian had been a leader in buying the Philadelphia
house and had contributed to the Washington house; now he and A. J.
Drexel successfully raised still another fund for Grant, with which he bought
an unpretentious but excellent house at 3 East Sixty-sixth Street. This was
the perfect Upper East Side address for a gentleman of affairs.[22]

From his Wall Street office, Grant continued to champion the cause of international free trade. In addition to his Mexican Southern Railroad post, he
was president of a company promoting construction of a canal across the
Isthmus in Central America, and later, in October 1882, he persuaded President Justo Rufino Barrios of Guatemala to allow a railroad extension running
250 miles into his country. The avenues of trade were to be extensive indeed.[23]

In 1882, while Grant was promoting his railroad, he was appointed by
President Chester A. Arthur to negotiate a reciprocal-trade agreement with
Mexico. He was joined in the negotiations by an old friend whom he had met
on his tour of the South in 1865. William H. Trescot of South Carolina had
led the negotiations which resulted in the dispossession of the freedmen from
the Sea Islands after the war, and he had lost none of his diplomatic skills.
The Mexican members of the commission charged with writing the treaty
were Estanislao Canedo and, once again, Matías Romero. The agreement,
known as the Grant-Romero Treaty, was concluded by the commissioners
on January 20, 1883. It established a list of products and manufactured goods
that could be imported into the respective countries free of tariff. To Grant's
chagrin, his prestige and long-term commitment to free trade did not sweep
away protectionist opposition. He was roundly criticized for having negotiated a treaty for his own personal gain, and after his death, the treaty was
rejected by the United States Senate.[24]

Things went no better in Grant's private undertakings. The initial capital
of the Mexican Southern Railroad carried the office expenses and paid
Grant's salary, but he saw none of that vast money that other railroad presi-

dents enjoyed. He never would. There was a great deal of negotiating for concessions, some surveying, and very little laying of track. There were no profits. Until the needed study of Jay Gould's mind and finances is made, we cannot know what game he was playing, but it is likely that he never intended to do his part in the arrangements and develop the northern branch of the road. Since profits depended on trade with the United States, this long connecting link was critical to Grant and Romero's hopes for the southern branch of the line, for which they were responsible in Oaxaca. What was more, two competing lines from Mexico City to the Rio Grande would very likely have outstripped the Mexican Southern Railroad even if Grant's other business misfortunes had not completed its descent into bankruptcy in 1884 and caused the revocation of the Mexican government's concession. Later, a narrow-gauge railroad was built from Mexico City to Oaxaca along the Mexican Southern route, and once subsidized and in rich British hands, this railroad paid dividends from 1897 to 1914. Nevertheless Pletcher concludes, "With no support other than that of the fickle opportunist Gould, it is highly doubtful that Grant could have done even this well." By 1883, Ulysses Grant was on his way to failure as a railroader. But he still lived in New York; he was accustomed to an office on Wall Street; and so he set out on yet another venture in his attempt to bring a fortune to the family. This time he would make his try in partnership with his son Ulysses S. Grant, Jr.[25]

Buck Grant was a rotund, cheerful young man with a fresh face and his father's coloring. He had received much the best education of anyone in the family, having attended Exeter, Harvard, and Columbia Law School, and on November 1, 1880, he married Fannie Josephine Chaffee. The bride's father, like the groom's, had clerked in a store, and Jerome B. Chaffee had also done some schoolteaching—one trade Grant had never tried—in Adrian, Michigan, on his way west from Lockport, New York. He had next tried Missouri, then Kansas, and finally Colorado, where he made a great deal of money in mining, land speculation, and banking. President of the First National Bank of Denver from 1865 to 1880, Chaffee was territorial delegate to Congress when Colorado was admitted to the Union, and became one of that state's senators. The marriage of Josephine and Buck was considered a fine one; there was no more comfortably placed young man in America in 1880 than Ulysses S. Grant, Jr.

Buck went into business. In 1881, with a hundred thousand dollars obtained from his father-in-law, he entered into partnership with Ferdinand Ward in a new Wall Street brokerage firm, Grant & Ward. Young and handsome, Ward was regarded as one of the rising stars on Wall Street. He was the son of a Baptist minister in Geneseo, New York; he had come to New York in 1875, taken a job as a clerk in the produce exchange, married Henriette Green, the daughter of the cashier (chief operating officer) of the Marine Bank, and, for a modest sum, bought a seat on the produce exchange. He also traded in securities in elevated railways, thus participating in the ur-

banization-suburbanization speculation which was the unglamorous source
of several great fortunes in the late nineteenth century. He was a man of great
expectations, and his financial marriage to Ulysses S. Grant, Jr., in 1881
seemed to promise vast prosperity.[26]

By 1883 the books showed that young Grant's initial investment had increased fourfold; he was on his way to being a millionaire. His father's Mex-
ican-railroad enterprise had not been equally successful, and Buck saw Grant
& Ward as the opportunity to be rich—to be secure—that his father had
looked for all his life. Ex-presidents are hard to place. As silent partners they
lend prestige and draw business, but one can never be certain they will
remain silent. Any number of the men who had subscribed to the fund for
the Sixty-sixth Street house could have taken Grant into their firms, but
none of them did. Instead, Grant was left in the embarrassing position of
being an object of charity. If he were to become rich, like them, he still, at
sixty, had to make his own start. The Mexican railroad, like the mines he had
seen in the West and had considered as his way to make money, had not
made him a rich man. Now his goodhearted, genial son was offering him his
chance. He took it, and invested a hundred thousand dollars in Grant &
Ward. (The name now took on a useful ambiguity; people assumed the general had been the founder.)[27]

Encouraged by the apparent strength of the firm, investors bought securities through Grant & Ward and, according to established Wall Street procedure, left them with the firm as collateral on loans with which they bought
still more securities. Grant & Ward, then, in a perfectly legal and normal
procedure, borrowed against the securities in order to invest for the firm's
own account. What was not legal was the fact that Ferdinand Ward was
rehypothecating the securities improperly by pledging the same stocks to
support more than one bank loan. He was doing so with the collusion of the
fourth partner in the firm, James D. Fish, who was also president of the
Marine Bank. And it was the Marine Bank that was making the loans, against
inadequate security.

If all of Grant & Ward's investments had been successful, if all the loans
had been repaid, no one would have needed to know that the security had
been inadequate. Indeed, *ex post facto*, it would not have been. The whole
point of capitalistic enterprise is to gain people's confidence and persuade
them to invest in ventures that will profit the entrepreneurs—the organizers
of the enterprise—and, concomitantly, society. If investors can be found to
build an elevated railway to the outskirts of a city, and more investors can be
found to build houses at the end of the line, and banks, appraising both investments, are willing to give mortgages on the houses, and salesmen can persuade people to have the confidence to buy a dream house on a remote sandy
stretch of, say, New York City's borough of Queens, then, all along the line,
the venture will have been a success. With confidence as the key commodity
for sale on Wall Street, it is not surprising that the men of that street were so

testy about talk of "confidence men" and so wary lest a gentleman break a rule of the club and shake the public's understandably tentative confidence in the investment business. The crises of 1869 and 1873 were, after all, not ancient history in 1884.

Many conservative businessmen suspected that the credit of Grant & Ward was unethically inflated. In a hypothecation agreement, the securities pledged are understood to support no other loan. Those pledged by Grant & Ward did support more than one loan, and Ferdinand Ward and James Fish knew it. But did the other partners, Ulysses S. Grant and Ulysses S. Grant, Jr., know it? With money rolling in from the flourishing young firm, was it possible that the two Grants did not guess that something dubious was under way? Not even Buck's fondest relatives ever claimed that he was a man of piercing intellect, but he could read, he was a lawyer, and the language of a hypothecation agreement, if turgid, is unequivocal. Of course it is possible that neither Buck nor his father looked at the transactions to which their partners, Ward and Fish, could, in perfectly standard fashion, sign the firm's name. But if Buck's father was not alert, what about his father-in-law, who was, after all, himself the president of a bank? And what about all of Grant's friends? Weren't people like Childs and Drexel and Hamilton Fish suspicious, and, if so, why didn't they say something to Ulysses and Julia?

It is not an easy problem. How does one tell a former president of the United States that his partner is doing something crooked, which is tantamount to saying that he himself is crooked? And if it would be hard indeed to say this to the general about himself, it would be harder still to say it to a doting father about his son. Horace Porter told of going to Sixty-sixth Street to try to do just that, only to find Ward present and exuding such confident charm that his courage faltered and he said nothing.[28]

On Sunday, May 4, 1884, Ward's own confidence faltered. He lived in Brooklyn Heights, but had spent this Sabbath morning at the office. He knew that the next morning he would be unable to cover the day loans he had taken at the end of the week; his only hope was one last display of confidence. He went uptown and told the general probably not all, but enough to persuade him that matters were at a crisis. Once more, Grant had the props pulled out from what had seemed to be as secure a fortress as those his friends inhabited. Once more, he was forced to be a funny little boy unable to trade like a man for a horse. William Henry Vanderbilt, almost the same age as Grant, had never fought any wars, and had never been president of the United States, but now Grant, in danger of disgrace, turned to this great monied patriarch as he had turned, in destitution, to his father in Covington a quarter of a century earlier. At the behest of a brassy young man, and to save his son, General Grant set out to rescue Grant & Ward. That Sunday afternoon, hat in hand, he went to Vanderbilt's house, and struggled lamely (he had fallen at Christmastime) up his fine steps to ask for a loan.[29]

The reasoning was that if Vanderbilt would show his confidence by giving

Ulysses Grant $150,000 on his name alone, then downtown, the next morning, the banks would agree to carry Grant & Ward until payment could be made. We know that Vanderbilt said yes to Grant, who left with a note for the $150,000—payable to him, not to Grant & Ward. But we do not know what Vanderbilt subsequently said to his own bankers. C. W. Moulton wrote his uncle William T. Sherman, who, as usual, was posted on everything going on in America, "The opinion on the Street is very unfriendly not only to the young men, but to the General. . . . The practice of *re-hypothecation* is looked upon here as an offense against the law and the ethics of mercantile dealing. No man or firm who have engaged in it have ever survived the condemnation that is placed upon it. There is much sympathy for the General, but it is mingled with much fault finding." Moulton's reading proved accurate. The good bankers elected not to save either Grant & Ward or the Marine Bank. Both failed, pulling several other brokerage houses and banks (and the Mexican Southern Railroad) down with them, and Ward fled the country. Fish was tried in 1885 and sent to jail, at a time when Grant was too ill to do more than submit a deposition.[30]

Not everyone was prepared to excuse the Grants, *fils et père*, as dolt and dupe. Hugh McCulloch, secretary of the treasury for Presidents Lincoln, Johnson, and Arthur, and a conservative banker, had admired Grant only for his ability as a warrior. When he looked back on Grant in 1889 he was critical indeed: "His name was known and respected throughout the world, but he was not content." Deprived of a third term as president, Grant was shunted into private life, and "his ambition now was to be rich. . . . For rich men he had great respect; for poor men, no matter how distinguished they might be by intellectual attainments, he had but little regard. He had felt the crushing influence of poverty for many years," and despite good salaries as general and president and "many valuable presents, he was, in comparison with most of his personal friends, poor. The love of money grew with the free use of it by himself, and by his observation of the influence which it commanded." And so he went "into a business for which he had no fitness, and with a man of no repute."[31]

McCulloch was not among those who believed that Grant should not be held responsible for his financial fate; neither were some newspaper writers. The *New York World* headed its story "Is Grant Guilty?" and the implication was that he was. Why weren't his involvements pursued as vigorously as were those of the hapless James Fish? Once again, Grant's eminence rescued him. He maintained a dignified silence, and the nation closed ranks around the belief that he was one who had been wronged, not a wrongdoer. One intelligent modern observer looks to psychology for a sensible explanation: ". . . the matter of General Grant was one of cognitive dissonance— Americans *wanted* to see Grant as a truly great hero, so they blocked out any conflicting information."[32]

Some of that dissonance could be seen in Grant's own mental processes.

As Moulton told Sherman, he seemed "to be a perfect child in financial matters." He had learned precisely nothing from Black Friday except that Jay Gould was still a rich man. He lacked discernment; he had an exceedingly limited moral sense. Or perhaps he was too simple to figure out who on Wall Street was ethical and who was not. There was something that Karl Marx would have recognized in Grant's upside-down sense of the capitalistic world he only half understood: To him, the man who won—who got rich and stayed rich—was the one who was moral and could make the judgments. All that mattered was success.[33]

Grant was destitute and on display as an object of national pity. Friends came to the Sixty-sixth Street house to offer their condolences as if someone in the family had died. When Matías Romero picked up his hat to leave, he quietly put a check for a thousand dollars in its place. (Julia claimed they considered it a loan and paid it back within a month.) Grant had been party to a financial debacle that mocked everything he had claimed to have saved the Union for. He had lowered himself—if not to the depth he had reached at Fort Humboldt, then to as great a degree of embarrassment as any nineteenth-century president had suffered. Not even Andrew Johnson, impeached, had been as humiliated. None had gone broke. But this very degree of humiliation laid the base for his last and greatest victory. He could treat his countrymen to another performance of heroism. He could publicly pull himself and his family up out of poverty. In May 1884, however, how to do so was not entirely clear.[34]

Nine years earlier, General Sherman had published his *Memoirs*. They were infused with the fire of the man and, in headlong prose, told well the story of his campaigns. Other generals had published their accounts of the war in magazine articles and books; reminiscences of the Civil War were a well-established genre of American writing. Before the failure of Grant & Ward, Robert U. Johnson, associate editor of *Century Magazine*, had tried to interest Grant in taking his turn at telling about the war. "It is all in Badeau," Grant had replied, referring to Adam Badeau's three-volume *Military History of Ulysses S. Grant*. Now, sensing that Grant might be more interested, Johnson approached Badeau, who was doing an article for *Century* on Grant, to see if he could persuade the general to write for the magazine. Whether persuaded by Badeau or by Johnson's own persistent calls on him, Grant did agree to try his hand at accounts of his battles.[35]

Grant had never before thought of himself as a writer, but he set to the task with the same lack of fuss that had characterized him twenty-one years earlier when he swiftly, clearly wrote his orders, revealing his remarkable grasp of realities, that first night in Chattanooga. The first draft of "Shiloh" reached the *Century* office on July 1; it was essentially a copy of Grant's official report of the battle. Johnson encouraged him to rewrite the piece to reflect his personal sense of what had gone on. Grant did so, and the article appeared in the February 1885 issue. During July he wrote "Vicksburg," working four hours a day, seven days a week. This diligence, and the fact that the prose was of excellent quality, made Johnson and his associates at *Century* become ambitious initially for a fuller series of articles on the war (which eventually resulted in the collection of memoirs by various veterans published as *Battles and Leaders of the Civil War*) and later for a single work by Grant on the whole war—on his whole life. They paid Grant $500 for each article, and as they began negotiating for the book they offered him the standard 10 percent royalty, which on the projected sales of 200,000 to 300,000 would bring $20,000–$30,000, about what Sherman told Grant he had made on his book. This would not suffice to pay back Vanderbilt or restore Grant's financial health and that of his sister Virginia Corbin, who had lost heavily in Grant & Ward, but it would give him and Julia a desperately needed income. And so, that summer at Long Branch he wrote his two articles, and considered writing a book.[36]

# XXVIII

## TO WRITE A BOOK:
## TO BE A MAN

He who has never failed somewhere, that man cannot be great. Failure
is the test of greatness.

— *Herman Melville*

Grant's whole character was a mystery even to himself—a combination
of strength and weakness not paralleled by any of whom I have read in
Ancient or Modern History. . . .

— *William Tecumseh Sherman*

IN LONG BRANCH in the summer of 1884, Ulysses Grant, at sixty-
two years and 186 pounds, was thirty pounds overweight; his lameness,
which stubbornly would not go away, was a typical ailment of the late-nine-
teenth-century gentleman who no longer got the exercise he needed. One day
at lunch, Grant complained of great pain in his throat as he ate a peach. It
seemed a minor matter at the time, but it was not just an annoyance; it was a
sign of cancer. For the next year, the nation watched its greatest hero die.

Still relatively young, Grant was to hear the sound of a crowd assembled
in his honor only once more. At the close of each summer, Ocean Grove, the
Methodist camp-meeting colony south of Long Branch, held a week of re-
vival services. One of Grant's rich Philadelphia friends, George H. Stuart,
an inveterate evangelical Christian who had sponsored every good cause from
freedom for slaves to fresh-air vacations for poor city children, invited the
general to a reunion in Ocean Grove of the veterans of the Civil War's Christian Commission. The commission, kin to the Young Men's Christian Association, had provided spiritual and morale-raising services during the war.
Stuart was proud indeed when the general agreed to attend still another ceremonial remembrance of wartime days.

Ten thousand people crowded down rush-matted sloping aisles to find folding chairs in the great tentlike structure that was the Ocean Grove auditorium, where the seaside revivals were held. Grant, still lame, came onto the platform leaning on Stuart's arm and made his way slowly to his chair. As he did so the "vast congregation" rose to its feet and "cheered with a vigor and a unanimity very uncommon in a religious assemblage." After a prayer and hymn, a Methodist preacher who had been a private during the war saluted him: "I was one of a million of your soldiers . . . ," and Stuart helped Grant to his feet. Almost inaudibly he said his thanks. The auditorium at Ocean Grove is a strangely affecting place; George W. Childs, who was present that summer evening, wrote that Grant "after saying a few words . . . utterly broke down, and the tears trickled on his cheeks. That was the last time he appeared in public."[1]

Julia's health, not his own, was on the general's mind early in September when he wrote a charming letter to a grandchild, Nellie's daughter, "My Dear Little Pet Vivian," full of news about the comings and goings of her cousins at the seaside cottage. He reported that "Grand-ma has been sick in bed for two days. But the Doctor says that it will not last long. She gets dizzy when she sits up, but feels very well when she is laying down. The Doctor says she does not take enough exercise. I think you will say so too." As for "Grand-pa," he was "writing his campaigns which he intends to publish in a book. It will," he predicted, "probably be a year yet before it will be ready." In his thinking, it was already a book.[2]

Julia's illness did indeed prove minor, but Grant's friends were greatly concerned about his throat, and George Childs arranged for him to see a Philadelphia physician, the first of many specialists to examine and prescribe for Grant as the disease progressed. This physician referred Grant to a New York doctor, but he was in Europe. When the Grants moved back to New York City in the fall and Grant finally went to see still a third doctor, John H. Douglas, the cancer was at least three months old. Surgery in 1884 was sufficiently advanced so that a carcinoma of the soft palate, the affected part of the throat, could have been completely excised. Late in the summer or very early in the fall the growth would have been about the size of a pea, on the surface, and removable. By the time Douglas entered the case, the growth must have been larger, perhaps as large as a plum, and deeply embedded in the tissue, and the chances for a successful operation and cure were slight. The doctor recalled that after the examination Grant asked if it was "cancer." Lying only to the extent that he did not use Grant's accurate word, Douglas replied, "General, the disease is serious, epithelial in character, and sometimes capable of being cured." "Epithelial," as the doctor used it, meant that unwanted cells lined the soft palate, but as both men were aware, the term was a euphemism for "cancerous." Grant knew what he was up against.[3]

He was going to die, and he was going to write a book. When Grant made his plans for writing in the fall of 1884, they included Adam Badeau. Badeau was a professional writer, and Grant trusted his judgment. Badeau had read the Shiloh and Vicksburg articles in manuscript that summer, and his comments had been helpful. Now, back in New York, Grant wrote on October 2 asking Badeau to come to the city, stay with them at 3 East Sixty-sixth Street, and work alongside him. Badeau happily accepted, but said he wanted to remain in the Adirondacks until he finished his own book, an exposé of diplomatic corruption in Cuba. On October 8, Grant wrote again; he had two articles that he would like Badeau to read, and though he said they could "rest two weeks longer," there was a restrained note of impatience in the note as he added, "But I will be glad to see you when you are ready to come. . . . There will be room for you and me both in my room. If there is not [,] a table can be put up in your bed-room."[4]

Adam Badeau was the strangest of the strange men who were close to Ulysses Grant. Born in New York City in 1831 and educated well in private schools, he was a skilled writer; his volume of essays, *The Vagabond*, contains interesting pieces on Charlotte Brontë, Edwin Booth (with whom Badeau spent an astonishing night in the rarely opened country house of Booth's father), George Bancroft, and "Myself." He went to war, served on the staff of General Thomas W. Sherman, and was wounded at Port Hudson. In 1864, he joined Grant's staff, and took part in the Wilderness campaign. An accomplished military historian, he published his three-volume *Military History of Ulysses S. Grant* in 1882. This was followed after Grant's death by his *Grant in Peace: From Appomattox to Mount McGregor*. Subtitled *A Personal Memoir*, this book is an odd collection of gossipy sketches concerning Grant's relationships with such diverse acquaintances as Sheridan, Stanton, Gladstone, Fish, and Romero. Since Badeau was away from Washington during most of Grant's presidency, the book includes almost no political history. There is neither acute analysis nor a firm narrative strand, and one is left knowing little of either Grant or Badeau.

Badeau was probably a homosexual, and in a world that accorded him limited license to express himself, he chose a derivative existence, being endlessly fascinated by society. His correspondence with his intimate friend Benjamin Moran, secretary of the legation in London, is awash with duchesses. He also allowed himself to enjoy the petty pleasure of hoisting himself up by cutting others down. His *Grant in Peace* is full of judgments on the gaucheries of people he met in Washington, such as the wife of the British minister: "Her ladyship, you see, was born in the middle class." In the winter preceding Grant's inaugural, when gossip about the new president was in great demand, Badeau chanced to be staying in the same boardinghouse in which Henry Adams had modest bachelor quarters. They shared a dining table, and Adams, pressing Badeau on one of his favorite subjects— Grant—did not fail to observe Badeau keenly at the same time. He found him "exceedingly social, though not in appearance imposing. He was stout;

his face was red, and his habits were regularly irregular; but he was very intelligent." Impatient for place, Badeau "resorted more or less to whiskey for encouragement, and became irritable, besides being loquacious. He talked much about Grant, and showed a certain artistic feeling for analysis of character, as a true literary critic would naturally do. Loyal to Grant, and still more so to Mrs. Grant, who acted as his patron, he said nothing, even when far gone, that was offensive about either, but he held that no one except himself and Rawlins understood the General."[5]

It is hard indeed to know why Grant was drawn to Badeau; the 105 letters that Grant wrote to him—and that Badeau proudly printed in *Grant in Peace*—are devoid of any hint of intimacy. But apparently Badeau was one of the members of Grant's staff who somehow managed to make Grant comfortable without in any way being a threat to him, one of those who could perhaps sense his power (and think they understood it), but were not in any way a psychological obstruction to him. Badeau was on Grant's army staff in 1869 and after the inaugural moved into the White House, living there until he won a consulship. Whether in army headquarters, the White House, or a legation office in some foreign land, Badeau was happy to run errands for Grant, and Grant felt comfortable asking him to do so. And the critical clue to understanding the difficult relationship between the two men is that both were writers.

Badeau did not pick up Grant's oblique hint that he was doing his own work; instead, he arrived hoping to win immortality by putting into literary form the words of the dying general. It did not occur to him that Grant could write a book. Despite the claim he had made to Henry Adams, Badeau never quite understood Grant. Indeed, he told Adams that during the war he and Rawlins and others on the staff "could never follow a mental process in his [Grant's] thought. They were not sure that he did think." It would have been closer to the truth to say that Grant himself did not know what he thought until he wrote it. Perhaps he should have banished cabinet meetings, as he had councils of war, and governed by penciled notes of instruction. For whether Grant could think or not, he could write—better than Badeau, in a style that was inimitable.[6]

The Grants' house on Sixty-sixth Street was beautifully placed, one door in from Fifth Avenue and in sight of Central Park. It was the solid reliable house the general and Julia had looked for all their lives. There was nothing strange about it. It had not the hand-crafted homemade quality of Hardscrabble, not the silly unreality of those subscription houses in Galena and Philadelphia and Washington, and none of the official nonsense of the White House. It was closest to the fine little house on High Street in Galena where they had lived so briefly in 1860–61. The New York house said that someone successful and stable lived in it. A sturdy flight of steps led up to the front door; inside were parlors and a dining room (with kitchen and servants' rooms below). On the second floor were good bedrooms for Julia and Ulysses, who had to have a separate room because of his illness, and at the front a fine study in which he did his writing. On the third floor were bedrooms for Ida and Fred and their children; on the fourth was space for servants and overflow grandchildren.

Grant sat at a large square table in the front room on the second floor, and worked with wonderful steadiness mornings and afternoons. Pain and doctors interrupted him, and so did a swirl of children and grandchildren, but nothing diverted him from his work. And no other person was indispensable to it. Even Badeau soon found that he was not necessary. With a clerk's mind, Colonel Fred was able to gather sources his father needed, and look up facts; Julia's eyes were weak, but the rest of the family were willing to read portions aloud, and both they and Julia could comment on them. Badeau could give good professional judgment on the manuscript as it progressed. He was useful, but not indispensable. The irritability his old friend Adams had spotted years ago reappeared; he came to resent and even to hate Fred, and he quarreled with Julia. When Nellie arrived in March, his bedroom was needed, and Badeau moved out of the house. By then, he had predicted (accurately) that Grant's book would compete with his own *Military History of Ulysses S. Grant*, published more than two years earlier. He was jealous not only of Fred and of Julia, but also, increasingly, of Samuel Clemens, who usurped his role as chief adviser. And Badeau was envious of the general himself. His own professional skill was not enough for him to dominate Grant in the writing world. If Badeau's work was good, Grant's, in a sense that Badeau refused to recognize or acknowledge, was great.

In November, far from having given up trying to have an imprint on events, Grant wrote a businesslike letter to John Russell Young in China, endorsing a trading venture in the Far East and stating, obviously for public consumption, "I believe . . . it is to the advantage of both China and Japan to look to the United States for anything which they must go abroad for." We, not the "strong European powers," should be getting that trade. Then, turning from commerce to politics and to more personal observations, he wrote, "Our election is over . . . the democratic party is to be restored . . . after . . . twenty-four years. It is to be seen now 'what they do with it.' " He said somewhat dutifully that he thought Blaine could have done a good job as president but, recalling another nominee of another day, observed that he thought Blaine's nomination a mistake, as there "has been no election since '72 when the republicans could have won so easily."[7]

Grant had an idea who might have done better at winning than Blaine, but politics were now behind him and the book lay ahead. He did not, however, have good arrangements for its publication. Back in September, he had told a grandchild of his writings, which he intended to publish "in a book"; at about the same time, on George Childs's porch at Long Branch, he asked Roswell Smith, president of the Century Company, with a certain guile, "Do you really think anyone would be interested in a book by me?" *Would anyone read*

*Napoleon on Austerlitz?* thought Smith, and he urged Grant to complete his work. When the publisher left Long Branch, he thought he had a deal, but he was not sure enough of the book to offer an advance. Smith reported to his associates, "When the book is ready he is to come to see us with it." He thought he had Grant sewed up.[8]

Smith, however, had not reckoned with one of the era's sharpest bucca-neers, a man who had shown his knowledge of the ways of the world in his own brilliant writings about its follies. That man—Samuel Clemens—was magnificently contemptuous of those who made their living as the publishers of books, precisely because he was so anxious to make sure that his own par-ticular living, for Mrs. Clemens and himself, was a handsome one. In No-vember, he got wind not only that his friend's book was going well but also that the people at the company that published *Century Magazine* were offering a good deal less than he and, one guesses, Grant thought it was worth, and he paid a call at Sixty-sixth Street.

In his wickedly triumphant account of how he bested the Century people, Clemens collapsed months of hard negotiating into two days. While suggest-ing that it was he who rescued Grant from a naive fall into Century's hands, he ignored the fact that the general was shopping around among several other publishers. One wonders, in fact, just who was conning whom in the conver-sations between Grant and Clemens. (Surely the core of the attraction which Ulysses Grant held for Samuel Clemens lay not in Grant's fame, although that mattered, but in Clemens's perception that he, and he alone, had been smart enough to figure out that Grant was no dumber than Tom Sawyer. Which is to say, not dumb at all—just stranded in a world that did not make much sense.) After he looked at the offer Century had made, Clemens said, he "explained that these terms would never do. . . . Strike out the ten per cent and put twenty per cent in its place. Better still, put seventy-five. . . . The General demurred, and quite decidedly. He said they would never pay those terms."[9]

Undaunted, Clemens argued his case strenuously, claiming Century's offer was an outrage to "such a colossus as General Grant." This was flatter-ing talk; nevertheless, the idea of renegotiating the contract "distressed Gen-eral Grant," who began wondering if, in fact, he had given Smith his word that Century would get the book. Grant, continued Clemens, thought this new contract proposal

> placed him in the attitude of a robber—robber of a publisher. I said that if he regarded that as a crime it was because his education was limited. I said it was not a crime and was always rewarded in heaven with two halos. Would be, if it ever happened.
>
> The General was immovable and challenged me to name the publisher that would be willing to have this noble deed perpetrated upon him. I named the American Publishing Company of Hartford. He asked if I

could prove my position. I said I could furnish the proof by telegraph in six hours—three hours for my despatch to go to Hartford, three hours for . . . jubilant acceptance to return by the same electric gravel train—that if he needed this answer quicker I would walk up to Hartford and fetch it.

Grant was right to be skeptical, for the American Publishing Company turned down the proposal. As Clemens chose to recall it: "I was fully expecting to presently hand that book to . . . [them] and enrich that den of reptiles—but the sober second thought came then. I reflected that the company had been robbing me for years and building theological factories out of the proceeds and that now was my chance to feed fat the ancient grudge I bore them."[10]

To exercise these urges he was already establishing his own publishing firm, Charles L. Webster & Company, to bring out *The Adventures of Huckleberry Finn*. Why he offered to give Grant's manuscript to the American Publishing Company is not clear; there was money to be made with the book, and now he offered Grant a $10,000 advance and talked of 75 percent royalties. Century, perhaps with an eye to the problems of finishing a dying man's book, had insisted that extraordinary costs would have to come out of Grant's share of the profits. These costs Clemens agreed to take on "out of my fourth." Grant was intrigued: "He laughed . . . and asked me what my profit out of that remnant would be. I said, a hundred thousand dollars in six months."[11]

The *Personal Memoirs of U. S. Grant* has had an interesting history. Clemens, who cannot be said to have been disinterested, claimed that the general's account of his campaigns was the greatest writing by a military man since Caesar wrote about Gaul. His subscription men crossed the country offering the volumes in a choice of three handsome bindings at three prices. Some of the better salesmen had pages of actual manuscript, with Grant's corrections penciled on them, bound in hard covers into a dummy book to use as an enticement. If the sales are calculated at an average of $5 a set for 300,000 sets, the gross income would have been $1,500,000. Out of this would have come the production costs and the commissions paid to the subscription men. Julia Grant is said to have received between $420,000 and $450,000, suggesting that the figure in the final contract was 30 percent for the Grants, which yielded certainly much more than $100,000 for the benevolent Mr. Clemens. The result was an astonishing number of two-volume sets sitting proudly on parlor tables in America in the 1880's. And what was more, the prose in the book was never totally forgotten. Gertrude Stein read hers and, with her penchant for strong people and taut prose, pronounced for Grant. Clemens was proud of the book on both literary and commercial grounds. He had the great satisfaction of writing the largest royalty check ever written, $200,000 payable to Julia Grant on February 27, 1886.

But in the fall of 1884 that was in the future; Ulysses Grant, with the prospect of munificent success but still without a contract, and in increasingly precarious health, pursued his writing. Late in November, in a slightly shaky hand, he wrote Nellie what must have been an exceedingly distressing letter for his daughter to receive. Except for a reference to an enclosed sample of lace from a dress that Julia was sending with Levi Morton, almost the whole of his note read, "I am still very lame and otherwise suffering. I have had a sore throat now for more than four months, and latterly I have been suffering from neuralgia. Last Friday I had three large double teeth pulled which I hope will cure the neuralgia, and the Doctor is making fair progress with the sore throat. The lameness is gradually improving." There were already rumors in the newspapers of his ill health, and they were confirmed in December by Grant's own candor when he wrote E. F. Beale, a slight acquaintance, saying that his painful throat made it impossible to keep an engagement in Hot Springs. Beale chose to document his intimacy with the general by releasing the note to a reporter, and Grant's illness was public. The cancer had not kept him from his writing, and the negotiations for the publication of his book went on. In November Samuel Clemens had proposed that Grant drop the Century people but the general was not yet won over to Clemens as his publisher, but unwittingly, Clemens had given his friend the confidence to raise the ante. In December, Grant wrote Andrew Carnegie, who had intervened in Scribner's behalf, that he could not sign a contract with that house without at least giving Century the chance to match it. Grant said the book would probably be finished by May, if it were not for his troubling health. He was, nonetheless, convinced that he would indeed finish it.[12]

In January 1885, Julia completed difficult arrangements with William H. Vanderbilt; as a result, he forgave his $150,000 loan, and the ceremonial gifts from the Grants' trip around the world were left in his possession (inaccessible to creditors), with the proviso that they go to the nation on Grant's death. The agreement meant both solvency and an end to the worrisome business of bankruptcy, but Julia, with no other business to do and no intellectual activity available to her, was left with fewer resources during the long months of the disease than her husband. He, though in pain and aware of the likelihood of his death, had the writing of his book to occupy him. In February he wrote Nellie that the throat condition—he never after the first instance called it cancer—was "very serious," that he had lost thirty pounds and had to see his doctors twice a day.

It would be very hard for me to be confined to the house . . . if it was not that I have become interested in the work which I have undertake[n]. It will take several months yet to complete the writing of my campaigns. The indications now are that the book will be in two volumes of about four hundred and fifty pages each. I give a condensed biography of my life up to the breaking out of the rebellion. If you ever take the time to read it you will find out what a boy and man I was before you knew me. I do not know whether my book will be interesting to other people or not, but all the publishers want to get it, and I have had larger offers than have ever been made for a book before. Fred helps me greatly in my work. He does all the copying, and looks up references for me.

A few days later Julia, distraught, wrote an old friend (herself close to death), "Genl Grant's health is our absorbing thought. Genl Grant is very, very ill. I cannot write how ill—my tears blind me." Grant himself had just told Nellie, "We have all been as happy as could be expected considering our great losses and my personal suffering. Philosophers profess to believe that what is is for the best. I hope it may prove so with our family." The "what is" for Ulysses S. Grant was not only his dying but his book, and now there was a real danger that he would not be able to finish it. The day he wrote Nellie, he had been to Dr. Douglas's office and had caught cold; thereafter he was treated at home. The ulceration of his throat grew much worse. In late February, a retinue of specialists confirmed that "the disease was epitheloma, or epithelial cancer of the malignant type, that was sure to end fatally." What Grant was told is not known, but he knew he was dying. Early in March he talked to Badeau about completing the book if he left it unfinished, but Clemens, although greatly distressed by his friend's appearance, expressed his faith that Grant would rally and finish it himself. And admirably, Clemens went ahead with the contract.[13]

Although exceedingly weak, Grant kept on writing. One day, as Clemens was chatting with him (and a sculptor Clemens admired worked on a fine bust of the general) Badeau came in, said, "I've been reading what you wrote this morning," and went on to compliment Grant for having made clear a wartime event that all other accounts had left in a muddle. There were, however, days when Grant could not work at all, and on March 26, he reached a dangerous point in his illness. An attempt to rally his spirits with a carriage ride through the park with his old friend Matías Romero produced fatigue instead. That evening, he had to give a deposition for the trial of James D. Fish, and Dr. Douglas complained the next morning that the lawyers had dangerously tired his patient. Indeed, on March 28 the doctors expected Grant to die. The family gathered, while an ostentatious and unctuous Methodist clergyman, John P. Newman, who had wormed his way into the family's confidence and persuaded them of the efficacy of baptism, performed this rite. Grant's sister Mary had devotedly prayed for her brother's conversion, but he had been assiduously indifferent. Now too weak to resist, he submitted to the ceremony, which later was widely acclaimed as having prolonged his life. On the same day he received the ministrations of the notable divine, Grant was also treated by Dr. George F. Shrady, and he rallied. Shrady later laconically recorded his judgment as to what had saved the general: "I was inclined to attribute the result to the brandy."[14]

One painful aspect of his disease in this period was severe coughing and vomiting, and Grant's debilitation was so great that it is difficult to account for the remarkable improvement in his condition which occurred. One medical scholar hypothesizes that "Grant bled into his tumor, this hemorrhage resulted in the death of many tumor cells, and Grant coughed up a lot of blood with dead cancer cells, vomited out a lot of blood with dead cancer cells, and probably also swallowed a lot of blood with dead and living cancer cells." This violent activity resulted, after the bleeding stopped, in a cancerous mass in the soft palate that was considerably smaller and less painful than it had been.[15]

In April, Grant was markedly better. He could go for drives, dine with the family, visit with friends, and work on his book. And the book became more and more important to him. Finally, there was something to be done that was worth doing. All the failures of his first forty years and the terrible successes of the next four, which had been given gaudy celebration for almost twenty more, yielded to a splendid struggle to create the *Personal Memoirs of U. S. Grant*. He pressed himself, not to write, for that he did with disconcerting ease, but to finish the book before he died. There was simple Grant logic in his determination. He was performing this task to support the family, and, of absolutely essential importance, there was fulfillment for him in the nature of the job itself. A cynic could say that without Donelson, Vicksburg, Chattanooga, the Wilderness and, of course, Appomattox, there could have been no book. He would be right. But neither would there have been a book—a good strong book—without Grant's magnificent eye and his clear rendering of what he saw into words. All his life he had struggled to get his story out, to get his life laid out before himself and before the world, so that in some way it could matter. Now—and only now—he succeeded.

The choice of publisher was announced by his son on March 2, 1885, in a businesslike letter sent to the rival houses which had lost the chance to publish the book: "Genl Grant's book will be published by Chas. L. Webster & Co." George Childs had come up from Philadelphia, reviewed the various offers, and, according to Clemens, pronounced, "Give the book to Clemens."[16]

William T. Sherman was no man for a euphemism: "I am sure Dr. Douglas told me there was no cancer—but Dr. Alexander says it *is* cancer, that it will gradually prevent his taking sufficient food, that he will gradually waste away and die." Sherman, without growing maudlin, regretted that he was no longer close to Grant personally; his concern for his old friend was great nevertheless, and he summed it up with his customary firmness: "I think it a matter of vital importance that he should complete his Memoirs." A year later Sherman wrote his nephew not to pay any attention to General Buell's anti-Grant account of Shiloh: "Let it fail still born. Thousands— millions—will read Grant's simple account who may never have the patience to compare the two accounts." He was referring not so much to Grant's article on the battle in the *Century Magazine* as to the *Memoirs*, which he knew would last.[17]

Grant matched Sherman in the ruthless realism with which he appraised his own illness and coming death. On June 17, he wrote a magnificent memorandum to his doctor, in which he told Douglas that he would die of "hemorage, strangulation, or exhaustion," and with mordant wit, gave the physician permission to bring in still another expert if "you are unwilling to have me go without consultation." He did, however, let Douglas know that he dreaded "more Drs. & more treatment & more suffering." It would have been splendid if such honesty from a man bent on so honest a task could have been rewarded by a dignified time in which to write and to die. Grant was not so lucky; first there was the business of Adam Badeau's jealousy of the book, and second there was the tinsel unreality of the place chosen for dying.[18]

On April 19, 1885, the *New York World* ran a column of gossip about Grant that included this statement: "Another false idea of Gen. Grant is given out by some of his friends, and that is that he is a writer. He is not a writer. . . . The work upon his new book about which so much has been said is the work of Gen. Adam Badeau." Samuel Clemens, furious, was ready to sue for libel. Grant worked for three hours on a letter to Charles L. Webster & Company, intended for publication, in which he discussed the charges made in the *World* and quietly stated, "The composition is entirely my own." Grant's statement appeared in the *New York Tribune* and the *New York Sun* on May 6. Meanwhile, on May 2, Badeau, with perverse perseverance, wrote Grant asking for additional payment for his services. Believing Fred would intercept the letter, he came to the house to present it to Grant himself. Badeau knew that advance sales were going well, and he wanted a thousand dollars a month to finish the book and 10 percent of the profits.[19]

On May 5, Grant wrote Badeau, ". . . you and I must give up all association as far as the preparation of any literary work goes which is to bear my signature." The controversy over whether he was able to write at all had stimulated Grant to prove he could. He admitted that Badeau had helped him in the writing, and that when he had been so ill in March he had expected Badeau to have to finish the book, but now, while saying he hoped they could remain friends, Grant warned that if the book was unfinished when he died, and Badeau insisted on completing it, he would face the enmity of the family. What was more, Grant intended to finish the book himself, and he rejected out of hand Badeau's claim to a percentage of the royalties. In 1888, Badeau sued the family for a share in the profits, and tried to cast Fred Grant in the role of the villain who had destroyed his relationship with the General. It was a thoroughly disagreeable and unsuccessful suit, but it came three years after Ulysses Grant could be touched by it.[20]

Summer was coming—Grant guessed it would be his last—and people outside of his family had thoughts about where he should spend it. As one gentleman put it: "I thought if we could get him to come to Mount McGregor, and if he should die there, it might make the place a national

shrine—and incidentally a success." The real-estate promoter was talking
about a cottage on the grounds of his resort hotel, Balmoral, a few miles
north of Saratoga Springs in the foothills of the Adirondacks. Shoddy exploitation followed Grant right to the grave. He was already the enshrined hero
of a noble cause and the wayward antihero of sham values.[21]

W. J. Arkell, an upstate New York butcher whose business had thrived,
had gone into Republican politics and into other ventures as well; these included publication of the *Albany Evening Journal* and, in 1881, resort real estate. After the Civil War, Saratoga Springs had become the most fashionable
mountain resort in the country, and exploitation of the lovely country to the
north was in full flower. Joining in, Arkell built a narrow-gauge railroad that
ran twelve miles from Saratoga Springs to Mount McGregor and then up a
spectacularly steep grade to the summit, where he built the Hotel Balmoral,
opened for the 1884 season. The resort was modeled on the successful and
beautiful Mohonk Mountain House, farther down the Hudson Valley;
rustic gazebos were placed along gently sloping paths where slow-paced
overdressed walkers could pause and admire lovely vistas. There were lakes
below, and the Saratoga battlefield, and to the north and west the mountain
peaks of the Adirondacks. The Mount McGregor Art Association was already in existence in 1883, and on its walls were Thomas Moran's *Hiawatha*
and, impressively for so new a gallery, one of the most famous of the paintings by the Grants' favorite artist, Albert Bierstadt—*The Rocky Mountains*,
bought for $1,500. In June 1885, advertisements appeared for "Hotel Bal-
moral, 1200 feet above the sea, on Mount McGregor . . . ('No Dew, No Ma-
laria, No Mosquitoes, Certain Relief from Hay Fever.')"[22]

In 1885, Joseph W. Drexel of New York City, the younger brother of the
head of the banking firm which had long curried Grant's favor, bought a cottage that had been moved to make room for the Balmoral. Apparently
Drexel, who summered in Saratoga Springs, thought of occupying it himself, but Arkell had a better idea. Drexel had known Grant both socially and
commercially in Long Branch and in New York—he was the first man Grant
approached when he took up a subscription for the pedestal of the Statue of
Liberty. Would it not, Arkell suggested to Drexel, be beneficial to the great
general to get to the mountain air and relieve his suffering? And would this
not make a success of the Balmoral, in which both the rich man from New
York and the more newly rich man from Canajoharie had invested?

Inexplicably, the Grants had decided to sell the lovely cottage in Long
Branch. On April 19 the *New York Tribune* reported that they would summer
in the Catskills, but a week later the destination was changed: "In the morning W. J. Arkell called and arranged definitely with the family for taking
General Grant to Mount McGregor. . . ." By June 14 the hot weather had
begun to bother the general, who was already suffering greatly. The cancer
had become rooted in deeper tissue, his neck was swollen, and he found it
painful and difficult to speak. William H. Vanderbilt lent his railroad car,

and on June 16 the general, Julia, Fred and Ida, Nellie, Dr. Douglas, Henry McQueeney (Grant's nurse), Harrison Tyrrell (his valet), and Julia's maid left Grand Central Station, traveled up the east side of the Hudson—in sight of West Point—crossed below Albany, and reached Saratoga Springs.[23]

All along the way, groups of people crowded the local stations to watch the great general in his splendid railroad car go by. At Saratoga Springs, he was cheered when, unaided, he got out and stepped over to the narrow-gauge railroad car that would take him to Mount McGregor. In a few minutes he stepped out again, exasperated by the bumbling efforts of Fred and the porters to transfer the huge chair in which he slept and the chair on which he propped his feet. The furniture finally in place, they moved on once more. The short final leg of the journey was a far cry from the trip Grant had made so long ago when, in pain from his injured leg, he had traveled alone in a railroad car from Nashville toward Chattanooga. This was a macabre holiday excursion. Drexel was aboard, as were reporters from newspapers all over the country, and Arkell "was thoughtfully attentive to all on the train over which he exercised supervision."[24]

Thomas M. Pitkin, in his admirable account of Grant's days at Mount McGregor, tells of Grant's annoyance with the smoke that wafted back into his railroad car from the little engine struggling up the mountain. Grant's car lurched as the grade-gaining curves were accomplished, and it was with considerable relief that he got out and, ignoring a hospital litter, made his way on foot to the ample, but not grand, cottage. There he found a good porch on three sides, which shaded and darkened the "reception room"—a correct term, as it turned out. The cottage's main room had been hastily converted from rusticity with veneers and wallpaper. The woodwork was pale blue, the new brick fireplace was Tuscan red, and the ceiling paper was "radiant with gold stars." On the figured carpet was a large sturdy writing table covered with green baize. Grant's bedroom, also newly papered and curtained, was on the first floor, as was Julia's room and that of Harrison Tyrrell. There were six rooms on the second floor for the rest of the family.[25]

Surely Grant had earned a rest, but he was tired of resting, of being out of sight. The crowds of people along the train's route all day had stimulated him. Instead of going straight into the house, he sat on the porch and visited with Drexel; then he went in, changed into a dress coat and top hat, and came out again. On display, he sat on the porch with others of the party until the supposedly nonexistent mosquitoes drove him inside. That porch became, in fact, as photographed as any in American history. Picture after picture shows the Grant family there, ridiculously overdressed in the best fashion of the day: Julia and her daughter and daughters-in-law in silk and bent-brimmed hats, the men in dress coats, and the general always with an excellent silk top hat and—the only sensible garment on display—a scarf at his neck. Nellie, whose three children were in England, had been with her father and mother since spring. Fred and Ida, who had established them-

*The family at Mount McGregor, 1885.* LIBRARY OF CONGRESS

selves as the premier branch of the family, were present with their two children—Julia, age nine, and Ulysses S. Grant, four. Jesse and his wife, Elizabeth, and their daughter, Nellie, who was nearly four, were also at Mount McGregor.*

It was there on the porch, as well as in the front room, that Grant received the flood of visitors who eagerly made the pilgrimage to gaze at the dying general. With the anticipatory clergyman John P. Newman in close attendance, there was a stream of Civil War generals, properly balanced Confederate to Union; of politicians, usually of respectably Republican stripe; and of vacationers from Saratoga Springs. The great man far outstripped any mountain scenery as the tourist attraction of the summer. "Every afternoon long lines" of these tourists "would walk past the cottage. Now and then Grant, sitting on the porch . . . writing or reading the newspapers, would look up and nod or wave his hand." A self-appointed Grand Army of the Republic veteran hovered around, to prevent the curious from actually going up onto the porch to peer into the door when, by poor luck, the general was not outside. Not all the tourists were idly curious. There was much genuine

* It is to be wondered how names were kept straight in the family. Repetition was rampant. Jesse, not Nellie, had a daughter Nellie; Fred, not Ulysses junior, was the father in 1881 of Ulysses 3rd, but Buck got even in 1893 by naming his second son after himself, so there was a fourth Ulysses. Fred's daughter, born in 1876, was Julia Grant; Buck's second daughter, born just before her grandfather died, was Julia Dent Grant. Things became hopeless in the next generation when a cousin, Helen Dent Wrenshall, called Nellie, married Chaffee Grant and (before she divorced him and married her sister-in-law Fannie Grant's ex-husband) had a daughter who gave one of her sons the name Grant and another the name Dent. By then, things were back almost to Cain and Abel.

affection and even reverence for the general. Simon Bolivar Buckner, the friend from Popocatepetl and enemy from Donelson, came to see him, and told reporters that his reunion with Grant was "too sacred" for him to discuss.[26]

Grant's need to be noticed, to be taken into account, had still not been sated. If he had sought seclusion in which to endure his pain and to complete his writing, it could have been found. Without question, the Fishes would have lent their place in Garrison, from which the public could easily have been barred; any number of Grant's other rich friends had mountain and lake hideaways that he could have borrowed. Clearly, he did not want to be hidden away to die in obscurity.

In a century that relished the spectacle of dying there was, in America at least, no deathwatch the equal of Grant's. Lincoln's had been dramatic and immensely affecting, but it had also been tragically brief. With Grant, the nation for eight months read almost daily in the newspapers of the progress of the disease, of the devouring of the victim by the unmentioned cancer, and of the valiant battle of the old warrior, before getting the news of his final surrender—or victory—depending on the reader's theology. When Grant's disease became known back in the fall of 1884, the house on Sixty-sixth Street had become the object of pilgrims intent on the traditional watch over the death of the great. During the crisis in March, reporters hovered and crowds gathered. One enterprising newspaperman bragged of having seduced a servant across the street in order to be able to peer down from her attic room into the Grant ménage. But the people gathered on Sixty-sixth Street were as nothing compared to the thousands rallied by energetic newspaper writers across the country to the pastime of waiting for the great general to die. Not until General Eisenhower's bowel movements gained public notice a century later were the American people given such graphic details about the health of a president.

Grant's publisher was eager to capitalize on the magnificent market created by the focus on his dying. In June, the first volume of the book was in press, and the stenographers and typesetters worked around the clock rushing the last of the copy of the second volume into print. Their problem was not that Grant would die before his work was done, but that he would keep working after they thought he was finished. He insisted on going over the proofs, and made intricate, careful changes. More than he had ever wanted anything, he wanted the book to be right.

Despite the visitors, or perhaps stimulated by them, Grant kept writing. Samuel Clemens had the publishing company send a stenographer, N. E. Dawson, to the cottage, and Grant told Fred to concentrate on checking sources for changes and additions. Each day, wrapped in a blanket on the porch, or settled in a chair in the house, Grant with pencil and pad wrote his strong, quiet prose. His medicine was cocaine (counteracted at night with morphine to enable him to sleep), and it is legitimate to ask if some of the quick directness as well as the blandness of the later sections of the *Memoirs* is not traceable to the drugs. The *non sequiturs* that nonetheless flow together, in the odd short concluding chapter, suggest that the drugs had some effect. But whether their effect is discounted or credited, there is a strength to Grant's narrative that argues against their being overvalued. He could sustain a story through two wars and eleven hundred pages. He had an extraordinary capacity to see certain of his life's experiences with a forbidding wholeness, and could carry that wholeness efficiently to the printed page.

The *Memoirs* begins with a tantalizingly brief account of his ancestry, boyhood, West Point years, and courtship. Then comes the masterful and thorough chronicle of the Mexican War. This is followed by a meager summary of the bleak days of the 1850's, with the rest—nearly two-thirds of the two volumes—devoted to a lucid account of the Civil War.[27]

Grant's story of the war does not have the flashes of fire of Sherman's *Memoirs*, or the novelist's details of Lew Wallace's *Autobiography*. There is none of the lavish social detail—and irony—of Mary Boykin Chesnut's great Civil

*Writing his memoirs, June 27, 1885, Mount McGregor.* LIBRARY OF
CONGRESS

War diary. Neither does Grant's story have the narrative thrust and rich texture of the best present-day account of the war, Shelby Foote's. But it is wonderfully clear. To read some of the tales of their battles written by other generals is mordantly amusing; they add more and more self-serving detail, only to end with a hopeless muddle. They create a metaphor for their own ineptitude, accomplishing exactly the opposite of what they set out to do. Grant avoided this. He apologized only for one hideously bloody day outside Vicksburg and for Cold Harbor, he bragged only in a most subtle and seemly fashion, and he left an indelible picture of himself as quietly competent. The book is, however, not merely an exercise in self-portrayal. Grant devoted excellent attention to theaters of the war in which he was not present (although Virginia, before he came east, is given short shrift). There is conciseness, totality, and strength, but what is perhaps most striking is the timeless quality of the prose. It has classical force.

Grant's sentences are not Stein's or Hemingway's. Where the simplest of declarative sentences would seem exactly what you would expect Grant to write, he often added a clause. And repeatedly these clauses have a kind of throw-away quality. Life is finally more absurd, more complex, more intricate than will satisfy those looking for a simple Grant. There is no account of events after the Civil War; the eight years of his presidency are ignored. This omission could be attributed to the obvious fact that he had run out of time, but nothing in the structure of the book suggests that the postwar presidential events had ever been part of his conception of the work. He edited those disappointing years out of his story. Instead, he told of the years in which he was alive—the years of the two wars, with the first, in which he was a young participant who fought and watched others fight, as a prelude to the second, in which he was of enormous and undoubted importance.

The "Conclusion" is the strangest part of the book. Grant dictated these last thirteen pages using notes he had written on a lined pad. Here he passed a kind of summary judgment on his nation and its place in the world. Ideas scarcely connect, and despite occasional hedging, the comments are the most unguarded in the book. It begins, "The cause of the great War of the Rebellion against the United States will have to be attributed to slavery." With that "have to be," Grant suggested that he almost begrudged the fact that his greatness stood on so ignoble a rock. He then devoted three paragraphs to slavery, concluding that it was a "degradation which the North would not permit any longer than until they could get the power to expunge [it]. . . ." The war was inevitable and, chillingly, he concluded that it was "probably well that we had the war when we did," since otherwise the prewar particularism of the states would have hindered national growth and we would have been behind the Europeans in world commerce. This placement of America in a global context reflects his trip. In addition, he staked a major claim for the United States as a world power: "Now it has shown itself capable of dealing with one of the greatest wars that was ever made, and our people

have proven themselves to be the most formidable in war of any nationality."
To this ominous assessment of the national character, he hastily added, "But
this war was a fearful lesson, and should teach us the necessity of avoiding
wars in the future."[28]

He next chided European nations for their "lack of conscience" during the
war, and then leaped to a relatively extended comment on his favorite foreign
country, Mexico. Here he reiterated the principle of the Monroe Doctrine,
without naming it. France was accorded the courtesy of being called "the
traditional ally and friend of the United States," but Louis Napoleon was
likened to Jefferson Davis (though the Confederate leader was not named)
and France to the South: "Like our own war between the States, the Franco-
Prussian war was an expensive one; but it was worth to France all it cost her
people," because it "was the completion of the downfall of Napoleon III." He
then passed judgment on one military man to whom he had never found it
flattering to be likened: "I never admired the character of the first Napoleon;
but I recognize his great genius. . . . The third Napoleon could have no
claim to having done a good or just act."[29]

He regretted the difficulties with England during the war, as "England and
the United States are natural allies," tied by blood. He saluted the people of
Manchester for a "demonstration in favor of the North at the very time when
their workmen were almost famishing." The British Empire also got high
marks: "England governs her own colonies, and particularly those embracing
the people of different races from her own, better than any other nation."
And he pursued the theme of different races: "It is possible that the question
of a conflict between races may come up in the future, as did that between
freedom and slavery before." In other—less bland—words, racial war was
possible. Continuing, he wrote, "The condition of the colored man within
our borders may become a source of anxiety, to say the least. But he was
brought to our shores by compulsion, and he now should be considered as
having as good a right to remain here as any other class of our citizens."
Then, in a *non sequitur*, he brought up his old idea of a black colony or state
for America: "It was looking to a settlement of this question that led me to
urge the annexation of Santo Domingo. . . . I took it that the colored people
would go there in great numbers, so as to have independent states [of the
Union] governed by their own race."[30]

Then Grant turned to his own race and his own torments: "After our
rebellion, when so many young men were at liberty to return to their homes,
they found they were not satisfied with the farm, the store, or the workshop
of the villages, but wanted larger fields." Those fields were, in this reverie,
the American West, and here for the first time he gave the Mexican War his
approval for having made so much of that territory free and clear for the
United States: "It is probable that the Indians would have had control of
these lands for a century yet but for the war. We must conclude, therefore,
that wars are not always evils unmixed with some good."[31]

With this compliment to war, he turned to a contemplation not only of the men who had fought with him but of other men he had encountered during his life, and presented a curious complex of conclusions about them. He was happy that people were no longer confined to their homes and caught in pockets of local idiom, but he was totally unsentimental about earlier free men in the West, the lonely and frequently alcoholic trappers. He saluted instead the single national idiom, the "commingling of the people," good railroads, and the maps which were his metaphor for the careful charted order that had been brought to the nation—". . . the country has filled up 'from the centre all around to the sea.' " Speaking again of the Civil War, he concluded that it "made us a nation of great power and intelligence. We have but little to do to preserve peace, happiness and prosperity at home, and the respect of other nations." And then, in one of his reversible sentences, he preached, "Our experience ought to teach us the necessity of the first; our power secures the latter." This homily out of the way, he turned to his concluding paragraphs.[32]

The great peroration ending "Let us have peace," because of its nobility and its very generality, has been taken as lifting Ulysses S. Grant's life above the private realm into a triumphant final resting place in the public sphere. But was that the message of his statement? Or was it, instead, his last sad attempt to escape his own personal past? R. C. Townsend has said of Sherwood Anderson, a writer who admired and perhaps even emulated Grant's writing, "But always he is saying that without the courage to risk failure and without the courage to admit to it a boy cannot become a man." Grant's book is the opposite of an admission of failure; it tells only of a boyhood shadowed with the fear of being mocked as a failure and of an adulthood in which success in two wars ensured adulation. And so the boy did not become a man; he never owned up to all those painful failures that had occurred before the Civil War and recurred after it. He never told the other ordinary American men that it was all right to fail, to be gentle; that a horse did not have to be bargained for or used, but could be enjoyed. Those other Americans did not know of any way to escape the frustration of ugly daily competitions except by going to war, and Ulysses Grant did not either. He never found out how to escape the taunts of the big boys who had succeeded in politics or business. He had tried their games and done badly at them.[33]

Then he wrote his book. The content of his homily at the end of the *Memoirs* is disappointing—the morphine did not help—but even in the worst of the tendentious passages there is a hint that he was still groping for a way to return the trust of the people who had fought alongside him and who, when the fighting was over, had called out to him, from crowds. "The war," he wrote, "has made us a nation of great power and intelligence." The simple authority of the statement disguises tragedy and folly; the power he spoke of is the worst legacy of Grant's war, and one looks in vain for evidence from Grant-era politics of the use of much intelligence. But it is that word "in-

telligence" that arrests us. Intelligently, Grant has taught us to trust the
quiet, direct language with which he told the story of his battles. His American plain speech seems right for a greater task. It is a language that argues
against the seductions of power and for the acceptance of a common humanity. If we put aside the obvious disharmonies that Grant ignored, the full passage can be seen as an attempt to say to his fellow Americans, almost privately, what much of his life as a public man had denied.

> I feel that we are on the eve of a new era, when there is to be great har-
> mony between the Federal and Confederate. I cannot stay to be a living
> witness to the correctness of this prophecy; but I feel it within me that it is
> to be so. The universally kind feeling expressed for me at a time when it
> was supposed that each day would prove my last, seemed to me the
> beginning of the answer to "Let us have peace."

Americans were being told that to be kind was a good thing. Kindness was
the homeliest of virtues; it had never been dishonored more than at Cold
Harbor, but now, in 1885, it was almost as if he were saying that as we commonly face death, so perhaps we can commonly find kindness for other
human transactions. His book gives us the quiet realistic words, and his life
gives us the experiences, with which we can look at failure. He is one of the
Americans who have given us a language for simple things, important things.
We need it for the immense task of making common ground with men like
those who understood him, and marched with him, and killed for him. And
still seek some place for being a man and a man's friend other than at war.[34]

A splendid example of Grant's ability to be true to a man he knew was
displayed in June 1885, when he was reading proofs of the book. He had
written an account of his first meeting with Secretary Stanton at Louisville in
the fall of 1863. He and Julia had gone out to visit relatives when word of the
worsening situation at Chattanooga reached Stanton and he sent aides scurrying through the city to find Grant. In his original draft, Grant wrote that
once he had been found, he went back to the hotel and found Stanton "pacing
the room rapidly in about the garb Mr. Davis was supposed to be wearing
subsequently, when he was captured in a dressing gown." In the proof he
deleted the passage beginning "in about the garb Mr. Davis was supposed to
be wearing" and inserted another in its place so that the printer would not
have to reset the whole page. (It was reset.) He did not know whether the
legend that Davis had worn women's clothing as he tried to escape in April
1865 was true, and would not suggest that it was. Nor would he imply that
Stanton was effeminate. This avoidance of a cheap anecdote is evidence of
the honesty that is a fundamental strength in Grant's book. Over the decades
since its publication there have been many insinuations that Grant had a
ghost writer. Clemens himself, if not Adam Badeau, has been mentioned in
conjectures about the book's authorship. The rumors are unfounded; Grant

wrote it. The fundamental evidence lies in his style, unchanged from that of the simple orders he wrote in pencil during the war, but if further proof be needed, it can be found in the handwritten pages of the draft and in the careful marginal corrections in his steady, clear writing.[35]

The book was now his life, but they took it away from him. On July 10, in one of the brave (and lucid) penciled notes with which he now "talked," he told his doctor that Buck had brought up the first volume, finished, and that in two weeks "if they work hard they can have the second vol. copied ready to go to the printer. *I will then feel that my work is done.*" (His publishers were keeping up with him; the date July 18 is penciled on drawings of the maps which were to be included in the second volume, and on the margin of a map in which two critical battle areas are mislabeled, a note to the printer by an editor says, "Wilderness must go where Spottsylvania is and Spottsylvania where indicated. *Please hurry.* CLW & Co.") Grant insisted on pressing ahead, reading the proofs of the second volume and making corrections on the stenographer's longhand draft of the final chapter. Fred Grant faced a cruel dilemma. Conventional wisdom argued that he should see that his father was not overtaxed (although he might have asked what he was saving his father for), and he decided to put a stop to the restless work on the book. Knowing his father could not live much longer and wanting him to have the satisfaction of thinking he had completed his work, Fred sent back the last of the proofs and copy to the publisher. What the colonel did not understand was that Grant did not see it as finished. He wanted to go on working and to know that after his death work on the book would continue. To Fred he wrote:

> If I should die here make arrangements for embalming my body and re-taining it for burial until pleasant weather in the fall. In that case you can continue your work and insure its being ready as fast as the printers can take it. This is my great interest in life, to see my work done. There is nothing in my condition that I know of except presentiment, on account of weakness to indicate that I may not as well live for the next three months as for the last five. Do *not* let the memory of me interfere with the progress of the book.[36]

Too late, Dr. Shrady, who was more sensitive than either Dr. Douglas or the family to the living still being done by the dying man, recognized that to deprive Grant of his writing had been a mistake. When the patient rallied re-markably on July 12—he was even able to talk in an almost normal voice to Nellie that Sunday morning—Shrady recommended that he read *The Auto-crat of the Breakfast-Table*, itself written by a doctor, and encouraged Fred to tell Grant that the relentless *Century Magazine* wanted still another article. The effort was gallant, but Grant recognized at last that he had no more work to do. He told Dr. Douglas, in another note, that he was pleased with the

*On the porch at Mount McGregor, July 19, 1885. Harrison Tyrrell is just inside the door.* LIBRARY OF CONGRESS

way he had written the section of the book on the Wilderness campaign and proud of the fifty pages he had added to the manuscript in a major revision—he had "done all of it over again from the crossing of the Rapidan . . . to Appomattox." All this had evidently been accomplished at Mount McGregor. "There is nothing more I should do to it now," he wrote on July 14, "and therefore I am not likely to be more ready to go than at this moment."[37]

Grant's consciousness of his coming death had a magnificence not matched at any other time in his life. In a wonderfully heightened intensity, his notes to his doctor show flashes of intelligence that leap past even the impressive power of the best prose of the *Memoirs*. One day in July—the note is undated but clearly near the end—he wrote, "I do not sleep though I sometimes doze a little. If up I am talked to and in my efforts to answer cause pain. The fact is I think I am a verb instead of a personal pronoun. A verb is anything that signifies to be; to do; or to suffer. I signify all three."[38]

On July 19, one last time in top hat and dress suit and slippers, with his round owlish spectacles on, he crossed his legs and read the paper in a wicker chair just outside the front door. The picture that was taken was his last. His cane rested on the chair next to him; Tyrrell, his valet, darkly in the doorway, was not four feet away. On the twentieth, bored or frightened, with nothing more he could write, he asked to get out of the house and was trundled in a Bath chair along a poorly graded path to the eastern outlook. When he got there he was tired and out of sorts and wanted to come back as soon as Tyrrell was rested enough to push the wretched contraption. They took another route, encountered railroad tracks, and the general had to get out and climb over them. When they reached the cottage he was exhausted. The following day he was so drowsy that Douglas thought he would die. But he did not die. Not malnutrition, massive bleeding, or pneumonia would rob the inexorable cancer of its power to destroy. The doctors, consciously or subconsciously, were practicing euthanasia with their injections of brandy and morphine and applications of cocaine, but Grant held on. The Reverend Dr. Newman hovered. The family gathered; Buck was summoned from New York. At eleven-thirty Grant whispered to the doctor that he wanted them all, including the minister, to go to bed.

The next day, July 22, Dr. Shrady and Buck arrived by special train. All of the general's children were now with him, and three of his grandchildren. So too was Julia. That evening a bed was brought down from the hotel, and Fred asked his father, who had not slept lying down in months, if he would give up his chairs and go to bed. The general finally surrendered and whispered that he would. His body was gaunt but his "beautiful hand," small and strong, clutched the blanket. He lasted the night, and early in the morning the exhausted family left his bedside, but the morphine was doing its work. It accumulated in Grant's brain and finally disabled the respiration and circulatory centers in the brain stem. At seven o'clock McQueeney, the nurse, ran for the doctor and for Tyrrell, who went up and hastily knocked on the bedroom doors. The family came downstairs. Julia had already come in to be with her husband. At 8:00 A.M. on July 23, 1885, Ulysses S. Grant died.[39]

There would be more crowds. Curious sightseers would come to Mount McGregor to look at the body, and a phalanx of generals, comrades and foes together, would ride up Fifth Avenue at his funeral. A decade later, some of these old soldiers would come back in the rain to dedicate Grant's Tomb, on a stretch above the Hudson River in New York City where he had probably never been. They said the weather was what kept the numbers down; still, some of his people did remember him, and they were there. But these were cheers that Grant would never hear. Now the silence was absolute.

# EPILOGUE

The old American note sounds in them, the sense of the "hard" life and
the plain speech.

— *Henry James on Grant's Letters*

JULIA GRANT lived for another seventeen years. She gave up the
house in New York, went back nearer the center of all she had loved as first
lady, and in 1895 bought a house at 2111 Massachusetts Avenue, in Washington. Nellie came to live with her, bringing her three teen-age children, so
there was not the whole of the loneliness that there might have been. Julia
wrote her *Memoirs*, obviously remembering Ulysses' and the money they
made. It is clear that she thought of selling them but was dissuaded, probably
by publishers troubled by both her sentimentality and her ruthless candor
about those who had not been sufficiently respectful of the general and of
her. People knew her manuscript existed, and were curious, but not until
1975 did it appear as a book.[1]

In 1902 Julia was seventy-six and comfortably rich, but her weight and inactivity caught up with her. On December 14, at 11:17 P.M., she died of a
heart disorder, aggravated by congested lungs. One of the headings in the
front-page obituary in the *New York Times* the next morning read, "A
WEALTHY WOMAN." She would have liked that, and she would have known
just how hard she had worked to deserve it. When her will was probated, the
assets came to $234,000 attributed by the *Times* in part to the subscriptions

raised for her husband, but primarily to the money that had come from his book. In addition, she had been receiving a five-thousand-dollar annual pension from the government. Nellie, unprovided for by the Sartorises, received the use of her quarter share of the estate. Julia's three sons were by then secure enough so that she could leave their shares in trust for their children's education. (One grandson, Buck's son Ulysses S. Grant, became a professor of geology and a productive scholar.) In a codicil to her will, Julia Grant left a piece of work given to her by the empress of Japan to the Metropolitan Museum of Art.[2]

Nellie and her daughter Rosemary were with Julia when she died; Buck and Jesse were at home in California, and Fred was on duty with the army in Texas. Jesse, who had always had his own sense of time, made it east only for the interment in New York. The other three children and several grandchildren were at the Metropolitan Methodist Church for the funeral. So was the president of the United States. Theodore Roosevelt came to honor Mrs. Ulysses S. Grant. Harrison Tyrrell, the man who had cared for her husband through his long, terrible illness, was old and ill himself—and disconsolate that he was unable to be present.[3]

Julia's family and her maid-secretary, Mary E. Coffey, took her body to New York. There, after another service, it was interred in the vast new mausoleum up on Riverside Drive in Morningside Heights. Grant's Tomb had been dedicated, and his body moved there after long temporary burial in Central Park, only in 1897. Fred had arranged a great parade of Union and Confederate veterans and martial younger soldiers riding in full splendor; President William McKinley and "the eminents" came at eleven for the ceremonies. It was to have been one last vast crowd for Ulysses, but the energy was not quite there: "The weather [raw and harsh] kept thousands away."[4]

When Julia was to be interred, electric lights were rigged in the tomb to illuminate the work of the men using a crane to hoist the immense bronze lid from the sarcophagus. When it was closed again, those two small simple people lay side by side in the vast, absurd, but somehow moving empty space of a tomb set on ground that had nothing to do with either of them. Once again they were in a house that was not quite their own. Legend had it that the idea of a single burial place had come to Ulysses when he was looking at the monuments to Ferdinand and Isabella in Spain.[5]

Fred, who lived until 1912, served as the executor of his mother's will and generally assumed the role of head of the family. There was at one time talk (nothing more) of pairing him with Robert Lincoln for an unbeatable Republican presidential slate, but his actual public career consisted of service under an appointment from President Benjamin Harrison as minister to Austria, and of a couple of years (1895–97) as commissioner of police in New York City. The quarrel between the Cubans and their Spanish governors that Ulysses Grant and John Rawlins once talked of settling still raged, and in 1898 Fred returned to the army for the Spanish-American War. That war

*The dedication of Grant's Tomb, 1897.* LIBRARY OF CONGRESS

did not, of course, bring his father's Santo Domingo under the sway of the
United States, but Fred did find himself in another part of the old Spanish
empire, the Philippines, and he and his fellow soldiers were active in the
repression of the people of those islands. Fred, now a major general, had
been back in the United States only briefly when his mother died. He and his
handsome and rich wife, Ida, had presided over their daughter's wedding to
Prince Michael Cantacuzene; their son, Ulysses S. Grant 3rd, married Elihu
Root's daughter, Edith. He too became a major general and, in turn, took
over his father's responsibilities as keeper of his grandfather's place in military history. His *Ulysses S. Grant: Warrior and Statesman* was published in
1969.

Buck recovered from the collapse of Grant & Ward with the help of the
Chaffee money. For a time he lived the life of a country gentleman in Mer-
ryweather, a stone and shingle house in Salem Center, New York, close to
the Connecticut border. He and Fannie had five children; when her health
deteriorated, they moved to San Diego. There Buck practiced law and invested $1,500,000 in the U. S. Grant Hotel. Although he aspired to the
Senate and was twice a delegate to Republican national conventions, the only
public office he held was that of assistant United States district attorney. His
wife, who had been an invalid, died in 1909. In 1913, he secretly married
America Workman Wills—they thus became U. S. and America Grant—and
later, he revealed that they were married and declared that she would inherit

two-thirds of his three million dollars. His children, unhappy at this sudden erosion of their own good fortune, did not attend the dinner at which the happy marriage was announced. But in time there were reconciliations, and the charming Buck, the most gregarious of the Grants, who died in 1929, is fondly remembered by his grandchildren.[6]

Nellie Grant had had enough of glamor back in 1874. After her divorce she had lived first with her mother; following her second marriage, to Frank Hatch Jones in 1912, she lived in Chicago. Smaller even than her mother and father, she had none of their resilience, and seemed somehow diminished by life. Her last long years were spent as an invalid in her house on Lake Shore Drive. She died in 1922. It was Nellie, not her brothers, who was built like and looked like Ulysses.[7]

When Jesse, the last surviving child, died in 1934, the *New York Times* described him as a "mining engineer" and a "wanderer." After scant schooling he went to Cornell, but left in 1877 to travel with his parents. Next, he had one unsuccessful year at Columbia Law School. He then roamed the United States and Mexico in search of investments like those which had so attracted and eluded his father. He was married to Elizabeth Chapman for more than three decades, and they had two children, but in 1914 he petitioned for divorce on the grounds of desertion. She objected, but in 1918 she did not contest a second petition. A week after the divorce, Jesse married Lillian Burns Wilkins. After she died of cancer in 1924 in Inwood-on-Hudson, Jesse went back to California, where he had long lived and at one time had managed Buck's hotel. In 1925 he published an affectionate reminiscence, *In the Days of My Father General Grant.*[8]

As if to prove that he was still the scamp who had ruffled Windsor Castle, Jesse became a Democrat. In 1908, at that bastion of the Democratic party the Manhattan Club, he announced that he was a candidate for the office of president of the United States. But he had to permit William Jennings Bryan the honor of being beaten by William Howard Taft, the son of his father's second-from-last secretary of war. Woodrow Wilson, born and brought up in the South, briefly thought of capturing the enemy, and Edward M. House lunched with Jesse Grant to discuss the possibility of his being named minister to China. According to House, Jesse claimed that "his father stood so high in China that his appointment would be particularly acceptable to them." House concurred (but Wilson did not make the appointment), and as they chatted he recollected that "Mrs. Phil Sheridan . . . thought Jesse more like his father than any of the Grant boys, and I take it this is true."[9]

The Grants' children all had children, and there are now a good many descendants of Ulysses and Julia. The general is still a great man in the family, but its members have had to live through a long decline in his reputation. Until Warren G. Harding's presidency, Grant was held to have misled the most corrupt administration in the nation's history. (Soiled though they were, neither Grant nor Harding would have even understood Richard

Nixon's unique contempt for democratic government.) Not only did Grant hold a low rank in ratings of the presidents, but even his military star dimmed in the twenties and thirties as the Civil War, in general, was valued less and the Lost Cause of the Confederacy, in particular, was celebrated more and more. In the shadow of the vanquished nobleman Robert E. Lee, "butcher Grant" did not appear as heroic as he once had. Fresh looks in the fifties and sixties at the plight of the descendants of the slaves freed in the Civil War brought Grant's stock partially back to value. Once more the Civil War was seen as part of a quest for freedom, and historians like Bruce Catton, writing enthusiastically about the war, celebrated Grant's role in it. In a somewhat contradictory way, Grant's record as a politician has also enjoyed rehabilitation. Conservative historians, dismissing the demise of Reconstruction as inevitable, and reassessing the Republican presidents between Abraham Lincoln and Theodore Roosevelt, have asked whether Grant's eight years, free of international war, were as bleak domestically as it has been common to assert. [10]

The present study will not sit well with either school of historians. Grant did not make war for reasons or in ways that ennoble the Civil War. He did not rise above limited talents or inspire others to do so in ways that make his administration a credit to American politics. If Ulysses Grant was, in any measure, "the concentration of all that is American" and we still believe in democracy, his story is troubling. In fact, it suggests that we must rethink both the worth of war and the uses we make of politics if we are to build a society in which a Ulysses Grant can be heard in a constructive way.

His voice is heard clearly in one realm. In 1962, Edmund Wilson in *Patriotic Gore* taught us to take Ulysses Grant seriously as a writer. All the present study has tried to do is to take him seriously as a man. Now, almost a century after he died, myths of glorification or denigration can be discarded. This is the generation of his grandchildren's grandchildren, and these Americans—who are not in all ways different from the person Grant was—deserve to know a man they would recognize if they met him in a crowd.

# Notes

*Chapter 1* CROWDS AND FAMILIES

1. *Newcastle Daily Chronicle*, Sept. 24, 1877.
2. Ibid.
3. Ibid.
4. Ulysses S. Grant, *Personal Memoirs of U. S. Grant*, 2 vols. (New York, 1885–86), 1:17.
5. Matthew Grant, Diary, Connecticut State Library, Hartford, Conn. In this quotation, the spelling stands as written. This practice is followed in the remainder of the book; in general, *sic* has been omitted.

   See also Roger Clap, *Memoirs of Captain Roger Clap* (Boston, 1731); Dorchester Town Records, Document 9-1880, in *Fourth Report of the Record Commissioners of the City of Boston*, 2d ed. (Boston, 1883), pp. 1, 6, 10, 12; T. M. Harris, "Chronological and Topographical Account of Dorchester," in *Collections of the Massachusetts Historical Society*, 10 (Boston, 1804):147–99, 154n.; Windsor Town Records, Connecticut State Library, typescript; Matthew Grant will, December 9, 1681, and inventory, January 10, 1681, Connecticut State Library.
6. Matthew Grant, Diary.
7. Edward Chauncey Marshall, *The Ancestry of General Grant, and Their Contemporaries* (New York, 1869); Hugh Montgomery-Massingberd, ed., *Burke's Presidential Families of the United States of America* (London, 1975), pp. 317–33.
8. *Connecticut Historical Society Collections*, vol. 9, *Rolls of Connecticut Men in the French and Indian War, 1755–1762* (Hartford, Conn., 1903), pp. 77–78, 121–23, 132; Action of the Connecti-

cut General Assembly, in "Colonial Wars," manuscript roll, Connecticut State Library, vol. 6, item 98. See also "Vital Records," Tolland, Conn.; "Colonial Wars," vol. 5, part 2, pp. 285, 328.

9.  USG, *Memoirs*, 1:18; Frank A. Burr, *A New, Original and Authentic Record of the Life and Deeds of General U. S. Grant* (Boston, 1885), p. 63.

    Noah could have left Coventry and gone to New Hampshire to enlist and thus be the same Noah who went to war, but records in Lyme suggest that their Private Grant was, indeed, another person, a farmer and logger who moved to Enosburg, Vermont. There is a Noah Grant "Detached until January 1779" in *Connecticut Historical Society Collections*, vol. 12, *Lists and Returns of Connecticut Men in the Revolution, 1775–1783* (Hartford, Conn., 1909), pp. 48, 132, but there is no record of this service in the Connecticut State Library or the National Archives—Dorothy W. Sears, Lyme Historians Inc., to the writer, April 27, 1975; Roll of the Militia Company in Lyme, 1776, Pay Roll, Receipt Roll, and Lists of Bedel's Regiment (1775–1776), National Archives, Washington, D.C.

10. Land Records, Town of Coventry, Town Clerk's Office, Coventry, Conn., vol. 8, p. 101. See also Land Grants, Town of Coventry, microfilm, Connecticut State Library; "Old Cemetery of North Coventry," Town Clerk's Office, Coventry, Conn., typescript; headstone, "Anna [Anne?] Richardson Grant," cemetery, Grant Hill. Had Ulysses Grant's grandfather been Captain Grant, the headstone most probably would have referred to her husband as "Captain" rather than "Mr." Grant.

11. *History of Portage County, Ohio* (Chicago, 1885), pp. 420–21. Noah Grant is said to have learned the leather business in John Brown's father's tannery.

12. USG, *Memoirs*, 1:20; County Records, Maysville, Kentucky.

13. *The History of Brown County, Ohio* (Chicago, 1883), p. 266; Henry Howe, *Historical Collections of Ohio*, 3 vols., with vols. 2 and 3 in one (Columbus, Ohio, 1889–91), 3:103.

14. Lloyd Lewis, *Captain Sam Grant* (Boston, 1950), pp. 27–28, 45, 48; clippings from the Georgetown, Ohio, *Castigator*, Cincinnati Historical Society.

15. Robert and Mary Belville to Samuel Simpson, Nov. 27, 1829, Cincinnati Historical Society; Mary Belville to Elizabeth Simpson, May 15, 1830, Cincinnati Historical Society; R. M. Griffith to Samuel Simpson, Jan. 30, 1830, Cincinnati Historical Society; USG to R. M. Griffith, Sept. 22, 1839, *The Papers of Ulysses S. Grant*, ed. John Y. Simon, 8 vols. to date (Carbondale, Ill., 1967–), 1:4–8.

16. *New York Times*, March 5, 1869.

17. Howe, *Historical Collections of Ohio*, 1:333.

18. USG to Jesse R. Grant, May 9, 1877, U. S. Grant Papers, Missouri Historical Society; *New York Times*, May 12, 1883.

19. USG, *Memoirs*, 1:26.

20. Ibid., p. 25. See also Lewis, *Captain Sam Grant*, p. 22.

21. USG, *Memoirs*, 1:29–30.

22. Ibid., pp. 27–29.

23. Ibid., p. 34.

## Chapter II   CADETSHIP AND COURTSHIP

1.  Ulysses S. Grant, *Personal Memoirs of U. S. Grant*, 2 vols. (New York, 1885–86), *1:* 37–38. See also *New York Times*, July 24, 1885.

2.  USG to R. M. Griffith, Sept. 22, 1839, *The Papers of Ulysses S. Grant*, ed. John Y. Simon, 8 vols. to date (Carbondale, Ill., 1967–), 1:4–8, 4n.; entry dated May 29, 1839, in "Descriptive Book of Candidates," manuscript, United States Military Academy (USMA) Library. Grant himself never used more than "S."; others converted the single letter to "Simpson."

3.  USG, *Memoirs*, 1:39; James Longstreet, interview in *St. Louis Globe Democrat*, July 24, 1885; USG, *Memoirs*, 1:38.

4. USG, *Memoirs*, 1:39; Stephen E. Ambrose, *Duty, Honor, Country: A History of West Point* (Baltimore, 1966), pp. 100–102.

5. USG to R. M. Griffith, Sept. 22, 1839, *Papers*, 1:4–8. See also James Lunsford Morrison, "The United States Military Academy, 1833–1866: Years of Progress and Turmoil" (Ph.D. diss., Columbia University, 1971), university microfilm 71-6230; USG, *Memoirs*, 1:39–40.

6. USG, *Memoirs*, 1:38. For a critique of West Point as an educational institution see Joseph Ellis and Robert Moore, *School for Soldiers: West Point and the Profession of Arms* (New York, 1974), pp. 12–13.

7. USG to R. M. Griffith, Sept. 22, 1839, *Papers*, 1:4–8; USG to Charles W. Ford, May 3, 1871, U. S. Grant Papers, Library of Congress. See also E. B. Strong to C. F. Smith, July 13, 1840, USMA Library; USG to C. F. Smith, undated, USMA Library; C. F. Smith to G. G. Waggam, July 16, 1840, USMA Library; J. G. Taylor to [the Superintendent], July 29, 1840, USMA Library; USG, *Memoirs*, 1:37–39.

8. USG, *Memoirs*, 1:39. See also USG to Carey & Hart, Mar. 31 and Apr. 8, 1843, *Papers*, 1:11.

9. Julia D. Grant, *Personal Memoirs of Julia Dent Grant*, ed. John Y. Simon (New York, 1975), p. 325. Legends have both Charles W. Eliot of Harvard and the younger Benjamin Silliman of Yale as the "old gentleman" of the evening. The story fits neither well; Julia Grant's nameless bore was probably someone else.

10. USG to R. M. Griffith, Sept. 22, 1839, *Papers*, 1:4–8.

11. Eight pieces of Grant's work are reproduced in *Papers*, 1:13–19.

12. USG, *Memoirs*, 1:40.

13. Ibid., p. 41.

14. Ibid., p. 44.

15. Julia D. Grant, *Memoirs*, pp. 35–36.

16. Ibid., pp. 39, 34.

17. Ibid., p. 43.

18. Ibid., pp. 43, 41, 42.

19. Julia Grant Cantacuzene, *My Life Here and There* (New York, 1921), p. 165; Julia D. Grant, *Memoirs*, p. 35.

20. Julia D. Grant, *Memoirs*, pp. 36, 46–47.

21. Ibid., pp. 46, 48; USG, *Memoirs*, 1:46–47.

22. Julia D. Grant, *Memoirs*, p. 49.

23. Ibid.

24. USG, *Memoirs*, 1:49–50.

25. Julia D. Grant, *Memoirs*, p. 50.

26. Jane Grant de MaCarty, in conversation with the writer, Aug. 16, 1974.

27. Ibid.

28. USG to Julia Dent, June 4, 1844, *Papers*, 1:23–27.

29. USG to Julia Dent, Jan. 12, 1845, ibid., p. 40.

30. USG to Julia Dent, July 11, 1845, ibid., pp. 50–51.

## *Chapter III* THE MEXICAN WAR

1. Ulysses S. Grant, *Personal Memoirs of U. S. Grant*, 2 vols. (New York, 1885–86), 1:170.

2. Russell F. Weigley, *The American Way of War: A History of United States Military Strategy and Policy* (New York, 1973).

3. James Longstreet interview with Hamlin Garland, ca. 1890, typescript, Doheny Library, University of Southern California. See also Frederick Merk, with Lois B. Merk, *Slavery and the Annexation of Texas* (New York, 1972); Karl Jack Bauer, *The Mexican War, 1846–1848* (*New York, 1974), pp. 32–43*, photograph following p. 202; USG, *Memoirs*, 1:61–83; *The*

*Papers of Ulysses S. Grant*, ed. John Y. Simon, 8 vols. to date (Carbondale, Ill., 1967–), 1:53–76.
4. USG, *Memoirs*, 1:75–76.
5. Ibid., p. 68.
6. Ibid., p. 53.
7. Ibid., p. 56.
8. USG to Julia Dent, May 3, 1846, *Papers*, 1:83–84.
9. USG, *Memoirs*, 1:92, 94–95.
10. USG to Julia Dent, May 11, 1846, Papers, 1:84–87; Albert D. Richardson, *A Personal History of Ulysses S. Grant* (Hartford, Conn., 1902), p. 86; USG, *Memoirs*, 1:96.
11. USG, *Memoirs*, 1:98.
12. USG to Julia Dent, May 11, 1846, *Papers*, 1:87–89.
13. USG, *Memoirs*, 1:106.
14. Ibid., pp. 110–11, 111–12.
15. Bauer, *Mexican War*, pp. 85–102; USG, *Memoirs*, 1:112–17.
16. USG, *Memoirs*, 1:117. See also Bauer, *Mexican War*, pp. 99–101.
17. USG to Julia Dent, Oct. 3 and Oct. 20, 1846, *Papers*, 1:112–13, 114–16.
18. USG to Julia Dent, Oct. 3 and Nov. 7, 1846, ibid., pp. 112–13, 116–18.
19. USG to John W. Lowe, May 3, 1847, ibid., pp. 135–37. See also USG to Julia Dent, Dec. 27, 1846, ibid., pp. 118–20.
20. USG, *Memoirs*, 1:123.
21. Weigley, *American Way of War*, pp. 70–76.
22. USG, *Memoirs*, 1:119, 118.
23. Bauer, *Mexican War*, p. 272.
24. USG, *Memoirs*, 1:132, 133. See also Weigley, *American Way of War*, p. 75.
25. USG, *Memoirs*, 1:157–59, 172.
26. USG to John W. Lowe, June 26, 1846, *Papers*, 1:94–98; USG to Julia Dent, Oct. 3, 1846, ibid., pp. 112–13.
27. USG, *Memoirs*, 1:92–93.
28. Ibid., pp. 138, 139, 123, 136–37, 139.
29. Ibid., pp. 180–84; Simon Bolivar Buckner, "A Visit to Popocatepetl," *Putnam's Weekly Magazine* 1 (Apr. 1853):408–16.
30. USG, *Memoirs*, 1:183–84.
31. Ibid., p. 184.
32. USG to Julia Dent, Mar. 22, 1848, Papers, 153–54. See also Howard T. Fisher and Marion Hall Fisher, eds., *Life in Mexico: The Letters of Fanny Calderón de la Barca* (New York, 1966).
33. USG to Julia Dent, Jan. 9, 1848, *Papers*, 1:148–50.
34. Simon Bolivar Buckner interview with Hamlin Garland, ca. 1890, typescript, Doheny Library, University of Southern California. See also *Papers*, 1:xxxiii.

Chapter *IV*   A  SOLDIER  BETWEEN  WARS

1. USG to Julia Dent, Aug. 7, 1848, *The Papers of Ulysses S. Grant*, ed. John Y. Simon, 8 vols. to date (Carbondale, Ill., 1967–), 1:163–64.
2. Julia D. Grant, *Personal Memoirs of Julia Dent Grant*, ed. John Y. Simon (New York, 1975), p. 56.
3. Ibid., p. 57. The grandmother, of whom Grant, too, was fond, was technically his stepgrandmother. Sarah Hale Simpson was not Hannah's mother, but John Simpson's second wife.—Ibid., p. 64n.
4. Ibid., p. 58.
5. Ibid.
6. Ibid.

7. Ibid., pp. 59–61; USG to O. F. Winship, Feb. 23, 1849, *Papers*, 1:175–77.
8. Julia D. Grant, *Memoirs*, pp. 59–60.
9. Ibid., pp. 60–61.
10. USG to Julia D. Grant, Aug. 3, 1851, *Papers*, 1:222–24. See also Julia D. Grant, *Memoirs*, pp. 65–66.
11. Julia D. Grant, *Memoirs*, pp. 65–66.
12. USG to Julia D. Grant, June 22, 1851, *Papers*, 1:211–12.
13. USG to Julia D. Grant, Aug. 3 and Aug. 10, 1851, ibid., pp. 222–24, 224–25. See also Julia D. Grant, *Memoirs*, pp. 69–70.
14. USG to Julia D. Grant, Aug. 3, 1851, *Papers*, 1:222–24; Julia D. Grant, *Memoirs*, p. 69; USG to Julia D. Grant, Aug. 3, 1851, *Papers*, 1:222–24.
15. Julia D. Grant, *Memoirs*, p. 71.
16. USG to Julia D. Grant, July 1, 1852, *Papers*, 1:242–44. See also USG sworn statement, June 27, 1848, ibid., pp. 162n.–163n.; USG to Julia D. Grant, June 20 and June 28, 1852, ibid., pp. 235–36, 239–41.
17. USG to Julia D. Grant, July 4, 1852, ibid., pp. 245–46.
18. Delia B. Sheffield, "Reminiscences of Delia B. Sheffield," *Washington Historical Quarterly* 15 (Jan. 1924):49–62.
19. Sheffield, "Reminiscences," pp. 52–53. Contract between Jose M. Saravia and USG, July 21, 1852, *Papers*, 1:249–50, 250n. See also Ulysses S. Grant, *Personal Memoirs of U. S. Grant*, 2 vols. (New York, 1885–86), 1:195–98; James Elderkin interview with Hamlin Garland, ca. 1890, typescript, Doheny Library, University of Southern California.
20. Sheffield, "Reminiscences," pp. 52–55.
21. USG to Julia D. Grant, Aug. 16 and Aug. 20, 1852, *Papers*, 1:254–56, 256–58; Julia D. Grant, *Memoirs*, p. 72.
22. USG to Julia D. Grant, Aug. 30, 1852, and June 28, 1853, *Papers*, 1:258–60, 303–5; Sheffield, "Reminiscences," pp. 59–61; John W. Emerson, "Grant's Life in the West and His Mississippi Campaigns," *Midland Monthly*, July 1897, pp. 3–9; Ripley's "Believe It or Not," 1974.
23. Emerson, "Grant's Life in the West," *Midland Monthly*, Aug. 1897, pp. 138–43.
24. USG to Julia D. Grant, July 15, 1852, *Papers*, 1:247–49.
25. Julia D. Grant, *Memoirs*, pp. 72–75.
26. Ibid., p. 75; USG to Julia D. Grant, Sept. 19, 1852, *Papers*, 1:265–67.
27. USG to Julia D. Grant, Dec. 3, 1852, Jan. 3 and Mar. 31, 1853, *Papers*, 1:274–76, 279–81, 296–98.
28. USG to Julia D. Grant, June 28 and July 13, 1853, ibid., pp. 303–5, 305–7. See also USG to Julia D. Grant, June 15, 1853, ibid., pp. 301–2.
29. USG to Julia D. Grant, Jan. 3, 1853, ibid., pp. 279–81.
30. USG, letter of recommendation for Margaret Getz, July 19, 1853, ibid., p. 308.
31. USG to Julia D. Grant, Feb. 2, 1853 [1854], ibid., pp. 316–18.
32. USG to Julia D. Grant, Feb. 6 and Mar. 6, 1854, ibid., pp. 320–22, 322–24. "Quit and" is a guess at two words deleted at his descendants' request.
33. USG to Julia D. Grant, Aug. 20, 1852, and Mar. 6, 1854, ibid., pp. 256–58, 322–24.
34. USG to Julia D. Grant, Mar. 6, 1854, ibid., pp. 322–24. See also Ulysses S. Grant 3rd, *Ulysses S. Grant, Warrior and Statesman* (New York, 1969), p. 95.
35. USG, *Memoirs*, 1:209, 210; Julia D. Grant, *Memoirs*, p. 75; USG to Julia D. Grant, Mar. 6, 1854, *Papers*, 1:322–24. See also Bruce Catton's introduction to Julia D. Grant, *Memoirs*, p. 3.
36. Ulysses S. Grant 3rd, *Ulysses S. Grant*, p. 98; Hamlin Garland's transcriptions of his interviews are in the Doheny Library, University of Southern California.
37. *Papers*, 1:328n.; USG to Samuel Cooper, Apr. 11, 1854 (twice), *Papers*, 1:328–29; James Elderkin interview with Hamlin Garland, ca. 1890, typescript, University of Southern California.

38. Andrew Ellison to Jefferson Davis, June 5, 1854, *Papers*, 1:330n.–331n.
39. Jefferson Davis to Jesse R. Grant, June 28, 1854, ibid. See also Davis to Andrew Ellison, June 7, 1854, ibid.; Jesse R. Grant to Davis, June 21, 1854, ibid.
40. Simon Bolivar Buckner interview with Hamlin Garland, typescript, ca. 1890, University of Southern California.
41. Julia D. Grant, *Memoirs*, p. 72; USG to Julia D. Grant, May 2, 1854, *Papers*, 1:332.

### Chapter V  GALENA

1. Julia D. Grant, *Personal Memoirs of Julia Dent Grant*, ed. John Y. Simon (New York, 1975), p. 76.
2. Ibid., p. 78. See also *The Papers of Ulysses S. Grant*, ed. John Y. Simon, 8 vols. to date (Carbondale, Ill., 1967–), 1:335n.
3. Julia D. Grant, *Memoirs*, pp. 78–79. See also Ulysses S. Grant, *Personal Memoirs of U. S. Grant*, 2 vols. (New York, 1885–86), 1:211.
4. USG to Jesse R. Grant, Dec. 28, 1856, *Papers*, 1:334–35; Julia D. Grant, *Memoirs*, p. 78.
5. USG to Jesse R. Grant, Dec. 28, 1856, and Feb. 7, 1857, *Papers*, 1:334–35, 336–37.
6. USG to Jesse R. Grant, Dec. 28, 1856, ibid., pp. 334–35. See also USG, *Memoirs*, 1:211; John W. Emerson, "Grant's Life in the West and His Mississippi Campaigns," *Midland Monthly*, Sept. 1897, p. 217.
7. USG to Jesse R. Grant, Feb. 7, 1857, *Papers*, 1:336–37, 337n.; USG to Mary Grant, Aug. 22, 1857, ibid., pp. 338–39. See also pawn ticket, Dec. 23, 1857, ibid., p. 339.
8. Julia D. Grant, *Memoirs*, p. 83; Emerson, "Grant's Life in the West," p. 213. See also USG to Jesse R. Grant, Oct. 1, 1858, *Papers*, 1:344; manumission order signed by USG, ibid., p. 347.
9. Emerson, "Grant's Life in the West," p. 214; Julia D. Grant, *Memoirs*, p. 85.
10. USG to Mary Grant, Mar. 21, 1858, *Papers*, 1:340–41.
11. USG to Mary Grant, Feb. 7, 1857, and Sept. 7, 1858, ibid., pp. 336–37, 343. See also USG to Jesse R. Grant, Mar. 12, 1859, ibid., pp. 345–46.
12. USG to Board of County Commissioners, Aug. 15, 1859, ibid., p. 348; USG to Jesse R. Grant, Aug. 20 and Sept. 23, 1859, ibid., pp. 350–51.
13. Julia D. Grant, *Memoirs*, p. 82. See also USG to Jesse R. Grant, Dec. 23, 1859, *Papers*, 1:352, 352n.
14. Julia D. Grant, *Memoirs*, p. 82; USG to Julia D. Grant, Mar. 14, 1860, *Papers*, 1:355–56.
15. USG to Julia D. Grant, Mar. 14, 1860, *Papers*, 1:355–56.
16. Hamlin Garland, *Ulysses S. Grant: His Life and Character* (New York, 1898), p. 148.
17. USG to Charles W. Ford, Dec. 10, 1860, U. S. Grant Papers, Library of Congress; Emerson, "Grant's Life in the West," *Midland Monthly*, Oct. 1897, pp. 316–25.
18. Lloyd Lewis, *Captain Sam Grant* (Boston, 1950), p. 376.

### Chapter VI  ESCAPING FROM THE ORDINARY

1. John W. Emerson, "Grant's Life in the West and His Mississippi Campaigns," *Midland Monthly*, Sept. 1897, p. 219, and Oct. 1897, p. 323.
2. Manumission order signed by USG, *The Papers of Ulysses S. Grant*, ed. John Y. Simon, 8 vols. to date (Carbondale, Ill., 1967–), 1:347.
3. USG to Jesse R. Grant, Sept. 23, 1859, ibid., pp. 351–52.
4. Albert D. Richardson, *A Personal History of Ulysses S. Grant* (Hartford, Conn., 1902), p. 167. See also Ulysses S. Grant, *Personal Memoirs of Ulysses S. Grant*, 2 vols. (New York, 1885–86), 1:215.
5. USG to Charles W. Ford, Dec. 10, 1860, U. S. Grant Papers, Library of Congress.

6. Ibid.
7. USG to Frederick Dent, Apr. 19, 1861, *Papers*, 2:3–4.
8. USG to Julia D. Grant, May 1, 1861, ibid., pp. 15–16; USG to Jesse R. Grant, May 6, 1861, ibid., pp. 20–22.
9. USG to Julia D. Grant, May 6, 1861, ibid., pp. 23–24.
10. Augustus Louis Chetlain, *Recollections of Seventy Years* (Galena, Ill., 1899), pp. 69–71.
11. Ibid., p. 70; "How Grant Got to Know Rawlins," *Army and Navy Journal*, Sept. 12, 1868, p. 53; USG, *Memoirs*, 1:231.
12. Augustus Louis Chetlain interview with Hamlin Garland, ca. 1890, typescript, Doheny Library, University of Southern California; USG to Jesse R. Grant, May 6, 1861, *Papers*, 2:20–22.
13. Chetlain interview with Garland.
14. Ibid.
15. USG to Jesse R. Grant, May 6, 1861, *Papers*, 2:20–22. See also USG to Lorenzo Thomas, May 24, 1861, ibid., pp. 35–36.
16. Chetlain interview with Garland; USG to Jesse R. Grant, May 30, 1861, *Papers*, 2:37.
17. USG to Julia D. Grant, June 17, 1861, *Papers*, 2:42–43, 43n.

### Chapter VII  W A R R I O R S

1. Adam Badeau, quoted in Russell F. Weigley, *The American Way of War: A History of United States Military Strategy and Policy* (New York, 1973), p. 150. See also "A Strategy of Annihilation: U. S. Grant and the Union," ch. 7 in Weigley, *American Way of War*.
2. William T. Sherman to O. O. Howard, May 17, 1865, Howard Papers, Bowdoin College Library.
3. USG to Julia D. Grant, Aug. 3, 1861, *The Papers of Ulysses S. Grant*, ed. John Y. Simon, 8 vols. to date (Carbondale, Ill., 1967–), 2:82–83.
4. USG to Julia D. Grant, June 26, 1861, ibid., pp. 49–51.
5. Lloyd Lewis, *Captain Sam Grant* (Boston, 1950), p. 430.
6. USG to Julia D. Grant, June 27, 1861, *Papers*, 2:52–53. See also USG to Julia D. Grant, June 26, 1861, ibid., pp. 49–51.
7. Philip Welshimer to his wife, June 25, 1861, ibid., p. 47n.; USG to Jesse R. Grant, July 13, 1861, ibid., pp. 66–67.
8. USG to Jesse R. Grant, July 13, 1861, ibid., pp. 66–67.
9. Julia D. Grant, *Personal Memoirs of Julia Dent Grant*, ed. John Y. Simon (New York, 1975), p. 92.
10. Ibid.; USG to Julia D. Grant, July 13, 1861, *Papers*, 2:69–70.
11. Julia D. Grant, *Memoirs*, p. 92; USG to Julia D. Grant, July 13 and July 19, 1861, *Papers*, 2:69–70, 72–73.
12. USG to Julia D. Grant, July 7, 1861, *Papers*, 2:59–60.
13. USG to Julia D. Grant, May 15, 1861, ibid., pp. 30–32. See also Kenneth P. Williams, *Lincoln Finds a General: A Military Study of the Civil War*, 5 vols. (New York, 1949–59), 3:16–17; USG to Mary Grant, Apr. 29, 1861, *Papers*, 2:13–15; *Papers*, 2:29n.
14. Ulysses S. Grant, *Personal Memoirs of U. S. Grant*, 2 vols. (New York, 1885–86), 1:249–50. See also Williams, *Lincoln Finds a General*, 3:42–43.
15. USG to Jesse R. Grant, Aug. 3, 1861, *Papers*, 2:80–81. See also John Y. Simon, "From Galena to Appomattox: Grant and Washburne," *Journal of the Illinois State Historical Society* 58 (Summer 1965):165–89.
16. USG to Jesse R. Grant, Aug. 3, 1861, *Papers*, 2:80–81.
17. USG to Julia D. Grant, Aug. 10, 1861, ibid., pp. 96–97; USG to Elihu B. Washburne, Sept. 3, 1861, ibid., pp. 182–83.
18. USG to Julia D. Grant, Aug. 10, 1861, ibid., pp. 96–97.

19. USG to Jesse R. Grant, Aug. 3, 1861, ibid., pp. 80–81; USG to Julia D. Grant, Aug. 26 and Aug. 4, 1861, ibid., pp. 140–41, 84–85.
20. James Harrison Wilson, *Life of John A. Rawlins* (New York, 1916), p. 31.
21. "How Grant Got to Know Rawlins," *Army and Navy Journal*, Sept. 12, 1868, p. 53.
22. Jacob Dolson Cox, "How Judge Hoar Ceased to Be Attorney-General," *Atlantic Monthly* 76 (Aug. 1895):164.
23. Albert D. Richardson, *A Personal History of Ulysses S. Grant* (Hartford, Conn., 1902), p. 155; *Papers*, 2:142n.
24. Theodore Lyman, *Meade's Headquarters, 1863–1865: Letters of Colonel Theodore Lyman from the Wilderness to Appomattox*, sel. and ed. George R. Agassiz (Boston, 1922), p. 81. See also Horace Porter, *Campaigning with Grant* (New York, 1897), p. 33; *Papers*, 6:294–96; Bruce Catton, *Grant Moves South* (Boston, 1960), p. 209.
25. Williams, *Lincoln Finds a General*, 3:37–42, 25.
26. USG to Julia D. Grant, Sept. 3, 1861, *Papers*, 2:180–81. See also Julia D. Grant, *Memoirs*, p. 93.
27. Frontispiece, *Papers*, 2.

## *Chapter VIII*  BATTLES

1. USG to Speaker of the Kentucky House of Representatives, Sept. 5, 1861, *The Papers of Ulysses S. Grant*, ed. John Y. Simon, 8 vols. to date (Carbondale, Ill., 1967–), 2:189.
2. USG, "Proclamation to the Citizens of Paducah," ibid., pp. 194–95. See also James Marshall-Cornwall, *Grant as Military Commander* (London, 1970), pp. 38–39; R. M. Kelly, "Holding Kentucky for the Union," in *Battles and Leaders of the Civil War*, ed. R. U. Johnson and C. C. Buel, 4 vols. (New York, 1887–88), 1:373–92.
3. E. B. Long, with Barbara Long, *The Civil War Day by Day: An Almanac, 1861–1865* (New York, 1971), pp. 135–36; Willie Lee Rose, *Rehearsal for Reconstruction: The Port Royal Experiment* (Indianapolis, 1964); Kenneth P. Williams, *Lincoln Finds a General: A Military Study of the Civil War*, 5 vols. (New York, 1949–59), 3:75–100; Marshall-Cornwall, *Grant*, pp. 40–44.
4. Chauncey McKeever to USG, Nov. 1, 1861, in United States War Department, *The War of the Rebellion: A Compilation of the Official Records of the Union and Confederate Armies* (Washington, D.C., 1880–1901), ser. 1, vol. 3, p. 267 (hereafter cited as *Official Records of the Rebellion* or *OR*). Ulysses S. Grant, *Personal Memoirs of U. S. Grant*, 2 vols. (New York, 1885–86), p. 271; USG to R. J. Oglesby, Nov. 6, 1861, *Papers*, 3:123.
5. USG, *Memoirs*, 1:278–79. See also Shelby Foote, *The Civil War: A Narrative*, 3 vols. (New York, 1958–74), 1:149–52; USG, report of Nov. 17, 1861, *OR*, ser. 1, vol. 3, pp. 267–72.
6. Leonidas Polk to Jefferson Davis, Nov. 8, 1861, *OR*, ser. 1, vol. 3, p. 304.
7. USG, report of Nov. 17, 1861, OR, ser. 1, vol. 3, pp. 267–72.
8. Grant, *Memoirs*, 1:281.
9. USG to Julia D. Grant, Oct. 6, 1861, *Papers*, 3:23.
10. USG, testimony before the House Select Committee on Government Contracts, ibid., pp. 90–98; Elihu B. Washburne to Salmon P. Chase, Oct. 31, 1861, ibid., p. 98n.
11. USG to Elihu B. Washburne, Nov. 20, 1861, ibid., pp. 204–7; Washburne to Abraham Lincoln, Nov. 23, 1861, ibid., p. 207n.
12. USG to Jesse R. Grant, Nov. 27, 1861, ibid., pp. 226–28.
13. USG to Mary Grant, Jan. 23, 1862, ibid., 4:96–97; *Papers*, 4:100n. See also USG to J. D. Kelton, Jan. 6, 1862, ibid., 3:375–76; USG, *Memoirs*, 1:287.
14. Samuel F. DuPont to Sophie DuPont, Apr. 29, 1862, in Samuel F. DuPont, *A Selection of His Civil War Letters*, ed. John D. Hayes, 3 vols. (Ithaca, N.Y., 1969), 2:20–22; U. S. Grant, *Memoirs*, 1:286–87.
15. USG, *Memoirs*, 1:287; Andrew Hull Foote to Henry W. Halleck, Jan. 28, 1862, *Papers*,

4:99n.; USG to Halleck, Jan. 28, 1862, ibid., p. 99; Henry W. Halleck to USG, Jan. 30, 1862, ibid., p. 104n.

16. Marshall-Cornwall, *Grant*, p. 56. See also maps of Henry and Donelson campaign in United States Military Academy, West Point, *The West Point Atlas of American Wars*, ed. Vincent J. Esposito, 2 vols. (New York, 1959), vol. 1, maps 25–30; Lew Wallace, *Lew Wallace: An Autobiography*, 2 vols. (New York, 1906), 1:365–81; W. H. L. Wallace to Ann Dickey Wallace, Feb. 7, 1862, Wallace-Dickey Family Papers, Illinois State Historical Society (ISHS).

17. George B. McClellan to Henry W. Halleck, Feb. 7, 1862, in Marshall-Cornwall, *Grant*, p. 56; USG to Mary Grant, Feb. 9, 1862, *Papers*, 4:179–80.

18. Wallace, *Autobiography*, 1:376.

19. Ibid., p. 377.

20. Ibid., p. 378. See also W. H. L. Wallace to Ann Dickey Wallace, Feb. 11, 1862, Wallace-Dickey Family Papers.

21. Foote, *Civil War*, 1:201–4.

22. USG, *Memoirs*, 1:307; Wallace, *Autobiography*, 1:411–12.

23. Wallace, *Autobiography*, 1:421, 413, 421.

24. USG, *Memoirs*, 1:307–8.

25. *West Point Atlas*, vol. 1, map 29; USG, *Memoirs*, 1:308–10.

26. USG, *Memoirs*, 1:310–15.

27. Hamlin Garland, *Grant: His Life and Character* (New York, 1898), p. 192. (There is a slightly different version in Garland's transcriptions of his interviews in the Doheny Library, University of Southern California.) See also USG, *Memoirs*, 1:312–13; Wallace, *Autobiography*, 1:427–32. The naval officer claimed he was suspended from active duty for two years for failing to take the prize for the Navy.

28. USG to Julia D. Grant, Feb. 16, 1862, *Papers*, 4:229–30; Charles A. Dana, *Recollections of the Civil War* (New York, 1899), pp. 10–14.

29. Wallace, *Autobiography*, 1:412.

30. USG to George W. Cullum, Feb. 28, 1862, *Papers*, 4:286–87.

31. Ibid.

32. Abraham Lincoln to Henry W. Halleck, Feb. 16, 1862, in *Collected Works of Abraham Lincoln*, ed. Roy P. Basler, 9 vols. (New Brunswick, N.J., 1953–55), 5:135.

33. Henry W. Halleck to George B. McClellan, Feb. 17, 1862, *OR*, ser. 1, vol. 7, p. 628. See also Bruce Catton, *Grant Moves South* (Boston, 1960), p. 188.

34. USG to Julia D. Grant, Mar. 1, 1862, *Papers*, 4:305–6.

35. Henry W. Halleck to George B. McClellan, Mar. 3, 1862, *OR*, ser. 1, vol. 7, pp. 679–80; McClellan to Halleck, Mar. 3, 1862, ibid.; Halleck to McClellan, Mar. 4, 1862, *Papers*, 4:320n.; Halleck to USG, Mar. 4, 1862, ibid., p. 319n. See also Catton, *Grant Moves South*, p. 197.

36. USG to Julia D. Grant, Feb. 22, 1862, *Papers*, 4:271–73.

37. USG to Flag Officer Andrew Hull Foote, Mar. 3, 1862, ibid., pp. 313–14; USG to Henry W. Halleck, Mar. 5, 1862, ibid., pp. 317–19.

38. USG to Julia D. Grant, Mar. 5, 1862, ibid., pp. 326–27.

39. USG to Charles F. Smith, Mar. 5, 1862 (thrice), ibid., pp. 321–24; USG to Julia D. Grant, Mar. 5, 1862, ibid., pp. 326–27; USG to Henry W. Halleck, Mar. 6, 1862, ibid., pp. 322n.–323n.

40. Henry W. Halleck to USG, Mar. 6, 1862, ibid., p. 331n.

41. USG to Henry W. Halleck, Mar. 7, 1862, ibid., p. 331. See also Andrew Hull Foote to Gideon Welles, Mar. 6, 1862, ibid., pp. 331n., 328n.–329n.; Benjamin P. Thomas and Harold M. Hyman, *Stanton: The Life and Times of Lincoln's Secretary of War* (New York, 1962), pp. 172–79; USG to Elihu B. Washburne, Mar. 22, 1862, Grant Papers, ISHS.

42. USG to John A. McClernand, Mar. 9, 1862, *Papers*, 4:338; McClernand et al. to USG, Mar. 9, 1862, ibid., p. 338n.; C. C. Marsh address to USG, Mar. 10, 1862, ibid., p. 376n.

43. Henry W. Halleck to USG, Mar. 6, 1862, ibid., pp. 353n.–354n.

44. Foote, *Civil War*, 1:318.
45. USG to Henry W. Halleck, Mar. 13, 1862, *Papers*, 4:353; Halleck to USG, Mar. 13, 1862, ibid., pp. 354n.–355n. See also USG to Halleck, Mar. 7 and Mar. 9, 1862, ibid., pp. 331, 334.
46. USG to Julia D. Grant, Feb. 22 and Feb. 24, 1862, ibid., pp. 271, 284.

## *Chapter IX* SHILOH

1. Henry W. Halleck to USG, Mar. 13, 1862, *The Papers of Ulysses S. Grant*, ed. John Y. Simon, 8 vols. to date (Carbondale, Ill., 1967–), 4:353n.–355n.
2. Albert Sidney Johnston to Soldiers of the Army of the Mississippi, quoted in Shelby Foote, *The Civil War: A Narrative*, 3 vols. (New York, 1958–74), 1:327.
3. USG to Henry W. Halleck, Apr. 5, 1862, *Official Records of the Rebellion (OR)*, ser. 1., vol. 10, pt. 1, p. 89.
4. Foote, *Civil War*, 1:319–51.
5. John A. Rawlins to USG, Apr. 1, 1863, *OR*, ser. 1, vol. 10, pt. 1, pp. 183–88; Lew Wallace to Edwin M. Stanton, July 18, 1863, ibid., pp. 188–89.
6. Ulysses S. Grant, *Personal Memoirs of U. S. Grant*, 2 vols. (New York, 1885–86), 1:344–45.
7. Ibid., p. 349; USG to N. H. McLean, Apr. 9, 1862, *OR*, ser. 1, vol. 10, pt. 1, pp. 108–11; Foote, *Civil War*, 1:346.
8. Howard C. Westwood to the writer, July 17, 1978; USG to Don Carlos Buell, Apr. 7, 1862, *Papers*, 5:20–21; Foote, *Civil War*, 1:327. See also Foote, *Civil War*, 1:350–51; USG, *Memoirs*, 1:368–69.
9. USG to N. H. McLean, Apr. 9, 1862, *OR*, ser. 1, vol. 10, pt. 1, pp. 108–11; USG to Don Carlos Buell, Apr. 7, 1862, *Papers*, 5:20–21; Lew Wallace, *Lew Wallace: An Autobiography*, 2 vols. (New York, 1906), 2:570; Oliver Wendell Holmes, Jr., *Touched with Fire: Civil War Letters and Diary of Oliver Wendell Holmes, Jr., 1861–1864*, ed. Mark DeWolfe Howe (New York, 1969), p. 45.
10. John A. McClernand to Abraham Lincoln, *OR*, ser. 1, vol. 10, pt. 1, pp. 113–14; Edwin M. Stanton to Henry W. Halleck, Apr. 23, 1862, *Papers*, 5:50n.–51n.; Wallace, *Autobiography*, 2:575–76; USG, *Memoirs*, 1:370.
11. USG, *Memoirs*, 1:374, 376; Wallace, *Autobiography*, 2:577. See also Don Carlos Buell to Adjutant General, United States Army, Aug. 1, 1862, *OR*, ser. 1, vol. 10, pt. 1, pp. 672–77.
12. USG, *Memoirs*, 1:376; Wallace, *Autobiography*, 2:581. Quaker guns are logs that from a distance look like cannon.
13. Henry W. Halleck to Edwin M. Stanton, June 4, 1862, *OR*, ser. 1, vol. 10, pt. 1, p. 669; USG, *Memoirs*, 1:382.
14. William Tecumseh Sherman, *Memoirs of General William T. Sherman*, 2 vols. (New York, 1875), 1:174.
15. O. O. Howard, "Grant at Chattanooga," in Military Order of the Loyal Legion of the United States, New York Commandry, *Personal Recollections of the War of the Rebellion*, 1st series (New York, 1891), p. 248.
16. Sherman, *Memoirs*, 1:255.
17. USG, *Memoirs*, 1:385; William T. Sherman to USG, June 6, 1862, Sherman, *Memoirs*, 1:256; USG to Elihu B. Washburne, July 22, 1862, *Papers*, 5:225–26.
18. USG to Elihu B. Washburne, June 19, 1862, *Papers*, 5:145–46, USG, *Memoirs*, 1:396.
19. Charles A. Dana, *Recollections of the Civil War* (New York, 1899), p. 15.
20. USG, *Memoirs*, 1:368, 397–98.

Chapter X  VICKSBURG

1. Charles S. Hamilton to USG, Nov. 9, 1862, *The Papers of Ulysses S. Grant*, ed. John Y. Simon, 8 vols. to date (Carbondale, Ill., 1967–), 6:286n.
2. USG to Stephen A. Hurlbut, Nov. 9, 1862, *Papers*, 6:283.
3. James Harrison Wilson interview with Hamlin Garland, ca. 1890, typescript, Doheny Library, University of Southern California.
4. USG to Joseph D. Webster, Nov. 10, 1862, *Papers*, 6:283n.; Charles A. Dana, *Recollections of the Civil War* (New York, 1899), p. 18; USG to William T. Sherman, Dec. 5, 1862, *Papers*, 6:393–95.
5. John A. Rawlins, General Order, Dec. 17, 1862, in Bertram Wallace Korn, *American Jewry and the Civil War* (Philadelphia, 1951), pp. 122–26.
6. USG to Henry W. Halleck, 7:45 P.M., Nov. 9, 1862, *Papers*, 6:288; Halleck to USG, Nov. 10, 1862, ibid., p. 288n. See also James B. McPherson to USG, 8:30 A.M., Nov. 9, 1862, ibid., p. 284n; USG to McPherson, Nov. 9, 1862, ibid., p. 285n.; USG to Charles S. Hamilton, Nov. 9, 1862, ibid., p. 285.
7. USG, General Orders 6, Nov. 11, 1862, ibid., pp. 294–95.
8. Shelby Foote, *The Civil War: A Narrative*, 3 vols. (New York, 1958–74), 2:60–65.
9. Ibid., p. 71.
10. USG to "Commanding Officer Expedition down Mississippi," quoted in Foote, 2:73; William T. Sherman to E. E. Sherman, Jan. 3, 1863, in Foote, 2:79.
11. USG to Henry W. Halleck, Nov. 15, 1862, *Papers*, 6:315. For the whole of this discussion of black refugees I am indebted to John Y. Simon's perceptive compilation of material in *Papers*, 6:315n.–317n.
12. John A. Rawlins, Special Order 17, Nov. 13, 1862, and Special Field Order 4, Nov. 14, 1862, *Papers*, 6:315n.–316n.
13. James M. Tuttle to Edwin M. Stanton, Sept. 18, 1862, ibid., p. 317n.; David Davis to Abraham Lincoln, Oct. 14, 1862, ibid.
14. John Eaton, with Ethel Osgood Mason, *Grant, Lincoln and the Freedmen* (New York, 1907); William S. McFeely, *Yankee Stepfather: General O. O. Howard and the Freedmen* (New York, 1970).
15. Eaton, *Grant, Lincoln and the Freedmen*, pp. 30–31.
16. Dana, *Recollections*, pp. 17–19.
17. Ibid., pp. 21, 28–30.
18. United States Military Academy, West Point, *The West Point Atlas of American Wars*, ed. Vincent J. Esposito, 2 vols. (New York, 1959), vol. 1, map 103.
19. Ulysses S. Grant, *Personal Memoirs of U. S. Grant*, 2 vols. (New York, 1885–86), 1:542–43.
20. Kenneth P. Williams, *Lincoln Finds a General: A Military Study of the Civil War*, 5 vols. (New York, 1949–59), 4:379.
21. USG, *Memoirs*, 1:524–26; Foote, *Civil War*, 2:372–73. See also James Marshall-Cornwall, *Grant as Military Commander* (London, 1970), pp. 113–14.
22. Foote, *Civil War*, 2:385.
23. John A. McClernand, Order 72, May 30, 1863, in *Official Records of the Rebellion* (*OR*), ser. 1, vol. 24, pt. 1, pp. 159–61. See also William T. Sherman to John A. Rawlins, June 17, 1863, ibid., pp. 162–63; Foote, *Civil War*, 2:421–22; Williams, *Lincoln Finds a General*, 4:409.
24. Kenneth P. Williams has an extensive and sarcastic account of the Cadwallader story that suggests that it was entirely a fabrication. He closes his essay with an irrelevant reference to Grant's courtesy to Lee at the McLean farmhouse and observes, "If the kindness that Grant habitually displayed during four bad years of war is not a precious part of the American heritage, we have lost all sense of values."—Williams, *Lincoln Finds a General*, 4:51; see also in Williams, 4:439–50, 577–83. Benjamin P. Thomas has been criticized for not fully annotating his edition of the Cadwallader manuscript, Sylvanus Cadwallader, *Three Years with*

*Grant* (New York, 1955). John Y. Simon discusses the incident in *Papers*, 8:322n.–325n. See also Foote, *Civil War*, 2:416–21.

25. Foote, *Civil War*, 2:417.
26. Cadwallader, *Three Years with Grant*, pp. 102–22.
27. Dana, *Recollections*, p. 83.
28. Ibid.
29. Foote, *Civil War*, 2:419; Cadwallader, *Three Years with Grant*, pp. 107, 109; Grant, *Papers*, 8:325n.
30. John A. Rawlins to USG, June 6, 1863, *Papers*, 8:322n.–323n.
31. Charles A. Dana to Edwin M. Stanton, July 13, 1863, in Dana, *Recollections*, p. 73.
32. William T. Sherman to John A. Rawlins, June 17, 1863, *OR*, ser. 1, vol. 24, pt. 1, pp. 159–63; William Tecumseh Sherman, *Memoirs of General William T. Sherman*, 2 vols. (New York, 1875), 1:356. See also Foote, *Civil War*, 2:421–22; Grant, *Memoirs*, 1:546–47.
33. USG to John A. McClernand, June 17, 1863, *OR*, ser. 1, vol. 24, pt. 1, p. 159; Foote, *Civil War*, 2:421–23.
34. Foote, *Civil War*, 2:608–12, 614; John C. Pemberton to USG, July 3, 1863, *Papers*, 8:455n.; USG to Pemberton, July 3, 1863, ibid., p. 455.
35. Ira Miltmore to his wife, July 4, 1863, Ira Miltmore Papers, Chicago Historical Society.
36. Theodore Lyman, *Meade's Headquarters 1863–1865: Letters of Colonel Theodore Lyman from the Wilderness to Appomattox*, sel. and ed. George R. Agassiz (Boston, 1922), p. 359.
37. Ibid.

## *Chapter XI*   CHATTANOOGA

1. Thomas Kilby Smith to his wife, Sept. 6, 1863, in Walter George Smith, *Life and Letters of Thomas Kilby Smith* (New York, 1898), pp. 328–29. See also Ulysses S. Grant, *Personal Memoirs of U. S. Grant*, 2 vols. (New York, 1885–86), 1:581; Shelby Foote, *The Civil War: A Narrative*, 3 vols. (New York, 1958–74), 2:774–75.
2. USG, *Memoirs*, 1:581.
3. Julia D. Grant, *Personal Memoirs of Julia Dent Grant*, ed. John Y. Simon (New York, 1975), pp. 121–23; USG, *Memoirs*, 1:504; Foote, *Civil War*, 2:784–85.
4. USG, *Memoirs*, 1:584. The decision to end the first volume at this point may not have been Grant's. Discussions of the editing of the *Memoirs* suggest that the location of the break shifted as the manuscript reached completion.
5. Ibid., 2:18.
6. Julia D. Grant, *Memoirs*, p. 123.
7. Ibid.; USG, *Memoirs*, 2:18–20.
8. USG, *Memoirs*, 2:19, 26.
9. Ibid., pp. 24–26.
10. Ibid., p. 27; Harvey Reid to Sarah Reid, Oct. 21, 1863, Huntington Library.
11. O. O. Howard, *Autobiography of Oliver Otis Howard*, 2 vols. (New York, 1907), 1:460; O. O. Howard, "Grant at Chattanooga," in Military Order of the Loyal Legion of the United States, New York Commandry, *Personal Recollections of the War of the Rebellion*, 1st series (New York, 1891), p. 246.
12. Howard, *Autobiography*, 1:460.
13. Howard, "Grant at Chattanooga," p. 247; Howard, *Autobiography*, 1:461. See also USG, *Memoirs*, 2:101–2.
14. Horace Porter, *Campaigning with Grant* (New York, 1897), p. 2.
15. Ibid., pp. 2, 5.
16. USG to Henry W. Halleck, Oct. 23, 1863, in *Official Records of the Rebellion*, ser. 1, vol. 31, pt. 1, p. 706.
17. Porter, *Campaigning*, pp. 6–7.

18. Ibid., p. 7.
19. William Tecumseh Sherman, *Memoirs of General William T. Sherman*, 2 vols. (New York, 1875), 1:357–58.
20. Bruce Catton, *Grant Takes Command* (Boston, 1969), pp. 49–58.
21. Sherman, *Memoirs*, 1:361; John A. Rawlins to M. E. Hurlbut, Nov. 16, 1863, Rawlins Papers, Chicago Historical Society.
22. Catton, *Grant Takes Command*, p. 65.
23. Howard, "Grant at Chattanooga," p. 250. See also Foote, *Civil War*, 2:834–69.
24. USG, *Memoirs*, 2:87.
25. Foote, *Civil War*, 2:862.
26. Julia D. Grant, *Memoirs*, p. 124.
27. USG, *Memoirs*, 2:102.
28. Ibid., pp. 42–43.
29. USG to William T. Sherman, Mar. 4, 1864, in Sherman, *Memoirs*, 1:398–99.

*Chapter XII* WASHINGTON AND THE WILDERNESS

1. Horace Porter, *Campaigning with Grant* (New York, 1897), pp. 21–22.
2. Theodore Lyman, *Meade's Headquarters, 1863–1865: Letters of Colonel Theodore Lyman from the Wilderness to Appomattox*, sel. and ed. George R. Agassiz (Boston, 1922), p. 80.
3. Ibid.; *Missouri Republican*, January 30, 1864. See also Ben Perley Poore and O. H. Tiffany, *Life of U. S. Grant* (Philadelphia, 1885), p. 100; William Makepeace Thayer, *From Tannery to the White House: The Life of Ulysses S. Grant* (Boston, 1887), pp. 260–61.
4. Gideon Welles, *Diary*, ed. by Howard K. Beale, assisted by Alan W. Brownsword, 3 vols. (New York, 1960), Mar. 9, 1864, 1:538–39; Porter, *Campaigning*, pp. 18–19.
5. Welles, *Diary*, Mar. 9, 1864, 1:538–39. See also Thayer, *Tannery to White House*, p. 270.
6. Welles, *Diary*, Mar. 9, 1864, 1:538–39; Ulysses S. Grant, *Personal Memoirs of U. S. Grant*, 2 vols. (New York, 1885–86), 2:115.
7. Julia D. Grant, *Personal Memoirs of Julia Dent Grant*, ed. John Y. Simon (New York, 1975), p. 127.
8. USG to William T. Sherman, Mar. 4, 1864, in William Tecumseh Sherman, *Memoirs of General William T. Sherman*, 2 vols. (New York, 1875), 1:398–99; Sherman to USG, Mar. 10, 1864, ibid., pp. 399–400.
9. William T. Sherman to USG, Mar. 10, 1864, ibid., pp. 399–400; USG, *Memoirs*, 2:146.
10. George Gordon Meade to M. S. Meade, Mar. 22, 1864, in George Meade, *The Life and Letters of George Gordon Meade*, 2 vols. (New York, 1913), 2:182.
11. USG to George Gordon Meade, Apr. 9, 1864, in USG, *Memoirs*, 2:135.
12. George Gordon Meade to M. S. Meade, Mar. 14, 1864, in Meade, *Life and Letters*, 2:177–78.
13. George Gordon Meade to M. S. Meade, Apr. 27 and Apr. 23, 1865, ibid., pp. 277, 275–76.
14. George Gordon Meade to M. S. Meade, Mar. 22, Mar. 29, and Apr. 24, 1864, ibid., pp. 182, 185, 191.
15. Charles A. Dana, *Recollections of the Civil War* (New York, 1899), p. 73; F. M. Pixley in the *San Francisco Bulletin*, quoted in the *Galena Gazette*, Sept. 27, 1864. See also Frederick Tracy Dent, Diary, June 4, 1864, Dent Papers, Morris Library, Southern Illinois University.
16. Lyman, *Meade's Headquarters*, p. 154. See also William E. Leuchtenberg, "The New Deal and the Analogue of War," in John Braeman, Robert H. Bremner, and Everett Walters, *Change and Continuity in Twentieth-Century America* (New York, 1964).
17. John A. Rawlins to James Harrison Wilson, Mar. 3, 1864, James Harrison Wilson Papers, Library of Congress.
18. Catton, *Grant Takes Command* (Boston, 1969), p. 107.
19. Ibid., pp. 107, 111–13; George T. Strong, *The Diary of George Templeton Strong*, ed. Allan Nevins and Milton H. Thomas, 4 vols. (New York, 1952), June 1, 1864, 3:453.

20. Porter, *Campaigning*, p. 111.
21. *Chicago Tribune*, quoted in the *Northwestern Gazette*, July 5, 1864, and June 7, 1864.
22. USG to Julia D. Grant, May 2, 1864, U. S. Grant Papers, Library of Congress (LC); Herman Melville, "The Armies of the Wilderness," in *Battle-Pieces and Aspects of the War*, ed. Sidney Kaplan (Gainesville, 1960), p. 99.
23. Melville, "The Armies of the Wilderness," *Battle-Pieces*, p. 101; F. M. Pixley in the *San Francisco Bulletin*, quoted in the *Galena Gazette*, Sept. 27, 1864.
24. United States Military Academy, West Point, *The West Point Atlas of American Wars*, ed. Vincent J. Esposito, 2 vols. (New York, 1959), vol. 1, map 122. See also Catton, *Grant Takes Command*, p. 193.
25. Shelby Foote, *The Civil War*, 3 vols. (New York, 1958–74), 3:278–317.
26. Lyman, *Meade's Headquarters*, p. 105.
27. USG to Julia D. Grant, May 13, 1864, U. S. Grant Papers, LC; Oliver Wendell Holmes, Jr., to his parents, May 16, 1864, *Touched with Fire: Civil War Letters and Diary of Oliver Wendell Holmes, Jr., 1861–1864*, ed. Mark DeWolfe Howe (New York, 1969), p. 121; Walt Whitman to his mother, May 13, 1864, in *The Wound Dresser* (New York, 1949), p. 182; Jedediah Hotchkis, diary entry for May 12, 1864, in *Make Me a Map of the Valley* (Dallas, 1969), p. 204.
28. James Ford Rhodes, *History of the United States, 1850–1877*, 7 vols. (New York, 1892–1906), 4:436; Strong, *Diary*, July 1, 1864, 3:463; *Collected Works of Abraham Lincoln*, ed. Roy P. Basler, 9 vols. (New Brunswick, N.J., 1953–55), 7:374n.; Abraham Lincoln to F. A. Conkling, June 3, 1864, ibid., 7:374.
29. USG, *Memoirs*, 2:212; Rhodes, *History of the United States*, 4:469.
30. Rhodes, *History of the United States*, 4:469.
31. George Gordon Meade to M. S. Meade, June 4, 1864, in Meade, *Life and Letters*, 2:200; USG to Meade, June 3, 1864, in Grant, *Memoirs*, 2:272–73. See also Catton, *Grant Takes Command*, p. 265; Charles A. Dana to Edwin M. Stanton, June 3, 1864, in *Official Records of the Rebellion (OR)*, ser. 1, vol. 36, pt. 1, pp. 87–88.
32. Catton, *Grant Takes Command*, p. 267. See also Martin T. McMahon, "Cold Harbor," in *Battles and Leaders of the Civil War*, ed. R. U. Johnson and C. C. Buel, 4 vols. (New York, 1887–88), 4:213; William Fanar Smith, "The Eighteenth Corps at Cold Harbor," ibid., 4:222; James Marshall-Cornwall, *Grant as Military Commander* (London, 1970), p. 177; William Swinton, *Campaigns of the Army of the Potomac* (New York, 1866), p. 481–92.
33. USG to Robert E. Lee and Lee to USG, June 5, June 6, and June 7, 1864, *OR*, ser. 1, vol. 36, pt. 3, pp. 600, 638–39, 666–67. See also Catton, *Grant Takes Command*, p. 267; Lyman, *Meade's Headquarters*, pp. 149–154; USG to Nellie Grant, June 4, 1864, in Catton, *Grant Takes Command*, p. 270; McMahon, "Cold Harbor," in *Battles and Leaders*, 4:219.
34. USG to Edwin M. Stanton, July 22, 1865, *OR*, ser. 1, vol. 36, pt. 1, p. 22. See also USG to Henry W. Halleck, June 5, 1864, ibid., pp. 11–12.
35. Lyman, *Meade's Headquarters*, p. 154.

Chapter XIII  PETERSBURG

1. Theodore Lyman, *Meade's Headquarters, 1863–1865: Letters of Colonel Theodore Lyman from the Wilderness to Appomattox*, sel. and ed. George R. Agassiz (Boston, 1922), p. 166.
2. Ibid., p. 170.
3. USG to Henry W. Halleck, July 14, 1864, Huntington Library (HL). See also E. B. Long, with Barbara Long, *The Civil War Day by Day: An Almanac, 1861–1865* (New York, 1971), pp. 535–37.
4. USG to Edwin M. Stanton, July 20, 1864, HL. It is Grant's hand that strikes "A. Lincoln" and replaces it with "E. M. Stanton."

5. USG to William T. Sherman, Mar. 4, 1864, in William Tecumseh Sherman, *Memoirs of General William T. Sherman*, 2 vols. (New York, 1875), 1:398-99; USG to Edwin M. Stanton, July 26, 1864, HL.
6. Shelby Foote, *The Civil War: A Narrative*, 3 vols. (New York, 1958-74), 3:531-38.
7. Foote, *Civil War*, 3:534.
8. Ibid., p. 535.
9. Ibid., p. 538.
10. USG to George Gordon Meade, Aug. 1, 1864, HL; Ulysses S. Grant, *Personal Memoirs of U. S. Grant*, 2 vols. (New York, 1885-86), 2:315; USG to Henry W. Halleck, Aug. 1, 1864, HL.
11. Abraham Lincoln, Aug. 19, 1864, in Long, *Civil War Day by Day*, pp. 557-58.
12. USG to Henry W. Halleck, Aug. 1, 1864, HL; Abraham Lincoln to USG, Aug. 3, 1864, in *Collected Works of Abraham Lincoln*, ed. Roy P. Basler, 9 vols. (New Brunswick, N.J., 1953-55), 7:476; USG to Philip H. Sheridan, Aug. 26, 1864, in *Official Records of the Rebellion (OR)*, ser. 1, vol. 43, pt. 1, p. 917.
13. USG to William T. Sherman, Aug. 7, 1864, HL.
14. USG to William T. Sherman, Aug. 9, 1864, HL.
15. USG to William T. Sherman, Aug. 9, 1864, HL; USG to Henry W. Halleck, Aug. 10, 1864, HL.
16. USG to Edwin M. Stanton, Aug. 11, 1864, HL; USG to Henry W. Halleck, Aug. 15, 1864, HL; USG to Philip H. Sheridan, Aug. 16, 1864, HL. See also George M. Frederickson, *The Inner Civil War: Northern Intellectuals and the Crisis of the Union* (New York, 1965), pp. 66-91.
17. George H. Mellish to his mother, Dec. 14, 1864, HL.
18. Walt Whitman, penciled item dated June 25, 1863, in "Hospital Note-Book," manuscript, HL.
19. USG to Philip H. Sheridan, Aug. 16 and Aug. 21, 1864, HL; USG to Abraham Lincoln, Aug. 17, 1864, HL; USG to Edwin M. Stanton, Aug. 21, 1864, HL.
20. USG to William T. Sherman, Aug. 18, 1864, HL; USG to Philip H. Sheridan, Aug. 26, 1864, HL.
21. USG to commander, Army of the Potomac, and all corps commanders, Sept. 2, 1864, HL.
22. USG to Edwin M. Stanton, Sept. 3, 1864, HL; USG to William T. Sherman, Sept. 4, 1864, HL.
23. USG to Henry W. Halleck, Sept. 21, 1864, HL.
24. USG, *Memoirs*, 2:332.
25. USG to Philip H. Sheridan, Sept. 22, 1864, HL. See also Long, *Civil War Day by Day*, p. 573.
26. USG to Philip H. Sheridan, Sept. 26, 1864, HL; USG to William T. Sherman, Sept. 26, 1864, HL; USG to Benjamin F. Butler, Sept. 27, 1864, HL; USG to Henry W. Halleck, Sept. 27, 1864 (twice), HL; USG to George Gordon Meade, Sept. 27, 1864, HL.
27. USG to William T. Sherman, Sept. 28, 1864, HL; USG to Edwin M. Stanton, Sept. 28, 1864, HL; USG to Henry W. Halleck, Sept. 28, 1864, HL.
28. USG to Joseph Barnes, Sept. 28, 1864, HL; USG to Benjamin F. Butler, Sept. 28, 1864, HL.
29. USG to Henry W. Halleck, Sept. 29, 1864, HL.
30. USG to Henry W. Halleck, Sept. 30, 1864, HL; USG to George Gordon Meade, Sept. 30, 1864, HL.
31. USG, *Memoirs*, 2:175-76.
32. USG to Edwin M. Stanton, Sept. 13, 1864, HL. Grant inserted (by asterisk) the sentence "Let them be undeceived" after he had crossed out an alternative insertion: "Undeceive them and you give a great triumph."
33. USG to George Gordon Meade, Sept. 20, 1864, HL; USG to Edwin M. Stanton, Sept. 20, 1864, HL.

34. USG to Edwin M. Stanton, Oct. 20, 1864, HL. See also Philip H. Sheridan, *Personal Memoirs of P. H. Sheridan*, 2 vols. (New York, 1888), 2:65–92.
35. USG to Henry W. Halleck, Oct. 21, 1864, HL.
36. USG to Edwin M. Stanton, Oct. 25 and Nov. 3, 1864, HL; Long, *Civil War Day by Day*, p. 592.
37. USG to Edwin M. Stanton, Nov. 9, 1864, HL; USG to Philip H. Sheridan, Nov. 10, 1864, HL.
38. USG to George H. Thomas, Nov. 15, 1864, HL; Thomas to USG in reply, *OR*, ser. 1, vol. 45, pt. 1, p. 895.
39. USG to George H. Thomas, Nov. 24, 1864, *OR*, ser. 1, vol. 45, pt. 1, p. 1014.
40. George H. Thomas to USG, Nov. 25, 1864, ibid., p. 1034.
41. USG to George H. Thomas, Nov. 27, 1864, ibid., p. 1083; Thomas to USG, Nov. 28, 1864, ibid., p. 1104. See also USG to Henry W. Halleck, Nov. 25, 1864, ibid., p. 1034.
42. George H. Thomas to USG, Dec. 1, 1864, ibid., pt. 2, p. 3; USG to Thomas, Dec. 2, 1864 (twice), ibid., p. 17.
43. USG to George H. Thomas, Dec. 5 and Dec. 6, 1864, ibid., pp. 55 and 70. See also Henry W. Halleck to USG, Dec. 5, 1864, ibid., p. 55; Halleck to Thomas, Dec. 9, 1864, ibid., p. 114; Thomas to Halleck, Dec. 6, 1864, ibid., p. 71.
44. USG to Edwin M. Stanton, Dec. 7, 1864, ibid., p. 84; USG to George H. Thomas, Dec. 8, 1864, ibid., p. 97; Henry W. Halleck to Thomas, Dec. 9, 1864, ibid., p. 114. See also Halleck to USG, Dec. 8, 1864, ibid., p. 96; USG to Halleck, Dec. 8, 1864, ibid., p. 96.
45. George H. Thomas to USG, Dec. 9, 1864, ibid., p. 115; USG to Thomas, Dec. 9, 1864, ibid., p. 115. See also draft of order, Dec. 9, 1864, ibid., p. 114.
46. USG to George H. Thomas, Dec. 11, 1864, ibid., p. 143. See also Thomas to Henry W. Halleck, Dec. 11, 1864, ibid.; Thomas to USG, Dec. 11, 1864, ibid.
47. George H. Thomas to F. L. Thomas, Dec. 15, 1864, ibid., p. 195.
48. USG to George H. Thomas, Dec. 15, 1864 (twice), ibid., p. 195; Thomas to Henry W. Halleck, Dec. 15, 1864, ibid., p. 194.
49. USG to George H. Thomas, Dec. 22, 1864, ibid., p. 307; Henry W. Halleck to Thomas, Dec. 31, 1864, ibid., p. 174.
50. USG to Julia D. Grant, Dec. 21, Dec. 22, and Dec. 26, 1864, U. S. Grant Papers, Library of Congress (LC).
51. USG to William T. Sherman, Dec. 18, 1864, in Sherman, *Memoirs*, 2:223–24.
52. William T. Sherman to USG, Dec. 24, 1864, ibid., pp. 224–26; USG to Julia D. Grant, Jan. 1, 1865, U. S. Grant Papers, LC.
53. USG to Julia D. Grant, Jan. 1, 1865, U. S. Grant Papers, LC.

*Chapter XIV* PEACE

1. Jubal A. Early, *War Memoirs*, ed. Frank E. Vandiver (Bloomington, Ind., 1960), pp. 389–95.
2. Jefferson Davis to Francis Preston Blair, Jan. 12, 1865, in James D. Richardson, ed., *A Compilation of the Messages and Papers of the Presidents, 1789–1897*, 10 vols. (Washington, D.C., 1896–99), 6:260–61.
3. Abraham Lincoln to Francis Preston Blair, Jan. 18, 1865, in Richardson, *Messages*, 6:261. All five participants in the peace conference wrote accounts of it. See William Henry Seward to Charles Francis Adams, Feb. 7, 1865, in George E. Baker, ed., *The Works of William H. Seward*, 5 vols. (New York, 1853–84), 5:171–75; Abraham Lincoln, in Richardson, *Messages*, 6:260–69, and *Peace*, 38th Cong., 2d sess., House Exec. Doc. 59, Feb. 10, 1865 (serial set 1229); Alexander H. Stephens, *A Constitutional View of the Late War between the States*, 2 vols. (Philadelphia, 1868–70), 2:576–630; Robert M. T. Hunter, "The Peace Commissions of 1865," *Southern Historical Society Papers* 3 (Apr. 1877):168–76; John A. Campbell, *Reminis-*

*cences and Documents Relating to the Civil War during the Year 1865*, pamphlet (Baltimore, 1886). The best modern account is Howard C. Westwood, "Lincoln and the Hampton Roads Peace Conference," *Lincoln Herald* 81 (Winter 1979):243–56.

4. Alexander H. Stephens to *Philadelphia Times*, undated draft of letter, Stephens Papers, Library of Congress (LC), quoted in Westwood, "Lincoln and the Hampton Roads Peace Conference"; O. B. Wil[l]cox to J. G. Parke, Jan. 29, 1865, forwarded by E. O. C. Ord to Edwin M. Stanton, Jan. 29, 1865, in *Collected Works of Abraham Lincoln*, ed. Roy P. Basler, 9 vols. (New Brunswick, N.J., 1953–55), 8:276; Stanton to Ord, Jan. 29 and Jan. 30, 1865, in Richardson, *Messages*, 6:262; Stanton to Ord, Jan. 30, 1865, in *Collected Works of Abraham Lincoln*, 8:277; USG to Alexander H. Stephens, John A. Campbell, and Robert M. T. Hunter, Jan. 31, 1865, in *Collected Works of Abraham Lincoln*, 8:279.

5. George Gordon Meade to M. S. Meade, Feb. 1, 1865, in George Meade, *The Life and Letters of George Gordon Meade*, 2 vols. (New York, 1913), 2:258–80; Stephens, *Late War*, 2:597. See also *Richmond Sentinel*, quoted in E. O. C. Ord to Edwin M. Stanton, Jan. 31, 1865, *Official Records of the Rebellion (OR)*, ser. 1, vol. 46, pt. 2, pp. 291–92.

6. Stephens, *Late War*, 2:597.

7. Ulysses S. Grant, *Personal Memoirs of U. S. Grant*, 2 vols. (New York, 1885–86), 2:421; George Gordon Meade to M. S. Meade, Feb. 1, 1865, in Meade, *Life and Letters*, 2:258–60.

8. George Gordon Meade to M. S. Meade, Feb. 1, 1865, in Meade, *Life and Letters*, 2:258–60.

9. Ibid.

10. Grant, *Memoirs*, 2:421–23. See also Westwood, "Lincoln and the Hampton Roads Peace Conference."

11. Julia D. Grant, *Personal Memoirs of Julia Dent Grant*, ed. John Y. Simon (New York, 1975), p. 138.

12. Hunter, "Peace Commissions," p. 172; David Homer Bates, *Lincoln in the Telegraph Office* (New York, 1907), pp. 126–29, 335–38. See also Campbell, *Reminiscences*.

13. Thomas T. Eckert to Abraham Lincoln, Feb. 1, 1865, in *Collected Works of Abraham Lincoln*, 8:281.

14. Alexander H. Stephens, undated manuscript, Stephens Papers, LC (brought to the writer's attention by Howard C. Westwood); Alexander H. Stephens, Robert M. T. Hunter, and John A. Campbell to USG, Feb. 1, 1865, *OR*, ser. 1, vol. 46, pt. 2, p. 342.

15. Alexander H. Stephens, undated manuscript, Stephens Papers, LC; Bates, *Lincoln in the Telegraph Office*, pp. 336–37; Thomas T. Eckert to Abraham Lincoln, Feb. 1, 1865, *OR*, ser. 1, vol. 46, pt. 2, p. 342. Bates quotes Eckert as saying he had been with Grant and reproved him in front of the Confederates. Stephens's account, written closer to the occasion, has Grant alone with them and does not mention the general's having been humiliated in their presence. In either case, they knew Eckert was trying to frustrate Grant's efforts to bring about the peace conference.

16. USG to Edwin M. Stanton, Feb. 1, 1865, in Richardson, *Messages*, 6:266.

17. Alexander H. Stephens, undated manuscript, Stephens Papers, LC.

18. Alexander H. Stephens, John A. Campbell, and Robert M. T. Hunter to Thomas T. Eckert, Feb. 2, 1865, in Richardson, *Messages*, 6:268.

19. Westwood, "Lincoln and the Hampton Roads Peace Conference," p. 15; Abraham Lincoln to USG, Feb. 2, 1865, in *Collected Works of Abraham Lincoln*, 8:256; Lincoln to House of Representatives, Feb. 10, 1865, ibid., p. 282; Lincoln to William Henry Seward, Feb. 2, 1865, ibid., p. 256. See also Thomas T. Eckert to Edwin M. Stanton, Feb. 1, 1865, *OR*, ser. 1, vol. 46, pt. 2, pp. 341–42.

20. Stephens, undated manuscript, Stephens Papers, LC; Campbell, *Reminiscences*; Stephens, *Late War*, 2:610–13.

21. Campbell, *Reminiscences*; Stephens, *Late War*, 2:610–13.

22. Campbell, *Reminiscences*. See also Stephens, *Late War*, 2:610–13.

23. Stephens, *Late War*, 2:614, 615n.

24. Ibid., pp. 610–13.

25. Ibid., p. 619; Julia D. Grant, *Memoirs*, pp. 137–38.

26. USG, *Memoirs*, 2:424.

27. Charles Francis Adams, Jr., to Charles Francis Adams, Feb. 7, 1865, and May 2, 1865, in Worthington C. Ford, ed., *A Cycle of Adams Letters, 1861–1865*, 2 vols. (Boston, 1920), 2:252–53, 267–69.

28. Charles Francis Adams, Jr., to Charles Francis Adams, Mar. 7, 1865, ibid., pp. 257–58.

29. Julia D. Grant, *Memoirs*, p. 141.

30. Gideon Welles, *Diary*, ed. by Howard K. Beale, assisted by Alan W. Brownsword, 3 vols. (New York, 1960), June 27, 1867, 3:121–22; USG to William T. Sherman, Feb. 7, 1865, W. T. Sherman Papers, LC.

31. USG to Elihu B. Washburne, Feb. 23, 1865, U. S. Grant Papers, Illinois State Historical Society (ISHS); George H. Mellish to his mother, Feb. 11, 1865, Huntington Library (HL); USG to Washburne, Feb. 23, 1865, U. S. Grant Papers, ISHS; USG to Abraham Lincoln, Mar. 20, 1865, in *Collected Works of Abraham Lincoln*, 8:367.

32. Julia D. Grant, *Memoirs*, p. 142.

33. Adam Badeau, *Grant in Peace: From Appomattox to Mount McGregor* (Hartford, Conn., 1887), p. 362; Julia D. Grant, *Memoirs*, pp. 146–47.

34. William Tecumseh Sherman, *Memoirs of General William T. Sherman*, 2 vols. (New York, 1875), 2:325.

35. Julia D. Grant, *Memoirs*, p. 150.

36. David Dixon Porter, "Account of Interview with Mr. Lincoln," in Sherman, *Memoirs*, 2:328–31.

37. Ibid., p. 329.

38. C. C. Carpenter, "President Lincoln in Petersburg," *Century Magazine* 40 (June 1890):306–7.

39. Edward H. Ripley, "The Occupation of Richmond," in Military Order of the Loyal Legion of the United States, New York Commandry, *Personal Recollections of the War of the Rebellion*, 3d series (New York, 1907), pp. 476–77.

40. Ibid., pp. 479–81.

41. Herman Melville, "The Fall of Richmond," in *Battle-Pieces and Aspects of the War*, ed. Sidney Kaplan (Gainesville, 1960), pp. 135–36; USG to Theodore S. Bowers, Apr. 3, 1865, HL; Julia D. Grant, *Memoirs*, p. 150.

42. Campbell, *Reminiscences*, p. 39.

43. Ibid., pp. 39–41.

*Chapter XV* "ON TO MEXICO"

1. USG to Robert E. Lee, Apr. 7 and Apr. 8, 1865, and Lee to USG, Apr. 7, 1865, in Ulysses S. Grant, *Personal Memoirs of U. S. Grant*, 2 vols. (New York, 1885–86), 2:625–26.

2. Theodore Lyman, *Meade's Headquarters, 1863–1865: Letters of Colonel Theodore Lyman from the Wilderness to Appomattox*, ed. George R. Agassiz (Boston, 1922), p. 354; Robert E. Lee to USG, Apr. 8, 1865, in USG, *Memoirs*, 2:627. See also ibid., p. 483; Horace Porter, *Campaigning with Grant* (New York, 1897), pp. 462–63; Bruce Catton, *Grant Takes Command* (Boston, 1969), p. 459.

3. USG to Robert E. Lee, Apr. 9, 1865, in USG, *Memoirs*, 2:627. See also Porter, *Campaigning*, p. 464.

4. Porter, *Campaigning*, pp. 464–66.

5. Ibid., pp. 466–68.

6. Ibid.

7. Charles Marshall, *An Aide-de-Camp of Lee*, ed. Frederick Maurice (Boston, 1927), p. 273; USG, *Memoirs*, 2:589.

8. Marshall, loyal to Lee's impeccable manners, contends that Lee did indeed remember Grant.—Marshall, *Aide-de-Camp of Lee*, p. 267.
9. USG, *Memoirs*, 2:492. See also Marshall, *Aide-de-Camp of Lee*, pp. 267–74; William Swinton, *Campaigns of the Army of the Potomac* (New York, 1866), p. 619.
10. USG, *Memoirs*, 2:495, 489. See also Marshall, *Aide-de-Camp of Lee*, p. 272.
11. USG, *Memoirs*, 2:498, 507; Porter, *Campaigning*, p. 493.
12. Gideon Welles, manuscript account of the period of Lincoln's death, Huntington Library (HL). See also Glyndon G. Van Deusen, *William Henry Seward* (New York, 1967), pp. 411–12.
13. Gideon Welles, *Diary*, ed. by Howard K. Beale, assisted by Alan W. Brownsword, 3 vols. (New York, 1960), Apr. 10 and Apr. 13, 1865, 2:278, 280.
14. Ibid., Apr. 7 and Apr. 14, 1865, 2:276, 280–83.
15. Ibid., Apr. 14, 1865, 2:280–83.
16. Ibid.
17. USG, *Memoirs*, 2:508; Julia D. Grant, *Personal Memoirs of Julia Dent Grant*, ed. John Y. Simon (New York, 1975), pp. 154–55; John Russell Young, *Around the World with General Grant*, 2 vols. (New York, 1879), 2:356.
18. Charles E. Bolles, "General Grant and the News of Mr. Lincoln's Death," in "Memoranda on the Life of Lincoln," *Century Magazine* 40 (June 1890):300–10. See also Julia D. Grant, *Memoirs*, p. 156.
19. Catton, *Grant Takes Command*, pp. 475–76; Julia D. Grant, *Memoirs*, pp. 155–56.
20. Julia D. Grant, *Memoirs*, pp. 155–56.
21. Ibid., pp. 156–57; Young, *Around the World*, 2:356; John Matthews, quoted in Louis J. Weichmann, *A True History of the Assassination of Abraham Lincoln and of the Conspiracy of 1865* (New York, 1975), pp. 139–41.
22. Julia D. Grant, *Memoirs*, pp. 145–57; Weichmann, *True History of the Assassination*; Ben Perley Poore and O. H. Tiffany, *Life of U. S. Grant* (Philadelphia, 1885), p. 255.
23. USG, *Memoirs*, 2:509. See also Welles, *Diary*, Apr. 15 and Apr. 16, 1865, 2:287–91.
24. Gideon Welles, manuscript account of the period of Lincoln's death. HL.
25. Benjamin P. Thomas and Harold M. Hyman, *Stanton: The Life and Times of Lincoln's Secretary of War* (New York, 1962), p. 406.
26. William T. Sherman to U. S. Grant, Apr. 28, 1865, in William Tecumseh Sherman, *Memoirs of General William T. Sherman*, 2 vols. (New York, 1875), 2:365–67; Herman Melville, "The Martyr," in *Battle-Pieces and Aspects of the War*, ed. Sidney Kaplan (Gainesville, 1960), pp. 141–42. See also O. O. Howard, *Autobiography of Oliver Otis Howard*, 2 vols. (New York, 1907), 2:155–56.
27. USG, *Memoirs*, 2:516. See also Thomas and Hyman, *Stanton*, p. 405; Welles, *Diary*, Apr. 21, 1865, 2:293–95.
28. USG, *Memoirs*, 2:516–17; Sherman, *Memoirs*, 2:358.
29. William T. Sherman to John A. Rawlins, May 22, 1865, HL.
30. *New York Times*, May 26, 1865.

*Chapter XVI* AFTER THE WAR

1. Julia D. Grant, *Personal Memoirs of Julia Dent Grant*, ed. John Y. Simon (New York, 1975), p. 157. See also *New York Times*, May 5, 1865; USG to Julia D. Grant, May 6, 1865, Huntington Library (HL).
2. Julia D. Grant, *Memoirs*, p. 157.
3. USG to Elihu B. Washburne, May 21, 1865, U.S. Grant Papers, Illinois State Historical Society (ISHS). See also *Galena Gazette*, June 6, 1865.
4. *New York Times*, June 8, 1865.
5. Ibid.

6. Ibid.
7. Ibid.
8. Ibid.
9. Ibid., June 9, 1865.
10. John Jay Cisco, quoted in George T. Strong, *The Diary of George Templeton Strong*, ed. Allan Nevins and Milton H. Thomas, 4 vols. (New York, 1952), June 1, 1864, 3:453.
11. Julia D. Grant, *Memoirs*, p. 162; Strong, *Diary*, Nov. 18, 1865, 4:50; *New York Times*, July 6, 1865. See also *Galena Gazette*, June 13 and June 20, 1865.
12. *Galena Gazette*, Aug. 19, 1865. See also William S. McFeely, *Yankee Stepfather: General O. O. Howard and the Freedmen* (New York, 1970), p. 109; *Galena Centennial Newspaper* (facsimile of an 1865 edition).
13. Joe Bascom to Henry Bascom, Sept. 21, 1865, Galena Public Library.
14. Joe Bascom to Henry Bascom, Aug. 29, 1865, Galena Public Library; *Galena Gazette*, June 20, 1865.
15. Mary Louise Williams to [no name], [Oct. 3, 1865?], Cincinnati Historical Society.
16. Ibid.
17. USG to Elihu B. Washburne, Oct. 8, 1865, U. S. Grant Papers, ISHS; Charles Sumner, in *Congressional Globe*, 39th Cong., 1st sess., pt. 1, p. 79, Dec. 19, 1865.
18. Gideon Welles, *Diary*, ed. by Howard K. Beale, assisted by Alan W. Brownsword, 3 vols. (New York, 1960), Dec. 15, 1865, 2:396–97.
19. *New York Times*, Dec. 11, 1865; the report is reprinted in Walter L. Fleming, *Documentary History of Reconstruction: Political, Military, Social, Religious, Educational, and Industrial, 1865–1906*, 2 vols. (Cleveland, 1906–7), 1:51–53.
20. Ibid.
21. Ibid.
22. Ibid.
23. Ibid.
24. Ibid.
25. Ibid. See also *New York Times*, Dec. 21, 1865.
26. Benjamin P. Thomas and Harold M. Hyman, *Stanton: The Life and Times of Lincoln's Secretary of War* (New York, 1962).
27. Ulysses S. Grant, *Personal Memoirs of U. S. Grant*, 2 vols. (New York, 1885–86), 2:551–53.
28. Ben Perley Poore and O. H. Tiffany, *Life of U. S. Grant* (Philadelphia, 1885), pp. 258–59; Jacob Gunn, in conversation with the writer, Apr. 28, 1969.
29. James A. Garfield, *The Diary of James A. Garfield*, ed. Harry J. Brown and Frederick D. Williams, 3 vols. (East Lansing, Mich., 1967–73), Dec. 8, 1875, 3:197. See also *New York Times*, Mar. 7 and Mar. 9, 1866.
30. *New York Times*, Mar. 7 and Mar. 9, 1866. See also *The Papers of Ulysses S. Grant*, ed. John Y. Simon, 8 vols. to date (Carbondale, Ill., 1967–), 5:103n.
31. *New York Times*, Apr. 6 and Apr. 7, 1866; Welles, *Diary*, Apr. 6, 1866, 2:477–78.
32. Welles, *Diary*, Apr. 6, 1866, 2:477–78; *New York Times*, Apr. 7, 1866.

*Chapter XVII* THE RISING MAN

1. *New York Times*, Aug. 7 and Aug. 8, 1866.
2. Ibid., Aug. 20 and Aug. 19, 1866.
3. USG to Elihu B. Washburne, Aug. 16, 1866, U. S. Grant Papers, Illinois State Historical Society (ISHS).
4. USG to Julia D. Grant, Aug. 31, 1866, from Albany, and Aug. 31, 1866, from Auburn, U. S. Grant Papers, Library of Congress (LC). See also *New York Times*, Sept. 1, 1866.
5. USG to Julia D. Grant, Sept. 4, 1866, U. S. Grant Papers, LC.
6. James Harrison Wilson to Orville E. Babcock, Sept. 11, 1866, Babcock Papers, Newberry Library, Chicago.

7. Ibid.
8. *Chicago Republican*, quoted in *Army and Navy Journal*, Sept. 22, 1866, p. 71.
9. USG to Julia D. Grant, Sept. 9, 1866, U. S. Grant Papers, LC; Daniel Ammen, *The Old Navy and the New . . . with an Appendix of Personal Letters from General Grant* (Philadelphia, 1891), p. 427.
10. USG to William T. Sherman, Oct. 15, 1866, W. T. Sherman Papers, LC. See also Sherman to Andrew Johnson, Feb. 11, 1866, ibid.; Daniel Butterfield to USG, Feb. 15, 1866, U. S. Grant Papers, ISHS; USG to Daniel Butterfield, Feb. 17, 1866, ibid.
11. Edwin M. Stanton to William Pitt Fessenden, Oct. 25, 1866, Huntington Library (HL); John Sherman to William T. Sherman, Oct. 26, 1866, W. T. Sherman Papers, LC.
12. Orville E. Babcock to Annie Campbell, Oct. 10 and Oct. 15, 1866, Babcock Papers, Newberry Library.
13. USG to Elihu B. Washburne, Oct. 23, 1866, U. S. Grant Papers, ISHS. See also Washburne to Orville H. Browning, Oct. 8, 1866, Browning Papers, ISHS; USG to Browning, Oct. 16, 1866, ibid.
14. *Baltimore Sun*, Oct. 20–Nov. 9, 1866; *New York Times*, Oct. 24–Nov. 9, 1866.
15. *Baltimore Sun*, Oct. 20–Nov. 9, 1866; *New York Times*, Oct. 24–Nov. 9, 1866.
16. *Baltimore Sun*, Oct. 20–Nov. 9, 1866; *New York Times*, Oct. 24–Nov. 9, 1866.
17. USG to Andrew Johnson, draft of letter, Oct. 24, 1866, U. S. Grant Papers, ISHS.
18. *Baltimore Sun*, Nov. 1–3, 1866.
19. Ibid., Nov. 4–9, 1866.
20. Ibid., Nov. 6, 1866.
21. Ibid., Nov. 7, 1866.
22. Gideon Welles, *Diary*, ed. by Howard K. Beale, assisted by Alan W. Brownsword, 3 vols. (New York, 1960), Nov. 17, 1866, 2:621.
23. USG to Daniel Ammen, Nov. 6, 1866, in Ammen, *Old Navy*, p. 533.
24. Welles, *Diary*, Dec. 24, 1866, 2:646.
25. Ibid., Jan. 4, 1867, 3:4–5.
26. *New York Times*, Jan. 10, 1867, cited in Welles, *Diary*, Jan. 10, 1867, 3:15; *Washington Star*, Jan. 8, 1867.
27. William T. Sherman to E. O. C. Ord, Dec. 26, 1865, W. T. Sherman Papers, Missouri Historical Society.
28. Welles, *Diary*, Feb. 15, 1867, 3:42. See also O. O. Howard to Edwin M. Stanton, Jan. 19, 1867, National Archives, Washington, D.C.
29. Welles, *Diary*, Feb. 16, 1867, 3:46.
30. Ibid., June 24, 1867, 3:118.
31. George W. Childs, *Recollections* (Philadelphia, 1890), p. 103. See also Welles, *Diary*, July 26, 1867, 3:140.
32. USG to Andrew Johnson, Aug. 1, 1867, LC; "Act Regulating the Tenure of Certain Civil Offices," March 2, 1867, *U.S. Statutes at Large*, vol. 14, p. 430.
33. USG to Andrew Johnson, Aug. 1, 1867, LC; Welles, *Diary*, Aug. 2, 1867, 3:155.
34. Thaddeus Stevens, quoted in the *New York Times*, May 7, 1866.
35. William B. Hesseltine, *Ulysses S. Grant, Politician* (New York, 1935), p. 88; John Lothrop Motley to his wife, Aug. 14, 1867, in *The Correspondence of John Lothrop Motley*, ed. George William Curtis, 3 vols. (New York, 1900), 2:283.
36. USG to Julia D. Grant, Aug. 5, 1867, LC.
37. John W. Forney, *Anecdotes of Public Men*, 2 vols. (New York, 1873–81), 1:288.
38. David Davis to J. M. Carlisle, July 29, 1867, HL; Forney, *Anecdotes*, 1:289.
39. Julia D. Grant, *Personal Memoirs of Julia Dent Grant*, ed. John Y. Simon (New York, 1975), p. 203; Forney, *Anecdotes*, 1:287.
40. Forney, *Anecdotes*, 1:287; William T. Sherman to I. H. Wilson, Oct. 18, 1867, W. T. Sherman Papers, Missouri Historical Society.
41. William T. Sherman to USG, Jan. 27, 1868, W. T. Sherman Papers, LC.
42. Robert C. Schenck to his daughter, Jan. 11, 1868, Schenck Papers, Rutherford B. Hayes

Library, Fremont, Ohio. See also *Congressional Globe*, 40th Cong., 2d sess., pt. 1, p. 456, Jan. 11, 1868.
43. William T. Sherman to USG, Jan. 27, 1868, W. T. Sherman Papers, LC.
44. Ibid.
45. Julia D. Grant, *Memoirs*, p. 166. See also *Congressional Globe*, 40th Cong., 2d sess., pt. 1, p. 473, Jan. 13, 1868.
46. Julia D. Grant, *Memoirs*, p. 166.
47. Benjamin P. Thomas and Harold M. Hyman, *Stanton: The Life and Times of Lincoln's Secretary of War* (New York, 1962), pp. 569–70.
48. Welles, *Diary*, Jan. 14, 1868, 3:261.
49. Ibid.
50. William T. Sherman to USG, Jan. 27, 1868, W. T. Sherman Papers, LC.
51. William T. Sherman to Andrew Johnson, Jan. 31, 1868, HL. See also *New York Times*, Feb. 5, 1868.
52. *New York Times*, Feb. 5, 1868. See also Welles, *Diary*, Feb. 4–8, 1868, 3:269–75.
53. John M. Schofield, *Forty-six Years in the Army* (New York, 1897), pp. 406–20.
54. Schofield, *Forty-six Years*, pp. 406–20; Welles, *Diary*, June 8, 1868, 3:380; George P. Brockway, "Toward a Political Interpretation of the Impeachment Trial of Andrew Johnson," unpublished article, pp. 7–12.


*Chapter XVIII*  THE PRESIDENT AND HIS CABINET

1. James Harrison Wilson to Frederick Tracy Dent, Mar. 4, 1868, Dent Papers, Morris Library, Southern Illinois University (SIU); USG to Charles W. Ford, Mar. 15 and Mar. 18, 1868, U. S. Grant Papers, Library of Congress (LC). See also *New York Herald*, May 2, 1868. Wilson had competitors; on June 20, 1868, the *New York Times* carried an advertisement for "The Cheapest Book Since the War: Coppee's Life of Grant: A Military Biography."
2. *New York Herald*, Mar. 12 and Mar. 14, 1868.
3. USG to Charles W. Ford, May 15, 1868, LC; Robert C. Schenck to his daughter, May 11, 1868, Schenck Papers, Rutherford B. Hayes Library, Fremont, Ohio; *New York Times*, May 16, 1868.
4. *New York Herald*, May 19, 1868. See also *New York Times*, May 19, 1868.
5. *New York Herald*, May 21, 1868.
6. *New York Herald*, May 22, 1868. See also *Dictionary of American Biography*, s.v. "Hawley, Joseph R."
7. Benjamin P. Thomas and Harold M. Hyman, *Stanton: The Life and Times of Lincoln's Secretary of War* (New York, 1962), p. 607.
8. *New York Herald*, May 30, 1868.
9. Ibid., June 6, 1868. See also ibid., June 7, 1868.
10. Ibid., July 2, 1868. See also ibid., Aug. 12, 1868.
11. Ibid., Aug. 14 and June 20, 1868; Charles H. Coleman, in *The Election of 1868: The Democratic Effort to Regain Control* (New York, 1933), p. 89, states that no Texas delegation was on the floor in Chicago. George T. Ruby was presumably a member of an unrecognized delegation. There were at least twelve black delegates to the convention.
12. Coleman, *Election of 1868*; William Gillette, *The Right to Vote: Politics and the Passage of the Fifteenth Amendment* (Baltimore, 1965), pp. 24, 26, 27, 47, 48n., 80, 105, 156; Edward McPherson, *The Political History of the United States of America during the Period of Reconstruction* (Washington, D.C., 1880), pp. 327–34, 374, 429, 450; Svend Petersen, *A Statistical History of the American Presidential Elections* (New York, 1963).
13. George S. Boutwell, *The Lawyer, the Statesman and the Soldier* (New York, 1887), pp. 170–71.

14. Coleman, *Election of 1868*, pp. 187–245.
15. William T. Sherman to USG, June 7, 1868, Huntington Library (HL); USG to Sherman, June 12, 1868, ibid. See also Sherman to USG, June 24, 1868, ibid.; *New York Times*, July 31, 1868.
16. *New York Times*, July 31, 1868; Orville E. Babcock to Annie C. Babcock, Aug. 21, 1868, Babcock Papers, Newberry Library, Chicago; *New York Times*, July 28, 1868.
17. *New York Times*, July 28, 1868.
18. Ibid., Aug. 14, 1868.
19. USG to Elihu B. Washburne, Sept. 23, 1868, U. S. Grant Papers, Illinois State Historical Society (ISHS); *New York Times*, Oct. 6, 1868.
20. Charlotte Perkins Gilman, *The Living of Charlotte Perkins Gilman* (New York, 1975), pp. 16–17.
21. William E. Chandler to Robert C. Schenck, Oct. 9, 1868, Schenck Papers, Rutherford B. Hayes Library; Chandler to Elihu B. Washburne, Oct. 19, 1868, Washburne Papers, LC.
22. William E. Chandler to Elihu B. Washburne, Oct. 19, 1868, Washburne Papers, LC; James G. Blaine to Washburne, Oct. 14, 1868, ibid.
23. "Reminiscences of Delia B. Sheffield," *Washington Historical Quarterly* 15 (Jan. 1924):62.
24. "Captain Grant of the Black Marines," in Irwin Silber, comp., *Songs America Voted By* (Harrisburg, Pa., 1971), p. 101; Francis H. Smith to Elihu B. Washburne, Nov. 8, 1868, Washburne Papers, LC.
25. J. D. Lee to [no name], Nov. [3 and 4], 1868, Washburne Papers, LC. See also Anson Stager to Elihu B. Washburne, Oct. 4, 1868, ibid.; *Galena Gazette*, Nov. 5, 1868; Petersen, *A Statistical History*, p. 41.
26. USG to J. Russell Jones, Nov. 4, 1868, U. S. Grant Papers, ISHS; *New York Herald*, June 20, 1868; *New York Times*, June 20, Dec. 28, and Dec. 29, 1868.
27. *New York Herald*, Jan. 2, 1869.
28. Ibid.
29. Orville H. Browning, *The Diary of Orville Hickman Browning*, ed. Theodore C. Pease and James G. Randall, 2 vols. (Springfield, Ill., 1925–33), Jan. 30, 1869, 2:237. See also *New York Herald*, Feb. 2 and Feb. 4, 1869.
30. *New York Herald*, Feb. 8, Feb. 24, and Mar. 1, 1869.
31. Gideon Welles, *Diary*, ed. by Howard K. Beale, assisted by Alan W. Brownsword, 3 vols. (New York, 1960), Mar. 4, 1869, 3:540–41. See also *New York Times*, Mar. 3, 1869; *New York Herald*, Mar. 5, 1869; Browning, *Diary*, Mar. 4, 1869, 2:243.
32. *New York Herald*, Mar. 5, 1869; *New York Times*, Mar. 5, 1869.
33. Jesse R. Grant to Frederick Tracy Dent, Feb. 4, 1869, Dent Papers, Morris Library, SIU.
34. *New York Herald*, Mar. 5, 1869.
35. Ibid.; USG, first inaugural address, Mar. 4, 1869, in James D. Richardson, ed., *A Compilation of the Messages and Papers of the Presidents, 1789–1897*, 10 vols. (Washington, D.C., 1896–99), 7:6–8. See also *New York Times*, Mar. 5, 1869.
36. USG, first inaugural address, Mar. 4, 1869, in Richardson, *Messages*, 7:6–8.
37. Ibid.
38. Ibid.
39. *New York Herald*, Mar. 5, 1869; *New York Times*, Mar. 5, 1869.
40. *New York Herald*, Mar. 5 and Mar. 6, 1869; *New York Times*, Mar. 5 and Mar. 6, 1869.
41. George T. Strong, *The Diary of George Templeton Strong*, ed. Allan Nevins and Milton H. Thomas, 4 vols. (New York, 1952), Mar. 3, 1869, 4:242.
42. Henry Adams to Charles Milnes Gaskell, Apr. 19, 1869, in *Letters of Henry Adams*, ed. Worthington C. Ford, 2 vols. (Boston, 1930), 1:156; Henry Adams to Charles Francis Adams, Jr., Feb. 3, 1869, ibid., 1:152; Henry Adams, *The Education of Henry Adams* (Boston, 1918), p. 262; *New York Herald*, Mar. 6, 1869. See also Henry Adams to Charles Francis Adams, Jr., Feb. 23, 1869, in *Letters*, 1:152.
43. *New York Herald*, Mar. 6, 1869.

44. Joseph Medill to Elihu B. Washburne, Mar. 5, 1869, Washburne Papers, LC. See also *New York Herald*, Mar. 6, 1869.
45. *New York Herald*, Mar. 6, 1869. See also *Dictionary of American Biography*, s.v. "Stewart, Alexander Turney."
46. *New York Herald*, Mar. 6, 1869.
47. John Burroughs interview with Hamlin Garland, ca. 1890, typescript, Doheny Library, University of Southern California.
48. *New York Herald*, Mar. 7, 1869; *Laws of the United States of America from the 4th of March, 1789, to the 4th of March, 1815*, 5 vols. (Washington, D.C., 1915), 1:644; Carl Schurz, *The Reminiscences of Carl Schurz*, 3 vols. (New York, 1907–8), 3:305.
49. Schurz, *Reminiscences*, 3:305–6. See also USG to the Senate of the United States, Mar. 6, 1869, in Richardson, *Messages*, 7:8–9; George H. Stuart, *The Life of George H. Stuart*, ed. Robert E. Thompson (Philadelphia, 1890).
50. USG to Elihu B. Washburne, Mar. 11, 1869, U. S. Grant Papers, ISHS; Welles, *Diary*, Mar. 5, 1869, 3:543.
51. USG to Elihu B. Washburne, Oct. 8, 1865, U. S. Grant Papers, ISHS; Schurz, *Reminiscences*, 3:305.
52. Julia D. Grant, *Personal Memoirs of Julia Dent Grant*, ed. John Y. Simon (New York, 1975), p. 188.
53. Hamilton Fish, Diary, Nov. 3, 1869, Fish Papers, LC.
54. USG to Hamilton Fish, Mar. 10, 1869, in Allan Nevins, *Hamilton Fish: The Inner History of the Grant Administration*, rev. ed., 2 vols. (New York, 1957), 1:112.
55. James Burke Chapin, "Hamilton Fish and American Expansion" (Ph.D. diss., Cornell University, 1971), pp. 26–27.
56. Henry Adams to Charles Frances Adams, Jr., Mar. 11, 1869, in *Letters of Henry Adams*, 1:152. See also David Ames Wells to T. H. Dudley, Feb. 13, 1869, HL.
57. Jacob Dolson Cox, "How Judge Hoar Ceased to Be Attorney-General," *Atlantic Monthly* 76 (Aug. 1895):164.
58. Ibid.
59. Ibid.
60. Ben Perley Poore and O. H. Tiffany, *Life of U. S. Grant* (Philadelphia, 1885), p. 157.
61. George W. Childs, "Mr. Childs' Recollections," in Frank A. Burr, *A New, Original and Authentic Record of the Life and Deeds of General U. S. Grant* (Boston, 1885), pp. 977–78. The painting, now at West Point, is reproduced in *The Papers of Ulysses S. Grant*, ed. John Y. Simon, 8 vols. to date (Carbondale, Ill., 1967–), 1:14.
62. Adams, *Education*, p. 265.
63. *New York Herald*, Mar. 6, 1869.
64. Welles, *Diary*, Mar. 5, 1869, 3:544.
65. Horace White to Elihu B. Washburne, Mar. 11, 1869, Washburne Papers, LC. See also *New York Herald*, Mar. 6–11, 1869.
66. Julia D. Grant, *Memoirs*, p. 173.
67. Ibid.
68. Ibid.
69. *New York Herald*, Mar. 11, 1869.

*Chapter XIX* ORIGINAL OCCUPANTS OF THIS LAND

1. USG, first inaugural address, Mar. 4, 1869, in James D. Richardson, ed., *A Compilation of the Messages and Papers of the Presidents, 1789–1897*, 10 vols. (Washington, D.C., 1896–99), 7:6–8.
2. Clarence King, *Mountaineering in the Sierra Nevada* (Boston, 1872), pp. 39–40.
3. Ibid.; George H. Stuart, *The Life of George H. Stuart*, ed. Robert E. Thompson (Philadelphia, 1890), p. 239.

4. King, *Mountaineering*, p. 292.
5. Francis Paul Prucha, *American Indian Policy in Crisis: Christian Reformers and the Indian, 1865–1900* (Norman, Okla., 1976), pp. 11–12.
6. Ibid., pp. 21–22; USG to William T. Sherman, Mar. 2, 1868, ibid., p. 23.
7. Robert M. Utley, "The Celebrated Peace Policy of General Grant," *North Dakota History* 20 (July 1953):121.
8. Arthur C. Parker, *The Life of General Ely S. Parker* (Buffalo, Buffalo Historical Society, 1919), pp. 77, 89; Lewis Henry Morgan, *League of the HO-DÉ-NO-SAU-NEE, Iroquois* (Rochester, N.Y., 1851). A thoroughly researched new biography of Parker is needed.
9. Parker, *Life*, p. 39.
10. Henry E. Fritz, *The Movement for Indian Assimilation, 1860–1890* (Philadelphia, 1963).
11. Robert Winston Mardock, *The Reformers and the American Indian* (Columbia, Mo., 1971), pp. 57–58.
12. Stuart, *Life*, p. 240.
13. Henry B. Whipple, quoted in Elsie Mitchell Rushmore, *The Indian Policy during Grant's Administrations* (Jamaica, N.Y., 1914), p. 26.
14. Lawrie Tatum, *Our Red Brothers and the Peace Policy of President Ulysses S. Grant* (1899; reprint ed., Lincoln, Nebr., 1970).
15. Mardock, *Reformers and the American Indian*, p. 130; Robert G. Athearn, *William Tecumseh Sherman and the Settlement of the West* (Norman, Okla., 1956), p. 278.
16. USG to George H. Stuart, July 22, 1871, in Mardock, *Reformers and the American Indian*, p. 106. See also *Investigation into Indian Affairs*, 41st Cong., 3d sess., House Report 39 (serial set 1464).
17. Parker, *Life*, pp. 221–23.
18. Ibid., p. 155.
19. John M. Blum et al., *The National Experience* (New York, 1963), p. 399.
20. Prucha, *American Indian Policy*, p. 403. See also Helen Hunt Jackson, *Century of Dishonor* (New York, 1881); Bernard W. Sheehan, *Seeds of Extinction: Jeffersonian Philanthropy and the American Indian* (Williamsburg, Va., 1973).
21. USG to Julia D. Grant, Mar. 19, 1853, in John Y. Simon, ed., *The Papers of Ulysses S. Grant*, 8 vols. to date (Carbondale, Ill., 1967–), 1:294–96.
22. *New York Herald*, May 26, June 2, June 6, and June 7, 1870.
23. *New York Herald*, June 7, 1870.

*Chapter XX*  A FRIDAY AND A FRIEND

1. *Gold Panic Investigation*, 41st Cong., 2d sess., House Report 31 (serial set 1436), pp. 168–69.
2. Walter T. K. Nugent, *The Money Question during Reconstruction* (New York, 1967).
3. *Gold Panic Investigation*, pp. 37, 171, 176.
4. Ibid., pp. 152–55, 242–46.
5. Ibid., pp. 171–72, 152–53.
6. Ibid., p. 152. See also ibid., pp. 243–44.
7. Ibid., p. 153.
8. Ibid., pp. 154, 437–44.
9. Ibid., p. 173. See also *Whisky Frauds*, 44th Cong., 1st sess., House Miscellaneous Doc. 186 (serial set 1706), pp. 369, 421–37.
10. *Gold Panic Investigation*, p. 155.
11. Ibid., pp. 444, 174. See also ibid., pp. 230–33, 444–49.
12. Ibid., pp. 444–45.
13. Julia D. Grant, *Personal Memoirs of Julia Dent Grant*, ed. John Y. Simon (New York, 1975), p. 182.
14. Gould and Corbin recollected the letter in almost precisely the same words: GOULD: " 'Tell your husband,' or 'Tell Mr. Corbin, that my husband is very much annoyed by your specu-

lations. You must close them as quick as you can.' "—*Gold Panic Investigation*, p. 157. COR-
BIN: "Tell your husband [or tell Mr. Corbin] that my husband is very much annoyed by
your speculations, and you must close them as quick as you can!"—*Gold Panic Investigation*,
p. 252 (phrase in brackets included in the testimony). Julia Grant, many years later, recalled
that she wrote, "The General says, if you have any influence with your husband, tell him to
have nothing whatever to do with ――― [her deletion in her manuscript]. If he does, he
will be ruined, for come what may, he (your brother) will do his duty to the country and the
trusts in his keeping." She added, "I signed 'Sis.' " The parenthetical "your brother"
suggests that she was reconstructing, not simply remembering.—Julia D. Grant, *Memoirs*,
p. 182.
15. *Gold Panic Investigation*, pp. 174-75.
16. Ibid., p. 251.
17. Ibid., pp. 252, 156.
18. Ibid., p. 159.
19. Ibid., p. 256.
20. Ibid., pp. 256, 342-63.
21. *New York Herald*, Sept. 1 and Sept. 8, 1869.
22. Ibid., Sept. 7, 1869. See also ibid., Sept. 2 and Sept. 6, 1869.
23. Ibid., Sept. 7, 1869.
24. Ibid., Sept. 7, 1869. See also ibid., Sept. 5, Sept. 6, and Sept. 8, 1869.
25. Ibid., Sept. 8, 1869.
26. Ibid.

*Chapter XXI*   ENGLAND AND SANTO DOMINGO

1. Adrian Cook, *The Alabama Claims: American Politics and Anglo-American Relations, 1865–1872*
   (Ithaca, N.Y., 1975), p. 89.
2. Hamilton Fish, Diary, Jan. 8, 1870, Fish Papers, Library of Congress.
3. Edward Thornton to Lord Clarendon, Jan. [?], 1870, Thornton Papers, Bodleian Library;
   Fish, Diary, Jan. 11, 1870.
4. Benjamin Moran to Adam Badeau, Jan. 29, 1870, Huntington Library (HL). See also
   Moran to Badeau, Feb. 12, Feb. 21, Feb. 24, Apr. 21, and Apr. 23, 1870, ibid.
5. *New York Herald*, Jan. 2, 1870. See also Sumner Welles, *Naboth's Vineyard: The Dominican
   Republic, 1844–1924*, 2 vols. (New York, 1928), 1:67.
6. Orville E. Babcock passport, Babcock Papers, Newberry Library, Chicago; Babcock to
   Annie C. Babcock, July 31, 1869, ibid. See also Fish, Diary, Apr. 6, 1869.
7. Copy of the Navy Department order to the *Tuscora*, Aug. 23, 1869, Babcock Papers, Newberry Library. See also Orville E. Babcock to "Sir," Sept. 4, 1869, ibid.
8. Orville E. Babcock to William L. Cazneau, [Sept. 1869], ibid.
9. Benjamin Moran to Adam Badeau, Dec. 22, 1869, HL.
10. J. C. Bancroft Davis, in David Herbert Donald, *Charles Sumner and the Rights of Man* (New
    York, 1970), p. 435; Edward L. Pierce, *Memoir and Letters of Charles Sumner*, 4 vols. (Boston,
    1877–93), 4:439.
11. John W. Forney to Orville E. Babcock, June 6, 1870, Babcock Papers, Newberry Library;
    Donald, *Sumner*, p. 436.
12. J. C. Bancroft Davis to Orville E. Babcock, Feb. 28, 1870, Babcock Papers, Newberry
    Library. See also Raymond H. Perry to Babcock, Jan. 20, 1870, ibid.; Perry to P. Soulier,
    Jan. 22, 1870, ibid.
13. *Davis Hatch*, 41st Cong., 2d sess., Senate Report 234 (serial set 1409), pp. i–xlvii, 1–268.
14. Charles Sumner to Orville E. Babcock, Mar. 10, 1870, Babcock Papers, Newberry Library;
    Edward Thornton to Lord Clarendon, Mar. 22 and Apr. 5, 1870, Thornton Papers, Bod-
    leian Library. See also Fish, Diary, Apr. 4, 1870.
15. Fish, Diary, Apr. 29, 1870; Edward Thornton to Lord Clarendon, May 17, 1870, Thornton

Papers, Bodleian Library. See also F. M. Kelley to Orville E. Babcock, Apr. 14 and May 4, 1870, Babcock Papers, Newberry Library.
16. Fish, Diary, May 6 and May 14, 1870.
17. Raymond H. Perry, in Fish, Diary, June 1, 1870; *Davis Hatch*, p. 209.
18. Jesse R. Grant, *In the Days of My Father, General Grant* (New York, 1925), p. 136; Edward Thornton to Lord Clarendon, June 14, 1870, Thornton Papers, Bodleian Library.
19. Fish, Diary, June 13, 1870.
20. Ibid., June 25, 1870.
21. *Davis Hatch*, pp. 210–11.
22. Jesse R. Grant, *In the Days of My Father*, p. 137; Adelbert Ames to Benjamin F. Butler, June 28, 1870, Ames Papers, Sophia Smith Collection, Smith College; Ames to Blanche Butler, June 28, 1870, ibid.
23. Fish, Diary, July 1, 1870; Edward Thornton to Edmund Hammond, Aug. 1, 1870, Thornton Papers, Bodleian Library.
24. Fish, Diary, July 1, 1870.
25. Ibid., June 27, July 14, 1870; Edward Thornton to Edmund Hammond, July 19, 1870, Thornton Papers, Bodleian Library; Hamilton Fish to Lyman Trumbull, Aug. 5, 1870, Trumbull Papers, Illinois State Historical Society (ISHS).
26. Fish, Diary, Oct. 21, 1870. See also Edwards Pierrepont to Julia D. Grant, Nov. 7, 1870, William R. Rowley Papers, ISHS.
27. Max Woodhull to Robert C. Schenck, Oct. 31, 1870, Schenck Papers, Rutherford B. Hayes Library, Fremont, Ohio.
28. Fish, Diary, Dec. 2, 1870; Max Woodhull to Robert C. Schenck, Dec. 3, 1870, Schenck Papers, Rutherford B. Hayes Library.
29. Fish, Diary, Dec. 4, 1870.
30. Ibid., Dec. 20, 1870.
31. Harris Fahnestock to Robert C. Schenck, Jan. 13, 1871, Schenck Papers, Rutherford B. Hayes Library. See also Edwards Pierrepont to Schenck, Dec. 16, 1870, ibid.; Moses H. Grinnell to Schenck, Dec. 19, 1870, ibid.; Schenck demand note for $25,000 payable to Jay Cooke, Dec. 27, 1870, ibid.; Jay Cooke to Schenck, Feb. 10, 1871, ibid.
32. Fish, Diary, Jan. 2, 1871.
33. USG, State of the Union address, December 5, 1870, in James D. Richardson, ed., *A Compilation of the Messages and Papers of the Presidents, 1789–1897*, 10 vols. (Washington, D.C., 1896–99), 6:99–100.
34. Lyman Trumbull to William Jayne, Nov. 18, 1870, Jayne Papers, ISHS.
35. *Congressional Globe*, 41st Cong., 3d sess., pt. 1, pp. 217–18, Dec. 21, 1870; Fish, Diary, Dec. 23, 1870.
36. *Congressional Globe*, 41st Cong., 3d sess., pt. 1, pp. 227–30, Dec. 21, 1870.
37. Pierce, *Sumner*, 4:437, 441.
38. *Congressional Globe*, 41st Cong., 3d sess., pt. 1, pp. 227–30, Dec. 21, 1870.
39. Edward Thornton to Lord Granville, Dec. 20, 1870, and Jan. 10, 1871, Thornton Papers, Bodleian Library.
40. Edward Thornton to Lord Granville, Feb. 14, 1871, Thornton Papers, Bodleian Library. See also Cook, *Alabama Claims*, pp. 158–59.
41. Fish, Diary, Apr. 8, 1871; John Morley, *The Life of William Ewart Gladstone*, 3 vols. (London, 1903), 2:402; Andrew Lang, *Life, Letters, and Diaries of Sir Stafford Northcote, First Earl of Iddesleigh* (Edinburgh, 1891), p. 232. See also Edward Thornton to Lord Granville, Apr. 2, 1872, Thornton Papers, Bodleian Library.
42. Lang, *Northcote*, pp. 232, 240.
43. Ibid., p. 241.
44. Fish, Diary, May 8, 1871.
45. Edward Thornton to Lord Granville, Feb. 6 and Feb. 20, 1872, Thornton Papers, Bodleian Library; Thornton to Edmund Hammond, July 2, 1872, ibid.
46. Cook, *Alabama Claims*, p. 244.

## Chapter XXII  DEMOCRACY

1. James Russell Lowell to Leslie Stephen, Mar. 25, 1870, in Martin Duberman, *James Russell Lowell* (Boston, 1966), p. 232; Moorfield Storey and Edward W. Emerson, *Ebenezer Rockwood Hoar: A Memoir* (Boston, 1911), pp. 203, 230.
2. "Mr. Hosea Biglow's Speech in March Meeting" (Apr. 5, 1866), in James Russell Lowell, *The Poetical Works of James Russell Lowell*, ed. Marjorie R. Kaufman (Boston, 1978), pp. 278, 280.
3. Ibid., pp. 280–81.
4. Ibid., p. 284.
5. Adelbert Ames to Blanche Butler, June 1, 1870, Ames Papers, Sophia Smith Collection, Smith College.
6. Adelbert Ames to Blanche Butler, Apr. 29, 1870, ibid.
7. Adelbert Ames to Blanche Butler, May 21 and June 18, 1870, ibid.
8. Blanche Ames Ames, *Adelbert Ames, 1835–1933: General, Senator, Governor* (North Easton, Mass., 1964).
9. Adelbert Ames to Blanche Butler, Apr. 26, 1870, Ames Papers, Sophia Smith Collection.
10. Adelbert Ames to Blanche Butler, Apr. 27, 1870, ibid.
11. Adelbert Ames to Blanche Butler, June 19, 1870, ibid.
12. Adelbert Ames to Blanche Butler, June 1, 1870, ibid.
13. Adelbert Ames to Blanche Butler, June 17, 1870, ibid.
14. Adelbert Ames to Blanche Butler, June 15, 1870, ibid.
15. Jacob Dolson Cox, "How Judge Hoar Ceased to be Attorney-General," *Atlantic Monthly* 76 (Aug. 1895):169.
16. Ibid., p. 169.
17. Ibid., pp. 169–70.
18. Ibid., p. 170. See also Hans L. Trefousse, *Ben Butler: The South Called Him Beast* (New York, 1957), p. 248.
19. Cox, "Judge Hoar," p. 170.
20. Ibid., p. 171.
21. Obituary notice in *The Dartmouth*, 4th series, 2 (Feb. 25, 1881):259–60.
22. George S. Boutwell, *Reminiscences of Sixty Years in Public Affairs*, 2 vols. (New York, 1902), 2:252; "Act to Enforce the Provisions of the Fourteenth Amendment . . . ," April 20, 1871, *U.S. Statutes at Large*, vol. 17, p. 13.
23. Amos T. Akerman to Foster Blodgett, July [?], 1871, Akerman Papers, Alderman Library, University of Virginia; Akerman to Garnet Andrews (Washington, Georgia), July 31, 1871, ibid.
24. Amos T. Akerman to USG, Aug. 5, 1871, ibid.; Akerman to Benjamin F. Butler, Aug. 9, 1871, ibid.
25. Allen W. Trelease, *White Terror: The Ku Klux Klan Conspiracy and Southern Reconstruction* (New York, 1971), pp. 402–8.
26. Amos T. Akerman to J. H. H. Wilcox, Aug. 16, 1871, Akerman Papers, Alderman Library.
27. Amos T. Akerman to E. P. Jackson, Aug. 18, 1871, ibid.
28. Amos T. Akerman to George S. Boutwell, Aug. 23, 1871, ibid.; Akerman to W. E. Walker (Trenton, N.J.), Sept. 8, 1871, ibid.; Akerman to R. A. Hill (Oxford, Miss.), Sept. 12, 1871, ibid.
29. Amos T. Akerman to B. D. Silliman, Nov. 9, 1871, ibid.
30. Amos T. Akerman to Lewis W. Merrill, Nov. 9, 1871, ibid.; *New York Tribune*, Nov. 13, 1871, in Trelease, *White Terror*, pp. 369–70; Akerman to A. H. Terry, Nov. 18, 1871, in Trelease, *White Terror*, pp. 402–3.
31. Amos T. Akerman to O. O. Howard, Nov. 9, 1871, Akerman Papers, Alderman Library.
32. Amos T. Akerman to Ebenezer Rockwood Hoar, Nov. 13, 1871, ibid.

33. Amos T. Akerman to Henry McNeal Turner, Nov. 16, 1871, ibid.
34. Amos T. Akerman to Benjamin Conley, Dec. 28, 1871, ibid. See also *New York Times*, Dec. 12, Dec. 13, Dec. 14, and Dec. 15, 1871; *New York Sun*, Dec. 1871.
35. Amos T. Akerman to Benjamin Conley, Dec. 28, 1871, Akerman Papers, Alderman Library; Akerman to Lewis W. Merrill, Jan. 8, 1872, ibid.; Akerman to "My dear Sir," Jan. 1, 1872, ibid.
36. Adelbert Ames to Blanche B. Ames, May 16, 1871, Ames Papers, Sophia Smith Collection.
37. Ibid.
38. *New National Era*, Jan. 6 and Jan. 19, 1871. See also *New York Times*, May 28, 1870.
39. Israel Smith to James Webster Smith, July 3, 1870, in *New National Era*, July 20, 1870. See also O. O. Howard to James Webster Smith, July 14, 1870, O. O. Howard Papers, Bowdoin College Library; Howard to the editor of the *New York Tribune*, July 8, 1870, ibid.; *New National Era*, Aug. 13, 1874; *Washington Evening Star*, July 1, 1870.
40. James Webster Smith to David Clark, June 29, 1870, in *New National Era*, July 14, 1870.
41. *New National Era*, Jan. 26, 1871; unidentified clipping, O. O. Howard Papers, Bowdoin College Library.
42. USG to William Worth Belknap, cited without date in *Illinois Guardian*, Aug. 14, 1872, clipping in O. O. Howard Papers, Bowdoin College Library. See also *New National Era*, Jan. 26, 1871; Blanche B. Ames to Sarah Butler, Sept. [?], 1870, Ames Papers, Sophia Smith Collection.
43. James Webster Smith to David Clark, June 29, 1871, O. O. Howard Papers, Bowdoin College Library. For the circumstances of the court-martial, see *New York Times*, July 15, Oct. 21, and Oct. 24, 1870; *New National Era*, Aug. 6 and Aug. 17, 1874.
44. Transcript of the court-martial of James Webster Smith, Oct. 21–24, 1870, together with the report of Joseph Holt to William Worth Belknap, Nov. 20, 1870, National Archives, Washington, D.C.
45. Ibid.
46. David Clark to O. O. Howard, June 21, 1871, O. O. Howard Papers, Bowdoin College Library. See also *New York Tribune*, June 14, 1871; O. O. Howard to David Clark, Jan. 27, 1871, O. O. Howard Papers, Bowdoin College Library (Howard wrote of "John Tappan" but it is likely he meant Lewis).
47. Peter S. Michie, "Caste at West Point," *North Atlantic Review* 130 (June 1880):609–11; *New York Times*, Aug. 12, 1874. See also Nancy Ledogar and Andrea Roschke, "Cadet Smith at West Point" (seminar paper, Mount Holyoke College, 1977); Walter Scott Dillard, "The United States Military Academy, 1865–1900: The Uncertain Years" (Ph.D. diss., University of Washington, 1972), ch. 8.
48. O. O. Howard to David Clark, June 24, 1871, O. O. Howard Papers, Bowdoin College Library; David Clark to O. O. Howard, July 1, 1871, ibid.

### *Chapter XXIII* GREATNESS

1. Carl Schurz to Jacob Dolson Cox, April 4, 1871, in Carl Schurz, *Speeches, Correspondence and Political Papers of Carl Schurz*, sel. and ed. Frederic Bancroft, 6 vols. (New York, 1913), 2:255. See also James Schouler, *History of the Reconstruction Period, 1865–1877* (New York, 1913), p. 218.
2. William Makepeace Thayer, *From Tannery to the White House: The Life of Ulysses S. Grant* (Boston, 1887).
3. Edward Thornton to Edmund Hammond, Aug. 6, 1872, Thornton Papers, Bodleian Library; George W. Childs, *Recollections* (Philadelphia, 1890), p. 75; James A. Garfield, *The Diary of James A. Garfield*, ed. Harry J. Brown and Frederick D. Williams, 3 vols. (East Lansing, Mich., 1967–73), Oct. 19, 1872, 2:104; *New York Herald*, Nov. 7, 1872.

4. Benjamin Helm Bristow to John Marshall Harlan, Dec. 4, 1872, Bristow Papers, Library of Congress (LC).
5. Ibid. See also Ross A. Webb, *Benjamin Helm Bristow: Border State Politician* (Lexington, Ky., 1969), p. 115.
6. Benjamin Helm Bristow to John Marshall Harlan, Dec. 4, 1872, Bristow Papers, LC; Susan B. Anthony, Diary, June 18, 1873, Anthony Papers, LC.
7. Julia D. Grant, *Personal Memoirs of Julia Dent Grant*, ed. John Y. Simon (New York, 1975), pp. 193–94.
8. Noah H. Swayne to Benjamin Helm Bristow, Sept. 15, 1873, Bristow Papers, LC.
9. Ibid.
10. C. H. Hill to Benjamin Helm Bristow, Sept. 20, 1873, ibid.; Hamilton Fish, Diary, Sept. 30, 1873, Fish Papers, LC.
11. Fish, Diary, Dec. 1, 1873.
12. Edwards Pierrepont to Benjamin Helm Bristow, Dec. 2, 1873, Bristow Papers, LC.
13. J. W. Stevenson to Benjamin Helm Bristow, Dec. 12, 1873, ibid.; C. H. Hill to Bristow, Dec. 19, 1873, ibid. See also Fish, Diary, Dec. 30, 1873.
14. C. H. Hill to Benjamin Helm Bristow, Dec. 13 and Dec. 19, 1873, Bristow Papers, LC.
15. Julia D. Grant, *Memoirs*, p. 194; David Davis to Benjamin Helm Bristow, Jan. 6, 1874, Bristow Papers, LC; Fish, Diary, Dec. 30, 1873.
16. Fish, Diary, Dec. 30, 1873, and Jan. 25, 1874. See also Allan Nevins, *Hamilton Fish: The Inner History of the Grant Administration*, rev. ed., 2 vols. (New York, 1957), 2:663.
17. *Nation*, Jan. 22, 1874, in Nevins, *Fish*, 2:664; J. W. Stevenson to Benjamin Helm Bristow, Jan. 9, 1874, Bristow Papers, LC; C. H. Hill to Bristow, Jan. 10, 1874, ibid.
18. David Davis to Benjamin Helm Bristow, Jan. 13, 1874, Bristow Papers, LC. See also draft of message withdrawing the Cushing nomination, Babcock Papers, Newberry Library, Chicago; Fish, Diary, Jan. 16, 1874.
19. Noah H. Swayne to B. H. Bristow, Jan. 20, 1874, Bristow Papers, LC.
20. USG, fifth annual message, Dec. 1, 1873, in James D. Richardson, ed., *A Compilation of the Messages and Papers of the Presidents, 1789–1897*, 10 vols. (Washington, D.C., 1896–99), 7:244.
21. Ibid., pp. 286–87.
22. Irwin Unger, *The Greenback Era: A Social and Political History of American Finance, 1865–1879* (Princeton, 1964), pp. 241–43.
23. Ibid.
24. George T. Strong, *The Diary of George Templeton Strong*, ed. Allan Nevins and Milton H. Thomas, 4 vols. (New York, 1952), June 8, 1874, 4:528. See also Unger, *Greenback Era*, p. 243; *Sanborn and Other Contracts*, 43d Cong., 1st sess., House Exec. Doc. 132, Feb. 16, 1874 (serial set 1808).
25. USG to Nathaniel Carlin, Oct. 27, 1873, Huntington Library (HL). See also Charles W. Ford to "whom it may concern," July 1, 1873, HL.
26. USG to Nathaniel Carlin, Nov. 28, 1873, ibid.
27. Ibid.
28. USG to John F. Long, July 20, 1874, ibid.
29. USG to Nathaniel Carlin, Dec. 26, 1874, ibid. See also USG to John F. Long, Nov. 29, 1874, ibid.
30. John F. Long to Nathaniel Carlin, Oct. 13, 1875, ibid.

### Chapter XXIV   WEDDING AND WHISKEY

1. Algernon Bertram Freeman-Mitford, Baron Redesdale, *Memories*, 2 vols. (London, 1915), 2:516; *New York Herald*, May 22, 1874.
2. Juliette M. Babbitt, "Nellie Grant Sartoris and Her Children," *Midland Monthly* 7 (Feb. 1897), 99–102.

3. Adelbert Ames to Blanche B. Ames, July 24, 1875, Ames Papers, Sophia Smith Collection, Smith College; Henry James to Alice James, May 19, [1879], in *The Letters of Henry James*, ed. Leon Edel, 2 vols. (Cambridge, Mass., 1974–75), 2:233–34.

4. *New York World*, Sept. 5, 1885.

5. Julia D. Grant to USG, May 22, 1875, U. S. Grant Papers, Library of Congress (LC); USG to Julia D. Grant, May 22, 1875, ibid.

6. James A. Garfield, *The Diary of James A. Garfield*, ed. Harry J. Brown and Frederick D. Williams, 3 vols. (East Lansing, Mich., 1967–73), 3:6; H. V. Boynton, "The Whiskey Ring," *North American Review* 123 (Oct. 1876):282. See also William S. McFeely, "Ulysses S. Grant, 1869–1877," in C. Vann Woodward, ed., *Responses of the Presidents to Charges of Misconduct* (New York, 1974), p. 136.

7. For an account of these events by one of the participants, see John McDonald, *Secrets of the Great Whiskey Ring; and Eighteen Months in the Penitentiary, Containing a Complete Exposure of the Illicit Whisky Frauds Culminating in 1875 . . . to Which Is Added the Author's Remarkable Experiences While a Convict . . .* (St. Louis, 1880).

8. Bluford Wilson, in *Whisky Frauds*, 44th Cong., 1st sess., House Miscellaneous Doc. 186 (serial set 1706), p. 355.

9. McDonald, *Secrets of the Great Whiskey Ring*, p. 140; Bluford Wilson, in *Whisky Frauds*, pp. 356–58.

10. Benjamin Helm Bristow, in *Whisky Frauds*, pp. 322–28; Marc Bloch, *Strange Defeat* (New York, 1968), p. 26.

11. Bluford Wilson, in *Whisky Frauds*, p. 355.

12. Hamilton Fish, Diary, May 22, 1875, Fish Papers, LC.

13. James Harrison Wilson interview with Hamlin Garland, ca. 1890, typescript, Doheny Library, University of Southern California.

14. Ibid.

15. USG to Elihu B. Washburne, Oct. 7, 1878, U. S. Grant Papers, Illinois State Historical Society; James Harrison Wilson interview with Hamlin Garland.

16. Bluford Wilson in *Whisky Frauds*, p. 359. See also Horace Porter, ibid., p. 542.

17 Bluford Wilson, ibid., p. 357. See also Fish, Diary, July 20 and July 21, 1875.

18. Bluford Wilson to John B. Henderson, Sept. 26, 1875, in *Whisky Frauds*, p. 550.

19. Edwards Pierrepont, ibid., pp. 2–3. The dating of the telegrams in the transcript of the congressional investigation is confusing; since Pierrepont was testifying in March 1876, the date of October 19, 1876, on one of the telegrams is obviously in error; others also appear misdated with respect to year. In the Bristow Papers in the Library of Congress, pencil copies of three of them are dated October 25, 27, and 28, 1873, suggesting that the conspirators were on guard two years before the prosecutions.

20. Edwards Pierrepont, in *Whisky Frauds*, p. 3.

21. Charles S. Bell, ibid., p. 123. See also Zachariah Chandler to Bell, Jan. 5, 1876, ibid., p. 113.

22. Fish, Diary, Dec. 21, 1875.

23. Charles S. Bell, in *Whisky Frauds*, p. 126. See also Elias W. Fox, ibid., pp. 335–43.

24. Bluford Wilson, ibid., p. 366.

25. Fish, Diary, Feb. 8, 1876.

26. Charles S. Bell, in *Whisky Frauds*, p. 114. See also Zachariah Chandler to Bell, Feb. 16, 1876, ibid., p. 117.

27. Fish, Diary, Mar. 1, 1876; Allan Nevins, *Hamilton Fish: The Inner History of the Grant Administration*, rev. ed., 2 vols. (New York, 1957), 2:803.

28. Bluford Wilson, in *Whisky Frauds*, p. 373.

29. USG, message to Congress, Jan. 13, 1875, in James D. Richardson, ed., *A Compilation of the Messages and Papers of the Presidents, 1789–1897*, 10 vols. (Washington, D.C., 1896–99), 7:307–8.

30. Ibid., pp. 308, 312.

31. Marshall Jewell to L. C. Fairchild, Dec. 28, 1874, in William B. Hesseltine, *Ulysses S. Grant, Politician* (New York, 1935), p. 353.
32. Adelbert Ames to Blanche B. Ames, Sept. 2, 1875, Ames Papers, Sophia Smith Collection. See also Vernon Lane Wharton, *The Negro in Mississippi, 1865–1890* (New York, 1965), pp. 181–98.
33. Adelbert Ames to Blanche B. Ames, Sept. 2, 1875, Ames Papers, Sophia Smith Collection.
34. Adelbert Ames to Blanche B. Ames, Sept. 3, 1875, ibid.
35. Adelbert Ames to Blanche B. Ames, Sept. 5, 1875, ibid. See also Helen Griffith, *Dauntless in Mississippi: The Life of Sarah A. Dickey, 1838–1904* (South Hadley, Mass., 1965).
36. Adelbert Ames to Blanche B. Ames, Sept. 6, 1875, Ames Papers, Sophia Smith Collection.
37. Adelbert Ames to Blanche B. Ames, Sept. 6 and Sept. 7, 1875, ibid.
38. Adelbert Ames to Blanche B. Ames, Sept. 10 and Sept. 17, 1875, ibid.
39. Adelbert Ames to Blanche B. Ames, Sept. 22 and Sept. 23, 1875, ibid.
40. Adelbert Ames to Blanche B. Ames, Sept. 26 and Oct. 4, 1875, ibid.
41. Griffith, *Dauntless in Mississippi*, p. 86; Adelbert Ames to Blanche B. Ames, Oct. 8, 1875, Ames Papers, Sophia Smith Collection.
42. Blanche B. Ames to Adelbert Ames, Oct. 10, 1875, Ames Papers, Sophia Smith Collection. See also Benjamin F. Butler to Adelbert Ames, Oct. 11, 1875, ibid.; John R. Lynch, *The Facts of Reconstruction* (New York, 1968), p. 151; Julius Eric Thompson, "Hiram R. Revels, 1827–1901: A Biography" (Ph.D. diss., Princeton University, 1973).
43. Adelbert Ames to Blanche B. Ames, Oct. 12, 1875, Ames Papers, Sophia Smith Collection.
44. Griffith, *Dauntless in Mississippi*, pp. 84–85; Adelbert Ames to Blanche B. Ames, Oct. 15, 1875, Ames Papers, Sophia Smith Collection.
45. Adelbert Ames to Blanche B. Ames, Oct. 28, 1875, Ames Papers, Sophia Smith Collection.
46. Adelbert Ames to Blanche B. Ames, Oct. 28 and Oct. 30, 1875, ibid.
47. Adelbert Ames to Blanche B. Ames, Nov. 4, 1875, ibid.

*Chapter XXV* WAIFS

1. James A. Garfield, *The Diary of James A. Garfield*, ed. Harry J. Brown and Frederick D. Williams, 3 vols. (East Lansing, Mich., 1967–73), January 2, 1876, 3:208; Rebecca Latimer Felton, *Country Life in Georgia in the Days of My Youth* (Atlanta, 1919), p. 133. See also Benjamin Brown French, Diary, Jan. 1, 1870, Library of Congress (LC).
2. Felton, *Country Life*, p. 133; *New York Tribune*, Mar. 3, 1876.
3. *New York Tribune*, Mar. 6, 1876.
4. *New York Times*, Oct. 15, 1890. There is no biography of Belknap, and the available information about him and his wives is sketchy.
5. *New York Times*, Oct. 15, 1890.
6. *Malfeasance of W. W. Belknap, Late Secretary of War*, 44th Cong., 1st sess., House Report 186, Mar. 2, 1876 (serial set 1708).
7. *Malfeasance of W. W. Belknap*, pp. 3, 4. The full investigation (with explicit testimony), the articles of impeachment, and the report of the Senate trial of William Worth Belknap are in *Malfeasance of W. W. Belknap* (cited in note 6); *Impeachment of W. W. Belknap*, 44th Cong., 1st sess., House Report 222, Mar. 8, 1876 (serial set 1708); *Impeachment of William W. Belknap*, 44th Cong., 1st sess., House Report 345, Mar. 30, 1876 (serial set 1709); *Report of the House Managers on the Impeachment of W. W. Belknap, Late Secretary of War*, 44th Cong., 1st sess., House Report 791, Aug. 2, 1876 (serial set 1713); "Proceedings in the Senate . . . Trial of William W. Belknap," *Congressional Record*, 44th Cong., 1st sess., vol. 14, pt. 7.
8. Robert C. Schenck to his daughter, July 27, 1870, Schenck Papers, Rutherford B. Hayes Library, Fremont, Ohio.
9. Hamilton Fish, Diary, Nov. 28, 1871, Fish Papers, LC; *Emma Mine Investigation*, 44th Cong., 1st sess., House Report 579, May 25, 1876 (serial set 1711).

10. Garfield, *Diary*, April 26, 1875, 3:67–68; *Surveys in the Territory of Wyoming*, 44th Cong., 1st sess., House Report 794, Aug. 2, 1876 (serial set 1714).

11. Benjamin Helm Bristow, in *Surveys in the Territory of Wyoming*, pp. 1, 2, 26.

12. Ibid., p. 4; Hamilton Fish, Diary, Apr. 29, 1875.

13. USG to Silas Reed, Aug. 7, 1875, in *Surveys in the Territory of Wyoming*, p. 4.

14. *Investigations of the Navy Department*, 44th Cong., 1st sess., House Report 784, July 22, 1876 (serial set 1712); *Deposits of Money by the Secretary of the Navy*, 44th Cong., 1st sess., House Report 789, Aug. 1, 1876 (serial set 1713); *Kittery Navy Yard*, 44th Cong., 1st sess., House Report 790, Aug. 1, 1876 (serial set 1713).

15. *Investigations of the Navy Department*, p. 159.

16. *New York Tribune*, Mar. 4, Mar. 6, and Mar. 9, 1876.

17. Ross A. Webb, *Benjamin Helm Bristow: Border State Politician* (Lexington, Ky., 1969), pp. 223–25; Garfield, *Diary*, Mar. 3, 1876, 3:243–44.

18. Garfield, *Diary*, Mar. 2, 1876, 3:242–43.

19. Fish, Diary, Mar. 3–4, 1876.

20. *New York Tribune*, Mar. 4, Mar. 6, and Mar. 9, 1876; USG to C. C. Augur, Sept. 15, 1867, Augur Papers, Illinois State Historical Society; Julia D. Grant, *Personal Memoirs of Julia Dent Grant*, ed. John Y. Simon (New York, 1975), pp. 189–92.

21. *Report of the House Managers on the Impeachment of W. W. Belknap*, House Report 791, Aug. 2, 1876.

22. William T. Sherman to John M. Schofield (reporting order to Gillem), Apr. 13, 1873, in *Modoc War*, 43d Cong., 1st sess., House Exec. Doc. 122, Jan. 4, 1874 (serial set 1607), p. 77; Alfred H. Lowe et al. to USG, July 12, 1873, in *Modoc War*, p. 310; USG, second inaugural address, Mar. 4, 1873, in James D. Richardson, ed., *A Compilation of the Messages and Papers of the Presidents, 1789–1897*, 10 vols. (Washington, D.C., 1896–99), 7:222. See also *New York Times*, Apr. 16, 1873, in Robert G. Ahearn, *William Tecumseh Sherman and the Settlement of the West* (Norman, Okla., 1956), p. 301.

23. James C. Olson, *Red Cloud and the Sioux Problem* (Lincoln, Nebr., 1965), pp. 171–75.

24. Ibid., pp. 175–89; Edgar I. Stewart, *Custer's Luck* (Norman, Okla., 1955), pp. 125–37.

25. Philip H. Sheridan to Alfred H. Terry, Nov. 9, 1875, Sheridan Papers, LC. The writer is indebted to Fred Nicklason for this citation.

26. Philip H. Sheridan to William T. Sherman, May 22, 1876, in Ahearn, *Sherman and the Settlement of the West*, p. 310. See also O. O. Howard, *Autobiography of Oliver Otis Howard*, 2 vols. (New York, 1907), 2:468–85.

27. Daniel H. Chamberlain to USG, July 22, 1876, in *Slaughter of American Citizens at Hamburgh, S.C.*, 44th Cong., 1st sess., Senate Exec. Doc. 95, Aug. 1, 1876 (serial set 1664), p. 4; USG to Chamberlain, July 26, 1873, ibid., p. 6.

28. Webb, *Benjamin Helm Bristow*, p. 240.

29. Ibid., pp. 250–51; Fish, Diary, June 20, 1876.

30. USG, State of the Union message, Dec. 5, 1876, in Richardson, *Messages*, 7:399.

31. Ibid., pp. 399–400.

32. Ibid., p. 400.

33. Ibid.

34. Ibid., p. 401.

35. Ibid.

36. Ibid., p. 402.

37. Ibid., p. 410.

38. Ibid., pp. 410–11.

39. Ibid., p. 412.

40. Ibid., p. 413.

41. Julia Grant Cantacuzene, *My Life Here and There* (New York, 1921), p. 7.

42. George W. Childs, *Recollections* (Philadelphia, 1890), p. 76.

43. Ibid., p. 77.

44. Ibid., p. 78.

45. C. Vann Woodward, *Reunion and Reaction: The Compromise of 1877 and the End of Reconstruction* (Boston, 1951), p. 108.
46. Ibid., p. 112; Childs, *Recollections*, p. 78.
47. Childs, *Recollections*, p. 80.
48. Woodward, *Reunion and Reaction*, p. 151.
49. Childs, *Recollections*, p. 81; *New York Herald*, Mar. 3, 1877. See also *New York Herald*, Mar. 4, 1877.
50. Julia D. Grant, *Memoirs*, p. 197. See also Daniel Ammen, *The Old Navy and the New . . . with an Appendix of Personal Letters from General Grant* (Philadelphia, 1891), p. 519.
51. Garfield, *Diary*, Mar. 5, 1877, 3:453–54.
52. *New York Herald*, Mar. 25, 1877; Julia D. Grant, *Memoirs*, pp. 196–97.

*Chapter XXVI* A R O U N D   T H E   W O R L D

1. John Russell Young, *Around the World with General Grant*, 2 vols. (New York, 1879), 1:409–10, and *passim* for the remainder of the chapter.
2. USG to Jesse R. Grant, May 9, 1877, U. S. Grant Papers, Missouri Historical Society; *New York Herald*, May 17, 1877. See also *New York Herald*, May 4 and May 15, 1877.
3. J. F. Packard, *Grant's Tour around the World* (Cincinnati, 1880), p. 108. This is one of several interesting pirate pieces; it contains a few things not in Young. See also *Times* (London), May 29 and May 30, 1877.
4. *Times* (London), May 31, 1877; *Morning Post* (London), June 1, 1877.
5. *Times* (London), June 4, 1877. See also *Times* (London), June 2, 1877; Young, *Around the World*, 1:19–20; duke of Wellington to the writer, May 23, 1979; Algernon Bertram Freeman-Mitford, Baron Redesdale, *Memories*, 2 vols. (London, 1915), 2:612.
6. Packard, *Grant's Tour*, pp. 57–63; *Times* (London), June 22, 1877; *Morning Post* (London), June 22, 1877.
7. *Morning Post* (London), June 22, 1877.
8. G. E. Buckle, *The Life of Benjamin Disraeli, Earl of Beaconsfield*, 6 vols. (London, 1920), 6:168. See also Anthony Trollope to Donald Currie, June 8, 1877, in B. A. Booth, ed., *The Letters of Anthony Trollope* (London, 1951), p. 372; *Times* (London), June 19 and June 21, 1877.
9. *Times* (London), June 16, 1877.
10. Ibid., June 4, 1877; USG to George W. Childs, June 10, 1877, in Packard, *Grant's Tour*, pp. 64–65.
11. *Times* (London), June 16, 1877.
12. USG to George W. Childs, June 10, 1877, in Packard, *Grant's Tour*, pp. 64–65.
13. Henry James to Alice James, May 19, [1879], in *The Letters of Henry James*, ed. Leon Edel, 2 vols. (Cambridge, Mass., 1974–75), 2:233. See also Juliette M. Babbitt, "Nellie Grant Sartoris and Her Children," *Midland Monthly* 7 (Feb. 1897), pp. 99–102.
14. Elizabeth Longford, *Queen Victoria: Born to Succeed* (New York, 1965), p. 420. See also Julia D. Grant, *Personal Memoirs of Julia Dent Grant*, ed. John Y. Simon (New York, 1975), pp. 206–8; Adam Badeau, *Grant in Peace: From Appomattox to Mount McGregor* (Hartford, Conn., 1887), pp. 282–89; *Times* (London), June 27 and June 29, 1877; *Morning Post* (London), June 28, 1877.
15. Jesse R. Grant, *In the Days of My Father, General Grant* (New York, 1925), p. 228; Longford, *Queen Victoria*, p. 420.
16. Badeau, *Grant in Peace*, p. 288.
17. USG to Ulysses S. Grant, Jr., July 2, 1877, Huntington Library. See also USG to Elihu B. Washburne, June 9, 1877, U. S. Grant Papers, Illinois State Historical Society (ISHS).
18. Packard, *Grant's Tour*, pp. 107–8.
19. *Newcastle Daily Chronicle*, Sept. 24, 1877, in Young, *Around the World*, 1:90–91.
20. Ibid., pp. 94–95, 98.
21. Ibid., 100–101.

22. John Russell Young, Diary, Oct. 29, 1877, Young Papers, Library of Congress (LC). See also Dossier 149793, (B$\frac{a}{1.099}$), "Grant, Président de la République des États-Unis," Préfecture de Police, Paris; Young, Diary, Oct. 31, 1877.

23. Young, *Around the World*, 1:156; Dossier 149793, "Grant,"; Dossier "Valentino" (B$\frac{a}{1.554}$) Préfecture de Police, Paris; Young, *Around the World*, 1:162.

24. Young, *Around the World*, 1:169, 175.

25. Ibid., pp. 193, 188.

26. Ibid., pp. 218–19.

27. Ibid., pp. 256, 274.

28. Ibid., p. 334.

29. Ibid., pp. 346, 354, 362.

30. Ibid., pp. 366, 368.

31. Edmund Wilson, *Patriotic Gore: Studies in the Literature of the American Civil War* (New York, 1962), p. 163.

32. Young, *Around the World*, 1:469.

33. Martin Duberman, *James Russell Lowell* (Boston, 1966), p. 293.

34. Young, *Around the World*, 1:413–14.

35. Ibid., p. 415.

36. Ibid., pp. 416–17.

37. Julia D. Grant, *Memoirs*, p. 246.

38. Young, *Around the World*, 1:592, 593, 599.

39. Ibid., p. 611; Lord Lytton to John Morley, quoted in Mary Lutyens, *The Lyttons in India* (London, 1979), p. 150. On the physical and psychological aspects of Grant's drinking, Solomon Cohen, M.D., to the writer, Dec. 12, 1979.

40. Young, *Around the World*, 2:138.

41. USG to John Russell Young, Mar. 4, 1879, Young Papers, LC.

42. USG to Elihu B. Washburne, Apr. 4, 1879, U. S. Grant Papers, ISHS; Young, *Around the World*, 2:316–18.

43. Julia Grant Cantacuzene, *My Life Here and There* (New York, 1921), p. 166; Young, *Around the World*, 2:372. See also "Report on the Famine in the Northern Provinces of China," (Hugh Fraser to the Earl of Derby) presented to the Houses of Parliament, written by W. F. Mayers, Chinese Secretary. This can be found in reports of American consular officials, Jan. 8–Oct. 4, 1878, Microcopy M92, Roll 49, National Archives, Washington, D.C. The American consuls reported on the famine with its "mortality that will be considered appalling by European standards." The report continued, "Were it not for the possession of improved weapons" mobs of starving people might have caused a severe political disturbance. The maps the consuls sent home indicate the Grants passed through the region of the famine; no comments are made on the coincidence of their visit.

44. Young, *Around the World*, 2:528–30.

45. USG to Elihu B. Washburne, Apr. 4, 1879, U. S. Grant Papers, ISHS; Packard, *Grant's Tour*, p. 827.

46. O. O. Howard, *Autobiography of Oliver Otis Howard*, 2 vols. (New York, 1907), 2:480; Young, Diary, Sept. 26, 1879, Young Papers, LC; Julia D. Grant, *Memoirs*, p. 311.

47. Ben Perley Poore and O. H. Tiffany, *Life of General Grant* (Philadelphia, 1885), pp. 458–59.

*Chapter XXVII* GRANT & WARD

1. William B. Hesseltine, *Ulysses S. Grant, Politician* (New York, 1935), p. 432.

2. John Russell Young, Diary, June 30, 1878, Young Papers, Library of Congress (LC); USG to Elihu B. Washburne, Oct. 7 and Dec. 24, 1878, U. S. Grant Papers, Illinois State Historical Society (ISHS); Hesseltine, *Ulysses S. Grant*, p. 433.

3. USG to Adam Badeau, Aug. 25, 1879, in Adam Badeau, *Grant in Peace: From Appomattox to Mount McGregor* (Hartford, Conn., 1887), p. 518.

4. Justin Kaplan, *Mr. Clemens and Mark Twain* (New York, 1968), p. 260; Badeau, *Grant in Peace*, p. 14. See also Samuel L. Clemens, *The Autobiography of Mark Twain*, ed. Charles Neider (New York, 1959), pp. 241–45.

5. Kaplan, *Mr. Clemens*, pp. 261–62, 263.

6. Hesseltine, *Ulysses S. Grant*, p. 435; T. L. Crowder, typescript [1880], U. S. Grant Papers, ISHS.

7. Crowder, typescript.

8. Badeau, *Grant in Peace*, p. 320; Julia D. Grant, *Personal Memoirs of Julia Dent Grant*, ed. John Y. Simon (New York, 1975), p. 321. See also Hesseltine, *Ulysses S. Grant*, pp. 321–33, 438.

9. Julia D. Grant, *Memoirs*, p. 321.

10. Ibid., pp. 321–22; *Galena Gazette*, June 8, 1880.

11. USG to Nellie G. Sartoris, June 27, 1880, U. S. Grant Papers, Chicago Historical Society; Julia D. Grant, *Memoirs*, p. 321.

12. USG to James A. Garfield, Aug. 5, 1880, Garfield Papers, LC.

13. Julia D. Grant, *Memoirs*, p. 322. See also USG to James A. Garfield, Sept. 19, 1880, Garfield Papers, LC; USG to Edwards Pierrepont, Sept. 10, 1880, U. S. Grant Papers, LC; USG to Julia D. Grant, Oct. 25, 1880, ibid.

14. USG to James A. Garfield, Sept. 19 and Nov. 11, 1880, Garfield Papers, LC.

15. USG to James A. Garfield, Jan. 26, 1881, ibid. See also USG to Garfield, Feb. 6, 1881, ibid.

16. USG to James A. Garfield, Apr. 24, 1881, ibid.

17. Ibid.; James A. Garfield to USG, May 15, 1881, Garfield Papers, LC.

18. Ben Perley Poore and O. H. Tiffany, *Life of U. S. Grant* (Philadelphia, 1885), p. 483.

19. David M. Pletcher, *Rails, Mines, and Progress: Seven American Promoters in Mexico, 1867–1911* (Ithaca, N.Y., 1958), p. 181.

20. Ibid., p. 150.

21. Osgood Hardy, "Ulysses S. Grant, President of the Mexican Southern Railroad," *Pacific Historical Review* 24 (1955):111–20.

22. Julia D. Grant, *Memoirs*, pp. 322–23.

23. Pletcher, *Rails, Mines, and Progress*, p. 164.

24. Ibid., pp. 171–77.

25. Ibid., p. 181.

26. Karen A. Wendell, "Grant & Ward: The Anatomy of a Fraud" (seminar paper, History Department, Smith College, Apr. 1977).

27. Ibid.

28. Hesseltine, *Ulysses S. Grant*, p. 446.

29. Ibid., p. 447.

30. C. W. Moulton to William T. Sherman, May 9, 1884, W. T. Sherman Papers, LC.

31. Hugh McCulloch, *Men and Measures of Half a Century* (New York, 1889), p. 360.

32. Wendell, "Grant & Ward," p. 15A.

33. C. W. Moulton to William T. Sherman, May 9, 1884, W. T. Sherman Papers, LC.

34. Julia D. Grant, *Memoirs*, p. 328.

35. Thomas M. Pitkin, *The Captain Departs: Ulysses S. Grant's Last Campaign* (Carbondale, Ill., 1973), p. 10.

36. Ibid., p. 12; Clemens, *Autobiography of Mark Twain*, p. 239.

*Chapter XXVIII*  TO WRITE A BOOK: TO BE A MAN

1. George H. Stuart, *The Life of George H. Stuart*, ed. Robert E. Thompson (Philadelphia, 1890), pp. 312–13, 313n.

2. USG to Vivian Sartoris, Sept. 7, 1884, U. S. Grant Papers, Chicago Historical Society.

3. Thomas M. Pitkin, *The Captain Departs: Ulysses S. Grant's Last Campaign* (Carbondale, Ill.,

1973), p. 24; Pitkin's book is an excellent treatment of Grant's death, and this account is largely drawn from it. On the course of Grant's illness, Solomon Cohen, M.D., to the writer, Jan. 8, 1980.

4. USG to Adam Badeau, Oct. 8, 1884, in Adam Badeau, *Grant in Peace: From Appomattox to Mount McGregor* (Hartford Conn., 1887), p. 565.

5. Badeau, *Grant in Peace*, p. 240; Henry Adams, *The Education of Henry Adams* (Boston, 1918), pp. 263–64. See also correspondence between Adam Badeau and Benjamin Moran, Huntington Library.

6. Adams, *Education*, p. 264.

7. USG to John Russell Young, [Nov. 1884?], Young Papers, Library of Congress (LC).

8. USG to Vivian Sartoris, Sept. 7, 1884, U. S. Grant Papers, Chicago Historical Society; Pitkin, *Captain Departs*, pp. 15–16.

9. Samuel L. Clemens, *The Autobiography of Mark Twain*, ed. Charles Neider (New York, 1959), p. 237.

10. Ibid., pp. 237–39.

11. Ibid., p. 240.

12. USG to Nellie G. Sartoris, Nov. 18, 1884, U. S. Grant Papers, Chicago Historical Society.

13. USG to Nellie G. Sartoris, Feb. 16, 1885, U. S. Grant Papers, Chicago Historical Society; Julia D. Grant to Mrs. W. S. Hillyer, Feb. 18, 1885, U. S. Grant Papers, Illinois State Historical Society (ISHS); Pitkin, *Captain Departs*, p. 26. See also William H. Vanderbilt to Julia D. Grant, Jan. 10, 1885, clipping in Francis Springer scrapbook, ISHS; Julia D. Grant to William H. Vanderbilt, Jan. 11, 1885, Grant Family Papers, Morris Library, Southern Illinois University (SIU).

14. Pitkin, *Captain Departs*, pp. 33–34.

15. Solomon Cohen, M.D., to the writer, Jan. 8, 1980.

16. Frederick D. Grant to A. D. Worthington, Mar. 2, 1885, Grant Family Papers, Morris Library, SIU; Clemens, *Autobiography*, p. 241.

17. William T. Sherman to J. E. Tourtelotte, Mar. 4, 1885, W. T. Sherman Papers, Missouri Historical Society; William T. Sherman to Sherman Moulton, Apr. 12, 1886, Huntington Library.

18. USG to John H. Douglas, June 17, 1885, U. S. Grant Papers, LC.

19. *New York World*, Apr. 19, 1885; *New York Tribune*, May 6, 1885; *New York Sun*, May 6, 1885. See also Pitkin, *Captain Departs*, pp. 37–38.

20. USG to Adam Badeau, May 5, 1885, in Pitkin, *Captain Departs*, p. 41. See also ibid., *passim*.

21. Ibid., p. 57.

22. Ibid., p. 56.

23. *New York Tribune*, Apr. 26, 1885, in Pitkin, *Captain Departs*, p. 58.

24. Pitkin, *Captain Departs*, p. 63.

25. Ibid., p. 61.

26. Ibid., p. 65; Robert Penn Warren, *The Legacy of the Civil War* (New York, 1961), p. 86.

27. The manuscript of the *Personal Memoirs* is on reels 5 and 6, U. S. Grant Papers, LC.

28. Ulysses S. Grant, *Personal Memoirs of U. S. Grant*, 2 vols. (New York, 1885–86), 2:542, 543, 544.

29. Ibid., pp. 546–47.

30. Ibid., pp. 549–50.

31. Ibid., p. 551.

32. Ibid., pp. 552, 553.

33. Ibid., p. 553; R. C. Townsend, "Sherwood Anderson: Trying to Be a Man," in *Trying to Be a Man*, forthcoming.

34. USG, *Memoirs*, 2:553.

35. The pages, with Grant's alterations, are in a salesman's dummy book for the *Personal Memoirs* at the Huntington Library.

36. USG to John H. Douglas, July 10, 1885, in Pitkin, *Captain Departs*, p. 84; manuscript of the

*Personal Memoirs*, reel 6, U. S. Grant Papers, LC; USG to Frederick D. Grant, [no date], in Pitkin, *Captain Departs*, p. 86.

37. USG to John H. Douglas, July 14, 1885, in Pitkin, *Captain Departs*, p. 87.
38. USG to John H. Douglas, [July ? 1885], Grant Papers, LC.
39. Julia Grant Cantacuzene, *My Life Here and There* (New York, 1921), p. 53. See also John H. Douglas, "Record of the Last Days of the Magnanimous Soldier U. S. Grant," John Hancock Douglas Papers, LC, published in the Appendix of Pitkin, *Captain Departs*, pp. 133–39.


EPILOGUE

1. Julia D. Grant, *Personal Memoirs of Julia Dent Grant*, ed. John Y. Simon (New York, 1975).
2. *New York Times*, Dec. 15, 1902. See also ibid., Dec. 16, Dec. 18, Dec. 21, and Dec. 27, 1902.
3. Ibid.
4. John Russell Young, Diary, Apr. 27, 1897, Young Papers, Library of Congress.
5. *New York Times*, Dec. 26 and Dec. 21, 1902.
6. Ibid., Nov. 11, 1909, Sept. 27, 1929; Jane Grant de MaCarty, in conversation with the writer, Aug. 16, 1974.
7. Frank Hatch Jones to N. H. Beauregard, Jan. 19, 1915, Missouri Historical Society.
8. *New York Times*, June 9, 1934. See also ibid., July 2, 1924.
9. Edward M. House, Diary, Jan. 10, 1913, Yale University Library; the writer is indebted to Wilton B. Fowler for this citation. See also *New York Times*, June 9, 1934.
10. For a favorable view of Grant during the war see Bruce Catton, *Grant Moves South* (Boston, 1960), and *Grant Takes Command* (Boston, 1969). For early and excellent statements of the revised view of post–Civil War politics see the essays in H. Wayne Morgan, ed., *The Gilded Age: A Reappraisal*, rev. ed. (Syracuse, 1963).

# Selected Bibliography

MANUSCRIPT COLLECTIONS

The collection of the Huntington Library, San Marino, California, contains papers of Ulysses S. Grant and Walt Whitman as well as of Simon Bolivar Buckner, Charles A. Dana, David G. Farragut, Henry W. Halleck, Joseph E. Johnston, George Gordon Meade, George H. Mellish, Benjamin Moran, E. O. C. Ord, Ely S. Parker, David Dixon Porter, Harvey Reid, Alexander R. Shepherd, Philip H. Sheridan, Thomas Kilby Smith, Edwin M. Stanton, Gideon Welles, David Ames Wells, James Harrison Wilson, and many other important observers of Grant's career.

Other major collections consulted include the following:

Akerman, Amos T.: Alderman Library, University of Virginia.

Ames, Adelbert: Sophia Smith Collection, Smith College.

Anthony, Susan B.: Library of Congress.

Arthur, Chester A.: Library of Congress.

Augur, Christopher Columbus: Illinois State Historical Society.

Babcock, Orville E.: Newberry Library, Chicago.

Bailey, Jacob Whitman: United States Military Academy Library.

Bayard, Thomas Francis: Library of Congress.

Blaine, James G.: Library of Congress.

Bristow, Benjamin Helm: Library of Congress.

Browning, Orville H.: Illinois State Historical Society.

Butler, Benjamin F.: Library of Congress.

Chandler, William E.: Library of Congress.

Chandler, Zachariah: Library of Congress.

Church, William C.: Library of Congress.

Conkling, Roscoe: Library of Congress.

Davis, David: Illinois State Historical Society.
Delafield, Richard: United States Military Academy Library.
Delano, Columbus: Library of Congress.
Dent, Frederick Tracy: Morris Library, Southern Illinois University.
Douglas, John Hancock: Library of Congress.
Fish, Hamilton: Library of Congress.
French, Benjamin Brown: Library of Congress.
Garfield, James A.: Library of Congress.
Garland, Hamlin: Doheny Library, University of Southern California.
Grant, Ulysses S.: Chicago Historical Society; Illinois State Historical Society; Library of Congress; Missouri Historical Society; Morris Library, Southern Illinois University; United States Military Academy Library.
Greeley, Horace: Library of Congress.
Grierson, Benjamin H.: Illinois State Historical Society.
Hancock, Winfield Scott: Illinois State Historical Society.
Harlan, John Marshall: Library of Congress.
Howard, O. O.: Bowdoin College Library.
Jayne, William: Illinois State Historical Society.
Johnson, Andrew: Library of Congress.
Lee, Robert E.: Illinois State Historical Society.
Lewis, Lloyd: Newberry Library, Chicago.
Lincoln, Abraham: Illinois State Historical Society.
McClernand, John A.: Illinois State Historical Society.
Miltmore, Ira: Chicago Historical Society.

Palmer, John M.: Illinois State Historical Society.
Parsons, Lewis B.: Illinois State Historical Society.
Rawlins, John A.: Chicago Historical Society; Illinois State Historical Society.
Ricks, Jesse Jay: Illinois State Historical Society.
Robb, Thomas P.: Illinois State Historical Society.
Rowley, William R.: Illinois State Historical Society.
Schenck, Robert C.: Rutherford B. Hayes Library, Fremont, Ohio.
Schurz, Carl: Library of Congress.
Sheridan, Philip H.: Library of Congress.
Sherman, William T.: Library of Congress; Missouri Historical Society.
Smith, Luther R.: Missouri Historical Society.
Stephens, Alexander H.: Library of Congress.
Stuart, George H.: Library of Congress.
Sumner, Charles: Library of Congress.
Thornton, Edward: Bodleian Library, Oxford University.
Trumbull, Lyman: Illinois State Historical Society.
Wallace, W. H. L.: Wallace-Dickey Family Papers, Illinois State Historical Society.
Washburne, Elihu B.: Library of Congress.
Webb, Alexander S.: Sterling Library, Yale University.
White, Horace: Illinois State Historical Society.
Wilson, James Harrison: Library of Congress.
Yates, Richard: Illinois State Historical Society.
Young, John Russell: Library of Congress.

BOOKS, ARTICLES, AND DISSERTATIONS

Aaron, Daniel. *The Unwritten War: American Writers and the Civil War.* New York, 1973.
Abbott, John S. C. *The History of the Civil War in America.* New York, 1863.
[Adams, Henry.] "American Finance, 1865–1869." *Edinburgh Review* 129 (Apr. 1869):504–33.
Adams, Henry. *The Education of Henry Adams.* Boston, 1918.
———. *Letters of Henry Adams.* Edited by Worthington C. Ford. 2 vols. Boston, 1930.
———. "The Session." *North American Review* 108 (Apr. 1869):610–40.
Ambrose, Stephen E. *Crazy Horse and Custer: The Parallel Lives of Two American Warriors.* Garden City, N.Y., 1975.
———. *Duty, Honor, Country: A History of West Point.* Baltimore, 1966.

————. *Halleck: Lincoln's Chief of Staff.* Baton Rouge, 1962.

————. *Upton and the Army.* Baton Rouge, 1964.

Ames, Adelbert. "The Capture of Fort Fisher." In Military Order of the Loyal Legion of the United States, Massachusetts Commandry, *Civil War Papers*, 1:269–95. Boston, 1900.

Ames, Blanche Ames. *Adelbert Ames, 1835–1933: General, Senator, Governor.* North Easton, Mass., 1964.

Ames, Blanche Butler, ed. *Chronicles from the Nineteenth Century: Family Letters of Blanche Butler and Adelbert Ames.* 2 vols. Clinton, Mass., 1957.

Ames, Charles Edgar. *Pioneering the Union Pacific: A Reappraisal of the Builders of the Railroad.* New York, 1969.

Ames, Mary Clemmer. *Ten Years in Washington: Life and Scenes in the National Capital, As a Woman Sees Them.* Hartford, Conn., 1874.

Ammen, Daniel. *The Old Navy and the New . . . with an Appendix of Personal Letters from General Grant.* Philadelphia, 1891.

Arnold, Matthew. *General Grant. With a Rejoinder by Mark Twain.* Edited and with an introduction by John Y. Simon. Carbondale, Ill., 1966.

Athearn, Robert G. *William Tecumseh Sherman and the Settlement of the West.* Norman, Okla., 1956.

Avery, I. W. *The History of the State of Georgia from 1850 to 1881.* New York, 1881.

Babbitt, Juliette M. "Nellie Grant Sartoris and Her Children." *Midland Monthly* 7 (Feb. 1897):99–102.

Bache, Richard Meade. *Life of General George Gordon Meade, Commander of the Army of the Potomac.* Philadelphia, 1897.

Badeau, Adam. *Grant in Peace: From Appomattox to Mount McGregor. A Personal Memoir.* Hartford, Conn., 1887.

————. *Military History of Ulysses S. Grant, from April, 1861, to April, 1865.* 3 vols. New York, 1882.

————. "The Mystery of Grant." *Cosmopolitan* 20 (Mar. 1896):483–92.

————. *The Vagabond.* New York, 1859.

Barber, John Warner, ed. *Connecticut Historical Collections.* New Haven, 1836.

Barnitz, Albert. *Life in Custer's Cavalry: Diaries and Letters of Albert and Jennie Barnitz, 1867–1868.* Edited by Robert M. Utley. New Haven, 1977.

Bates, David Homer. *Lincoln in the Telegraph Office.* New York, 1907.

Bates, Edward. *The Diary of Edward Bates, 1859–1866.* Edited by Howard K. Beale. Washington, D.C., 1933.

*Battles and Leaders of the Civil War.* Edited by R. U. Johnson and C. C. Buel. 4 vols. New York, 1887–88.

Bauer, Karl Jack. *The Mexican War, 1846–1848.* New York, 1974.

Beale, Howard K. *The Critical Year: A Study of Andrew Johnson and Reconstruction.* New York, 1930.

Belz, Herman. *Emancipation and Equal Rights: Politics and Constitutionalism in the Civil War Era.* New York, 1978.

————. *A New Birth of Freedom: The Republican Party and Freedmen's Rights, 1861–1866.* Westport, Conn., 1976.

————. *Reconstructing the Union: Theory and Policy during the Civil War.* Ithaca, N.Y., 1969.

Benedict, Michael Les. *A Compromise of Principle: Congressional Republicans and Reconstruction, 1863–1869.* New York, 1974.

————. *The Impeachment and Trial of Andrew Johnson.* New York, 1973.

Benson, Harry King. "The Public Career of Adelbert Ames, 1861–1876." Ph.D. dissertation, University of Virginia, 1975.

Blaine, James G. *Twenty Years of Congress: From Lincoln to Garfield.* 2 vols. Norwich, Conn., 1884–86.

Blassingame, John W. *Black New Orleans, 1860–1880.* Chicago, 1973.

Boatner, Mark M., III. *The Civil War Dictionary.* New York, 1959.

Bolles, Charles E. "General Grant and the News of Mr. Lincoln's Death." In "Memoranda on the Life of Lincoln," *Century Magazine* 40 (June 1890):309–10.

Bonadio, Felice A. *North of Reconstruction: Ohio Politics, 1865–1870*. New York, 1970.

Boutwell, George S. *The Lawyer, the Statesman and the Soldier*. New York, 1887.

———. *Reminiscences of Sixty Years in Public Affairs*. 2 vols. New York, 1902.

Bowers, Claude G. *The Tragic Era: The Revolution after Lincoln*. New York, 1929.

Boyd, James Penny. *The Life of William T. Sherman*. Philadelphia, 1891.

Boynton, H. V. "The Washington 'Safe Burglary' Conspiracy." *American Law Review* 11 (Apr. 1877):401–46.

———. "The Whiskey Ring." *North American Review* 123 (Oct. 1876):280–327.

Brock, W. R. *An American Crisis: Congress and Reconstruction, 1865–1867*. New York, 1963.

Browning, Orville H. *The Diary of Orville Hickman Browning*. Edited and with an introduction and notes by Theodore C. Pease and James G. Randall. 2 vols. Springfield, Ill., 1925–33.

Brownlow, William Gannaway. *Sketches of the Rise, Progress and Decline of Secession*. Philadelphia, 1862.

Burne, Alfred Higgins. *Lee, Grant and Sherman: A Study of Leadership in the 1864–65 Campaign*. Aldershot, England, 1938.

Burr, Frank A. *A New, Original and Authentic Record of the Life and Deeds of General U. S. Grant*. Boston, 1885.

Butler, Benjamin F. *Autobiography and Personal Reminiscences of Major-General Benj. F. Butler; Butler's Book*. Boston, 1892.

Cadwallader, Sylvanus. *Three Years with Grant*. Edited by Benjamin P. Thomas. New York, 1955.

Campbell, John A. *Recollections of the Evacuation of Richmond, April 2d, 1865*. Pamphlet. Baltimore, 1880.

———. *Reminiscences and Documents Relating to the Civil War during the Year 1865*. Pamphlet. Baltimore, 1886.

Cantacuzene, Julia Grant. *My Life Here and There*. New York, 1921.

Carpenter, John A. *Ulysses S. Grant*. New York, 1970.

Carr, Julian S. *The Hampton Roads Conference*. Pamphlet. Durham, N.C., 1917.

Catton, Bruce. *Grant Moves South*. Boston, 1960.

———. *Grant Takes Command*. Boston, 1969.

———. *U. S. Grant and the American Military Tradition*. Boston, 1954.

Chamberlain, Joshua L. "Appomattox." In Military Order of the Loyal Legion of the United States, New York Commandry, *Personal Recollections of the War of the Rebellion*, 3d series, pp. 260–80. New York, 1907.

Chapin, James Burke. "Hamilton Fish and American Expansion." Ph.D. dissertation, Cornell University, 1971.

Charnwood, Godfrey Rathbone Benson, first baron. *Abraham Lincoln*. London, 1917.

Chase, Salmon P. "Diary and Correspondence of Salmon P. Chase." In American Historical Association, *Annual Report . . . for the Year 1902*. Vol. 2. Washington, D.C., 1903.

———. *Inside Lincoln's Cabinet: The Civil War Diaries of Salmon P. Chase*. Edited by David Herbert Donald. New York, 1954.

Chetlain, Augustus Louis. *Recollections of Seventy Years*. Galena, Ill., 1899.

Chidsey, Donald Barr. *The Gentleman from New York: A Life of Roscoe Conkling*. New Haven, 1935.

Childs, George W. *Recollections*. Philadelphia, 1890.

———. *Recollections of General Grant*. Philadelphia, 1885.

Church, William Conant. *Ulysses S. Grant and the Period of National Preservation and Reconstruction*. New York, 1897.

Cleaves, Freeman. *Meade of Gettysburg*. Norman, Okla., 1960.

——— *Rock of Chickamauga: The Life of George H. Thomas*. Norman, Okla., 1948.

Clemens, Samuel L. [Mark Twain]. *The Autobiography of Mark Twain*. Edited by Charles Neider. New York, 1959.

————. *Mark Twain in Eruption.* Edited and with an introduction by Bernard De Voto. New York, 1940.

————. *Mark Twain's Autobiography.* Introduction by Albert Bigelow Paine. 2 vols. New York, 1924.

————. *Mark Twain's Letters.* Edited by Albert Bigelow Paine. 2 vols. New York, 1917.

Coben, Stanley. "Northeastern Business and Radical Recons'ruction: A Re-examination." *Mississippi Valley Historical Review* 46 (June 1959):67–90.

Coleman, Charles H. *The Election of 1868: The Democratic Effort to Regain Control.* New York, 1933.

Conger, Arthur L. *The Rise of U. S. Grant.* New York, 1931.

Conkling, Alfred R. *The Life and Letters of Roscoe Conkling, Orator, Statesman, Advocate.* New York, 1889.

Connelly, Thomas Lawrence. *The Marble Man: Robert E. Lee and His Image in American Society.* New York, 1977.

————. *The Politics of Command: Factions and Ideas in Confederate Strategy.* Baton Rouge, 1973.

————. "Robert E. Lee and the Western Confederacy: A Criticism of Lee's Strategic Ability." *Civil War History* 15 (June 1969):116–32.

Conway, Alan. *The Reconstruction of Georgia.* Minneapolis, 1966.

Conway, Moncure D. *Autobiography, Memoirs, and Experiences of Moncure Daniel Conway.* 2 vols. Boston, 1904.

Cook, Adrian. *The Alabama Claims: American Politics and Anglo-American Relations, 1865–1872.* Ithaca, N.Y., 1975.

Coolidge, Louis Arthur. *Ulysses S. Grant.* Boston, 1917.

Coppée, Henry. *General Thomas.* New York, 1893.

————. *Grant and His Campaigns: A Military Biography.* New York, 1866.

Cox, Jacob Dolson. "How Judge Hoar Ceased to Be Attorney-General." *Atlantic Monthly* 76 (Aug. 1895):162–73.

Cox, Lawanda C. *Politics, Principle, and Prejudice, 1865–1866: Dilemma of Reconstruction America.* Glencoe, Ill., 1963.

Craven, Avery. *The Coming of the Civil War.* New York, 1966.

————. *Reconstruction: The Ending of the Civil War.* New York, 1969.

Crenshaw, W. V. "Benjamin F. Butler: Philosophy and Politics, 1866–1879." Ph.D. dissertation, University of Georgia, 1976.

Cruden, Robert. *The Negro in Reconstruction.* Englewood Cliffs, N.J., 1969.

Cunliffe, Marcus. *Soldiers and Civilians: The Martial Spirit in America, 1775–1865.* Boston, 1968.

Current, Richard N. *Old Thad Stevens: A Story of Ambition.* Madison, Wis., 1942.

Curry, Richard O. "The Abolitionists and Reconstruction: A Critical Appraisal." *Journal of Southern History* 34 (Nov. 1968):527–45.

Curtis, Newton Martin. "The Capture of Fort Fisher." In Military Order of the Loyal Legion of the United States, New York Commandry, *Personal Recollections of the War of the Rebellion,* 3d series, pp. 25–51. New York, 1907.

Dana, Charles A. *Recollections of the Civil War.* New York, 1899.

————, and Wilson, James Harrison. *The Life of Ulysses S. Grant, General of the Armies of the United States.* Springfield, Mass., 1868.

Davis, J. C. Bancroft. *Mr. Fish and the Alabama Claims: A Chapter in Diplomatic History.* Boston, 1893.

————. *Mr. Sumner, the Alabama Claims, and Their Settlement.* New York, 1878.

Davis, Jefferson. *The Rise and Fall of the Confederate Government.* New York, 1881.

Dillard, Walter Scott. "The United States Military Academy, 1865–1900: The Uncertain Years." Ph.D. dissertation, University of Washington, 1972.

Dodge, Grenville M. "Personal Recollections of General Grant and His Campaigns in the West." In Military Order of the Loyal Legion of the United States, New York Commandry, *Personal Recollections of the War of the Rebellion,* 3d series, pp. 347–72. New York, 1907.

————. *Personal Recollections of President Abraham Lincoln, General Ulysses S. Grant, and General William T. Sherman.* Council Bluffs, Iowa, 1914.

————. "Personal Recollections of Some of Our Great Commanders in the Civil War." In Military Order of the Loyal Legion of the United States, New York Commandry, *Personal Recollections of the War of the Rebellion,* 3d series, pp. 207–27. New York, 1907.

Donald, David Herbert. *Charles Sumner and the Rights of Man.* New York, 1970.

————. *Lincoln Reconsidered: Essays on the Civil War Era.* New York, 1956.

————. *The Politics of Reconstruction, 1863–1867.* Baton Rouge, 1965.

————, ed. *Why the North Won the Civil War.* Baton Rouge, 1960.

Dorris, Jonathan T. *Pardon and Amnesty under Lincoln and Johnson: The Restoration of the Confederates to their Rights and Privileges, 1861–1898.* Chapel Hill, N.C., 1953.

————. "Pardoning the Leaders of the Confederacy." *Mississippi Valley Historical Review* 15 (June 1928):3–21.

————. "Pardon Seekers and Brokers: A Sequel to Appomattox." *Journal of Southern History* 1 (Aug. 1935):276–92.

Duberman, Martin. *Charles Francis Adams, 1807–1886.* Boston, 1961.

————. *James Russell Lowell.* Boston, 1966.

Dunning, William A. *Reconstruction, Political and Economic, 1865–1877.* New York, 1907.

DuPont, Samuel F. *A Selection of His Civil War Letters.* Edited by John D. Hayes. 3 vols. Ithaca, N.Y., 1969.

Durbin, E. F. M., and Bowlby, John. *Personal Aggressiveness and War.* London, 1939.

Durden, Robert F. *James Shepherd Pike: Republicanism and the American Negro, 1850–1882.* Durham, N.C., 1957.

Early, Jubal A. *War Memoirs.* Edited and with an introduction by Frank E. Vandiver. Bloomington, Ind., 1960.

Eaton, Dorman B. *Civil Service in Great Britain: A History of Abuses and Reforms and Their Bearing upon American Politics.* New York, 1881.

Eaton, John, with Mason, Ethel Osgood. *Grant, Lincoln and the Freedmen.* New York, 1907.

Ellis, John B. *The Sights and Secrets of the National Capital.* Chicago, 1869.

Ellis, Joseph, and Moore, Robert. *School for Soldiers: West Point and the Profession of Arms.* New York, 1974.

Ellis, Richard N., ed. *The Western American Indian.* Lincoln, Nebr., 1972.

Emerson, John W. "Grant's Life in the West and His Mississippi Campaigns." *Midland Monthly* 6–11 (Oct. 1896–May/June 1899).

[Federal Writers' Project, Work Projects Administration.] *Entertaining a Nation: The Career of Long Branch.* Bayonne, N.J., 1940.

Fels, Rendig. *American Business Cycles, 1865–1897.* Chapel Hill, N.C., 1959.

Felton, Rebecca Latimer. *Country Life in Georgia in the Days of My Youth.* Atlanta, 1919.

————. *My Memoirs of Georgia Politics.* Atlanta, 1911.

Fessenden, Francis. *Life and Public Services of William Pitt Fessenden.* 2 vols. Boston, 1907.

Ficklen, John Rose. *History of Reconstruction in Louisiana (through 1868).* Johns Hopkins University Studies in Historical and Political Science, series 28. Baltimore, 1910.

Fiske, A. S. *Our Dead Hero.* Pamphlet. Ithaca, N.Y., 1885.

Foner, Eric. *Free Soil, Free Labor, Free Men: The Ideology of the Republican Party before the Civil War.* New York, 1970.

Foote, Henry S. *War of the Rebellion; or, Scylla and Charybdis.* New York, 1866.

Foote, Shelby. *The Civil War: A Narrative.* 3 vols. New York, 1958–74.

Ford, Worthington C., ed. *A Cycle of Adams Letters, 1861–1865.* 2 vols. Boston, 1920.

Forgie, George B. *Patricide in the House Divided: A Psychological Interpretation of Lincoln and His Age.* New York, 1979.

Forney, John W. *Anecdotes of Public Men.* 2 vols. New York, 1873–81.

Fowler, Wilton B. "A Carpetbagger's Conversion to White Supremacy." *North Carolina Historical Review* 43 (July 1966):286–304.

Franklin, John Hope. *Reconstruction after the Civil War*. Chicago, 1961.

Frederickson, George M. *The Inner Civil War: Northern Intellectuals and the Crisis of the Union*. New York, 1965.

Freeman, Douglas Southall. *R. E. Lee: A Biography*. 4 vols. New York, 1934–35.

Fritz, Henry E. *The Movement for Indian Assimilation, 1860–1890*. Philadelphia, 1963.

Frost, John. *The Mexican War and Its Warriors*. New Haven and Philadelphia, 1848.

Fuller, J. F. C. *The Generalship of Ulysses S. Grant*. New York, 1929.

———. *Grant and Lee: A Study in Personality and Generalship*. Bloomington, Ind., 1957.

———. *A Military History of the Western World*. 3 vols. New York, 1954–56.

Garfield, James A. *The Diary of James A. Garfield*. Edited and with an introduction by Harry J. Brown and Frederick D. Williams. 3 vols. East Lansing, Mich., 1967–73.

———. *The Works of James Abram Garfield*. Edited by Burke A. Hinsdale. 2 vols. Boston, 1882–83.

Garland, Hamlin. *Hamlin Garland's Diaries*. Edited by Donald Pizer. San Marino, Calif., 1968.

———. *Ulysses S. Grant: His Life and Character*. New York, 1898.

Gates, Paul W. "Federal Land Policy in the South, 1866–1888." *Journal of Southern History* 6 (Aug. 1940):303–30.

Gerteis, Louis S. *From Contraband to Freedman: Federal Policy toward Southern Blacks, 1861–1865*. Westport, Conn., 1973.

Gillette, William. *Retreat from Reconstruction, 1869–1879*. Baton Rouge, 1979.

———. *The Right to Vote: Politics and the Passage of the Fifteenth Amendment*. Baltimore, 1965.

Ginker, P. R.; Spregel, J. P.; and Major, M. C. *Men under Stress*. Philadelphia, 1945.

Goetzmann, William H. *Army Exploration in the American West, 1803–1863*. New Haven, 1960.

———. *When the Eagle Screamed: The Romantic Horizon in American Diplomacy, 1800–1860*. New York, 1966.

Goldhurst, Richard. *Many Are the Hearts: The Agony and the Triumph of Ulysses S. Grant*. New York, 1978.

Gordon, John B. *Reminiscences of the Civil War*. New York, 1903.

Gorham, G. C. *Life and Public Services of Edwin M. Stanton*. 2 vols. Boston, 1899.

Grant, Arthur H. *The Grant Family: A Genealogical History of the Descendants of Matthew Grant . . .* Poughkeepsie, N.Y., 1898.

Grant, Frederick D. "A Boy's Experience at Vicksburg." In Military Order of the Loyal Legion of the United States, New York Commandry, *Personal Recollections of the War of the Rebellion*, 3d series, pp. 86–100. New York, 1907.

Grant, Jesse R. *In the Days of My Father, General Grant*. New York, 1925.

Grant, Julia D. *Personal Memoirs of Julia Dent Grant*. Edited by John Y. Simon. New York, 1975.

Grant, Ulysses S. "The Battle of Shiloh." *Century Magazine* 29 (Feb. 1885):593–613.

———. *Conversations and Unpublished Letters*. Edited by Michael J. Cramer. New York, 1897.

———. *General Grant's Letters to a Friend* [Elihu B. Washburne], *1861–1880*. Introduction and notes by James Grant Wilson. New York, 1897.

———. "Grant's Letters to His Missouri Farm Tenants." Edited by LeRoy H. Fischer. *Agricultural History* 21 (1947):26–42.

———. *Letters of Ulysses S. Grant to His Father and His Youngest Sister, 1857–78*. Edited by Jesse Grant Cramer. New York, 1912.

———. *The Papers of Ulysses S. Grant*. Edited by John Y. Simon. 8 vols. to date. Carbondale, Ill., 1967—.

———. *Personal Memoirs of U. S. Grant*. 2 vols. New York, 1885–86.

———. "The Siege of Vicksburg." *Century Magazine* 30 (Sept. 1885):752–65.

Grant, Ulysses S., 3rd. *Ulysses S. Grant, Warrior and Statesman*. New York, 1969.

Green, Constance McLaughlin. *The Secret City: A History of Race Relations in the Nation's Capital*. Princeton, 1967.

Green, Horace. *General Grant's Last Stand: A Biography*. New York, 1936.

Gresham, Matilda McGrain. *Life of Walter Quintin Gresham, 1832–1895*. 2 vols. Chicago, 1919.

Griffith, Helen. *Dauntless in Mississippi: The Life of Sarah A. Dickey, 1838–1904.* South Hadley, Mass., 1965.

Grinker, Roy R., and Spiegel, John P. *Men Under Stress.* Philadelphia, 1945.

Hardy, Osgood. "Ulysses S. Grant, President of the Mexican Southern Railroad." *Pacific Historical Review* 24 (1955):111–20.

Harris, William C. *The Day of the Carpetbagger: Republican Reconstruction in Mississippi.* Baton Rouge, 1979.

———. *Presidential Reconstruction in Mississippi.* Baton Rouge, 1967.

Hart, Albert Bushnell. *Salmon Portland Chase.* Boston, 1899.

Haworth, Paul L. *The Hayes-Tilden Disputed Election of 1876.* Cleveland, 1906.

Hay, John. *Lincoln and the Civil War in the Diaries and Letters of John Hay.* Selected and with an introduction by Tyler Dennett. New York, 1939.

Hayes, Rutherford B. *Diary and Letters of Rutherford Birchard Hayes, Nineteenth President of the United States.* Edited by Charles R. Williams. 5 vols. Columbus, Ohio, 1922–26.

Headley, P. C. *The Hero Boy; or, The Life and Deeds of Lieut.-Gen. Grant.* New York, 1864.

———. *The Life and Campaigns of General U. S. Grant.* New York, 1868.

Healy, G. P. A. *Reminiscences of a Portrait Painter.* Chicago, 1894.

Henry, George Selden, Jr. "Radical Republican Policy toward the Negro during Reconstruction, 1862–72." Ph.D. dissertation, Yale University, 1963.

Henry, Robert Selph. *The Story of the Mexican War.* Indianapolis, 1950.

Hesseltine, William B. *Ulysses S. Grant, Politician.* New York, 1935.

Hewitt, Abram S. *Selected Writings of Abram S. Hewitt.* Edited by Allan Nevins, with an introduction by Nicholas M. Butler. New York, 1937.

Hirshon, Stanley P. *Grenville M. Dodge, Soldier, Politician, Railroad Pioneer.* Bloomington, Ind., 1967.

*The History of Brown County, Ohio.* Chicago, 1883.

Hittle, J. D. *The Military Staff: Its History and Development.* 3d ed. Harrisburg, Pa., 1961.

Hoar, George F. *Autobiography of Seventy Years.* 2 vols. New York, 1903.

Hobsbawm, E. J. *The Age of Capital, 1848–1875.* New York, 1975.

Hoeveler, J. David, Jr. "Reconstruction and the Federal Courts: The Civil Rights Act of 1875." *Historian* 31 (Aug. 1969):604–17.

Holt, Thomas. *Black over White: Negro Political Leadership in South Carolina during Reconstruction.* Urbana, Ill., 1977.

Hoogenboom, Ari. *Outlawing the Spoils: A History of the Civil Service Reform Movement, 1865–1883.* Urbana, Ill., 1961.

Hoppin, James Mason. *Life of Andrew Hull Foote.* New York, 1874.

Horn, Stanley F. *The Army of Tennessee: A Military History.* New York, 1941.

Hotchkiss, Jedediah. *Make a Map of the Valley.* Edited by A. P. McDonald. Dallas, 1976.

Howard, Michael. *Studies in War and Peace.* New York, 1971.

Howard, O. O. *Autobiography of Oliver Otis Howard, Major General, United States Army.* 2 vols. New York, 1907.

Howland, Edward. *Grant as a Soldier and Statesman.* London, 1868.

Hyman, Harold M. "Johnson, Stanton and Grant: A Reconsideration of the Army's Role in the Events Leading to Impeachment." *American Historical Review* 66 (Oct. 1960):85–100.

———. *A More Perfect Union: The Impact of the Civil War and Reconstruction on the Constitution.* New York, 1973.

Jackson, Helen Hunt. *Century of Dishonor.* New York, 1881.

Jellison, Charles A. *Fessenden of Maine: Civil War Senator.* Syracuse, 1962.

Johnson, Willis Fletcher. *Life of Wm. Tecumseh Sherman.* Philadelphia, 1891.

Johnston, Joseph E. *Narrative of Military Operations Directed during the Late War between the States.* Bloomington, Ind., 1959.

Jomini, Antoine Henri. *Summary of the Art of War.* . . . New York, 1854.

Jones, George R. *Joseph Russell Jones.* Chicago, 1964.

Jones, J. William. *Life and Letters of Robert Edward Lee.* New York, 1906.

Jordan, David M. *Roscoe Conkling of New York: Voice in the Senate.* Ithaca, N.Y., 1971.

Keegan, John. *The Face of Battle.* London, 1976.

Kincaid, Larry G. "Victims of Circumstance: An Interpretation of Changing Attitudes toward Republican Policy Makers and Reconstruction." *Journal of American History* 57 (June 1970):48–66.

King, Charles. *The True Ulysses S. Grant.* Philadelphia, 1914.

Korn, Bertram Wallace. *American Jewry and the Civil War.* Philadelphia, 1951.

Krug, Mark M. *Lyman Trumbull: Conservative Radical.* New York, 1965.

Kutler, Stanley I. *Judicial Power and Reconstruction Politics.* Chicago, 1968.

Lang, Andrew. *Life, Letters, and Diaries of Sir Stafford Northcote, First Earl of Iddesleigh.* Edinburgh, 1891.

Lansden, John McMurray. *A History of the City of Cairo, Illinois.* Carbondale, Ill., 1976.

Latham, Henry. *Black and White: A Journal of a Three Month's Tour in the United States.* London and Philadelphia, 1867.

Leech, Margaret. *Reveille in Washington, 1860–1865.* New York, 1941.

Leslie, Leigh. "Grant and Galena." *Midland Monthly* 4 (Sept. 1895):195–215.

Lewis, Lloyd. *Captain Sam Grant.* Boston, 1950.

Lincoln, Abraham. *Collected Works of Abraham Lincoln.* Edited by Roy P. Basler. 9 vols. New Brunswick, N.J., 1953–55.

Litwack, Leon. *Been in the Storm So Long: The Aftermath of Slavery.* New York, 1979.

Long, E. B., with Long, Barbara. *The Civil War Day by Day: An Almanac, 1861–1865.* New York, 1971.

Longford, Elizabeth. *Queen Victoria: Born to Succeed.* New York, 1965.

Longstreet, James. *From Manassas to Appomattox: Memoirs of the Civil War in America.* New York, 1969.

Loth, David G. *Public Plunder: A History of Graft in America.* New York, 1938.

Lothrop, Thornton Kirkland. *William Henry Seward.* Boston, 1899.

Low, W. A. "The Freedmen's Bureau and Civil Rights in Maryland." *Journal of Negro History* 37 (July 1952):221–47.

Lowell, James Russell. *The Poetical Works of James Russell Lowell.* Edited and with an introduction by Marjorie R. Kaufman. Boston, 1978.

Lowenfels, Walter, ed. *Walt Whitman's Civil War.* New York, 1961.

Luvaas, Jay. *The Military Legacy of the Civil War.* Chicago, 1959.

Lyman, Payson W. *The Career and Character of Gen. Ulysses S. Grant. An Address Delivered in the Cong'l. Church, Belchertown, at the Grant Memorial Service, August, 1885. . . .* Belchertown, Mass., 1885.

Lyman, Theodore. *Meade's Headquarters, 1863–1865: Letters of Colonel Theodore Lyman from the Wilderness to Appomattox.* Selected and edited by George R. Agassiz. Boston, 1922.

Lynch, John R. *The Facts of Reconstruction.* New York, 1968.

Macartney, C. E. N. *Grant and His Generals.* New York, 1953.

Mahan, Dennis H. *An Elementary Treatise on Advanced-Guard, Out-Post, and Detachment Service of Troops. . . .* New York, 1847.

Mann, Charles S. "The Bucks and Montgomery County Kindred of General U. S. Grant." In *Historical Sketches: A Collection of Papers Prepared for the Historical Society of Montgomery County, Pennsylvania, 1915,* pp. 218–36. Norristown, Pa., 1925.

Mantell, Martin E. *Johnson, Grant, and the Politics of Reconstruction.* New York, 1973.

Mardock, Robert Winston. *The Reformers and the American Indian.* Columbia, Mo., 1971.

Marshall, Charles. *An Aide-de-Camp of Lee.* Edited by Frederick Maurice. Boston, 1927.

Marshall, Edward Chauncey. *The Ancestry of General Grant, and Their Contemporaries.* New York, 1869.

Marshall-Cornwall, James. *Grant as Military Commander.* London, 1970.

Martin, Asa Earl. *After the White House.* State College, Pa., 1951.

Mayer, George H. *The Republican Party, 1854–1964.* New York, 1967.

Mayes, Edward. *Lucius Q. C. Lamar: His Life, Times, and Speeches, 1825–1893.* Nashville, 1896.

McCabe, James Dabney [Edward Winslow Martin]. *Behind the Scenes in Washington.* New York, 1873.

McCall, Samuel Walker. *Thaddeus Stevens.* Boston, 1899.

McClellan, Carswell. *The Personal Memoirs and Military History of U. S. Grant versus the Record of the Army of the Potomac.* Boston, 1887.

McCormick, Robert R. *Ulysses S. Grant: The Great Soldier of America.* New York, 1934.

McCulloch, Hugh. *Men and Measures of Half a Century.* New York, 1889.

McDonald, John. *Secrets of the Great Whiskey Ring; and Eighteen Months in the Penitentiary, Containing a Complete Exposure of the Illicit Whisky Frauds Culminating in 1875 . . . to Which Is Added the Author's Remarkable Experiences While a Convict. . . .* St. Louis, 1880.

McElroy, Robert M. *Levi Parsons Morton: Banker, Diplomat and Statesman.* New York, 1930.

McFeely, William S. "Andrew Johnson" and "Ulysses S. Grant." In C. Vann Woodward, ed., *Responses of the Presidents to Charges of Misconduct.* New York, 1974.

———. *Yankee Stepfather: General O. O. Howard and the Freedmen.* New York, 1970.

McKinney, Francis F. *Education in Violence: The Life of George H. Thomas and the History of the Army of the Cumberland.* Detroit, 1961.

McKitrick, Eric L. *Andrew Johnson and Reconstruction.* Chicago, 1960.

McPherson, Edward. *The Political History of the United States of America during the Great Rebellion.* Washington, D.C., 1865.

———. *The Political History of the United States of America during the Period of Reconstruction.* Washington, D.C., 1880.

McPherson, James M. *The Abolitionist Legacy: From Reconstruction to the NAACP.* Princeton, 1975.

———. *Marching toward Freedom: The Negro in the Civil War.* New York, 1968.

———. *The Struggle for Equality: Abolitionists and the Negro in the Civil War and Reconstruction.* Princeton, 1964.

McWhiney, Grady, ed. *Grant, Lee, Lincoln and the Radicals: Essays on Civil War Leadership.* Evanston, Ill., 1964.

Meade, George. *The Life and Letters of George Gordon Meade.* 2 vols. New York, 1913.

Merk, Frederick, with Merk, Lois B. *Slavery and the Annexation of Texas.* New York, 1972.

Miers, Earl Schenck. *The Web of Victory: Grant at Vicksburg.* New York, 1955.

Montgomery, David. *Beyond Equality: Labor and the Radical Republicans, 1862–1872.* New York, 1967.

Monton, Charles. "A Boy of Shiloh." In Military Order of the Loyal Legion of the United States, New York Commandry, *Personal Recollections of the War of the Rebellion,* 3d series, pp. 52–69. New York, 1907.

Morgan, H. Wayne, ed. *The Gilded Age: A Reappraisal.* Rev. ed. Syracuse, 1963.

Morrison, James Lunsford. "The United States Military Academy, 1833–1866: Years of Progress and Turmoil." Ph.D. dissertation, Columbia University, 1971.

Moss, Michael E. *Robert W. Weir of West Point.* West Point, N.Y., 1976.

Motley, John Lothrop. *The Correspondence of John Lothrop Motley.* Edited by George William Curtis. 3 vols. New York, 1900.

Nash, Howard P. *Stormy Petrel: The Life and Times of General Benjamin F. Butler, 1818–1893.* Rutherford, N.J., 1969.

Nevins, Allan. *Abram S. Hewitt, with Some Account of Peter Cooper.* New York, 1935.

———. *Hamilton Fish: The Inner History of the Grant Administration.* Rev. ed. 2 vols. New York, 1957.

Niven, John. *Gideon Welles, Lincoln's Secretary of the Navy.* New York, 1973.

Nugent, Walter T. K. *Money and American Society, 1865–1880.* New York, 1968.

———. *The Money Question during Reconstruction.* New York, 1967.

Oates, Stephen B. *With Malice Toward None: The Life of Abraham Lincoln.* New York, 1977.

Oberholtzer, Ellis Paxson. *A History of the United States since the Civil War.* 5 vols. New York, 1917–37.

Olson, James C. *Red Cloud and the Sioux Problem*. Lincoln, Nebr., 1965.

Osthaus, Carl R. *Freedmen, Philanthropy, and Fraud: A History of the Freedman's Savings Bank*. Urbana, Ill., 1976.

Owens, Kenneth N. *Galena, Grant, and the Fortunes of War: A History of Galena, Illinois, during the Civil War*. DeKalb, Ill., 1963.

Owsley, Frank L. *King Cotton Diplomacy: Foreign Relations of the Confederate States of America*. Chicago, 1931.

Packard, J. F. *Grant's Tour around the World, with Incidents of His Journey through England, Ireland, Scotland. . . .* Cincinnati, 1880.

Palmer, Loomis T. [ L. T. Remlap], ed. *The Life of General Grant*. Chicago, 1885.

Parker, Arthur C. *The Life of General Ely S. Parker, Last Grand Sachem of the Iroquois and General Grant's Military Secretary*. Buffalo, Buffalo Historical Society, 1919.

Payne, Darwin. "Camp Life in the Army of Occupation: Corpus Christi, July 1845 to March 1846." *Southwestern Historical Quarterly* 73 (Jan. 1970): 326–42.

Pendel, Thomas F. *Thirty-six Years in the White House*. Washington, D.C., 1902.

Pepper, George W. *Personal Recollections of Sherman's Campaigns, in Georgia and the Carolinas*. Zanesville, Ohio, 1866.

Perman, Michael. *Reunion without Compromise: The South and Reconstruction, 1865–1868*. Cambridge, Eng., 1973.

Phelps, Charles A. *Life and Public Services of General Ulysses S. Grant, from his Boyhood to the Present Time*. Boston, 1868.

Phillips, Ulrich B., ed. *The Correspondence of Robert Toombs, Alexander H. Stephens and Howell Cobb. Annual Report of the American Historical Association for the Year 1911*. Vol. 2. Washington, D.C., 1913.

Pierce, Edward L. *Memoir and Letters of Charles Sumner*. 4 vols. Boston, 1877–93.

Pike, James S. *The Prostrate State: South Carolina under Negro Government*. New York, 1874.

Pitkin, Thomas M. *The Captain Departs: Ulysses S. Grant's Last Campaign*. Carbondale, Ill., 1973.

Pletcher, David M. *Rails, Mines, and Progress: Seven American Promoters in Mexico, 1867–1911*. Ithaca, N.Y., 1958.

Polakoff, Keith Ian. *The Politics of Inertia: The Election of 1876 and the End of Reconstruction*. Baton Rouge, 1973.

Pollard, E. A. *Southern History of the War*. 4 vols. New York, 1863–66.

Poore, Ben Perley. *Perley's Reminiscences of Sixty Years in the National Metropolis*. 2 vols. Philadelphia, 1886.

———, and Tiffany, O. H. *Life of U. S. Grant*. Philadelphia, 1885.

Porter, David Dixon. *Incidents and Anecdotes of the Civil War*. New York, 1891.

Porter, Horace. *Campaigning with Grant*. New York, 1897.

Post, James Louis, comp. *Reminiscences by Personal Friends of Gen. U. S. Grant and the History of Grant's Log Cabin*. St. Louis, 1904.

Post, Robert C., ed. *1876: A Centennial Exhibition*. Washington, D.C., 1976.

Potter, David M. *The Impending Crisis, 1848–1861*. New York, 1976.

———. *Lincoln and His Party in the Secession Crisis*. New Haven, 1962.

Powell, Lawrence N. "The American Land Company and Agency: John A. Andrew and the Northernization of the South." *Civil War History* 21 (Dec. 1975):293–308.

———. *New Masters: Northern Planters during the Civil War and Reconstruction*. New Haven, 1980.

Powell, William H. *A History of the Organization and Movements of the Fourth Regiment of Infantry, U.S. Army, from May 30, 1796, to December 31, 1870*. Washington, D.C., 1871.

Pratt, Fletcher. *Stanton, Lincoln's Secretary of War*. New York, 1953.

Pressly, Thomas J. *Americans Interpret Their Civil War*. New York, 1962.

Prickett, Robert C. "The Malfeasance of William Worth Belknap, Secretary of War, October 13, 1869, to March 2, 1876." *North Dakota History* 17 (Jan. 1950):5–51.

Priest, Loring Benson. *Uncle Sam's Stepchildren: The Reformation of United States Indian Policy, 1865–1887*. New Brunswick, N.J., 1942.

Prucha, Francis Paul. *American Indian Policy in Crisis: Christian Reformers and the Indian, 1865–1900.* Norman, Okla., 1976.

Rahill, Peter J. *The Catholic Indian Missions and Grant's Peace Policy, 1870–1884.* Washington, D.C., 1953.

Randall, J. G., and Donald, David [Herbert]. *The Civil War and Reconstruction.* Boston, 1961.

Redesdale, Algernon Bertram Freeman-Mitford, baron. *Memories.* 2 vols. London, 1915.

Reed, Rowena. *Combined Operations in the Civil War.* Annapolis, 1978.

Reid, Harvey. *The View from Headquarters: Civil War Letters of Harvey Reid.* Edited by Frank L. Byrne. Madison, Wis., 1965.

Reid, Wemyss. *Life of . . . William Edward Foster.* 2 vols. London, 1888.

Reid, Whitelaw. *After the War: A Tour of the Southern States, 1865–1866.* New York, 1965.

———. *Ohio in the War: Her Statesmen, Her Generals, and Soldiers.* 2 vols. Cincinnati, 1868.

Remlap, L. T., ed. *The Life of General U. S. Grant.* Chicago, 1885.

Republican Party, National Committee. *Life and Services of General U. S. Grant, Conqueror of the Rebellion and Eighteenth President of the United States.* Washington, D.C., 1868.

Rhodes, James Ford. *Historical Essays.* New York, 1909.

———. *History of the United States, 1850–1877.* 7 vols. New York, 1892–1906.

Richardson, Albert D. *A Personal History of Ulysses S. Grant.* Hartford, Conn., 1902.

Richardson, James D., ed. *A Compilation of the Messages and Papers of the Presidents, 1789–1897.* 10 vols. Washington, D.C., 1896–99.

Riegel, R. E. "The Missouri Pacific Railroad to 1879." *Missouri Historical Review* 18 (1923–24):3–26.

Ripley, C. Peter. *Slaves and Freedmen in Civil War Louisiana.* Baton Rouge, 1976.

Robins, Edward. *William T. Sherman.* Philadelphia, 1905.

Rose, Willie Lee. *Rehearsal for Reconstruction: The Port Royal Experiment.* Indianapolis, 1964.

Ross, Ishbel. *The General's Wife: The Life of Mrs. Ulysses S. Grant.* New York, 1959.

Rushmore, Elsie Mitchell. *The Indian Policy during Grant's Administration.* Jamaica, N.Y., 1914.

Sadler, Christine. *Children in the White House.* New York, 1967.

Schofield, John M. *Forty-six Years in the Army.* New York, 1897.

Schouler, James. *History of the Reconstruction Period, 1865–1877.* New York, 1913.

Schurz, Carl. *Intimate Letters of Carl Schurz, 1841–1869.* Translated and edited by Joseph Schafer. Madison, Wis., 1928.

———. *The Reminiscences of Carl Schurz.* 3 vols. New York, 1907–8.

———. *Speeches, Correspondence and Political Papers of Carl Schurz.* Selected and edited by Frederic Bancroft. New York, 1913.

Scudder, Horace Elisha. *James Russell Lowell: A Biography.* 2 vols. Boston, 1901.

Sefton, James E. "The Impeachment of Andrew Johnson: A Century of Writing." *Civil War History* 14 (June 1968):120–47.

———. *The United States Army and Reconstruction, 1865–1877.* Baton Rouge, 1967.

Seward, Frederick William. *Reminiscences of a War-Time Statesman and Diplomat, 1830–1915.* New York, 1916.

Seward, William Henry. *The Works of William H. Seward.* Edited by George E. Baker. 5 vols. New York, 1853–84.

Sharkey, Robert P. *Money, Class, and Party: An Economic Study of Civil War and Reconstruction.* Baltimore, 1959.

Shaw, John M. "The Life and Services of General John A. Rawlins." In *Glimpses of the Nation's Struggle.* 3d series. St. Paul, 1893.

Sheehan, Bernard W. *Seeds of Extinction: Jeffersonian Philanthropy and the American Indian.* Williamsburg, Va., 1973.

Sheffield, Delia B. "Reminiscences of Delia B. Sheffield." *Washington Historical Quarterly* 15 (Jan. 1924):49–62.

Sheridan, Philip H. *Personal Memoirs of P. H. Sheridan, General, United States Army.* 2 vols. New York, 1888.

Sherman, Hoyt. "Personal Recollections of General Grant." *Midland Monthly* 9 (Apr. 1898):325–27.

Sherman, John. *Recollections of Forty Years in the House, Senate, and Cabinet.* 2 vols. New York, 1895.

Sherman, William Tecumseh. *Home Letters of General Sherman.* Edited by M. A. DeWolfe Howe. New York, 1909.

———. *Memoirs of General William T. Sherman.* 2 vols. New York, 1875.

———. *The Sherman Letters: Correspondence between General and Senator from 1837 to 1891.* Edited by Rachel Sherman Thorndike. New York, 1894.

Shy, John W. *A People Numerous and Armed: Reflections on the Military Struggle for American Independence.* New York, 1976.

Silber, Irwin, comp. *Songs America Voted By.* Harrisburg, Pa., 1971.

Silbey, Joel H. *A Respectable Minority: The Democratic Party in the Civil War Era, 1860–1868.* New York, 1977.

Simon, John Y. "From Galena to Appomattox: Grant and Washburne." *Journal of the Illinois State Historical Society* 58 (Summer 1965):165–89.

Slattery, Charles Lewis. *Felix Reville Brunot, 1820–1898.* London, 1901.

Slayden, Ellen Maury. *Washington Wife: Journal of Ellen Maury Slayden from 1897–1919.* New York, 1963.

Smith, Goldwin Albert. *The Treaty of Washington, 1871: A Study in Imperial History.* Ithaca, N.Y., 1941.

Smith, Justin H. *The War with Mexico.* 2 vols. New York, 1919.

Smith, Walter George. *Life and Letters of Thomas Kilby Smith.* New York, 1898.

Speer, Emory. *Lincoln, Lee, Grant, and Other Biographical Addresses.* New York, 1909.

Sproat, John G. *The Best Men: Liberal Reformers in the Gilded Age.* New York, 1968.

———. "Blueprint for Radical Reconstruction." *Journal of Southern History* 23 (Feb. 1957):25–44.

Stampp, Kenneth M. *The Era of Reconstruction, 1865–1877.* New York, 1965.

Starr, Stephen Z. *Jennison's Jayhawkers: A Civil War Cavalry Regiment and Its Commander.* Baton Rouge, 1973.

Stephens, Alexander H. *A Constitutional View of the Late War between the States: Its Causes, Character, Conduct and Results Presented in a Series of Colloquies at Liberty Hall.* 2 vols. Philadelphia, 1868–70.

Stewart, Edgar I. *Custer's Luck.* Norman, Okla., 1955.

Stickles, Arndt Mathias. *Simon Bolivar Buckner: Borderland Knight.* Chapel Hill, N.C., 1940.

Storey, Moorfield, and Emerson, Edward W. *Ebenezer Rockwood Hoar.* Boston, 1911.

Stouffer, Samuel A., et al. *Studies in Social Psychology in World War II.* Princeton, 1949–50.

Strode, Hudson. *Jefferson Davis.* 3 vols. New York, 1955–64.

Strong, George T. *The Diary of George Templeton Strong.* Edited by Allan Nevins and Milton H. Thomas. 4 vols. New York, 1952.

Stuart, George H. *The Life of George H. Stuart.* Edited by Robert E. Thompson. Philadelphia, 1890.

Sumner, Charles. *Republicanism vs. Grantism. Speech . . . Delivered May 31, 1872.* New York, 1872.

———. *The Works of Charles Sumner.* 15 vols. Boston, 1875–94.

Swift, John Lindsay. *About Grant.* New York, 1880.

Swinney, Everette. "Enforcing the Fifteenth Amendment, 1870–1877." *Journal of Southern History* 28 (May 1962):202–18.

Swinton, William. *Campaigns of the Army of the Potomac.* New York, 1866.

Sword, Wiley. *Shiloh: Bloody April.* New York, 1974.

Szabad, Imre. *Le Général Grant, Président de la République Américaine.* Paris, 1868.

Tansill, Charles C. *The United States and Santo Domingo, 1798–1873: A Chapter in Caribbean Diplomacy.* Baltimore, 1938.

Tatum, Lawrie. *Our Red Brothers and the Peace Policy of President Ulysses S. Grant.* 1899. Reprint, with foreword by Richard N. Ellis. Lincoln, Nebr., 1970.

Taylor, Richard. *Destruction and Reconstruction: Personal Experiences of the Late War.* New York, 1879.

Thayer, William Makepeace. *From Tannery to the White House: The Life of Ulysses S. Grant.* Boston, 1887.

Thomas, Benjamin P. *Abraham Lincoln: A Biography.* New York, 1952.

———, and Hyman, Harold M. *Stanton: The Life and Times of Lincoln's Secretary of War.* New York, 1962.

Thomas, Wilbur D. *General George H. Thomas, the Indomitable Warrior, Supreme in Defense and in Counterattack: A Biography.* New York, 1964.

Thompson, Julius Eric. "Hiram R. Revels, 1827–1901: A Biography." Ph.D. dissertation, Princeton University, 1973.

Trefousse, Hans L. "The Acquittal of Andrew Johnson and the Decline of the Radicals." *Civil War History* 14 (June 1968):148–61.

———. *Ben Butler: The South Called Him Beast.* New York, 1957.

———. *Benjamin Franklin Wade: Radical Republican from Ohio.* New York, 1963.

———. *Impeachment of a President: Andrew Johnson, the Blacks and Reconstruction.* Knoxville, 1975.

———. *The Radical Republicans: Lincoln's Vanguard for Racial Justice.* New York, 1968.

Trelease, Allen W. *White Terror: The Ku Klux Klan Conspiracy and Southern Reconstruction.* New York, 1971.

Tyler, Mason Whiting. *Recollections of the Civil War.* Edited by William S. Tyler. New York, 1912.

Unger, Irwin. *The Greenback Era: A Social and Political History of American Finance, 1865–1879.* Princeton, 1964.

United States Military Academy, West Point. *The Centennial of the United States Military Academy at West Point, New York.* 2 vols. Washington, D.C., 1904.

———. *The West Point Atlas of American Wars.* Edited by Vincent J. Esposito. 2 vols. New York, 1959.

United States War Department. *The War of the Rebellion: A Compilation of the Official Records of the Union and Confederate Armies.* Washington, D.C., 1880–1901. Customarily cited as *Official Records of the Rebellion.*

Utley, Robert M. "The Celebrated Peace Policy of General Grant." *North Dakota History* 20 (July 1953):121–42.

Van Deusen, Glyndon G. *Horace Greeley: Nineteenth-Century Crusader.* New York, 1964.

———. *William Henry Seward.* New York, 1967.

Vandiver, Frank E. *Jubal's Raid: General Early's Famous Attack on Washington in 1864.* New York, 1960.

Van Horne, Thomas B. *History of the Army of the Cumberland.* 2 vols. Cincinnati, 1875.

———. *The Life of Major-General George H. Thomas.* New York, 1882.

Voegeli, V. Jacque. *Free but Not Equal: The Midwest and the Negro during the Civil War.* Chicago, 1967.

Walke, Henry. "The Gun-Boats of Belmont and Fort Henry." In *Battles and Leaders of the Civil War,* edited by R. U. Johnson and C. C. Buel, 1:358–67. New York, 1887.

Walker, Cam. "Corinth: The Story of a Contraband Camp." *Civil War History* 20 (March 1974):5–22.

Wallace, Lew. *Lew Wallace: An Autobiography.* 2 vols. New York, 1906.

Warmoth, Henry Clay. *War, Politics and Reconstruction: Stormy Days in Louisiana.* New York, 1930.

Warner, Ezra J. *Generals in Blue: Lives of the Union Commanders.* Baton Rouge, 1964.

Warren, Robert Penn. *The Legacy of the Civil War: Meditations on the Centennial.* New York, 1961.

Washburn, Wilcomb E. *The Indian in America.* New York, 1975.

Webb, Ross A. *Benjamin Helm Bristow: Border State Politician.* Lexington, Ky., 1969.

Wecter, Dixon. *The Hero in America: A Chronicle of Hero Worship.* New York, 1941.

Weichmann, Louis J. *A True History of the Assassination of Abraham Lincoln and of the Conspiracy of 1865.* New York, 1975.

Weigley, Russell F. *The American Way of War: A History of United States Military Strategy and Policy.* New York, 1973.

——. *History of the United States Army.* New York, 1967.

——. *Quartermaster General of the Union Army: A Biography of M. C. Meigs.* New York, 1959.

——. *Towards an American Army: Military Thought from Washington to Marshall.* New York, 1962.

Weinstein, Allen. *Prelude to Populism: Origins of the Silver Issue, 1867–1878.* New Haven, 1970.

——. "Was There a 'Crime of 1873'? The Case of the Demonetized Dollar." *Journal of American History* 54 (Sept. 1967):307–26.

Welles, Gideon. *Diary.* Edited by Howard K. Beale, assisted by Alan W. Brownsword. 3 vols. New York, 1960.

Welles, Sumner. *Naboth's Vineyard: The Dominican Republic, 1844–1924.* 2 vols. New York, 1928.

Wells, O. V. "The Depression of 1873–1879." *Agricultural History* 11 (1937):237–49.

Westwood, Howard C. "Lincoln and the Hampton Roads Peace Conference." *Lincoln Herald* 81 (Winter 1979):243–56.

Wharton, Vernon Lane. *The Negro in Mississippi, 1865–1890.* New York, 1965.

White, Horace. *The Life of Lyman Trumbull.* Boston, 1913.

Wiley, Bell Irvin. *The Common Soldier of the Civil War.* New York, 1977.

——. *The Life of Billy Yank, the Common Soldier of the Union.* Indianapolis, 1952.

——. *The Life of Johnny Reb, the Common Soldier of the Confederacy.* Indianapolis, 1943.

Williams, Kenneth P. *Lincoln Finds a General: A Military Study of the Civil War.* 5 vols. New York, 1949–59.

Williams, T. Harry. *McClellan, Sherman and Grant.* New Brunswick, N.J., 1962.

Williamson, Joel. *After Slavery: The Negro in South Carolina during Reconstruction, 1861–1877.* Chapel Hill, N.C., 1965.

Wilson, Edmund. *Patriotic Gore: Studies in the Literature of the American Civil War.* New York, 1962.

Wilson, James Grant. *General Grant.* New York, 1897.

——. *The Life and Public Services of Ulysses Simpson Grant.* New York, 1885.

Wilson, James Harrison. *The Life of Charles A. Dana.* New York, 1907.

——. *Life of John A. Rawlins: Lawyer, Assistant Adjutant-General, Chief of Staff, Major General of Volunteers, and Secretary of War.* New York, 1916.

——. *Under the Old Flag.* 2 vols. New York, 1912.

Winks, Robin W. *Canada and the United States: The Civil War Years.* Baltimore, 1960.

Wister, Owen. "Ulysses S. Grant." In *Beacon Biographies of Eminent Americans,* edited by M. A. DeWolfe Howe. Boston, 1911.

——. *Ulysses S. Grant.* Boston, 1901.

Wolf, Lucien. *Life of the First Marquess of Ripon.* . . . 2 vols. London, 1921.

Woodward, C. Vann. *American Counterpoint: Slavery and Racism in the North-South Dialogue.* Boston, 1971.

——. *The Burden of Southern History.* Baton Rouge, 1960.

——. *Reunion and Reaction: The Compromise of 1877 and the End of Reconstruction.* Boston, 1951.

——, ed. *Responses of the Presidents to Charges of Misconduct.* New York, 1974.

Woodward, William E. *Meet General Grant.* New York, 1928.

Woodworth, Charles Louis. *A Commemorative Discourse on the Work and Character of Ulysses Simpson Grant.* Pamphlet. Boston, 1885.

Wright, A. O. *General Grant's Military Service.* Pamphlet. n.d.

Young, John Russell. *Around the World with General Grant.* 2 vols. New York, 1879.

Young, Mary E. "Congress Looks West: Liberal Ideology and Public Land Policy in the Nineteenth Century." In *The Frontier in American Development.* Edited by David M. Ellis. Ithaca, N.Y., 1969.

Zimmerman, Joan Grace. "Free Soil for the South? Views of the Economic Future of the Sea Islands, 1861–1867." M.A. thesis, University of Virginia, 1973.

# Index

Page entries in **boldface** refer to illustrations

Harland, James, 342
Harrison, Benjamin, 519
Harrison, William Henry, 161
Hartranft, John F., 454
Haruko, empress of Japan, 475, 519
Hatch, Davis, 341–42, 343–44, 345
Hawley, Joseph R., 276, 277
Hayes, Rutherford B., 279, 431, 484, 485
  election of, 441, 445–48
  inauguration of, 448–49
  as president, 456, 460, 468
Healy, G. P. A., 212, **213**, 464
Hellman, Lillian, xi
Henderson, John B., 410
Henry, Fort, battle of, 97–98, 103, 107
*Hepburn* v. *Griswold*, 387
Herzog, Jacques, 465
Hesseltine, William B., 478–79
Hewitt, Abram S., 430
Hewitt, James, 42
Hewitt, Richard M., 202
Hill, A. P., 166, 175
Hill, C. H., 390, 392
Hillyer, W. S., 85, 87–88, 93, 119, 125
Hindes, Samuel, 254
Hitler, Adolf, 68
Hoar, Ebenezer Rockwood, 356–59, 372–73, 374
  background of, 301–2
  dismissal of, 362, 363, 364–66
  in Grant's cabinet, 291, **291**, 300, 301, 302, 344, 345, 368
  nominated to Supreme Court, 387, 389
Hoar, Samuel, 301–2
Hoge, Solomon L., 375
Holmes, Oliver Wendell, 152, 302
Holmes, Oliver Wendell, Jr., 116, 169
Homer, Winslow, **261**
Hood, John Bell, 177, 181, 185, 191–93, 194
Hooker, Joseph, 114, 148, 163, 166, 168, 341
  Grant's first meeting with, 144
Hooker, Thomas, 4
House, Edward M., 521
Howard, Bronson, 232
Howard, Jacob M., 266
Howard, Michael, 375
Howard, O. O., 278, 286, 428, 476–77
  in Civil War, 118–19, 144–45, 148, 177, 194
  as head of Freedmen's Bureau, 127, 236, 239, 240, 259, 260, 312, 377, 438
  in Indian affairs, 312, 438
  integration of West Point and, 377–78, 379
Howe, Timothy, 388
Hugo, Victor, 464
Humboldt, Fort, Grant stationed at, 49, 52–55, 67, 106, 493
Hunt, Lewis Cass, 52
Hunt, Ward, 330, 386–87
Hunter, David, 89, 94
Hunter, Robert M. T., 199–201, 202–5, 206–8
Huntington, Collis P., 282, 373, 374, 487
Hurlbut, Stephen A., 123, 128
Hyman, Harold M., 242

Indian agents, 308, 312–13
Indians, American, 289, 299, 305–18, 436–38, 443
  cheated by merchants, 313, 314–15, 428, 432, 436, 437

  in delegations to White House, 317, 318, 437
  extermination of, 305, 307, 308, 313, 316, 317, 436, 438
  Grant's Peace Policy and, 308–9, 310–11, 312–13, 314, 316–17, 436, 438
  peace commission for (1867), 307–8
  Quaker Policy and, 308
  reservations for, 308, 309, 312, 316
  wars against, 316, 332, 436–38
  westward migration and, 306–7, 308, 436
Inflation Bill (1874), 395–97
Ingalls, Rufus, 20, 51, 55, 87, 157, 340, 343
*Inner History of the Grant Administration, The* (Nevins), 296
*In the Days of My Father General Grant* (Jesse Root Grant), 521

Jackson, Andrew, 23, 161, 198, 346, 367, 406, 447
Jackson, Claiborne, 82
Jackson, E. P., 371
Jackson, Helen Hunt, 316
Jackson, Thomas J., 20, 166
James, Henry, 400, 401, 403, 458, 518
James, William, 197
Japan, Grants in visit to, 474–76, **475**, 478, 479
Jefferson, Thomas, 295, 453
Jerome, William, 250–51
Jewell, Marshall, 302, 418
Johnson, Andrew, 143, 224, 226, 230, 233, 245, 246, 254–56, 277, 286, 288, 292, 293, 348, 385–86, 395, 492
  abandoned by Grant, 269–71, 274, 284
  absent from Grant's inauguration, 286–87, 289
  Cooper Union rally for, 233, 234–35
  foreign policy under, 334, 337–38
  Grant almost sent to Mexico by, 221, 256–57
  impeachment of, 248, 259, 272, 273, 274–76, 277, 290, 298, 389, 435, 493
  political tour of, 250–52, 253
  Reconstruction policies of, 226–27, 238, 240, 241, 242, 247–50, 252, 258, 259–61, 262–63, 298, 307, 357, 365
  Stanton removed from office by, 247–48, 252–53, 257, 262, 263–64, 266–71, 273, 274, 275, 298, 300
Johnson, Reverdy, 249–50, 268–69, 334
Johnson, Robert U., 493–94
Johnson-Clarendon Convention, 334, 349
Johnston, Albert Sidney, 112, 113, 115, 117, 158
Johnston, Joseph E., 130–31, 136, 177
  Sherman's Carolinas campaign against, 208, 212, 223, 227–29
Jomini, Antoine Henri, 15, 104
Jones, Frank Hatch, 521
Jones, John Percival, 486
Jones, J. Russell, 163–64, 284, 399
Jones, William, 62, 63, 69
Joseph, chief of Nez Percé, 438
Joyce, William, 409, 411
Juárez, Benito Pablo, 257, 486
Judd, Norman B., 326
Julia (slave), 62, 126
Justice Department, U.S., 439
  creation of, 368, 424

Kaplan, Justin, 480–81
Kellogg, William Pitt, 418
Kelly, Rachel, 5